CANADIAN EDITION

Biological Anthropology

THE NATURAL HISTORY OF HUMANKIND

Craig Stanford UNIVERSITY OF SOUTHERN CALIFORNIA
John S. Allen UNIVERSITY OF IOWA
Susan C. Antón NEW YORK UNIVERSITY
Nancy C. Lovell UNIVERSITY OF ALBERTA

Toronto

Library and Archives Canada Cataloguing in Publication

Biological anthropology : the natural history of humankind / Craig Stanford ... [et al.]. -- Canadian ed.

Includes bibliographical references and index.
ISBN 978-0-13-613912-6

1. Physical anthropology--Textbooks. I. Stanford, Craig B. (Craig Britton), 1956-

GN25.B55 2009 599.9 C2007-907509-6

ISBN-13: 978-0-13-613912-6
ISBN-10: 0-13-613912-4

Vice President, Editorial Director: Gary Bennett
Senior Acquisitions Editor: Laura Paterson Forbes
Marketing Manager: Sally Aspinall
Senior Developmental Editor: Jennifer Murray
Production Editor: Gex Publishing Services, Mary Ann Field
Copy Editor: Gex Publishing Services
Proofreader: Gex Publishing Services
Production Coordinator: Peggy Brown
Composition: Gex Publishing Services
Photo Research: Terri Rothman
Art Director: Julia Hall
Cover and Interior Design: Anthony Leung
Cover Image: Veer Inc.

1 2 3 4 5 12 11 10 09 08

Printed and bound in United States.

CBS: For Erin, Gaelen, Marika, and Adam

JSA: For my wife, Stephanie Sheffield,
and our sons, Reid and Perry

SCA: For Mr. Carl, My Folks, and
the wet noses of Four Dog Farm

NCL: For Dennis, Lisa, and Sara

Brief Contents

Contents

PREFACE

Biological anthropology, traditionally known as physical anthropology, has evolved over the past 20 years into the study of the evolutionary biology of humankind based on the fossil record of our ancestors, human skeletal biology, the genetics of individuals and populations, the biology and behaviour of our primate relatives, the nature of human adaptation to a variety of physical environments, and the biology of human behaviour. Our book combines up-to-date, comprehensive coverage of these topics with a modern biological approach that includes fields that have become major areas of research in recent years. Though comprehensive, the book is written as accessibly as possible to be useful from community college to research-oriented university levels. We four coauthors conduct our research in four of the main areas of biological anthropology: the human fossil record (Susan Antón), primate behaviour and ecology (Craig Stanford), human biology and the brain (John Allen), and modern human skeletal biology and bioarchaeology (Nancy Lovell). This has allowed us to provide a specialist approach to each of the broad divisions of the field covered by the text.

Undergraduate enrolment in introductory biological anthropology courses has increased sharply as biological anthropology has become one way to fulfil the basic natural science requirement at many colleges and universities. We believe the new audience and the changing field have created a need for a text such as this one, integrating traditional physical anthropology with a modern Darwinian framework.

The authors are anthropologists with extensive backgrounds in both biological and social sciences and are both teachers and researchers. In a field changing as rapidly as human evolutionary science is today, we feel it is critical for active researchers to produce textbooks that serve the needs of students. In addition to the strong biological orientation of the book, we try to frame questions about humankind in light of our understanding of culture and the ways in which culture interacts with biology to create the template for human nature.

We have also tried to keep polemic out of the book; in a field famous for intellectual disagreements over the meaning of fossils or interpretations of Darwinian theory, it is essential to provide students with well-rounded views of the evidence. There are places where, because of the introductory nature of the text, we have not delved deeply into the details of some debates, but we have nevertheless tried to balance multiple views of ongoing unresolved questions.

HIGHLIGHTS OF THE CANADIAN EDITION

This first Canadian edition presents Canadian data and examples (on topics such as cloning, obesity, and DNA fingerprinting) and incorporates the results of research being done by Canadian biological anthropologists and affiliated scientists. In this text you will find reference to the work of Canadian primatologists Linda Fedigan, Biruté Galdikas, Lisa Gould, and Mary Pavelka (Chapters 7 and 8); palaeoprimatologist Mary Silcox (Chapter 9); geochemists Henry Schwarcz and Jack Rink (Chapter 13); biomedical anthropologists Ann Herring, Tina Moffat, and Eric Roth (Chapter 16); skeletal biologists Richard Lazenby, Nancy Lovell, Susan Pfeiffer, and Christine White (Chapter 18) and forensic anthropologists Owen Beattie, Tracy Rogers, and Mark Skinner (Chapter 18); as well as reference to the cutting edge work in forensic and ancient DNA analysis that is being undertaken at the University of Alberta, Lakehead University, and McMaster University.

In addition, the Canadian edition includes a chapter on human skeletal biology (Chapter 18), a topic not usually covered in introductory biological anthropology texts. The text also features biomedical anthropology and the behaviour and biology of modern people, including an extensive discussion of the human brain.

FORMAT OF THE BOOK

The book is organized in much the same way that we have taught introductory courses in biological anthropology. We have different backgrounds within biological anthropology but a common intellectual thread, which is the heart and soul of any book on biological anthropology: the theory of evolution by natural selection. This is the unifying aspect of each chapter, and indeed for the entire discipline. Part I, Foundations (Chapters 1 and 2) reflects this. The text begins with an overview of biological anthropology, including a brief history of the field. Chapter 2 reviews the roots of evolutionary thinking and how it became central to biological anthropology. Part II, Mechanisms of Evolution (Chapters 3 through 6) reviews at length the mechanisms of evolution and describes the applications of modern genetic research techniques in unravelling some of the mysteries of human evolution. Chapters 3 and 4 review cellular, molecular, and population genetics. Chapter 5 takes the discussion of genetics into modern evolutionary theory: the formation of species and the central topics of natural selection and adaptation. Chapter 6 surveys the field of human adaptation and the ways in which evolutionary forces mould human populations.

Part III, Primates (Chapters 7 and 8) is about the living nonhuman primates. We review their classification, their anatomical and behavioural adaptations, and their social life. We cautiously use the behaviour of living monkeys and apes to understand what their ancestors, and therefore ours, may have been like.

Part IV, The Fossil Record (Chapters 9 through 14), describes the fossil record for humanity. We begin with the environmental context in which fossils are found and describe the periods of Earth's history during which primates arose, and review primate evolution (Chapter 9). We discuss the anatomical transition from an ape to human ancestor (Chapter 10), a change that set off a cascade of effects that we feel to the present day. Chapter 11 describes the most up-to-date information on the earliest known hominids in Africa. Chapter 12 introduces the genus *Homo* and the causes and consequences of dispersal from Africa. Chapters 13 and 14 cover the more recent hominid fossils, including Neandertals, and the origins of our own species. We have tried to provide up-to-the-minute information on the discovery of new human fossils.

Part V, Biology and Behaviour of Modern Humans (Chapters 15 through 18) is about the biology of modern people. We include coverage of the human brain and its evolutionary aspects (Chapter 15), biocultural issues of biomedical anthropology (Chapter 16), the biocultural aspects of the lives of traditional foraging people (Chapter 17), and the biocultural analysis of the skeletal remains, archaeological and forensic, of modern humans (Chapter 18).

The appendices offer reference material on the primate skeleton (Appendix A), additional material on the Hardy–Weinberg equilibrium (Appendix B), and metric to imperial conversion factors (Appendix C).

SPECIAL FEATURES

As you read the book, you will notice a few special features in addition to the main body of text. We begin each chapter with a short **vignette** depicting the main topic of the chapter. Some of these are quotes taken from famous works by biological anthropologists, such as Canadian primatologist Birutė Galdikas describing a day with orangutans at the beginning of Chapter 8. For other chapters, one of the authors has written a short description of how someone studying human fossils, for example, might experience a day in the field. In a few chapters, we depict the lives of early humans drawn from our imagination, fleshed out with details as accurate as our science currently possesses. You should use the vignettes as a way to get a feel for the chapter topics and as an enjoyable and informative reflection on the text material.

We have also presented some material in **boxes** inset into each chapter, such as the profile of Canadian anatomist Davidson Black, who studied the fossil remains of "Peking Man" in China. The purpose of the boxes is to expand on text material or call your attention to current events connected to our field, to emerging debates, or sometimes just to fascinating side stories. The material in the boxes is generally distinct from that in the text.

Other special features of the text are a margin **glossary** to define new terms as students encounter them and a complete glossary at the back of the book. Each chapter is summarized by a list of questions and answers, and each chapter also ends with several **critical thinking questions** intended to provoke as well as summarize. We have listed a few **suggested readings** with each chapter, with an emphasis on books that are highly readable, nontechnical accounts that an introductory student may want to pursue. And the book contains a **bibliography** of all the references used and cited in the text.

ILLUSTRATIONS

Illustrations play a major role in any textbook, and they are crucial learning tools in introductory science texts. The publisher and authors have worked together to try to provide you with the best possible photos and drawings of every topic covered in the book. Many of the photographs were taken by the authors, and others were contributed by other biological anthropologists. Pearson Education has worked hard to produce some of the finest images of everything from molecular genetics to stone tools that have ever been published in a biological anthropology textbook. The maps have been specifically created for this book by Dorling Kindersley, a leading publisher of atlases for both the educational and consumer markets. These maps describe the geography of everything from the distribution of living primates in the world today to the locations of the continents in the distant past. We authors worked with the publisher to be sure all information in this text is depicted accurately and clearly, and we hope you will gain a better understanding of the text by studying the visual material as well.

Special two-page feature illustrations appear in a number of chapters, especially in Part IV, and provide a snapshot of evolutionary development through time. These special feature illustrations provide a concise way for the reader to easily grasp the evolutionary changes through a vast sweep of time that are presented in greater detail in the text.

A Note about Language Authors must make decisions about language and terminology, and textbook authors make those choices with the knowledge that they may be influencing the mindset of a generation of young scholars. Some of these choices are modest. For instance, we use the modern spelling *Neandertal* instead of the traditional German spelling *Neanderthal*. Other language choices are more central to the subject matter. Perhaps the most significant choice we have made is with regard to primate classification. Although the primate order historically has been subdivided into anthropoids (the apes and monkeys, including us) and prosimians (the "lower" primates, including lemurs, galagos, lorises, and tarsiers), the majority of scholars today think this dichotomy does not reflect evolutionary reality as well as a subdivision into haplorhines and strepsirhines. Haplorhines include all anthropoids and tarsiers, and strepsirhines include all prosimians except tarsiers. We discuss this distinction in some depth in Chapter 7 and use the terms *strepsirhine* and *haplorhine* rather than *prosimian* and *anthropoid*. In another case, we have opted to use the more traditional family-level designation *hominid* to refer to humans and our ancestors rather than the alternative tribal-level *hominin*, which is less broadly used in the literature. We discuss this classification in Chapter 10.

Regarding Abbreviations and Time Because of the plethora of sometimes conflicting abbreviations used to refer to time throughout the text, we have attempted to spell out time ranges (e.g., "millions of years ago" or "thousands of years ago"). Where this is not feasible, such as in tables, we use the abbreviations most common to anthropology textbooks (*mya* for "millions of years ago" and *kya* for "thousands of years ago"). However, students should note that the standard usage in geology and palaeontology is *Ma* (mega-annum) and *ka* (kilo-annum).

SUPPLEMENTAL RESOURCES

The ancillary materials that accompany *Biological Anthropology* are part of a complete teaching and learning package and have been carefully created to enhance the topics discussed in the text.

Instructor Resource CD-ROM This CD pulls together all the supplements available to instructors, including the Instructor's Resource Manual, PowerPoint Presentations, and Test Item File.

Instructor's Resource Manual For each chapter in the text, this valuable resource provides a detailed outline, list of objectives, discussion questions, and classroom activities.

PowerPoint Presentations This instructor resource contains key points and notes to accompany each chapter in the text.

Test Item File Test questions in multiple-choice and short answer formats are available for each chapter; the answers to all questions are page referenced to the text. The Test Item File is also available electronically as a MyTest.

MyTest A powerful assessment generation program, MyTest helps instructors easily create and print quizzes, tests, and exams. Questions and tests can all be authored online, allowing flexibility and the ability to efficiently manage assessments at anytime, from anywhere.

Companion Website This online study guide provides unique support to help students with their studies in biological anthropology. Featuring a variety of interactive learning tools, including online quizzes with immediate feedback, this site is a comprehensive resource organized according to the chapters in the Canadian edition of *Biological Anthropology*. It can be found at www.pearsoned.ca/stanford.

ACKNOWLEDGMENTS

Textbooks require the collaboration of many people with many areas of expertise, and this book made good use of all those involved. The process begins with each author compiling his or her notes from years of teaching biological anthropology and thinking about how the course could be more effectively taught. Over the years the students in our courses have helped us to assess what did and did not work in conveying the information and excitement of biological anthropology, and for this we are extremely grateful.

For the Canadian edition, Nancy Lovell is grateful to her collaborators at Pearson Education Canada: Christine Cozens, acquisitions editor, and Jennifer Murray, senior developmental editor, for her patience and diplomacy. She owes a debt of gratitude to Kelly Morrison, senior project manager, Deborah Cooper-Bullock, copy editor, and Terri Rothman, picture research and permissions.

For their constructive reviewing of the manuscript of the Canadian edition, we thank the following reviewers:

Miguel Bombin, Laurentian University
Brenda Clark, Camosun College
Julie L. Cormack, Mount Royal College
David Ebert, University of Saskatchewan

Paul A. Erickson, Saint Mary's University
Carol MacLeod, Langara College
Moira McLaughlin, St. Thomas University
Koumari Mitra, University of New Brunswick
Andrew Nelson, University of Western Ontario
Hugh Notman, University of Calgary
Jennifer Ramsay, Simon Fraser University
Michael Schillaci, University of Toronto Scarborough
Sabine Stratton, Kwantlen University College
Jill Taylor-Hollings, Lakehead University
Gary G. Tunnell, Malaspina University College
Jocelyn S. Williams, Trent University

We've made a great effort to produce a comprehensive and fully accurate text, but as in any book's first edition, errors may remain. We would be grateful for comments or corrections from students and instructors using *Biological Anthropology*. And we hope you find this account of human evolution as fascinating and compelling as we do.

Craig Stanford
John S. Allen
Susan C. Antón
Nancy C. Lovell

About the Authors

Craig Stanford is a professor of anthropology and biological sciences at the University of Southern California (USC), where he also directs the Jane Goodall Research Center and chairs the Department of Anthropology. He has conducted field research on primate behaviour in South Asia, Latin America, and East Africa. He is well known for his long-term studies of meat-eating among wild chimpanzees in Gombe, Tanzania, and of the relationship between mountain gorillas and chimpanzees in the Impenetrable Forest of Uganda. He has authored or coauthored more than 100 scientific publications. Craig has received USC's highest teaching awards for his introductory *Biological Anthropology* course. In addition, he has published seven books on primate behaviour and human origins, including *Significant Others* (2001) and *Upright* (2003). He and his wife, Erin Moore, a cultural anthropologist at USC, live in South Pasadena, California, and have three children.

John Allen is a research scientist and adjunct associate professor in the Department of Neurology at the University of Iowa College of Medicine. Previously, he was a faculty member in the Department of Anthropology at the University of Auckland, New Zealand, for several years. His primary research interests are the evolution of the human brain and behaviour, and behavioural disease. He also has research experience in molecular genetics, nutritional anthropology, and the history of anthropology. He has conducted fieldwork in Japan, New Zealand, Papua New Guinea, and Palau. He has received university awards for teaching introductory courses in biological anthropology both as a graduate student instructor at the University of California and as a faculty member at the University of Auckland. John and his wife, Stephanie Sheffield, have two sons, Reid and Perry (the Berry).

Susan Antón is an associate professor in the Center for the Study of Human Origins, Department of Anthropology at New York University, where she also directs the M.A. program in Human Skeletal Biology. Her field research concerns the evolution of genus *Homo* in Indonesia and human impact on island ecosystems in the South Pacific. She is best known for her work on *H. erectus* and dispersal. She is joint editor of the *Journal of Human Evolution*. She received awards for teaching as a graduate student instructor at the University of California and was Teacher of the Year at the University of Florida. She has been twice elected to *Who's Who Among America's Teachers*. Susan and her husband, Carl Swisher, a geochronologist, raise Anatolian shepherd dogs.

Nancy Lovell is a professor of anthropology at the University of Alberta. Her research, funded largely by the Social Sciences and Humanities Research Council of Canada, concerns the skeletal biology of ancient peoples, particularly how their skeletons reveal aspects of the interrelationships between culture, environment, and health. She has excavated ancient cemeteries in Egypt and Pakistan, and has studied human skeletal remains from ancient Egypt and Mesopotamia, the Indus Valley Civilization, and from historic cemeteries of the fur trade period in western Canada. A continuing interest is the expression of trauma and disease in the skeletal remains of free-living apes and monkeys and how this reflects social behaviour and may help us understand selective pressures in primate and hominid evolution. She teaches a variety of courses in biological anthropology, including the evidence for diseases in antiquity, the excavation and analysis of human skeletal remains from archaeological sites, and mortuary archaeology.

A Great Way to Learn and Instruct Online

The Pearson Education Canada Companion Website is easy to navigate and is organized to correspond to the chapters in this textbook. Whether you are a student in the classroom or a distance learner you will discover helpful resources for in-depth study and research that empower you in your quest for greater knowledge and maximize your potential for success in the course.

[www.pearsoned.ca/stanford]

Enter

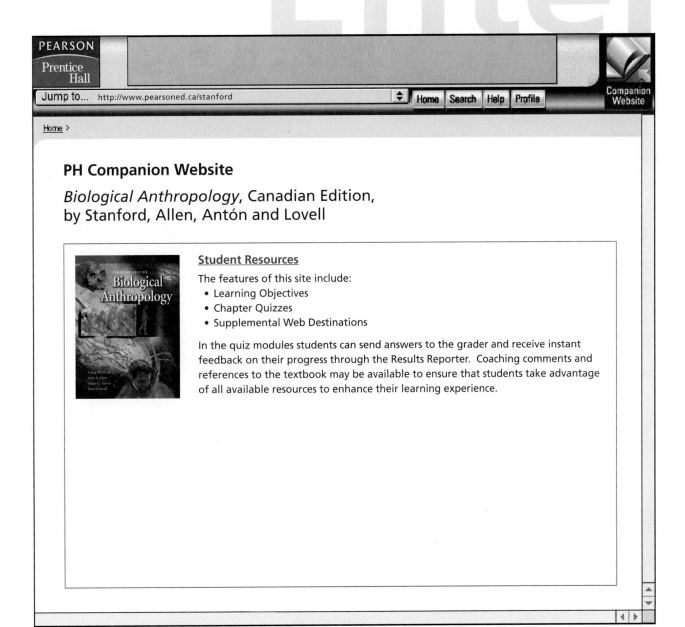

PEARSON Prentice Hall

Jump to... http://www.pearsoned.ca/stanford

Home Search Help Profile

Companion Website

Home >

PH Companion Website

Biological Anthropology, Canadian Edition, by Stanford, Allen, Antón and Lovell

Student Resources

The features of this site include:

- Learning Objectives
- Chapter Quizzes
- Supplemental Web Destinations

In the quiz modules students can send answers to the grader and receive instant feedback on their progress through the Results Reporter. Coaching comments and references to the textbook may be available to ensure that students take advantage of all available resources to enhance their learning experience.

PART I

FOUNDATIONS

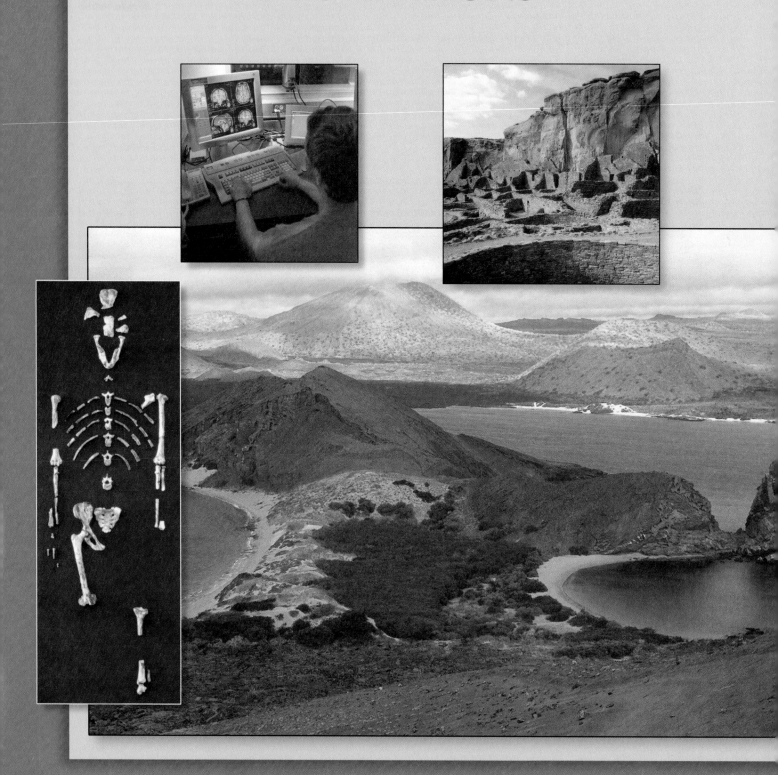

Chapter 1

Introduction: What Is Biological Anthropology?

On a sunny morning in East Africa, with the temperature already climbing past 30° Celsius (90°F), a scientist stands in a shallow pit, carefully examining the dusty ground. All around her are the tools of her trade: shovels, dental picks, whisk brooms, surveying equipment. Something glinting in the morning light catches her eye. She bends over to examine a tiny fragment of whitish bone, then another and another. Realizing that her week of hard, sweaty work has just paid off, she beckons her assistants to see the prize, then carefully begins to map the spot for the work that now begins: unearthing the fossilized skeleton of an ancient primate, perhaps the forerunner of all modern apes. Weeks later, after returning to the capital city and its museum, the scientist compares the new fossils with previously collected specimens. She finds that a few of the pieces her team has excavated fit together with the long-neglected bones of a fossil ape discovered at the site in the 1930s. The scientist devotes long hours to studying every

Chapter Outline

THE SCOPE OF BIOLOGICAL ANTHROPOLOGY

Palaeoanthropology • Skeletal Biology and Human Osteology • Primatology • Human Biology

THE ROOTS OF MODERN BIOLOGICAL ANTHROPOLOGY

BIOLOGICAL ANTHROPOLOGY TODAY

detail of the skeleton. A new picture emerges: This ancient ape may have been the first to come down from the trees and venture forth on the ground below.

A FEW HUNDRED KILOMETRES (MILES) AWAY, another scientist sits in the tall grass of a high mountain meadow. All around him are massive, shaggy-haired mountain gorillas, happily munching on wild celery. A bright-eyed baby gorilla ambles up to the scientist and toys with the laces of his boot, then runs quickly back to its mother. Two silverbacks, majestic 180-kilogram (400-lb) males wearing saddles of grey hair across their backs, sit like enormous statues a few yards away. The scientist uses the tools of his trade: a notebook and checklist to record behaviour, plus a handheld global positioning system unit to map the animals' travels. As the gorilla group finishes its lunch, the silverbacks get up and head off into the forest, bulldozing a trail that the females, babies, and scientist obediently follow.

AT THE SAME TIME, HALF A WORLD AWAY, a third scientist is sitting in a laboratory intently studying a computer monitor. He looks at a three-dimensional, high-resolution image of a human brain. Millimetre by millimetre, he examines the frontal lobe, a region of the brain thought to be of key importance in the evolution of modern people. By moving the screen cursor slightly, he can study the brain's surface from every possible angle, making virtual slices through it to study its internal organization. Unlike skulls, brains do not become preserved as fossils, so the scientist uses images of the brains of living humans and other primates to reconstruct the way in which the brains of long-dead ancestors may have been organized.

What do these three scientists—one studying ancient fossils, another observing primate behaviour, and the third studying the evolution of the human brain—have in common? They are biological anthropologists, engaged in the scientific study of humankind (from *anthropos*, meaning human, and *-ology*, the study of). Despite our exalted intellect, our mind-boggling technology, and our intricately complex social behaviour, we are nonetheless biological creatures. Humans are primates and share a recent ancestry with the living great apes. Like the apes, we are the products of millions of years of evolution by natural selection.

The famed geneticist Theodosius Dobzhansky once said, "Nothing in biology makes sense except in the light of evolution." Biological anthropologists spend their careers trying to understand the details of the evolutionary process and the ways in which the process has shaped who we are today. They use a central, unifying set of biological principles in their work, first set down by Charles Darwin nearly 150 years ago. The frequency of a particular trait and the genes that control it can change from one generation to the next; this is **evolution**. This elegantly simple idea forms the heart and soul of **biological anthropology**.

The evolutionary process usually is slow and inefficient, but over many generations it can mould animals and plants into a bewildering variety of forms. Our ancestry includes many animals that little resemble us today. Biological anthropology is particularly concerned with the evolutionary transformations that occurred over the past 6 million years, as an apelike **primate** began to walk on two legs and became something different: a **hominid**. From the perspective of evolutionary theory, humans are like all other biological species, the product of the same long process of **adaptation**.

THE SCOPE OF BIOLOGICAL ANTHROPOLOGY

The scope of biological anthropology is vastly wider than the study of primates, fossils, and brain evolution. Any scientist studying evolution as it relates to the human species, directly or indirectly, could be called a biological anthropologist. This includes a number of related disciplines.

PALAEOANTHROPOLOGY

When an exciting new fossil of an extinct form of human is found, palaeoanthropologists usually are responsible (Figure 1.1). **Palaeoanthropology** is the study of the fossil record for humankind, and fossilized remains are the direct physical evidence of human ancestry. The discovery of skeletal evidence of new ancestral species, or additional specimens of existing species, revises our view of the human family tree. Discoveries of hominid fossils—some as famous as Peking Man or Lucy (Figure 1.2) but many less known—have profoundly changed the way we view our place in nature. Palaeoanthropology also includes the study of the fossil record of the other primates—apes, monkeys, and prosimians—dating back at least 65 million years. These early fossils give us key clues about how, where, and why hominids evolved millions of years later. There are fossil sites producing important fossils all over the world, and with more and more students and researchers searching, our fossil history grows richer every year. In fact, although the first half of the twentieth century witnessed discoveries of new human fossils every decade or so, the pace of discovery of new species of fossil humans has accelerated rapidly in recent years. This is because more students and researchers are searching for fossils and because global and regional political changes have allowed researchers into areas that were long off limits because of civil war or political unrest.

Palaeoanthropological research begins in the field, where researchers search the landscape for new discoveries. Much of the scholarly work then takes place in museums and university laboratories around the world, where the specimens are archived and preserved for detailed study. Because we can safely assume that the evolutionary process taking place in the present also took place in the past, the study of the meaning of human and nonhuman primate fossils proceeds from comparisons between extinct and living forms. For example, the presence of large canine teeth in the male specimens of a fossil monkey species implies that in life, the species lived in multiple male groups in which males competed for mates, because major differences in canine tooth size between males and females indicates mate competition in living monkeys.

evolution A change in the frequency of a gene or a trait in a population over multiple generations.

biological anthropology The study of humans as biological organisms, considered in an evolutionary framework; sometimes called physical anthropology.

primate Member of the mammalian order Primates, including prosimians, monkeys, apes, and humans, defined by a suite of anatomical and behavioural traits.

hominid A member of the primate family Hominidae, distinguished by bipedal posture and, in more recently evolved species, large brain.

adaptation A trait that increases the reproductive success of an organism, produced by natural selection in the context of a particular environment.

palaeoanthropology The study of the fossil record of ancestral humans and their primate kin.

FIGURE 1.1 Palaeoanthropologist Jane Moore maps sites at Kanapoi, Kenya.

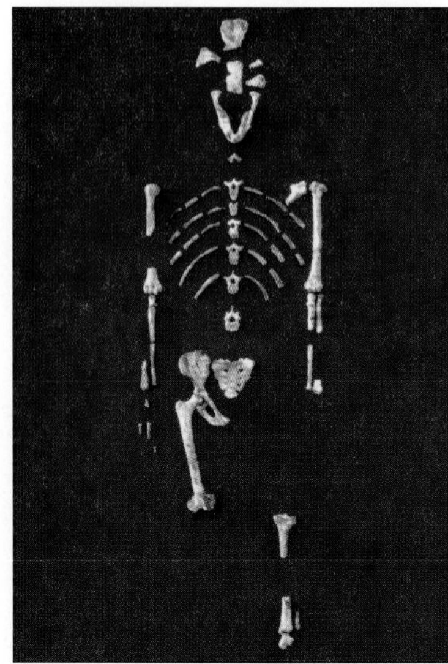

FIGURE 1.2 Lucy, a partial hominid skeleton.

As the fossil record has grown, we have begun to see that the evolutionary history of our species is extremely complicated; most lineages are now extinct, but many thrived for millions of years. The ladder of progress notion—an older, more linear view of our ancestry in which each species evolved into more complex forms—has been replaced by a family tree with many branches.

SKELETAL BIOLOGY AND HUMAN OSTEOLOGY

Osteology is the study of the skeleton. The first order of business when a fossil is discovered is to figure out what sort of animal the fossil—often a tiny fragment—may have been in life, so osteologists must possess extraordinary skills of identification and a keen spatial sense of how a jigsaw puzzlelike array of bone chips fits together when they are trying to understand the meaning of fossils they have found (Figure 1.3).

Among the first generation of biological anthropologists were the *anthropometrists*, who made detailed measurements of the human body in all its forms, and their work is still important today. Understanding the relationship between genetics, human growth and stature, and geographic variation in human anatomy is vital to identifying the origins and patterns of human migration across the globe during prehistory, for example. When a 9000-year-old skeleton was discovered some years ago on the banks of the Columbia River in the Pacific Northwest, osteologists with expertise in human variation in body form were among those who sought to identify its biological affinities.

Skeletal biology and osteology are terms that often are used interchangeably. In the past, osteologists were concerned mainly with visually observable anatomical features, but they now have a broader focus that includes an understanding of the patterns and processes of human growth, physiology, and development, including bone chemistry and cellular processes.

Palaeopathology, a specialization within skeletal biology, is the study of disease in ancient human populations, as evidenced by telltale signs on the skeleton. Palaeopathologists are interested in research questions such as the effects of status differences on health and nutrition, evidence for interpersonal violence in past societies, and how sedentism and increased population density can affect the patterns of infectious disease.

osteology The study of the skeleton.

palaeopathology The study of diseases in ancestral human populations.

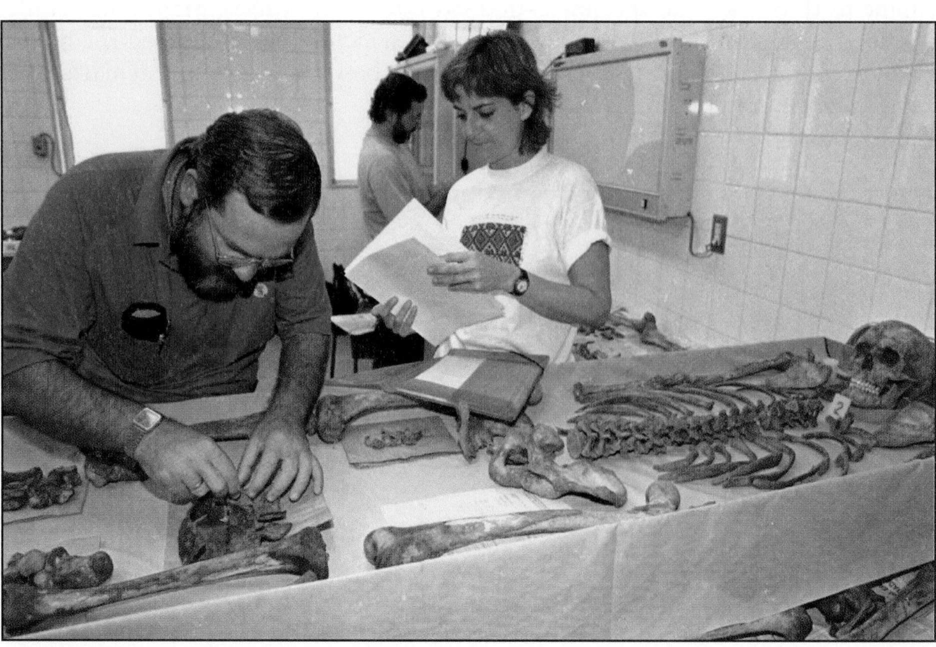

FIGURE 1.3 An osteologist at work.

Biological anthropologists also play roles in our daily lives. **Forensic anthropology** is another specialization within skeletal biology and is a contemporary application of biological anthropology. Forensic anthropologists apply the same methods and knowledge that are used to determine the sex and estimate the age at death of an ancient skeleton to historical and criminal investigations (Figure 1.4). During the war crime investigations into mass graves in Bosnia, forensic anthropologists were called in to help identify victims, as they also were after the terrorists' attacks in New York, Washington, and Pennsylvania on September 11, 2001 (Figure 1.5).

PRIMATOLOGY

Primatology is the branch of biological anthropology that is best known to the public through the highly publicized work of renowned primatologists Jane Goodall, Dian Fossey, and Biruté Galdikas. Primatologists study the anatomy, physiology, behaviour, and genetics of both living and extinct monkeys, apes, and prosimians. Behavioural studies of nonhuman primates in their natural environments gained prominence in the 1960s and 1970s, when the pioneering work of Jane Goodall was publicized widely in the United States and elsewhere. In the early days of primate behaviour study, the researchers were mainly psychologists. Behavioural studies of nonhuman primates in their natural environments, as opposed to zoos and laboratories, gained prominence during the 1960s and by the late 1960s biological anthropology had become the domain of primate behaviour study, especially in North America.

Primatologists study nonhuman primates for a variety of reasons, including the desire to learn more about their intrinsically fascinating patterns of behaviour (Figure 1.6). Within an anthropological framework, primatologists study the nonhuman primates for the lessons they can provide on how evolution has moulded the human species. For example, male baboons fight among themselves for the chance to mate with females. They are also much larger and more aggressive than females. Do larger, more macho males father more offspring than their smaller and gentler brothers? If so, these traits seem to have appeared slowly through generations of evolutionary change, and the size difference between males and females is the result of selection for large body size. Then, what about the body size difference between men and women of our own species? Is it the result of competition between men in prehistory, or perhaps a preference by women in prehistory for tall men? The clues that we derive about human nature

forensic anthropology The study of human remains applied to a legal context.

primatology The study of the nonhuman primates and their anatomy, genetics, behaviour, and ecology.

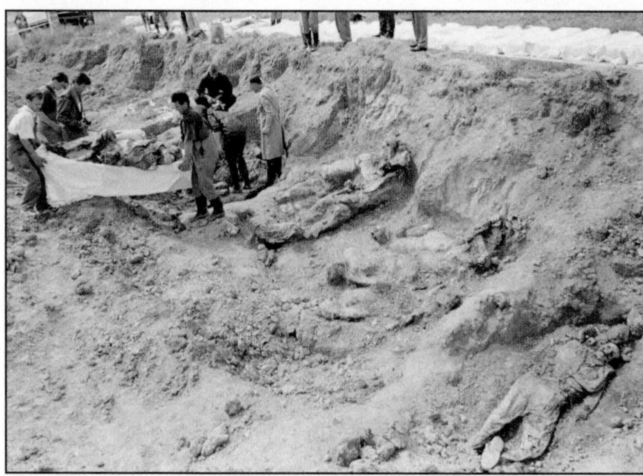

FIGURE 1.4 Forensic anthropologists help to identify victims of war in Bosnia.

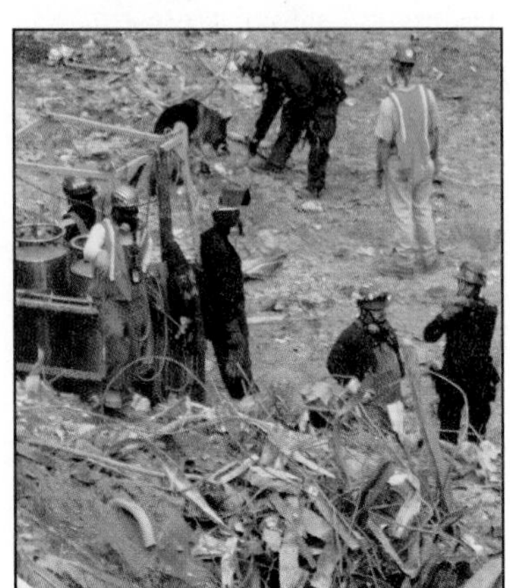

FIGURE 1.5 Recovery team at work at the World Trade Center Ground Zero following the September 11, 2001, attack.

from the behaviour and anatomy of living primates must be interpreted cautiously but can be vitally important in our understanding of who we are and where we came from.

Biological anthropologists trained as primatologists find careers not only in universities but also in museums, zoos, and conservation agencies. Many important wildlife conservation projects seeking to protect endangered primate species are being carried out around the world by biological anthropologists.

HUMAN BIOLOGY

In addition to palaeoanthropology and primatology, biological anthropologists span a wide range of interests that are often labelled **human biology**. Some work in the area of *human adaptation*, learning how people adjust physiologically to the extremes of Earth's physical environments. For instance, how are children affected by growing up high in the Andes mountain range of South America at elevations over 4270 metres (14 000 ft)? Other human biologists work as *nutritional anthropologists*, studying the interrelationship of diet, culture, and evolution. Biological anthropologists interested in demography examine the biological and cultural forces that shape the composition of human populations. Other biological anthropologists are particularly interested in how various hormones in the human body influence human behaviour and how, in turn, the environment affects the expression of these hormones. The study of *human variation* deals with the many ways in which people differ in their anatomy throughout the world.

human biology Subfield of biological anthropology dealing with human growth and development, adaptation to environmental extremes, and human genetics.

At an earlier time in history, the scholarly study of physical traits such as height, skull shape, and especially skin colour was tainted with the possibility that researchers had some racially biased preconceptions. Today, biological anthropologists are interested in human variation, both anatomical and genetic, because it offers clues about the evolution and adaptation of the human species. For example, understanding when, where, and how people left Africa and colonized Europe, Asia, and eventually the New World can tell us a great deal about the roots of modern languages, diseases, population genetics, and other topics of great relevance in the world today.

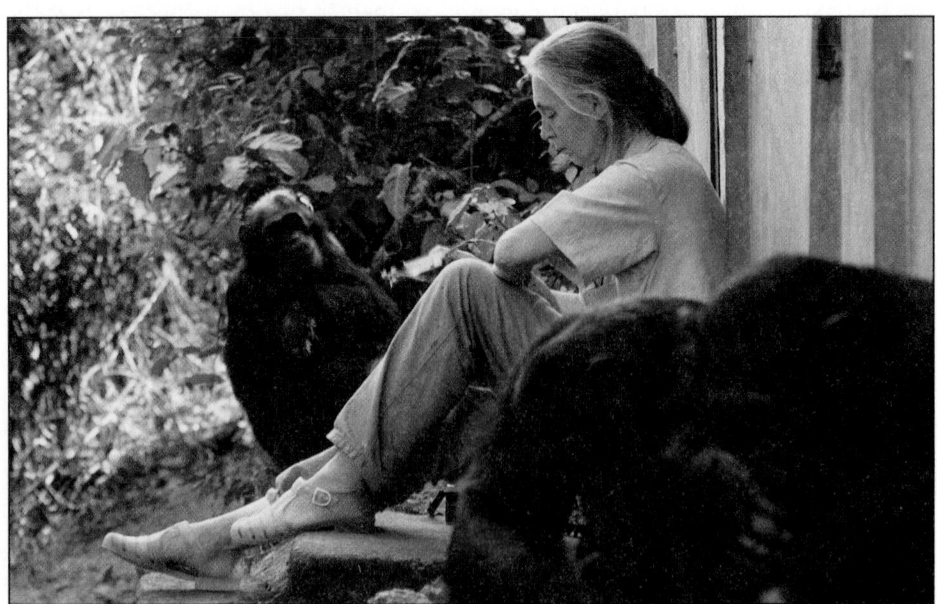

FIGURE 1.6 Jane Goodall is a pioneering primatologist whose studies of wild chimpanzees changed our view of human nature.

Many contemporary biological anthropologists are interested in research problems that require an understanding of both biological and cultural factors. Biological anthropologists with these interests sometimes are called *biocultural anthropologists*. One area in which a biocultural perspective is vitally important is *biomedical anthropology* (Figure 1.7). Biomedical anthropologists might study how human cultural practices influence the spread of infectious disease and how the effects of pollution or toxins in the environment affect human growth. Biomedical anthropologists are particularly interested in looking at the effects that adopting an urbanized (and Western) lifestyle has on people who have lived until recently under more traditional, non-Western conditions. The expression of many human diseases is influenced by genetic factors, and biomedical anthropologists often look at the long-term evolutionary consequences of disease on human populations.

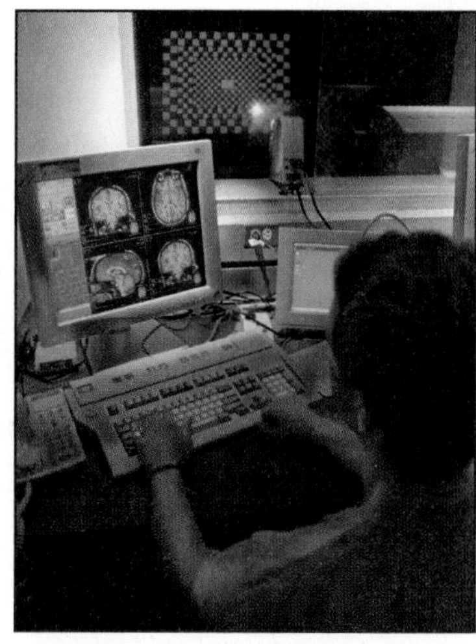

FIGURE 1.7 Biomedical anthropologists study, among other things, the human brain.

Finally, an increasing number of biological anthropologists work in the field of genetics (Figure 1.8). *Molecular anthropology* is a genetic approach to human evolutionary science that seeks to understand the differences in the genome between humans and their closest relatives, the nonhuman primates. Because genetic inheritance is the basis for evolutionary change, a geneticist is in a perfect position to be able to address some of the fundamental questions about human nature and human evolution. We know that the human DNA sequence is extremely similar to that of an ape, but what exactly does this mean? At which points do the differences result in some key shift, such as language? These are some of the questions that may be answerable in the very near future with the help of anthropological geneticists.

THE ROOTS OF MODERN BIOLOGICAL ANTHROPOLOGY

In 1856, the fossil of an ancient human ("Neandertal Man") was discovered in Germany (Schaaffhausen, 1858). Three years later, Charles Darwin published *On the Origin of Species*. Darwin's work had a greater immediate impact than the Neandertal's appearance because it was some time before scientists agreed that the Neandertal was an ancient human rather than just an odd-looking modern one. Darwin's introduction of an evolutionary perspective made many of the old debates about human origins irrelevant. After Darwin, scientists no longer needed to debate whether humans originated via a single creation or the different races were created separately (*monogenism* versus *polygenism*); the study of the natural history of humans became centred on the evolutionary history of our species. Human variation was the product of the interaction between the biological organism and the environment. Apes and monkeys—the nonhuman primates—became our "cousins" almost overnight.

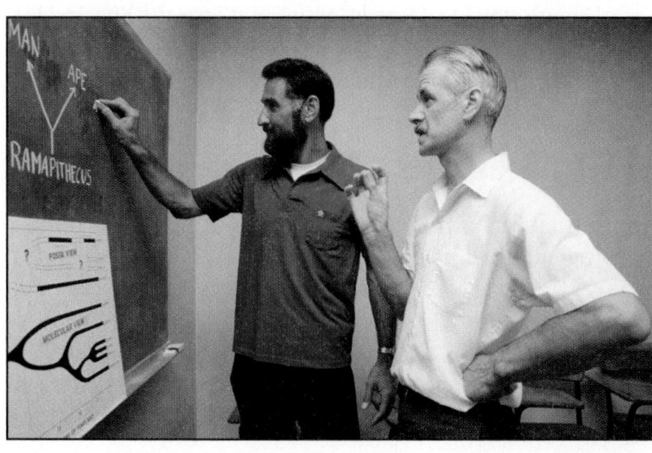

FIGURE 1.8 Vincent Sarich and Allan Wilson helped pioneer the molecular anthropological approach to studying primate and human evolution.

The field known in North America as **physical anthropology** was established as an academic discipline in the second half of the nineteenth century (Spencer, 1997). In France, Germany, and England, it was called simply *anthropology*. Most early physical anthropologists were physicians who taught anatomy in medical schools and had an interest in human variation or evolution. In the first half of the twentieth century, much of physical anthropology was devoted to measuring bodies and skulls (*anthropometry* and *craniometry*), with particular attention paid to the biological definition of human races. Physical anthropologists also studied the comparative anatomy of nonhuman primates and the limited fossil record of humans and other primates.

By the mid-twentieth century, a new physical anthropology emerged, led by a generation of scholars who were trained as anthropologists first and foremost and who in turn trained hundreds of graduate students who benefited from the expansion of higher education fuelled by the Baby Boom generation. The new physical anthropology, whose main architect was Sherwood Washburn of the University of Chicago and later of the University of California, Berkeley, embraced the dynamic view of evolution promoted by the adherents of the neo-Darwinian synthesis. This synthesis of genetics, anatomy, ecology, and behaviour with evolutionary theory emerged in the biological sciences in the 1930s and 1940s. In the new physical anthropology, primates were not simply shot and dissected; their behaviour and ecology were studied in the natural environment as well as in the laboratory (Goodall, 1963). The study of human races as pigeonholed categories gave way to the study of evolving populations, with a particular emphasis on how human populations adapt to environmental conditions. The field of palaeoanthropology was revolutionized by the introduction of new dating techniques and the adoption of a multidisciplinary approach to understanding ancient environments. Molecular genetics research in anthropology gave us a whole new way to reconstruct the biological histories of human populations and of primate species as a whole (Goodman, 1962; Sarich and Wilson, 1967).

Today, biological anthropology embraces a wide variety of approaches with the goal of answering a few basic questions: What does it mean to be human? How did we become who we are today? How does our biological past influence our lives in the environments of the present? What is the place of human beings in nature?

As we will see in the coming chapters, the interplay between biology and culture provides many of the most intriguing and perplexing clues about the roots of our humanity. It also creates many of the most intense debates. For example, for decades scholars have debated whether genes or the environment have played the more important role in moulding intelligence and other human qualities.

The dichotomy between biological and cultural influences on humankind is a false one, as we examine in detail later in the book. In earliest humans, biological evolution produced the capacity for culture: Intelligence had to evolve before learned traditions such as tool using could flourish, as we see in wild apes today. Our biology produced culture, but culture can also influence biology. We study these patterns under the rubric of **biocultural anthropology**.

physical anthropology The study of humans as biological organisms, considered in an evolutionary framework. Now also referred to as biological anthropology.

biocultural anthropology The study of the interaction between biology and culture, which plays a role in most human traits.

BIOLOGICAL ANTHROPOLOGY TODAY

Anthropologists no longer limit themselves to academic studies of people in remote corners of the world, and biological anthropologists are no exception. Biological anthropologists who undertake field studies of African hunter-gatherers with purely academic scholarly research questions in mind often become advocates for indigenous people. Because local people who cannot read or write usually lack the ability to speak out effectively against their government, biological anthropologists often end up on the front line of efforts to protect the culture, language, and way of life of

Box 1.1 A Paradigm Split in Anthropology?

A *paradigm* is a conceptual framework that allows scholars to make sense of existing information. It is the rules and methods by which a scientist works. Newtonian physics is a paradigm; so is Freudian psychology. Darwin's theory of evolution is the paradigm anthropologists have used for a century and a half to make sense of the natural world. But in the first decade of the twenty-first century, the field of anthropology is experiencing sharp growing pains. Many cultural anthropologists have come to reject biological influences on human behaviour, and a debate over paradigms has ensued. During most of the twentieth century, all anthropologists shared a common mindset: that we can study human societies scientifically by gathering information about them and testing ideas in much the same way that scientists in other fields work. In the 1960s, a cultural anthropologist might have gone off to rural Africa to spend a year studying the religious practices and beliefs of a tribal culture there; she made an educated guess about the reasons that a given religious ritual was performed and then collected data to test her hypothesis or idea. She would then come home and write a book that would become the authoritative work on the subject, partly because the culture she studied would not have had literate scholars of its own.

In the past decade, there has been a movement to reconsider the role that the anthropologist plays in describing a culture. A white male anthropologist from an urban background will have a very different perspective on the culture under study than a Black female anthropologist from a rural background. If these two anthropologists, both highly trained in the practice of ethnography, see the same culture differently, what does this say about the notion of objective science? The view that scholarly study is subject to the biases inherent in the background and philosophy of the researcher is part of a worldview called *postmodernism*, in which a new age of scholars seek to "deconstruct" the conclusions of an earlier generation of anthropologists. The benefit of this approach is the open acknowledgement that an observer brings his or her own background into a scientific question. We are never fully objective observers of events around us: Postmodernists reflect on their own role in these events and in how they tend to interpret them. Postmodernism has had a profound impact on how cultural anthropology and the other subfields of anthropology are practised today in North America and abroad. It has meant that some of the new generation's cultural scholars regard the time-honoured ethnographies of the past with scepticism. One healthy result has been an increase in importance of ethnographies written by minority scholars, especially those who are from the culture they study.

The result of this paradigm shift is that many anthropology departments in Canadian universities are split between cultural and biological approaches to their research. Biological anthropologists are universally empirical, testing hypotheses within an objective scientific framework. Many cultural anthropologists now reject this framework, preferring to interpret what they see in other cultures in light of issues of power, gender, and ethnicity.

Although some see this split as a natural outgrowth of the fields, most anthropologists savour the cross-fertilization of ideas that occurs when cultural and biological perspectives are present in the same academic program.

such groups, whether they are hunter-gatherers in the Amazon basin or war refugees in central Africa.

Likewise, some of the most important primate conservation projects, such as the protection of mountain gorillas in Rwanda or chimpanzees across Africa, began as the result of long-term field studies by anthropologists, who later became environmental activists. Today, as tropical forests are felled at an increasing rate and primates everywhere are threatened with imminent extinction, primatologists often form the backbone of tropical forest conservation efforts, working with conservation groups and local governments to set aside protected land for the long-term preservation of primate biodiversity. For example, primatologist Karen Strier began a study of one of the most endangered primates in the world, the muriqui of the Atlantic coastal forests of Brazil, as a graduate student at Harvard University. Some 20 years later, she continues to conduct research at the same site but has also helped to persuade the local landowners, as well as the Brazilian government, to actively help ensure the continued survival of the species.

Palaeoanthropologists often are as active in preservation movements to protect the natural fossil heritage of the countries in which they work as they are in the research itself. And geneticists, while probing the mysteries of the DNA molecule, contribute to important advances in biomedical research. Applied biological anthropologists with training in forensic techniques were deeply involved in the recovery efforts at Ground Zero of the World Trade Center after the terrorist attacks of September 11, 2001. These efforts, and many others like them, are an essential part of what biological anthropologists do in the modern world.

SUMMARY

1. **How is anthropology different from other disciplines that involve the study of humankind?**

   Anthropology is the study of humankind in a cross-cultural perspective. Anthropologists study cultures in far-flung places, and they also study subcultures in our own society, typically immersing themselves in other cultures in ways scholars in other disciplines do not.

2. **What exactly is culture, and why do anthropologists care so much about it?**

   Culture is a set of learned behaviour traditions. Every human group has its own distinctive culture, which includes its collective values and beliefs. Our capacity for culture itself is biological, and the evolution of intelligence in humans that allowed us to learn much of our behaviour is a defining feature of our humanity.

3. **How does biological anthropology differ from the other subfields of anthropology?**

   Biological anthropology is the study of humans as biological creatures. It is the study of where we came from, our evolution, and how our biology interacts with our culture today. Biological anthropology is one of anthropology's four subfields, along with archaeology, cultural anthropology, and linguistic anthropology.

4. **What is the central unifying theory of biological anthropology?**

CRITICAL THINKING QUESTIONS

1. For centuries, people have argued about whether biology or culture is the more important influence on human behaviour, intelligence, and a wide range of other human qualities. This has sometimes been called the genes–environment debate or the nature–nurture debate. Why is the dichotomy between biology and culture a false one? Considering any human trait, from aggression to intelligence to courtship, how might human biology and culture interact with each other?

2. How might a forensic anthropologist be useful to a palaeoanthropologist? Can you think of other special training, apart from that described in this chapter, that someone studying the human fossil record might want to have to more fully understand what he or she is studying?

KEY TERMS

evolution	adaptation	forensic anthropology
biological anthropology	palaeoanthropology	primatology
primate	osteology	human biology
hominid	palaeopathology	physical anthropology

SUGGESTED READING

Darwin, Charles. (1859). *On the Origin of Species by Means of Natural Selection; or, The Preservation of Favoured Races in the Struggle for Life*. Murray, London, England.

Mead, Margaret. (1972). *Blackberry Winter: My Earlier Years*. William Morrow & Company, New York, NY.

Spencer, Frank. (1997). *History of Physical Anthropology*. Routledge, New York, NY.

Chapter 2

Origins of Evolutionary Thought

Chapter Outline

IN 2005, PROFESSOR BRIAN ALTERS of McGill University in Montreal took the stand as an expert witness in a high-profile U.S. federal trial, *Kitzmiller et al. v. the Dover District Board of Education*, in which a heated debate about the nature of public education and science had erupted. The town of Dover, Pennsylvania, had become a battleground in the war that *creationists* (people who prefer religious explanations for the origins of humankind) have waged against the teaching of evolution in public schools. A specialist in science education, Professor Alters was among several experts to testify that the theory of intelligent design (see Box 2.1) was not a scientific theory. The legal battle ended when the judge concluded that intelligent design was based on theology, not science, and thus it could not be taught in a science classroom because the United States Constitution separates the workings of church and state. Repeated United States Supreme Court rulings have held that the teaching of theological beliefs in public school science classrooms is unconstitutional. The U.S. courts have also stated that evolution is the unifying principle of the life sciences, without valid competition in a science curriculum from theological explanations.

IN CANADA, THE ROLE OF RELIGION in public education has also garnered some debate. Attempts to introduce religion into the public school system have been legally opposed in Canada also, but the reasoning for the opposition in Canada is different from the reasoning in the United States. Separation of the workings of the church and government is not part of the Canadian constitutional experience; however, according to the *Canadian Charter of Rights and Freedoms* one religion must not be given a position of dominance in a public school (although some provinces subsidize religious schools through the historical precedents set by the laws in place when they joined Confederation) and so the multicultural realities of Canadian society are protected in school curricula and practices throughout the country. For example, Canadian courts have ruled that requiring students to recite the Lord's Prayer, a Christian practice, violates the rights of students who are not Christians or who do not wish to practise their religion in public.

For centuries, people considered the Earth to be young and life on it to be unchanging. Perhaps this is because the reality of evolutionary change is inconceivable to some people. You can't see it, touch it, or sense it happening in any way, unlike more easily perceived physical laws such as gravity. The 80-year human life span is far too short to watch evolution, a process that typically happens on a scale of thousands of years. The enormous time scale of evolution is one reason that religious fundamentalists in North America argue that evolution is "only a theory," and therefore they campaign for equal time in public schools for biblical explanations for the origins of life and humankind. As we shall see in this chapter, evolution is a theoretical framework that is the only way to make sense of the tremendous amount of evidence that surrounds us. Fossilized dinosaur bones and ancient hominid skulls are evidence of evolution. But so are a disease's resistance to antibiotics and a pest's resistance to pesticides.

In this chapter we will examine the history of ideas about how life came to be and the proponents and opponents of evolutionary theory and fact.

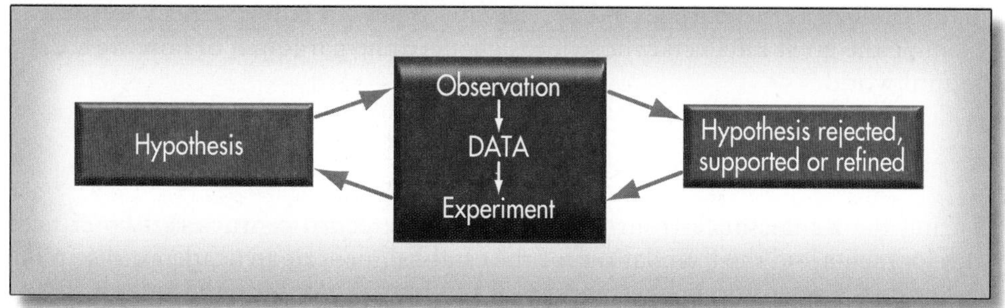

FIGURE 2.1 The Scientific Method.

We will also consider the issue of creationist opposition to evolutionary science. Biological anthropologists, as human evolutionary scientists, often find themselves on the front line of the debate between science and creation. First, we need to consider what science is and how it works.

WHAT IS SCIENCE?

Science is a process, not a result. The process involves **deduction** and **observation**, formulating a **hypothesis** or preliminary explanation, testing, and **experimentation**, or the collection of evidence (**data**) that either supports or refutes the hypothesis. This is the **scientific method** (Figure 2.1). It is the way scientists proceed when they have a question that needs answering or a possible explanation for a natural phenomenon that needs testing. Suppose a scientist proposes that the reason that humans walk upright and apes do not is that walking upright uses less energy (in the form of calories burned) per kilometre (mile) of walking, thereby giving early humans who stood up to walk an advantage over their ape ancestors (Rodman and McHenry, 1980). This is the hypothesis. The scientist would then gather quantitative evidence—the data—to test this hypothesis. He might compare the caloric output of two-legged and four-legged walking by having a human and a chimpanzee walk on a treadmill while measuring the oxygen consumption of each. If chimpanzees were discovered to be less efficient walkers than humans, then the hypothesis would be supported. Of course, there are always alternative hypotheses; perhaps another researcher would argue that chimpanzees are *more* efficient walkers than other four-legged animals, in which case a whole new study that measures the walking efficiency of many other animals will be needed before the first researcher can truly stake his claim.

Science is an empirical process that relies on evidence and experimentation. Science is not a perfect process, because data can be subject to differences in interpretation. But science has the essential property of being *self-correcting*. If one scientist claims to have found evidence that the Earth is flat but others claim it is round, this question can be resolved by examining all the data, which can be published for the scientific world to scrutinize. If the data supporting the flat-Earth hypothesis are weak and the weight of scientific evidence indicates that Earth is round, the flat-Earth research will be ignored or overturned. In other words, the hypothesis that the Earth is flat is **falsifiable**. Such falsifiability is a defining trait of science. It means that a scientist rarely claims to have "proven" anything. Instead, results are presented and a hypothesis is either supported or rejected. Falsifiability is also a primary reason why science is such a powerful way to understand the world around us: The opportunity always exists for others to come along and correct earlier mistakes. This can be a long, slow process. Once a **paradigm**—a conceptual framework useful for understanding a body of evidence—is in place, it may take a great deal of conflicting evidence and debate between scientists before

deduction A conclusion that follows logically from a set of observations.

observation The gathering of scientific information by watching a phenomenon.

hypothesis A preliminary explanation of a phenomenon. Hypothesis formation is the first step of the scientific method.

experimentation The testing of a hypothesis.

data The scientific evidence produced by an experiment or by observation, from which scientific conclusions are made.

scientific method Standard scientific research procedure in which a hypothesis is stated, data are collected to test it, and the hypothesis is either supported or refuted.

falsifiable Can be shown to be false.

paradigm A conceptual framework useful for understanding a body of evidence.

that paradigm is overturned and replaced by a new one. In the next section we examine the great intellects whose ideas changed the paradigm of how we see the natural world.

THE ROOTS OF MODERN SCIENCE

During the Renaissance (fourteenth through sixteenth centuries), two critical developments laid the foundation for the establishment of an academic discipline devoted to a scientific understanding of the human condition (Hodgen, 1964; Rowe, 1965). First, Renaissance scholars developed a strong sense of time, their own past, and the process whereby that past is reconstructed. They also developed a sense of cultural variation as they came to realize that the people of antiquity were not like them.

Second, the Renaissance coincided with the first circumnavigation of the globe and the European discovery and exploration of the New World. European naturalists got their first look at thousands of exotic plant and animal species at about the same time that they were trying to be more systematic and accurate in describing the natural world around them. Europeans were exposed to a greater range of human variation, both biological and cultural, than they ever knew existed. Questions were raised as to the basic humanity of First Nations peoples: Did they possess souls? Could their origins be traced to Adam and Eve and the Garden of Eden? Could they be converted to Christianity? The church was definitive on this issue: By proclamation of Pope Paul III in 1537, the Indians of the New World were declared to be, in the eyes of the church, "truly men," sharing a common creation with all other men. This was used as the rationale for converting the First Nations peoples to Christianity. The declaration that the people of the New World were indeed people, however, did not prevent their enslavement or exploitation by Christian colonizers.

If most natural historians and philosophers of the time believed that there was a single creation event, when did they think this happened? Anglican Archbishop James Ussher (1581–1656) calculated the date of the creation of Earth using the only evidence of the age of Earth available to him: the Old Testament of the Bible. By counting backward using the ages of the main characters as given in the books of the Old Testament, Ussher arrived at 4004 BC as the year of the creation. Although it sounds a bit silly today, Ussher had no other chronological evidence available to him. He knew that Adam had lived to a ripe old age and begat Cain and Abel; the cumulative ages of these founders and all their descendants added up to about a 5500-year history of the world. Ussher's date provided the timeframe for understanding the natural history of Earth for more than two centuries and to this day is accepted by fundamentalist Christian creationists as a reasonably accurate estimate for the age of Earth.

During this period of European history the church exerted enormous influence over scientific thinking. When Italian mathematician Galileo Galilei (1564–1642) turned his homemade telescope to the night sky in 1609 and saw that the giant planet Jupiter had four large moons orbiting it, he immediately realized that he had proof of Copernicus' sun-centred theory of a century earlier. The universe was not, as church doctrine held, Earth-centred and stationary; the planets of the solar system were obviously in orbit around our sun. But believing this was heresy, and Galileo spent years under house arrest by order of the pope for publishing his findings in 1610. The law of the church was simple and steadfast: God created Earth and everything on it, and life on Earth had remained unchanged since the moment of the creation.

Over time, with the advent of more powerful telescopes and with the work on motion and gravity by German mathematician and astronomer Johannes Kepler

(1571–1630) and English physicist Isaac Newton (1642–1727), it became more difficult for the church to argue against the burgeoning evidence of a sun-centred solar system constantly in orbital motion. The official doctrine that humans were the centre of creation and that all forms of life existed today in the form they always had, however, remained firmly entrenched.

FIGURE 2.2 Carolus Linnaeus.

LINNAEUS AND THE NATURAL SCHEME OF LIFE

In the seventeenth and eighteenth centuries, naturalists became more concerned with developing classification schemes for naming and organizing plants and animals. Nevertheless, they did not part company with the theological view of a static, unchanging world and supported the notion of the basic unity of humankind via monogenesis, the Biblical orthodoxy that all humans were derived from a single creation. The classification scheme we use in the biological sciences today (now called the *Linnaean system*) dates from this period.

Anglican minister John Ray (1627–1705) was the first naturalist to use the terms *genus* and *species* to designate types of animals and plants. Later, Carolus Linnaeus (1707–1778), an eminent Swedish botanist (Figure 2.2), used the physical characteristics of plants and animals to assign them to a scheme of classification. The science of classifying and naming living things that Linnaeus invented is called **taxonomy**. Sorting organisms into categories was a vital way to make sense of their patterns of relationship, so he applied a hierarchy of names to the categories of similarity, which today we call the Linnaean hierarchy. The two-level genus-species labels, or **binomial nomenclature**, were at the heart of taxonomy; a **taxon** is any group of organisms in one division of this formal hierarchy. Linnaeus followed the naming pattern of the ancient Greeks by using Greek and Latin languages for his scheme. But Linnaeus was intellectually hidebound by his theology. He believed firmly in the immutability of species—that each species existed as a completely separate entity from every other species and that God fixed these separations. Influenced further by his belief that apes and humans could not be closely related by common descent, Linnaeus assigned people to the family Hominidae and great apes to the family Pongidae. This separation stands to this day although, as we shall see, it may not be justifiable on biological grounds.

taxonomy The science of biological classification.

binomial nomenclature Linnaean naming system for all organisms, consisting of a genus and species label.

taxon A group of organisms assigned to a particular category.

THE ROAD TO THE DARWINIAN REVOLUTION

In the eighteenth and early nineteenth century, a number of European natural historians made their mark by explaining the nature of the diversity of flora and fauna on Earth. Some of these people directly influenced Darwin's thinking decades later; most were also following in Linnaeus' taxonomic footsteps. Prominent among these were three eminent French natural historians.

Comte de Buffon Georges-Louis Leclerc, Comte de Buffon (1707–1788) accepted the notion of biological change in general. Buffon (Figure 2.3) observed that animals that migrate to new climates often change in response to new environments; although like others of his day he knew no specifics about the mechanism of change. He famously claimed that the animals of the New World were weaker and smaller than their counterparts in the Old World, a result of a generally less healthy and productive environment. Thomas Jefferson vigorously refuted this claim in his *Notes on the State of Virginia* (1787).

FIGURE 2.3 Comte de Buffon.

Georges Cuvier By the turn of the nineteenth century, discoveries of dinosaur bones across western Europe had made it difficult for biblically driven scholars

FIGURE 2.4 Georges Cuvier.

catastrophism Theory that there have been multiple creations interspersed by great natural disasters such as Noah's flood.

theory of inheritance of acquired characteristics Discredited theory of evolutionary change proposing that changes that occur during the lifetime of an individual, through use or disuse, can be passed on to the next generation.

Lysenkoism Soviet-era research program that tried to apply Lamarckian thinking to agricultural production.

FIGURE 2.5
Jean-Baptiste Lamarck.

to continue to deny the importance of change to the history of Earth. Georges Cuvier (born Jean-Léopold Cuvier; 1769–1832) rose rapidly in the ranks of the world's foremost natural scientists at the Natural History Museum of Paris, where he spent his entire career. Cuvier (Figure 2.4) was a steadfast opponent of the modern concept of evolutionary change. The existence of extinct creatures such as dinosaurs was a large problem for Cuvier and other creationist scientists of the day because they presented compelling evidence of a past world very different from that of the present day. Cuvier and his supporters advocated a theory now known as **catastrophism**, in which cataclysmic disasters were believed to have wiped out earlier forms of life on Earth and prepared the way for newly created forms.

Jean-Baptiste Lamarck In 1809, Lamarck (1744–1829) proposed his **theory of inheritance of acquired characteristics**, which is today often called simply *Lamarckism.* Lamarck (Figure 2.5) argued that all organisms make adjustments to their environment during their lifetime that could be passed on to their offspring, making those offspring better adapted to their environment. It relied on the concept of *need and use.* For example, if an animal that lived by the seashore spent much of its time swimming in the ocean, its offspring, according to Lamarck, would be better swimmers than its parents had been. In postulating this sort of evolutionary process, Lamarck made one laudable breakthrough and one major error. The breakthrough was seeing the crucial relationship between the organism and its environment. But the fundamental error was thinking that evolutionary change could occur during the lifetime of an individual. This error is easily seen by taking Lamarck's theory to its logical extension: If a mouse loses its tail to a cat, does the mouse later give birth to babies lacking tails? Likewise, no amount of bodybuilding will enable you to give birth to muscular children.

Larmarck's idea is often ridiculed today, but it was a brilliant notion in light of the evidence of evolutionary change available in the eighteenth century. Lamarck knew nothing about the mode of inheritance—genes—and his theory of the inheritance of acquired characteristics served as a natural antecedent to Darwin's theories (Figure 2.6).

The so-called **Lysenkoism** incident in the twentieth century illustrated the failure of Lamarck's theory in a dramatic way. Trofim Lysenko, although never formally educated in biology, was one of the top-ranking botanists in the Soviet Union from the 1930s to 1960s. He argued that Darwinian thinking was inherently capitalist in its focus on the individual struggle for existence.

Lysenko campaigned successfully for a Lamarckian (he called it Stalinist-Marxist) model of evolution to be applied to Soviet agricultural production. He took the environmental focus of Larmarck's work to an illogical extreme. For years Soviet scientists stored winter wheat grain at low temperatures, on the theory that such exposure during the seeds' lifetime would create a new generation of wheat that was cold tolerant, thereby turning the colder parts of the Soviet Union into a new breadbasket. Of course, the experiment was an embarrassing and tragic failure. Soviet biology was set back decades (many of their best genetic scientists were exiled to concentration camps, never to be seen again), and Lysenkoism is a good example of why political ideology should never drive scientific practice.

THE UNIFORMITARIANS: HUTTON AND LYELL

At about the same time that Lamarck's ideas were being debated, a key piece of the evolution puzzle fell into place. Along the rocky Scottish seacoast, James Hutton (1726–1797) spent his career studying, among other things, the layering of rock formations. One of the fathers of modern geology, Hutton saw clear evidence of past worlds in the upthrusting of the earth. A devout Christian, Hutton attempted to shoehorn his observations into a biblical framework; however, he did assert a

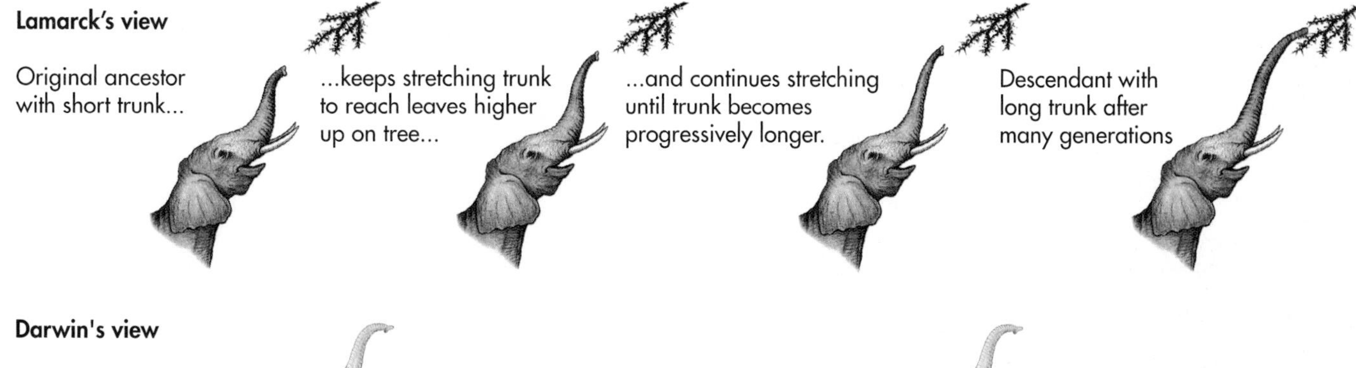
Lamarck's view
Original ancestor with short trunk...
...keeps stretching trunk to reach leaves higher up on tree...
...and continues stretching until trunk becomes progressively longer.
Descendant with long trunk after many generations
Darwin's view
Original group with variation in trunk length.
Natural selection favours longer trunks.
The favoured characteristic is passed on to the next generation in greater proportion than the shorter trunk.
After many, many generations, group is still variable, but showing a general increase in trunk length.

FIGURE 2.6 Lamarckian and Darwinian views of evolution.

central principle that stands to this day: **uniformitarianism.** Hutton asserted that the geological processes that drive the natural world today are the same as those that prevailed in the past. Hutton was not prepared to extend this theory to the living world; that was left for Charles Darwin many years later. But his views of the changing Earth strongly influenced a generation of geologists.

uniformitarianism Theory that the same gradual geological process we observe today was operating in the past.

Charles Lyell (1797–1875), another British geologist, was a strong proponent of uniformitarianism, arguing that slow, gradual change was the way of the physical world and that if one looked in older and older rock sediments, one would find increasingly primitive forms of life. Although an ardent creationist, Lyell (Figure 2.7) became the leading geologist of his day; through his research and his prominence in the social hierarchy of nineteenth-century London, Lyell exerted an enormous influence over his academic peers. His acquaintance with Darwin certainly was a strong influence on the latter's evolutionary ideas. His book *Principles of Geology*, published in three volumes beginning in 1830, was a work that Darwin carried and read time and again during his voyage of discovery on the sailing ship HMS *Beagle*. Lyell played a key role in convincing both the scientific world and the public that the Earth's history could be understood only in the context of deep, ancient changes in geology, which necessarily cast creationist explanations for life in a different, more dubious light.

FIGURE 2.7 Charles Lyell.

THE DARWINIAN REVOLUTION

Charles Darwin (1809–1882) was one of six children (Figure 2.8). An ardent naturalist from an early age, Darwin wandered the English countryside in search of animals and plants to study. However, he was a lacklustre student. When Darwin was 16, his father sent him to study medicine at the University of Edinburgh. Uninterested in his studies and appalled at the sight of surgery, young Darwin did not fare well academically. He did, however, make his initial contacts with evolutionary theory, in the form of Lamarck's ideas about evolutionary change.

Darwin subsequently left Edinburgh and headed to Cambridge University, where he planned to study for the ministry in the Church of England. He received a degree in 1831, but more importantly continued his studies in the natural sciences

FIGURE 2.8 Charles Darwin.

and left Cambridge more eager for adventure and natural history study than for the ministry. Two key events in Darwin's career took place there. One of his professors at Cambridge was John Henslow, a botanist and eminent naturalist who deeply influenced Darwin's scientific thinking. Second, Darwin read the travel and natural history accounts of the renowned German explorer and scientist Baron Friedrich Heinrich Alexander von Humboldt and was greatly inspired by them.

In the summer of 1831, while Darwin was on a natural history field trip in Wales, Henslow was meeting with Captain Robert Fitzroy (1805–1865). Fitzroy, an officer in the Royal Navy and himself a keen amateur naturalist, was planning a voyage to map the coastlines of the continents, particularly South America, on the sailing ship HMS *Beagle*. He had invited Henslow to accompany him, but Henslow turned down the offer and put Darwin's name forward. Charles Darwin thus departed in December 1831 as the "gentleman" amateur naturalist aboard the *Beagle*, a trip that changed not only Darwin but also modern science. It also changed Captain Fitzroy, whose deep Christian beliefs eventually led him to regret his decision to take Darwin along on the voyage.

THE GALÁPAGOS

It's hard for us to fully appreciate today what a rare gift a trip around the world was for a naturalist in the early nineteenth century. The 22-year-old Darwin, who had left the British Isles only once before his voyage on the *Beagle*, spent 5 years of his life exploring the seacoasts of South America, Australia, and Africa, with many stops along the way (Figure 2.9). From 1831 to 1836, unburdened by other

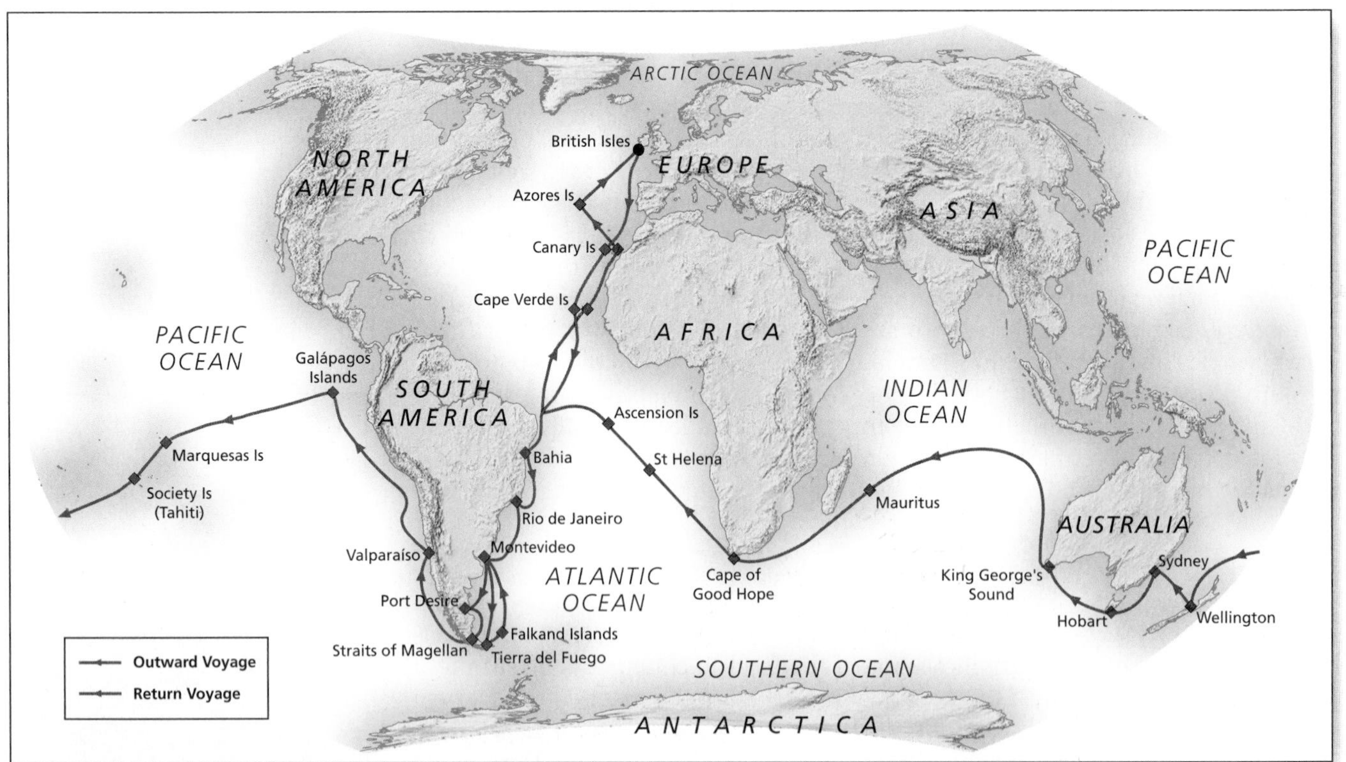

FIGURE 2.9 Map of Darwin's voyage on the HMS *Beagle*.

FIGURE 2.10 Darwin was deeply influenced by his stop in the Galápagos Islands, isolated volcanic rocks off the coast of Ecuador.

distractions, he was able to devote most of his waking hours to observing myriad plants and animals in their natural environment.

Contrary to the popular image of Darwin spending 5 years at sea, most of his time was spent on land expeditions or in seaside ports in South America. He rode horses in Patagonia, trekked in the Andes, and explored oceanic islands in the Atlantic and Pacific oceans. Of these oceanic island stops, one had a profound influence on Darwin: the Galápagos Islands.

The *Beagle* dropped anchor amid a cluster of rocky islands 965 kilometres (600 mi) off the coast of Ecuador on September 15, 1835. The two dozen Galápagos Islands, most of them tiny lumps of rock, are of recent volcanic origin (Figure 2.10). Most of the islands are rather barren, possessing only a few species of large animals, most notably reptiles and birds. Darwin was amazed by the bizarre and oddly approachable animal life of the islands, including iguanalike lizards that dived into the sea to forage for seaweed and enormous tortoises that weighed more than 180 kilograms (400 lb) (Darwin, 1839) (Figures 2.11 and 2.12).

Each of the Galápagos Islands had its own varieties of animals. There was a distinctive variety of giant tortoise on each, many of which still survive today. It was the birds, however, that provided Darwin with the key piece of evidence for his eventual theory of evolution. Each of the islands has a distinct species of finch. Some live on the arid rocky islets, and others on lusher parts of the island group. There are finches with rather generic-looking beaks, finches with long slender beaks, and finches with remarkably large, strong beaks. Altogether, Darwin collected at least 13 different varieties of small, brownish or black finches in the islands, skinning them and packing them into crates to carry back to the British Museum in London.

There are many myths about the influence the Galápagos had on Darwin. He certainly did not immediately formulate the theory of natural selection upon

FIGURE 2.11 Darwin observed that tortoises on islands with trees tend to have shells that allow them to reach up to browse.

FIGURE 2.12 Tortoises living on islands where the main foods are grasses lack such saddle-shaped shells.

spending a month there. In fact, Darwin left the Galápagos an uneasy creationist, his heretical ideas taking shape only months and years later (Larson, 2001). And although history often records Darwin immediately recognizing something of evolutionary importance when he began to see the variations among finch species, this was not the case. Darwin collected hundreds of the little birds but never saw the importance of their small differences in appearance. In fact, he never even labelled the specimens as to the specific island on which he collected them. It was ornithologist John Gould in London who studied the expedition's collection of finches, now stuffed, and realized that they could be sorted into an array of different species according to island. In his published journal of the voyage of the *Beagle*, written the year after he returned home, Darwin said,

> Seeing this gradation and diversity of structure in one small, intimately related group of birds, one might really fancy that from an original paucity of birds in this archipelago, one species had been taken and modified for different ends. (Darwin, 1839)

In light of a discovery by Gould on bill differences, Darwin realized the importance of the finches for his budding theory. He surmised that the various animal varieties of the Galápagos, from giant tortoises to mockingbirds, were probably descended from a very small number of creatures that had reached the islands (presumably from the South American mainland) long ago and had then diversified in response to the different island habitats they found there (Figure 2.13). Darwin referred to this process of many species emerging from one or few ancient ones, like the spokes of wheel emerging from the hub, as **adaptive radiation**. The process of biological change in a species by which such a radiation occurs, Darwin referred to as **natural selection**. In fact, the Galápagos were the perfect setting for Darwin to see evolution in action. Because they are islands, isolated from the mainland, and because they are relatively young, they are biologically simple. Only a few species had managed to reach the islands. Perhaps the ancestors of the finches had been blown off course while flying in a storm and ended up there; ocean currents probably had carried the tortoises and iguanas there as they floated or clung to pieces

adaptive radiation The diversification of one founding species into multiple species and niches.

natural selection Differential reproductive success over multiple generations.

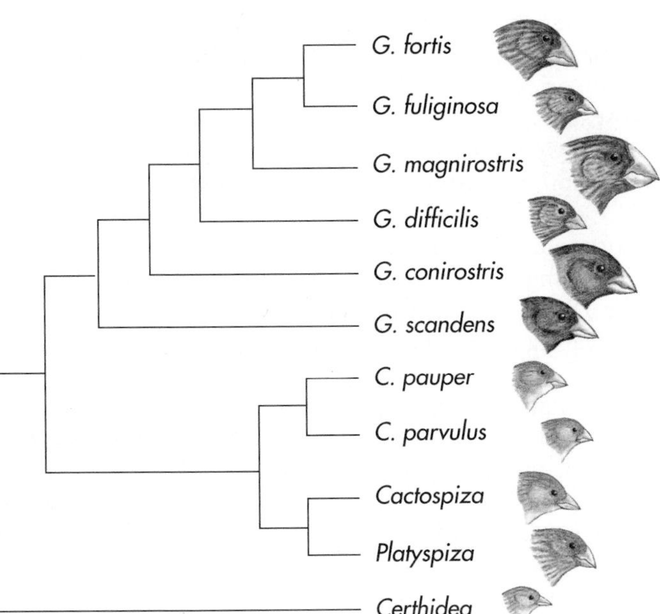

FIGURE 2.13 Darwin's finches: Adaptive radiation of bill types.

of driftwood. Finding rocky islets that had food and shelter but few competitors, the species flourished, and eventually their descendants had radiated into the available space in the archipelago.

In setting out his theory of evolution, Darwin used what he had learned from the Galápagos in three ways. First, he observed that isolated oceanic islands seem to hold many species found nowhere else, many of them closely related. Second, isolated islands often lack whole groups of animals found on the mainland; for example, the Galápagos Islands lack any large mammals. Darwin therefore suggested that because only a few tenacious species reach such islands, others fill the place of missing species. In the Galápagos, the place of land mammals may be taken by gigantic tortoises and oversized iguanas. Third, the distinctive animals and plants of isolated islands tend to resemble close relatives on the mainland, even when the environment of the island differs greatly from that of the mainland.

REFINING THE THEORY OF EVOLUTION BY NATURAL SELECTION

Home in England, Darwin took up a life of nature study, contemplation, and writing in the village of Downe, some 24 kilometres (15 mi) south of London. Beset by a variety of health problems, he rarely left Downe and was bedridden for long periods. But he spent years developing his theory of natural selection, drawing extensively on the parallel process of artificial selection. When animal breeders try to develop new strains of livestock, they select the traits they want to enhance and allow only those individuals to breed. For example, a farmer who tries to boost milk production in Guernsey cows must allow only the best milk producers to breed, and over many generations milk production will indeed increase. Darwin developed friendships with some of the local breeders of fancy pigeons and drew on their work to elaborate on his theory of natural selection. Pigeons, horses, cows, dogs—all are fine examples of what selective breeding can achieve in a few generations. What artificial breeders do in captivity natural selection does in the wild, with one key exception. The animal breeder chooses certain traits, such as floppy ears or a long tail, and pushes the evolution of the breed in that direction generation after generation (Figure 2.14). Breeders have a goal in mind with respect to animal form or function. Natural selection has no such foresight. Instead, it moulds each generation in response to current environmental conditions.

As Darwin worked his theories into publishable form, he had frequent discussions with his two closest colleagues. One of these was Joseph Hooker, Henslow's brother-in-law and a well-known botanist. The other was T. H. Huxley (Figure 2.15), an ally whose support Darwin relied on time and again during his life after the publication of *On the Origin of Species* and who remained a loyal advocate of Darwinian theory long after the author's death. Darwin was content to ruminate on his ideas, reworking them over and over and publishing only short sketches of the theory in the 1840s, even as his friends pushed him to go public. For years Darwin demurred, fearing the public reaction to his controversial, potentially heretical idea.

In 1858 an event occurred that galvanized Darwin into action. He received a letter and manuscript from Alfred Russel Wallace (1823–1913; see Figure 2.16), another field biologist then collecting plant and animal specimens in Indonesia. Wallace had come up with his own version of the theory of evolution by natural selection and was writing to Darwin for advice as to whether the idea was sound

(a)

(b)

(c)

(d)

FIGURE 2.14 Species of horses: (a) zebra, (b) Przewalski's horse, (c) Mongolian ass, and (d) thoroughbred race horse.

and worthy of publication. With prodding from Hooker and Huxley, Darwin wrote up his own theory and readied it for publication.

Twelve hundred copies of *On the Origin of Species* were published on November 24, 1859, and quickly sold out of every bookshop in London. Alongside the expected best-sellers that autumn—Charles Dickens' *Tale of Two Cities* and Alfred Lord Tennyson's *Idylls of the King*—it was a surprise hit. Darwin wrote, as did many scientific authors of his day, with both a scientific audience and the reading public in mind. He was immediately besieged by letters and requests for personal appearances. He turned down most of the opportunities to speak publicly but received and wrote hundreds of letters in the next few months. Darwin was suddenly one of the most famous men in the world.

FIGURE 2.15
Thomas H. Huxley.

In presenting his theory of evolution by natural selection as laid out in *On the Origin of Species*, Darwin explained his three observations and two deductions:

Observation 1. All organisms have the potential for explosive population growth that would outstrip their food supply. Darwin took this idea directly from Malthus, who had been concerned with human population growth. A female bullfrog may lay 100 000 eggs every spring, but we don't see bullfrogs hopping everywhere. Even humans, with their very low reproductive potential compared with most animals, can undergo exponential population growth, as evidenced by the global population explosion.

Observation 2. But when we look at nature, we see populations that are roughly stable.

Deduction 1. Therefore, there must be a struggle for existence. That is, the bullfrog's 100 000 eggs may yield no more than a handful, or even just one, adult frog. This, Darwin labelled *natural selection* to parallel the term *artificial selection* in use by animal breeders of the period.

Observation 3. Nature is full of variation. Even in one animal group, every individual is slightly different from every other individual. If you look closely enough, even a basketful of uniform-looking bullfrogs will resolve into myriad small differences in size, shape, colour, and other features.

Deduction 3. Therefore, some of these variations must be favoured, and others must be disfavoured, in a process we can call natural selection.

This elegantly simple set of ideas is the heart of evolutionary theory. Far from the eternally static cubbyholes that most earlier thinkers had conceived, species were dynamic units, constantly in flux in response to changing environments and the unceasing pressure of competitors (Figure 2.17). Natural selection was a filtering process in which unfavourable traits lost the race with more favourable traits. As Darwin saw it, natural selection is all about reproductive success. Therefore, the time-honoured definition of natural selection as "survival of the fittest" is misleading. That phrase was coined by social theorist Herbert Spencer and does not apply well to natural selection. It is much more about the number of offspring an organism leaves in the next generation who themselves survive to reproductive age, a measure we call **fitness**, a biological measure of reproductive success (not a reference to physical fitness). This can be measured, and the qualities that contribute to reproductive success can often be determined. Natural selection can therefore be succinctly defined as differential reproductive success across multiple generations and among the individuals of a given population of animals or plants.

fitness Reproductive success.

FIGURE 2.16
Alfred Russel Wallace.

For natural selection to work, three preconditions must be met (Figure 2.18). First, *the trait in question must be inherited*. For example, if you incubate the eggs of some animals, such as reptiles, at temperatures that are too high or too low, the resulting baby will have odd colour patterns. These are not genetic and so are not

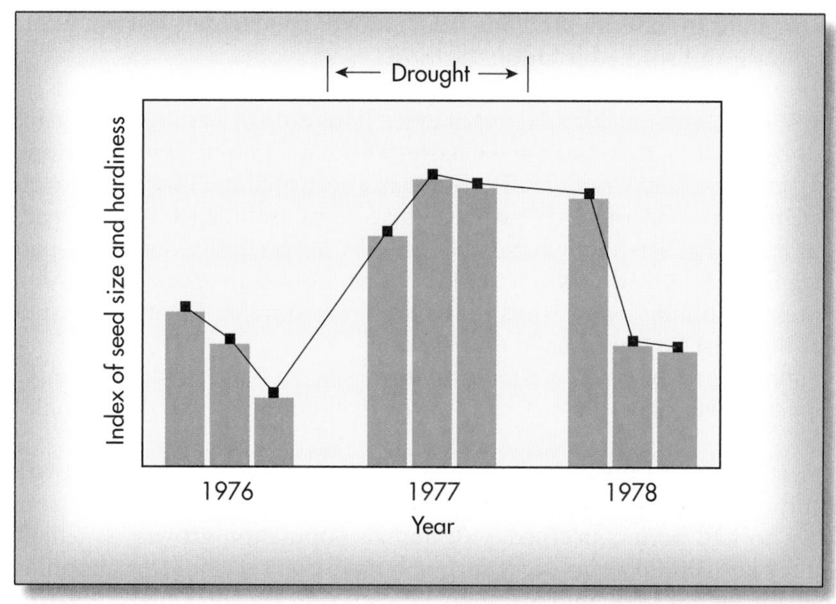

FIGURE 2.17 Index of seed size and hardiness prior to, during, and after drought. A thicker seed coat and an increased ratio of seed weight/(seed length × seed width) serve as buffers against drought.

under the control of natural selection. Second, *the trait in question must show variation between individuals.* Natural selection cannot distinguish good from bad traits if all individuals are genetically identical clones. This is rarely the case in nature, where variants abound, and is the key difference between organisms that reproduce by asexual splitting, such as amoebas, and higher animals that reproduce sexually. Higher animals are all genetically unique, so their traits can be selected or not selected. Third, *the filter between the organism and its genetic makeup is the environment, which must exert some pressure in order for natural selection to act.* Many scholars believe that humans evolved rapidly in part because the environment in which our ancestors lived underwent many dramatic fluctuations caused by world climate swings.

population An interbreeding group of organisms.

mutation An alteration in the DNA, which may or may not alter the function of a cell. If it occurs in a sex cell (i.e., sperm or egg), it may be passed from one generation to the next.

Evolution is about change. Although in common English usage *evolution* sometimes is used to describe the changes an individual goes through in the course of a lifetime ("in my evolution as an artist . . ."), in biology this is never the case. It is a change in a **population** (a breeding group of organisms of the same kind) in the frequency of a trait or a gene from one generation to the next. The currency of change is the genetic material, in which alterations in the DNA sequence provide the raw source of variation—**mutation**—on which natural selection can act. Whereas evolution happens at the level of the population, natural selection occurs at the level of the individual organism. As we will see,

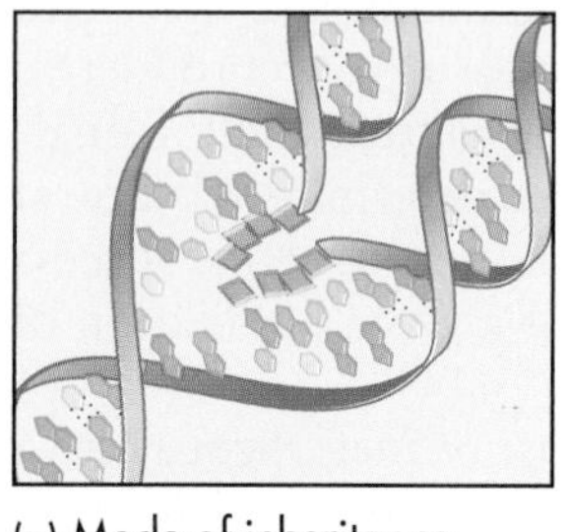

(a) Mode of inheritance

(b) Variation among individuals

(c) Environmental pressure

FIGURE 2.18 The prerequisites needed for natural selection to occur.

this has important implications for understanding how the evolutionary process produces the myriad forms we see in nature.

THE RESPONSE TO DARWIN

Although many people think that Darwin's (and Wallace's) theory of evolution by natural selection was a dramatically new view that replaced the old view of immutability, this is only partly true. Scholars had held evolutionary views for generations; recall Lamarck and his many advocates right up to the time of Darwin. Darwin simply offered a mechanism, one so elegantly simple and effective that many scholars were surprised that they had not themselves seen it.

But the response to Darwin by some scholars was not immediate acceptance. The church and many religious people were offended and outraged by the implication that there was no meaning to existence other than the random sorting of traits by natural processes. Even in the scientific community, there were many holdouts who continued to argue for other forms of evolutionary change into the mid-twentieth century. For instance, Louis Agassiz of Harvard University was one of America's most prominent naturalists around the time of the publication of *On the Origin of Species*. Darwin's book rendered Agassiz's work on animal classification instantly obsolete. Agassiz not only repudiated natural selection but also set out to refute it (Larson, 2001). He offered his own view, based on Cuvier's theory of catastrophism and multiple new creations, to explain the appearance of fossil animals that no longer existed. Agassiz fought Darwin relentlessly, motivated by both professional jealousy and a deeply held belief that natural selection's failure to invoke the power of a divine creator made it fatally flawed. He mounted expeditions to the Galápagos and elsewhere to seek evidence that natural selection was wrong. He seized on Darwin's prediction that the creatures of the Galápagos, ridiculously tame and approachable in the 1830s, would evolve a fear of humans once they had been hunted for generations. Agassiz tried to demonstrate that the creatures' continued tameness in the 1860s showed that Darwinian theory must be flawed. Most other naturalists chastised Agassiz for this futile attempt to refute natural selection since intense hunting of the Galápagos animals had begun only a century earlier. Agassiz's death after his return from the 1873 expedition silenced his voice of opposition.

Failure to accept natural selection came from other scientific quarters as well. Neo-Lamarckian views surfaced in the decades after the publication of the *Origin* and persisted well into the twentieth century. Darwin himself, challenged repeatedly by critics and hampered by the general lack of understanding of genetic transmission, acknowledged that Lamarckian mechanisms might have some role in evolutionary change. Not until the so-called neo-Darwinian modern synthesis of the 1940s and 1950s, when Ernst Mayr and other biologists integrated ecology with Darwinian theory, genetics, anatomy, and other fields, did the full weight and influence of Darwin pervade the biological sciences and, by extension, the field of biological anthropology.

THE SCIENCE AND CREATIONISM QUESTION

Ever since the publication of *On the Origin of Species*, a small but vocal minority in the United States and Canada has argued against the teaching of the principles of evolution. They argue instead for a biblical, creationist view of the origin of species and humanity. But what exactly is a *creationist?* A scientist who studies the origins of the known universe but who believes that the universe may have been created 14 billion years ago by a single supernatural force is a creationist. So is a fundamentalist who believes that the Earth and every living thing on it were created in six days, that dinosaurs and other extinct animals never existed, and that we are all descendants of Adam and Eve. Creationism is a belief in a single creative force in the universe.

The ongoing conflict between evolution and creationism lies in the claim by some fundamentalist religious groups that the creation story in the Book of Genesis is a viable alternative to science as the explanation for how humans came to be. These groups argue that evolution is a theory that has no more scientific validity than biblical explanations for origins of life and people. The intellectual centrepiece of their thinking is that the Earth is very young (that is, it is approximately the age calculated by Ussher) and that the sedimentary layers of the Earth that provide scientists with evidence of antiquity, and also yield most of our fossils, were really the product of Noah's flood and are of recent origin. They consider the species found alive today and in the most recent fossil beds to be the species that could swim well enough to escape the rising flood waters. Not surprisingly, this belief can be easily overturned by quick examination of the fossil record and by the study of radiometric dating of the age of the Earth's layers.

A religious belief in a divine creation relies entirely on faith. The sole evidence of this faith is the Book of Genesis in the Old Testament of the Bible. Although the Bible is a profoundly important book, its contents are not testable evidence. Nowhere in the evaluation of the truth of the Old Testament does the scientific method come into play; either you accept the reality of the Old Testament or you don't. A literal interpretation of Genesis would mean accepting a six-day creation. However, many Christians accept the Old Testament as a powerful and important work that is not intended to be taken literally. The problem that most scientists have with teaching religion in public schools therefore is not due to lack of respect for religion—some are quite religious themselves—but rather that science classes are intended to teach children how to think like scientists (Figure 2.19).

creation science A creationist attempt to refute the evidence of evolution.

intelligent design A creationist school of thought that proposes that natural selection cannot account for the diversity and complexity of form and function seen in nature.

The political agenda of some anti-evolution fundamentalist groups belies their stated belief in offering diverse approaches to human origins. Religious fundamentalists often support the teaching of the Judeo-Christian creation story as fact but do not want to allow other creation stories to be taught alongside them in classrooms. Christianity, Judaism, and Islam are creationist faiths: They identify a single creator. Other major religions of the world, such as Hinduism, do not accept a single creator. Fundamentalists fight politically for the right to teach the Judeo-Christian belief system in public schools but generally do not support and sometimes even oppose teaching other religious points of view.

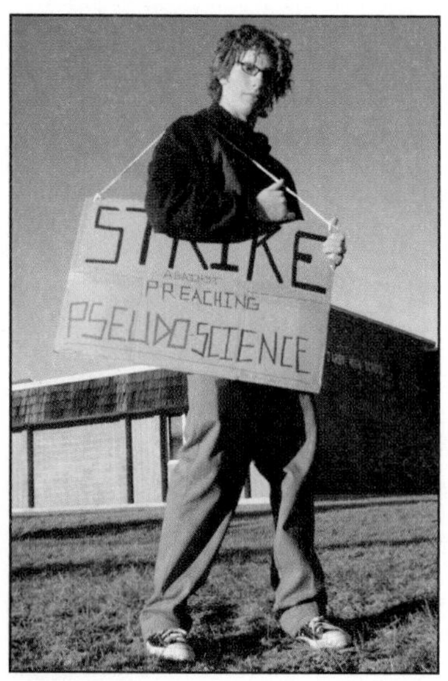

FIGURE 2.19 A student protesting the teaching of creationism.

All the pieces of evidence for evolution, from fossils to DNA, are facts that add up to a body of evidence for a scientific theory without viable competitors. In recent years, however, challenges have come to evolution in the form of new incarnations of creationism. **Creation science** is one approach taken by fundamentalists. Recognizing that the Old Testament is not scientific evidence for life's origins, many creationists have argued in the negative, trying to refute the voluminous evidence for evolution. They ask why there are gaps in the fossil record; where, they ask, are the intermediate forms that ought to exist between *Homo erectus* and modern humans? Don't these gaps support the notion of a divine power moulding our species? The fossil record is fragmentary and always will be because of the low odds of fossils being formed, preserved, and then found millions of years later. Creationists seize on this fragmentariness, attempting to portray early humans as apes and later humans as aberrant forms of modern people. In the resulting gap they argue that God must have played his hand. As we shall see in later chapters, the fossil record for human ancestry is rich, with a progression of brain size and anatomical changes bridging the apes, early hominids, and modern humans. Creation science is a denial of science rather than science itself and has not been any more successful than were earlier approaches by creationists. In recent years other attempts have been made to resurrect creationism in science education. **Intelligent Design** is one such school of thought (Box 2.1).

The relationship between the church and the teaching of evolution remains an uneasy one even in the twenty-first century. Pope John Paul II stated publicly that the Roman Catholic Church accepts the reality of evolution, even though the essence of humanity is still maintained to be a divine product.

Most biological scientists have deep respect for all religious beliefs; however, scientists want creationist thinking to be excluded from science curriculum in government-supported schools because that is the place where children are being trained to think like scientists. In addition, the *Canadian Charter of Rights and Freedoms* ensures that the rights of those of other religious faiths, or those without religious faith, must be fully respected. Biological anthropology links social science and biological science and because of this there is an enduring tension that affects our discussions of topics such as evolution. As scientists, we deal with theories and laws, with observation and experimentation. As anthropologists we

Box 2.1 What Is Intelligent Design?

Intelligent design is an attempt to repackage creationist ideas in a way that might be more palatable for society and the scientific community. Instead of arguing outright for a biblical or divine basis for life, intelligent design advocates claim they have evidence that evolution by natural selection cannot fully explain the diversity of form and function that exists in nature. This school of thought is fond of using the argument of "irreducible complexity": There are aspects of the design of some organisms that are so complex that gradual, successive small modifications of earlier forms could not have produced them. If removal of one part of an organism's adaptive complex of traits causes the entire complex to cease functioning, advocates of intelligent design say, then a supernatural force must have been the actual creator. The example of a mousetrap is often cited. Without each essential feature of a mousetrap—the wooden platform, the spring mechanism, and the latch holding it—the device fails to function at all. Intelligent design advocates say that unless the trap was assembled all at once, it would be useless and therefore could not be created by natural selection. Michael Behe, a biologist and an influential advocate of intelligent design who seeks to reconcile evolution with religious faith, has claimed that there are examples of irreducible complexity in biology that make natural selection an inadequate mechanism for all change. For instance, Behe claims that the working of cells at the biochemical level, in which cellular function can occur only after numerous working integrated parts are in place, might be an example of irreducible complexity (Behe, 1996).

Unfortunately for adherents of intelligent design, their few examples of irreducible complexity have been met with refutations in scientific literature. Michael Ruse, a Fellow of the Royal Society of Canada and formerly a professor at the University of Guelph, is a well-known evolutionary historian and philosopher who has refuted many of the anti-Darwinian arguments. Behe himself acknowledges that whereas gradual Darwinian change by natural selection can be studied and tested using the scientific method, intelligent design cannot. By definition, if the original design is supernatural, understanding this design must be beyond the reach of science or rational explanation. In other words, the intelligent design movement asks us to accept on blind faith that supernatural forces are at work in designing life. Rather than offering rational explanations for features that might challenge Darwinian theory, advocates of intelligent design offer criticisms that cannot be addressed by further research. The whole belief system of intelligent design therefore stands well outside of science in the realm of faith rather than offering a scientific alternative to evolution by natural selection.

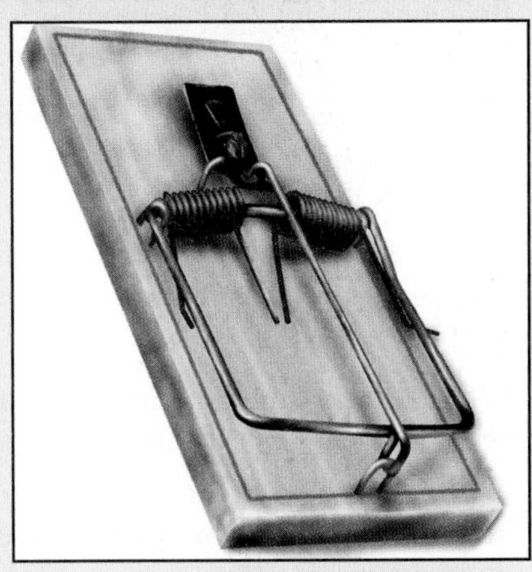

FIGURE A A mousetrap.

As the latest addition to the beliefs of the creationist movement, intelligent design is unlikely to go away any time soon. Indeed, because it is an intellectual, if not scientific, approach to evolutionary change, it is held by some academics, including university-level science instructors. Because instructors in universities can cite the legal right of academic freedom, the teaching of intelligent design belief, even though it lies outside the sciences, is hard to prevent.

are also social scientists and thus recognize the importance of the historical, philosophical, and socio-cultural contexts of our scientific data as well as our scientific theories and laws. As anthropologists we recognize that different cultures and different religions may have explanations for the origin of the Earth and the organisms that inhabit it. We respect the fact that the Cree have an explanation and that Hindus have a different explanation, but we explore those explanations not in biological anthropology classes but in classes such as the anthropology of religion. We do not present these as alternatives to evolutionary theory in the science classroom and encourage students to choose among them. Neither do we debate creation versus evolution or the merits of intelligent design in the science classroom, because these are not scientific controversies. They are, however, socio-cultural controversies and so it behooves us to understand what they are about.

SUMMARY

1. **What are the key features that distinguish the scientific from the religious view of the origins of life?**

   Science is a form of inquiry based on hypothesis testing via evidence collection. It is falsifiable and self-correcting. Religious ideology is based on faith and religious texts; it cannot be tested in an empirical way.

2. **Before Darwin, why was the notion of evolutionary change forbidden?**

   The church had decreed that the world was created by God and had existed in its original form until the present; to contradict that was heresy punishable by imprisonment or worse.

3. **What is catastrophism, and can you think of a modern idea that is similar to it?**

   Catastrophism is the eighteenth-century theory that natural disasters had wiped out life on parts of the Earth multiple times, and each time new forms of life moved in from other regions. This would account for the existence of past life forms that no longer exist without invoking evolutionary change. A similar modern idea is that the extinction of the dinosaurs was caused by a catastrophic mechanism, such as an asteroid impact or widespread volcano activity.

4. **How did the false view of evolution expressed in Lamarckian theory differ from Darwinian theory?**

   Lamarck proposed that the use of a trait could influence an offspring's phenotype in the next generation. Darwin showed that change could occur across generations based only on the selective retention of some traits and the filtering out of others.

5. **How was Darwin's *On the Origin of Species* influenced by his association with geologist Charles Lyell?**

   Darwin carried Lyell's book *Principles of Geology* with him during his voyage on the HMS *Beagle*. Lyell, the leading geologist of his day, played a key role in convincing both the scientific world and the public that the Earth's history could be understood only in the context of the long time frame of geological changes.

6. **What are the three conditions necessary for natural selection to work?**

   Natural selection can occur only if a trait can be inherited, there is variation within a population, and there is pressure from the environment.

CRITICAL THINKING QUESTIONS

1. Was it really so absurd for Bishop James Ussher to come up with a date of 4004 BC as the moment of creation? If you had only your own intuition and observation to guide you, how could you prove to others that the world is round or that the Earth is ancient? This leads to the question, What exactly is a fact?
2. How would you handle the science versus creationism issue?
3. Despite Linnaeus' contribution to the study of animal and plant life through the invention of the classification scheme we call taxonomy, his approach hampers us today in understanding what a species is. Why do you think this is true?

KEY TERMS

deduction
observation
hypothesis
experimentation
scientific method
data
falsifiable
paradigm
taxonomy
binomial nomenclature
taxon
catastrophism
theory of the inheritance of acquired characteristics
Lysenkoism
uniformitarianism
adaptive radiation
natural selection
fitness
population
mutation
creation science
intelligent design

SUGGESTED READING

Brooks, J. L. (1984). *Just before the Origin*. ToExcel Publishing, New York, NY.

Browne, Janet. (1995). *Charles Darwin: Voyaging*. Alfred A. Knopf, New York, NY.

Browne, Janet. (2002). *Charles Darwin: The Power of Place*. Alfred A. Knopf, New York, NY.

Dennett, Daniel C. (1995). *Darwin's Dangerous Idea*. Simon and Schuster, New York, NY.

Ruse, Michael. (2006). *Darwinism and its Discontents*. Cambridge University Press, New York, NY.

Weiner, J. (1994). *The Beak of the Finch*. Vintage Books, New York, NY.

PART II
MECHANISMS OF EVOLUTION

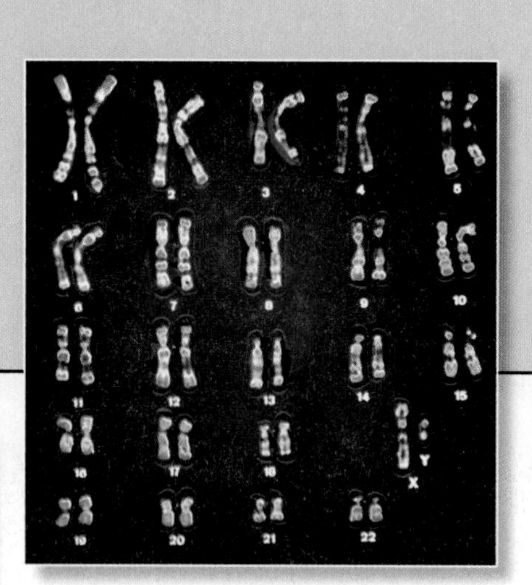

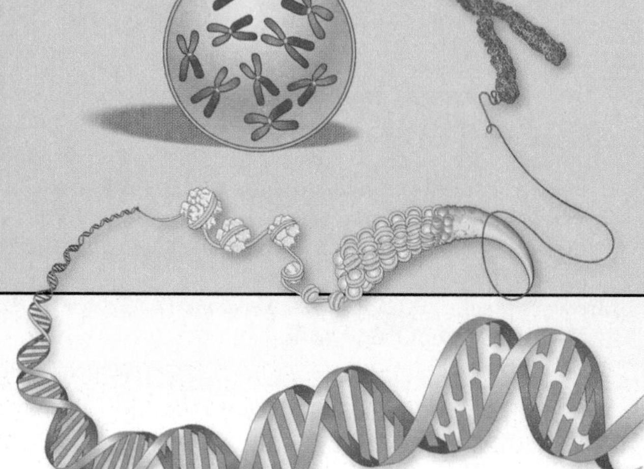

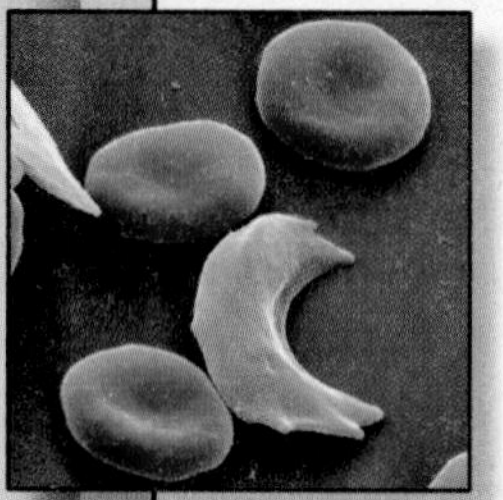

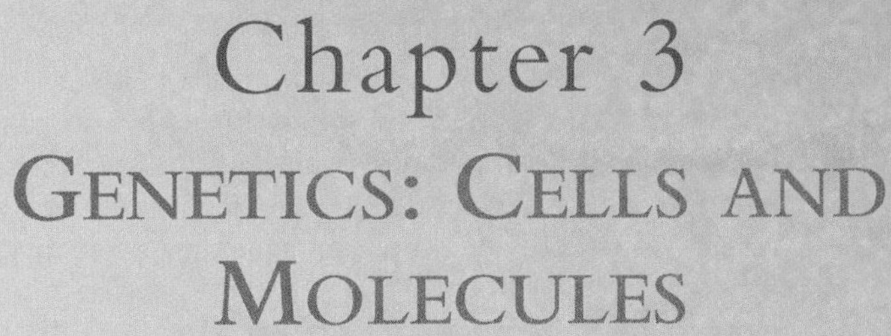

Chapter 3
Genetics: Cells and Molecules

On a spring day in 1900, an English scientist named William Bateson was riding on a train to London. Although relatively young, Bateson was widely recognized among scientists interested in heredity and evolution. He had conducted field and experimental research on both plants and animals and had been involved in theoretical debates about the nature of evolutionary change. Bateson was heading to London to give a talk to the Royal Horticultural Society. In Darwin's time, inheritance was thought to result from the "blending" of some material from each parent. But in his talk to the society in the previous year, Bateson had argued that if the mechanisms of heredity were ever to be worked out, it would only be through the careful breeding of plants or animals, with precise recording of the expression of characters in parent and offspring generations. The expression of these characters would have to be statistically analyzed to make sense of the patterns of hereditary transmission.

As he rode on the train, Bateson read a scientific paper by Gregor Mendel, a biologist and Augustinian monk. The paper, in an obscure

journal, had been published 35 years earlier but had only recently been referred to in a publication by Hugo de Vries, a Dutch botanist.

As HE READ MENDEL'S PAPER, one word came to Bateson: remarkable. Mendel had conducted a long series of painstaking hybridization experiments using the common garden pea. Bateson was impressed by the scale of the experiments, Mendel's description of them, and, most particularly, the analysis of the results Mendel provided. Bateson immediately recognized that the research program he had so boldly advocated the year before had been implemented more than four decades earlier by Mendel.

BATESON HAD ALREADY PREPARED HIS TALK to the Royal Horticultural Society, but after arriving in London he hurriedly added a long section to the end discussing and lauding Mendel's work. During his presentation, he admitted some puzzlement as to how research as significant as Mendel's could be all but forgotten or unnoticed for so many years. He proclaimed that Mendel's ideas would "play a conspicuous part in all future discussions of evolutionary problems." Bateson was confident that the "laws of heredity" were finally within reach.

Chapter Outline

Bateson returned home a self-avowed "Mendelian" and, within two years, published a book-length defence of "Mendelism." He devoted the rest of his career to the promotion of Mendel's ideas and to explaining what Mendelism meant to understanding evolutionary change. Strictly speaking, Bateson did not rediscover Mendel. Rather, he did something that was even more important: He recognized the significance of the rediscovery of Mendel and that a whole new science—genetics (a term Bateson coined for "the study of heredity")—was at hand.

Over the past hundred years, the modern science of *genetics* has developed to give us a much better understanding of the biological processes underlying heredity. We need to understand genetics if we are to understand how evolution happens because genetic variation provides the raw material for evolutionary change. In this chapter, we begin our exploration of genetics—which will continue in Chapter 4—with a historical look at the study of heredity and an overview of genetic science today. We will then look at the fundamental building block of life, the cell, and consider its structure and function. Then we will discuss DNA, the genetic material itself, and how it carries out the important functions of replication and protein synthesis. We conclude the chapter with a discussion of the molecular methods biological anthropologists use to study human and primate evolution.

GENETICS

In the nineteenth and early twentieth centuries, scientists embraced ideas about heredity that were ill-conceived or later proved to be simply wrong.

One such nineteenth-century notion was **blending inheritance.** Blending inheritance was based on two assumptions: Each parent contributes equally to the offspring, and these contributions are halved at each successive generation. The first assumption is valid. The second assumption only *appears* to be valid, based on selected observations. Blending inheritance was commonly used in the late nineteenth century as an argument against evolution by natural selection because it was thought that it would be virtually impossible to select for any trait if it was being "blended out" with each passing generation (Figure 3.1). The logic for this argument went as follows: Suppose a trait appeared in a population that greatly enhanced the fitness

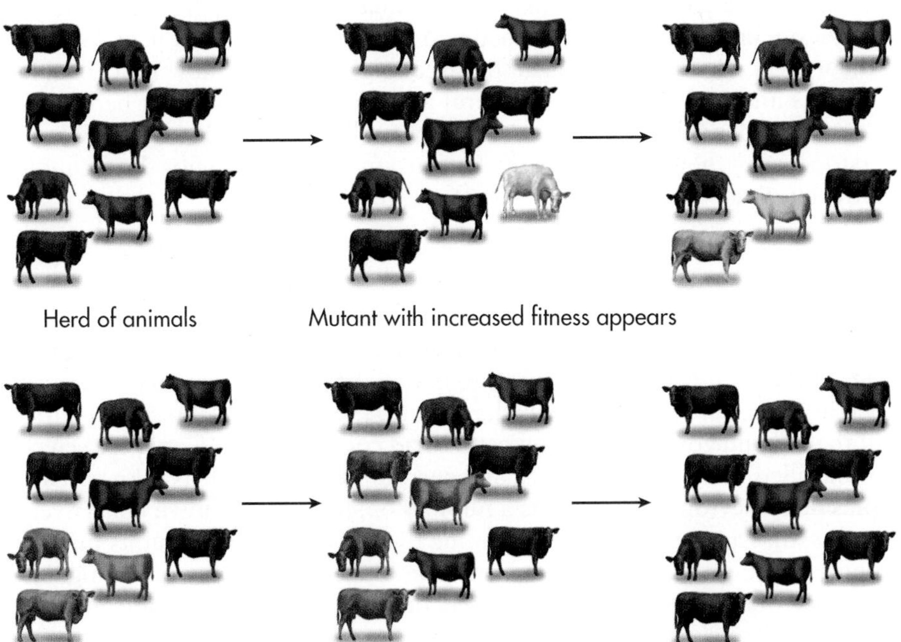
Herd of animals
Mutant with increased fitness appears
With each passing generation, the advantageous feature is "blended out".

FIGURE 3.1 Blending inheritance formed the basis of 19th-century critiques of evolution by natural selection.

of the individual who possessed it. With blending inheritance, it would be expected that if this individual mated with an individual who did not possess that advantageous trait, their offspring would represent some intermediate form between the phenotypes of the parent. As such, the offspring would not have the fitness advantage possessed by the parent with the new trait. With each passing generation, the advantageous trait would be diminished, blended out of existence. It was very difficult to see how natural selection could work under such circumstances, although convoluted and wholly speculative theories of inheritance were offered to try to counter this argument.

blending inheritance
A discredited nineteenth-century idea that genetic factors from the parents averaged-out or blended together when they were passed on to offspring.

Gregor Mendel's careful experimental work demonstrated the non-blending nature of heredity. He demonstrated that inheritance did not involve the blending of substances, but that traits are passed on by individual particles; he called these particles "factors" and we call them "genes." (The term *gene* was coined in the early 1900s by a Danish botanist named Wilhelm Johannsen, as an abbreviation of the term *pangen*. Pangen was first used by Hugo de Vries in 1889 to describe the particulate unit of inheritance that was being passed on from generation to generation. Neither Johannsen nor any of his colleagues at that time knew exactly what a gene was in a biochemical sense.) Mendel (Figure 3.2) also gave us a basic model for how traits are inherited, based on traits that are controlled by a single gene.

FIGURE 3.2 Gregor Mendel.

The twentieth century saw a steady increase in our understanding of the biological mechanisms underlying heredity, with the gene evolving from a theoretical construct to a well-described biochemical entity. The first modern evolutionary synthesis connected the discovery of the units of evolution, genes, with Darwin's mechanism of evolution by natural selection, and incorporated the mathematics of population genetics. Dobzhansky's work on fruit flies is often considered the first comprehensive neo-Darwinian approach to evolutionary theory and is well known to many biology students, although several other scholars are also credited as architects of the modern synthesis. More recently, a second synthesis, that of evolutionary biology with molecular genetics, has been recognized, and the modern synthesis continues to be developed and refined in the light of new discoveries and theoretical advances (see Suggested Reading). We move now to a consideration of cells and molecules, the structural and biochemical bases of heredity and variation that Mendel and the scientists of the early 1900s could not possibly have understood since they had neither the background knowledge nor the technology to study inheritance at the chemical level.

eukaryote A cell that possesses a well-organized nucleus.

nucleus In eukaryotic cells, the part of the cell in which the genetic material is separated from the rest of the cell (cytoplasm) by a plasma membrane.

cytoplasm In a eukaryotic cell, the region within the cell membrane that surrounds the nucleus; it contains organelles, which carry out the essential functions of the cell, such as energy production, metabolism, and protein synthesis.

prokaryotes Single-celled organisms, such as bacteria, in which the genetic material is not separated from the rest of the cell by a nucleus.

somatic cells The cells of the body that are not sex cells.

gametes The sex cells: sperm in males and eggs (or ova) in females.

stem cells Undifferentiated cells found in the developing embryo that can be induced to differentiate into a wide variety of cell types or tissues. Also found in adults, although adult stem cells are not as totipotent as embryonic stem cells.

deoxyribonucleic acid (DNA) A double-stranded molecule that is the carrier of genetic information. Each strand is composed of a linear sequence of nucleotides; the two strands are held together by hydrogen bonds that form between complementary bases.

proteins Complex molecules formed from chains of amino acids (polypeptide) or from a complex of polypeptides. They function as structural molecules, transport molecules, antibodies, enzymes, and hormones.

THE CELL

Humans have eukaryotic cells, or **eukaryotes**, which possess a well-organized **nucleus** that contains the cell's genetic material. The outer boundary of the cell is defined by a *plasma membrane*, which regulates the transport of material into and out of the cell and governs communication and coordinated activity between cells. The fluid-filled space within the cell and surrounding the nucleus is known as the **cytoplasm.** The cytoplasm contains a number of structures, known collectively as *organelles*, that are essential in maintaining the cell and carrying out its functions. In contrast, the **prokaryotes**, which include bacteria and blue-green algae, are single-celled organisms in which the genetic material is not separated from the rest of the cell by a nucleus.

Our eukaryotic cells include gametes and somatic cells. Gametes are the germ cells that are directly involved in propagation or reproduction. In animals, male gametes are called sperm and female gametes are called ova. **Somatic cells** are simply the cells of the body that are not **gametes**. Complex organisms have a variety of somatic cell types. Humans have around 200 different types of tissues, each of which is composed of a characteristic somatic cell type (Klug and Cummings, 2003). We have nerve cells, muscle cells, skin cells, bone cells, cells that secrete hormones, and so on. At the earliest stages of its development, the human embryo contains a population of cells known as **stem cells**. These cells are *totipotent*, which means they can differentiate into any of the somatic cell types found in the foetus or adult. Stem cells are also found in adults, but adult stem cells can differentiate into a more limited variety of cell types (Stewart and Pryzborski, 2002).

Stem cell research has become an important and controversial topic in recent years. Given their totipotent capacity, embryonic stem cells may be useful for treating diseases that are characterized by the loss of specific types of cells. An example of this is *Parkinson's disease*, a nervous system disorder characterized by movement problems, which is caused by the loss of a certain population of cells in the brain. It is hoped that embryonic stem cells may be able to replace (that is, take on their form and function) the specific cells lost in Parkinson's disease. The controversy surrounding embryonic stem cell research lies in the fact that human embryos (produced in the laboratory through in vitro fertilization) historically have been the only source of totipotent stem cells; after the stem cells are removed, the embryos are no longer viable. This controversy may well be eliminated by future research, however: recent advances indicate that non-embryonic cells from the amniotic fluid surrounding a foetus can be removed without harming the foetus and can be differentiated into muscle, bone, and nerve cells (De Coppi et al., 2007). Research is also being done on adult stem cells to see whether they can be coaxed into forming a greater variety of cell types than they would under more natural conditions.

CELL ANATOMY

It should come as no surprise that different types of cells have different anatomies, which serve the functional or structural needs of a particular tissue. Nonetheless, almost all somatic cells share a host of characteristics that can be represented in

Box 3.1 The Study of Genetics

If a scientist says that he or she works on the genetics of an organism, this can mean several different things. Biological organisms differ greatly from one another, ranging from the very simple (such as a bacterium) to the very complex (such as a mammal), and the role genetics plays in influencing what an animal is and does varies correspondingly. In complex animals, genetics can be approached from several different levels, depending on what aspect of the organism is of interest. These include the following:

Cellular and molecular genetics. Cellular and molecular genetics involves the study of genetics at the level of the basic building blocks of bodies (cells) and at the most fundamental level of genetic transmission (the DNA molecule). We often hear about exciting advances in molecular genetics in the news as scientists attempt to devise genetic therapies for disease or determine the precise makeup of our DNA and that of other animals.

Classical or Mendelian genetics. Classical genetics, such as that done by Mendel or Johannsen, involves looking at *pedigrees* of related individuals (plant or animal) and tracking how various traits are passed from one generation to the next. Although pedigree studies go back to the beginning of genetic science, they are still essential in the age of molecular genetics. After all, we are usually not interested in the variation of the molecules per se but in the observable traits they influence. These traits must first be identified as genetic features using pedigree analysis or a related technique.

Population genetics. Biological species usually are divided into populations composed of groups of individuals who associate more with one another than with members of another population. Different populations within species almost always vary at the genetic level. By examining the genetic variation within and among populations (at both the molecular level and at the level of observable traits), we can gain insights into the evolutionary history of those populations and of the species as a whole.

Phylogenetics. This field is concerned with determining evolutionary relationships between species, usually by constructing treelike diagrams that visually indicate how closely or distantly species are related to one another. Although traditionally it has been done by comparing observable traits, over the last 30 years the methods of molecular genetics have come to the forefront of phylogenetic analysis.

Behavioural genetics. When one honeybee transmits information to another honeybee about the location of a flower, the behaviour of both honeybees is under strong genetic control. When we look at other animals, especially animals that engage in more complex forms of behaviour that may involve learning, the role of genetics is more difficult to ascertain. Behavioural genetics involves trying to understand how the behaviour of animals, including humans, is influenced by genetics. It is a controversial field, especially in regard to human behaviour, because human behaviour is especially complex and is the product of multiple, interacting influences.

the figure of a generic cell. Although gametes share some of the characteristics of somatic cells, there are also some fundamental differences, which we'll discuss separately.

In most eukaryotic cells (Figure 3.3), the most prominent structure in the cytoplasm is the nucleus. The nucleus is bounded by its own membrane or envelope, which separates its contents from the rest of the cytoplasm. Within the nucleus, the hereditary material, **deoxyribonucleic acid (DNA)**—the substance that genes are made of—is found. DNA is a double-stranded complex molecule. Two of the primary functions of DNA are making **proteins** for the body, or **protein synthesis**, and cellular replication. Another complex molecule, **ribonucleic acid (RNA)**, which is similar structurally to DNA but is single stranded, is also found in large quantities in the nucleus and in the cytoplasm. RNA is essential for carrying out the protein synthesis function of DNA.

Floating in the cytoplasm of the cell are several other important structures or organelles. These structures are analogous to the organs of the body, and they are responsible for functions such as metabolizing nutrients and eliminating waste, energy synthesis, and protein synthesis. The **mitochondria** (sing. *mitochondrion*) are capsule-shaped organelles that number in the hundreds or thousands in each cell. Mitochondria are the site where a series of metabolic reactions take place and are known as the "powerhouse" of the cell. Another important feature of mitochondria

protein synthesis The assembly of proteins from amino acids, which occurs at ribosomes in the cytoplasm and is based on information carried by messenger RNA.

ribonucleic acid (RNA) Single-stranded nucleic acid that performs critical functions during protein synthesis and comes in three forms: messenger RNA, transfer RNA, and ribosomal RNA.

mitochondria Organelles in the cytoplasm of the cell where energy production for the cell takes place. Contains its own DNA.

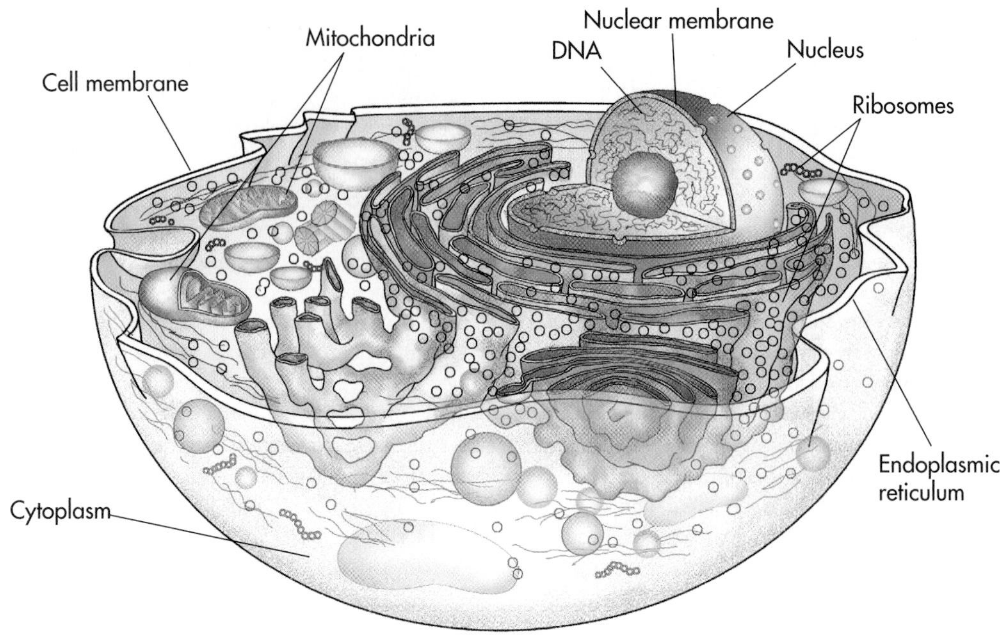

FIGURE 3.3 A typical eukaryotic cell.

is that they have their own DNA, which is not contained in a nucleus and is different from the DNA found in the nucleus of the cell. *Mitochondrial DNA* (mtDNA) has proved to be an important tool in evolutionary and anthropological research.

The **endoplasmic reticulum** (**ER**) is another organelle found in the cytoplasm. The ER is a complex structure, with a folded-sheet appearance. It provides increased surface area within the cell for metabolic reactions to take place. Some of the endoplasmic reticulum has a knobby appearance; the knobs are **ribosomes**, the site in the cell where proteins are synthesized. Molecules of ribosomal RNA (rRNA) form a large component of ribosomes. The synthesis of ribosomes begins in the nucleus but can be completed only in the cytoplasm. Because completed ribosomes cannot pass through the nuclear membrane, protein synthesis always occurs in the cytoplasm.

DNA STRUCTURE AND FUNCTION

Hereditary material—DNA—has to be able to do three things. First, it must be able to make copies of itself, or *replicate*, so that it can be passed from generation to generation. Second, it has to be able to make proteins, which are the most important components of cells. Third, it must coordinate the activity of proteins to produce bodies, or at least have some way to translate the information it carries about making bodies into growing actual bodies (that is, development). As it turns out, the chemical structure of DNA lends itself to self-replication and to carrying the information necessary for making proteins; however, the third function—directing development—is much more complex and is beyond the scope of this text.

endoplasmic reticulum (ER) An organelle in the cytoplasm consisting of a folded membrane.

ribosomes Structures composed primarily of RNA, which are found on the endoplasmic reticulum. They are the site of protein synthesis.

nucleotide Molecular building block of nucleic acids DNA and RNA; consists of a phosphate, sugar, and base.

DNA STRUCTURE I: THE MOLECULAR LEVEL

The structure of the DNA molecule is a double helix, resembling a ladder twisted around its central axis. The basic unit of DNA (and RNA) is a molecule called a **nucleotide** (Figure 3.4). A nucleotide consists of three parts: a sugar, a phosphate group, and a nitrogenous **base**, either adenine (A), thymine (T), cytosine (C), or guanine (G). The DNA molecule is assembled from four different nucleotide units, which vary according to the base they carry. DNA consists of two separate strands, corresponding to the two sides of the ladder, each of which is made up of a chain of

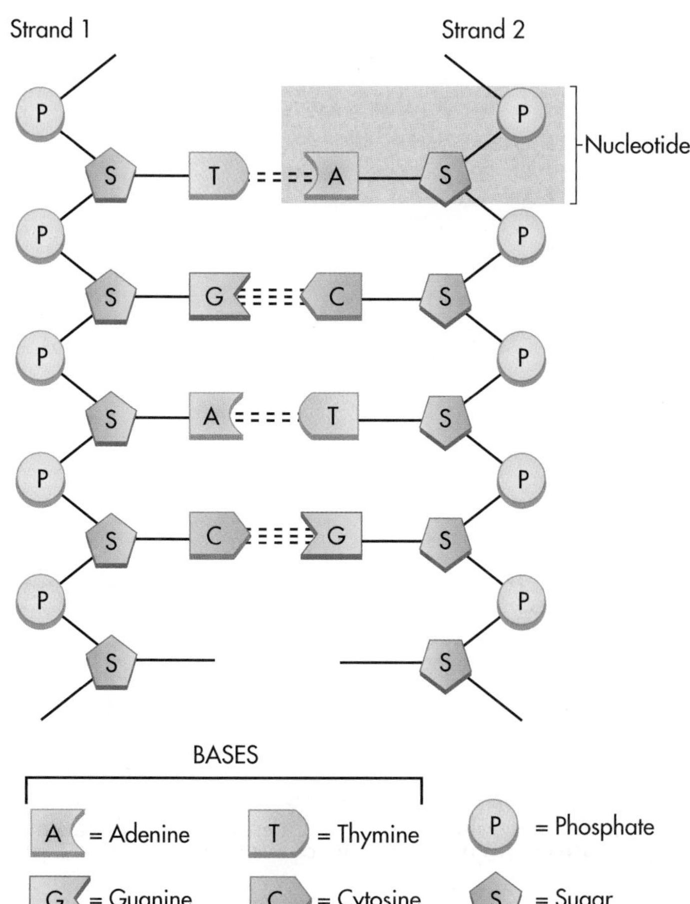

FIGURE 3.4 The nucleotide structure of DNA. The dashed lines between the A-T and C-G pairings indicate hydrogen bonds.

nucleotides (Figure 3.5). The sugar of one nucleotide bonds to the phosphate group of the next one; thus, each side of the DNA ladder is composed of alternating sugar and phosphate molecules. The bases point toward the centre of the ladder and form its rungs. The rungs are formed by two bases, one projecting from each side of the ladder. The elucidation of this structure of DNA by James Watson and Francis Crick in 1953, aided by Maurice Wilkins and Rosalind Franklin (Figure 3.6) launched the modern era in molecular genetics and led to a Nobel Prize in Medicine in 1962.

The bases are paired only in A-T or T-A and G-C or C-G combinations. For example, if there is a sequence of nucleotides on one side of the DNA that goes ATCGATCG, then on the other side of the ladder, the sequence will be TAGCTAGC. The Human Genome Project is an ongoing effort to find the sequence of these chemical building blocks that make up the genes and to map the location of genes on chromosomes. The Project began in 1990 and in 2003 published a draft sequence of the human **genome**, with further refinements published in 2006. Canada is only one of the many countries that have contributed to this project. Over 30 genes have been pinpointed and associated with breast cancer, muscle disease, deafness, and blindness. In addition, the DNA sequences underlying such common diseases as cardiovascular disease, diabetes, arthritis, and various cancers are being identified by the data generated by the Human Genome Project (for further information, see the Project's Web site at www.ornl.gov/sci/techresources/Human_Genome/home.shtml).

base Variable component of the nucleotides that form nucleic acids DNA and RNA. In DNA, the bases are adenine, guanine, thymine, and cytosine. In RNA, uracil replaces thymine.

genome The hereditary information of an organism, encoded in the DNA (or, for some viruses, RNA)

DNA FUNCTION I: REPLICATION

The paired nature of the DNA molecule makes it possible for the molecule to make copies of itself during cell division. Simply put, the DNA molecule, or a portion of

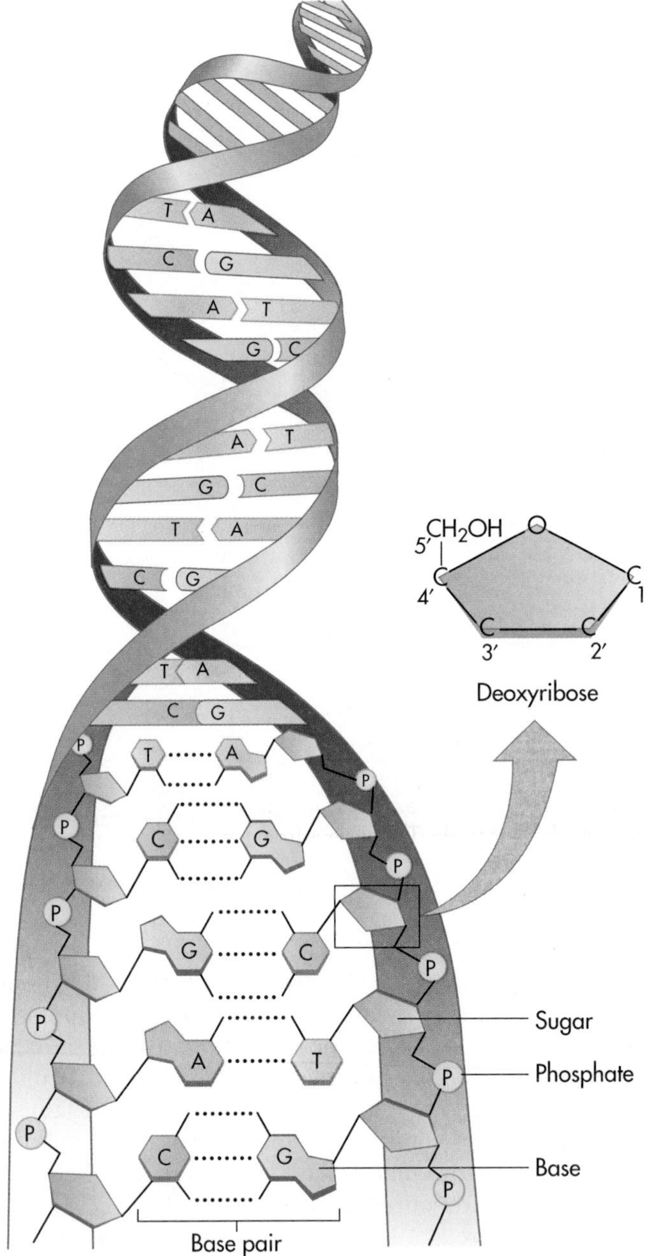

FIGURE 3.5 The double-helix structure of DNA. RNA is very similar to DNA except that it is a single-stranded molecule, and the thymine in DNA is replaced by uracil (U), which also bonds to adenine.

it, divides into two separate strands. After separation, each of the strands serves as a template for the assembly, nucleotide by nucleotide, of a new complementary strand of DNA. When the process is completed, there are two copies of the mother DNA molecule, each of which is made up of one original side and one newly synthesized side.

Errors in DNA replication can have important consequences for the survival of an organism. If these errors in DNA replication are not corrected, they can lead to permanent changes in the DNA of a cell. These changes are known as mutations. Mutations can alter cell function in many different ways. For example, a mutation can transform a cell, causing it to replicate at an accelerated rate; such uncontrolled cell growth is the basis of cancer. Mutations that occur in gametes can be passed from one generation to the next and may have profound effects on the biology of offspring.

Box 3.2 Cloning Controversies

In September 2000, a cloned Holstein calf, named Starbuck II, was born in St. Hyacinthe, Quebec, through the combined efforts of L'Alliance Boviteq Inc., the Centre d'insémination artificielle du Québec, and the Faculté de médecine vétérinaire de l'Université de Montréal. The calf was cloned from a frozen skin cell obtained from the prize-winning bull Hanoverhill Starbuck before he died in 1998.

The process of cloning is straightforward, which is not to say that it is easy (Solter, 2000). First, the nucleus of a somatic cell (which contains a copy of all the genetic material of an individual) is carefully removed. Often the cell comes from a cell line that has been established in a laboratory, not directly from the body. At the same time, the nucleus of an egg (or *oocyte*) is carefully removed, preserving the cell membrane and the cytoplasm as much as possible. The nucleus from the somatic cell is then transferred to the oocyte either mechanically via microinjection or by using an inactivated virus as a carrier for the genetic material. Once the new nucleus is introduced to the egg, the egg is *activated*, which initiates the development of the embryo. In normal fertilization, the introduction of the sperm to the egg causes activation. In cloning, an electrical current applied to the egg (with the new nucleus) activates the egg. It is possible to use a fertilized egg that has already been activated (after the removal of both the egg and sperm nuclei), but they are harder to come by than unfertilized eggs. Activation is essential to reprogram the donor nucleus away from whatever its original function was and toward the development of a new individual. Once the embryo begins to develop, the egg can be implanted into a surrogate mother, and the pregnancy proceeds in the usual way.

The creation of Starbuck II took 68 attempts at producing viable embryos. Fifteen surrogate mothers were used. Six pregnancies survived to 60 days; only one went to term.

Sheep, cows, mice, and pigs have all been cloned. For each group, the success rate of growing a clone (egg with a new nucleus) to adulthood is about 1%. The live birth rate is perhaps twice as high as this, but a number of cloned newborns have problems and die before adulthood.

Another problem that arises with cloned individuals is that even if they survive to adulthood, they do not live as long. In a study of cloned mice, it was found that only two of twelve cloned mice lived as long as 800 days, compared with ten of thirteen control mice (Ogonuki et al., 2002). A cloned sheep lived less than 7 years, whereas sheep usually live to be 11 to 12 years (Coghlan, 2003). Scientists are not yet sure why this happens. At one time it was thought that the short life span of cloned individuals involved structures called *telomeres*, which are pieces of DNA that cap the ends of chromosomes and which may become shortened after each cloning. The length of telomeres is believed to be related to aging, so shortened telomeres could make producing offspring more difficult. But in some cases the telomeres actually appear to be longer with each generation, so that's not likely the problem.

Why do we need cloning? Agricultural scientists are working on cloning to develop methods for efficiently propagating animals that have desired characteristics. After all, sexual reproduction leads to an inefficient genetic mixing (recombination or crossing over) every generation. Sperm from Starbuck II, for example, has been used to sire offspring, and it has been reported recently that his progeny have normal chromosomal stability, growth, and physical, hematological, and reproductive parameters (Ortegon et al., 2006).

Other scientists see cloning as a potential tool to save endangered or even extinct species, such as the giant panda or the extinct Tasmanian wolf (Mazurek, 1999). The largest wild populations of our closest relatives, the chimpanzee and gorilla, declined by one-half between 1983 and 2000 (Walsh et al., 2003), and the development of efficient cloning techniques may someday help save these threatened species.

Arguments in favour of human reproductive cloning are harder to come by. The poor survival rate of cloned individuals from other mammal species is reason enough to consider human reproductive cloning to be an unethical undertaking. Canada banned human cloning in 2004, citing concerns over sex selection of offspring and commercialization of sperm and eggs, among other issues.

Many consider therapeutic cloning, however, to be a different matter. Imagine a patient who has a disease that may be curable by the introduction of a working cell type to replace cells that are nonfunctional or have been destroyed. Somatic cells from that patient could be used to make cloned embryos. At a very early stage of development (the blastocyst stage), embryonic stem cells could be recovered and then coerced in the lab into growing into the cell type the patient needs. Once a population of these cells has grown, they are transferred to the patient. Because the patient is the original source for the cells, there would be no worry about immunological rejection. It is clear that even if some countries ban therapeutic cloning, other countries will work hard to develop this technique.

FIGURE A Starbuck II, a cloned Holstein calf.

(a)

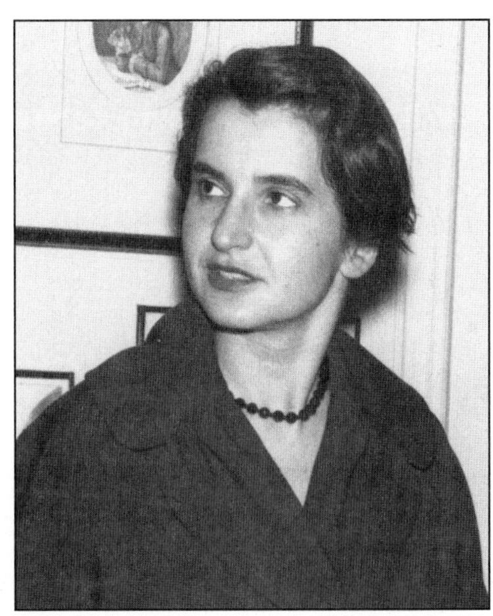

(b)

FIGURE 3.6 (a) Some of the 1962 Nobel Prize winners. Francis Crick is at far left, Maurice Wilkins is next to Crick, and James Watson is third from the right. Also pictured are Nobel Laureates John Steinbeck (Literature), and Max Perutz and John Kendrew (Chemistry). (b) Rosalind Franklin made an essential contribution to the discovery of DNA structure but died four years before these Nobel Prizes were awarded.

DNA FUNCTION II: PROTEIN SYNTHESIS

haemoglobin Protein found in red blood cells that transports oxygen.

hormone A natural substance (often a protein) produced by specialized cells in one location of the body that influences the activity or physiology of cells in a different location.

enzyme A complex protein that is a catalyst for chemical processes in the body.

amino acids Molecules that form the basic building blocks of protein.

polypeptide A molecule made up of a chain of amino acids.

genetic code The system whereby the nucleotide triplets in DNA and RNA contain the information for synthesizing proteins from the 20 amino acids.

codon A triplet of nucleotide bases in messenger RNA that specifies an amino acid or the initiation or termination of a polypeptide sequence.

Proteins are the workhorse molecules of biological organisms and the most common large molecules found in cells. Structural tissues, such as bone and muscle, are composed primarily of protein. Proteins such as **haemoglobin**, a protein molecule in red blood cells, bind to oxygen and transport it throughout the body, while other transport proteins facilitate the movement of molecules across cell membranes. Some proteins function as **hormones** and hormone receptors and regulate many bodily functions. Antibodies or immunoglobulins are proteins of the immune system, which our bodies use to fight disease or any biochemical invader. The largest class of proteins in the body are the **enzymes**. These proteins lower the activation energy of (*catalyze*) countless biochemical reactions in cells. Many biochemical reactions happen at physiological temperatures (body temperature) only if catalyzed by enzymes. So enzymes are essential for life.

Proteins are complex molecules made up of smaller molecules known as **amino acids**. Amino acids share a common chemical structure that allows them to bond to one another in long chains. There are twenty different amino acids that function as building blocks for proteins. Of these twenty, nine are essential amino acids (Laidlaw and Kopple, 1987). This means they cannot be synthesized by the body and must be obtained from protein in the diet. The nonessential amino acids can be synthesized from the essential amino acids.

A typical protein may be made up of a chain of 200-amino acids; such a chain can also be called a **polypeptide**. Any combination of the twenty different amino acids may go into this chain. Thus the number of possible 200-amino acid proteins that may be generated from the twenty kinds of amino acids is immense (20^{200}). At a primary level, proteins differ from one another by length and by the sequence of amino acids in the polypeptide chain. However, protein structures generally are much more complex than a simple linear chain. The sequence of amino acids in a polypeptide governs how the chain may be folded in space or how it may associate with other polypeptide chains to form a larger, complex protein. For example, the protein haemoglobin is composed of four separate polypeptide chains, which in conjunction assume a complex three-dimensional form. The form that a protein takes is integral to its function.

Because proteins are made of chains of amino acids, the structure and function of proteins are determined by the sequence of amino acids in their polypeptide chains. The structure of DNA, in which different bases are lined up in sequence, is ideal for carrying other kinds of sequential information, such as the sequence of amino acids in a protein. The system that has evolved to represent protein amino acid sequences in the base pair sequence of DNA is known as the **genetic code**.

There are twenty different amino acids in proteins, but there are only four different bases in DNA. Obviously, there are not enough types of bases to represent each amino acid. If two bases in sequence were used to represent an amino acid, there would still be only sixteen possible combinations (4^2), which is not enough to represent the twenty amino acids. However, three bases in sequence produce sixty-four (4^3) unique triplet combinations—more than enough to have a unique triplet sequence of bases represent each of the twenty amino acids. The genetic code therefore consists of three-base sequences, called **codons**, each of which represents a single amino acid. There is *redundancy* in the code: Given that there are sixty-four possible codons and only twenty amino acids, most of the amino acids are represented by more than one codon. Three of the codons do not code for any amino acid but instead signal that the protein chain has come to an end; they are called termination codons. Another codon typically serves as an initiation codon, signalling the beginning of a polypeptide chain.

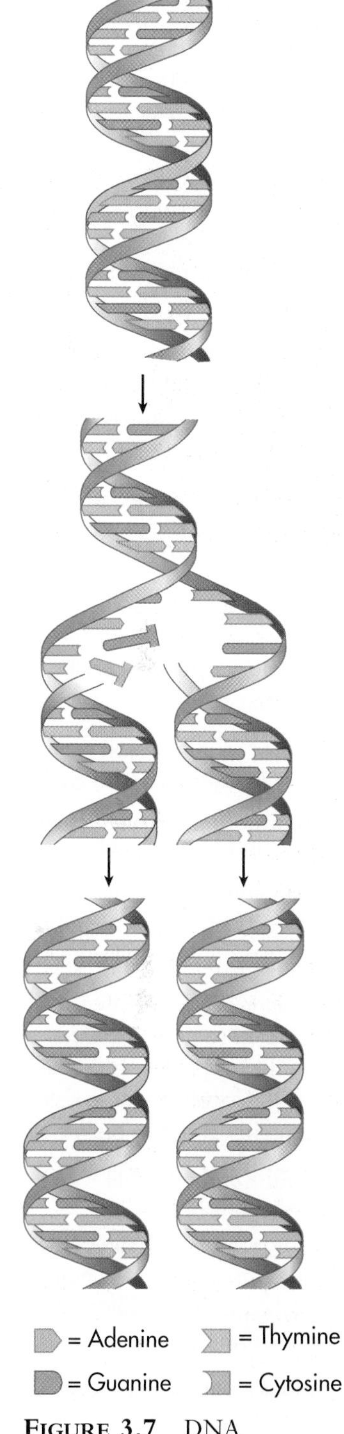

Figure 3.7 DNA replication.

The information to make proteins is represented, via the genetic code, in the sequence of bases in a portion of a DNA molecule. The part of a DNA molecule that contains the information for one protein (or for one polypeptide chain that makes up part of a protein) is called a **gene**. One DNA molecule can have many genes arrayed along its length. Given the triplet codons of the genetic code, a protein with 300 amino acids would need 900 bases to represent it (not including initiation or termination signals) in a gene. A single gene can consist of hundreds of thousands of bases, and current estimates are that human beings have between 30 000 and 40 000 genes in total.

So how does the information to make a protein, encoded in the DNA, actually become a protein? It involves two steps, *transcription* and *translation*, along with the participation of RNA molecules with specialized functions. Transcription occurs in the nucleus of the cell, while translation (protein synthesis) occurs in the cytoplasm. Each step is mediated by specialized enzymes.

Transcription begins when the two DNA strands split apart in a region where a gene is represented on one of the strands. The whole molecule does not split apart because only the region where the gene is located must be read. When the DNA molecule separates, the strand corresponding to the gene can serve as a template for the synthesis of a single-stranded RNA molecule. As mentioned previously, RNA is a nucleic acid, like DNA. At the site of the gene, a complementary RNA molecule is synthesized: In effect, the information of the gene is transcribed from the language of DNA to the related language of RNA. When an RNA molecule has been synthesized that corresponds to the entire gene, it separates from the DNA and exists as a free-floating, single-stranded molecule. The two strands of the DNA reattach to each other, returning the DNA to its intact double helix structure. The free RNA molecule is called **messenger RNA (mRNA)**. This is an appropriate name because the mRNA carries the information of the gene from the nucleus of the cell to the cytoplasm, which is where protein synthesis or translation takes place.

gene The fundamental unit of heredity. It consists of a sequence of DNA bases that carries the information for synthesizing a protein (or polypeptide), and occupies a specific chromosomal locus.

Protein synthesis occurs at ribosomes, where the information the mRNA carries is translated into a protein molecule. The mRNA is read at the ribosome, from beginning to end, two codons at a time. At this point in the process, another critical molecule enters the picture: **transfer RNA (tRNA)**. The job of tRNA is to transport a single, specific amino acid to the ribosome, so that it can be attached to the growing protein chain. The tRNA has a three-base region called the

messenger RNA (mRNA) Strand of RNA synthesized in the nucleus as a complement to a specific gene (transcription). It carries the information for the sequence of amino acids to make a specific protein into the cytoplasm, where at a ribosome it is read and a protein molecule is synthesized (translation).

transfer RNA (tRNA) RNA molecules that bind to specific amino acids and transport them to ribosomes to be used during protein synthesis.

chromatin The diffuse form of DNA as it exists during the interphase of the cell cycle.

mitosis Somatic cell division in which a single cell divides to produce two identical daughter cells.

meiosis Cell division that occurs in the testes and ovaries that leads to the formation of sperm and ova (gametes).

chromosome Discrete structures composed of condensed DNA and supporting proteins.

centromere Condensed and constricted region of a chromosome. During mitosis and meiosis, this is the location where sister chromatids attach to one another.

diploid number Full complement of paired chromosomes in a somatic cell. In humans, the diploid number is 46 (23 pairs of different chromosomes).

haploid number The number of chromosomes found in a gamete, representing one from each pair found in a diploid somatic cell. In humans, the haploid number is 23.

homologous chromosomes Members of the same pair of chromosomes (or autosomes). Homologous chromosomes undergo crossing over during meiosis.

anticodon that is complementary to the codon on the mRNA. When an mRNA codon (ACU, for example, which corresponds to the DNA triplet TGA) is read at the ribosome, a tRNA with the anticodon UGA temporarily aligns to the mRNA and brings the amino acid into position. Then the next codon on the mRNA is read, and a second tRNA brings the appropriate amino acid into position next to the first amino acid. Once the two amino acids are next to each other, a chemical reaction requiring energy occurs, and a bond is formed between the two amino acids. The ribosome then moves down one codon, while the growing peptide chain moves in the opposite direction.

This process continues until the entire mRNA has been read and the complete protein (or polypeptide chain) has been assembled. A single mRNA molecule can be read by several ribosomes at the same time, and thus one mRNA molecule can lead to the synthesis of several copies of the same protein molecule.

Of course in the real world of cells, protein synthesis is a bit more complicated than outlined here. For example, most of our DNA does not code for anything, but as we will see later, this noncoding DNA has important ramifications for a variety of genetic processes.

DNA Structure II: Chromosomes and Cell Division

We have 2 to 3 metres (6.6 to 9.8 ft) of DNA in the nucleus of each somatic cell. Most of the time, the DNA in these cells exists in dispersed, uncoiled strands, supported by proteins. DNA in this state is called **chromatin**. However, during **mitosis** and **meiosis**, the two processes of cell division or replication, the chromatin condenses and coils into larger, tightly wound, discrete structures called **chromosomes** (which, like chromatin, are composed of DNA and supporting proteins) (Figure 3.8). Because chromosomes are visible under the light microscope, scientists were able to study them and learn something about genetic mechanisms before DNA was identified. Each chromosome has a distinctive size and shape. The shape is determined in part by the position of the **centromere**, a condensed and constricted region of chromosomes that is of critical importance during cell replication. The size is determined by the size (in numbers of base pairs) of the DNA molecule that makes up the chromosome.

Except for the gametes or sex cells, each somatic cell in an individual's body has the same number of chromosomes. In fact, chromosome number is a constant across entire species. Most organisms have two copies of each chromosome in each cell; in each of these pairs of chromosomes, one is maternally derived and the other is paternally derived. The total number of chromosomes in each somatic cell is called the **diploid number**. Sex cells have only half as many chromosomes as somatic cells (one copy of each chromosome), so the total number of chromosomes in a sex cell is known as the **haploid number**. In a diploid cell, the members of each pair of chromosomes are known as **homologous chromosomes**.

The genes are distributed across the chromosomes, and the locations of specific genes can be mapped to specific chromosomes. Sometimes the term **locus** (pl. *loci*) is used interchangeably with the term *gene*. More specifically, we can think of the locus as the location of a gene on a chromosome. Because somatic cells have two copies of each chromosome, they also have two copies of each gene, one at each locus. Genes come in different versions, called **alleles**. For example, there might be a gene for eye colour, but it could have two alleles, one for brown and one for blue; the locus of this gene could be mapped to a specific chromosome. A real example involves the ABO blood type system (which is discussed in more detail in Chapter 4). At that locus (which is on chromosome 9), there are three possible alleles, called A, B, and O, which determine blood type. When an individual has the same allele for a gene at each locus on each chromosome, this individual is called **homozygous** for that gene (Figure 3.9). If the individual has different alleles of the gene at each locus, then he or she is **heterozygous** for that gene. When we consider that each individual has thousands of genes, each of which may be

Nucleus
The genetic material of somatic cells is packaged into discrete chromosomes in the nucleus. Diploid organisms have two copies of each chromosome.
Somatic Cell
Nucleus
Chromosome
Chromosomes are made of DNA and protein. Genes are located on the chromosomes, and defined by nucleotide base pair sequences. Humans have 23 different chromosomes (haploid number; diploid number is 46), which have from 300+ to 2000+ genes each.
Chromosome structure
Chromosomes become visible (under the microscope) during mitosis, or cell division. This occurs as the diffuse DNA condenses around proteins known as histones into tightly wound structures that form the subunits of the chromosomes.
DNA structure
Each strand of DNA is composed of long sequences of nucleotide bases. The two strands of DNA are held together by weak hydrogen bonds that form between complementary bases from each strand.
DNA
Gene structure
A gene is a sequence of nucleotide bases on a strand of DNA that contains the information to make a protein.

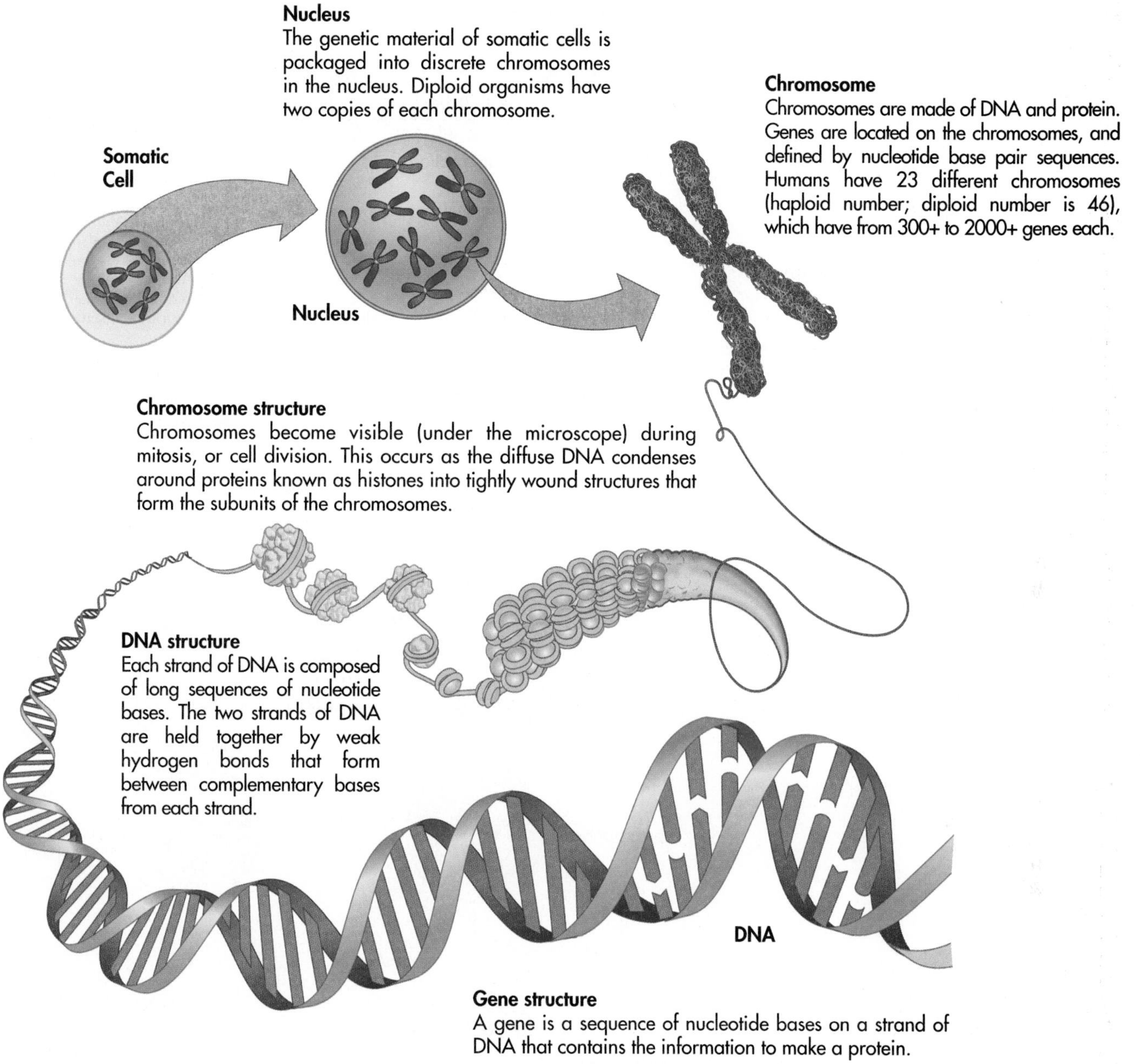

FIGURE 3.8 Chromosome structure.

represented by several alleles, it is easy to see that the number of possible different combinations of alleles is enormous.

Mitosis As stated previously, mitosis is the process whereby a somatic cell replicates, leading to the formation of two identical daughter cells. Mitosis is the basis of all cell proliferation, which can occur in the context of the growth of an organism, during healing, or during any physiological process in which new cells are needed to replace the loss of cells (Figure 3.10).

The ongoing process of cell division and nondivision is known sometimes as the *cell cycle*. The cell cycle can be divided into several stages. The *interphase* is the stage of a cell's life when it is not involved in mitosis; instead, most of its energies are devoted to metabolism and growth. Although the interphase is not part of mitosis, an important premitotic activity occurs toward the end of interphase: The DNA is replicated in preparation for mitosis. During interphase, DNA is packaged into chromatin, and discrete chromosomes are not visible.

locus The location of a gene on a chromosome. The locus for a gene is identified by the number of the chromosome on which it is found and its position on the chromosome.

alleles Alternative versions of a gene. Different alleles are distinguished from one another by their different affects on the phenotypic expression of the same gene.

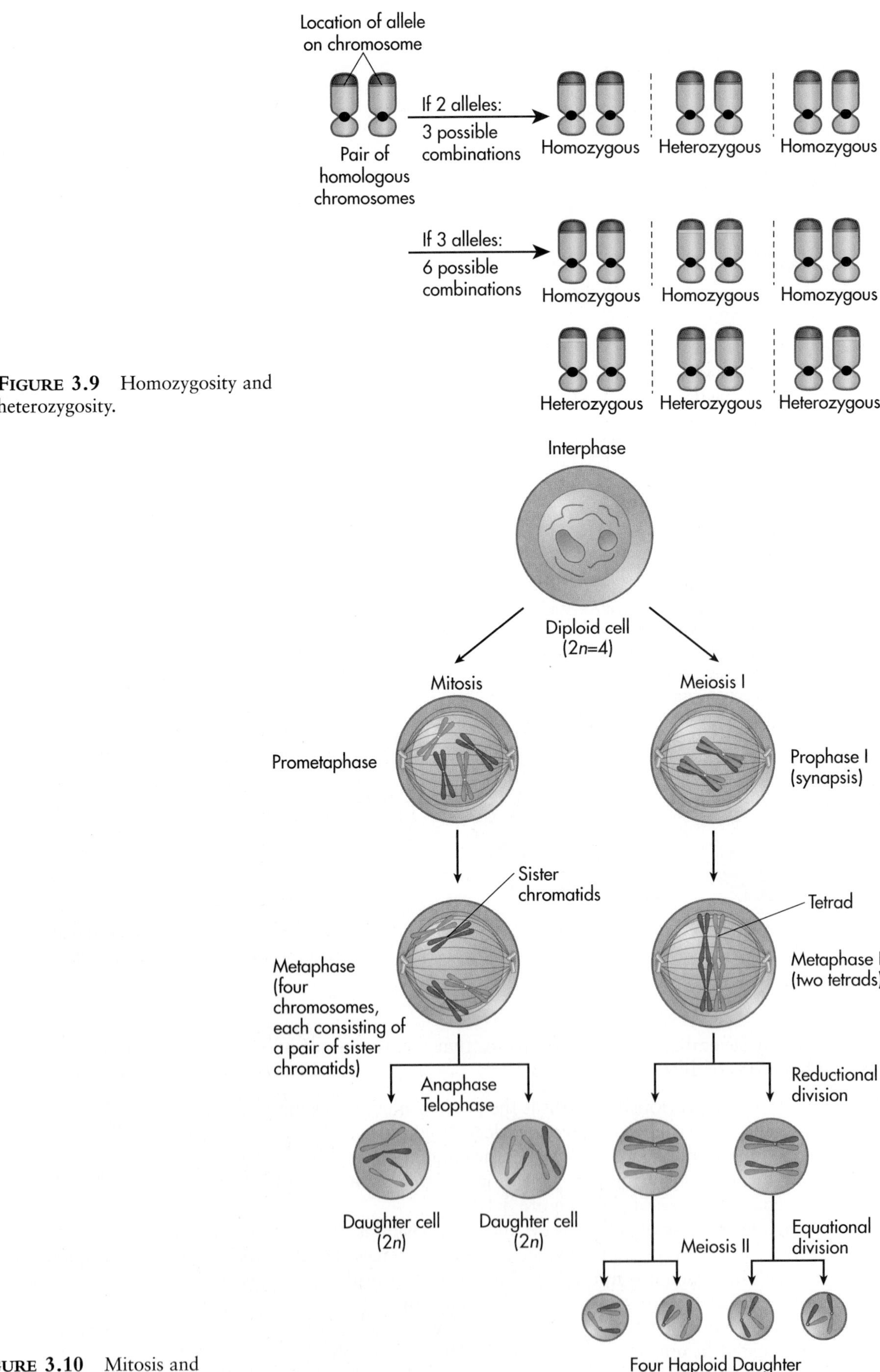

FIGURE 3.9 Homozygosity and heterozygosity.

FIGURE 3.10 Mitosis and meiosis.

The first stage of mitosis is the *prophase*. Three important things happen during the prophase:

1. The nuclear envelope breaks down and disappears.
2. The diffuse chromatin fibres condense and begin to form dense chromosomes. The individual chromosomes actually are doubled chromosomes, composed of two identical sister *chromatids*.
3. The polar orientation of the cell for the division into two daughter cells is established. The prophase often takes up at least half of the process of mitosis.

After prophase, the chromosomes migrate to the equatorial centre of the cell, where they line up in an orderly fashion. When they have reached this position, the cell is in the *metaphase*. The *anaphase* follows the metaphase as the sister chromatids split apart and migrate to opposite ends of the cell. This is usually the shortest part of mitosis. Once the anaphase is completed, there will be a complete diploid complement of *daughter chromosomes* at each end of the cell.

The final stage of mitosis is the *telophase*. During this period, the cytoplasm is split in two, resulting in the complete separation of the two daughter cells, each with its daughter chromosomes. Once the separation is complete, the chromosomes uncoil into chromatin, and the nucleus of the cell forms around the genetic material. The new cell then enters interphase, restarting the cell cycle.

Meiosis The process of meiosis (Figure 3.10) leads to the formation of the gametes (sperm in males and eggs in females), which are cells that have the haploid number of chromosomes (that is, one copy of each chromosome as opposed to the two copies of each found in diploid somatic cells). Meiosis occurs only in the testes of males and the ovaries of females. Like mitosis, meiosis begins with diploid cells, but through an additional cell division, haploid gametes eventually result. The sex cells must be haploid because when the sperm and egg unite to form the **zygote** (fertilized egg), the resulting zygote should re-establish the diploid number of chromosomes.

The first meiotic prophase is similar in some ways to prophase in mitosis but with some critical differences. It is similar in that the replicated DNA condenses into chromosomes, and sister chromatids form. However, unlike in mitosis, in meiosis the double-stranded homologous chromosomes pair up, forming units that are in effect made up of four chromatids (that is, two pairs of sister chromatids); this unit is known as a *tetrad*. At this stage, an important process called **crossing over** occurs. Crossing over is the process whereby genetic material is exchanged between pairs of homologous chromosomes. This process results in a **recombination** of alleles on the chromosomes.

Crossing over is extremely important because it enables new genetic combinations (although not new genes) to be assembled along each chromosome. Crossing over increases the available genetic variability in a population, thereby increasing the amount of variability available for natural selection to act on. The rate of evolution in sexually reproducing species therefore is much faster than in asexually reproducing species. Without sexual reproduction, it is likely that the complexity of plant and animal life on Earth could never have been achieved. Only mutation can provide wholly novel new variants in a population, but the new combinations of genes that arise from sexual reproduction are of critical importance in evolution by natural selection. One advantage of nonsexual reproduction is that it is possible to make sure that an exact copy of a parent is created. Although this would not be an advantageous long-term evolutionary strategy, some people today think that there may be commercial and other reasons to develop artificial cloning techniques.

After crossing over occurs in the first meiotic prophase, a metaphase follows and tetrads align along the equator of the cell. During the *first meiotic division* (also known as the *reduction division*), the chromatid tetrads split, and a double-stranded chromosome is sorted into each daughter cell. This is very different from

homozygous Having the same allele at the loci for a gene on both members of a pair of homologous chromosomes (or autosomes).

heterozygous Having two different alleles at the loci for a gene on a pair of homologous chromosomes (or autosomes).

zygote A fertilized egg.

crossing over Exchange of genetic material between homologous chromosomes during the first prophase of meiosis; mechanism for genetic recombination.

recombination The rearrangement of genes on homologous chromosomes that occurs during crossing over in meiosis. It is the source of variation arising out of sexual reproduction; it is important for increasing rates of natural selection.

BOX 3.3 Biochemical Individuality

Individual human beings differ from one another in physical appearance. Even identical twins have subtle physical differences that allow others to tell them apart. But individuality extends to the biochemical and genetic levels as well. We are as much unique individuals at the biochemical level as at the anatomical level.

In the 1950s, biochemist Roger Williams wrote a monograph called ***Biochemical Individuality*** in which he argued, based on innumerable biochemical measures, that everyone deviated from the norm in some way. In other words, at the biochemical level, everyone was an individual. For example, Williams measured amino acid secretion in saliva. He found that every individual secreted a different combination of amino acids and in different amounts. There were amino acids that were secreted by a small percentage of the people, while other amino acids were more commonly secreted. Williams pointed out that people varied from one another in levels of enzymatic activity, nutritional metabolism, and many other phenotypic expressions of biochemical processes.

Williams's work anticipated later developments in genetics that made it possible to develop unique biochemical profiles for every individual. These methods have come to be used in a variety of forensic settings, especially in the analysis of blood (*forensic serology*). The ability of investigators to identify different alleles of proteins provides a valuable tool for individual identification. Blood types, such as the ABO system, represent one such allelic system, but several other proteins that can be isolated from blood samples also show allelic variation. These proteins allow individual identification because it is very unlikely that two individuals will share exactly the same combination of alleles from a number of variable proteins. For example, if we examine ten blood proteins, each with two alleles that are represented in the population at a frequency of 0.5, the chance that any two individuals from that population will have the same combination of ten alleles is 0.5^{10}, or about 0.00098. If you add some more proteins or if the individual has some alleles that are very rare in the population, you can develop an allelic profile that is unique among the entire human population. It is important to keep in mind that the allele frequencies used to make these calculations must be derived from the individual's own biological population because allele frequencies vary from population to population.

Over the last 20 years, a technique known as *DNA fingerprinting* has been developed to further refine the ability of investigators to make individual genetic identifications (Jeffreys et al., 1985). DNA fingerprinting is based on the fact that there are segments of DNA (called *minisatellites*) dispersed throughout the genome at different loci, which are composed of different numbers of repeated base-pair sequences. These sequences do not code for anything and are highly variable. When the DNA from an individual is digested using an enzyme called a *restriction endonuclease*, a unique pattern of DNA fragments derived from these minisatellites will emerge for each individual (Figure A). Canadian legislation that allowed the creation of a National DNA Databank was passed in 2000. DNA samples can be collected from convicted criminal offenders and the resulting DNA profiles can be used only for law enforcement purposes (strict guidelines regarding genetic privacy are specified in the *DNA Identification Act*). The databank has assisted law enforcement agencies by helping to eliminate suspects, identify suspects, and link crimes, and by the spring of 2007 more than 7000 matches had been made between crime scenes and convicted offenders.

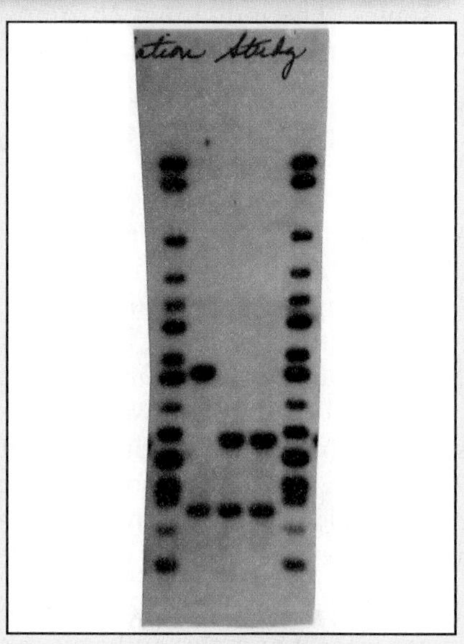

FIGURE A DNA fingerprint.

what happens in mitosis. In mitosis, the doubled-chromosomes separate so that each daughter cell winds up with one paternally derived chromosome and one maternally derived chromosome, just as the mother cell had. In the first meiotic division, one daughter cell has two copies of the maternal chromosome and the other has two copies of the paternal chromosome (although after crossing over, of course, they are no longer identical to the parental chromosomes).

Once the first cell division is complete and after another round of prophase and metaphase, the *second meiotic cell division* occurs. During this division, the paired chromatids split—as they do in mitosis—resulting in a total of four haploid gametes (two from each of the two daughter cells of the first meiotic division) with only one copy of each chromosome.

Different Kinds and Numbers of Chromosomes As mentioned previously, chromosomes come in different sizes and shapes, and different species have different numbers of chromosomes. Humans have 23 different chromosomes (haploid number) and a diploid number of 46. Of the 46 chromosomes in humans, 44 can be distributed into 22 homologous pairs. These are called **autosomes**. The 23rd pair is the **sex chromosomes**. In mammals, the sex chromosomes are labelled X and Y, and the autosomes are numbered (in humans, from 1 to 22). Mammalian males have one X chromosome and one Y chromosome, whereas females have two X chromosomes. Because females have only X chromosomes, it is the sex cells of the male, who can produce gametes with one X and one Y chromosome, that determine the sex of the offspring.

Even closely related species can have different numbers of chromosomes. In chimpanzees, our closest living biological relatives, the haploid number is 24 chromosomes, and the diploid number is 48. At some point since humans and chimpanzees last shared a common ancestor, the packaging of DNA into chromosomes changed. As it turns out, the other great apes, the gorilla and orangutan, to which we are also closely related, have the same number of chromosomes as a chimpanzee. Thus, along our unique evolutionary lineage, humans had a fusion of two chromosomes, resulting in the loss of one chromosome. Note that this does not mean a loss of DNA because chromosomes are indicative only of the packaging, but not the amount, of DNA. We do not know whether the fusion of these two chromosomes was a critical event in human evolutionary history. Among the gibbons—small-bodied Asian apes—there are several species whose diploid chromosome numbers vary from 38 to 52, and yet in physical appearance and behaviour the species are not all that different from one another (Marks, 1992). Certainly they are nowhere near as different from one another as humans are from any of the great apes.

Chromosomal Abnormalities In humans, individuals with abnormalities in chromosome number usually suffer from a range of medical and developmental problems; chromosomal abnormalities probably are also a common cause of miscarriages. **Nondisjunction errors** that occur during meiosis result in the misdistribution of chromosomes to the sex cells (that is, one receives both copies of the chromosomes and the sister cell receives none). If fertilization occurs with either of these sex cells, this leads to an inappropriate number of chromosomes in the fertilized egg, or zygote. For example, *trisomy* occurs when there is an extra chromosome, resulting in three copies of the chromosomes rather than a pair.

Down syndrome, or *trisomy 21*, occurs when an individual has three rather than two copies of chromosome 21. Individuals with Down syndrome share a constellation of features, including a common facial anatomy and head shape, short stature, a furrowed tongue, and short, broad hands with characteristic palm and fingerprint patterns. People with Down syndrome also show retarded physical and mental development, and they are also prone to heart disease and leukaemia. Another striking feature of Down syndrome is that as people with the condition age, they almost always develop *Alzheimer's disease*, the most common form of age-related dementia. Alzheimer's disease is characterized by the development of microscopic plaques in the brain (which cause the death of neurons); a primary component of these plaques is a protein called *beta-amyloid*. As it turns out, the gene for beta-amyloid is on chromosome 21. The susceptibility of people with Down syndrome to Alzheimer's disease probably is a result of the over expression of this gene caused by the fact that three copies are present rather than two.

It is important to keep in mind that for most chromosomes, monosomy or trisomy is incompatible with life. Down syndrome is the exception rather than the rule. The rate for Down syndrome is only 0.05% in pregnancies in 20-year-old women but rises to 3% in women over 45. When you consider that all of the chromosomes are vulnerable to trisomy, it is easy to see why it is so difficult for older women to produce a viable zygote (Figure 3.11). Studies show that about 2%

autosomes Any of the chromosomes other than the sex chromosomes.

sex chromosomes In mammals, chromosomes X and Y, with XX producing females and XY producing males.

nondisjunction error The failure of homologous chromosomes (chromatids) to separate properly during cell division. When it occurs during meiosis, it may lead to the formation of gametes that are missing a chromosome or have an extra copy of a chromosome.

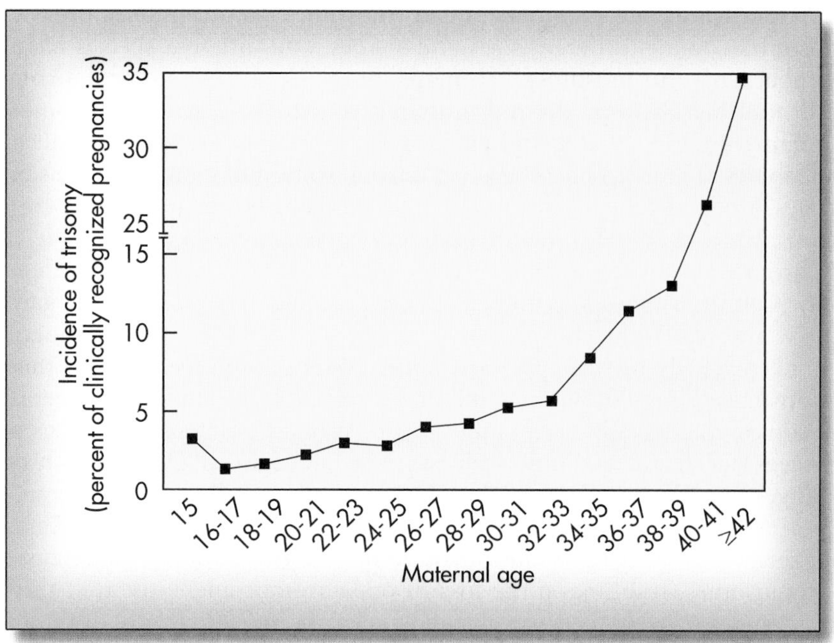

FIGURE 3.11 Increased risk of trisomy with maternal age.

of all recognized pregnancies (including those that result in miscarriage) in women 25 years or younger are trisomic for some chromosome; this compares with 35% in pregnancies in women over 40 years (Hassold and Hunt, 2001). Nondisjunction errors obviously are more common with increasing maternal age; currently there is little evidence that increasing paternal age is also a factor.

MOLECULAR TOOLS FOR BIOANTHROPOLOGICAL RESEARCH

Understanding genetics is critical to understanding evolutionary phenomena such as adaptation and the biological histories of populations and species. Over the years biological anthropologists have used a variety of molecular genetics techniques to study the natural history of people and other primate species. The application of these techniques to anthropological problems and issues will be considered in later chapters.

INDIRECT METHODS

The ultimate indirect method to study genetics is to look at the visible *phenotype:* the anatomy and physiology of an organism. But as we will discuss in more detail in Chapter 4, individual organisms are a result of complex interactions between genes and the environment. Molecular structures provide a more straightforward way to compare populations or species because they are not strongly influenced by environmental variables.

In terms of molecular analysis, indirect methods are useful only for looking at molecular differences *between* species. *Within* a species, the differences are too subtle for indirect methods to detect. But within-species variation can be very important. We know that allele frequencies vary between human populations, as in the case of the ABO blood type system. The most commonly used method for uncovering protein variation (that is, allelic variation) is *protein electrophoresis.* Proteins vary not only by size but also by electrical charge, which is determined by the amino acid composition of the protein. If you place small amounts of a protein in a thin sheet of agarose gel and run an electric current through it, the proteins will migrate across the gel, driven by the current. The protein can be visualized on the gel by using a variety of dyes. This technique is useful for detecting protein and allelic variation because different versions of a protein migrate at different speeds across the gel, depending on their amino acid composition. For example, an individual who is heterozygous at some locus may produce two different bands on a gel, reflecting the two slightly different versions of the same protein his body produces. Electrophoresis techniques are also widely used in experiments involving DNA and RNA.

Direct Sequencing Methods

In recent years, advances in molecular genetics techniques have allowed the direct sequencing of molecules such as DNA. However, the direct study of genetic structures extends back almost a century. *Cytogenetics*, the study of chromosome structure, has long been available as a way of comparing different species. Besides chromosome number, species vary in the size and shape of their chromosomes. In addition, when stains are used, banding patterns on chromosomes emerge under the microscope that can also be used to provide insights into the relationships between species and to track evolutionary events.

Although *protein sequencing* is another direct method that has been used for evolutionary research, *DNA sequencing*—determining the actual base sequence of a gene or stretch of DNA—is by far the most widely used tool in molecular anthropology today. DNA sequencing provides the most direct kind of evidence about the genetic makeup of individuals and species, and it can yield insights about both coding and noncoding regions of the genome. The automated methods currently used to directly sequence DNA are beyond the scope of this text, but it is important to know that the development of these methods in the 1970s and 1980s made possible much of the "molecular revolution" at the end of the twentieth century. Without automated DNA sequencing, for example, it would have been impossible for molecular biologists to sequence the entire genomes of humans, rats, and other species.

PCR, Mitochondrial DNA, and Ancient DNA

In addition to automated DNA sequencing, the other essential tool of the molecular revolution is a technique known as the **polymerase chain reaction (PCR)** (Mullis, 1990). The key feature of PCR is that an extraordinarily small amount of DNA can be used to make millions or even billions of copies of a specific DNA segment.

PCR allows the recovery of DNA sequences from miniscule samples, such as a single hair or dried saliva on an envelope obtained at a crime scene. In biological anthropology, PCR often is used to study evolutionary patterns in mitochondrial DNA and nuclear DNA recovered from bone, or *ancient DNA*.

Mitochondrial DNA As you recall, the mitochondria are the organelles found in cells in which energy metabolism occurs. **Mitochondrial DNA (mtDNA)** is a circular structure of about 16 600 base pairs. Each mitochondrion may have several copies of its DNA, and because each cell can have hundreds or thousands of mitochondria, each cell also has hundreds or thousands of mtDNA copies. Although there are several genes in the mtDNA genome, there are also regions that do not code for anything. These regions are highly variable, so they tend to evolve quickly. They are very useful for looking at evolutionary patterns between closely related species, or even between populations within a single species. These regions are so variable that families may have mutations or sequences specific to them. Sequences of these highly variable mtDNA regions therefore are very important in forensic investigation because they allow otherwise unidentifiable pieces of tissue or bodily fluids to be linked to a known individual (provided an appropriate DNA sample from the individual or a relative is available for comparison). Lakehead

polymerase chain reaction (PCR) Method for amplifying DNA sequences using the Taq polymerase enzyme. Can potentially produce millions or billions of copies of a DNA segment starting from a very small number of target DNA.

mitochondrial DNA (mtDNA) Small loop of DNA found in the mitochondria. It is clonally and maternally inherited.

University's Paleo-DNA Laboratory was the first university-affiliated laboratory in Canada to become accredited by the Standards Council of Canada (SCC) for forensic DNA testing. The lab conducts research and teaching on both nuclear and mitochondrial DNA analysis on a variety of sample types.

There are two important things to keep in mind about mtDNA. First, unlike nuclear DNA, mtDNA has no exchange (crossing over) between maternal and paternal DNA as it is passed down through the generations. Instead, mtDNA is passed on clonally from generation to generation. Second, mtDNA is passed on only through the mother because an offspring's mtDNA comes from the mitochondria floating in the cytoplasm of the egg. The mitochondria of the sperm are concentrated in the tail region of the cell and are not injected into the egg with the nuclear DNA at fertilization. All of your mtDNA came from your mother, and if you are a male, you are an mtDNA evolutionary dead-end. The Y chromosome acts as the male version of the mtDNA: It undergoes minimal recombination and is passed on only through males. It is also being used in evolutionary studies of populations.

Ancient DNA Bones up to 100 000 years old can yield DNA. Because the DNA in bone often is fragmentary or degraded, PCR is essential for recovering ancient DNA sequences. In most cases, the DNA amplified from bone is mtDNA. Because there are thousands of copies of mtDNA per cell, there are potentially many more individual copies of mtDNA than nuclear DNA in bony remains, which may be used as a target for amplification (Figure 3.12). Both mtDNA and nuclear DNA from fossil and archaeological remains can be analyzed to help us learn more

1) Excavation of bone

(Clean and dry conditions)

2) Selection of sample

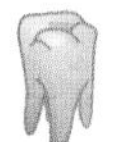
Tooth

Intact bone fragment
0.5–1.0 grams of sample sufficient
3) Clean and grind sample:
removal of surface or drill into bone

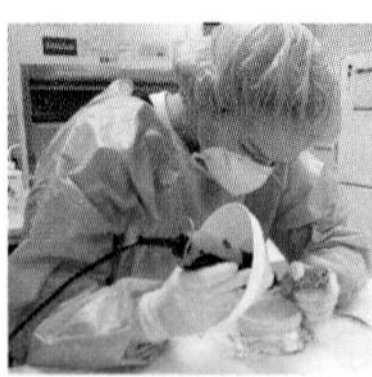
4) Chemicals and enzymes applied to
extract fragmentary DNA

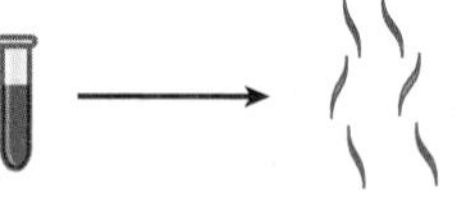
5) PCR-primers selected to amplify relatively short
(<1000 BP) DNA section

target
in intact
DNA
DNA fragments
from ancient DNA
6) Sequencing of amplified DNA

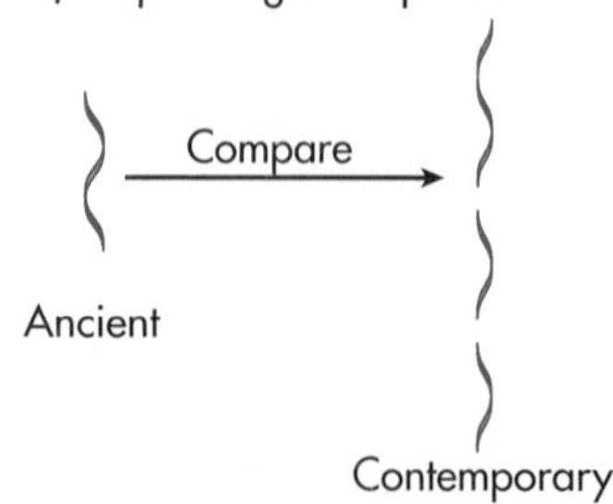
Compare
Ancient
Contemporary

FIGURE 3.12 Recovery process of ancient DNA.

about genetic relationships in the past. As we will discuss in Chapter 14, recovery of DNA from one extinct hominid species, the Neandertals, has shed new light on our evolutionary relationship with this close cousin of modern humans. And in Chapter 18 we will explore the uses of ancient DNA in the study of the movement of past peoples and their relationships to living groups.

Because the recovery of DNA in bone often involves pushing the PCR technique to its limits, contamination is a major worry. If the PCR primers find complementary DNA sequences to which to attach, amplification of DNA will occur, even if it is not the target sequence. This is especially a concern if one is looking at human bones because the experimenters themselves become the source of contamination: The primers designed to work on the ancient sample might also work on the researcher's DNA. Given the sensitivity of PCR, even a single molecule of contamination can distort the results of an experiment. Researchers and students at the Ancient DNA Centre in the Department of Anthropology at McMaster University and at the Ancient DNA Facility in the Department of Archaeology at Simon Fraser University have studied aspects of preservation and contamination of ancient DNA in order to improve the techniques of analysis (Pääbo et al., 2004; Yang and Watt, 2005). As well, some molecular archaeologists specialize in looking at the ancient DNA from fish and other items in the diets of prehistoric and historic human groups, such as salmon remains from the coast of British Columbia (Cannon and Yang, 2006). Because these molecular archaeologists are not studying human remains, any human DNA that they find can be recognized as a contaminant from the excavators or the laboratory workers.

In this chapter, we have reviewed some of the most fundamental aspects of life on Earth. Although humans may in some ways be unique among our planet's life forms, molecular genetics reaffirms the evolutionary continuity between us and other organisms, ranging from bacteria to plants to all other animals.

SUMMARY

1. **What are the different levels at which scientists study genetic phenomena?**

   Genetics can be studied at the cellular and molecular, individual, population, and species levels. The genetic bases of physical and behavioural traits of an organism can also be studied. The ultimate goal of genetic science is to understand how genes interact with one another and the environment to produce complex organisms. This requires an understanding of genetic expression at each level.

2. **What did Mendel's experiments on the garden pea show us about the nature of genetic transmission?**

   Mendel's work demonstrated first and foremost the particulate nature of genetic inheritance: There was no "blending" of the basic genetic factors (that is, genes) during sexual reproduction.

3. **Why is the cell called the fundamental building block of life?**

   All the different tissues and structures of the body are composed of cells. Although the cells from different tissues become specialized and differ substantially in appearance, all cells have a similar basic design. Even single-cell organisms have the same basic structure as cells from more complex, multicellular life forms.

4. **What is the difference between prokaryotes and eukaryotes?**

   Prokaryotes, such as bacteria, are single-celled life forms in which the genetic material is not contained within a nucleus in the cytoplasm. In eukaryotes, the genetic material is contained within a structure in the cytoplasm known as the nucleus. Eukaryotes include single-celled and multicelled life forms, including all complex plants and animals.

5. **What are DNA and RNA? What functions do they serve in the cell?**

   In both prokaryotes and eukaryotes, the genetic material is composed of DNA. DNA is a double-stranded nucleic acid made up of a sequence of bases. The sequence of bases is used to carry the information (in genes) to synthesize proteins and direct growth and development through cellular replication. RNA is a single-stranded nucleic acid. Different kinds of RNA (for example, messenger RNA, transfer RNA, and ribosomal RNA) have specific roles in protein synthesis.

6. **What are proteins, and what functions do they serve in living organisms? How are proteins synthesized?**

   Proteins are large molecules composed of amino acids. An amino acid chain is also known as a polypeptide; a protein may be formed from several polypeptide chains. Protein synthesis occurs via a two-step process occurring in the nucleus and cytoplasm. Transcription occurs in the nucleus and involves the synthesis of an mRNA molecule that is complementary to the base sequence of a gene. The mRNA molecule carries the genetic information to make a protein from the nucleus to the cytoplasm. At ribosomes located in the cytoplasm, translation occurs, a process in which the information carried by the mRNA is read and a polypeptide or protein is assembled. The language of protein synthesis that allows the conversion of DNA base pair sequences into protein amino acid sequences is known as the genetic code.

7. **How are mitosis and meiosis different from each other? How does crossing over during meiosis increase genetic variability?**

   Mitosis is the process of somatic cell replication in which the diploid chromosome number is maintained in each of the daughter cells after a cell divides. Meiosis is the process of cellular replication that results in the production of sex cells, or gametes. Meiosis has one more step of cell division than mitosis, which results in four daughter cells with the haploid number of chromosomes. If chromosomes cross over each other during meiosis, new combinations of genes on the chromosomes are created. These new combinations are expressed as new variants on which natural selection can work.

8. **Why is mitochondrial DNA important in the recovery of ancient DNA?**

   DNA in bony remains degrades over time and becomes fragmented. In order for DNA to be recovered from bone, the PCR method is used to amplify target sequences. Because there are thousands of copies of mtDNA per somatic cell, target sequences from mtDNA are more likely to be present intact than target sequences from nuclear DNA (for which only one or two copies would be present per cell).

CRITICAL THINKING QUESTIONS

1. Mendel often is said to have been "ahead of his time." Why? Do you think such a delay between the discovery and the recognition of the discovery could happen today?
2. What is a gene? Compare physical and theoretical definitions. How do you think laypeople conceive the gene and how it works?
3. What do you think about the ethics of cloning and stem cell research? Should they be allowed to continue, or be restricted by society and the government?

KEY TERMS

prokaryotes
eukaryotes
nucleus
cytoplasm
somatic cells
gametes
stem cells
genome
deoxyribonucleic acid (DNA)
proteins
protein synthesis
ribonucleic acid (RNA)
mitochondria
endoplasmic reticulum (ER)
ribosomes
nucleotide
base
enzyme
haemoglobin
hormone
amino acids
polypeptide
genetic code
codon
gene
messenger RNA (mRNA)
transfer RNA (tRNA)
chromatin
mitosis
meiosis
chromosome
centromere
diploid number
haploid number
homologous chromosomes
locus
alleles
homozygous
heterozygous

zygote
crossing over
recombination
autosomes
sex chromosomes
nondisjunction error
polymerase chain reaction (PCR)
mitochondrial DNA (mtDNA)

SUGGESTED READING

Huxley, J. S. (1942). *Evolution: The Modern Synthesis*. Allen and Unwin, London, England.

Maddox, Brenda. (2003). *Rosalind Franklin: The Dark Lady of DNA*. Perennial, New York, NY.

Mayr, E., and Provine, W. B. (editors). (1980). *The Evolutionary Synthesis: Perspectives on the Unification of Biology*. Harvard University Press, Cambridge, MA.

Ridley, Matt. (2000). *Genome*. HarperCollins, New York, NY.

Watson, James D. (2001). *The Double Helix: A Personal Account of the Discovery of the Structure of DNA*. Touchstone Books, New York, NY.

Chapter 4

Genetics: From Genotype to Phenotype

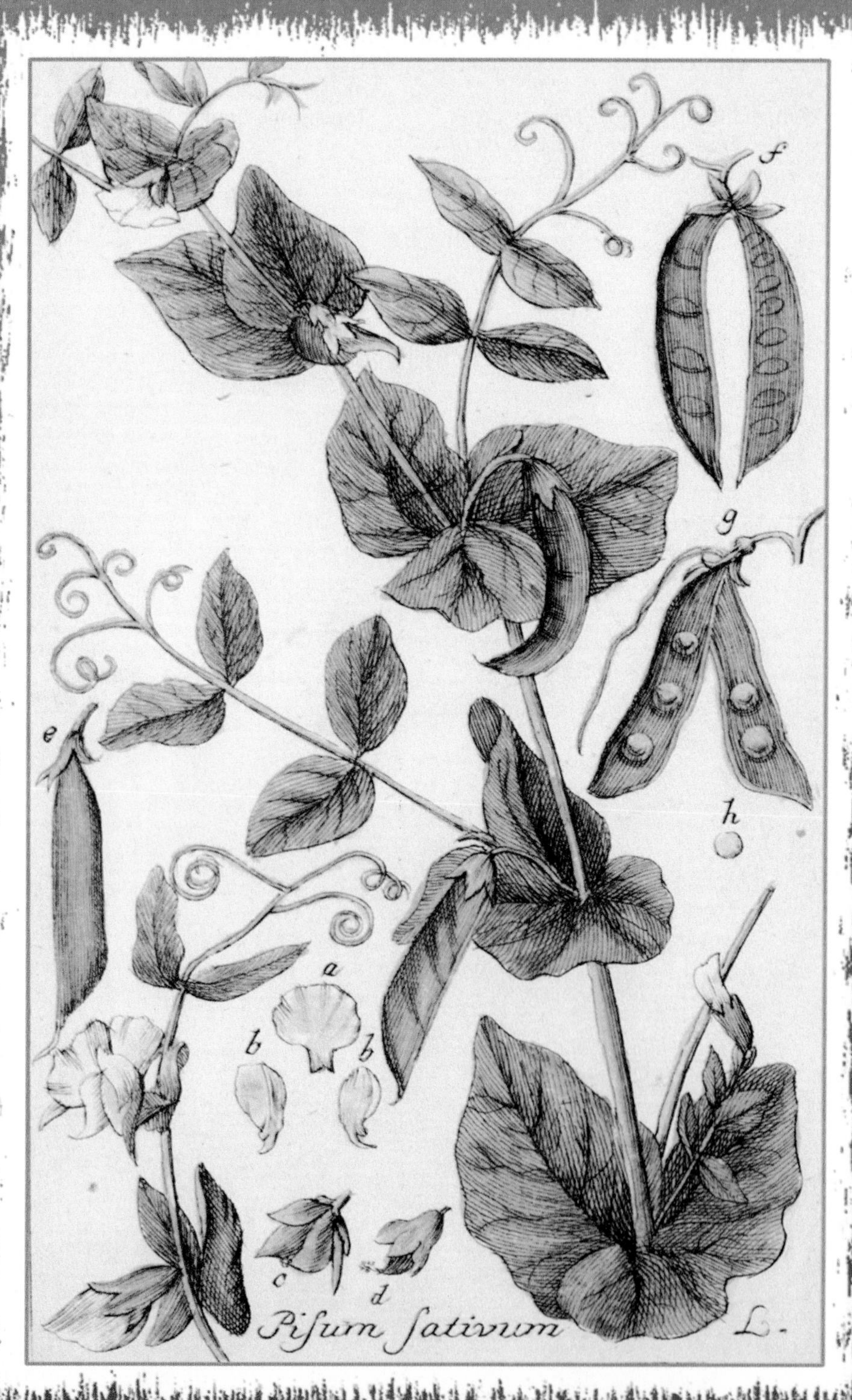

IN 1959, AT THE AGE OF FOURTEEN, Leilani Muir was sexually sterilized under Alberta's *Sterilization Act*. Passed in 1928, the *Sterilization Act* was based on the principals of eugenics, a broad social and intellectual movement grounded in an enthusiasm for Mendelism that incorporated Darwin's ideas of selection. *Eugenics*, a term coined in 1883, was derived from a Greek root meaning "good in birth" or "noble in heredity." Eugenics was based on a misconception of heredity that assumed that parents inevitably passed on their characteristics to their offspring. Proponents of eugenics believed that if only those people with desirable genes bore children, the human race as a whole would improve. Thus, the Alberta government and pressure groups sought to limit the reproduction of many people, including new immigrants, alcoholics, epileptics, unwed mothers, First Nations peoples, the poor, and the "feebleminded." Women's suffrage and temperance groups had a major influence in Alberta, where Canada's first woman magistrate, Emily Murphy and suffragist Liberal MLA Nellie McClung promoted the benefits of sterilization.

THE EUGENICS MOVEMENT WAS WIDESPREAD. By 1928, 2 Canadian provinces and 28 American states had passed sterilization laws. By 1935, Norway, Sweden, Denmark, and Switzerland had followed. Germany did the same, and sterilization became a tool of the Nazis.

THE *STERILIZATION ACT* WAS REPEALED IN ALBERTA in 1972 on the grounds that it violated fundamental human rights. In 1996, Leilani Muir was awarded more than $700 000 in damages after suing the province for wrongful sterilization and wrongful confinement in a provincial school for "mental defectives." In succeeding years over 1200 victims brought suits for similar losses against the Alberta government, which has attempted in the past 10 years to redress the harm caused by the ***Sterilization Act***.

Chapter Outline

The eugenics movement called for deliberate intervention in the "natural" evolutionary processes that were ongoing in human populations. This intervention could take either positive or negative forms. In many countries, many upper-class people believed that there was a disturbing trend for the better-educated, more intelligent, and sensitive young people to marry later and to have fewer children than the less-educated, coarser, and less intelligent lower classes. Positive eugenics was devoted to reaching out to the "right kind" of people and encouraging them, for the sake of the "race," to have more babies.

Negative eugenics was far less benign and had more serious and long-standing consequences. It focused on removing the "wrong kind" of people from the population by preventing them from having children, banning their entry into a country, expelling them from a country, or killing them. In the United States, legislation in the 1920s allowed the involuntary sterilization of "mental defectives" and the exclusion of immigrants from certain (that is, non–northern European) countries; both actions were strongly influenced by an ideology of negative eugenics. In Nazi Germany, the implementation of the "final solution"—the genocidal killings of Jews, Gypsies, and others whom the Nazis considered undesirable—was the most horrifying form of negative eugenics.

Although the popularity of the eugenics movement has waned, controversies over doctrines of racial superiority, the inheritance of traits such as intelligence, and the ethics of stem-cell research, cloning, and prenatal genetic counselling continue to appear in the public media and in scholarly publications. Even as we learn more about genetics, new questions and ethical debates arise.

Human genetics encompasses a wide range of phenomena, which are of evolutionary, cultural, and medical significance. As we cover these diverse topics in this chapter, it is useful to keep in mind the universality of the system of inheritance shared by all forms of life. In Chapter 3, we discussed the cellular and molecular bases of heredity. In this chapter, we explore in greater detail the observable effects of genes on the bodies and behaviour of animals, including humans. As we will see, the relationship between gene and structure is very simple and straightforward sometimes and is much more complex at other times.

FROM GENOTYPE TO PHENOTYPE

How do we make the connection between genes and the physical traits we can observe? As we learned in Chapter 3, DNA functions include replication and protein synthesis. But DNA must do more than this: The genetic information of the DNA must somehow be translated into the physical reality of working bodies. Even today, as some investigators deduce the base composition of the entire human genome, we are far from understanding the exact molecular mechanisms linking genes to bodies.

The local control of gene expression is reasonably well understood. Genes that contain information to make proteins are called **structural genes**. Structural genes are surrounded by *regulatory regions*, sequences of bases that are important in initiating, promoting, or terminating transcription. If these regulatory regions are altered or missing, the expression of the gene can be affected. Beyond these regulatory regions, however, there must also be **regulatory genes** that further guide the expression of structural genes.

Structural genes may be quite similar across divergent (but related) species, so regulatory genes probably are critical in determining the form an organism, or species, takes. For example, two species may have several differences in the structural gene for some protein. Given the redundancy of the genetic code and the fact that the function of a protein may not change even with one or more amino acid substitutions, the structural protein may function in the same way in both species despite the changes at the structural gene level. A single change in a regulatory gene, however, could result in the synthesis of the protein being shut down in one species while it is maintained in the other. This could lead to major differences between the two species in anatomy, physiology, or behaviour. Recent estimates indicate that DNA base sequences in humans and chimpanzees are 95% identical (including coding and noncoding regions) (Britten, 2002). The small number of differences between human and chimpanzee DNA indicates that the physical and behavioural differences between the species result primarily from regulatory rather than structural genes (Figure 4.1).

When Wilhelm Johannsen introduced the term *gene* in the early twentieth century (see Chapter 3), he introduced two other terms that remain in use today: **genotype** and **phenotype**. The genotype is the set of specific genes (or alleles) an organism carries; it is the genetic constitution of that organism. The phenotype is the observable physical feature of an organism that is under some form of genetic control or influence. In some cases, the relationship between genotype and phenotype is direct: The observed phenotype is a direct product of the underlying alleles. In other situations, the genotype interacts with factors in the environment to produce a phenotype. In phenotypes that are the result of complex gene–environment interactions, it can be difficult to ascertain the contributions

structural genes Genes that contain the information to make a protein.

regulatory genes Genes that guide the expression of structural genes, without coding for a protein themselves.

genotype The genetic makeup of an individual. *Genotype* can refer to the entire genetic complement or more narrowly to the alleles present at a specific locus on two homologous chromosomes.

phenotype An observable or measurable feature of an organism. Phenotypes can be anatomical, biochemical, or behavioural.

FIGURE 4.1 Genetically closely related species can have profound anatomical differences, as this movie still from the 1938 film *Her Jungle Love*, featuring Dorothy Lamour and one of her chimpanzee co-stars, indicates.

each makes to the variation we observe. Two divergent examples of the relationship between genotype and phenotype in humans are the ABO blood type system and obesity.

THE ABO BLOOD TYPE SYSTEM

The **ABO blood type system** illustrates a straightforward relationship between genotype and phenotype. The ABO system, which is important in typing for blood transfusions, refers to a protein found on the surface of red blood cells that is coded for by a gene located on chromosome 9. This gene has three alleles: A, B, and O. A and B stand for two different versions of the protein, and O stands for the absence of the protein (more precisely, A and B represent versions of the protein modified by enzymes from a common precursor, whereas O has only the precursor version of the protein). Because we are diploid organisms, we have two copies of each gene, one on each chromosome. As we discussed in Chapter 3, if an individual has the same allele of the gene on each chromosome, he or she is said to be homozygous for that gene. If the alleles are different, then the individual is heterozygous. In many cases, the phenotypic expression of the alleles for a gene depends on whether the genotype is heterozygous or homozygous.

An allele that must be present on both chromosomes to be expressed (that is, homozygous) is called a **recessive** allele (or gene). In the ABO system, O is a recessive allele: In order for it to be expressed, you must be homozygous for O (that is, have two copies of it). An allele that must be present at only one chromosomal locus to be expressed is called a **dominant** allele (or gene). Both A and B are dominant to O and **co-dominant** with each other: Only one copy is needed (see Table 4.1). As you can see, there are six possible genotypes and four possible phenotypes. Even though this example illustrates a direct relationship between genotype and phenotype, knowing an ABO blood type does not necessarily tell you what the underlying genotype is if you are type A or B. But no amount of environmental intervention will change your blood type. The phenotype is a direct product of the genotype.

ABO blood type system Refers to the genetic system for one of the proteins found on the surface of red blood cells. Consists of one gene with three alleles: A, B, and O.

recessive In a diploid organism refers to an allele that must be present in two copies (homozygous) in order to be expressed.

dominant In a diploid organism, an allele that is expressed when present on only one of a pair of homologous chromosomes.

co-dominant In a diploid organism, two different alleles of a gene that are both expressed in a heterozygous individual.

OBESITY: A COMPLEX INTERACTION

Obesity provides another example of the complex interaction between genes, environments, and phenotypes (and is discussed further in Chapter 16). Studies have shown that some people with an obese phenotype, defined as some percentage of body

TABLE 4.1 ABO Blood Type System Genotypes and Phenotypes

	GENOTYPE	PHENOTYPE
Homozygous	AA BB OO	Type A Type B Type O
Heterozygous	AO BO AB	Type A Type B Type AB

weight greater than population norms or ideals, are in some way genetically predisposed to such a condition. Recent research in both lab animals and humans indicates that there are specific genes that are critical to regulating appetite, which would be an important factor in overall body development. Some individuals have alleles for these genes that make it difficult for them to regulate their appetites (Figure 4.2). Genes that regulate fat storage, metabolism, and so on, would also be critical in the development of an obese phenotype. If we could look at all the genes underlying the development of body size and shape, we might be able to come up with combinations of alleles that might indicate that an individual is prone to developing obesity.

Of course, the development of obesity depends on the availability of food in the environment. No one becomes obese, even those in possession of alleles predisposing them to obesity, if there is not enough food to maintain an adequate body weight. On the other hand, the obese phenotype in some modern populations—such as those in industrialized nations that are characterized by abundant food and sedentary lifestyles—is becoming so common that the environment is unleashing the potential for obesity in the majority of people rather than in the small number who may be exceptionally prone to developing the condition. This "epidemic of obesity"—which is associated with increased rates of heart disease and diabetes, among other medical conditions—probably is a clear example of the mismatch between the environment in which humans evolved and the environment in which people in developed countries now live. People in general are genetically adapted for an environment where food is not so plentiful and where simply accomplishing everyday tasks uses a substantial amount of energy. The obesity phenotype is the product of genes and the environment even in people who do not have an "obesity genotype."

Despite the very different biological levels at which they are expressed, both ABO blood types and obesity are phenotypes. They are both measurable traits that are under a greater or lesser degree of genotypic control. However, in neither case does the observation of the phenotype necessarily provide an unequivocal understanding of the underlying genotype.

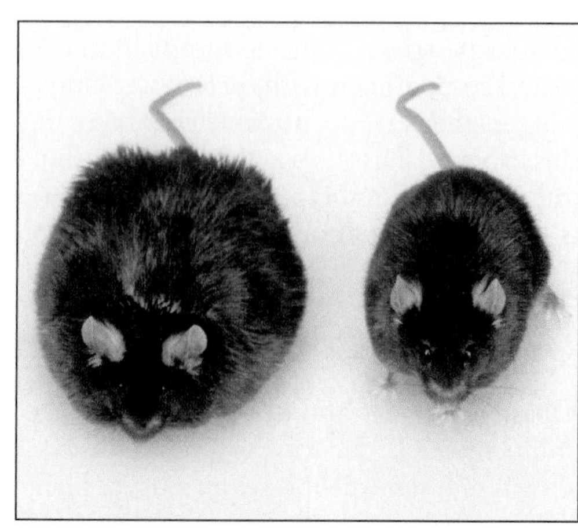

FIGURE 4.2 Laboratory mice demonstrate that genetic differences can have profound effects on the propensity to gain weight.

MENDELIAN GENETICS

Gregor Mendel conducted plant breeding experiments in the garden of the abbey in which he lived and taught. These experiments were conducted on different varieties of the common garden pea (genus *Pisum*). He crossed plants that exhibited different expressions of a trait, crossed hybrids with each other, and crossed hybrids with the original plants, carefully recording the transmission of several characters across generations. As it turned out, the garden pea was an ideal organism for elucidating the particulate nature of genetic transmission. Its best feature is that it displays two alternative phenotypes, or *dichotomous variation*, for several different and independent traits, such as seed colour, pod shape, and flower colour. These traits are monogenic and appear in one distinct form or the other with no apparent blending.

In his simplest experiments, Mendel looked at the expression of just one trait at a time in the first generation (the F_1 generation) when he crossed two lines that were true-breeding; a true-breeding line is one that reliably produced the same phenotype generation after generation. In the next stage of the experiment, he bred the F_1 generation plants with themselves and looked at the distribution of characters in the second generation (F_2) (Figure 4.3). He obtained similar results for each feature he examined:

1. Although the F_1 generation plants were the result of crosses between different true-breeding lines, only one of the parental generation traits was expressed. For none of the seven traits he examined did Mendel find evidence of blending inheritance.
2. In the F_2 generation, the version of the trait that had disappeared in the F_1 generation returned, but was found in only one quarter of the offspring plants. The other three quarters of the plants were the same as those in the F_1 generation. In other words, there was a 3:1 ratio in the expression of the original parental lines. Mendel called the version of the trait that appeared in the F_1 generation dominant, and the trait that reappeared (as one-quarter of the total) in the F_2 generation was called recessive.

From these basic observations, Mendel developed a series of postulates (or laws or principles) that anticipated the work of later generations of geneticists.

MENDEL'S POSTULATES

In the postulates listed (Klug and Cummings, 2003), the Mendelian insight is in italics while the modern interpretation of his insight is discussed below it.

1. *Hereditary characteristics are controlled by particulate unit factors that exist in pairs in individual organisms.*
The unit factors are genes, and they exist in pairs because in diploid organisms, chromosomes come in pairs. Each individual receives one copy of each chromosome from each parent, thus he or she receives one of his or her pair of genes from each parent. Different versions of the genes (alleles) may exist. An individual may have two that are the same (homozygous) or two that are different (heterozygous).

2. *When an individual has two different unit factors responsible for a characteristic, only one is expressed and is said to be dominant to the other, which is said to be recessive.*
In heterozygous individuals, those who have different versions of a gene on each chromosome, the allele that is expressed is dominant to the allele that is not expressed. Thus in Mendel's experiments, round seed form was dominant to wrinkled seed form, yellow seed colour was dominant to green, and so on. Mendel did not examine a co-dominant character, such as AB in the ABO blood type system.

CHARACTER	CONTRASTING TRAITS	F_1 RESULTS	F_2 RATIO
SEEDS	round/wrinkled	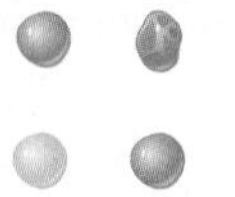 all round	3 round:1 wrinkled
	yellow/green	all yellow	3 yellow:1 green
PODS	full/constricted	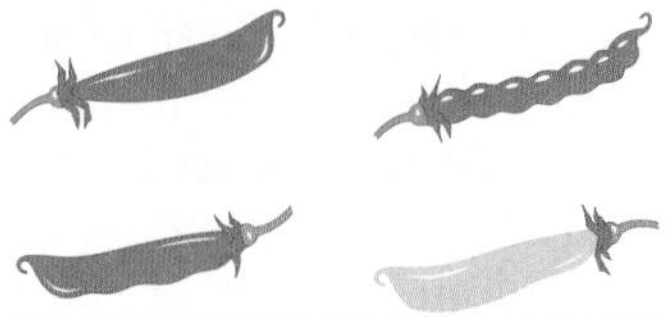 all full	3 full:1 constricted
	green/yellow	all green	3 green:1 yellow
FLOWERS	violet/white	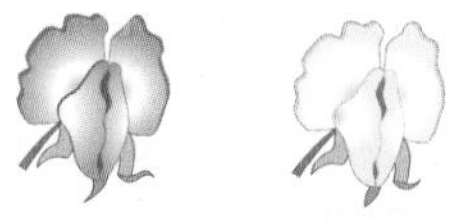 all violet	3 violet:1 white
STEM	axial/terminal	 all axial	3 axial:1 terminal
	tall/dwarf	 all tall	3 tall:1 dwarf

FIGURE 4.3 The traits Mendel used in his experiments, and the results of the F_1 and F_2 generation crosses.

Mendel's law of segregation The two alleles of a gene found on each of a pair of chromosomes segregate independently of each other into sex cells.

Mendel's law of independent assortment Genes found on different chromosomes are sorted into sex cells independently of one another.

linkage Genes that are found on the same chromosome are said to be linked. The closer together two genes are on a chromosome, the greater the linkage and the less likely they are to be separated during crossing over.

3. *During the formation of gametes, the paired unit factors separate, or segregate, randomly so that each sex cell receives one or the other with equal likelihood.* This is known as **Mendel's law of segregation**, and it reflects the fact that in diploid organisms, the chromosomes in a pair segregate randomly into sex cells during meiosis. Mendel formulated this law based on his interpretation of the phenotypes expressed in the F_1 (100% of which had the dominant phenotype) and F_2 generations (dominant:recessive phenotype ratio of 3:1). It is easy to understand Mendel's insight if we use a kind of illustration known as a *Punnett square*, named after British geneticist R. C. Punnett (1875–1967).

The Punnett square allows us to illustrate parental genetic contributions to offspring and the possible genotypes of the offspring (Figure 4.4). For example, in the cross between green peas and yellow peas, yellow is dominant to green. Let us call the alleles G and g, for the dominant yellow seed and recessive green seed, respectively. The yellow seed parent can contribute only the G allele and the green seed parent can contribute only the g allele to the offspring. In the Punnett square, you can see that all the offspring will be heterozygous Gg. Because G is dominant to g, all of the offspring have yellow seeds. Now, if we cross the heterozygous offspring (Gg) of the F_1 generation with each other, we get three possible genotypes: GG (25%), gg (25%), and Gg (50%). As we can see from the Punnett square, 75% of the offspring will produce yellow seeds and 25% of them will have green seeds. Thus the 3:1 phenotypic ratio of Mendel's F_2 generation is obtained. Punnett squares are quite handy and can be used to illustrate the parental contributions to offspring for any gene.

4. *During gamete formation, segregating pairs of unit factors assort independently of one another.*
This is known as **Mendel's law of independent assortment** (Figure 4.5). Mendel did a series of more complex pea breeding experiments known as *dihybrid crosses* that looked at the simultaneous transmission of two of the seven genetic characters of peas. For example, Mendel looked at how both seed colour and seed shape might be transmitted across generations. What he found was that the unit factors (alleles) for different characters were transmitted independently of each other. In other words, the segregation of one pair of chromosomes into two sex cells does not influence the segregation of another pair of chromosomes into the same sex cells.

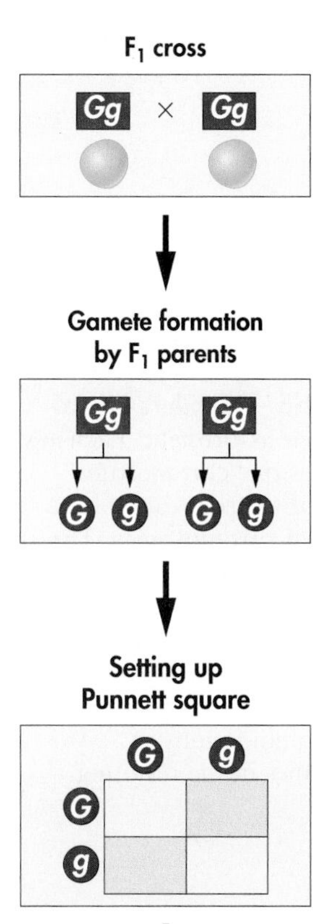

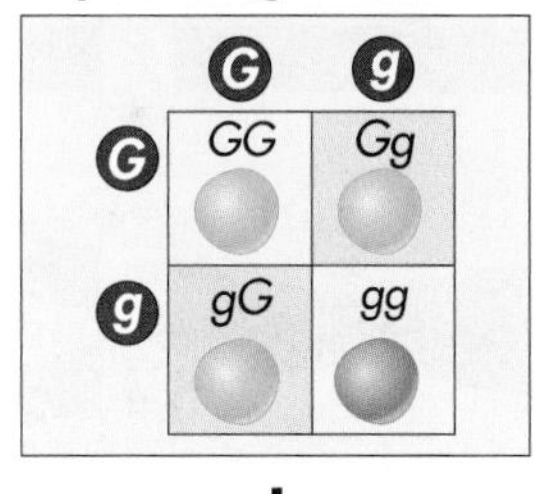

Figure 4.4 The Punnett square demonstrates how the F_2 ratio arises from an F_1 X F_1 cross.

Linkage and Crossing Over

The law of independent assortment applies only to genes that are on different chromosomes. Because the chromosome is the unit of transmission in meiosis, genes that are on the same chromosome should segregate together and find themselves in the same sex cells. This is known as **linkage**. A chromosome may have thousands of genes, and these genes are linked together during meiosis by virtue of being on the same chromosome.

However, decades of genetic research on fruit flies and other organisms have shown that independent assortment of genes on the same chromosome is not only possible but relatively common. How does this happen? It occurs through the process of crossing over, or recombination, which we discussed in Chapter 3. As you recall, during meiosis there is a physical exchange of genetic material between nonsister chromosomes (that is, the chromosomes that originally came from different parents), so that a portion of one chromosome is replaced by the corresponding segment of the other homologous chromosome. Through this process of crossing over, new allele combinations are assembled on the recombinant chromosomes (Figure 4.6). The likelihood of any two genes on a chromosome being redistributed through crossing over is a function of distance, or how far apart they are physically along the length of the chromosome. Genes that are located near one another on a chromosome are more strongly linked than genes that are far apart and thus are less likely to be separated or "independently assorted" during meiosis through crossing over.

Given the obvious complexities that linkage and crossing over introduce to the genetic process, it may occur to you that Mendel was not only extraordinarily insightful but also a bit lucky. How did he get such consistent results for seven different genes without being distracted or derailed by linkage or crossing over? As it happens, the garden pea has seven chromosomes, and Mendel looked at seven genes; it is easy to assume that this is the reason why Mendel had no problems with linkage. Two of the genes Mendel looked at were on chromosome 1 of the pea, and three others were on chromosome 4; the other two were alone on chromosomes 5 and 7, respectively (Blixt, 1975). The two genes on chromosome 1 are so far apart that very little linkage is detected between them (due to crossing over), and the same is true for some of the gene combinations on chromosome 4. In addition, one of the characters on chromosome 4 (pod shape) is also controlled by a gene on chromosome 6, and we do not know which gene Mendel was using. Some have accused Mendel of detecting linkage but ignoring it in his published work, but a recent re-analysis of these claims supports the view that Mendel did not have to deal with linkage because he never observed it (Fairbanks and Rytting, 2001).

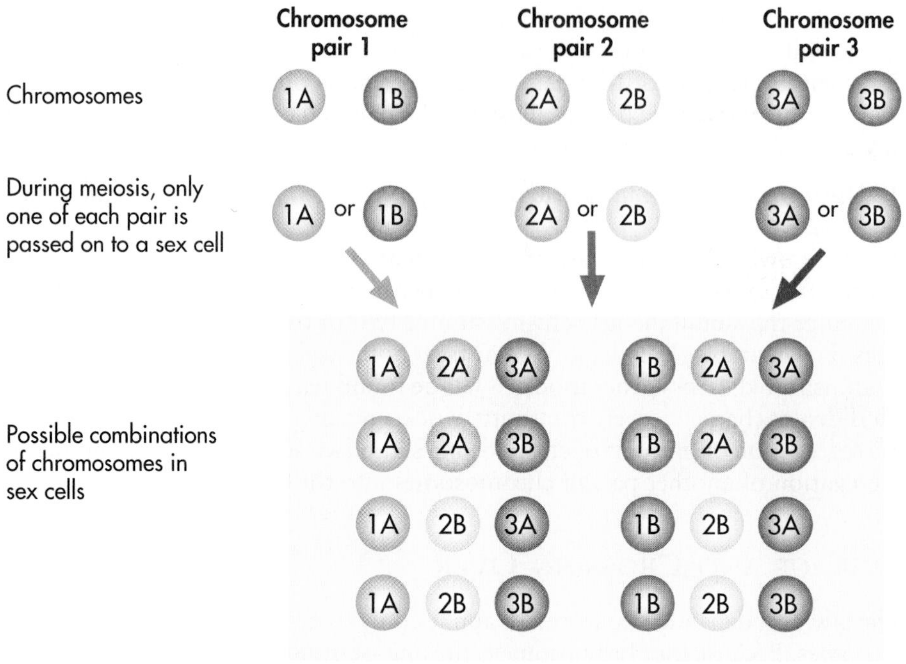

Chromosome pair 1 | Chromosome pair 2 | Chromosome pair 3

Chromosomes: 1A 1B | 2A 2B | 3A 3B

During meiosis, only one of each pair is passed on to a sex cell: 1A or 1B | 2A or 2B | 3A or 3B

Possible combinations of chromosomes in sex cells:

1A 2A 3A | 1B 2A 3A
1A 2A 3B | 1B 2A 3B
1A 2B 3A | 1B 2B 3A
1A 2B 3B | 1B 2B 3B

FIGURE 4.5 Mendel's law of independent assortment. Each sex cell receives one chromosome (either A or B) from each of the three paired chromosomes. The assortment of one pair of chromosomes is not influenced by either of the other chromosome pairs, hence "independent assortment." There are eight possible combinations of chromosomes in the resulting sex cells.

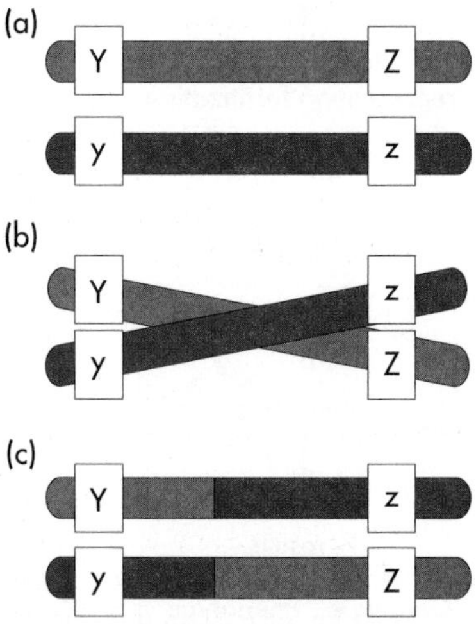

(a) Y Z / y z
(b) Y z / y Z
(c) Y z / y Z

FIGURE 4.6 Crossing over during meiosis leads to allele combinations in sex cells that are not present in the parent chromosomes. (a) A pair of homologous chromosomes is represented, carrying alleles YZ and yz respectively. (b) Crossing over occurs during meiosis. The more distant from each other two genes are on a chromosome, they more likely they are to be separated during meiosis. (c) Two recombinant chromosomes, with allele combinations of Yz and yZ, may now be passed into sex cells.

MUTATION

Given that Mendel did not know about the biochemical mechanisms of heredity, he was not too concerned with mutations as we know them. A mutation is any change in a DNA sequence that becomes established in a daughter cell. Any time somatic cells divide, a mutation may occur and be passed to the daughter cells. However, mutations that occur in sex cells are especially important because they can be passed to subsequent generations and will be present in all cells of the bodies of offspring. Mutations can occur in any part of the DNA, but obviously those that occur in structural or regulatory genes are more likely to have an impact.

POINT MUTATION AND SICKLE CELL DISEASE

There are several different kinds of mutations. A **point mutation** occurs when a single base in a gene is changed. A number of diseases can be attributed to specific point mutations in the gene for a protein. One of the most well-known and anthropologically important is the mutation that results in **sickle cell** disease (the evolutionary mechanisms for its prevalence in certain populations is discussed in Chapter 6). Sickle cell disease is caused by an abnormal form of the protein haemoglobin, which is the protein that transports oxygen throughout the body in red blood cells (it makes up 95% of the protein found in a red blood cell). Haemoglobin molecules normally exist separately in the red blood cell, each binding to a molecule of oxygen. In sickle cell disease, the haemoglobin molecules are separate from one another when they bind oxygen, but upon the release of oxygen, the abnormal haemoglobin molecules stick together, forming a complex structure with a helical shape. These long helical fibre bundles deform the red blood cells from their normal, platelike shape to something resembling a sickle, hence the name of the disease (Figure 4.7).

Red blood cells, which lose their nucleus not long after they are formed, are remarkably flexible and malleable in order to squeeze through tiny blood vessels. In contrast, sickled red blood cells lose this flexibility. They clump together in small blood vessels and impair circulation in capillaries; they also collect in the spleen,

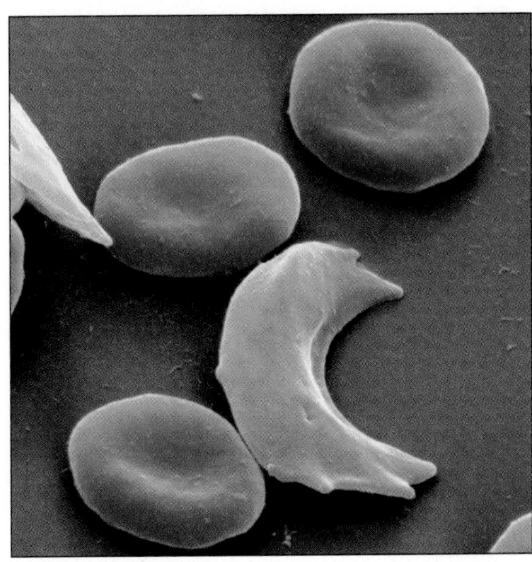

FIGURE 4.7 Normal and sickle-shaped red blood cells.

causing damage to that organ. The sickling also damages the red blood cells themselves. If a sickled red blood cell can make it back to the lungs and become reoxygenated, then the cell returns to its normal shape and can be used to transport oxygen. But repeated sickling shortens the life span of the red blood cells, contributing to the development of anaemia. In addition, abnormal complexes of haemoglobin cause the body's immune system to make antibodies against these cells, further exacerbating the anaemia. During periods of oxygen stress, such as during exercise, there is an increase in the formation of sickle cells. Sickle cell disease is characterized by chronic anaemia, but the secondary effects of the circulation of sickled cells can also be deadly during a crisis.

Haemoglobin (Hb) is a protein. The normal, adult haemoglobin is called HbA. The sickle cell haemoglobin, or HbS, is one amino acid different from HbA: The sixth amino acid in HbA is glutamic acid, whereas in HbS it is valine. This amino acid substitution is caused by a mutation in the codon from CTC to CAC. Out of 438 bases, this is the only change. A striking feature of the mutation in sickle cell is that it does not directly affect the ability of the haemoglobin to carry oxygen but rather causes the haemoglobin molecules to stick together, leading to the deformed cell shape. Of course, a mutation that rendered a red blood cell totally incapable of carrying oxygen probably would be directly fatal.

Sickle cell disease appears in people who are homozygous (have two copies) for the HbS allele. A disease of this kind that is caused by being homozygous for a recessive, disease-causing allele is known as an **autosomal recessive disease**. People who are heterozygous HbA HbS produce enough normal haemoglobin to avoid the complications of sickle cell disease under most circumstances, but they are *carriers* of the disease: They do not suffer from the disease but can pass on the allele that causes the disease. If a carrier mates with another individual who is a heterozygous carrier, then following Mendelian laws, there is a 25% chance that the offspring will be a homozygous sufferer of the disease.

TRINUCLEOTIDE REPEAT DISEASES

In addition to point mutations, another common kind of mutation involves the **insertion mutation** or **deletion mutation** of several bases in sequence. In the last decade, at least 16 genetic diseases have been found to be caused by a specific kind of insertion mutation, which involves the multiple, repeated insertion of trinucleotide (three-base) repeat sequences (Fischbeck, 2001). The best known of the **trinucleotide repeat diseases** may be *Huntington disease*, a degenerative neurological disorder that is caused by a dominant allele: It is an **autosomal dominant disease**.

point mutation A change in the base sequence of a gene that results from the change of a single base to a different base.

sickle cell disease An autosomal recessive disease caused by a point mutation in an allele that codes for one of the polypeptide chains of the haemoglobin protein.

autosomal recessive disease A disease caused by a recessive allele; one copy of the allele must be inherited from each parent for the disease to develop.

insertion mutation A change in the base sequence of a gene that results from the addition of one or more base pairs in the DNA.

deletion mutation A change in the base sequence of a gene that results from the loss of one or more base pairs in the DNA.

trinucleotide repeat diseases A family of autosomal dominant diseases that is caused by the insertion of multiple copies of a three-base pair sequence (CAG) that codes for the amino acid glutamine. Typically, the more copies inserted into the gene, the more serious the disease.

autosomal dominant disease A disease that is caused by a dominant allele: Only one copy needs to be inherited from either parent for the disease to develop.

The gene that causes Huntington disease is located on chromosome 4. In most individuals, a trinucleotide sequence, CAG, which codes for the amino acid glutamine, is repeated usually 10 to 35 times. In contrast, people who have Huntington disease have 40 to 120 CAG repeats. Usually Huntington disease is thought of as a disease that strikes people in middle age, with a gradual onset of symptoms, including loss of motor control and ultimately dementia. However, there is variability in the age of onset, and it is directly related to the number of CAG repeats a person is carrying. If someone has more than 80 repeats, the age of onset could be in the teenage years, whereas someone with 40 repeats may not show signs of illness until he or she reaches 60 years of age. In addition, the more repeats, the more severe the disease. About half of the known trinucleotide repeat diseases are characterized by CAG repeats.

MUTATIONS: BAD, NEUTRAL, AND GOOD

The idea that mutations are bad pervades our popular culture. After all, you would probably not consider it a compliment if someone called you a mutant. However, although several diseases arise as a result of mutations in normal genes, it is important to keep in mind that the vast majority of mutations probably are neutral.

Mutations that occur in noncoding regions are by definition neutral because they make no contribution to the phenotype. Mutations that occur in a gene but do not alter the amino acid in a protein also have no phenotypic effect. These kinds of mutations are common because of the redundancy in the genetic code. On top of that, proteins can endure amino acids substitutions without changes in function. There are usually some parts of a protein that are more critical to function than other parts. Amino acid substitutions in noncritical parts of a protein may not affect the function of the protein at all. In fact, protein variation in nature is extensive, and in many cases it does not appear to have any functional consequence. If protein function is not affected, then there is likely to be no change to the physiology or anatomy of the organism.

Finally, a mutation may affect the anatomy or physiology of an organism and still have no direct affect on the fitness of an individual. A famous example of such a trait is the *Habsburg face*, which is composed of a characteristic combination of facial features, including a prominent lower lip (hence the name *Habsburg jaw*, by which it is also known). This trait is found in many European noble families, and its transmission has been traced over 23 generations (Wolff et al., 1993). Because these European nobles were painted and sculpted with some regularity, there are many accurate historical representations of people with this condition (Figure 4.8). It is caused by an autosomal dominant allele.

FIGURE 4.8 King Charles V, Holy Roman Emperor and ruler of Spain from 1516–1556, possessed the distinctive Habsburg jaw.

Can mutations be good? Absolutely. Mutations are the ultimate source of variation, and variation is the raw material on which evolution acts. Without mutation, there could be no natural selection. Although chromosomal processes such as crossing over create new allele combinations and thereby increase phenotypic variability, mutation is the only source for new alleles that can be combined in novel ways. "Good" mutations—those that increase an organism's chance of surviving and reproducing—do not have to be common. The process of natural selection makes their spread throughout a population possible. Once this happens, they are no longer considered to be mutations but are the normal or wild type (Figure 4.9).

If we focus on any given gene, we will find that mutations are not very common. However, if we consider the genome as a whole, then mutations are not so hard to find. The calculation of mutation rate is very complicated. It is made even more complicated by the fact that the mutation rate varies between species, and within species different genes appear to undergo spontaneous mutation at different rates (Eyre-Walker and Keightley, 1999).

Many autosomal dominant disorders (such as *achondroplasia*, a disorder characterized by dwarfism caused by impaired long bone growth) occur at rates on the order of 1 in 10 000 births, and they result almost entirely from new mutations. Let us suppose that the mutation rate in humans for any given gene averages about

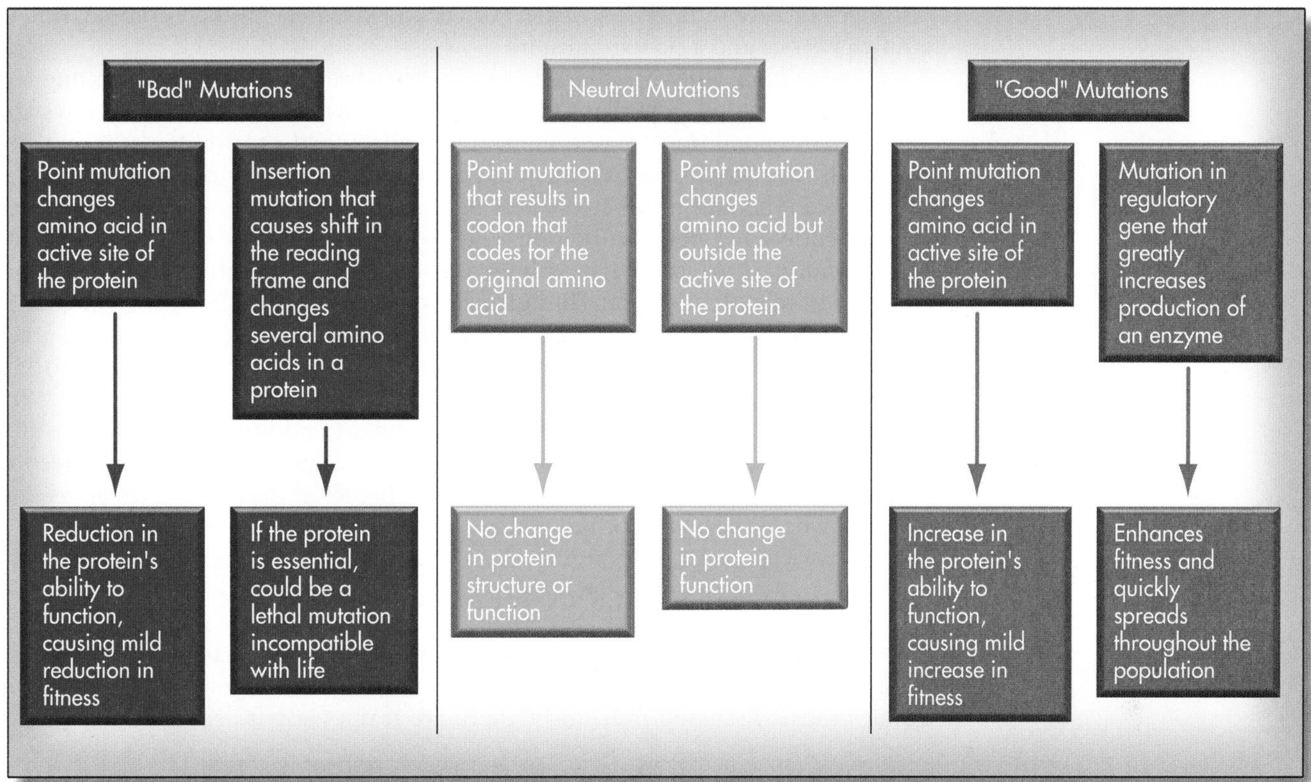

FIGURE 4.9 "Bad," neutral, and "good" mutations.

1 in 10 000 per generation (a very rough estimate). That might not seem very high, but when we consider that humans have two copies each of 30 000–40 000 genes, then it is likely that every individual carries a mutation in some gene. And if we search in a population of individuals, the chance of finding mutations in more than one gene is very high indeed.

X-LINKED DISORDERS

We discussed chromosomal mutations or abnormalities in an earlier section. However, there is one class of gene mutations that is directly related to chromosome structure. These are the **X-linked disorders**. As discussed in Chapter 3, the sex chromosomes in human males are XY, and in human females they are XX. The Y chromosome is very small compared with other chromosomes and contains a small number of genes. In contrast, the X chromosome contains a large number of genes.

Because human males have only one copy of the X chromosome, they are susceptible to a host of diseases that are caused by mutations in X chromosome genes. These diseases are much less common in females because they are essentially autosomal recessive disorders and will appear in a female only when they are present in two copies. Female children of affected males are all carriers of the condition because one of their X chromosomes is a copy of their father's (only) X chromosome. **Pedigrees** of families affected by X-linked disorders show a typical pattern whereby the disorders appear to skip a generation. If a male has an X-linked disorder, he cannot pass it on to his sons because he does not pass an X chromosome to them. His daughters will not have the disease but will be carriers. Their sons then have a 50% chance of getting the disorder because they have a 50% chance of receiving the affected X chromosome.

X-linked disorders that cause death before reproductive age are never seen in females because they are on X chromosomes that are never transmitted to the next generation. A female can develop an X-linked disorder if her father has one of the

X-linked disorders Genetic conditions that result from mutations to genes on the X chromosome. They are almost always expressed in males, who have only one copy of the X chromosome; in females, the second X chromosome containing the normally functioning allele protects them from developing X-linked disorders.

pedigree A diagram used in the study of human genetics that shows the transmission of a genetic trait over several generations of a family.

disorders and her mother is a carrier (or via an extremely unlikely combination of family genetics and a new mutation).

Haemophilia, a disease characterized by the absence of one of the clotting factor proteins in blood, is perhaps the most well-known X-linked disorder. Boys and men with this condition are very vulnerable to haemorrhage and severe joint damage. With advances in the treatment of haemophilia, males with the condition are able to live long and productive lives. Several of the male descendants of Queen Victoria suffered from this condition (Figure 4.10). *Red colour blindness* and *green colour blindness* are both also X-linked disorders and therefore are much more common in men than women. In European-derived populations, the frequency in men is about 7% and in women is about 0.4%. The genes affecting red and green colour vision are located next to each other at one end of the X chromosome (Vollrath et al., 1988). The high frequency of colour blindness may reflect the absence of selective pressure against the condition. In addition, studies of the alleles of colour-blind individuals indicate that those alleles have all arisen via recombination events. Recombination rates often are higher at the end of a chromosome, which is where the genes for red and green colour vision are located.

Mendelian Genetics in Humans

Over the past century, hundreds of conditions and diseases have been catalogued in humans that can be explained in terms of Mendelian genetic transmission. Besides those discussed previously, there are traits (such as ear lobe form—free

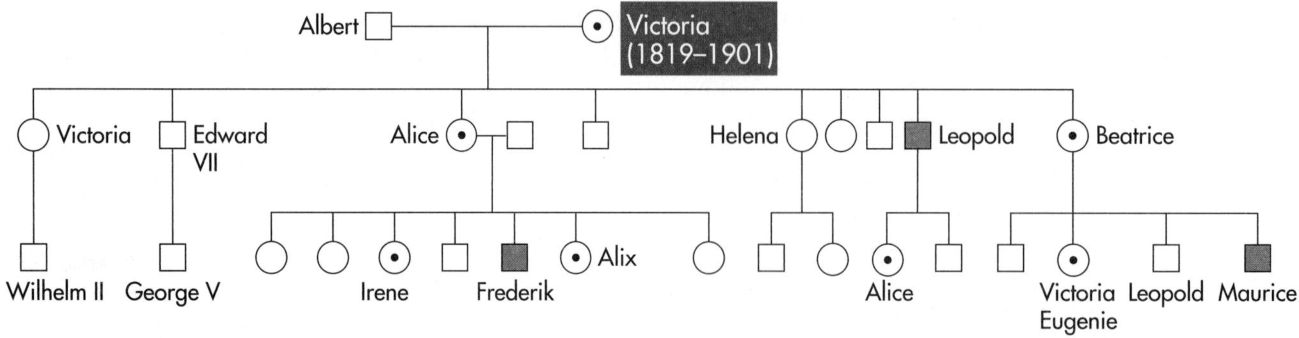

FIGURE 4.10 Queen Victoria and her family and a pedigree showing the transmission of haemophilia in the British royal family. Females are denoted by circles, and those who are carriers of the gene for haemophilia are identified by a dot within the circle. Males are represented by boxes, and males with haemophilia have shaded boxes.

hanging is dominant to the recessive attached form) that appear to conform to simple Mendelian rules of transmission. The Online Mendelian Inheritance in Man (OMIM) Web site (www3.ncbi.nlm.nih.gov/Omim/) provides an extraordinary database on genetic conditions in humans, from the most innocuous to the most lethal. An examination of this database conveys a sense of the complexity inherent in studying even the simplest genetic conditions. Even such classic examples as ear lobe form are not necessarily as clear-cut as they have appeared to be (although the dominant–recessive model works well enough for them).

GENETICS BEYOND MENDEL

Mendelian genetics provided a beginning for our understanding of the biological mechanisms of heredity and evolution. By studying the genetics of phenotypes that are determined by a single gene, which have a small number of alleles, scientists have gained a significant understanding of many other more complex biological phenomena. However, it is important to keep in mind that a single-gene, dominant–recessive model of heredity cannot explain much of the biological world we see around us. As Kenneth Weiss (2002, p. 44) has pointed out, although Mendelian genetics provides a foundation for understanding heredity, "a misleading, oversimplified, and overdeterministic view of life is one of the possible consequences." Not long after the rediscovery of Mendel, the overly enthusiastic application of Mendelian principles to human affairs, in combination with certain political and nationalistic movements, had a number of important consequences, as described at the beginning of this chapter.

Mendelian genetics is most useful in examining characters for which there are different and nonoverlapping phenotypic variants. This is called **qualitative variation**. Seed colour in peas or the different phenotypes in the ABO blood system are examples of qualitative variation. In contrast, **quantitative variation** refers to continuous variation for some trait, which emerges after we measure a character in a population of individuals. It is not possible to divide the population into discrete groups reflecting one variant or another because the variation is overlapping. For many characters, if we measure enough individuals, we find that there is a normal (or bell-shaped) distribution in the individual expression of the character. Individuals who have extremely high or low measurements are most rare, and individuals who have measurements near the population mean, or average, are most common. Stature in humans is a classic example. Very short and very tall people are much less common than people of average height. Stature is influenced by genes, but except for rare kinds of dwarfism, the phenotypic distribution of stature in humans does not lend itself to a simple Mendelian explanation.

Stature and other complex phenotypes, such as the timing of puberty, skin colour, and eye colour, are **polygenic traits**. Their expression depends on the action of multiple genes, each of which may have more than one allele. The more genes and alleles that contribute to a polygenic trait, the more genotypes—and phenotypes—are possible. Thus when continuous variation for a trait is observed in a population (whether or not it is normally distributed), it is much more likely to be caused by polygenic inheritance rather than a single gene effect.

Just as one trait can be the result of the interaction of more than one gene, one gene can have multiple phenotypic effects (Figure 4.11). This is called **pleiotropy**. For example, the gene that causes achondroplasia has the paradoxical effect of shortening limb length while also leading to larger than average head size (megalencephaly). Artificial breeding for docility in foxes leads to the development of coat colours not found in wild foxes; this is undoubtedly a pleiotropic effect of whatever genes underlie that behavioural pattern. As we will discuss later in the text, aging patterns in humans may best be explained as resulting from the pleiotropic effects of genes selected for their effectiveness during the reproductive phase of life.

qualitative variation Phenotypic variation that can be characterized as belonging to discrete, observable categories.

quantitative variation Phenotypic variation that is characterized by the distribution of continuous variation (expressed using a numerical measure) within a population (for example, in a bell curve).

polygenic traits Phenotypic traits that result from the combined action of more than one gene; most complex traits are polygenic.

pleiotropy The phenomenon of a single gene having multiple phenotypic effects.

POLYGENIC TRAITS, THE PHENOTYPE, AND THE ENVIRONMENT

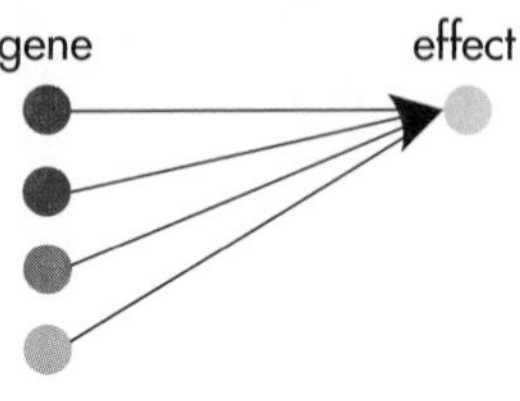
(a) Polygenic trait: many genes contribute to a single effect.
gene
effect

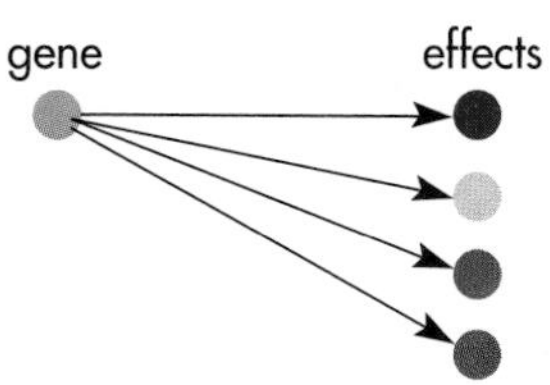
(b) Pleiotropy: one gene has multiple effects.
gene
effects

FIGURE 4.11 Contrasting (a) polygenic and (b) pleiotropic effects.

Bell curve distributions for the expression of a trait may result from polygenic inheritance. However, phenotypes, especially complex phenotypes, tend to be the result of an interaction between the genotype and the environment. The variation we observe in the expression of a complex trait may result from genetic factors or environmental factors that may influence phenotypic expression.

When scientists investigate the relative contributions of genes and environment to the production of the phenotype, they often use a statistical concept called **heritability**. If we look at variation for some trait in a population, we can be certain that the total variation we observe is caused by some combination of environmental and genetic factors. Heritability is a measure of the proportion of the total variation observed in a population that can be attributed to genetics rather than to the environment:

$$\frac{\text{Variability caused by genetics}}{\text{Variability caused by genetics} + \text{Variability caused by the environment}}$$

Heritability can range from 0 to 1. It is easy to measure heritability if you can control all the critical factors in the environment, as a scientist working on a short-lived experimental animal might be able to do. In humans, heritability is more difficult to measure because we obviously cannot use humans in breeding experiments.

There are several methods for using pedigree and adoption data to estimate heritability in human populations. The most commonly used is the **twin method**. As is well known, there are two kinds of twins: *identical* or *monozygotic (MZ) twins* and *fraternal* or *dizygotic (DZ) twins*. Monozygotic twins are genetically identical to each other, and they are the result of the fertilization of a single egg that splits into two embryos very early in development. Dizygotic twins result from the separate fertilization of two eggs during the same ovulatory cycle. They are no more alike than any other full siblings, and they share, on average, half of their genes.

If two twins share a common phenotype or if both get a certain disease, we say that they are *concordant* for that trait; if the twins are dissimilar, then they are *discordant*. Twins raised together typically share a similar environment. If we compare the MZ and DZ concordance for a trait, a significantly higher concordance rate in the MZ twins indicates that genetic factors may be important in the expression of that trait. Both MZ and DZ twins share a common environment (some critics have argued that MZ twins may share a more similar environment than DZ twins, which may be true, but how much this may contribute to similarities or differences must be assessed for each condition examined), but MZ twins share a much stronger genetic link than DZ twins. For example, concordance for ABO blood type is 100% in MZ twins and 66% in DZ twins. This indicates that blood type is totally under genetic control. Allergy patterns have a concordance rate of 59% in MZ twins and 18% in DZ twins. This indicates that genetics plays an important role in developing allergies. However, the fact that the concordance rate is not 100% in MZ twins indicates that the environment plays a substantial role as well. Many complex diseases such as schizophrenia and heart disease have MZ and DZ concordance rates that indicate that both genetic and environmental factors play a role in their expression.

heritability The proportion of total phenotypic variability observed for a given trait that can be ascribed to genetic factors.

twin method A method for estimating the heritability of a phenotypic trait by comparing the concordance rates of identical and fraternal twins.

Although concordance rates cannot be used directly to compute heritability values, they can be incorporated into mathematical models for estimating heritability. In addition, they indicate the possible roles of genetic and environmental factors in the expression of a trait or disease, providing useful directions for future research or intervention.

Heritability is an extremely important tool in trying to understand genetic influences on complex phenotypes. However, the discovery of significant heritability for a trait does not provide information about which or even how many genes are responsible for a phenotype. Heritability is a population statistic and provides no direct insight into individual genetic mechanisms. Also, heritability does not provide an absolute measure of the genetic contribution to the development of a phenotype. It is a relative statistic that measures the influence of genetics in a specific environment. If that environment is highly variable and most of the variation results from environmental factors, then the heritability will be low. On the other hand, if the environment is uniform and all members of the population are affected equally by environmental factors, then heritability will be high. As variation caused by environmental factors decreases, any remaining variation we observe can result only from genetic factors. Thus heritability changes with changing environments, even as the genetics remain the same.

Heritability and IQ Test Score Performance

Perhaps the most well-known and controversial use of heritability statistics has been in the study of variation in IQ test score performance (Mackintosh, 1998). Let us consider them as a measurement that exhibits continuous variation in human populations, with a normal distribution. Innumerable studies of the heritability of IQ test score in industrial societies have been conducted over the years, and they almost all agree that genetics is an important factor in producing the variation observed within populations (heritability ranges from 0.3 to 0.75). Most scientists, although not all, interested in IQ test score would agree that in a population with an absolutely uniform environment, you would still observe variation for IQ test score performance, which would result from genetic factors.

Most people would not argue with the idea that genetics and environment both play some role in IQ test score performance. But what does heritability tell us about an issue of anthropological importance: ethnic differences in IQ test score performance? Much empirical evidence demonstrates that American whites score on average about 100 (the designed mean for the test) on IQ tests, American blacks score substantially lower (7 to 12 points less), and Asian Americans score somewhat higher (about 5 points higher, with most of the difference occurring on the nonverbal portions of the test). Do the heritability studies of IQ test score performance indicate that the ethnic differences we observe result from genetic differences? No. Heritability scores apply only *within* a population or environment, not *between* populations. Heritability may give us some insight into the production of variation within each ethnic group, but it cannot be used to address issues of population variation between groups. The variation between groups could result from genetics, the environment, or both, but heritability scores, whether high or low, have no bearing on between-group differences.

In fact, it is theoretically possible that you could observe within-group heritabilities of 0 for some trait, whereas the between-group differences could result entirely from genetic factors. For example, imagine that we have two distinct populations, one with a substantially greater mean stature than the other one. Let's say that this difference in stature reflects the presence of "tall" alleles in one population that are absent in the other. If in both populations access to food while growing up is highly variable, then within each population the distribution of stature would result primarily from environmental factors (that is, food availability). There would still be a difference in mean stature between the populations, caused entirely by genetics. However, if we measured heritability within each population separately, we would find that little of the observed variation could be ascribed to genetics (that is, heritability would be low). Thus low within-group heritability does not mean that between-group differences cannot be caused by genetic differences, and vice versa.

PHENYLKETONURIA: ILLUSTRATING MENDELIAN AND POST-MENDELIAN CONCEPTS

Before the advent of universal neonatal screening for the condition (Lindee, 2000), **phenylketonuria (PKU)** was one of the most common causes of mental retardation. Pedigree studies have shown that the transmission of PKU appears to follow classic Mendelian rules. It is caused by a recessive allele and therefore is seen only in people who are homozygous for this allele. People who have just one copy of the allele are heterozygous carriers of the condition.

Individuals with PKU accumulate large quantities of the amino acid phenylalanine in the blood (up to forty times the normal amount) (Scriver et al., 1985). In newborns and infants, a high level of phenylalanine is toxic to the developing nervous system. The most prominent feature of the PKU phenotype is mental retardation, which is a direct result of the neurotoxic effects of high levels of phenylalanine. However, people with PKU also tend to have light skin and hair and abnormal gait, stance, and sitting posture, among other characteristic features. It is quite clear that the allele for PKU has multiple pleiotropic effects.

At a biochemical level, PKU is the result of a deficiency of an enzyme, *phenylalanine hydroxylase*, which converts phenylalanine to another amino acid, tyrosine. Phenylalanine builds up in the bloodstream because the PKU phenylalanine hydroxylase either is inactive or has much lower than normal activity. Because the phenylalanine is not converted to tyrosine, people with PKU also tend to have less tyrosine available for metabolic reactions. Tyrosine is the starting point for the body's synthesis of melanin, which is one of the most important components of skin pigment. This explains one of the pleiotropic effects of the PKU allele: Light skin and hair is a result of low tyrosine levels and low production of melanin.

Over the past 20 years, there have been many advances in our understanding of the molecular genetics of PKU. The gene for phenylalanine hydroxylase has been localized to chromosome 12, and hundreds of different point mutations in the gene have been identified. The effects of these mutations on phenylalanine hydroxylase activity vary tremendously, with some of them rendering the enzyme inactive, whereas others show no effect or only a mild depression in activity (Benit et al., 1999). The variability in the alleles of the phenylalanine hydroxylase gene explains why PKU exhibits a good deal of phenotypic variability. Remember that PKU is an autosomal recessive disorder: Individuals who have one normal phenylalanine hydroxylase allele are phenotypically normal.

Screening for PKU in newborns is done by assessing phenylalanine levels in the blood not long after birth. Profoundly elevated levels of phenylalanine indicate the presence of PKU and the need for dietary intervention. This intervention takes the form of drastically reducing the amount of phenylalanine in the diet. This is easier said than done because phenylalanine is an important component of proteins found in meat, fish, eggs, cheese and other milk products, legumes, and some cereals. Babies with PKU must take special formula that provides calories and essential nutrients, and children with the condition must adhere to a very limited diet. They must also learn to be wary of dietary additives such as the artificial sweetener aspartame, which is composed of phenylalanine and aspartic acid. The good news is that when they become adults, most PKU sufferers can adopt a normal diet because their nervous system is no longer developing. However, if a woman with PKU wants to become pregnant, she must resume the restricted diet, or the elevated levels of phenylalanine in her blood will damage the developing nervous system of her developing child.

phenylketonuria (PKU) Autosomal recessive condition that leads to the accumulation of large quantities of the amino acid phenylalanine, which causes mental retardation and other phenotypic abnormalities.

PKU provides a striking example of the relationships between genotype, phenotype, and the environment. People with PKU are different from other people because they have two copies of an abnormal allele for a single enzyme. If they grow up in a typical dietary environment—which is basically the dietary environment you have if you live on the planet Earth—their nervous systems will not develop normally and they will have a seriously dysfunctional phenotype. On the other hand, if we place children with PKU in a different, highly artificial nutritional environment, they will develop normally.

Genes and Environments

When we hear the word *environment* we usually think about the world around us—things such as the air and water, trees and other plants, and all the other creatures with which we share the world. But from a gene's perspective, the environment is made up mainly of other genes. Concepts such as pleiotropy and polygenic inheritance emphasize that the genetic environment is just as critical to the production of phenotypes as any other kind of environment.

Mendelian concepts such as independent assortment and segregation were useful in establishing the activities of genes in isolation from one another. This was essential for doing away with concepts such as blending inheritance. But it is clear that the challenge of genetics in the twenty-first century will be to determine how genes work together, not separately, to produce complex phenotypes in the context of complex environments.

SUMMARY

1. **What is the difference between structural genes and regulatory genes?**

   Structural genes carry the information to make proteins. Regulatory genes guide the expression of structural genes. Given that the DNA of humans and chimpanzees is so similar—their DNAs are about 95% identical—many scientists believe that changes in regulatory genes have been critical in producing the profound physical and behavioural differences between the species.

2. **What are genotypes and phenotypes?**

   The genotype consists of the specific genes (or alleles) an organism carries; it is the genetic constitution of an individual. The phenotype is an observable or measurable feature of an organism. Phenotypes can be anatomical, biochemical, or behavioural. If we look at the expression of a phenotype among a group of organisms in a population, we will probably see some variation. This variation could be caused by genetic factors; individuals may have different genotypes that influence the expression of the phenotype differently. It could also be caused by environmental factors if the expression of the phenotype changes with changes in the environment. In many cases, the observed phenotypic variation is caused by a combination of genetic and environmental factors.

3. **What is heritability?**

   Heritability is a measure of the proportion of the total phenotypic variation that is caused by genetics. It can range from 0 to 1. For example, in a population where all organisms have exactly the same environment, all observed variability would have to be caused by genetic factors, and the heritability would be 1.

4. **What are X-linked disorders?**

   X-linked disorders are diseases or conditions that are almost always seen in males and appear in pedigrees to skip a generation after their appearance in a male sufferer. An X-linked disorder is caused by a mutation in a gene on the X chromosome. If a woman carries this mutated allele on one of her X chromosomes, she does not develop the disease because she also has a normal allele on the other X chromosome. However, if her son receives a copy of the mutant allele from his mother, he will develop the disease because he has only the single copy of the X chromosome (along with the Y chromosome). Because he can pass on an X chromosome only to his daughters, they will be carriers of the condition but will not suffer from it, and they can later pass it on to their sons. Therefore, it appears to skip a generation. Haemophilia is the best-known X-linked condition.

5. **Compare and contrast polygenic traits and pleiotropy.**

   Polygenic traits are those that are the product of the action of more than one gene, each of which may have more than one allele. Observed quantitative variation in a polygenic trait often follows a bell curve distribution because of the many possible genotypes that may underlie the expression of single phenotype. Pleiotropy is the converse: A single gene can influence more than one phenotypic trait. This is seen in the condition known as achondroplasia, in which several changes in the phenotype result from a change in a single allele.

CRITICAL THINKING QUESTIONS

1. What is the role of genetic knowledge in our day-to-day lives? Should information about the alleles we carry be available to employers or health insurance providers?
2. Would you want to know if you are carrying an allele that might cause you to have a fatal illness 20 years from now?

KEY TERMS

structural genes
regulatory genes
genotype
phenotype
ABO blood type system
recessive
dominant
co-dominant
Mendel's law of segregation
Mendel's law of independent assortment
linkage
point mutation
sickle cell disease
autosomal recessive disease
insertion mutation
deletion mutation
trinucleotide repeat diseases
autosomal dominant disease
X-linked disorders
pedigree
qualitative variation
quantitative variation
polygenic traits
pleiotropy
heritability
twin method
phenylketonuria (PKU)

SUGGESTED READING

Dawkins, R. (1989). *The Selfish Gene*, New edition. Oxford University Press, Oxford, England.

Mackintosh, N. J. (1998). *IQ and Human Intelligence*. Oxford University Press, Oxford, England.

Mendel, G. (1866). Versuche über Plflanzenhybriden (Experiments in plant hybridization). *Verhandlugen des nature-forschenden Vereines in Brünn, Bd. IV für das Jahr* 1865, 3–47. (English translation available at www.esp.org/foundations/genetics/classical/gm-65.pdf.)

Provine, W. B. (1971). *The Origins of Theoretical Population Genetics*. University of Chicago Press, Chicago, IL.

Chapter 5

The Forces of Evolution and the Formation of Species

THE LITTLE BOAT SLOSHES DANGEROUSLY CLOSE to the cliffs of a tiny islet, little more than a rock among the Galápagos Islands. The passengers—biologists and their students—carefully climb the rocky shoreline. For the next six months they live like monks, watching the tiny finches that are the major inhabitants of the island of Daphne Major. They catch the birds in mist nets, and measure their beaks, feet, wings, and everything in the finches' island habitat.

THE SCIENTISTS COME AND GO FOR 30 YEARS, spanning about 30 generations of finches and a large portion of their own life. The island is subjected to a terrible drought. The drought is followed by several years of plentiful rainfall, turning the island green and lush. Throughout these periods of plenty and famine, the scientists dutifully collect their birds and record their measurements.

THEN ONE DAY THEY NOTICE THAT SOMETHING astounding is happening. The dimensions of the beaks of the finches have changed in direct relationship to the periods of drought and plenty. When food is scarce, the major available seeds are thick-shelled and very tough to crack. The birds that were born with minutely larger, stronger beaks survive better and leave more baby finches than their smaller-beaked neighbours. When the rains come again and food is plentiful, the trend reverses. The evidence is indisputable: The species is evolving. In the span of just a few years, climate and food conditions have changed the appearance of the tiny finches because finches with stronger beaks are better able to crack open hard-shelled seeds and therefore produce more offspring than their smaller-beaked neighbours.

Chapter Outline

Demonstrating natural selection in the wild is not easy. It takes many generations and a great deal of tedious field research. However, the results show the truth of Darwin's ideas. The now-famous field study just described, conducted by biologists Peter and Rosemary Grant, is one of the best demonstrations of evolution by natural selection under natural conditions. In this chapter we will examine the principles of the evolutionary process. These include but are not limited to Darwinian natural selection. We will consider where variation in nature comes from and how the forces of evolution act on this variation to mould the form and function of animals and plants. We also examine another important question: What is a species?

HOW EVOLUTION WORKS

We speak of the forces of evolution as those factors occurring in natural populations that cause changes in gene frequencies over multiple generations. These include both adaptive and nonadaptive causes. Natural selection is the most cited cause of evolution, and much evidence suggests that it is the most important force. But, as we will see, several other causes of evolutionary change exist as well. Moreover, evolution can occur only in the presence of a source of variation, which is mutation.

Where Does Variation Come From?

In Chapter 3, we saw that alterations occur in the DNA sequence during the course of replication, changing the allelic expression at a given locus. A change in a base on the DNA molecule is a *point mutation.* Larger-scale errors during replication can result in *chromosomal mutations*, when entire chunks of chromosomes are transposed with one another. Such changes in the genetic material, whether large or small, are the source of new variation. Mutations of great significance occur very rarely. Many mutations are neutral and have no effect on the offspring's viability, survival, and reproduction. Only through the accumulation of mutations do new traits enter a population, allowing natural selection and other evolutionary forces to filter out undesirable traits and perpetuate favourable ones.

How Natural Selection Works

Natural selection takes the package of traits each animal or plant inherits from the previous generation and then tweaks it in response to the current environment. Natural selection is not simply about genes and traits. The environment is the filter through which traits—and the genes that control their expression—are selected. As we saw in Chapter 4, each organism's genetic makeup, or genotype, is fixed from conception. Natural selection acts on the organism's phenotype, the actual expression of the alleles present in the genotype. The environment can play a critical role in how the genotype is expressed, even when basic Mendelian principles are operating at single gene loci.

Populations evolve as the frequency of certain genes changes; individual organisms don't evolve. The result is that the frequency at which a gene or a trait governed by genes occurs in a population changes over time. This change generally happens very slowly, although it can be seen easily when researchers study animals with very short generation lengths, such as fruit flies or mice, or when animal breeders take selection into their own hands and choose which animals will breed and which will not. In this latter case, selection is not necessarily based on survival and reproductive value of traits. For instance, cattle breeders may select cows for milk production, or they may select them for purely aesthetic reasons such as body size, temperament, or colour. The process is analogous to natural selection, as Darwin himself understood.

The case of natural selection pushing the size of finch beaks larger and stronger when food is scarce and pushing it back the other way when food is plentiful is an example of **directional selection** (Figure 5.1). Of course, it could also be the case that selection is intense for certain beak dimensions when times are lean, and this pressure is diminished when the rains come again. A relaxation of selection pressure in a population might be difficult to distinguish in nature from selection in the opposite direction from earlier generations.

If natural selection can drive gene frequencies in a certain direction by elaborating or eliminating a certain trait, can it also be responsible for keeping populations uniform? It can, by a process known as **stabilizing selection**. The first demonstration of stabilizing selection was an early study of natural selection in the wild. In the winter of 1898, 136 house sparrows were found lying on the icy ground the morning after a severe snowstorm in Providence, Rhode Island. Seventy-two of the birds recovered; the other sixty-four died of exposure to the frigid conditions. A biologist found that surviving birds were smaller-bodied and had shorter wings than those that died, and they were more similar to the average size of birds in the local population. We don't know why smaller-bodied birds survived the storm better but we can say that birds that deviated greatly from certain sizes and shapes were not favoured by natural selection.

There are many such examples of natural selection in populations of wild animals. Showing natural selection at work in a human population is far more difficult: People

directional selection Natural selection that drives evolutionary change by selecting for greater or lesser frequency of a given trait in a population.

stabilizing selection Selection that maintains a certain phenotype by selecting against deviations from it.

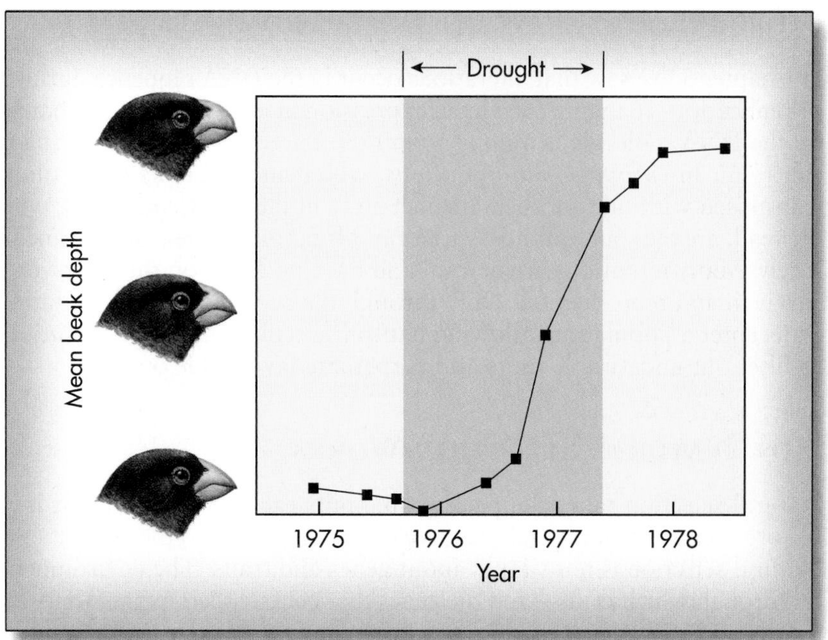

FIGURE 5.1 Directional selection pushes a phenotype one way or another.

reproduce slowly and have fairly long generational lengths. One well-documented case of natural selection in human populations is birth weight (Figure 5.2). Low birth weight, defined as weight less than 2500 grams, is associated with about 75% of early infant death in both Canada and the United States and is the principal risk factor for deaths occurring during the first month of life (da Silva, 1994). Natural selection seems to play a role at the time of birth, favouring survival of infants who are healthy, as indicated by a lack of congenital abnormalities and by an optimal range of birth weights. Over human history, natural selection operated on birth weights and perhaps on other factors related to birth weight. Birth weights that deviated far from the mean were selected against, producing a normal distribution

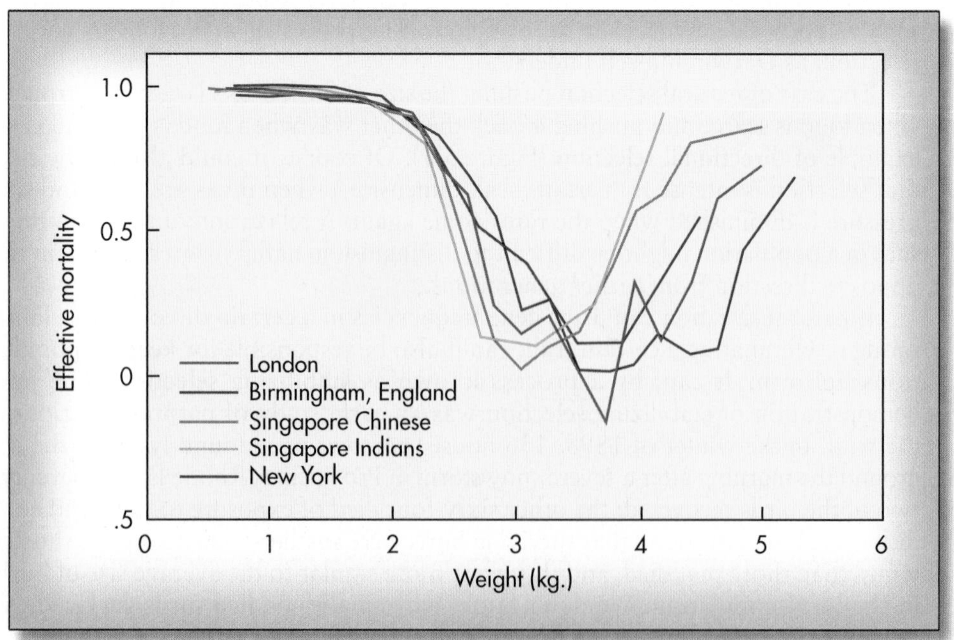

FIGURE 5.2 The birth weight of human infants is tightly constrained by natural selection. Note the high mortality of newborns of very high or low body weight based on hospital records.

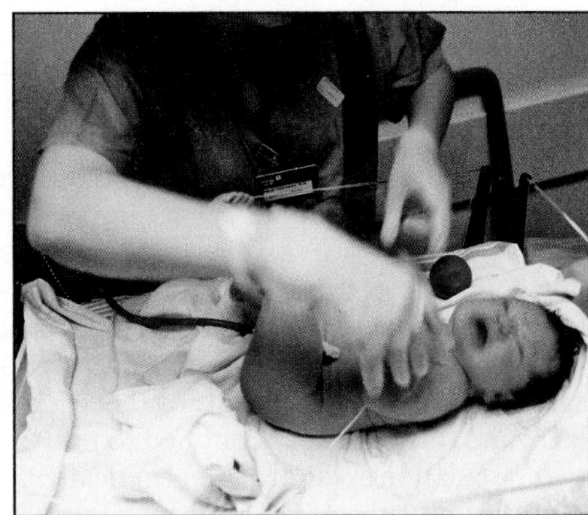

FIGURE 5.3 Human infants are like all other placental mammals, except they are born at a less developed state. Low birth weight newborns may need medical care to survive.

of birth weights with a well-defined optimum. We must remember that humans have a cultural, as well as physical, environment, and so in recent years we have seen a decrease in the mortality of low birth weight infants because of medical interventions (Figure 5.3). Conversely, we have also seen increases in the number of low birth weight babies because of cultural influences: in developed countries such as Canada, maternal cigarette smoking is the greatest direct cause of low birth weight (da Silva, 1994; Muscati et al., 1994). Alcohol consumption and drug abuse during pregnancy have also been linked to low birth weight, and low socio-economic status can contribute through inadequate nutrition, poor living conditions, and a lack of prenatal care (da Silva, 1994; Health Canada, 2003).

OTHER WAYS IN WHICH EVOLUTION HAPPENS

The power of natural selection remains a topic of debate. Some scholars argue that natural selection alone cannot account for the rapid evolution of wholesale changes in anatomy that we sometimes observe. These critics are not creationists; they simply question whether natural selection can or should be expected to have produced all the myriad traits we see in nature. There are at least two other important natural processes that produce evolutionary change in populations that are unrelated to natural selection: gene flow and genetic drift.

GENE FLOW

When humans or other animals migrate from one place to another, or when wind carries airborne seeds hundreds of kilometres from where the parent tree stands, **gene flow** has occurred. *Migration* refers to whole animals on the move; *gene flow* refers to the genetic material they carry with them in their genotypes. The exchange of genes between populations in different geographic locations can produce evolutionary change, as can stopping the exchange of genes between two areas. Movements, both permanent and temporary, of people to new locales have characterized human history. These migrations have become widespread and rapid as regional and global transportation has improved in recent centuries. When migrants produce offspring in new populations, whether they remain in the population long term or not, their genes enter the new gene pool and provide biological diversity and new traits that may eventually change the evolutionary character of the population. An excellent example of how gene flow can change a population occurred in 1789, when the crew of the British sailing ship H.M.S. *Bounty* mutinied against Captain William Bligh. Surviving crew members ended up on Pitcairn Island

gene flow Movement of genes between populations.

in the South Pacific and one sailor named Adams ended up as a permanent resident. Over the ensuing years, Adams fathered many children, and his genes, including those for his blue eyes, became widespread in the population of Pitcairn.

The cessation of gene flow can be just as important an evolutionary force as gene flow itself. If a population receives genetic contributions (*admixture*) from other nearby populations for a long period of time, it may create one large gene pool spread across two areas through extensive interbreeding. Suppose that interbreeding stops because of changes in social behaviour (two neighbouring tribes go to war, and all exchange between them is halted for centuries) or changes in geography (a flood creates a wide river barrier between the two populations). In either case the lack of gene flow means that random mutations that were formerly passed back and forth are now confined to only one population. As they accumulate, the two populations will diverge genetically and perhaps anatomically as well.

Studies of the genetics of human and other populations have generally concluded that despite our long-standing belief that **inbreeding**, or reproduction between close kin, is always bad for the health of a population, very limited amounts of gene flow can eliminate the harmful effects of inbreeding. A study of rhesus macaque monkeys conducted in the mountains of Pakistan showed only limited migration between breeding groups. Nonetheless, very limited gene flow from males who immigrated to the valley where the study was conducted were enough to maintain high levels of genetic diversity (Melnick and Hoelzer, 1996). Studies such as this do not imply that inbreeding is normal and healthy, only that a low level of immigration apparently can offset its harmful effects in a population. Inbreeding is discussed further in Chapter 17.

GENETIC DRIFT

Despite the importance of selection pressure on animal phenotypes, evolution can also result from nothing more than chance. **Genetic drift** is a change in the frequency of a gene in a population over time caused entirely by random factors. The odds that genetic drift will have great importance in changing the frequency of a trait are greatest in very small populations.

Although on average each cross of two people who are heterozygous for a trait should produce half heterozygous children, one-quarter homozygous dominant, and one-quarter homozygous recessive (recall Mendelian crosses from Chapter 4), this does not always occur. At a population level, genetic drift brings about evolutionary change through the same principle of alleles appearing or disappearing by random chance. This is important mainly in small populations, where an allele can easily disappear entirely or become prevalent in all individuals (going to *fixation*, in genetic terms). The smaller the population, the larger the potential affect of genetic drift on gene frequencies. Distinguishing drift from the effects of natural selection is not always easily done because selection in a small population would have similar visible results to the gene pool.

There are many examples of genetic drift in human and other mammalian populations, most often caused by another aspect of genetic drift, called **founder effect**. When a small subset of a much larger population becomes isolated or cut off from genetic contact with its parent gene pool, its gene pool consists only of the genotypes of the individuals in the new, small subpopulation. Only through a long and slow accumulation of mutations can the genetic diversity of the subset increase. If you and a boatload of fellow travellers were stranded permanently on a desert island, the genetic makeup of the new human population of that island would consist only of the combined genotypes of all the passengers. Founder effect and gene flow often are linked, as in the case of the Pitcairn Islanders receiving new residents in the form of the *Bounty* mutineers. The combination of immigration and very small population size of the island enabled the genes of one British mutineer to become widespread in a short period of time.

inbreeding Mating between close relatives.

genetic drift Random changes in gene frequency in a population.

founder effect A component of genetic drift theory, stating that new populations that become isolated from the parent population carry only the genetic variation of the founders.

Some immigrant populations to Canada who have chosen to live in closed societies experience the effects of genetic drift. The Hutterian Brethren, or Hutterites, are members of a pacifist religion that evolved in Europe as an outgrowth of the Protestant Reformation of the early 1500s. An estimated 30 000 Hutterites now live in colonies of about 100 persons in Alberta, Manitoba, and Saskatchewan (there are also other colonies in the north central and western United States). Hutterite colonies are usually large-scale, highly mechanized, mixed-agricultural producers. Although families usually have their own homes, meals are taken together and property is owned communally. Young men and women typically marry between the ages of 20 and 24 and may choose a spouse from their home colony or another colony. Limb girdle muscular dystrophy (LGMD), a muscular system disorder, has a high prevalence among Hutterites. LGMD affects the voluntary muscles around the hip and shoulder regions, and the heart and breathing muscles also may be involved. Because of the small and relatively closed nature of the Hutterite populations, and because they have kept excellent records of births, deaths, and marriages, researchers have been able to study the genetics of this disorder. The Molecular Genetics and Human Disease Group at the University of Manitoba has identified two different genes that lead to this type of muscular dystrophy within the Hutterite population (Frosk et al., 2005). Records indicate that one or a few Hutterite individuals carried these genes with them from Europe to North America and, by virtue of their high reproductive rate (Hutterite women have an average of 10 to 12 children), spread the gene rapidly through the very small founding population.

A phenomenon associated with the founder effect that can bring about evolutionary change is a **genetic bottleneck**. A bottleneck occurs when a large, genetically diverse population undergoes a rapid reduction in size and then increases again (Figure 5.4). When the population size declines, a large percentage of the alleles present may be lost, and after the bottleneck, only the accumulation of mutations will rebuild genetic diversity. If, for example, a gene for disease resistance that existed in the population before the bottleneck is lost, the disease could devastate the surviving populations. Hundreds of generations will have to pass before mutations can begin to restore this diversity.

Natural selection is not the only mechanism by which evolution can occur, although it is considered by most researchers to be the predominant way the variation present in nature is moulded into new forms.

genetic bottleneck Temporary dramatic reduction in size of a population or species.

sexual selection Differential reproductive success within one sex of any species.

Sexual Selection: Darwin's Other Great Idea

In his second book, *The Descent of Man*, published in 1871, Darwin extended his evolutionary principles directly to humankind. In it, he explained another major evolutionary force: nonrandom mating brought about by **sexual selection**. Social

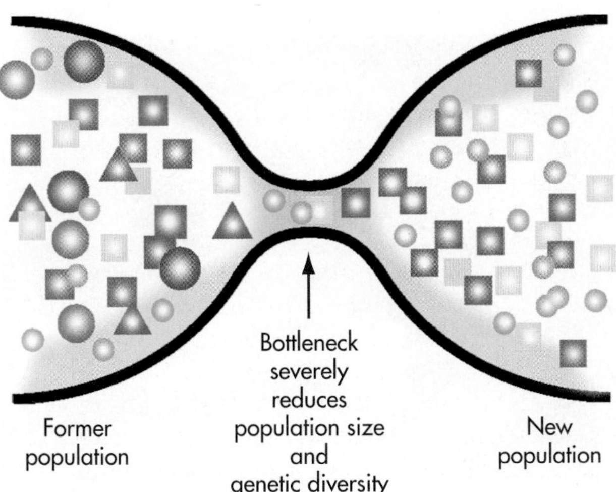
Bottleneck severely reduces population size and genetic diversity
Former population
New population

Figure 5.4 A genetic bottleneck reduces a population temporarily to very low levels, removing much of its genetic diversity.

sexual dimorphism Difference in size, shape, or colour, between the sexes.

animals don't mate and bear offspring simply because they bump into each other like balls on a pool table. Females choose particular males as their mates, and they make their choices based on natural variations in male traits (Figure 5.5).

Darwin identified two components to sexual selection: the struggle between males to gain access to mates and the struggle by a female to choose the right mate. Sexual selection can be defined as differential reproductive success among the members of the same sex within a given species. Female choice of particular genetically based male traits, such as antlers or large muscles or bright colours, leads to the evolution of males that exhibit those traits because these males enjoy greater reproductive success. Many animal traits that we once believed had evolved to allow males to defend themselves and their group against predators, such as horns and antlers, are now believed to be the products of sexual selection.

Although Darwin considered sexual selection to be an aspect of natural selection, the two forces can operate independently and even in opposition. Although early research on the topic tended to focus on competition between males for mates and assumed that male competition was the driving force behind sexual selection, scientists today recognize that the opposite is more likely. Females of many animal species drive evolutionary change through their selection of certain male phenotypes. Increased male body size is a common outcome of sexual selection; in a few primate species, males are nearly twice as large as females. This results from female choice for larger body sizes, and implies competition between males for access to females. **Sexual dimorphism**, a difference in size, shape, or colour between the sexes, usually is brought about by evolutionary changes in male appearance caused by female mate preferences.

But why should females prefer large-bodied males? Females are thought to be under selection pressure to choose a male that offers her a direct benefit, such as help in offspring rearing or protection against predators. She may use physical features of the male to judge his quality in these areas (Kirkpatrick, 1982). If the capacity for judging males on this basis evolves in females, then males are expected to evolve more and more elaborate features to impress females. Or females may choose males by selecting for indirect benefits. In species where males offer nothing to a female except their genes at conception, we expect a female to choose a mate based on his genetic quality. To judge a potential mate's genetic quality, a female may use a male's ornamental features as clues. Among birds, for example, brightly coloured feathers may indicate a male's underlying genetic health. Sexual selection is currently a hot research area for evolutionary biologists, and new discoveries are being made all the time.

Why is it that males compete for females, and females choose male traits, rather than the other way around? The theory of sexual selection proposes that

FIGURE 5.5 A male peacock displays his genetic worth for a female.

the sex with the more limited **reproductive potential** should be competed over by the sex with the greater reproductive potential. For nearly all higher animals, this means that females are competed over by males because females are the limited commodity that males need to achieve reproductive success. Whereas a male mammal's fitness often is limited only by access to females, a female must bear most of the costs of reproduction: gestation, lactating, and nurturing. Her level of *parental investment* is far greater than that of males.

The difference in reproductive potential in males and females can be dramatic in a slow-reproducing animal such as humans. Consider the maximum number of children you've ever heard of a woman giving birth to. The *Guinness Book of World Records* cites an eighteenth-century Russian woman who is alleged to have had 69 children. By contrast, the same source confirms the maximum recorded children for a man to be 888. In addition to the disparity in reproductive potential, males and females often differ greatly in their **reproductive variance**, the degree of variation from the mean of a population in the reproductive potential of one sex compared with the other. One consequence of a female's lower reproductive potential—she can be fertilized only once in each breeding season—is that whereas nearly all the females find mates, many males fail to find females. This reproductive asymmetry between males and females holds major consequences for how males and females behave toward one another during courtship, as we will see in Chapter 8.

CLASSIFICATION AND EVOLUTION

In order to understand the natural world, we categorize plants and animals according to the similarities of their features. The science of taxonomy that Linnaeus devised forms the basis for the study of biological classification today, although Linnaeus' scheme did not incorporate modern notions of evolutionary change.

TAXONOMY AND SPECIATION

Linnaeus classified species in much the same way that we all classify things in our everyday lives, lumping types together based on physical characteristics that were readily apparent to the eye.

However, animal or plant species are dynamic units, always changing in ways that may be too small or slow for us to see in comparing any two or three generations. Furthermore, species themselves don't care whether we can identify them; animals themselves determine the boundaries of species units by their willingness to mate or not with animals from other similar species. Our natural tendency to treat species as distinct, separate categories even when this does not reflect biological reality has contributed to great confusion about species and their formation.

Linnaeus established a hierarchy of categories to classify all living things (Table 5.1). Each of these levels of the hierarchy is like a set of nested Russian dolls. As one descends the categories, the distinctions between related forms become increasingly smaller. The only "natural" category is the species. All others are a taxonomist's way of making sense of the evolutionary past of clusters of related species. Notice that humans and chimpanzees are classified in the same taxonomic categories until the level of the family, and if Linnaeus had not been so driven by theology he would have placed us in the same family. Tortoises, in contrast, are separated from humans and chimpanzees at the level of the class. To Linnaeus, this indicated that tortoises had been created in a different image than primates in God's plan. Today, we recognize that the class-level distinction indicates distant evolutionary relatedness.

reproductive potential The possible offspring output by one sex.

reproductive variance A measure of variation from the mean of a population in the reproductive potential of one sex compared with the other.

TABLE 5.1 The Linnaean Hierarchy

LINNAEAN CATEGORY	HUMAN	CHIMPANZEE	TORTOISE
Kingdom	Animalia	Animalia	Animalia
Phylum	Chordata	Chordata	Chordata
Class	Mammalia	Mammalia	Reptilia
Order	Primates	Primates	Testudines
Family	Hominidae	Pongidae	Testudinidae
Genus	*Homo*	*Pan*	*Manouria*
Species	*Homo sapiens*	*Pan troglodytes*	*Manouria emys*

Evolutionary biologists use a variety of methods to determine relationships between related evolutionary groups. Today the study of taxonomy usually is called **systematics**. Systematists rely on the principle of **homology**, the notion that similar features in two related organisms look alike because of a shared evolutionary history. The bones of your arm have homologous counterparts in the flukes of a whale; despite the whale's aquatic lifestyle, its evolution as a land animal is revealed in the bones it shares with all other land animals. On the other hand, some features are similar because of similar patterns of use rather than shared ancestry. Bird, bat, and fly wings are all used for flight and are **analogous** traits but they evolved independently (Figure 5.6).

We use anatomical *characters*, meaning physical features, to categorize organisms. Two principles are commonly used. First, all organisms are composed of many *ancestral* (historically also referred to as *primitive*) characters or traits, inherited from ancestors they share with living relatives. Second, organisms also possess *derived* characters: features that are evolved from the ancestral condition. The designation of ancestral or derived is relative to the comparison being made. For example, if comparing mammals to reptiles, the fur or hair of mammals is a derived trait; it is shared by mammals but not by reptiles because mammals have evolved from the ancestral condition. However, when comparing different mammals, for example a cat and a baboon, the fact that they both have fur now is classified as a shared ancestral trait.

By identifying the derived characters, systematists can begin to establish a family tree, or *phylogeny*, of the degree of evolutionary relatedness of one form to another. Phylogenies are the evolutionary histories of groups of related organisms, illustrated in a way that the relationship and the time scale of splitting between ancestors and descendants is shown.

Another brand of evolutionary classification is called **cladistics** (from the Greek word *clados*, meaning "branch"), a science of classification in which certain traits are considered more evolutionarily important and informative than others. After establishing which traits are ancestral and which are derived, cladists then analyze the uniquely derived characters. If a cladist is trying to build a taxonomy of all monkeys, he or she will study the anatomies of enough known species to identify which traits are shared by all and which are possessed by only a few species. If a cluster of species displays a trait that no other group displays, then this *clade*, or cluster of species linked by a set of unique traits, can be studied further to distinguish which traits of the cluster are ancestral and which are derived. The cladist might identify monkeys that possess a grasping tail as a clade and then try to determine the evolutionary path by which grasping tails evolved, studying the presence or absence of other traits in the same clade in which the grasping tail appears. The result of this analysis is a **cladogram**, or branching order of the origins of

systematics Branch of biology that describes patterns of organismal variation.

homology Similarity of traits resulting from shared ancestry.

analogous Having similar traits due to similar use, not due to shared ancestry.

cladistics Method of classification using ancestral and derived traits to distinguish patterns of evolution within lineages.

cladogram Branching diagram showing evolved relationships among members of a lineage.

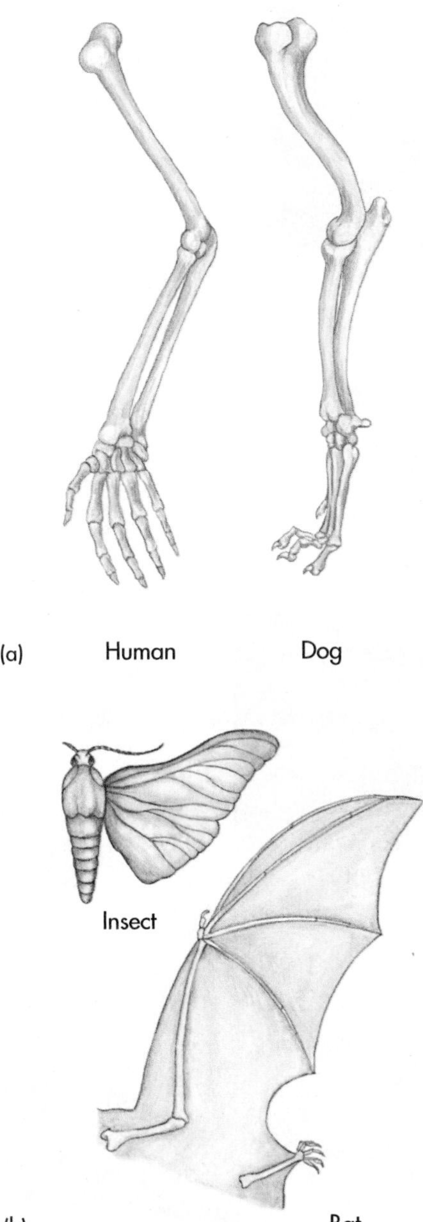

FIGURE 5.6 (a) Homologous traits, such as the bones of the arms of a human and the limbs of a dog, are similar due to shared ancestry. (b) Analogous traits, such as the wings of an insect and the wings of a bat, evolved independently but serve a similar function.

the lineage of monkeys (Figure 5.7). A cladogram does not depict the distance in time between the clades, only the relative degree of anatomical and evolutionary difference.

You may see that there is at least one potential problem with this approach. What about the possibility that the trait in question, a monkey's prehensile tail, evolved twice? The separate, **convergent evolution** of very similar traits is a confounding factor in cladistic analyses. One way around this problem is to make a very reasonable assumption: A given feature is unlikely to have evolved twice independently in the same lineage or to have disappeared and then re-evolved later in the same lineage. This is called the *law of parsimony*, which argues that one should always seek the simplest explanation for a natural phenomenon.

convergent evolution Similar form or function brought about by natural selection under similar environments rather than shared ancestry.

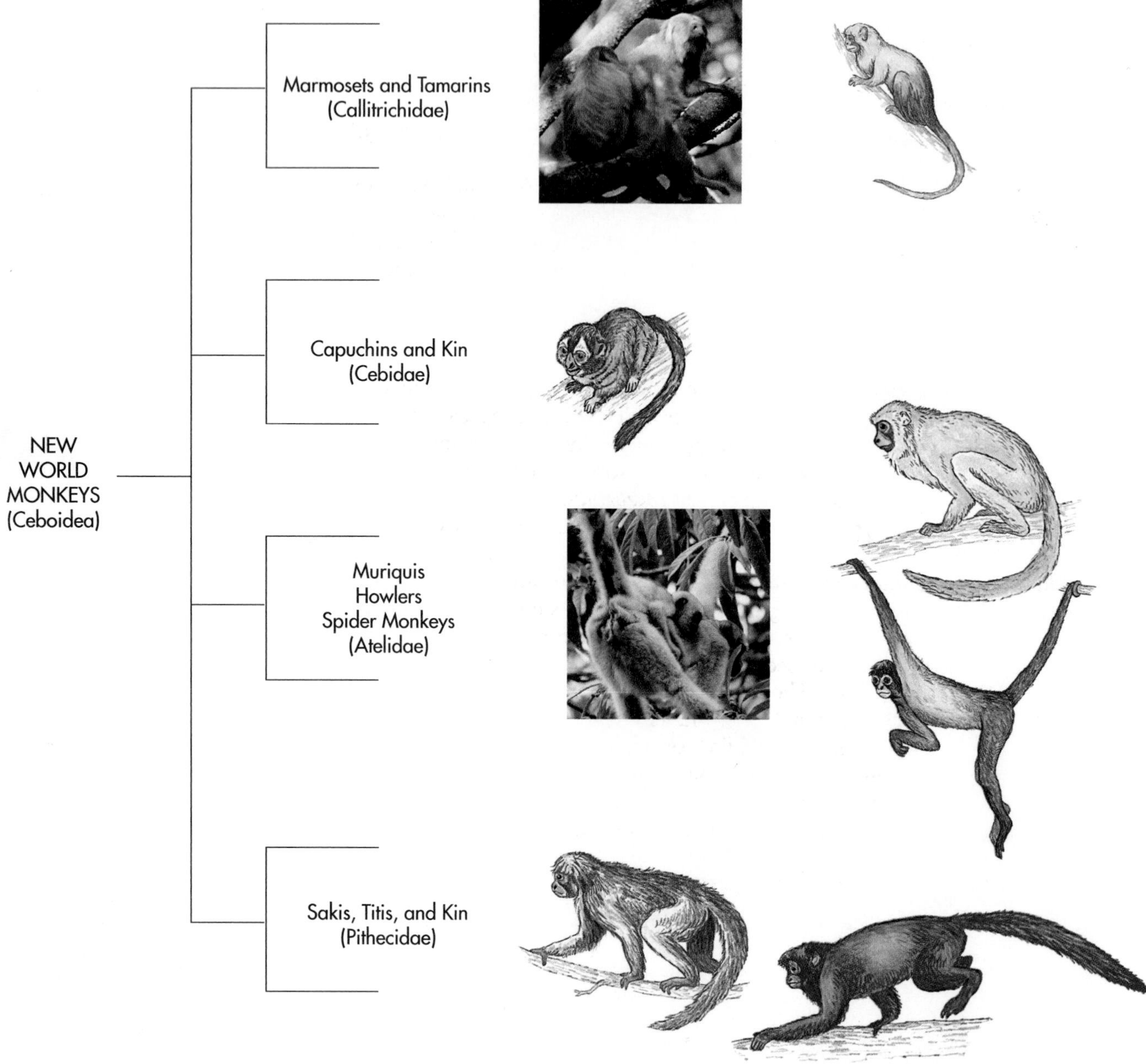

FIGURE 5.7 Example of a cladogram, or branching order, of the New World monkey Superfamily Ceboidea. A cladogram is a family tree but does not show evolutionary time scales.

A second approach to systematics is called *phenetics*, or numerical taxonomy. Pheneticists use all traits that link two organisms, not worrying whether they are similar because of homology or analogy. Phenetics relies solely on numerically describing degrees of similarity and difference between organisms, without biases created by knowing some groups are more closely related than others. Unrelated animals sometimes are lumped in the evolutionary group under this scheme. Taxonomies created by phenetics often differ in important ways from those assembled by cladists or other systematists. Phenetics has largely been superseded by cladistics for research into evolutionary relationships among species and most scholars studying nonhuman primate and human evolution use the principles and language of cladistics in their work.

What Is a Species?

There is no issue more confusing to both students and scientists of evolution than the question "What is a **species**?" In Linnaeus' time the answer was easy: Species were fixed pigeonholes without evolutionary pasts or connections to other species in the present. But ever since Darwin, we recognize that species are dynamic, ever-changing entities, and finding a consensus on concepts of species has proved vexing. The formation of new species, or **speciation**, is a fundamental evolutionary process.

Species are difficult to define because of the amount of variation found in nature. What we call species tend to be overlapping categories, rather than completely distinct units. Modern evolutionary biologists can use DNA analysis and studies of physiology, ecology, and behaviour, yet the problem of defining "species" remains.

A Guide to Species Concepts

Evolutionary biologists have a wide variety of species concepts from which to choose. The most widely used definition of species is the **biological species concept**, which defines species as "groups of actually or potentially interbreeding natural populations which are reproductively isolated from other such groups" (Mayr, 1942, 1963). This definition has two key phrases. *Reproductive isolation* is at the heart of this concept. If two types of related animals can be distinguished absolutely, then they must have been reproductively isolated for some period of time. But the phrase *actually or potentially* indicates that populations of animals that could cross-breed to create hybrid offspring in nature but don't should be considered separate species, so the definition refers to *natural populations* only.

Consider lions and tigers. They seem to be two obviously distinct species, but their differences are only skin deep. The two species are closely related, and if housed together in the same zoo exhibit, a male lion and female tiger will produce a hybrid cub as will a male tiger that mates with a lioness. These hybrid cubs are fully fertile and can be bred to one another or to a lion or tiger to produce another generation of tiger–lion hybrids. In the one natural habitat the two species share (the Gir Forest in western India), lions and tigers have never been seen mating. So are lions and tigers considered separate species according to the biological species concept? The answer is yes, because in nature the species are reproductively isolated: There is no overlap between the two species' phenotypes and no evidence of them interbreeding naturally. There are many such examples of animals that do not ever meet in nature, because they live thousands of kilometres apart or occupy different niches in the same habitat, but hybridize readily if placed in the same cage or pond. Nevertheless, these have been traditionally considered separate species.

Reproductive Isolating Mechanisms

If species are reproductively isolated from other species, then what factors keep species apart? Such mechanisms can be sorted into two categories: premating isolating mechanisms and postmating isolating mechanisms. Such **reproductive isolating mechanisms (RIMs)** have been built into the phenotypes of animals to prevent them from accidentally mating with members of another, similar species. Such a mistaken hybrid mating in most cases would be a wasted reproductive effort, and natural selection promotes mechanisms to prevent such matings. Premating barriers to accidental cross-species breeding include, for example, habitat isolation and mechanical incompatibility (especially of the reproductive system), while postmating barriers include conditions such as biochemical incompatibility of the sperm and egg and the reproductive sterility of the hybrid offspring.

There are many alternatives to the biological species concept; no fewer than 25 definitions of *species* have been proposed in scientific literature.

species An interbreeding group of animals or plants that are reproductively isolated through anatomy, ecology, behaviour, or geographic distribution from all other such groups.

speciation Formation of one or more new species via reproductive isolation.

biological species concept Defines species as interbreeding populations reproductively isolated from other such populations.

reproductive isolating mechanisms (RIMS) Any factor—behavioural, ecological, or anatomical—that prevents a male and female of two different species from hybridizing.

evolutionary species concept Defines species as evolutionary lineages with their own unique identity.

ecological species concept Defines species based on the uniqueness of their ecological niche.

recognition species concept Defines species based on unique traits or behaviours that allow members of one species to identify each other for mating.

The **evolutionary species concept** is used by many scientists who study the fossil record and therefore cannot directly observe the reproductive isolating mechanisms on which the biological species concept relies. Proponents of the evolutionary species concept consider the enormous geologic time needed to establish the evolutionary history of a species to be an important criterion of a species. Its proponents say that a species should be not only phenotypically distinct from all other species but also that it should have its own evolutionary identity (Simpson, 1961). The **ecological species concept** says that a species should occupy its own unique ecological niche, or role, that distinguishes it clearly from all other species (Van Valen, 1976). This concept has never been widely applied, although it may be useful in distinguishing species that are very similar genetically and anatomically but differ in how they divide up the resources in their habitat.

The most influential current alternative to the biological species concept is the **recognition species concept** (Paterson, 1986). It argues that the emphasis on reproductive isolation found in the biological species concept is flawed in that such isolation may be only a side effect of the splitting of two populations into separate species for other reasons. The recognition species concept states that species have their own unique systems for recognizing mates. For example, galagoes (bush babies) are small nocturnal primates that use calls to recognize one another in dark tropical forests. Each species has a unique set of calls that apparently prevents accidental matings between members of different galago species. Studying these calls with an emphasis on how galagoes of one species find each other for mating uses the principle of the recognition species concept.

The difficulties raised by applying multiple species concepts create problems for anthropologists trying to understand the human fossil record. Just as species in the present day are best seen as dynamic entities that overlap genetically in many cases, drawing the line in history where one species has evolved into another species often is problematic. We will see later in the text that some early human species can be considered one species or four species depending on which taxonomist one listens to and which species concept that taxonomist uses.

In addition to confusion over species concepts, interpreting fossils is complicated by individual variation. If we identify a species in the fossil record, some individuals will look more alike than others because of random variation of the kind that makes one person taller or thinner than another today. And often whole populations, the breeding subunits of each species, look a bit different from other populations of the same species. For example, lowland gorillas in western Africa (Figure 5.8) exist in multiple separate populations, which show a startling degree of genetic divergence. In fact, some western lowland gorilla populations are as different from one another genetically as gorillas are from chimpanzees. Their genetic diversity has prompted some scientists to propose splitting lowland gorillas into at least two species, although this remains controversial. This implies a very long

FIGURE 5.8 Most of the world's remaining gorillas are western lowland gorillas.

history of separation among the populations. However, despite this genetic divergence, western lowland gorillas all look very much alike; in other words, their phenotypes have remained the same.

anagenesis Evolution of a trait or a species into another over a period of time.

cladogenesis Evolution through the branching of a species or a lineage.

allopatric speciation Speciation occurring via geographic isolation.

parapatric speciation Speciation occurring when two populations have continuous distributions and some phenotypes in that distribution are more favourable than others.

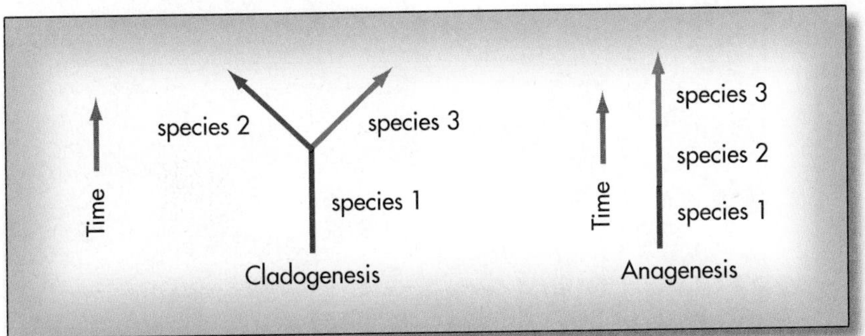

The Origin of Species: How Species Are Formed

The process of speciation can occur in a variety of ways. One species can evolve into another over time, a process known as **anagenesis.** In this mode of change, Species 1 would slowly become Species 2, and Species 1 would no longer exist or be identifiable in the fossil record (Figure 5.9). The question then becomes when taxonomists should stop referring to the species as 1 and begin calling it 2. Species 1 might also branch into two or more new species, a process called **cladogenesis.** In cladogenesis, Species 1 might or might not still exist as one of the new array of species.

Beyond these two general modes of evolutionary change, there are specific processes by which new species are formed. One of these is **allopatric speciation** (Mayr, 1942). In allopatric speciation, the trigger to the emergence of new species is geographic separation between two populations of the same species (Figure 5.10). Such circumstances of isolation and divergence happen frequently in nature; islands and river course changes both create fragmented animal habitats that lead to allopatric speciation all the time.

Scientists studying the great apes believe the closely related chimpanzee and bonobo may have been formed when the great Congo River split and isolated two populations of an ape species that was their common ancestor (Figure 5.11). Apes do not swim, and with a lack of gene flow over thousands of generations, two apes with differing anatomies and behaviour emerged where there had been one.

Natural processes are not the only factors that create geographic isolation. In the eastern slopes of the Rocky Mountains, human-led development in the valleys for transportation corridors, recreation, and housing have fragmented populations of grizzly bears by interfering with the animals' mobility. Although male bears continue to migrate, the movement of females is more restricted, particularly in terms of crossing the TransCanada Highway. The fragmentation has created relatively small sub-populations, some of which exhibit reduced genetic diversity in the maternal lines (Herrero, 2005; Proctor et al., 2004).

A second process of species formation is **parapatric speciation**, which appears to be a much less important force than allopatric speciation. When two populations occur adjacent to each other, with continuous gene flow back and forth between them, speciation of one from the other is nevertheless possible, especially if one or both species occur over a very large geographic area. This can make one part of a population remote enough from another that new traits can appear, and over time parts of the original populations diverge more than others. Often, a zone of overlap remains where the new populations, now two species, continue to interbreed.

Figure 5.9 Two modes of evolutionary change. (a) In cladogenesis, one species branches into multiple new species. (b) In anagenesis one species evolves into another new species over time.

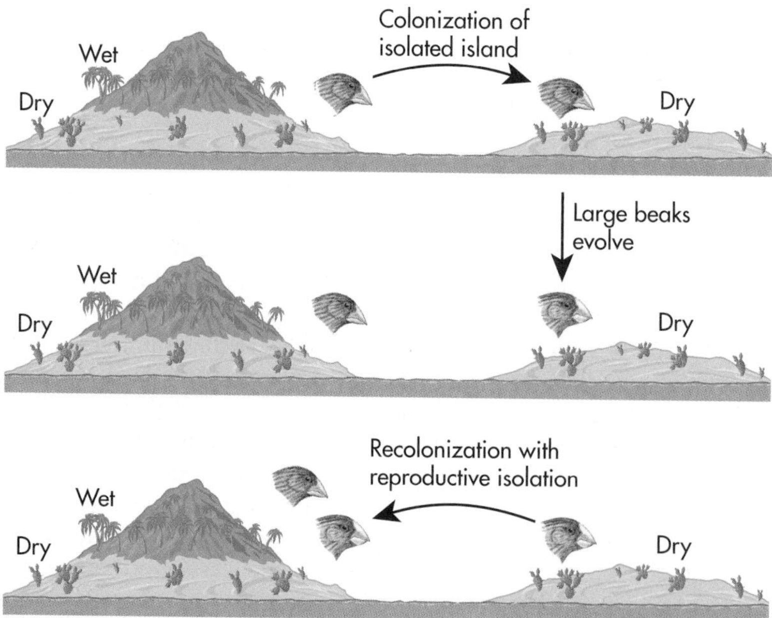

FIGURE 5.10 How allopatric speciation works.

sympatric speciation Speciation occurring in the same geographic location.

Such hybrid zones are confusing to evolutionary biologists because they can remain stable, without disappearing or growing, over many years. In northeastern Africa, a hybrid zone exists between savannah and hamadryas baboons. In the strip of arid land that is the hybrid zone, but nowhere outside of it, baboons exist that share a mosaic of traits between the two species. These traits are not only morphological ones such as hair colour or body size; they include aspects of mating behaviours in hybrids that resemble a mixture of the behaviour of both species. Such hybrids therefore allow primatologists to better understand the degree of genetic influence over particular traits.

Another mode of speciation is **sympatric speciation.** In theory, sympatric speciation occurs when multiple phenotypes exist in a single species, some of which have greater reproductive success than others. No spatial separation of the parent species is needed. The most common cases of sympatric speciation in nature are

(a)

(b)

FIGURE 5.11 Chimpanzees (a) and bonobos (b) likely diverged from a common ancestor due to allopatric speciation in central Africa.

found in plants, in which a single mistake made during reproduction produces large-scale chromosomal mutation. The mutation isolates a whole new form of plant reproductively from its neighbours, thereby creating a new species, which can lead to very rapid speciation because of its dramatic genetic effects.

gradualism Darwinian view of slow, incremental evolutionary change.

macroevolution Evolution of major phenotypic changes over relatively short time periods.

punctuated equilibrium Model of evolution characterized by rapid bursts of change, followed by long periods of stasis.

The Tempo of Speciation

When Darwin considered evolution by natural selection, he considered mainly one kind of change. Lineages of animal and plant species evolve slowly, gradually evolving into new species over vast periods of Earth's history. This is known as **gradualism** and is widely accepted as the most important and prevalent type of biological evolution. Although Darwin knew about the occurrence of mutations that differed radically in colour or shape from their parents, he considered these extremely rare aberrations. Darwin and most biologists since have accepted gradualism based on the occurrence of so many intermediate forms in the fossil record and the intricate relationships between an organism's adaptations, which imply small incremental evolutionary changes because rapid major changes would disrupt the way an organism functions.

Given this evidence of gradual evolution, how do we explain the presence of gaps in the fossil record? Creationists point to these gaps as evidence that a divine power has created at least some species, and therefore they lack an evolutionary history. Scientists point out that the fossil record is fragmentary, and if complete it would reveal all the gradual changes that evolution has produced.

An alternative explanation for gaps in the fossil record is **macroevolution**, meaning rapid, large-scale evolutionary changes. The most commonly cited mode of macroevolution is **punctuated equilibrium** (Eldredge and Gould, 1972). The theory of punctuated equilibrium holds that most species' phenotypes remain static, changing very little over long periods of time. These long periods of stasis are punctuated by bursts of evolutionary change that happen rapidly (Figure 5.12). Such a process would produce gaps in the fossil record because intermediate forms would occur only in brief windows in time. The theory's advocates claim that this may explain large gaps in the fossil record for the most ancient invertebrates, in which wholesale changes in the phenotypes of lineages appear suddenly and without evidence of immediate ancestors.

Punctuated equilibrium is a variation on the traditional Darwinian theory of gradual evolutionary change. Most scientists studying the fossil record of more recent animal life are sceptical of punctuated evolution, for at least two reasons. First, in cases where abundant fossils are discovered for a lineage of animals,

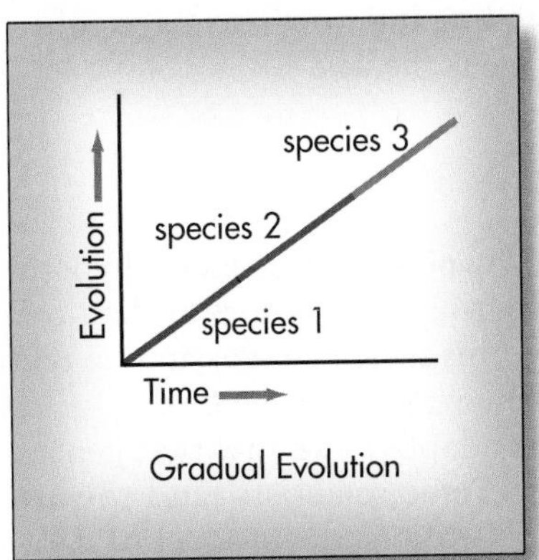

(a)

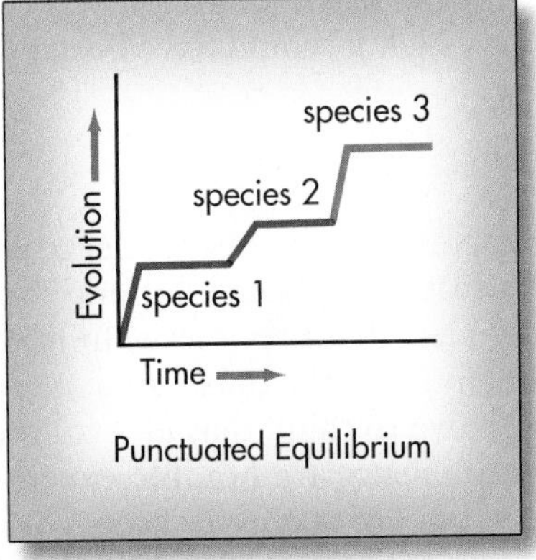

(b)

FIGURE 5.12 The tempo of evolution. (a) Gradual evolution involves small, steady changes over a long period. (b) Punctuated equilibrium involves long periods of stasis punctuated by bursts of change.

adaptationism A premise that all aspects of an organism have been moulded by natural selection to a form optimal for enhancing reproductive success.

evidence of gradual change exists. Second, much evidence exists that indicates that species change slightly over time without evolving into new species, as opposed to the claim of punctuated equilibrium theorists that species remain static for long periods.

However, scientists who study the deep history of life on Earth have a very different view of punctuated equilibrium. The fossil record of very primitive life forms living hundreds of millions of years ago provides strong evidence that punctuated equilibrium might have been an important mode of speciation. Most evidence of punctuation events comes from patterns of wholesale changes in communities of ancient marine animals, in which large-scale change can be seen in short periods of time. Punctuated equilibrium is a good example of how scientists' views differ widely depending on their perspective of nature. Those looking at only recent evolution on Earth see little evidence of punctuation events, whereas those studying enormously long time scales and more complete fossil records see ample evidence.

As we saw in Chapter 1 and will examine in detail in the next section, adaptation is a fundamental aspect of evolution by natural selection. Many scientists question whether punctuated equilibrium can account for the ever-present force of adaptation in nature.

ADAPTATION

Adaptations are evolved phenotypic traits that increase an organism's reproductive success. The concept of adaptation is central to modern biology, but it is also much debated. Some evolutionary biologists consider any well-designed trait an organism possesses to be an adaptation. Others use a stricter definition: They consider an adaptation to be a trait that evolved for a purpose and that is still serving that purpose. A trait that evolved for a purpose other than what it does today would not be considered an adaptation.

For instance, we can be sure that the wings of birds did not evolve for flight. We know this because natural selection sorts among the available adaptive advantages an organism possesses *in each generation.* There would have been no selective advantage to an ancient bird in having wings that were just slightly adapted for flight. Instead, wings must have evolved for another function entirely and then were co-opted for flight. Some evolutionary theorists think that feathered wings were initially adaptive as organs that absorbed solar radiation, allowing a protobird to bask in the sun and warm up more effectively (as some birds use them today). As feathered wings evolved, they became useful for gliding and then eventually were modified for powered flight (Figure 5.13). As in other cases of explaining retrospectively the origin of an adaptation, finding intermediate stages of its evolution during which it would have been adaptive is the key.

FIGURE 5.13 A feathered dinosaur.

IS EVERYTHING ADAPTIVE?

As we saw in Chapter 2, evolutionary science works by posing a reasonable hypothesis to explain a feature or behaviour and then figuring out the sort of data one needs to collect to test that hypothesis. In practice, this means that assuming that a trait may be adaptive at the outset of a study is the way to proceed.

It would be naive to think that all evolution is adaptive; we saw that genetic drift and its components are notable exceptions. Some scientists tend toward **adaptationism**, accepting that every aspect of an organism is the product of natural selection or sexual selection. Others, including members of one school we can

Box 5.1 What Would Populations Be Like If Evolutionary Change Never Occurred?

We can examine mathematically what populations would be like if evolutionary change didn't occur, and the experiment is extremely useful for understanding the **null hypothesis** that natural selection and other evolutionary forces have no effect on a population. In 1908, English mathematician G. H. Hardy published a short article in the journal *Science* that played a vital role in the reconciliation of Mendelian and Darwinian views of nature. It also laid the foundations for the modern field of population genetics and other mathematical approaches to understanding evolution.

Before 1908, geneticists struggled with concepts of equilibrium in biological populations. At what point would genetic stability be reached in these dynamic populations? Looking at it from the simplest perspective of one gene with two alleles (one dominant and one recessive), it was argued that equilibrium would be reached in a population when there was a 3:1 ratio of the dominant to the recessive phenotype (Yule, 1902). Most geneticists with practical experience knew this was wrong but did not know how to prove it was wrong. This is where Hardy stepped in.

Suppose we have a population of diploid, sexually reproducing organisms. Assume that this population is not subject to any evolutionary forces that might lead to changes in allele frequencies: no mutation, no natural selection, no migration. Assume that the population is infinitely large (that is, no genetic drift) and that mating is random (that is, allele frequencies cannot be influenced by assortive or disassortive mating practices). This is obviously an "ideal" population, but that is not a problem, as we will see. Let us take the case of a single gene A with two alleles, A_1 and A_2. The frequencies of these alleles in the population can be represented by p and q, respectively (see also Appendix B). By definition, $p + q = 1$.

Hardy showed that after one generation, the genotype frequencies in the population can be represented by a simple quadratic equation:

$$(p + q)^2 = p^2 + 2pq + q^2 = 1$$

This means that the frequencies of the homozygous genotypes A_1A_1 and A_2A_2 are $p2$ and $q2$, respectively, and the frequency of the heterozygote A_1A_2 is $2pq$. No matter what values p and q have, if the assumptions of no evolution, infinitely large population, and random mating hold, these allele (and genotype) frequencies will not change over generations of breeding. The population is in equilibrium, at least for this single gene or locus.

Despite the fact that ideal populations rarely exist in nature, Hardy's equation, which later became known as the **Hardy–Weinberg equilibrium**, has proved to be valuable in many ways. It can be mathematically expanded to model the distribution of more complex genetic systems, including polygenic traits and those for which more than two alleles exist. One can also use it to calculate approximate allele frequencies based on knowledge of the phenotypic frequency of a homozygous recessive trait. For example, there is a chemical called phenylthiocarbamide (PTC), which can be tasted by about 75% of the European population but cannot be tasted by the other 25%. It is known that this is controlled by a single gene with two alleles, where "tasting" is dominant to "nontasting." Thus the allele frequency of "nontasting" (homozygous recessive) equals the square root of 0.25, or 0.5.

Finally, although ideal populations rarely exist, the allele distributions of many genes often are found to be in equilibrium. Of course, when we find an allele distribution that is not in equilibrium that can be the most exciting finding of all: It may mean that an evolutionary force is at work in the population, waiting to be uncovered by a curious investigator.

FIGURE A G. H. Hardy.

Hardy's article put to rest any ideas of "blending" inheritance. He demonstrated not only that in the absence of evolution allele frequencies are in equilibrium but also that phenotype frequencies are in equilibrium. There would be no averaging out of beneficial traits, which for many years was the standard argument against Darwinian evolution by natural selection.

And who is Weinberg? Hardy did not know Wilhelm Weinberg, a German physician, who in 1908—and some months before Hardy—presented an equilibrium model of allele frequency stability identical to Hardy's. Weinberg published several articles on population genetics in 1909, many of which anticipated later developments in the field. They were all ignored and therefore had no influence on the development of population genetics. It was many years later, after the rediscovery of Weinberg's work, that the Hardy equilibrium became universally known as the *Hardy–Weinberg equilibrium*.

null hypothesis The starting assumption for scientific inquiry that one's research results occur by random chance. One's hypothesis must challenge this initial assumption.

Hardy-Weinberg equilibrium The theoretical distribution of alleles in a given population in the absence of evolution, expressed as a mathematical equation.

reductionism Paradigm that an organism is the sum of many evolved parts and that organisms can best be understood through an adaptationist approach.

kin selection Principle that animals behave preferentially toward their genetic kin.

inclusive fitness Reproductive success of an organism plus the fitness of its close kin.

call *holism*, are sceptical that natural selection is all-powerful and consider many apparent adaptations to be merely the byproduct of other evolutionary changes.

These two schools of thought represent very different ways of understanding how evolution works. Adaptationists tend toward **reductionism,** trying to understand the function of each component of an organism in order to understand the organism as a whole. They make the working assumption that each part of the organism is adaptive. Holists claim that reductionists oversimplify the nature of adaptation and see natural selection in places where it had not occurred. Adaptationists respond that assuming that traits are adaptive is the only rational starting point for using the scientific method to test their hypotheses. Just as there are both evolved and immediate causes in biology, there are both adaptive and nonadaptive explanations for what an organism looks like. Using an adaptive, reductionist framework as a starting point for investigating those traits is the best, and perhaps the only, way to conduct scientific research into human evolutionary biology. The holistic approach cautions us against assuming that all features of an organism are adaptive. But in practise, biological anthropologists tend to begin with adaptive hypotheses and test them until they appear to be poor explanations for a phenomenon, and then turn to other possible explanations.

LEVELS OF SELECTION

A final consideration about the nature of selection and evolution is the level at which evolution by natural selection occurs. Darwin considered an individual's lifetime reproductive success as the bottom line for natural selection.

More recent evolutionary thinkers argue that selection may operate at other levels as well. Social animals such as primates behave in ways that benefit their close relatives, often to the detriment of their nonrelatives. Such behaviour, called **kin selection,** is part of a larger concept known as **inclusive fitness.** Instead of considering only an animal's own reproductive success, evolutionary biologists realized that the reproductive success of one's kin also matters because it can contribute indirectly to the animal's fitness by helping its offspring survive and reproduce. Inclusive fitness predicts that social animals should behave less competitively toward close kin because of their shared genes.

The field of study that incorporates the concepts of inclusive fitness and kin selection is *sociobiology* (see also Chapter 17). The majority of scientists who study animal social behaviour in the wild today use an evolutionary framework to understand why animals behave as they do. Because full siblings share more of their genetic material than distant cousins, we can make predictions about how animals will behave in nature. For example, food-sharing between chimpanzees is far more likely to occur between close relatives than between nonrelatives. Ground squirrels sitting near their burrows give piercing alarm calls when hawks or coyotes appear. Isn't this altruistic behaviour hard to explain in Darwinian terms because the call attracts attention to the caller, making him more likely to be eaten than his neighbour? Researchers found that alarm calls are given mainly when the nearest neighbour is a close relative; when a squirrel is sitting near nonrelatives, he is the first animal to flee into the burrow when danger approaches (Figure 5.14) (Sherman, 1977).

FIGURE 5.14 Ground squirrel predator warnings illustrate how kin selection may work.

The closer the degree of kinship, the more likely altruistic behaviour becomes, and the more likely an animal is to engage in dangerous behaviour to help its kin (Figure 5.15). This principle guides much of the modern-day research into the social behaviour of our closest relatives.

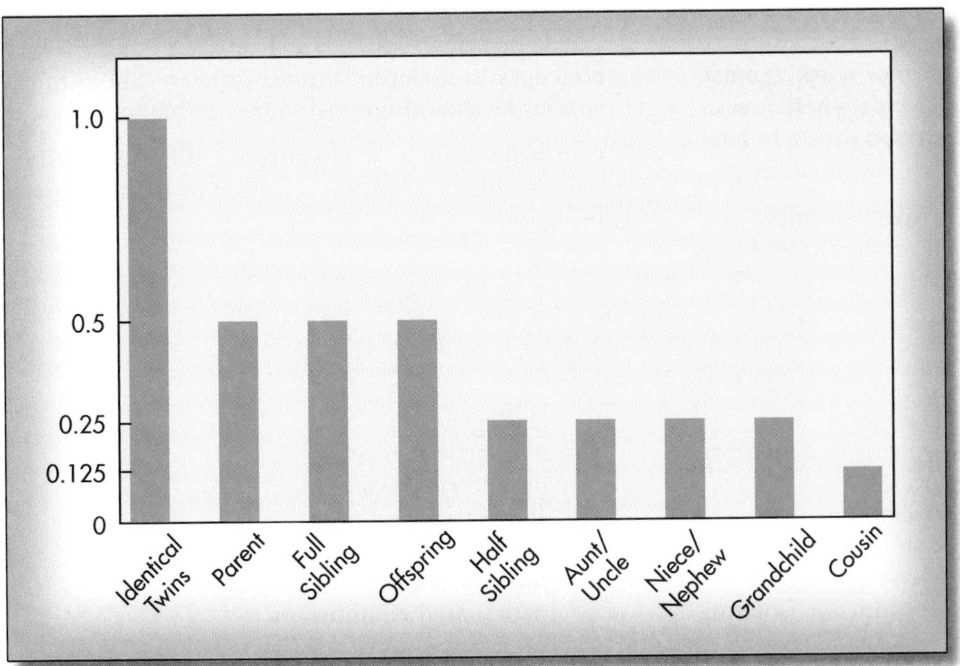

FIGURE 5.15 Coefficients of relatedness: How kin selection works.

SUMMARY

1. **How does natural selection work to mould adaptations?**

   Natural selection filters genetically inherited traits by favouring some phenotypes in a given environment and disfavouring others. The process perpetuates and enhances mutations that have positive effects on an organism's survival and reproduction. The same process can remove harmful or nonadaptive traits from a population.

2. **What is the goal of taxonomic analysis?**

   Taxonomists attempt to categorize organisms based on their phenotypes. Cladists use ancestral and derived traits to separate lineages and to sort members of a single lineage.

3. **What is the difference between Linnaeus' way of classifying species and our modern notion of species?**

   Linnaeus used a typological pigeonholing scheme for sorting species by similarities to other species. Modern evolutionary biologists recognize that species are dynamic entities that are in flux.

4. **Are there nonadaptive modes of evolution?**

   Genetic drift, including the founder effect, is an example of evolution without adaptation.

5. **How does population size affect the impact of random forces such as genetic drift?**

   Genetic drift and other random factors are much more powerful in very small populations because traits can become fixed (100% occurrence) or lost more easily.

6. **Does sexual selection ever work against the effect of natural selection? How?**

   Sexual selection promotes the elaboration of male traits that enhance reproductive success but not necessarily phenotypic traits that enhance survival. In some cases sexual selection appears to favour traits that adversely affect survival.

7. **What is the reproductive asymmetry between males and females?**

   Males typically have a far greater potential for reproductive success than females and also a far greater variance in mating and reproductive success.

8. **How can we resolve the paradox of animals behaving altruistically toward one another when Darwin predicted that all behaviour should enhance one's own reproductive success?**

   Through kin selection, animals act in ways that enhance their own fitness. When an animal shares genes with another through kinship, altruistic or cooperative behaviour helps the giver as well as the recipient of the cooperation.

9. **Is every aspect of an organism adaptive?**

   As an initial working hypothesis, we can presume that a trait evolved to enhance an organism's fitness; this is the reductionist approach. We attempt to understand adaptations by considering each element of an organism's phenotype as the product of natural selection.

CRITICAL THINKING QUESTIONS

1. How can sexual selection sometimes work against natural selection? How can we decide whether sexual selection is a part of or acts in opposition to natural selection?
2. How should we choose which species concept to apply? Is it acceptable to use different species concepts in different circumstances? Shouldn't a species be unambiguously identifiable in all cases?
3. Can behaviour be a phenotype? What conditions must be met for natural selection to mould a given behaviour?

KEY TERMS

directional selection
stabilizing selection
gene flow
inbreeding
genetic drift
founder effect
genetic bottleneck
sexual selection
sexual dimorphism
reproductive potential
reproductive variance
systematics
homology
analogous
cladistics
cladogram
convergent evolution
species
speciation
biological species concept
reproductive isolating mechanisms (RIMs)
evolutionary species concept
ecological species concept
recognition species concept
anagenesis
cladogenesis
allopatric speciation
parapatric speciation
sympatric speciation
gradualism
macroevolution
punctuated equilibrium
adaptationism
reductionism
null hypothesis
Hardy–Weinberg equilibrium
kin selection
inclusive fitness

SUGGESTED READING

Andersson, M. (1994). *Sexual Selection.* Princeton University Press, Princeton, NJ.
Endler, J. (1986). *Natural Selection in the Wild.* Princeton University Press, Princeton, NJ.
Hey, J. (2001). The mind of the species problem. *Trends in Ecology and Evolution* 16: 326–329.
Lipo, C.P., O'Brien, M. J., Shennan, S.J., and Hawthorne, C. M. (2006). *Mapping Our Ancestors: Phylogenetic Methods in Anthropology and Prehistory.* Aldine de Gruyter, New York, NY.
Mayr, Ernst. (2001). *What Evolution Is.* Basic Books, New York, NY.
Weiner, Jonathan. (1994). *The Beak of the Finch.* Vintage Books, New York, NY.
Williams, G. C. (1966). *Adaptation and Natural Selection.* Princeton University Press, Princeton, NJ.

Chapter 6

Human Variation: Evolution, Adaptation, and Adaptability

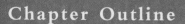

Chapter Outline

In the northern reaches of the Northwest Territories, approaching the Beaufort Sea, temperatures in late September are usually below freezing. The biological anthropologist would have preferred to collect his samples during the warmer summer months, but his negotiations with the band council had gone more slowly than he had expected. He was relieved that he had finally convinced the chief, councillors, and other members of the First Nations community that a genetic study of their group would have both scientific and social benefits for them.

Obtaining permission to collect the samples and conduct the study had not been easy. The anthropologist had explained that his work would provide a "biological snapshot" of the group today, to which future generations could refer for scientific, cultural, or medical reasons. Although he could not promise immediate health benefits as a result of his work, he pointed out that he was creating a genetic database that could be important in the future and that it would belong to the First Nations community.

But the First Nations peoples had been misled and lied to in the past, and this First Nations community was understandably hesitant to agree to this study. For example, in a highly publicized case of a violation of research ethics, a biological anthropologist had collected blood samples from the Ahousaht First Nation of British Columbia in the 1980s for a study of the high incidence of rheumatic disease in the population. When the anthropologist failed to find any genetic markers to show a predisposition to rheumatic disease he dropped the study but later used the blood in research on the antiquity of Aboriginal peoples in North America.

For the Ahousaht, the research was not only irrelevant (since they believe they have been on the West Coast since time immemorial), it was also a contravention of the forms they had signed giving consent for their blood to be used in research. Those forms promised that their blood would be used only for the research of rheumatic disease and that the research would be the first step in establishing therapy programs to assist those suffering from the debilitating effects of the disease.

This kind of experience with scientific research was not unique to the Ahousaht. For decades the treatment of First Nations peoples in the interests of science had taught them not to trust researchers.

An official federal policy governing the specifics of participants' consent to studies was published in 1998. Guidelines to promote the ethical conduct of research involving human subjects had been published in the 1970s, but increasing concern about ethical research led to the formation, in 1994, of a working group that was asked to develop an official policy. The result was the *Code for Ethical Conduct for Research Involving Humans* (Canadian Institutes of Health Research; Natural Sciences and Engineering Research Council of Canada; Social Sciences and Humanities Research Council of Canada, *Tri-Council Policy Statement: Ethical Conduct for Research Involving Humans.* 1998 [with amendments in 2000, 2002, and 2005]). This Code requires researchers applying for funding from the Canadian Institutes of Health Research, the Natural Sciences and Engineering Research Council of Canada, or the Social Sciences and Humanities Research Council of Canada to obtain consent from participants before research begins. Researchers must also obtain new consent when the purpose of their study, or their use of previously collected data (including interviews and all other kinds of data, not just tissue samples), changes.

NOT ONLY DO BIOLOGICAL ANTHROPOLOGISTS have a scientific responsibility to conduct research capably, but they also have an ethical responsibility: researchers contribute to human welfare by acquiring knowledge and applying it to human problems, but they are obligated to protect the dignity and preserve the well being of human research participants.

The origins of biological anthropology go back to the first half of the nineteenth century, an era when evolution had yet to be accepted by most natural historians and fossils representing human ancestors were all but unknown. At that time, biological anthropology was essentially the study of human variation. Unlike the modern anthropologist described in the vignette, most of the earliest anthropologists did not go into the field to meet their research subjects. Instead, they relied on travellers' accounts of exotic peoples from faraway places and waited in their universities, hospitals, and museums for specimens, such as skeletal remains, to be sent to them.

Today, the study of human variation covers a wide range of topics, encompassing population genetics and the evolutionary history of human populations, how natural selection influences human biology, and how humans biologically and culturally adapt to environmental stress. However, before considering how biological anthropologists now approach the topic of human variation, it is important to examine past approaches, many of which were centred on the concept of race and the goal of racial classification.

HUMAN VARIATION AT THE INDIVIDUAL AND GROUP LEVEL

It is obvious that modern humans show substantial *individual variation*. Except for identical twins, our genetic differences alone make each of us unique. At the anatomical and behavioural levels, even identical twins are not truly identical. Twins reared in different environments develop different phenotypic characteristics despite having the same genotype (although they may still be more similar to each other than two people picked at random). The "twin environment" itself leads to the development of variation: In the uterus, one twin often receives more nutrients than the other, leading to a difference between the two in birth weight. Thus, it is clear that human phenotypes are shaped by both genetic and environmental factors.

Human variation can also be measured at the *group level*. In Chapter 5, we discussed sexual dimorphism. Some of the variation we observe in the human species results from the fact that men and women vary in the expression of certain phenotypic features, such as body size. Another profound source of variation at the group level is age. Children differ in many ways from adults, and younger adults differ from older adults. Phenotypic traits that vary according to age are very common. Body size is again an obvious one but all sorts of anatomical, physiological, and behavioural features change as we age.

For as long as the field has existed, variation at the *population level* has been of particular interest to biological anthropologists. Humans have long noticed that people from different populations may look different from one another. They also noticed that they may behave differently. The science of anthropology developed to systematically examine biological and cultural differences observed among different human populations. *Homo sapiens* is a **polytypic species**, one that is divided into local populations that differ by one or more phenotypic traits. As anthropology has developed over the years, methods for disentangling genetic, cultural, and environmental factors responsible for producing population variation have become more refined (Figure 6.1).

polytypic species Species that consist of a number of separate breeding populations, each varying in some genetic trait.

FIGURE 6.1 Humans vary according to age, sex, and population of origin.

WHAT IS A POPULATION?

The word *population* often is used to describe groups or communities of animals that are identifiable within a species (Figure 6.2). As we discussed in Chapter 5, a biological population is a group of potentially interbreeding individuals. From the perspective of an individual organism, it will find its reproductive mates among the other members of its population. As you will see, *population* can be a very flexible term.

Many other terms have also been suggested for groups below the species level. Population geneticists have used several that emphasize that populations are assemblages of genes as well as individuals: *gene pool, local Mendelian population*, and *panmictic unit* (a local population in which mating is completely random) (Mettler et al., 1988). In general, geneticists use the term **deme** to refer to populations that are being defined in terms of their genetic composition (such as allele frequencies). All of these terms are meant to convey the notion that although these groups are in some way stable and identifiable, they are by no means genetically impermeable. After all, we study gene flow *among* populations.

deme A local, interbreeding population that is defined in terms of its genetic composition (for example, allele frequencies).

subspecies A group of local populations that share part of the geographic range of a species, and can be differentiated from other subspecies based on one or more phenotypic traits.

race In biological taxonomy, it is the same thing as a subspecies; when applied to humans, it sometimes incorporates both cultural and biological factors. The term is not used by biological anthropologists today.

Subspecies is another term some biologists use to describe variation below the species level. A subspecies is defined as a group of local populations that share part of the geographic range of a species and can be differentiated from other subspecies based on one or more phenotypic traits (in rare cases, a subspecies could consist of a single local population). Theoretically, the identification of a subspecies is done somewhat more formally than the identification of a population. In the biological sciences, the term **race** has been used interchangeably with *subspecies.* As we will see in this chapter, however, the historical use of the race concept in anthropology has not been a simple matter of identifying biological subspecies. In the past, some anthropologists subscribed to the idea that human races, like biological subspecies, correspond to groups of populations that are found in or derived from a particular geographic area.

All terms used to describe groups of individuals or populations within species share some basic shortcomings. There can be no objective way to decide how much variation (genetic or anatomical) is enough to consider two groups worthy of separate identification, nor is it possible to declare that all individuals in a geographic area are by definition members of a single population. For some scientists, these shortcomings are so problematic that they would never formally identify any group

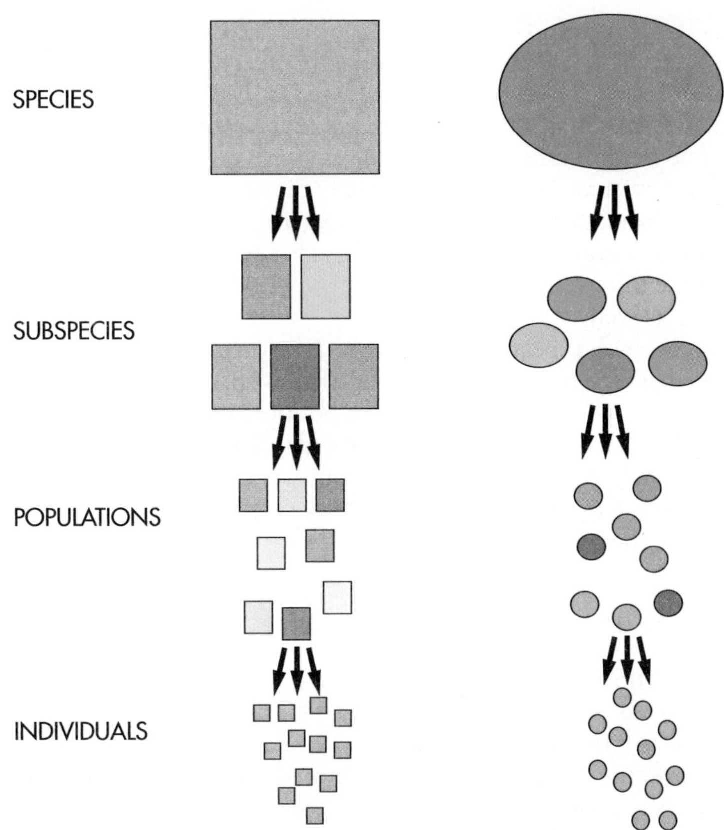

FIGURE 6.2 Species, subspecies, populations, and individuals. Species are reproductively isolated from one another, but all members of a species can interbreed.

below the species level. Most species are made up of distinct local groups of individuals who tend to interbreed within their group, however, and may be genetically or anatomically distinct from other such groups.

The identification of particular populations can depend on the research questions in which a particular scientist is interested. For example, if a scientist were interested in studying the effects of geographic isolation on gene flow in urban-dwelling ground squirrels, then his populations might be groups of squirrels living in different city blocks. If another scientist wanted to know about the long-term evolution of North American squirrels, she might identify populations based on samples taken from large geographic areas, and so her populations would be very different from those identified in a small city environment. To some extent, then, the identification of populations is a pragmatic matter depending on what hypothesis is being tested or which genetic phenomenon is being investigated.

Modern bioanthropological, medical, and genetic researchers also seem to apply the term *population* in a pragmatic way. For example, investigations of diseases in Canada often are conducted by measuring the rates in different groups that have biological, historical, and cultural relevance in this setting. Thus, a study may compare rates of diabetes in Aboriginal Canadians and first-generation Canadians of South Asian ancestry. An anthropologist investigating the evolution of modern humans as a species might not find these categories useful, nor would a geneticist who is looking at gene flow between Asian and North American populations. But, the issues being examined and the groups accessible for research influence how populations are identified.

HISTORICAL PERSPECTIVES ON HUMAN VARIATION

The most basic and universal classification of human variation at the group level is "us" and "them." The field of **ethnobiology** is dedicated to understanding the different systems that cultures have developed to classify the objects and organisms in the world around us (Berlin, 1992; Atran, 1998). One thing that ethnobiology makes clear is that human beings are masters at making up categories and classifications in which to place things. It comes as no surprise that humans have made efforts to classify people as well.

One problem that has arisen repeatedly in the investigation of variation within our species is that in the past the pragmatic concerns of some people were centred on identifying inferior and superior races, and using politically motivated, scientific racism to reinforce and justify the prevailing social order. The science of anthropology was born in the nineteenth century when there were incendiary debates about the moral and scientific correctness of slavery. Was it the natural right of a "superior race" to enslave the members of an "inferior race"?

THE RACE CONCEPT IN THE TWENTIETH CENTURY

Racial issues were of critical importance during World War II. In Depression-era Germany, the Nazi party rose to power on the basis of an ideology that celebrated "Aryanism," a form of racism that was, in effect, a mythical rendering of the racial history of northern Europeans. The Aryan myth celebrated the "true" German as being the member of a "superior race" and was used to justify the subjugation and ultimately the extermination of "inferior races," such as Jews and Gypsies (Roma). Nazi ideology tapped into and amplified prejudices that had long existed, and the Nazis themselves acted on these impulses on an unprecedented scale.

In Canada, prior to World War II more than 22 000 individuals of Japanese origin lived in British Columbia; 60% of them had been born in Canada. They earned their living as fishers, farmers, and small business owners. Some served with the Canadian Expeditionary Force during World War I. But for decades they had suffered the sting of racism, which reached a critical point when Canada declared war on Japan in December 1941 (Adachi, 1977; National Association of Japanese Canadians, 2008; Sunahara, 2004; Ward, 1990). After the declaration of war, persons of Japanese origin, including those who were Canadian citizens, were required to register with the government as Enemy Aliens. In the following months and years these people were forced to leave the west coast of Canada and were interned in camps. Most men were sent to work on road camps in the Rockies while women and children were sent to detention camps in the interior of British Columbia, although some families stayed together by agreeing to work on sugar beet farms in Alberta and Manitoba where labour shortages existed. Fishing boats, homes, cars, and other types of property were confiscated and sold. After Japan surrendered in September 1945, the camps were closed but the discrimination continued. It was not until four years after the war ended that all restrictions were lifted and Japanese Canadians were given the right to vote. In 1984, a national effort sought acknowledgement of and redress for the injustices committed against Japanese Canadians, and in 1988, the Canadian government officially acknowledged the injustices and apologized. The prime minister signed a compensation package giving $21 000 to each internee's survivor, a package that amounted to about $12 million overall.

Since the end of World War II (1939–1945), there has been an increasing awareness of **racism**, scientific and otherwise. At one level, racism is simply prejudice against a person based on his or her heritage. The basis of such prejudice is the idea that important qualities of an individual (such as intellect, physical ability, and temperament) are biologically determined by his or her membership in a specific

ethnobiology The study of how traditional cultures classify objects and organisms in the natural world.

racism A prejudicial belief that members of one group are superior in some way to those of another because of their ancestry, usually geographically or ethnically defined.

ancestral group, whether that group be of geographic origin, such as Asian, or of ethnic origin, such as Ukrainian. **Ethnic groups** are separated from one another primarily by social barriers, which may lead to biological differentiation or be a marker of biological difference. Although the term *ethnic group* has come into widespread usage, often as a replacement for *race*, it is far from ideal for use in biologically oriented research because it explicitly incorporates socio-cultural factors into group identification.

In recent decades there has also been an increased recognition of the impact of political and cultural factors on "objective" science. While gendered approaches to science and medicine have been central to scholarly studies for several decades, it is only more recently that social scientists have turned their attention to the study of "race in science," that is, how biological sciences, including biological anthropology and medicine, use race as a category in research. For example, race is used as a category in medical studies that compare the rates of diabetes in First Nations Canadians and non–First Nations Canadians, or the rates of heart disease in American Blacks and American Hispanics. As we learn in this course, such categorization is problematic not only on a genetic basis, but also because of the role of socio-cultural environmental factors in the expression of human health. (For students interested in the study of the use of race in science, the History Department at the University of Toronto sponsors an informative Web site at http://www.racesci.org/home.html).

POPULATION GENETICS

The field of **population genetics** is concerned with uncovering genetic variation within and among populations of organisms. In Chapter 5 we discussed several evolutionary processes, such as natural selection, gene flow, and genetic drift, which are all studied by population geneticists. Studying the dynamic distribution of alleles across populations can require complex mathematical tools (Cavalli-Sforza et al., 1994), many of which are derived from the Hardy–Weinberg equilibrium (see Chapter 5 and Appendix B). Although discussing these tools in detail is beyond the scope of this text, we will consider some of the results they have produced.

Population genetics is concerned primarily with **microevolution**, or evolutionary processes that occur within a species and which we can observe over two or three generations (in contrast to *macroevolution;* see Chapter 5). With increasingly sophisticated molecular biological techniques now available, the line between microevolutionary and macroevolutionary studies is becoming less clear-cut.

POLYMORPHISMS: ABO AND OTHER BLOOD TYPE SYSTEMS

If we look at a population and find that there are at least two alleles present for a given gene, and the alleles are both present at a frequency greater than 1%, then we can say that the population is **polymorphic** for that gene. The term is also used to describe variation at the more observable phenotypic level (see Chapter 4). For example, in a population where both blue- and brown-eyed people live, we can say that it is polymorphic for eye colour, assuming that it is a genetic feature and that both phenotypes are present at a frequency of at least 1%. Many protein polymorphisms have no phenotypic effect other than the fact that they are slightly different versions of the same protein. The 1% figure is used as a cutoff because it is substantially above the level you would expect if a rare allele or phenotype were present simply because of the occurrence of mutations.

Different populations can be polymorphic for the same trait or gene but differ in the frequency of alleles. In Chapter 4 we discussed the ABO blood type system, which is a classic example of a polymorphic genetic system. It is interesting to note that ABO distribution initially was of little interest to many anthropologists because it did not correlate particularly well with traditional notions of racial

ethnic group A human group defined in terms of sociological, cultural, and linguistic traits.

population genetics The study of genetic variation within and among groups of organisms.

microevolution The study of evolutionary phenomena that occur within a species.

polymorphic Two or more distinct phenotypes (at the genetic or anatomical levels) that exist within a population.

BOX 6.1 Traits in Folk Racial Taxonomies

A few key traits loom large in the folk racial taxonomies that have been used in Western cultures over the past 200 years. Even if the race concept itself is not considered valid in biological anthropology, what about the features people have been focusing on for so many years? What is their biological relevance or irrelevance?

Skin Colour Skin colour is perhaps the most important morphological feature in social racial categories. Variation in human skin colour is of no small biological significance. Because humans do not have fur, our skin is more directly exposed to the environment, and skin colour probably is influenced by natural selection. Many of the insights we have about the evolution of skin colour come from looking at the associations of skin colour with various medical conditions (such as severe sunburn, cancer, and vitamin synthesis), so we will discuss it in more detail later in the text.

On a global scale, skin colour is not a particularly good indicator of geographic origins. Populations from different parts of the world may have similar skin colours because they share a common environmental feature, namely the intensity of sunlight exposure. Very dark-skinned populations can be found in parts of Africa, southern India, and Melanesia, but these populations do not share a recent common ancestry compared with other populations. The amount of variation in skin colour of people classified as "white Canadians" is substantial and reflects the diverse population origins (in terms of sunlight exposure, among other things) of this "race," which ranges from the Middle East and Mediterranean regions to South and West Asia and the far north of Europe.

Eye Form Northern and eastern Asians, as well as some of their descendant populations in the New World, have a high frequency of a morphological feature known as an ***epicanthic fold***. This is the classic racial marker of "Oriental" or "Mongoloid" populations, although it can appear in individuals from other parts of the world. The epicanthic fold is a small flap of skin extending from the eyelid to the bridge of the nose (Figure A). It has no known biological function. Alice Brues (1977) suggests that it is a secondary anatomical feature that results from a combination of a fatty eyelid and a low nasal bridge, both of which, she argues, may reflect adaptations to cold. She points out that epicanthic folds are more common in women than men in some North American Aboriginal populations and in children rather than adults in European populations; both patterns may be a function of the relative development of the nasal bridge.

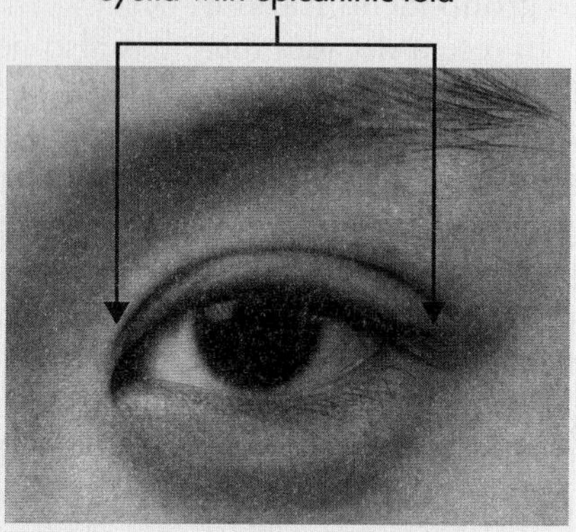

FIGURE A An epicanthic fold is a small flap of skin at the inner corner of the eye.

Today, biological anthropologists do not typically use the term race, preferring almost always to use the term population. But if biological anthropologists do not use the term race, does that mean that races do not exist? In a formal sense, the answer is "yes," but the word race is commonly used every day, by all sorts of people, in all kinds of contexts. These people are talking about something, and other people understand to what they are referring, so in that sense races must exist. Population-level biological differences do exist and are often quite significant, but they are most valuable to us when considered in their social and environmental context.

---

classification (Boyd, 1950). In Figure 6.3 *clinal* maps of the distribution of the ABO alleles throughout the world's populations are presented. A **cline** represents the distribution of a genotype or phenotype across geographical space.

cline The distribution of a trait or allele across geographical space.

The clinal maps in Figure 6.3 clearly illustrate that the ABO system is highly polymorphic across the species but that some populations are essentially monomorphic for type O, including several South American Indian groups. The allele frequencies for A and B never exceed 50% and typically are much lower than this. High A frequencies are found in some European populations, in some North American First Nations groups, in Inuit living in arctic North America and Greenland, and in some Australian Aborigine tribes. High B frequencies are found in central Asia, especially in the Himalayan region, declining gradually as one moves away from this high-frequency zone. There are also pockets of high B frequency in sub-Saharan Africa. The B allele is almost entirely absent from the Americas or Australia. One worldwide estimate for the frequencies of the three alleles is 62.5% O, 21.5% A, and 16.0% B (MacArthur and Penrose in Harrison et al., 1988).

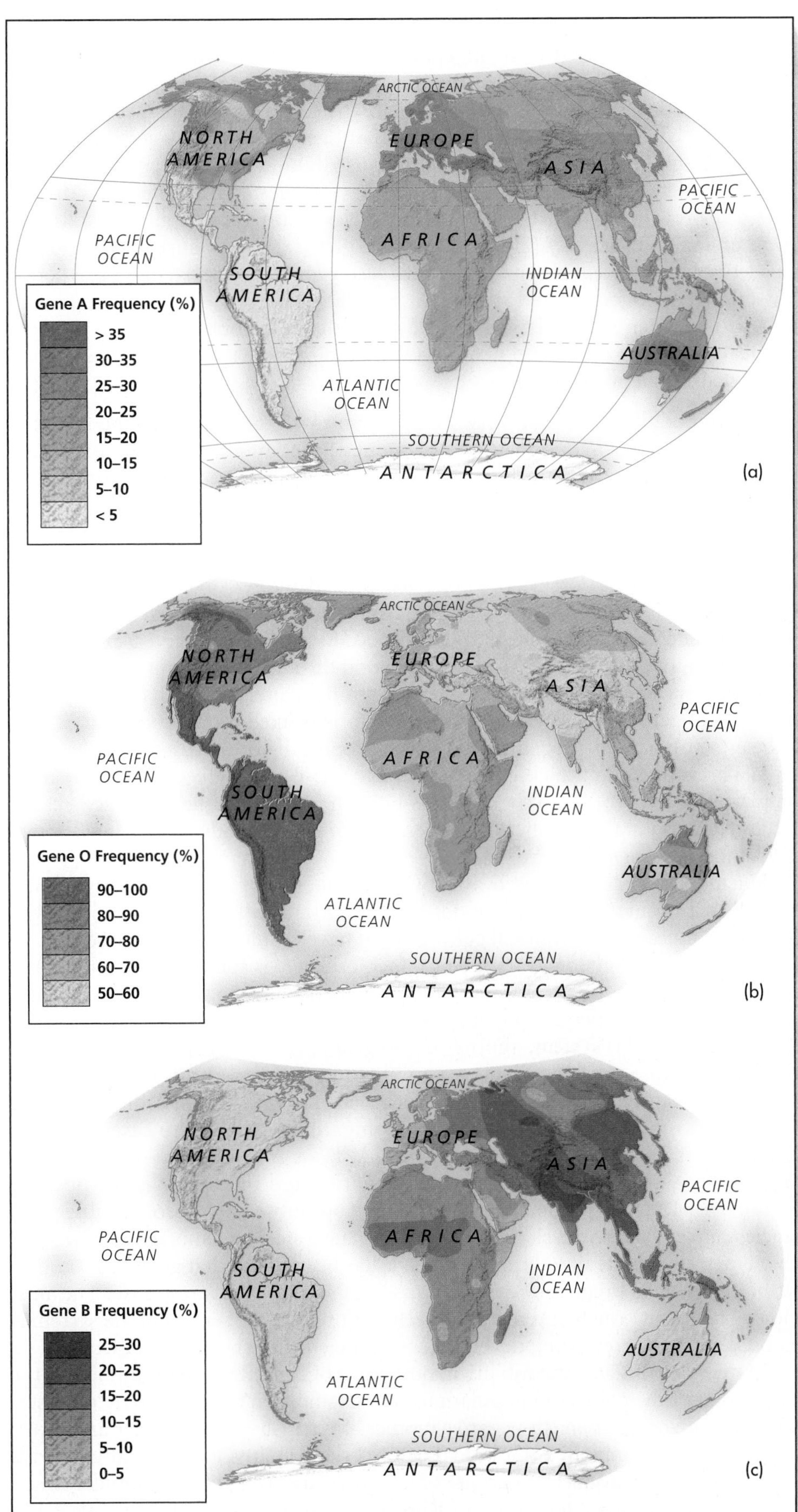

FIGURE 6.3 Clinal maps of ABO allele distributions in the indigenous populations of the world. (a) Frequency distribution of the *A* allele. (b) Frequency distribution of the O allele. (c) Frequency distribution of the *B* allele.
Source: Adapted from Mourant et al, 1976.

The distribution of ABO alleles in populations raises some interesting evolutionary issues. Why are the polymorphisms maintained in different populations? Why do we not see more alleles at fixation in different populations because of the effects of genetic drift or bottlenecks? Why are the A and B allele frequencies always less than 50%? Recent research on A and B antigens strongly suggests that natural selection has influenced their population distribution in some way (Koda et al., 2001). Over the years, several investigators have suggested that infectious disease plays a key role in the distribution of ABO alleles in different populations. Robert Seymour and his colleagues (2004) recently suggested that a balance between A and B alleles is maintained in populations with a heavy load of bacterial disease, whereas O would be expected to predominate in populations that are more vulnerable to viral disease. Their mathematical genetic models suggest that the relative frequencies of A, B, and O alleles are maintained by the relative impact of bacterial and viral diseases in a population.

Maternal–Foetal Incompatibility Another factor that influences the distribution of ABO alleles in a population arises out of the immune response of a pregnant woman and how it influences the health of her foetus. **Maternal–foetal incompatibility** occurs when a mother has type O blood and her infant has type A, B, or AB or when a woman has type A and the infant has type B and vice versa. In the case of a type O mother and a type B infant (the father must carry an B allele), because the mother does not possess the B antigen on her red blood cells, she will make anti-B antibodies upon exposure to the foetus's blood. For much of the pregnancy, the maternal and foetal blood do not mix; however, at birth the mother is almost always exposed to foetal blood through ruptures in tissues caused by the delivery or separation of the placenta from the uterine wall. Upon exposure to the B antigen, the mother's immune system is primed to produce anti-B antibodies. In subsequent pregnancies, the red blood cells of foetuses that carry the B allele are subject to attack by the maternal anti-B antibodies, which can cross the placental barrier. When the infant is born, he or she can be anaemic because of the reduction in the number of oxygen-carrying red blood cells. This is known as *haemolytic anaemia.*

Haemolytic anaemia caused by ABO maternal–foetal incompatibility is rare, and when it occurs it is usually mild. It is important to keep in mind, however, that a mild illness in a traditional culture could have far more serious consequences than it would in a contemporary medical facility. There is some evidence that ABO incompatibilities can have a damaging effect early in pregnancy, resulting in a higher rate of spontaneous abortion (Bottini et al., 2001).

The **rhesus (RH) system**, another blood group, is of particular clinical importance because maternal–foetal incompatibility in this system leads to the development of a much more severe form of anaemia in the newborn, a disease called *erythroblastosis fetalis*, than does ABO incompatibility. Similar to cases in which the mother is type O and the infant is type A, B, or AB, maternal–foetal incompatibility arises when the mother is Rh-negative and the infant is Rh-positive (Figure 6.4). The first pregnancy usually is fine, but subsequent incompatible pregnancies can lead to the development of severe haemolytic anaemia in the newborn, which may necessitate blood transfusions. It has been found that giving the mother antibodies early in pregnancy can suppress her immunological response: The antibodies "intercept" the foetal red blood cells before the mother's immune system is exposed to them, preventing development of anaemia in the at-risk newborn.

Maternal–foetal incompatibility in both the ABO and Rh systems influences the distribution of their alleles in populations. For example, in the Rh system, only heterozygous offspring of an Rh-negative mother and an Rh-positive father are at risk of developing anaemia. In a traditional culture, these infants would be at great risk of dying without reproducing. Because of factors such as genetic drift, founder effect, and genetic bottlenecks, high rates of Rh-negative or Rh-positive individuals could

maternal–foetal incompatibility Occurs when the mother produces antibodies against an antigen (for example, a red blood cell surface protein) expressed in the foetus that she does not possess.

rhesus (Rh) system Blood type system that can cause haemolytic anaemia of the newborn through maternal-foetal incompatibility if the mother is Rh-negative and the child is Rh-positive.

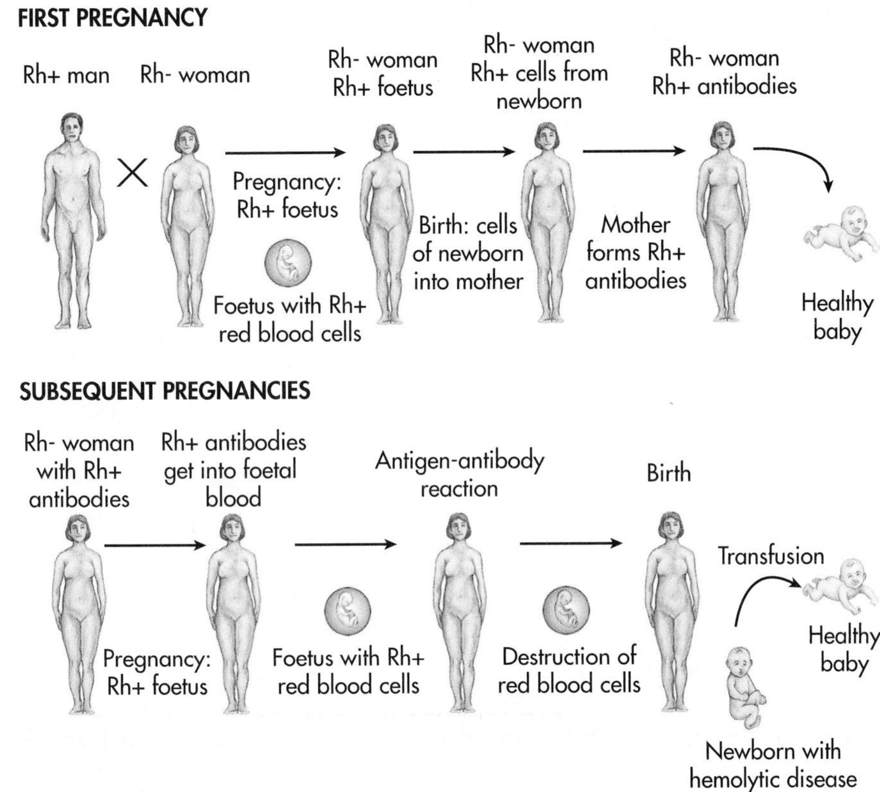

FIGURE 6.4 Maternal-foetal incompatibility in the Rh system.

evolve. However, only one population has a majority of Rh-negative individuals: the Basques of southern France and northern Spain. The Basque population was historically isolated and is well known for having a language unrelated to any other in Europe. Although one might predict that Rh-negative alleles should go to fixation, there is enough admixture with the predominantly Rh-positive surrounding populations that this seems unlikely.

The Human Leukocyte Antigen (HLA) System Besides the ABO and Rh systems, several other blood systems are used in population genetic studies. These include the Diego, Duffy, Kell, Kidd, Lewis, Lutheran, and MNS systems. A different class of blood group markers is formed by the **human leukocyte antigen (HLA) system.** These antigens are proteins found on the surface of white rather than red blood cells. There are many classes of white blood cells, all of which are critical in the immune system's response (an elevated white blood cell count indicates that the body is fighting an infection). As most people know, the ABO antigens are critical for determining who can donate blood to whom. The HLA system is critical in matching donors and hosts for organ and skin transplants.

The HLA system is organized into two classes, more than a dozen loci, and hundreds of alleles (Meyer and Thomson, 2001). These genes are all located on the short arm of chromosome 6. Besides their critical importance in tissue typing for transplantation, HLA-A and HLA-B have also been used extensively in population genetics studies. Different HLA alleles are also associated with increased susceptibility to different diseases. Many of these are **autoimmune diseases,** those in which the pathological process involves the body's immune system attacking its own tissues. For example, *celiac disease* is an autoimmune disorder characterized by a digestive intolerance to gluten, a protein found in wheat, rye, and barley. Celiac disease causes damage to the small intestine, preventing the absorption of nutrients through its walls. The highest rates of celiac disease are found in Europe, where screening of newborns for the disease is routine in some countries (Volta et al., 2001).

human leukocyte antigen (HLA) system Class of blood group markers formed by proteins expressed on the surface of white blood cells (leukocytes).

autoimmune diseases Occur when a body's immune system attacks its own tissues.

Negative selection operates on the HLA alleles that are associated with the development of serious genetic diseases. However, some HLA alleles are associated with protection from a variety of infectious diseases, including malaria, HIV, hepatitis B, and bacterial diseases (Cooke and Hill, 2001). The high degree of variability within the HLA system is evidence in itself that natural selection and other nonrandom evolutionary forces have been critical in shaping the distribution of its alleles (Meyer and Thomson, 2001).

GENE FLOW AND PROTEIN POLYMORPHISMS

Because allele frequencies for countless proteins vary from population to population, genetic polymorphisms can be used to look at patterns of gene flow and migration from one population to another. For example, because the A and B alleles are so rare in indigenous South American populations, the ABO system can be used to measure gene flow or admixture with European or African populations that have migrated to the region since 1500 A.D. This is despite the fact that on a worldwide basis, there is much overlap in the distribution of ABO alleles in different populations.

The history of the human species has been characterized by events involving migration and gene flow. Even when there are cultural prohibitions against mating with others outside the group, there is ample evidence that such matings occur. Official written records do not always indicate the scope of admixture between distinct cultural groups living in the same area.

Gene Flow in Contemporary Populations Countless gene flow studies have been done on populations throughout the world. For example, the complex origins of the Hungarian people, who live in central Europe at the crossroads between Asia and Europe, have recently been examined using a variety of classic (protein) markers (Guglielmino et al., 2000). One Hungarian ethnic group, the Örség, were found to be particularly closely related to populations from the Ural Mountains in Central Asia. Hungarian is a non–Indo-European language of Uralic origin, and these results confirmed oral histories and traditions that linked the Örség to populations that had migrated from the Ural region in the ninth century.

Numerous studies have also been done to trace the complex genetic history of Jewish populations in western Eurasia and Africa. The migrational history of Jews is complex, dating back to the *diaspora* (dispersal of the Jews from ancient Palestine to Babylonian exile in 586 B.C.). The diaspora became a permanent feature of Jewish life and included events such as the expulsion of Jews from Spain in 1492. Gene flow studies have produced conflicting results, some indicating substantial admixture between Jewish and other populations located in an area and others indicating much less gene flow. More recently, Y-chromosome markers have provided new insights into the histories of some Jewish populations. The Lemba, or "Black Jews," of southern Africa have a long oral tradition of Jewish ancestry (Figure 6.5). Consistent with this tradition, genetic studies indicate that about half of the Y-chromosomes in the Lemba population are of Semitic origin (Spurdle and Jenkins, 1996).

Morphological Features and Gene Flow Morphological features (such as eye or hair colour) are rarely used today to study gene flow between populations. There are several reasons for this: Many morphological features have complex genetics, thus making patterns of inheritance difficult to discern; their expression in an individual may be highly subject to environmental factors during development; and more so than genetic markers, morphological markers may be subject to the forces of natural selection, leading, for example, to convergent evolution. Of course, even with our ability to recover ancient DNA, morphological features may be all we have to study gene flow in past populations.

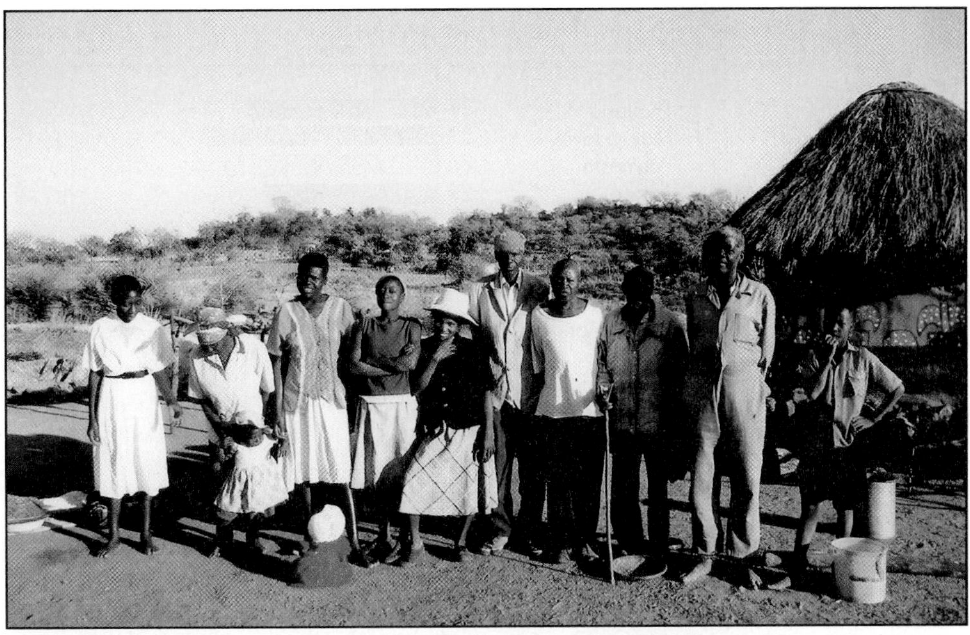

FIGURE 6.5 Members of the Lemba ethnic group from southern Africa.

One set of morphological features, dental traits, has been extensively used to study gene flow in skeletal populations. Some discrete dental traits appear to be transmitted in a simple genetic fashion, are resistant to environmental factors (except wear), and can be easily examined in large numbers of skeletal specimens. Christy Turner (1989, 1990) has argued that a constellation of dental features, known collectively as *sinodonty*, links northern Asian populations with the populations of the New World. Not all North American populations have high frequencies of sinodonty, but because it is absent elsewhere, it provides evidence of a migrational link or gene flow between the northern Asian and Native American populations. East Asian, Australian Aborigine, and Ainu (Aboriginal Japanese) populations exhibit a different dental pattern, which Turner calls *sundadonty.* Turner used eight dental features to distinguish sinodonts from sundadonts. For example, shovel-shaped incisors are more common among sinodonts than sundadonts, and four-cusped lower molars (cusps are the bumps on the chewing surfaces of molars; five is the typical number) are significantly more common in sundadonts than sinodonts (Figure 6.6). Turner places the origins of sinodonty at 18 000 years ago or earlier in northern China.

POLYMORPHISMS AND PHYLOGENETIC STUDIES

Allele frequencies, haplotype frequencies, and DNA and protein sequence information can all be used to construct an evolutionary tree, or **phylogeny**, relating populations (if frequency data are used) or individuals from different populations (if sequence data are used). Morphological characteristics, such as the dental traits described above, serve as proxies for genotypes and enable researchers to examine the relatedness of archaeological populations through phylogenetic trees, an approach that will be described in more detail in Chapter 18. The statistical mathematics underlying the construction of these trees is beyond the scope of this text, but the basic principles are not.

Constructing a Phylogenetic Tree Any phylogenetic tree aims to cluster closely related populations together (Figure 6.7). Closely related populations share a *branch:* a lineage or a clade (see Chapter 5). Branching points, or *nodes*, in the

phylogeny An evolutionary tree indicating relatedness and divergence of taxonomic groups.

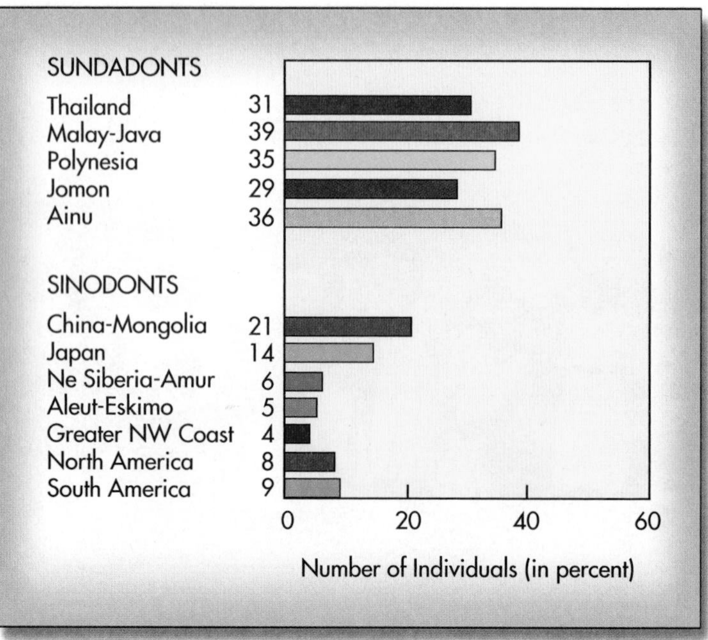

FIGURE 6.6 Number of lower molar cusps is one of the features used to distinguish sundadonts from sinodonts. Graph shows that 4-cusped molars are more common in sundadont populations rather than sinodont populations.

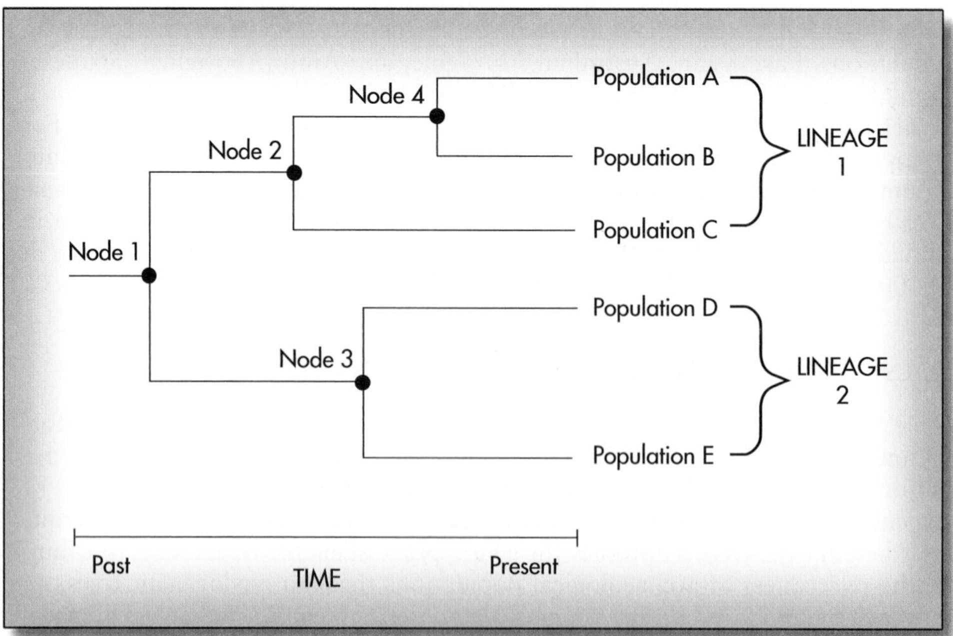

FIGURE 6.7 A generic phylogenetic tree. Populations A, B, and C share a lineage (or clade) and are more closely related to one another than populations D and E of lineage 2. Populations A and B share a more common ancestor (at node 4) with each other than they do with population C. The last time all five populations shared a common ancestor was at node 1.

tree should be placed with as high degree of statistical certainty as possible. These nodes represent evolutionary events leading to the separation of any pair (or groups) of populations. Longer branches and deeper nodes indicate that more evolution has occurred and thus that more time has elapsed since the separation of the two populations (assuming that evolutionary change is occurring at similar rates in different populations, which is not always the case when a nonneutral trait is being used). Whatever the source of data, the overriding concern in constructing an evolutionary tree is that it should be parsimonious. In other words, the phylogenetic tree produced from a dataset should be the one that incorporates the fewest number of evolutionary steps or events.

Phylogenetic trees are not precise reconstructions of evolutionary events. They are hypotheses about the way evolution happened, inferred from genetic or other kinds of data collected from living or extinct populations. Even a tree that is statistically rigorous may be subject to different kinds of interpretation.

A Genetic Tree of the World's Populations Geneticist Luigi Luca Cavalli-Sforza and colleagues (1994) provided an extensive analysis of the distribution of 120 alleles (29 of which come from the HLA system) in 42 populations throughout the world. The selection of these 42 populations was based on several criteria, not least important of which was the availability of genetic data for inclusion in the analysis. They provide a good sample of the world's populations as they were distributed at the arbitrary cutoff date of 1492 A.D. The phylogenetic tree of these 42 populations divides into nine major clusters: Africans (sub-Saharan), Caucasoids (Europeans), Caucasoids (non-Europeans), northern Mongoloids (excluding arctic populations), northeast Asian arctic populations, southern Mongoloids (mainland and island Southeast Asia), New Guineans and Australians, inhabitants of the minor Pacific islands, and Americans (Figure 6.8).

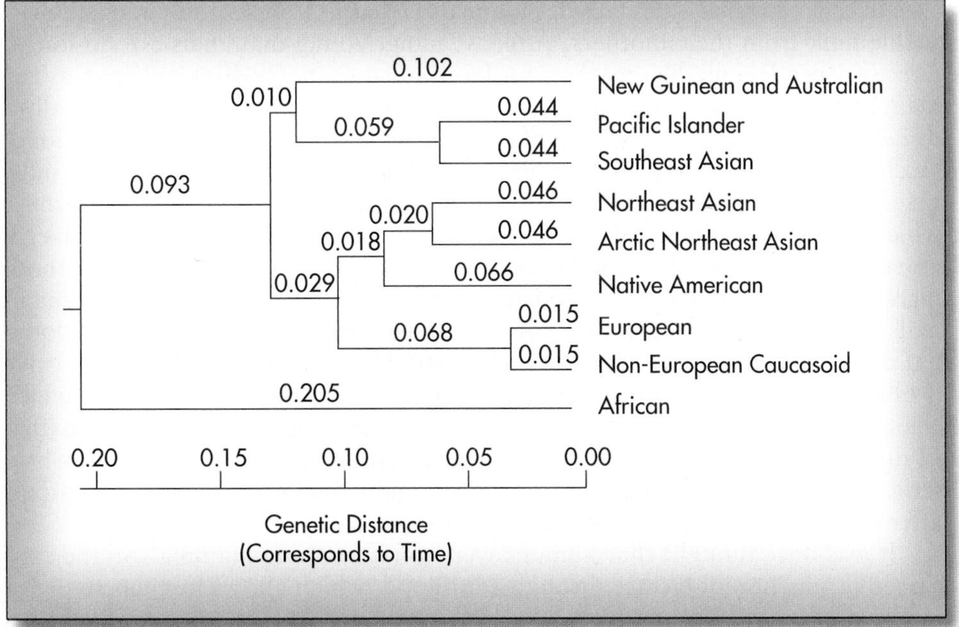

FIGURE 6.8 Phylogenetic tree based on the distribution of 120 alleles in 42 populations from around the world, clustered into 9 major groups.
Source: Cavalli-Sforza et al., 1994.

Although slightly different trees result depending on the method used and how the populations are constructed, some basic conclusions are possible. First, the deep separation of the African populations from others is an indication that this reflects the earliest genetic event in human history. This event could have happened outside Africa, although palaeontological evidence indicates that modern humans evolved first in Africa, followed by migration to other parts of the world (discussed later in the text). A northern Eurasian cluster clearly includes both Caucasoid and northeast Asian (including arctic and American) populations. The relationships between Australians, New Guineans, and southeast Asians are less clear-cut. One tree groups the southeast Asians with the Australians and New Guineans, and another places them as an early split from the northern Eurasian cluster. Given the complex patterns of population movements throughout Southeast Asia and Melanesia into Polynesia and Micronesia, it is not surprising that unambiguous clusters are not always possible.

POLYMORPHISMS AND NATURAL SELECTION IN HUMAN POPULATIONS

We have already discussed several examples of the effects of natural selection on polymorphisms in human populations. For example, negative selection probably is also working to reduce the frequencies of any number of HLA alleles associated with the development of autoimmune diseases, which may have initially reached high frequencies because of genetic drift or founder effects. On the contrary, it is clear that some HLA variants confer resistance to various infectious diseases. Why don't these variants go to fixation? If they confer resistance to a serious disease, then why do they remain polymorphisms rather than becoming a monomorphism? We will address this issue, but first let us look at a straightforward example of natural selection that has led to the evolution of a polymorphism at the species level.

THE EVOLUTION OF LACTOSE TOLERANCE

One of the main characteristics of mammals is that newborns and young animals suckle milk from their mothers. After weaning, young mammals are no longer directly dependent on their mothers for food, and most never drink milk again. The main carbohydrate in mammal milk is a sugar called *lactose*. Lactose is actually a *disaccharide*—or a sugar made up of two smaller sugars—composed of the monosaccharides glucose and galactose. In order for lactose to be metabolized, it must first be split into glucose and galactose; this is done by an enzyme called *lactase*, which is present in the small intestine of most young mammals. As mammals get older, their bodies shut down production of lactase, so older mammals cannot digest lactose. As adults, they are *lactose malabsorbers*. Indeed, many older mammals suffer gastric distress if they consume milk, with symptoms such as abdominal distention, flatulence, cramps, acidic stools, and diarrhea. These digestive problems are caused by the accumulation of lactose in the small intestine, which changes the osmotic activity in that part of the gut, leading to an influx of fluid (that is, diarrhea), and excess lactose in the large intestine, which is fermented by bacteria in the colon (that is, gas production). An individual who has these symptoms after consuming milk products is **lactose intolerant.**

lactose intolerant The inability to digest lactose, the sugar found in milk; most adult mammals (including humans) are lactose intolerant as adults.

It was once thought that humans were unique among mammals in the continued production of lactase through adulthood, which allows humans to digest lactose (milk products) as adults. However, research in the 1960s on European and African Americans demonstrated that only *some* humans were lactose tolerant as adults (Cuatrecasas et al., 1965). Indeed, as more research was done, it was discovered that most people in the world are lactose intolerant as adults and that lactase production is a highly polymorphic trait across the human species (Allen and Cheer, 1996). Table 6.1 presents lactose absorption rates for populations throughout the world. High-absorber populations are concentrated in Europe or in populations with a high degree of European admixture (such as Polynesian populations in New Zealand). In addition, some African ethnic groups, such as the Tussi, Fulani, and Hima, also have high rates of lactose tolerance (the African figures in the table are for countries, not ethnic groups). Other populations, such as many in Asia, some African, and many Native American groups, have very low frequencies of lactose absorbers.

The Genetics of Lactase Production The genetics of lactase production is reasonably well understood. The lactase gene is located on chromosome 2. Continued lactase production in adulthood is caused by a dominant allele (called the *lactase persistence allele*, or *LCT*P*), so heterozygous and homozygous individuals with this allele can produce lactase. The lactase enzymes produced by lactose tolerant and lactose intolerant adults are identical in structure and function, although there are many "silent mutations" in the base pair sequence that can be used for phylogenetic studies of this locus (Hollox et al., 2001). Variants that are located in regions of the chromosome that are several thousand base pairs away from the lactase gene itself cause the differentiation between lactase persistent and lactase nonpersistent individuals (Enattah et al., 2002). These regions clearly have a regulatory function (as yet undetermined) in the timing of lactase synthesis.

TABLE 6.1 Lactose Absorption Rates in Different Populations

POPULATION	PERCENTAGE OF LACTOSE ABSORBERS
AFRICA	
Bantu (West Africa)	4
Watutsi (East Africa)	83
Nilotic (Sudan)	39
Indigenous South African	17
ASIA	
Southern Indian	33
Japanese	0
Thai	2
Taiwan Chinese	0
EUROPE	
British	94
German	85
Swedish	100
Italian	25–50
NORTH AMERICA	
European American	80–94
African American	25–30
Apache	0
Chippewa	30
PACIFIC	
Fijian	0
New Zealand Maori	36
Aboriginal Australian	16
Papua New Guinean	11

Source: Allen and Cheer, (1996); Molnar, (2002).

Explanations for the Lactase Polymorphism Lactose tolerant individuals are found at high frequency in populations with a long history of dairying and using milk products (Simoons, 1970; McKracken, 1971; Durham, 1991). There has been strong selection for LCT*P in these populations. In nondairying populations, the distribution of **haplotypes** associated with lactase nonpersistence are consistent with evolution primarily by genetic drift (Hollox et al., 2001). The *cultural historical hypothesis* proposes that in populations where animals were domesticated and milk products used (dating back to about 9000 B.C. in the Middle East), there has been strong selection for lactase tolerant individuals (Simoons, 1970; McKracken, 1971). Milk is a valuable food providing both carbohydrates and proteins, and in an environment where other nutritional resources might be scarce, individuals who could digest milk as adults would have a substantial survival advantage. Modest selective advantages (relative increases in fitness) of 5 to 10% could account for the high frequencies of lactose tolerance found in northern European populations over a period of about 6000 years (Aoki, 1986; Feldman and Cavalli-Sforza, 1989).

There are populations in which dairying is present but lactose tolerance frequencies are low, such as those in central and southern Asia. In many of these populations, milk is not drunk raw but is processed into yogourt or cheese. In the making of yogourt and cheese, bacteria are used to convert lactose to lactic acid. Thus the ability to digest lactose is not critical in obtaining the nutrients from these products, and lactose tolerant individuals historically have had no selection advantage in these populations.

The evolution of lactose tolerance is a clear-cut example of the interaction of biological and cultural factors in shaping microevolutionary processes within our species.

BALANCED POLYMORPHISMS: SICKLE CELL AND OTHER CONDITIONS

In any population, the polymorphism for lactose digestion ability in adulthood can be explained in terms of cultural practices, natural selection, gene flow, and genetic drift. There are no particular reasons for a population to be polymorphic for this feature: Some populations approach 100% lactose tolerant, and others approach 100% lactose intolerant. However, when we look at other genetic systems and populations, it appears that there are polymorphisms that are quite stable and are not the result of obvious historical factors. Something is preventing alleles from going to fixation or being lost. This is called a **balanced polymorphism.** A fascinating aspect of microevolution is the attempt to explain mechanisms underlying balanced polymorphisms.

The large number of variants present in the HLA system may be evidence of a balanced polymorphism in this genetic system. If HLA variants are useful for conferring resistance to infectious diseases, then some HLA polymorphisms may be maintained as a **frequency-dependent balanced polymorphism** (Cooke and Hill, 2001). In this situation, an allele (or trait) has an advantage in a population relative to other alleles until it reaches a certain frequency in the population. If it becomes more common than this frequency, it loses its advantage, and the balanced polymorphism is maintained. In the HLA system, an HLA variant may confer resistance to a specific infectious disease. While it is rare in the population, it will have an advantage because the infectious agent itself has not evolved to overcome whatever defence it confers. However, as the resistant variant becomes more common in the population, there will be selection on the infectious agent to adjust to it. Eventually, a frequency will be reached at which the disease-resistant variant loses its advantage. A high degree of polymorphism in a population may result as this process is repeated for multiple alleles, and the resulting polymorphism is stable or balanced.

haplotypes Combinations of alleles (or at the sequence level, mutations) that are found together in an individual.

balanced polymorphism A stable polymorphism in a population in which natural selection prevents any of the alternative phenotypes (or underlying alleles) from becoming fixed or being lost.

frequency-dependent balanced polymorphism Balanced polymorphism that is maintained because one (or more) of the alternative phenotypes has a selective advantage over the other phenotypes only when it is present in the population below a certain frequency.

Heterozygous Advantage It has been noted that genetic diversity in breeding plants and animals often results in improved yields; this is called hybrid vigour or *heterosis*. It is assumed that this may result from a high frequency of heterozygosity at many loci underlying a complex genetic trait. However, **heterozygous advantage** has been observed in much simpler genetic contexts. In a one-gene, two-allele situation, a balanced polymorphism will be maintained if the heterozygotes have a selective advantage over both of the homozygotes. This is just the opposite of what happens in cases of maternal–foetal incompatibility, which actually works against the maintenance of a polymorphism.

heterozygous advantage With reference to a particular genetic system, the situation in which heterozygotes have a selective advantage over homozygotes (for example, sickle cell disease); a mechanism for maintaining a balanced polymorphism.

The classic example of a balanced polymorphism maintained by heterozygous advantage is the high frequency of the *sickle cell trait* in some populations with endemic *malaria*. In Chapter 4, we discussed the molecular and cellular genetics of sickle cell disease, which is caused by an abnormal haemoglobin protein, HbS (as opposed to the normal HbA), that impairs the ability of red blood cells to deliver oxygen to the tissues of the body. It is an autosomal recessive disease, and people who are heterozygotes are carriers of the condition. In a nonmalarial environment, the carriers show few signs of illness, although they may be slightly at risk in low-oxygen environments.

Malaria may have killed more people—especially children—than any other infectious disease. According to the World Health Organization, more than 40% of the world's population lives in malarial regions, it affects 300 to 500 million people per year, and it kills a million children per year under the age of 6 in Africa alone. In addition, chronic malaria has incalculable negative economic, social, and political effects. There is no doubt that malaria has exerted a strong selection pressure on human populations for many thousands of years.

Malaria is caused by protozoa from the genus *Plasmodium*. Of the 120 species in this genus, four cause malaria: *P. malariae, P. vivax, P. falciparum*, and *P. ovale*. The symptoms of malaria include fever, anaemia, inflammation of the spleen, and headache. Cerebral malaria is especially serious and may lead to insanity, unconsciousness, and death.

Humans are infected with the *Plasmodium* parasite via the bite of a female *Anopheles* mosquito, which is an essential carrier or *vector* of the disease. The *Plasmodium* life cycle requires both human and mosquito hosts. Because malaria depends on the mosquito for its spread from human host to host, the ability of the mosquito to survive and breed is a critical factor in local patterns of malarial expression. For example, in regions that have a pronounced dry season, mosquito breeding is highly seasonal, and malaria does not become a stable and constant aspect of life. In contrast, malaria is endemic in wet, equatorial climates in Africa and Southeast Asia, where mosquito breeding continues year-round.

FIGURE 6.9 Slash and burn agriculture in Africa.

Although human intervention has worked to limit the range of malaria, human cultural practices have also helped to increase its impact on human populations. The development of slash-and-burn agriculture in Africa led to the clearing of tropical forests, an increase in the amount of standing, stagnant water, and higher human population densities (Figure 6.9) (Livingstone, 1958). All of these worked to increase the disease's spread. In addition, the disrupted tropical forest conditions favoured the breeding of a particular species of mosquito, *A. gambiae*, which is the vector for *P. falciparum*, which in turn causes the most lethal form of malaria. This was the context for the evolution of high frequencies of the HbS allele (Allison, 1954).

In malarial environments, individuals who are heterozygous HbS HbA have higher reproductive fitness than either HbA HbA or HbS HbS homozygotes (Figure 6.10). Individuals who are homozygous HbS HbS have sickle cell anaemia, a disease that, in traditional settings, drastically shortens the life span, precluding reproduction. However, heterozygous individuals with the sickle cell trait are more resistant to developing malaria than homozygous HbA HbA individuals because of the presence of abnormal haemoglobin in the red blood cells of heterozygous individuals, though not enough to affect human physiology in any meaningful way, seriously affects the life cycle of the *P. falciparum* parasite. In these malarial regions, heterozygote individuals are overrepresented in populations over age 45, indicating their enhanced survival. The HbS allele cannot go to fixation because the homozygotes are seriously impaired. Thus the HbA–HbS polymorphism is maintained by heterozygous advantage.

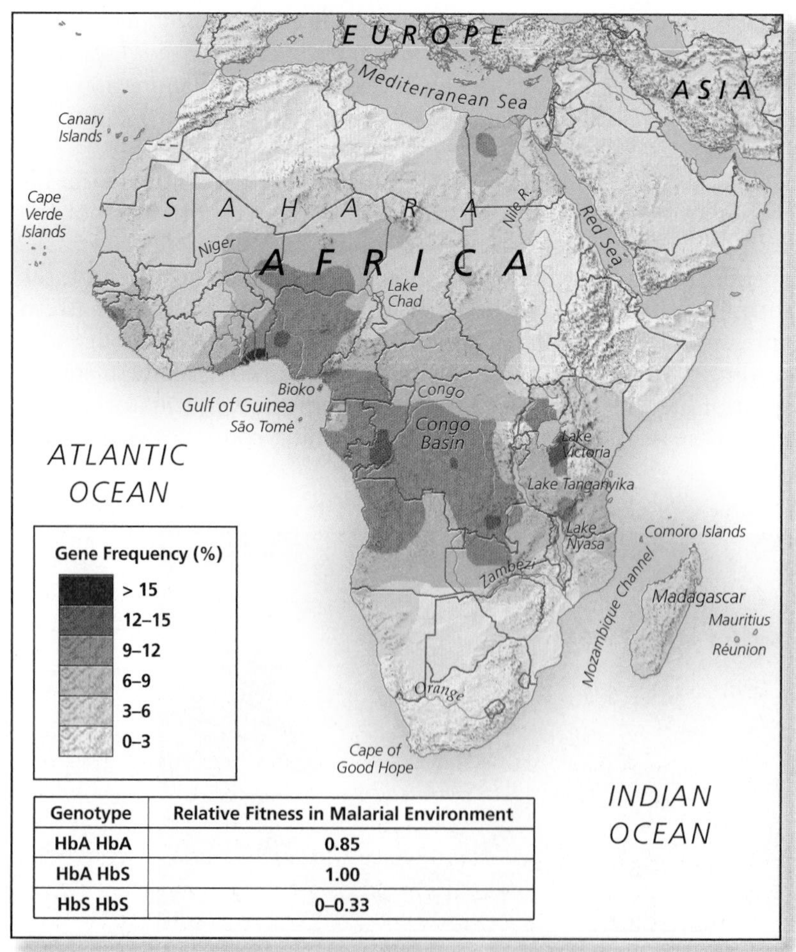

Genotype	Relative Fitness in Malarial Environment
HbA HbA	0.85
HbA HbS	1.00
HbS HbS	0–0.33

FIGURE 6.10 Clinal map of the distribution of HbS in Africa.

Sickle cell carrier frequencies are almost 40% in some African populations. High HbS frequencies are also found in Mediterranean, Middle Eastern, and Indian populations, reflecting former and present malarial loads in these regions. African Americans also have a high frequency of HbS, which reflects their ancestral populations. However, without malaria in the environment, heterozygotes are no longer at an advantage, and the frequency of HbS is declining because of the reduced fitness of HbS homozygotes.

ADAPTATION AND ADAPTABILITY

A variant that can be demonstrated to increase fitness in a specific environment (such as the ability to digest lactose as an adult) is an adaptation in the classic evolutionary sense. However, adaptation is a more general phenomenon. All organisms exhibit some degree of *biological plasticity:* an ability on the part of individuals to physiologically respond to changes in the environment. This is obvious in poor environments; for example, if there is not enough food, an animal will become thinner. When the phenotype of an organism reflects *positive* changes that arise in the context of short- or long-term exposure to a set of environmental conditions, this is called **adaptability**. Differences in environments can thus lead to population-level differences as individuals within the populations biologically adapt to local conditions. Because of biological plasticity and adaptability, populations may phenotypically differentiate from one another without any underlying changes to the genotypes.

Adaptation and adaptability are not always separate and distinct issues. The ability of a phenotype to respond differently to different environments an organism may encounter in a lifetime may in itself be an adaptation. When we look at different populations adapting to similar environmental conditions, one population may have adapted to the environment in a more genetic sense, whereas the other may be adapting in the context of biological plasticity. Or populations may vary in their adaptability to specific environmental conditions depending on the biological variation present in those populations.

LEVELS OF ADAPTABILITY

The process of very short-term changes in physiology that occur in response to changes in environmental conditions is called **acclimatization**. We are all familiar with acclimatization. When people from sea level move to high altitude, they have to cope with a reduction in the amount of oxygen available in the atmosphere. Initially, the body physiologically adapts by breathing more quickly and increasing its heart rate. Over time, more profound changes in the body occur, such as an increase in red blood cell production, which allows the individual to cope with a lower-oxygen environment. Tanning is another example of acclimatization. The transient darkening of the skin in lighter-skinned individuals is an acclimatization response to increased ultraviolet radiation in the atmosphere.

In contrast to acclimatization, adaptability refers to the physiological changes that arise in individuals who have lived their entire lives under a certain set of environmental conditions (Figure 6.11). Thus their bodies reflect the influence of the environment on their development as they were growing up and the long-term effects of continued exposure to such an environment.

Again, acclimatization, adaptability, and genetic adaptation are all interacting forces in the production of individual phenotypes. They reflect different mechanisms that organisms possess to adapt to the environments in which they live. Humans also use cultural adaptations to cope with the environment (Box 6.2). These cultural adaptations can interact with biological adaptations to shape patterns of human variation.

adaptability The ability of an individual organism to make positive anatomical or physiological changes after short- or long-term exposure to stressful environmental conditions.

acclimatization Short-term changes in physiology that occur in an organism in response to changes in environmental conditions.

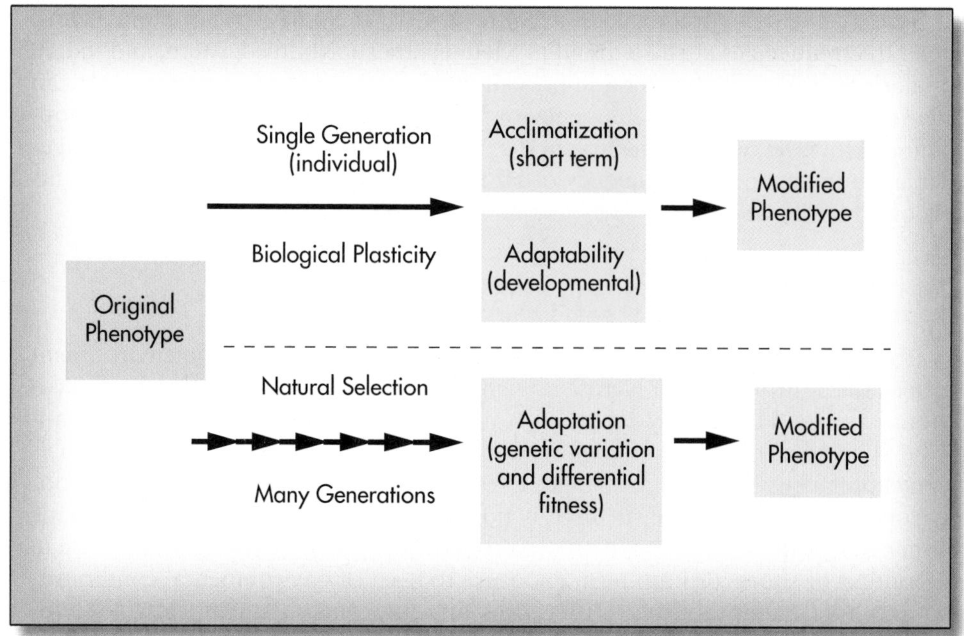

FIGURE 6.11 Adaptability and adaptation.

HEAT AND COLD

From the arctic to the desert, humans live in a vast array of thermal environments, some of them with marked seasonality. One way we cope with changes in ambient temperature is through the cultural adaptation of wearing more or less clothing. But in addition to clothing, humans display a variety of physiological adaptations to heat and cold, some of which reflect adaptations of a genetic kind, whereas others are better described in terms of acclimatization and adaptability (Moran, 2000; Beall and Steegman, 2000).

When people get too hot, the body responds through a process of *vasodilation* and sweat. Vasodilation (which appears as flushing in lighter-skinned people) increases blood flow to the surface of the body, which allows heat from the core of the body to be dissipated into the environment. The primary mechanism for dissipating heat at the surface of the body is sweating. The evaporation of 1 litre of sweat removes 560 kcal of heat from the body, and people can sweat up to 4 litres/hour (Beall and Steegman, 2000). Heat stroke—when the core temperature of the body reaches 41°C (105.8°F)—is a serious condition, with the depletion of fluid from the body unleashing a cascade of events that ultimately leads to the coagulation of blood and the death of brain tissue. Even today, heat waves in urban environments kill hundreds or even thousands of people. Heat is a strong selective force.

Cold is also a strong selective force in environments where temperatures go significantly below freezing. Death from hypothermia is likely to result if the body's core temperature falls between 31 to 32°C (88 to 90°F). Because the body's reaction to cold is to decrease blood flow to the periphery—*vasoconstriction*—in order to maintain core temperature, frostbite, resulting in serious damage to the appendages and face, is another serious consequence of prolonged exposure to cold. Another basic acclimatization mechanism to cold is shivering. A decline of the body's core temperature by 2 to 3°C brings on the shivering response, which generates heat.

Humans can cope with temperatures in the freezing range via a combination of shivering and vasoconstriction. Subcutaneous fat also helps insulate the core of

Box 6.2 Technology and Extreme Environments

Human beings have had thousands of years to adapt to certain kinds of natural environments. However, our technological prowess allows us both to exploit and to create new environments. These new environments require a physiological response from our bodies if we are to survive within them and it will be interesting to see what the long-term effects of exposure to these environments will be.

A *zero-gravity* or *microgravity* environment is one of the most exotic to which any human being would have to adapt (Williams, 2003) (Figure A). Since the advent of extended (weeks and months) stays in space, with the Skylab and Mir programs and the development of the International Space Station, dozens of people have had to deal with how their bodies react to an environment essentially free of the effects of gravity. Over time, people in a microgravity environment have muscle atrophy and experience loss of muscle strength. There are also cardiovascular changes, which can affect the ability to maintain blood pressure after one returns to Earth. The most critical change may be the loss of calcium in bone. In certain bones, prolonged microgravity exposure causes calcium levels to drop two standard deviations below normal levels. Although this loss is mostly reversible when one returns to gravity, it is not known what the effects would be after a very long-range flight, such as would be needed for a mission to Mars. Another medical issue that arises with prolonged microgravity exposure involves how the symptoms of various diseases might be influenced by bodily changes. For example, physicians recognize appendicitis by the presence of pain in a certain part of a patient's abdomen (although it varies widely). In space, the effects of microgravity on both the structure and function of the gastrointestinal tract could totally change how appendicitis presents to physicians (Williams, 2003).

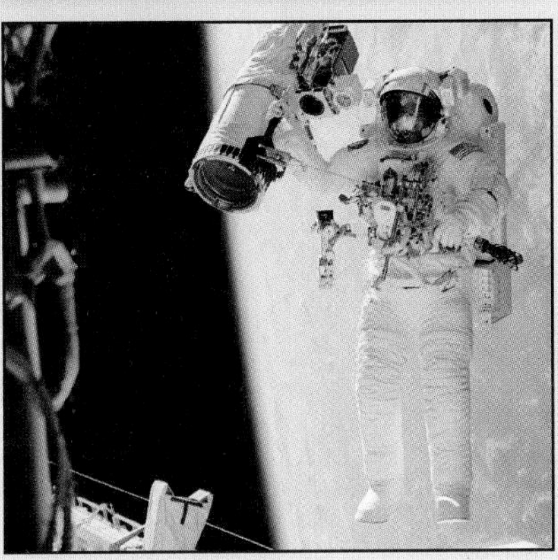

FIGURE A A human in a microgravity environment.

In contrast to the small numbers of people affected by the space environment, billions of people around the world are subject to the effects of industrial pollution in the environment, and it has been argued that polluted environments, as much as high-altitude or hot or cold climates, should be considered extreme environments to which humans must adapt (Schell and Hills, 2002). Air pollutants, such as carbon monoxide, sulphur dioxide, and ozone, contribute to increased mortality rates and may also affect prenatal and postnatal growth. Exposure to lead, mercury, and other substances may also affect growth and have cognitive effects. Industrial pollution has been a problem for some human populations for more than 150 years. And even as some parts of the developed world clean up their air and water, people living in developing countries are increasingly being exposed to toxic substances in their environments while in westernized countries the human biology of pollution exposure interacts with social issues such as access to food, health care, and adequate housing.

the body from the external cold. Populations vary in how these mechanisms are used to deal with cold. Arctic Inuit populations, who must deal with extreme cold, use cultural adaptations such as clothing, combined with biological adaptations, such as subcutaneous fat storage and vasoconstriction, to cope with cold on an ongoing basis. At the other extreme, desert-dwelling Australian Aborigines must cope with a great range of temperatures on a daily and seasonal basis. In winter, they sleep in near-freezing temperatures uncovered and without shelter. They cope with the cold by using an extreme vasoconstriction response, which causes the skin surface temperature to fall. Given that the temperatures they must cope with are not severely cold, frostbite does not occur, and they conserve energy while maintaining adequate core body temperatures. It is assumed that the adaptive responses seen in these populations are a result of both genetic adaptation and the process of developmental adaptability.

Bergmann's rule Stipulates that body size is larger in colder climates to conserve body temperature.

Allen's rule Stipulates that in warmer climates, the limbs of the body are longer relative to body size to dissipate body heat.

BODY SIZE AND SHAPE

In the nineteenth century, two biologists, Carl Bergmann (1814–1865) and Joel Asaph Allen (1838–1921), looked at the relationship between body size and climate in a wide range of mammals. They found that within polytypic species, there were predictable relationships between body form and proportions and temperature. **Bergmann's rule** (1847) focuses on body size. He found that the colder the climate, the larger the body. This makes geometric sense in that as volume increases, surface area decreases as a proportion of the volume. This would decrease the rate of heat dissipation through the surface, which helps to maintain a higher core temperature. **Allen's rule** (1877) focuses on the appendages of the body. For example, limbs should be longer relative to body size in warmer climates because that would help to dissipate heat, whereas shorter limbs in colder climates would conserve body heat. An example of Bergman's and Allen's rules can be found in comparing artic and desert hares (Figure 6.12). The ears of the desert hare are much longer than those of the arctic hare and the body much leaner and rangier; both are features that dissipate heat.

Do Allen's and Bergmann's rule hold for human populations? In general, yes. If we look at humans adapted to extreme environments, such as Inuit in the Arctic and Nilotic peoples from East Africa, we see that the Inuit body seems to be structured to conserve heat, whereas the African body is designed to dissipate heat (Figure 6.13). Looking at a broad range of populations, there is a general trend among humans for larger body size and greater sitting height (that is, body length) to be associated with colder climates, whereas relative span (fingertip to fingertip length divided by height) tends to be greater in warmer temperatures (that is, longer appendages relative to body size) (Roberts, 1978).

LIVING AT HIGH ALTITUDE

Humans originally evolved in a warm, humid climate, which was at low altitude. But millions of people today live at very high altitudes of 3500 to 4000 m (11 600 to 13 200 ft), in environments that are typically dry and cold (Figure 6.14). Another major difference between high- and low-altitude environments is that atmospheric

(a)

(b)

FIGURE 6.12 Bergmann's and Allen's rules expressed in 2 rabbit species. (a) A snowshoe hare. (b) A desert-living black-tailed jackrabbit.

(a) (b)

FIGURE 6.13 Bergmann's and Allen's rule expressed in 2 human populations.
(a) Sudanese tribesman have body types adapted to warm climates. (b) Inuit people have body types adapted to cold climates but also rely extensively on cultural adaptations, such as clothing, in order to survive in their environment.

pressure is much less at high altitude. Although oxygen makes up the same proportion of the air at high and low altitude (21%), the lower pressure means that haemoglobin molecules in red blood cells take in fewer oxygen molecules with each breath—about one-third less at 4000 m (13 200 ft) than at sea level (Harrison

FIGURE 6.14 Anthropologist Andrea Wiley (left) investigates the effects of high-altitude living on reproductive health in Ladakh, India.

et al., 1988; Beall, 2001). The effects of altitude on oxygen availability start to become an issue at around 2500 m (8200 ft).

Any person accustomed to breathing at sea level who goes to one of these high-altitude locations is at risk of *hypoxia*, or "oxygen starvation." Immediate acclimatization to hypoxia involves increasing heart and breathing rates in order to increase circulation of oxygen. This is only a temporary solution, and the long-term effects of increased lung ventilation include headaches, tunnel vision, and fainting. Haemoglobin concentrations are increased by initially reducing the volume of blood plasma, followed by an increase in the production of red blood cells. Over time, the maximal oxygen consumption capacity reduces, which is an adaptation to the reduction in oxygen available. There are few indications that high altitude alone poses any particular long-term health problems. Growth is slower in children, but the total growth period is prolonged, so overall size is not decreased (Frisancho and Baker, 1970). High altitude has been no barrier to the development of large-scale, well-populated civilizations.

The inhabitants of three high-altitude populations have been extensively studied to determine the mechanisms underlying adaptation to hypoxia. These include Andean populations in South America, Tibetans in south Asia, and Ethiopians in Africa (Beall, 2001; Beall et al., 2002). A striking result of these studies is that there does not appear to be a single way in which humans adapt to high altitude: A variety of mechanisms or combinations of mechanisms are observed. In particular, researchers believe that Tibetans have a unique adaptation of oxygen uptake or delivery (Beall et al., 2002). Future research will therefore attempt to determine the biological mechanisms underpinning the high altitude adaptation of Tibetans, as well as understand the evolutionary processes that produced these different patterns in order to explain how and why several successful adaptations evolved among human populations.

Adaptability to Water

There are no human populations that live under water. However, there are populations whose inhabitants traditionally have made a living on what they can harvest from the sea. Some tribal groups in Southeast Asia have long been known for their diving and swimming ability, which they use to collect shells, clams, and sea cucumbers (Gislén et al., 2003). The Moken are one such group living in coastal areas of Burma and Thailand. Moken children are expert divers and are noted for their ability to locate objects under water without the benefit of diving goggles or masks (Figure 6.15).

Being terrestrial animals, humans are not well adapted to seeing under water. We lose about two-thirds of our focusing power under water, which explains why everything appears blurry to us and it is almost impossible to pick out small objects. Given this limitation, the ability of Moken children to pick out small objects under water is remarkable. A study comparing a group of Moken children with a group of European children found that both groups of children had equivalent vision out of the water, but the underwater visual acuity of the Moken children was twice as good as that of the European children (Gislén et al., 2003).

How do they see under water? The eye focuses through a process known as accommodation, which involves, among other things, constricting the pupil. Unlike European children, Moken children accommodate under water by constricting their pupils. Underwater environments typically are darker than open-air environments, so the natural response of the pupil is to expand under water, not constrict. Somehow, accommodation in Moken children takes precedence over pupil expansion to compensate for the reduction in light. Furthermore, underwater pupil constriction and accommodation in the Moken children are at the known limits of human performance for children their age.

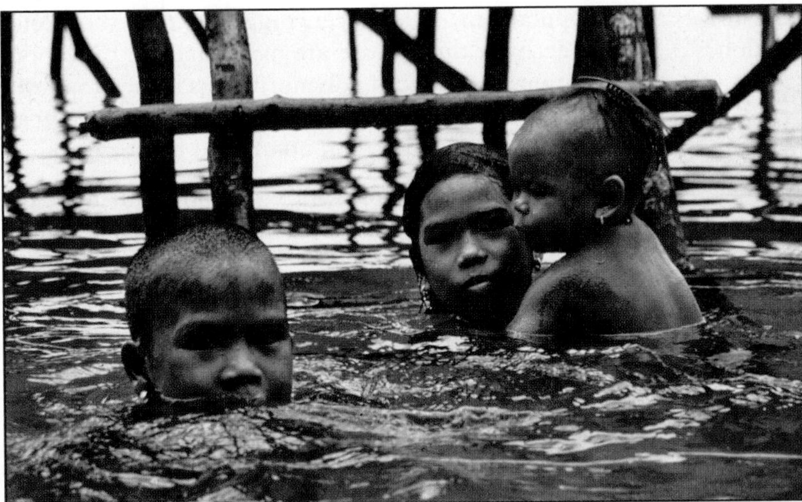

FIGURE 6.15 Moken children can see small objects under water.

As in other examples of coping with extreme environments, it is not clear whether the Moken ability to see under water results from a genetic adaptation or is an example of human adaptability or acclimatization. People can be taught to voluntarily accommodate to some extent, so this may simply represent an extreme version of that kind of learning. On the other hand, given their traditional lifestyle, the ability to accommodate under water may have been strongly selected for.

Human variation is a truly multifaceted topic. It goes right to the heart of what it is to be a human being. Although in the past some scientists looked at human variation as a means of dividing our species into competing groups, contemporary views emphasize differences without resorting to division. Human diversity is a beautiful thing, and that diversity reflects our extraordinary ability to adapt to different environments and our penchant for migrating across great swaths of the planet. Our individual biologies reflect where we came from, in both a genetic and environmental sense. We are all products of a dual heritage.

SUMMARY

1. **Why do we say that *Homo sapiens* is a polytypic species?**

   A polytypic species is one that can be divided into local populations that differ from each other by more than one phenotypic trait. Human populations exhibit substantial population-level diversity, which can be observed both genetically and anatomically.

2. **How do the biological and genetic definitions of *population* differ?**

   The classic biological definition of population focuses on the organism: A population is a potentially interbreeding group of individuals. A genetic population—sometimes called a deme—is defined in terms of that genetic composition of a group of animals, expressed, for example, in terms of allele frequencies. Both viewpoints agree that populations defined within a species are fluid and that gene flow or migration can occur between populations.

3. **Compare and contrast the terms *race* and *subspecies*.**

   A subspecies is defined as a group of local populations within a species that share a geographic range and can be distinguished from other subspecies based on one or more phenotypic traits. In biology, a subspecies is the same thing as race. Historically, however, many classifications of human races, both formal and informal, have incorporated behavioural, cultural, and sociological factors that have extended the definition of human race beyond that of a biological subspecies.

4. **What is maternal–foetal incompatibility, and how does it influence allele frequencies in a population?**

   Maternal–foetal incompatibility arises in the context of the ABO blood type system and, more critically (from a medical point of view), in the Rh system. It occurs when the mother does not possess a red blood cell surface protein, while the foetus does (inherited from the father). In the case of an Rh-negative mother, the Rh-positive foetus causes her to create antibodies against the Rh-positive blood cells. Although the first incompatible pregnancy usually is normal, in subsequent incompatible pregnancies, the mother's immune system will produce antibodies that attack the red blood cells of the infant, resulting in severe anaemia of the newborn.

5. **Why did lactose tolerance evolve in some human populations?**

   Mammals typically lose the ability to digest lactose, the sugar found in milk, after weaning. Most humans share this mammalian characteristic. However, in human populations that have a long history of dairying, a high frequency of individuals continue to produce the enzyme lactase through adulthood, and they can therefore digest lactose as adults. In these populations it is likely that lactose tolerance is an adaptation that has been selected for in an environment where raw milk products are available and consumed.

6. **What characterizes sickle cell anaemia?**

   Sickle cell anaemia is an autosomal recessive disease whose disease-causing alleles are found in higher than expected frequency (given the low fitness of homozygous individuals who have the diseases) in certain populations. It has been suggested that the alleles underlying this disease are maintained in these populations as balanced polymorphisms by heterozygous advantage. Sickle cell carriers are more resistant to developing malaria than unaffected homozygotes.

7. **What role does temperature play in influencing the distribution of body size and shape in the human species?**

   In cold climates, body heat must be conserved, whereas in hot climates, it is necessary to dissipate heat. Bergmann's rule states that animals in colder climates should have larger bodies because the greater the volume, the smaller the relative surface area and the less loss of heat through the body's surface. Allen's rule states that in hotter climates, appendages should be longer compared with the size of the body because that will increase surface area and promote heat dissipation. These rules are expressed in human populations adapted to extreme temperatures, such as in the arctic Inuit and Nilotic tribes of Africa.

8. **Why are high-altitude environments considered to be stressful?**

   Humans originally evolved in warm and humid environments at low altitude. High-altitude environments tend to be dry and cold. In addition, the decrease in atmospheric pressure at higher altitudes reduces the ability of haemoglobin molecules to carry oxygen. This becomes an issue at altitudes greater than 2500 m (8200 ft). Individuals from different high-altitude populations (Andes, Tibet, Ethiopia) have different physiological adaptations to high-altitude conditions.

CRITICAL THINKING QUESTIONS

1. How is the concept of race currently being used in your community? Are you comfortable with its usage? Is it consistent with what we know about human biological variation?
2. In what ways is natural selection acting on human populations today? Is it possible to identify these selective forces now, or can it be done only retrospectively after their effects are more apparent?

KEY TERMS

polytypic species
deme
subspecies
race
ethnobiology
racism
ethnic group
population genetics
microevolution
polymorphic
cline
maternal–foetal incompatibility
rhesus (Rh) system
human leukocyte antigen (HLA) system
autoimmune disease
phylogeny
lactose intolerant
haplotypes
balanced polymorphism
frequency-dependent balanced polymorphism
heterozygous advantage
adaptability
acclimatization
Bergmann's rule
Allen's rule

SUGGESTED READING

Cavalli-Sforza, L. L., and Cavalli-Sforza, F. (1996). *The Great Human Diasporas: The History of Diversity and Evolution*. Perseus, Reading, MA.

Kagawa, J. (1983). *Obasan*. Penguin Canada, Toronto, ON.

Kogawa, J. (1994). *Itsuka*. Anchor Books, New York, NY.

Molnar, S. (2005). *Human Variation: Races, Types, and Ethnic Groups*, 6th edition. Prentice Hall, Upper Saddle River, NJ.

Montagu, A. (1974). *Man's Most Dangerous Myth: The Fallacy of Race*, 5th edition. Oxford University Press, London.

Turner, T. (editor). (2005). *Biological Anthropology and Ethics: From Repatriation to Genetic Identity*. State University of New York Press, Albany, NY.

PART III

PRIMATES

Chapter 7
The Primates

Ranomafana National Park in Madagascar is a range of rugged, rain-soaked hills and rushing streams, and is home to some of the world's most unusual, beautiful, and endangered primates. We've come here to spend a few days looking for them.

Unlike monkeys and apes, which are active in the daytime and sleep all night, many of the most interesting primates in Madagascar are nocturnal. Finding them means hiring a guide who can lead us with his headlamp along muddy trails in the rainy dark. We have high hopes of seeing some of the forest's more exotic residents, such as aye-ayes, dwarf lemurs, and avahis. For several hours we follow in our guide's footsteps as the beam of his light falls across prehistoric-looking chameleons clinging to tree limbs along our path.

Around midnight we cross our umpteenth muddy ravine, and I am cold and tired and beginning to privately curse my guide for leading me on this wild primate chase. Just then he stops and points at the tree branches overhead. Looking up, I see movement in the foliage and spot several small rat-sized creatures bounding about. We stare at them, and one stares back. It's a mouse lemur, one of the world's smallest primates, weighing in at only a few ounces.

If I were not in Madagascar, I would assume it was a rodent. But due to Madagascar's isolation, natural selection took the primate path in an idiosyncratic direction, and primates evolved along some bizarre

lines. I reflect on the difference between a mountain gorilla, with a close genetic kinship to me, and this little creature that seems more rat than primate. But the mouse lemur is just as much a primate as the gorilla is; the two species share an ancestor that lived over 60 million years ago before they and the monkeys and apes went separate evolutionary ways. If we look back far enough into Earth's past, this tiny mammal's ancestor and my ancestor are the same.

The mouse lemur takes a last look at us, its eyes glowing in the beam of our headlamps, then turns and bounces off into the rainy night.

—Craig Stanford, Madagascar, August 1998

Chapter Outline

Biological anthropologists are interested in nonhuman primates for three reasons. First, as our closest living kin, nonhuman primates share with us a recent ancestry. By carefully testing hypotheses about their diet, social behaviour, and anatomy, we can reconstruct aspects of how extinct primates, including hominids, probably behaved. In other words, studying nonhuman primates offers us a window onto our own evolutionary past.

Anthropologists also want to know how the forces of natural selection and sexual selection moulded our ancestors after the human lineage split from the rest of the primate order. Therefore, when we study nonhuman primates we are studying not just the animals but also the evolutionary process itself.

Finally, biological anthropologists study nonhuman primates simply because they are intrinsically fascinating animals. Most living nonhuman primate species are under threat of extinction because human activities are destroying their habitat and the animals themselves. To develop strategies for primate conservation, we must first have detailed information about primates' habitat needs and behavioural biology. Only with this knowledge can we hope to ensure their survival.

This chapter introduces the nonhuman primates, their habitat, and their anatomical and ecological adaptations. After considering the place of the order Primates among the mammalian orders, we examine the suite of traits that characterizes the order. We then survey primate taxonomy and general traits of the major primate groups. In the latter part of the chapter, we turn to the topic of primate ecology—the role of nonhuman primates in tropical ecosystems—and look at the ecological factors that have moulded primate behaviour.

THE PRIMATE RADIATION

About 5 to 10 million species of animals and plants inhabit Earth today. Only a tiny fraction of these, about 4000 species, are mammals. Taxonomists divide the mammals into three groups:

1. The **metatheria**, or marsupials, reproduce without use of a placenta. Instead, their offspring are born in an almost embryonic state. They leave the mother's reproductive tract and crawl into her pouch, where they attach themselves to a nipple. After a further period of development, the offspring leave the pouch at a well-developed stage. Metatheria include kangaroos (Figure 7.1), koalas, opossums, and a

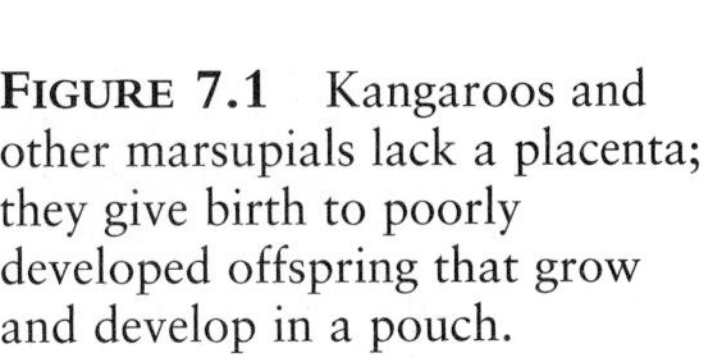

FIGURE 7.1 Kangaroos and other marsupials lack a placenta; they give birth to poorly developed offspring that grow and develop in a pouch.

FIGURE 7.2 Most modern mammals are placentals.

wide variety of other mammals, most of which are confined to Australia and nearby islands.

2. The **prototheria** are the monotremes, a small and unusual taxonomic group that includes only the Australian platypus and echidna. These species reproduce by egg-laying, but they nurse their young with milk in the manner of other mammals. Palaeontologists believe that monotremes were more diverse and numerous in the past than they are today.
3. The **eutheria**, or placental mammals (Figure 7.2), include some two dozen orders, one of which is the order Primates. Primates and other placental mammals reproduce by means of internal fertilization, followed by implantation of the fertilized zygote on the wall of the uterus. The developing embryo is nourished via thickened tissue that connects the circulatory system of the mother with that of her offspring. The pattern of reproduction, length of gestation, and degree of development of the newborn offspring vary widely among placental forms.

THE EXTRAORDINARY DIVERSITY OF NONHUMAN PRIMATES

Some 250 species of nonhuman primates are currently recognized but including all the minor taxonomic variations of these species, there are more than 350 varieties, or *taxa* (Groves, 2001). This is a small percentage of overall mammalian diversity, but nonhuman primates nonetheless exhibit an amazing variety of size and form. Adult body weights range from less than 40 grams (2 oz) in mouse lemurs to more than 200 kilograms (450 lb) in gorillas (Figure 7.3). Body shapes range from the graceful arm-swinging gibbon to the bizarre aye-aye.

WHAT EXACTLY IS A PRIMATE?

Primates are mammals with grasping hands, large brains, a high degree of learned rather than innate behaviour, and a suite of other traits. However, the primates are a diverse group, and not all species share the same suite of traits. The order Primates is divided into two suborders: the **Strepsirhini**, or **strepsirhine** primates

metatheria Mammals that reproduce without a placenta, including the marsupials.

prototheria Mammals that reproduce by egg-laying, then nurse young from nipples. The Australian platypus and echidna are the only living monotremes.

eutheria Mammals that reproduce with a placenta and uterus.

strepsirhine (Strepsirhini) Infraorder of the order Primates that includes the prosimians, excluding the tarsier.

FIGURE 7.3 Primate body size and shape vary widely from the 200-kilogram (450-lb) gorilla to the 40-gram (2-oz) mouse lemur.

haplorhine (Haplorhini) Infraorder of the order Primates that includes the anthropoids and the tarsier.

prosimian Member of the primate suborder Prosimii that includes the lemurs, lorises, galagos, and tarsiers.

anthropoid Members of the primate suborder Anthropoidea that includes the monkeys, apes, and hominids.

(lemurs, lorises, and galagos), and the **Haplorhini,** or **haplorhine** primates (tarsiers, monkeys, apes, and humans) (Figure 7.4). We should not consider strepsirhines more primitive than haplorhines; both groups have been evolving on their own paths for more than 60 million years. But many of their adaptations are clear holdovers from the early days of the Primate order. The strepsirhine–haplorhine classification system reflects genetic relationships and was developed in the late eighteenth century, long after Linnnaeus's earlier primate taxonomy. Many taxonomists use another traditional naming system, which is based on aspects of anatomy, for the major primate groups: the **prosimian** and **anthropoid** suborders. We'll see how the strepsirhine–haplorhine classification differs from the prosimian–anthropoid classification later in the chapter.

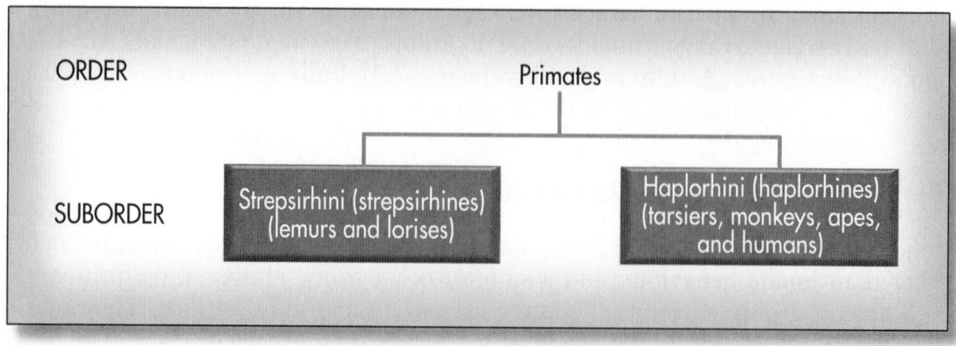

FIGURE 7.4 The major groupings of living primates.

Anatomical Traits

We distinguish primates from other mammals by a set of traits that all primates share.

Grasping Hands with Opposable Thumbs or Big Toes The grasping hand with opposable thumb is believed to be the fundamental primate adaptation, although some prosimians don't fully exhibit this trait. Like most other mammals, primates typically have five digits per hand or foot. Having a thumb and big toe that are anatomically opposed to the other four digits allows primates to grasp objects with greater precision than other mammals. In some primates, such as colobine monkeys, gibbons, and spider monkeys, the four fingers are so elongated or the thumb is so reduced that the digits do not meet, rendering them less useful for gripping. Nonhuman primates also have an opposable hallux (the big toe).

For example, an ape uses its feet in much the same way that we use our hands. Humans have instead evolved a foot in which all the toes line up in the same plane, at the cost of a loss of dexterity of the foot.

Flattened Nails The primate grasping hand has flattened nails at the ends of the digits instead of claws. This is the case for all primates except one group, the marmosets and tamarins. In addition, many strepsirhines have a combination of nails and a single clawed digit on their hands and feet.

Forward-Facing Eyes with Stereoscopic Vision Consider the way you see the world and compare it with the view of most other mammals. For example, a horse has eye sockets mounted on either side of its head. It has a field of vision that extends nearly 360 degrees, except for a blind spot directly behind. However, the horse's forward vision is not very good because the fields of vision of its two eyes don't fully overlap in front. Now consider your own vision. Like those of nonhuman primates, your eyes are mounted flush on the front of your head (Figure 7.5); your peripheral vision to the sides and behind you is severely constrained by this anatomy. But your forward field of vision is covered by both

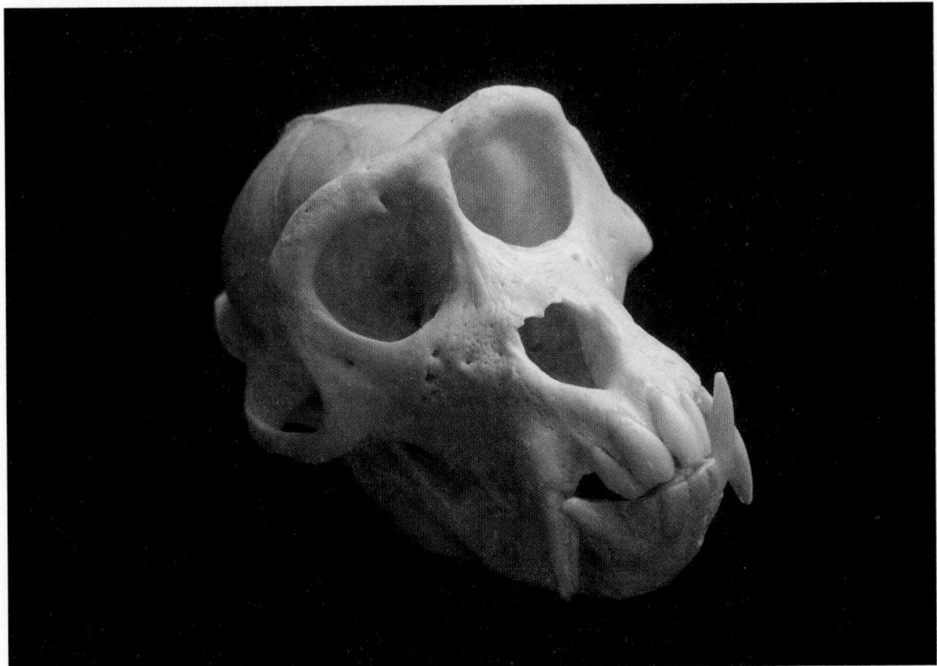

Figure 7.5 The primate skull is characterized by a forward-facing eye and enclosed bony eye orbits.

arboreal hypothesis Hypothesis for the origin of primate adaptation that focuses on the value of grasping hands and stereoscopic vision for life in the trees.

visual predation hypothesis Hypothesis for the origin of primate adaptation that focuses on the value of grasping hands and stereoscopic vision for catching small prey.

eyes. This stereoscopic view enables you to have excellent *depth perception* because the overlapping fields of vision provide a three-dimensional view of the world.

Enclosed Bony Eye Orbits in the Skull Primates also have an apparent anatomical adaptation to the importance of vision: enclosed (or partially enclosed) bony eye orbits (sockets) in the skull, which may protect the eye more effectively than the open orbit of lower mammals (Figure 7.5). This orbital closure is more complete in haplorhines than it is in strepsirhines.

Petrosal Bulla The petrosal bulla is the tiny bit of the skeleton that covers and protects parts of the inner ear. Its importance to primate taxonomists is that this is the single bony trait that is shared by all primates, living or extinct, which occurs in no other mammalian group. When a fossil of questionable status is uncovered, researchers examine the ear portion carefully in search of the petrosal bulla.

Stereoscopic vision, grasping hands, opposable thumbs, and nails rather than claws seem like an obvious suite of adaptations to life in the trees. This was the thinking of the scientists who proposed the **arboreal hypothesis** in the 1920s, which was widely accepted and stood unchallenged for a half-century. But in the 1970s some key flaws in that model were noted. Squirrels, for example, lack the primate stereoscopic vision and grasping hand with nails, yet they scamper up and down trees with great agility. To understand primate origins, then, we should consider how the very earliest primates and their close kin lived. The fossil record shows that early on, primates were anatomically very much like modern insectivores, which live in the tangled thickets that grow around the base of tropical forest trees and stalk and capture insects and other fast-moving prey. These creatures are a useful analog for early primates in the **visual predation hypothesis,** which proposes that forward-facing eyes, depth perceptive vision, and grasping hands for catching their prey, not for climbing in trees, were the key adaptations of ancient primates (Cartmill, 1974). Many predators have forward-facing eyes—eagles, owls, and cats, for instance—and this is thought to aid them in precisely homing in on their prey.

The arboreal hypothesis and the visual predation hypothesis are not mutually exclusive; at some point ancient nonhuman primates did indeed live in the trees. Variants of these two theories have been put forward, including the proposal that excellent stereoscopic vision and grasping hands were essential for foraging for flowering plants, which arose during the same geologic period in which early primates emerged (Sussman, 1991).

Generalized Body Plan The primate body plan is generalized, not specialized. Many mammals have extremely specialized body designs; consider a giraffe's neck, a seal's flippers, or an elephant's trunk. Primates typically lack such specializations. Their generalized body plan gives them versatility; most primate species engage in a wide variety of modes of travel, for instance, from arm-swinging (in apes) to running, leaping, and walking.

Because primates evolved from ancient mammalian stock, they have inherited the many traits of that lineage. All nonhuman primates are quadrupeds, designed for moving about using all four limbs, but there is great variation in the way they use their limbs (Figure 7.6). Many strepsirhines move by *vertical clinging and leaping* (VCL). Their hind limbs are longer than their front legs. This allows them to sit upright against a tree trunk or bamboo stalk, then launch themselves from a vertical posture through the air, turning as they leap and landing upright against a nearby upright support. For instance, sifakas bound from tree trunk to tree trunk at high speed using this locomotor technique.

Contrary to the commonly depicted image of them swinging through treetops, monkeys actually walk and run (on the ground and in trees) in much the same way that dogs, cats, and other four-legged mammals do. Rather than arm-swing, monkeys run and leap along branches, their arms and legs moving in a limited plane of motion. The palms of the hands and feet make contact with the surface they are walking on. The skeleton of a monkey such as a baboon, which lives both on the ground and in trees, shows this clearly (Figure 7.6). The running motion of any four-legged animal, whether a dog or a monkey, features a limited range of motion of the limbs, which are adapted for fast forward running, not three-dimensional climbing. The shoulder blade, or scapula, is oriented vertically across the upper arm and shoulder, allowing the arms to swing back and forth in a rapid pendulum motion but not rotate.

By contrast, an ape's arm has a full range of motion (Figure 7.6). As we shall see, this is an adaptation to arm-hanging for feeding. Arm-hangers need a scapula that is oriented across the back rather than on the sides of the upper arms to allow this freedom of motion. Apes also possess a cone-shaped rib cage and torso, long, curved digit bones, small thumbs, and long arms to aid in arm-swinging.

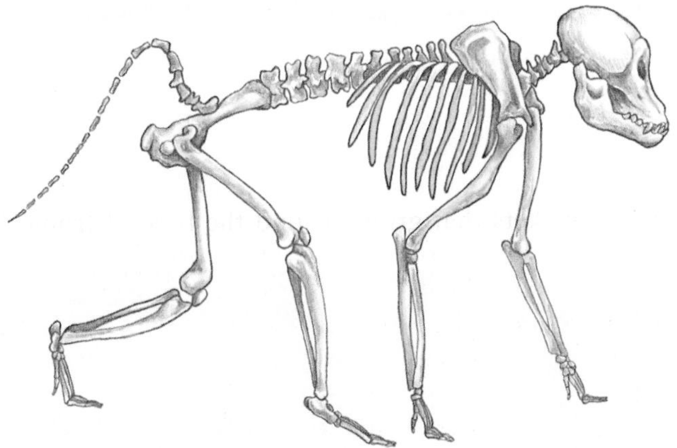

(a) Skeleton of a terrestrial quadruped

Baboon

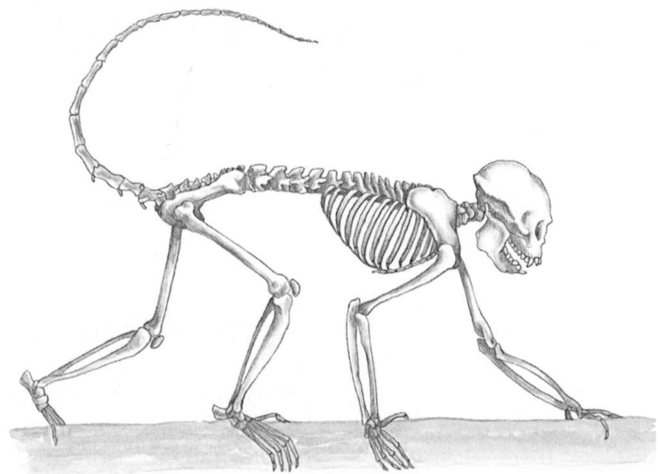

(b) Skeleton of an arboreal quadruped

Uakari

FIGURE 7.6 The Primate order displays a diversity of ways of moving around.

(c) Skeleton of a vertical clinger and leaper

Indri

(d) Skeleton of a brachiator

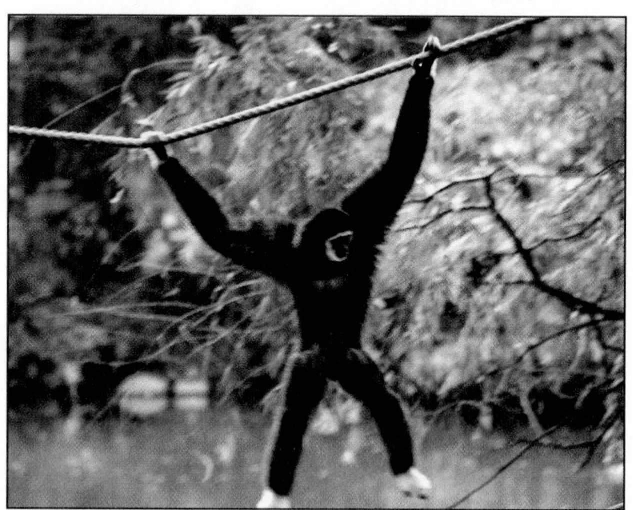

Gibbon

FIGURE 7.6 *(continued)*

Generalized Teeth Teeth are an extraordinarily important part of a nonhuman primate from an anthropologist's perspective. Their shape tells us a great deal about everything from a species' diet to its mating system. Most nonhuman primates eat a diet that is some combination of leaves, fruit, and other plant products, with occasional animal protein in the form of insects, small mammals, or other animals. Only one, the tarsier, eats mainly animal protein.

Scientists believe that nonhuman primates have undergone an evolutionary reduction in the degree of specialization of the teeth, evident in the small canines and incisors and the rounded molars of most of them. If we consider the **dental arcade**, the arc of teeth along either the bottom or top of the mouth, beginning at the midline of the mouth there are four types of teeth arranged in the following dental formula: two incisors, one canine, two premolars (what your dentist calls bicuspids), and three molars (Figure 7.7). The exceptions to this pattern are most of the New World monkeys, which have a third premolar, and the strepsirhines, which have varying dental formulas.

Activity Patterns Most primate species are active during daylight hours, possess colour vision, and have limited olfactory senses. Although many strepsirhines are **nocturnal** (active at night), all haplorhines except one, the night monkey *Aotus*, are **diurnal** (active during the daylight hours). Primates made a fundamental shift from a nocturnal lifestyle that relied on their sense of smell to a visually based diurnal one. Diurnal animals have a greater need for colour vision, and haplorhine primates in particular use their eyes to find plant foods, including brightly coloured fruits, in a complex forest environment. At the same time, diurnal primates evolved complex patterns of visual communication, such as bright colours and communicative behaviours, in place of the scent-marking communication that nocturnal primates use. Other nonhuman primate species are active mainly at dusk and dawn, and others are active irregularly throughout the day and night.

dental arcade The parabolic arc that forms the upper or lower row of teeth.

nocturnal Active at night.

diurnal Active during daylight hours.

neocortex The part of the brain that controls higher cognitive function; part of the cerebrum.

Life History Traits

The life history of mammals—their trajectory from conception to death—varies widely. In general, mammals that reproduce slowly, live long lives, and acquire information about their world through learning and not their genes, have delayed maturation and drawn-out life histories. Primates take this trend to an extreme.

Single Offspring Nearly all primates give birth to single offspring. Many mammals, especially smaller species, give birth to litters or twins. The only exception among nonhuman primates is the marmosets and tamarins, which give birth to twins. Single births, combined with the long maturation period and the amount of time and energy mothers invest in their offspring, represent a strategy in which investment of time and energy in a few babies has replaced the more primitive mammalian pattern of litters of offspring that receive less intensive care.

Large Brains Primates have large brains. They possess a high degree of *encephalisation*, or evolved increase in the volume of the **neocortex** of the brain,

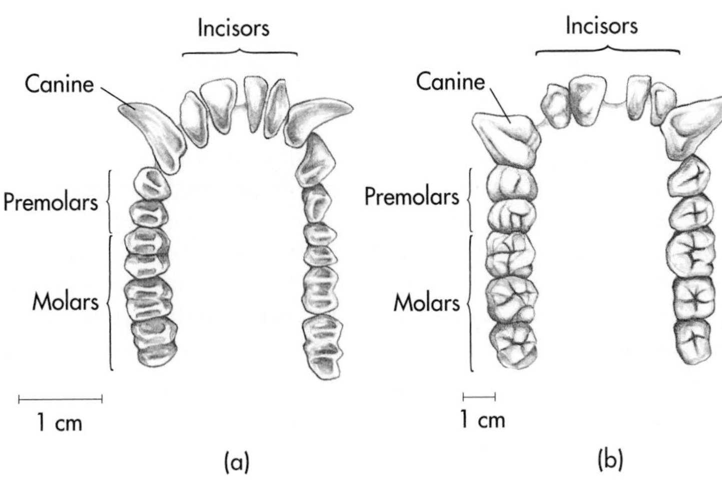

FIGURE 7.7 The primate dental formula illustrated for (a) the lower dentition of an Old World monkey and (b) the upper dentition of a gorilla.

ontogeny The life cycle of an organism from conception to death.

sociality Group living, a fundamental trait of haplorhine primates.

which is involved in higher cognitive processes. This is more obvious in the brains of haplorhine primates than in strepsirhines, and we see it in the greater number of convolutions that compose the ridges and fissures (sulci and gyri) of the brain's surface. These convolutions increase the effective surface area of the brain and are believed to contribute to higher cognitive function.

There is much debate among scientists about the reasons for the evolutionary expansion of brain volume in primates and for the survival value of a big brain itself. The primate brain is such a large, metabolically expensive organ to grow and maintain that it must have important survival and reproductive benefits. More on brain anatomy and function is in Chapter 15.

Extended Ontogeny Primates live by learned behaviours as much as they do on hard-wired instinct. For example, many primates live in social groups, so a baby monkey or ape must learn how to be a member of a social group if it intends to successfully court a mate and rear offspring itself; these are largely learned behaviours. Thus it is important for primates to be socialized within their communities, a process that can take up a large proportion of their infancy and maturation.

Although many animals have longer life spans than primates, primates are notable for the extended length of each stage, from infancy to adulthood, of their life cycle (Figure 7.8). The life cycle is also called **ontogeny**. The gorilla life span is about 20 times longer than that of a mouse, but the time it takes from gestation to sexual maturity is almost 80 times longer (about 15 years, compared with 10 weeks). Why?

Consider the sort of information a growing primate must learn in order to survive in the world. In addition to learning how to find food and water, the primate must learn how to live in a social group. The process of learning to live in a group is a long one, and the behaviours involved tend not to be purely instinctual. An infant monkey or ape reared in isolation will end up severely deficient in the social skills it needs to be part of a social group. Parental investment in the infant is dramatically greater in primates than it is in rodents or most other mammals because social skills require years of maturation and practice.

Behavioural Traits

Sociality, or the characteristic of living in groups, is perhaps the most fundamental social adaptation that characterizes most primates. It is the adaptation by which a primate survives and reproduces because it provides the animal with ready access to mates and may help it find food and avoid predators.

Of the haplorhine primates, only one—the orangutan—is not normally found in a social group of some sort. There are many variations in sociality among the nonhuman primates, and we will examine the diversity of social grouping patterns in detail in Chapter 8.

All the characteristics in the previous descriptions do not apply to every primate species. Many strepsirhines are nocturnal and solitary, navigating by olfaction, whereas others are highly social, diurnal, and visually oriented. Strepsirhines often possess a mixture of primate traits, such as a combination of claws and nails on the hands. Don't make the mistake of thinking that lemurs and their kin are "less evolved" or more primitive than monkeys. The simple fact is that monkeys and strepsirhines share a common ancestor, and after the split between the two lineages, each group evolved in separate lines. Natural selection favoured diurnality and sociality more in monkeys than it did in strepsirhines.

A GUIDE TO THE NONHUMAN PRIMATES

As we discussed earlier, we consider the nonhuman primates as two major groups within the order Primates: the suborders Strepsirhini and Haplorhini (Figure 7.9). Alternately the primates can be subdivided into suborders Prosimii and Anthropoidea. Recall that the Linnaean system for naming includes not only order, family, genus, and species but also higher and lesser categories (see Chapter 5). So primate families that are anatomically similar are lumped in the same superfamily, and subgroups of

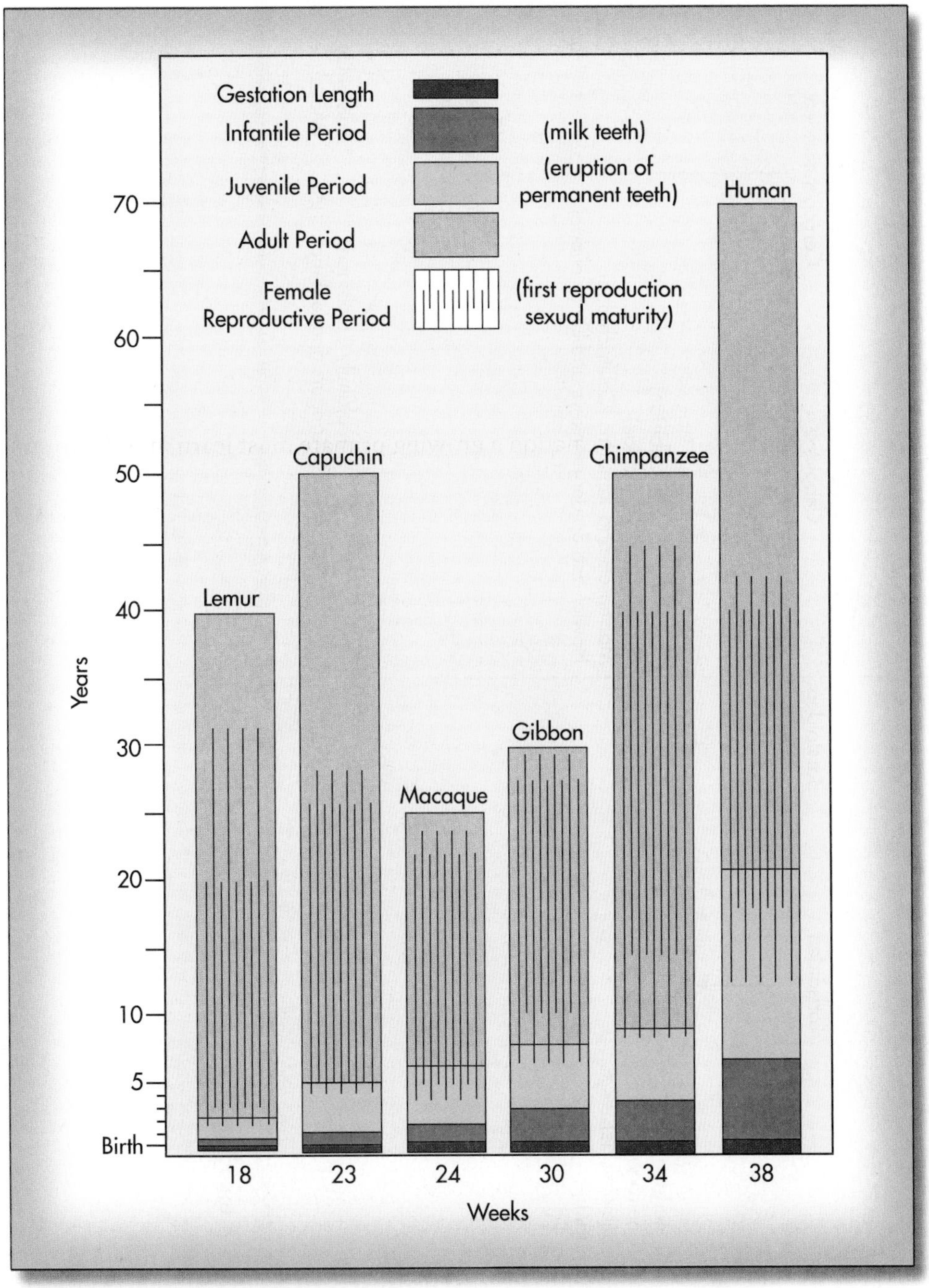

FIGURE 7.8 Primates exhibit prolonged life histories, spending more time in each stage of life than most other mammals do.

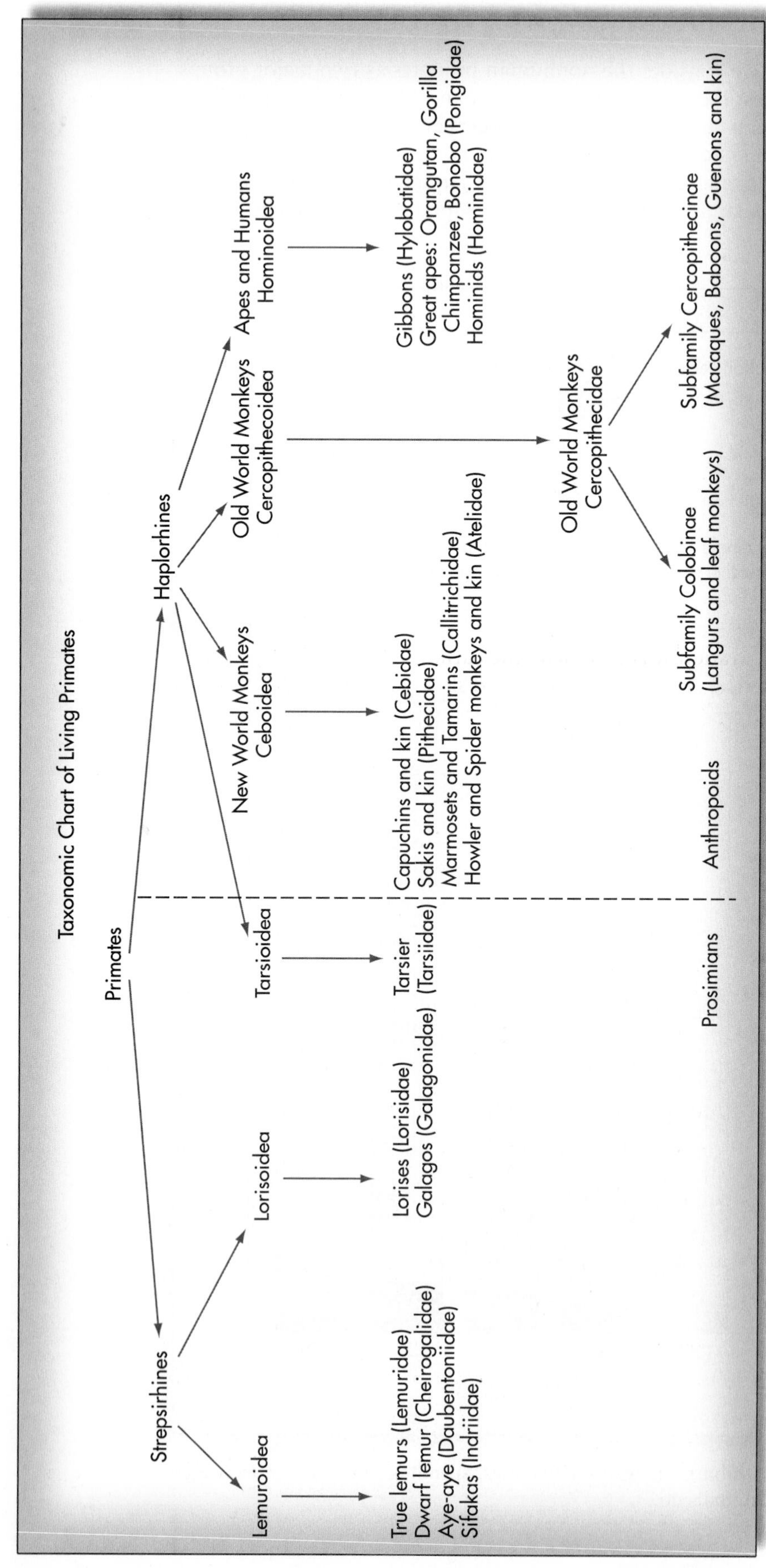

FIGURE 7.9 A taxonomic chart of the living primates.

families are called subfamilies. Not all taxonomists agree on how to classify the primates, and one nonhuman primate, the tarsier, straddles the two suborders. The geographic distribution of nonhuman primates is presented in Figure 7.10.

The Strepsirhines

The primates of the suborder Strepsirhini include the lemurs of Madagascar and the lorises and galagos of mainland Africa and tropical Asia. Linnaeus originally subdivided the primates into two major groups—the prosimians (sometimes called the lower primates) and the anthropoids (higher primates)—based on a number of anatomical features. *Strepsirhine* and *prosimian* are not completely synonymous; one prosimian primate, the tarsier, is a haplorhine, not a strepsirhine. But all strepsirhines and prosimians share some common anatomical features: a reliance on olfaction, nocturnality, and a lack of complex social behaviour patterns. Their incisor teeth protrude from the front of the mouth to form a comblike surface, known as the *tooth comb*, used for grooming. Many also have specialized clawed toes that serve as grooming tools.

The Lemurs The superfamily Lemuroidea is found only on Madagascar. The fourth largest island on Earth, Madagascar is home to perhaps the best example of an adaptive radiation we know of among living nonhuman primates (Figure 7.11). Madagascar broke away from the eastern coast of the continental mainland of Africa, through the process of continental drift, beginning some 100 million years ago. By the time the separation was complete, the earliest members of the primate order had evolved in Africa. As Madagascar drifted slowly out of contact with the rest of Africa, the primitive primates stranded on its land mass began to evolve without gene flow from other primates.

Over time, these animals developed a wide range of adaptations to exploit the many available habitats and niches on Madagascar. In the absence of large predators (there are no big carnivores or large eagles on the entire island), a diverse array of forms radiated from the ancestral colonizing forms (Figure 7.12). Sadly, many of those species are now extinct, presumably because of hunting by people, who arrived on the island beginning 1500 to 2000 years ago.

There are four families of lemurs alive today, which range in size from the 40-gram (20-oz) mouse lemur to the 8-kilogram (20-lb) indri.

The Lorises The lorises are a diverse group of strepsirhines in tropical Africa and Asia (Figure 7.13).

Lorises (Figure 7.14) and galagos (Figure 7.15) probably resemble the primitive ancestors of modern haplorhines. They communicate both vocally and olfactorily, by scent-marking objects in their environment. They are nocturnal and largely solitary and spend their nights feeding on fruits and hunting for insects and other small animals.

Lorises are slow-moving, deliberate stalkers, capturing small prey. In contrast, galagos are active, leaping animals (using VCL) that range in size from a housecat to a rat and generally are more insectivorous than lorises.

The Haplorhines

The nonhuman primates of the suborder Haplorhini include the tarsier, New World monkeys, Old World monkeys, apes, and hominids. The tarsier is a haplorhine but also a prosimian. It is closely related to the anthropoids but occupies an evolutionary status intermediate between the lower and higher primates. Haplorhines possess the full suite of adaptations that characterize the living primates. Without exception haplorhines are guided more by vision than by olfaction. This emphasis on vision is reflected in the full closure of the back of

Figure 7.10

A WORLD MAP OF LIVING NONHUMAN PRIMATES

NORTH AND SOUTH AMERICA

Primates in the New World tend to be small-bodied compared to those elsewhere. All species are primarily arboreal, and some have grasping tails to aid in tree-top feeding. New World primates are found from central Mexico to Argentina, and in some equatorial forests numerous species can be found sharing the same habitat.

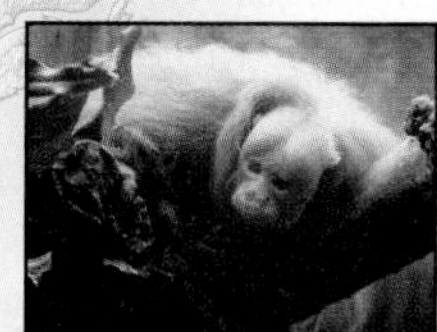

UAKARI Native to seasonally flooded rain forests

MURIQUI Highly endangered, the largest New World monkey

GOLDEN LION TAMARIN One of Brazil's endangered primates

EUROPE AND ASIA

Nonhuman primates are found across tropical Asia, occurring as far north as central Japan (the Japanese macaque). They occur in only the tiniest bit of Europe, on the island of Gibraltar (where they may have been introduced by people). Asia is the home of gibbons and orangutans, many species of Old World monkeys (the langurs, leaf monkeys and macaques) plus numerous strepsirhines.

DeBrazza's Guenon A diverse group found in African forests

Galago Live in many African forests; Also called bushbabies

Golden Snub-Nosed Monkey One of China's beautiful and endangered primates

Savanna Baboon Baboons are found across subsaharan Africa

Chimpanzee Found in suitable habitat across equatorial Africa

Hanuman Langurs Found all across the Indian Subcontinent

Lar Gibbon Found in forests from India through Southeast Asia

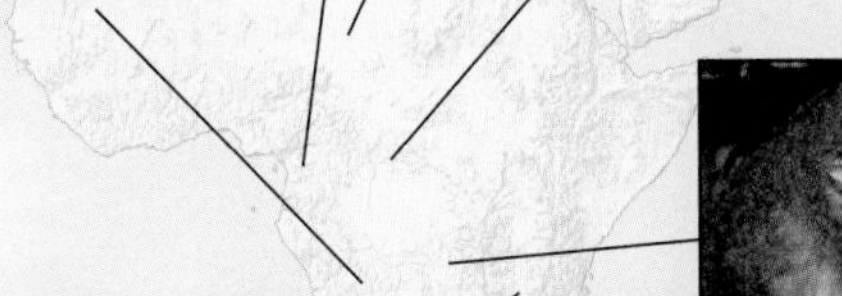

Lorises The only Strepsirhine primates in Africa and mainland Asia

Gorillas Live in both lowland and mountain forests

Tarsier The only entirely carnivorous primate, found in Southeast Asia rain forests

Lion-Tailed Macaque One of the world's most threatened primates, found in hilly forests of Southern India

Red-Bellied Lemur Found only on Madagascar

Orangutan Live only on the Islands of Sumatra and Borneo in Indonesia

AFRICA

Primates are found across sub-Saharan Africa and also in small areas of northwestern Africa and in the Arabian peninsula. Primate biodiversity peaks in the central African Congo Basin, where more than fifteen species can be found in the same tropical rain forest habitat. Africa provides primate habitat ranging from rain forest to savannah to high mountain meadows, across a vast area. Moreover, since humans evolved in Africa, we can study African primates with an eye toward learning something about the environment of the human past.

FIGURE 7.11 Lemurs are found only in Madagascar.

FIGURE 7.12 The ring-tailed lemur is the best-known of the Madagascar primates.

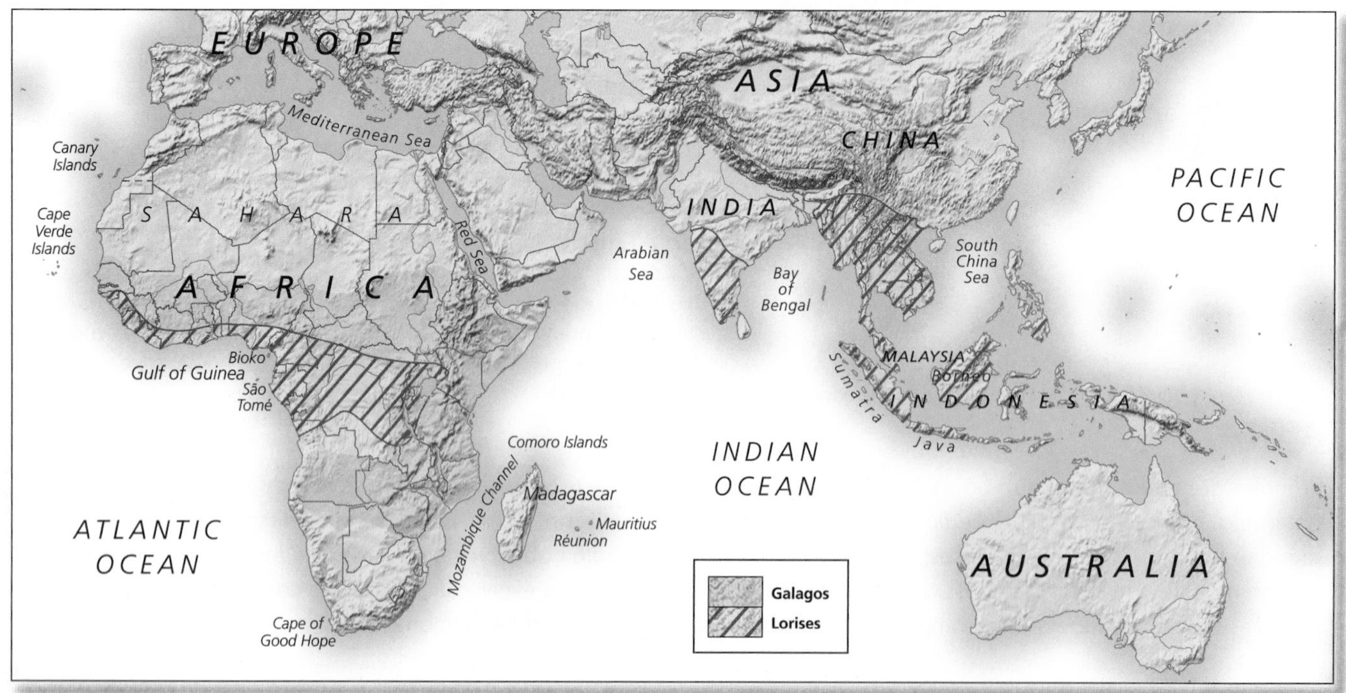

FIGURE 7.13 The distribution of lorises and galagos.

Figure 7.14 A loris.

Figure 7.15 A galago, or bushbaby.

their eye orbits, providing bony protection for the eye that strepsirhines and most other mammals lack. Living haplorhines also possess a lower jaw that is fused at the midline in adulthood; in prosimians and most other mammals the jaw is two pieces joined in the middle with cartilage.

With few exceptions, haplorhines are diurnal. And with one exception (the orangutan), they live in social groups. The ratio of brain to body size in haplorhines is higher than in strepsirhines; cognition is part of the haplorhine suite of adaptations. Cognition also is related to the degree of social complexity we observe among haplorhines, greater than what we usually see among the strepsirhines. The haplorhines include all extinct forms of hominids, as well as humans.

The Tarsiers Tarsiers possess a mixture of traits of anthropoid and prosimian primates, but they are generally considered to be closer to anthropoids (Figure 7.16). The several species of tarsier recognized today live in Indonesia and nearby island groups (Figure 7.17). They occupy an owl-like ecological role as nocturnal predators on small vertebrates and are the most highly carnivorous of all nonhuman primates, eating small prey such as lizards, frogs, and insects. They live in monogamous pairs, are exclusively nocturnal, and park their young in tree nests while out foraging (Gursky, 1994, 1995).

The New World Monkeys

Platyrrhini Infraorder of the order Primates that is synonymous with the New World monkeys, or ceboids.

The New World monkeys are classified in the infraorder **Platyrrhini** (referring to the flat shape of the nose). They live in the tropical and subtropical forests of the Western Hemisphere, from Argentina northward to within around 500 kilometres of the

Figure 7.16 The tarsier is a haplorhine, and may represent an evolutionary bridge between lower and higher primates.

FIGURE 7.17 The distribution of the tarsier.

U.S. border in the state of Veracruz, Mexico (Figure 7.18). All the New World monkeys share three features:

- *Small body size.* The largest New World monkey, the muriqui, weighs only about 12 kilograms (25 lb). The smallest, the marmosets and tamarins, range from 0.6 kilograms (1.5 lb) down to less than 100 grams.
- *Three premolar teeth.* Whereas all other haplorhine primates have two premolars (bicuspids) in each quadrant of the mouth, New World monkeys have three.
- *Arboreality.* Even though there are large stretches of grassland in parts of South America, there are no primarily terrestrial New World nonhuman primates, (as opposed to Africa, where baboons and other nonhuman primates make use of open country). Some New World monkeys have grasping **prehensile tails;** this trait is an adaptation to feeding, allowing a monkey to hang beneath slender branches to reach food (Figure 7.19).

THE OLD WORLD MONKEYS

The Old World monkeys, along with the apes and humans, are in the infraorder **Catarrhini** (or primates with downward-facing nostrils). Old World monkeys occur in many parts of Africa and Asia and also in small areas of the Middle East (Figure 7.20 and Figure 7.21). Old World monkeys have exploited a wider variety of habitats than their New World counterparts, occupying every ecological setting from tropical rain forest to savannah to desert.

As a family, the Old World monkeys share *ischial callosities:* thickened calluses on the rump that presumably make sitting on rough surfaces more comfortable. They also possess double-ridged molar teeth. These *bilophodont molars* are believed to be an evolutionary advance for biting through fibrous plant material. Old World monkeys display a greater size range than New World monkeys, from

prehensile tail Grasping tail possessed by some species of New World monkeys.

Catarrhini Infraorder of the order Primates that includes the Old World monkeys, apes, and hominids.

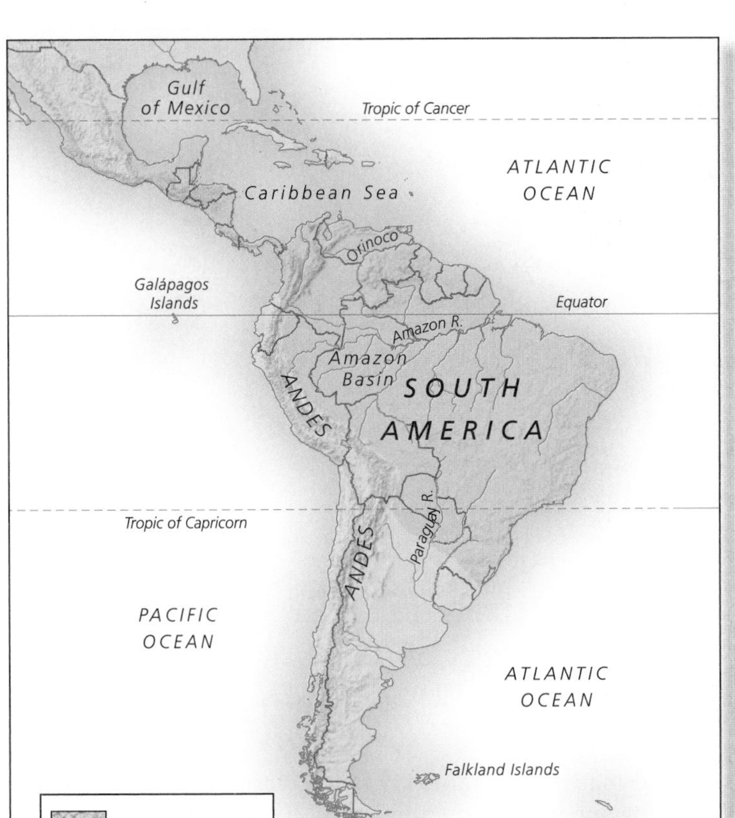

FIGURE 7.18 Distribution of the Ceboidea, or New World monkeys.

0.8-kilogram (2-lb) talapoins (*Miopithecus talapoin*) to 32-kilogram (70-lb) baboons (*Papio* ssp.)(Figure 7.22). Some groups also display a greater degree of sexual dimorphism than we see in any New World monkey species.

THE HOMINOIDS

The apes and humans, past and present, are classified in the superfamily Hominoidea. This includes the ape families **hylobatid (Hylobatidae)** and **pongid (Pongidae)** and the human family **hominid (Hominidae)**. As we saw earlier, had Linnaeus not been so bound by his theology, humans and apes probably would have been placed in the same family, based on their many shared anatomical traits.

hylobatid (Hylobatidae) Member of the gibbon, or lesser ape, family.

pongid (Pongidae) One of the four great apes species: gorilla, chimpanzee, bonobo, or orangutan.

hominid (Hominidae) Member of our own human family, past or present.

FIGURE 7.19 A prehensile tail is an adaptation to grasping branches for support while feeding.

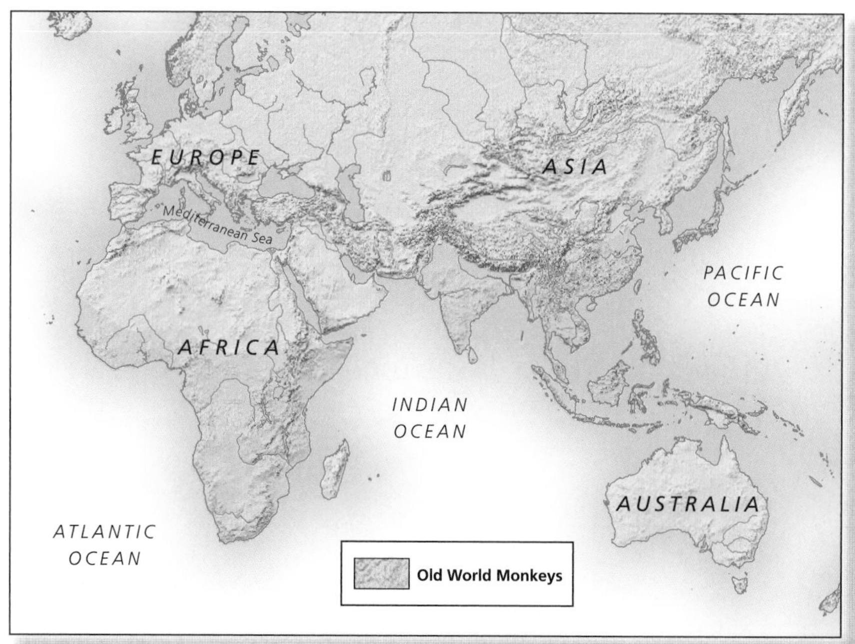

FIGURE 7.20 Distribution of the Old World monkeys.

The hominoids extend many haplorhine traits: increased brain volume and intelligence, extended ontogeny, increased complexity of social interactions, and large body size. The hylobatids, or gibbons, often are called the lesser apes, based on minor anatomical differences from the four pongids, or great apes: the chimpanzee, bonobo, gorilla, and orangutan.

Apes and humans share several key postcranial anatomical traits. Foremost among these is the suspensory, rotating shoulder apparatus that allows for arm-hanging and arm-swinging, or **brachiation**. The anatomy that allows a quarterback to throw a football or a gymnast to perform on the high bar is the same as that which allowed fossil apes to hang from branches in the canopy of ancient forests (Figure 7.23), although it probably did not evolve for the purpose. Instead, researchers believe that arm-hanging initially was adaptive for suspending a large-bodied ape underneath a tree limb from which ripe fruit was growing. A branch that could not support the weight of an ape walking on top of it could support the same weight hung beneath it. In this way, the rotating shoulder of the ape may have an evolved function similar to that of the prehensile tail of many New World monkeys. Like humans, apes lack tails.

brachiation Mode of arm-hanging and arm-swinging that uses a rotating shoulder to suspend the body of an ape or hominid beneath a branch or to travel between branches.

FIGURE 7.21 The Hanuman langur, a widely distributed Asian colobine.

FIGURE 7.22 Baboons are African cercopithecines.

FIGURE 7.23 All living apes possess rotating, suspensory shoulders, as do humans.

The four great apes move about by a modified form of quadrupedalism called knucklewalking (Figure 7.24) or, in the case of the orangutan, fist-walking.

Gibbons Gibbons live in Asian tropical and subtropical forests from easternmost India and Bangladesh through mainland Southeast Asia and the Indonesian archipelago (Figure 7.25). They range in size from about 4 to 12 kilograms (10 to 20 lb).

Gibbons are rain forest canopy inhabitants, their bodies well adapted for a highly arboreal existence of brachiating among and hanging beneath tree limbs (Figure 7.26). They possess long arms, extremely elongated fingers, shortened thumbs, and a suspensory shoulder designed for treetop life. Most gibbon species

FIGURE 7.24 Great apes knucklewalk when travelling on the ground.

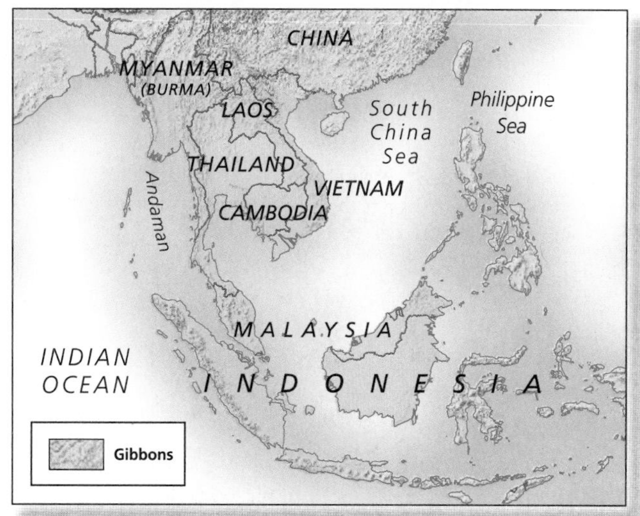

FIGURE 7.25 Distribution of the gibbons.

FIGURE 7.26 Gibbons are lesser apes, and live in the forests of South and Southeast Asia.

frugivorous An animal that eats a diet composed mainly of fruit.

are highly **frugivorous**, or fruit-eating, using their high-energy diet to engage in a high-energy lifestyle of brachiating and singing. They are among the most vocal of all nonhuman primates; their whooping songs are given from morning until night and serve as declarations of territorial boundaries for other members of their species. Mated pairs also sing duets that reinforce the bond between male and female.

Orangutans Orangutans (*Pongo pygmaeus*) are the most enigmatic of all the hominoid primates. These red apes are among our closest living kin and among the largest-brained animals on Earth. But compared with other apes, they are largely solitary. Found in the rapidly disappearing rain forests of the Indonesian islands of Sumatra and Borneo (Figure 7.27), orangutans are large-bodied and extremely sexually dimorphic. Males may weigh 78 kilograms (200 lb), more than twice the size and weight of adult females (Figure 7.28).

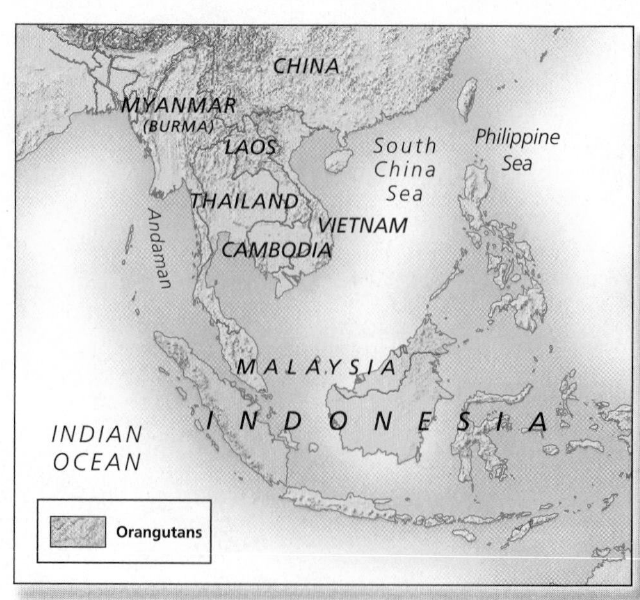

FIGURE 7.27 Orangutans are limited to the islands of Sumatra and Borneo, where their numbers are rapidly declining.

Orangutans are highly arboreal, travelling slowly through the forest canopy in search of fruit. Adult females and their dependent offspring occupy territories that they defend from other adult females. Adult males attempt to maintain control over a number of female territories, moving over a much larger area to attempt to monopolize them for mating purposes. Surplus males that cannot obtain access to their own females live as transients, attempting to approach females without being detected by the resident adult male. Resident adult males use resonating, loud calls to warn transients away.

Orangutan reproduction is strongly influenced by the food supply. *Mast-fruiting*, the unpredictable ripening of many fruit trees at the same time in Indonesian rain forests, triggers ovulation among female orangutans (Knott, 1998). At times of fruit abundance, orangutans form temporary associations of several individuals, presumably for mating purposes.

When times are lean, orangutans cope with the lack of fruit by feeding on whatever foods are available, including tree bark. They possess thickened molar enamel, unlike that of the African apes, which may be an adaptation to eating seeds and unripe fruits (Leighton, 1993). Sumatran orangutans have been seen to use twigs to probe tree holes for insects or honey, sticks (stripped of bark) to dislodge seeds in ripe fruit, and leafy branches to scoop water (McConkey, 2005).

Orangutans share the extended ontogeny of the other great apes; females reach sexual maturity between the ages of 11 and 15 and males reach maturity at 15. The interval between successive births is longer in orangutans than in any other primate, nearly 8 years (Galdikas and Wood, 1990). When females mature, they disperse from their mother's territory to a nearby area to establish themselves as breeding adults. Males disperse more widely and often are alone for long periods (Delgado and van Schaik, 2000).

FIGURE 7.28 Orangutan males are twice the size and weight of females.

Gorillas The largest primates are gorillas, weighing more than 200 kilograms (400 lb) in the wild (Figure 7.29). Gorillas today have a severely fragmented geographic distribution (Figure 7.30). Most of the estimated 80 000 gorillas in equatorial Africa

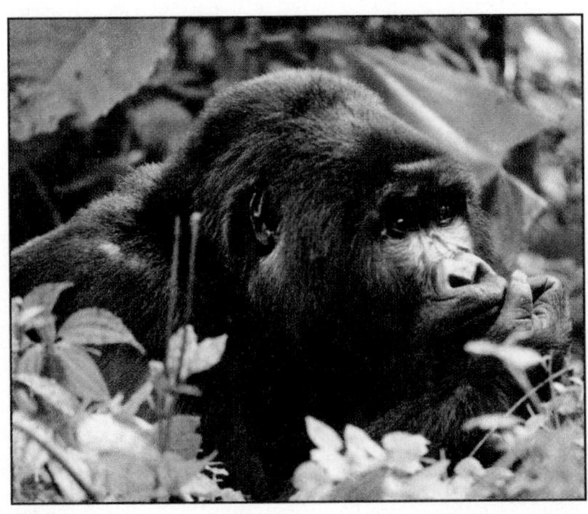

FIGURE 7.29 Gorillas are the largest primate.

FIGURE 7.30 Distribution of the African great apes.

Box 7.1 The Impending Extinction of the Great Apes?

For more than 20 million years, apes have flourished in the tropical forests of the Old World. But today, throughout their geographic distribution in equatorial Africa and Southeast Asia, the great apes are in grave peril of extinction. For the most critically endangered, the orangutan and bonobo, this could mean extinction in the wild within your lifetime. Can this be prevented? Conservation efforts must begin with an understanding of the threats to the endangered species. These threats exist in several key areas:

- *Habitat destruction* The loss of tropical forest habitat is the single greatest factor causing the decline in nonhuman primate populations worldwide (Figure A). From Congo to Indonesia, forest clearing is accelerating, and with it comes the loss of thousands of animal and plant species. Forests are cut by local farmers so they can plant crops, but forests are also cut by government-sanctioned logging companies in many regions.

Recent estimates on the Indonesian island of Sumatra place the loss of orangutan habitat at 80% in the past two decades, and the population declined 45% just from 1993 to 1999 (van Schaik et al., 2001). At current rates of habitat loss, the 20 000 orangutans remaining in the wild face extinction within 15 years.

FIGURE A The destruction of tropical forests, the habitat of living great apes, continues at an alarming rate.

- *Bushmeat* A major cause of population decline among apes in central and western Africa is the bushmeat trade. Bushmeat is simply the meat of any wild animal that is eaten by people.

In Africa, the smoked flesh of gorillas, chimpanzees, and bonobos is highly valued. People have been hunting and eating apes for thousands of years, but recently the pattern has changed. No longer is ape hunting practised only by local villagers trying to put some protein in their children's stomachs. As international logging companies from Europe cut logging roads deep into pristine rain forests, they create a pipeline by which ape carcasses can be easily transported from remote areas. Businessmen in towns and cities pay hunters to send them as many apes as they can kill, the meat of which is sold on the black market, and sometimes in the open market, for several times the price of beef. In Africa, government officials and wealthy people exhibit their affluence by serving ape meat to visitors, occasionally including stunned foreigners.

are lowland gorillas and live in forests across central and western Africa. Lowland gorillas are extraordinarily diverse genetically, and some isolated populations are being elevated to full species status on the basis of the degree of their divergence from other gorillas (Gagneux et al., 1996). In eastern Africa, mountain gorillas also live in a highly fragmented distribution, but their overall numbers are far lower. Only 600 remain in the wild in two mountain ranges, the Virunga Volcanoes and the Bwindi Impenetrable Forest, along the border of Uganda, Rwanda, and the Democratic Republic of the Congo (Box 7.1). The two populations are nearly identical genetically and were separated by forest clearing only in the last several hundred years (Garner and Ryder, 1996; Stanford, 2001). Between the ranges of western lowland and mountain gorillas live eastern lowland gorillas, which occur across a wide elevational range in eastern Congo. Only a few thousand eastern lowland gorillas are believed to remain in the wild.

Gorillas are extremely sexually dimorphic, with males outweighing females by more than 50%. In their mid-teen years, males reach sexual maturity and acquire a grey saddle of hair on their backs, hence the label *silverback* for an adult male gorilla and *blackback* for an adolescent male. Females give birth about every four years. At or after sexual maturity, females tend to migrate to other groups, often in the company of sisters or close female kin.

Apes have withstood low levels of hunting for millennia, but the recent intense pressure, combined with the very slow reproductive rate of the great apes (perhaps one baby every four years), has resulted in dramatic population decline even in forests that have seen little human use. Stopping the bushmeat trade entails not only law enforcement but also a change in cultural values so that Africans do not consider the eating of apes to be a status symbol. Working for the Jane Goodall Institute and the World Wildlife Fund, Christina Ellis (Bachelor of Arts, University of Alberta; Master in Environmental Studies, York University) has worked closely with communities and other stakeholders to improve education efforts and to develop viable alternatives to the bushmeat trade.

- *International zoo, laboratory, and pet trade* Despite increased public awareness of the evils of taking apes from the wild, poaching for the live animal trade still occurs. Hundreds of baby orangutans are caught every year to be sold illegally as pets in Southeast Asia. Some years ago, conservationists estimated that there were more baby orangutans being kept as household pets on the island of Taiwan than were being born in all of Borneo each year. For every baby entering the pet trade alive, many others die before reaching the market.

Biruté Galdikas, a professor at Simon Fraser University, is dedicated not only to understanding the nature of the orangutan but also to preserving its rapidly diminishing natural habitat. She began her field study in Tanjung Puting, Indonesian Borneo, in 1971, and has spent most of each year since then in the field. She is President of Orangutan Foundation International, which sponsors a number of initiatives in Tanjung Putting, including health care and rehabilitation for orangutans that have been confiscated from the pet trade.

Although most labs in Europe and North America now use captive-bred apes, gorillas, and chimpanzees are poached sometimes for their value as laboratory animals in other countries and for sale to unscrupulous zoos.

- *Disease* Emerging viruses, including ebola and anthrax, have recently been discovered in wild ape populations and pose a great threat.

What can we do? The first step is habitat protection. Many conservation organizations work to preserve ape populations. This goal can be achieved only by providing local people with an economic incentive to protect the animals and other forest resources. Because apes are valued as tourist attractions, ecotourism sometimes provides that incentive.

In Bwindi Impenetrable National Park in southwestern Uganda, tourists pay up to $350 per hour to view wild mountain gorillas. A percentage of this fee goes to local villages for building and staffing clinics and funding other entrepreneurial endeavours. Ecotourism does not work everywhere, however, and is highly vulnerable to the political instability that plagues much of Africa. In addition, close contact between tourists and apes increases the risk of disease transmission from us to them. Most wild ape populations have no immunity to flus, colds, and other human diseases that, because of their genetic kinship with us, they easily catch.

Conservationists must provide a simple economic rationale for local people and governments: How will protecting the forest and its inhabitants, rather than destroying them, help people living near great apes? The answer to nonhuman primate protection lies in improving the living conditions of people. Scientists from wealthier countries help to train students in countries where apes live to become conservation leaders themselves. In this way, we hope to help people in Asia and Africa preserve their natural heritage for future generations.

Gorillas live in highly cohesive groups, ranging in size from several animals to several dozen. Males have two reproductive options. They can remain in their birth group, waiting to join the ranking silverback as a breeding adult male someday (or wait for him to die or be driven out). Alternatively, they can emigrate and attempt to find mates elsewhere. Young silverbacks often spend months or years on their own or live in bachelor groups of other silverbacks. Such bachelors wait for opportunities either to take over a male–female group by driving out the resident silverback or to steal a female or two away from an established group. Contrary to the image of a "harem" of females led by a single silverback male, many gorilla groups have two or more silverbacks.

Our view of gorillas as slow-moving, terrestrial leaf-eaters was shaped by the pioneering study of mountain gorillas begun by Dian Fossey in the Virunga Volcanoes. Fossey established a research camp in the mountains of Rwanda and began to document the daily lives of her study subjects: the mountain gorillas ate a diet that was nearly 100% high-fibre, poor-quality plants, for which they foraged slowly, almost exclusively on the ground (Fossey, 1983).

As more recent studies of gorillas elsewhere in Africa have been carried out, it has become clear that most wild gorillas do not behave much like those in the Virungas. Gorillas in other forests, including mountain gorillas in the Bwindi

fission–fusion Form of mating system seen in chimpanzees, bonobos, and a few other primates in which there are temporary subgroups but no stable, cohesive groups.

Impenetrable Forest (Uganda), climb trees readily and often are seen feeding on fruits more than 30 metres (100 ft) from the ground. At Bai Hokou in the Central African Republic, lowland gorillas eat a highly varied diet containing many fruit species and walk nearly 3 kilometres (2 miles) per day in search of food (Remis, 1997b; Goldsmith, 1999). It appears that gorillas all over Africa prefer to eat fruit but can fall back on fibrous leaves as a staple when fruit is not widely available.

Socially, lowland gorillas appear to forage in a more dispersed way than mountain gorillas and may live in less cohesive groups (Remis, 1997a). In some sites in central Africa, lowland gorilla groups use open swampy clearings to gather and feed, even wading into water in search of aquatic plants to eat.

Chimpanzees Chimpanzees (*Pan troglodytes*) and bonobos (*Pan paniscus*) are our closest living relatives. The genetic similarity between a chimpanzee and us is greater than the chimpanzee's evolutionary affinity to a gorilla. The most abundant of the three living African apes, with a total wild population estimated at 150 000 to 200 000, chimpanzees are extraordinarily adaptable animals, found across equatorial Africa from lowland rain forest to nearly open grasslands. Males may weigh up to 68 kg (150 lb) and are 10 to 15% larger and heavier than females.

Unlike most nonhuman primates, chimpanzees do not live in cohesive, stable social groups but rather in a multimale, multifemale community called a **fission–fusion** mating system. A community may number 20 to 120 individuals, in which the only stable unit is a mother–offspring pair. Its members come together in unpredictable social groupings to form foraging subgroups, the size and composition of which seem to be determined by a combination of fruit distribution and the presence of fertile females (Figure 7.31). The community occupies a territory, which is defended by its males with great ferocity.

Within the community, males and females have very different social behaviour patterns. Males tend to be highly social with one another, forming strong, long-lasting coalitions that they use to try to control females, patrol, and hunt. These alliances are not necessarily based on genetic relatedness among the males (Goldberg and Wrangham, 1997). Females travel more independently, apparently in order to avoid feeding competition from other adults. After an 8-month pregnancy, a 4-year infancy, and a prolonged juvenile period, a female chimpanzee reaches sexual maturity at about age 12. After this time, most females begin to visit neighbouring communities, eventually settling there as breeding adults. Males remain in their birth community their entire lives, reaching maturity at 15 years of age. In the wild, chimpanzees live to a maximum age of 45; in captivity some have been known

FIGURE 7.31 Chimpanzees live in complex kin groups in which life-long bonds and individual personalities play key roles, as in human societies.

to reach 60 years of age.

Chimpanzees eat a highly diverse diet that is composed mainly of ripe fruit. They also relish meat, in the form of monkeys, wild pigs, young antelope, and other small animals. In some forests, chimpanzees kill and eat hundreds of animals every year (Stanford, 1998a). Anthropologists find chimpanzee hunting behaviour intriguing as a model for how early hominids may have behaved.

Chimpanzees also eat leaves and other plant products, plus insects such as termites and ants, which they extract from termite mounds using hand-fashioned tools (Figure 7.32) Some West African chimpanzee populations use stones and clubs collected from the forest floor to crack open hard-shelled nuts. Tool use is not genetic, although the intellectual capacity to understand how a tool is used certainly is. Patterns of tool use and meat-eating vary across Africa and are prime examples of another aspect of chimpanzee sophistication: culture (Whiten et al., 1999). More than any animal other than humans, chimpanzees live by learned traditions and pass these traditions on to their offspring.

Bonobos Bonobos (*Pan paniscus*), sometimes called pygmy chimpanzees because of their slightly more slender build, are close relatives of chimpanzees and are classified in the same genus (Figure 7.33). They exhibit more modest sexual dimorphism than the other great apes. Males and females have similar body sizes but males have larger skulls and canine teeth. They occur only in a limited region south of the Congo River in the Democratic Republic of the Congo, mainly in lowland rain forest habitat. Their total population is estimated at only about 25 000. Far less is known about bonobos than about chimpanzees; the first detailed field studies began only in the 1980s.

Bonobos eat a largely fruit diet but rely more on leafy plant material from the forest floor than chimpanzees do. Their more consistently available food supply may allow bonobos to live in larger parties than do chimpanzees (Malenky et al., 1994). Although they hunt and kill other mammals, bonobos do not necessarily eat them. At Lilungu, bonobos have been observed capturing young monkeys and using them as playthings, then releasing them unharmed after they became bored with their prey (Sabater-Pi et al., 1993). At other sites, however, bonobos catch and eat small antelopes (Hohmann and Fruth, 1993).

Like chimpanzees, bonobos live in large, fluid social groupings we call communities. Males remain in the community of their birth, whereas females migrate between communities after sexual maturity. Males engage in border clashes with males from neighbouring communities (Kano, 1992). But there are some striking

FIGURE 7.32 Wild chimpanzees make and use simple tools to obtain food, learning tool-making from one another.

FIGURE 7.33 Bonobos are close relatives of chimpanzees, and of humans.

ecology The study of the interrelationships of plants, animals, and the physical environment in which they live.

differences between bonobo and chimpanzee societies. Unlike female chimpanzees, female bonobos forge strong bonds and use female coalitions to prevent males from dominating them. Immigrant females ally themselves with individual resident females and slowly extend their social network (Furuichi, 1987). Females achieve dominance status in bonobo communities far beyond that of female chimpanzees (Parish, 1996).

Bonobos have become well known to the public because of reports of their hypersexuality. The contrast between their behaviour and that of chimpanzees has led to a debate over which species is the better model for how early humans may have behaved. Bonobos are said to be closer in sexual behaviour and biology to humans than any other animal. Whether this is fully accurate has been questioned by a number of researchers.

In addition to their interesting behaviour patterns in the wild, bonobos have been the subjects of exciting research on the origins of human language. Kanzi, a male bonobo at Georgia State University, understands several hundred words in spoken English and communicates using a symbol board (Savage-Rumbaugh and Lewin, 1994).

PRIMATE ECOLOGY

It's important to remember that primates are first and foremost parts of ecosystems. A revolution has taken place in the way we see primates and other animals in their natural habitat, as a result of advances in the field of ecology. **Ecology** is the study of the interrelationships of animals, plants, and their physical environment. The environment provides the template on which natural selection moulds behaviour. At the same time, primates influence the ecology of many tropical forests, as dispersers of seeds and even as pollinators of flowering plants. Primate behaviour evolved in direct response to environmental pressures, and we can understand most aspects of primate behaviour only in the context of the natural environment in which the primate evolved.

Several key ecological factors have shaped the evolution of nonhuman primates and continue to shape them today. Finding and eating food is a constant, chronic concern that occupies much of the day for nonhuman primates. They are bound by the same equation that faces all other wild animals: The energy that is expended to find food (calories burned) must be balanced by the quantity (calories consumed) and quality (nutrients such as fats, proteins, and carbohydrates) of the food eaten (Figure 7.34). This need is even greater for females because of the physical cost of reproduction. To understand how nonhuman primates live, we must therefore understand something about the nature and distribution of their favourite foods and how that affects aspects of their behaviour. In this section we consider primate ecology, which will allow us, in Chapter 8, to understand how primate social systems may be adapted to the environment.

FIGURE 7.34 Like all animals, primates must balance their calories expended searching for food with calories, protein, fat, and other nutrients obtained.

DIET

Most primates are *herbivores*, living largely on a plant food diet. Exceptions to this pattern are many of the lower primates, which eat insects as a substantial portion of the diet, and a few higher primates (including humans) that also eat meat. Only one primate group is entirely carnivorous: the tarsier of Southeast Asia, which subsists on insects, lizards, frogs, and other small animals. For the rest, much of the diet is composed of two items: fruits and leaves.

We tend to think of the natural world in a very human-centric way. But for a moment, consider a tropical forest from the point of view of a tree. As a tree, you produce several products that are highly valued by the animals with which you share the forest: fruit, leaves, flowers, seeds, and so forth. All around you there are birds, monkeys, and small mammals that hunger after the fruit you produce. There are also millions of leaf-eating insects, monkeys, and other animals that eat your leafy foliage. But fruit and leaves have very different values to the potential herbivore. Leaves are the factories of a tropical tree; they take in sunlight and synthesize energy for the tree by the process of photosynthesis. For this reason, if a horde of insects or leaf-eating monkeys comes along and eats all its leaves, the tree will be unable to produce energy or obtain the nutrients it needs. At best it will have to endure a difficult period until new leaves can be grown, and at worst it could die. So ecologists predict that natural selection should endow trees with the means to protect their leaves.

Fruits have a very different value. They are the vessels that hold the seeds, which are the reproductive opportunities for the tree—its embryos for the next generation. Therefore, it's beneficial for the fruit of a tree to be eaten by animals, carried away somewhere, and then excreted out so that its seeds can germinate on the forest floor some distance away. Whereas trees and leaf-eaters, or **folivores**, are in a constant evolutionary battle, trees and fruit-eaters, called *frugivores*, are in a long-running symbiosis. So ecologists predict that natural selection should build traits into fruit that encourage frugivores to seek out the fruit crop and eat it.

There is abundant evidence that this is exactly what has happened. Consider how you choose a peach in the market that is ripe and ready to eat. First you look at it; is it orange and red, or still green? Then you touch it; is it soft, or still rock hard? Finally, you may smell it; does it have a pleasant, sweet smell? Wild primates use exactly the same criteria for choosing their fruits in tropical forests. And all these qualities—bright colour, soft texture, and a good smell—were built into fruits by natural selection to convince frugivorous animals that they are delicious, nutritious, and ready to be eaten. These signals show a foraging primate that the fruit contains high levels of carbohydrate in the form of sugars, providing a caloric boost for an active day of foraging. Certainly brightly coloured fruit did not evolve solely in response to primates; many birds eat fruit too, and their ancestors predate those of modern primates. But like birds, many primates are colour-visioned fruit foragers.

Fruit-eating primates reap the benefit of a carbohydrate-rich diet, but at a cost. Fruits are temporary tree products that ripen and rot quickly, so fruit availability is far less predictable than leaf availability. And fruit is sought after by a wide range of animals because of its high caloric content. A primate must be able to efficiently locate fruits and then compete successfully for access to them. Fruits also tend to be patchily distributed on the tree.

Leaves are an entirely different story when it comes to foraging. Leaves are found everywhere in a tropical forest, so you might think all a monkey has to do is reach out and pluck its breakfast, but a tropical forest is not the cornucopia of food that it might appear. Leaves tend to be poor sources of nutrients and calories compared with fruits, but they can contain large amounts of protein. Because leaves are such a valuable and dependable resource, trees protect them against folivores in a variety ways. First, many leaves are coated with bristles, spines, or hairs that make them difficult or painful to ingest. A primate must also have a digestive system designed to cope with *fibre*. Young tender leaves contain minimal fibre because the cell walls in each leaf have not yet built up layers of cellulose and hemicellulose that later become the structural support of the plant (Figure 7.35). Mature leaves are tougher and highly fibrous.

In addition to physical barriers, folivorous primates must cope with chemical defences that plants put into their leaves. Leaves often contain an array of chemicals, called **secondary compounds** (because they are the byproducts of plant metabolism), which are toxic or at least indigestible to a primate. We're all familiar with secondary compounds; the reason tea becomes bitter when brewed too long is the presence of *tannins* in the tea leaves. Alkaloids and phenols are other secondary compounds commonly found in tropical forest foliage. The presence of secondary

folivores Animals who eat a diet composed mainly of leaves, or foliage.

secondary compounds Toxic chemical compounds found in the leaves of many plants which the plants use as a defence against leaf-eating animals.

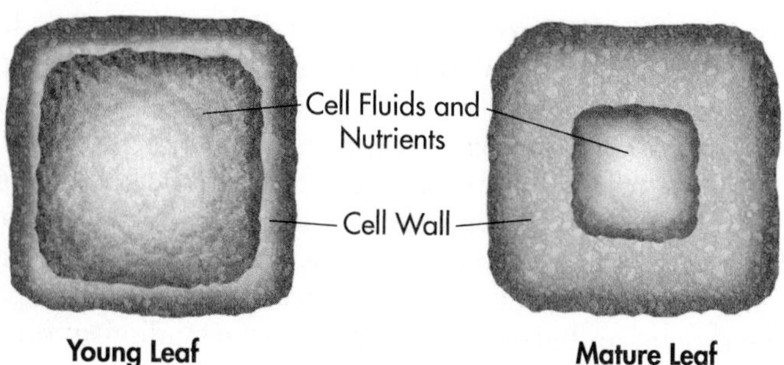

FIGURE 7.35 Comparison of a tender and mature leaf. As leaves mature, they become fibre-filled and harder to digest.

compounds is greatest in mature trees growing in poor soil, apparently because the tree needs to protect its leaves most in circumstances where nutrients for new growth are most limited.

THE CYCLES OF A TROPICAL FOREST

Tropical trees do not influence primate behaviour only by the nutritional content of their food products. The distribution of foods is also profoundly important. Many tropical forest trees have *asynchronous cycles*, meaning that while one individual tree is laden with ripe fruit, the other trees of the same species standing nearby have no fruit at all. This is apparently an evolved strategy to protect trees by preventing predators ranging from insects to monkeys from homing in on a whole stand of trees and devouring all of their leaves in one swoop.

The diversity of tree species and the existence of asynchronous cycles in the tropics mean that wild primates must know their habitats intimately to find food. Climate seasonality is another very important dietary factor to primates because they must locate tender new leaves and ripening fruit before other animals in the forest find it.

In addition to leaves and fruit, most primates eat at least small quantities of other foods. Many species eat insects and other small invertebrates such as spiders, grubs, scorpions, and (for those living near water) crayfish and crabs. And a few species, primarily the marmosets and tamarins, rely on another source: the resin that flows from tree trunks. A final source of nutrition for wild primates is the meat of other mammals. Chimpanzees are the most avid hunters of mammalian prey, but many other species hunt as well.

In general, the largest-bodied primates rely the least on insect prey, although a few primates, such as chimpanzees and capuchin monkeys, forage for insects very intensively and at times consume large numbers of them. Gorillas don't eat many insects, and very small-bodied primates rarely eat large quantities of leafy matter. This is because of the time and energy needed to make a living on these diets in relation to the time and energy needed to properly digest leaves, fruits, and live prey. The very largest primates tend to be folivorous, although there are exceptions.

DIET AND ACTIVITY BUDGETS

activity budget The pattern of waking, eating, moving, socializing, and sleeping that all nonhuman primates engage in each day.

In nature, there are only so many hours of daylight during which a diurnal primate can make its living. A primate's **activity budget** allows it to compensate for calories expended with calories consumed. Diurnal primates forage during the day, nocturnal primates come out of hiding at night, and *crepuscular* primates forage at dawn and dusk. *Cathemeral* primates have irregular active periods during both the day and night. Each activity period has its share of foods available and predators lurking to catch unwary prey.

Activity budgets are tightly linked to dietary quality. Primates that live on high-fibre, low-calorie diets also tend to be more sedentary than those living on a high-fruit diet.

As you can see, primates are a highly diverse group of mammals that are subject to many of the same evolutionary and ecological principles that guide the lives of other mammals. However, nonhuman primates have two adaptations—sociality and large brains—that set them apart from nearly all other animals. The social complexity of the hominoids does not apply to all taxa. We see it to its greatest extent in chimpanzees, bonobos, and human societies. Anthropologists study ape behaviour because, in addition to being intrinsically fascinating, apes are among the most intelligent animals with which we share the planet. Only in great apes do we see tool technologies that resemble simple versions of human tool industries, lethal aggression between communities that resembles human warfare, and cognitive development, including language acquisition, that parallels that of children.

In the next chapter, we will examine nonhuman primate social behaviour and cognition to see what they tell us about human evolution.

SUMMARY

1. **What characteristics distinguish nonhuman primates from other mammals?**

   Primates share a suite of characteristics: grasping hand and opposable thumb, stereoscopic vision, single births, sociality, large brain–body size ratio, extended ontogeny, visually oriented daytime activity, nails instead of claws, and an enclosed bony eye orbit.

2. **What are the main hypotheses that account for the origin of primates?**

   The arboreal hypothesis was the first theory put forward to explain primate origins. This centred on the role of stereo vision and the grasping hand in life in the trees. The leading alternative theory is the visual predation hypothesis, which is based on the likely predatory behaviour of the earliest nonhuman primates.

3. **Why is the diversity of lemurs on Madagascar today only a shadow of lemur diversity in the past?**

   The largest lemur species went extinct not long after human arrival on Madagascar about 1500 to 2000 years ago. The species found there today are mainly the smaller species, presumably less desirable as food and so less hunted.

4. **What is the taxonomic position of the tarsier?**

   The tarsier is a haplorhine, linking it to the anthropoid primates, but it retains many prosimian characters, such as a combination of nails and claws on its feet. Therefore, it may represent an evolutionary bridge between the prosimian and anthropoid primates.

5. **What is an ape?**

   An ape is an anthropoid primate with a suspensory shoulder anatomy that allows brachiation. Apes also lack tails, have large brains, and exhibit a highly elaborated degree of social complexity.

6. **Why is it a mistake to think of a tropical rain forest as a cornucopia of food available for wild nonhuman primates?**

   Plant foods in tropical forests are protected by a variety of adaptations, from high fibre content to bristles to chemical defences. In addition, tropical forest trees often produce leaves and fruit at different times, making it difficult for nonhuman primates to predict when they can harvest the tree's products.

7. **Why would primates of different species associate together despite increased feeding competition?**

   Primates of different species may capitalize on the food-finding and predator detection abilities of other species, which may outweigh the disadvantages of being in a larger group.

CRITICAL THINKING QUESTIONS

1. We say that primates are the most highly social animals on Earth. But many animals, from fish to birds to hoofed mammals, live in enormous herds, flocks, or schools that are far larger than any primate group. What is the difference between those sorts of groups and those in which nonhuman primates live?

2. Chimpanzees and bonobos are very similar anatomically but quite different behaviourally. Based on what you learned about species concepts in Chapter 5, should they be considered separate species or merely variants of a single species? Why?

3. Why should we consider the primate body plan to be a series of evolutionary compromises?

KEY TERMS

metatheria
prototheria
eutheria
strepsirhine (Strepsirhini)
haplorhine (Haplorhini)
prosimian
anthropoid
arboreal hypothesis
visual predation hypothesis
dental arcade
nocturnal
diurnal
neocortex
ontogeny
sociality
Playtrrhini
prehensile tail
Catarrhini
hylobatid (Hylobatidae)
pongid (Pongidae)
hominid (Hominidae)
brachiation
frugivorous
fission–fusion
ecology
folivores
secondary compounds
activity budget

SUGGESTED READING

Caldecott, Julian, and Miles, Lera (editors). (2005). *World Atlas of Great Apes and Their Conservation*. University of California Press, Berkeley, CA.

Cheney, Dorothy, and Seyfarth, Robert M. (1991). *How Monkeys See the World*. University of Chicago Press, Chicago, IL.

Goodall, Jane. (1986). *Chimpanzees of Gombe*. Harvard University Press, Cambridge, MA.

Stanford, Craig. (2001). *Significant Others*. Basic Books, New York, NY.

Strier, Karen. (2003). *Primate Behavioral Ecology*, 2nd edition. Allyn & Bacon, Boston, MA.

Chapter 8

Primate Behaviour

Chapter Outline

I was checking my watch and entering the date in my notebook when I heard the telltale sound of branches snapping. I whirled around. The leaves of a large tree just off the trail were shaking. I spied an orangutan female with an infant on her shoulder rapidly climbing up the trunk. She must have seen me first, because she began moving away, high in the trees. But I was on dry ground, not in the swamp or on the river, which meant I could follow her.

"Beth," as we named her, showed her displeasure at our presence by dropping branches, hooting, and kiss-squeaking, but she did not flee, as other wild orangutans had. Rather she stopped a short distance away and began to eat something unidentifiable high in the tree. Beth was a medium-sized female orangutan, weighing perhaps seventy or eighty pounds. Like Alice [another orangutan] who inhabited the same area, she had high, wide cheekbones, but with a distinctive furrow under one eye. Her face was placid, almost expressionless. Her infant, whom we named "Bert," was a small ball of orange fuzz on her shoulders; she herself was dark red. After staring at us intently for more than a minute, Beth began to construct a small day nest, bending and twisting branches into a circular platform and covering it with a cushion of leafy twigs. Sitting in her nest, Beth continued to vocalize and shake branches at us. Occasionally she stopped to bend a new branch into her nest. Then, less than fifteen minutes later, she left the day nest and moved slowly on through the trees.

During the ten hours we followed Beth that day, I recorded the beginning and end of each bout of activity. Noting the time, I wrote down everything she ate, what the fruit or bark looked like, how she had extracted or prepared this food, how high she was in the trees, how far she travelled between various fruit trees and vines, and her interaction with her infant son, filling nearly thirty pages of my notebook.

That first day, Beth travelled less than half a mile. Nonetheless, I was exhausted. The intense concentration was enormously wearying. My neck ached from continuously looking up into the treetops. But I didn't dare take my eyes off her for fear I would miss something important.

I was overjoyed: for the first time I had followed a wild orangutan for an entire day.

—Biruté Galdikas, *Reflections of Eden* (1995)

Watching nonhuman primates is one thing, understanding their behaviour is another. But observation of behaviour is at the heart of the subfield of biological anthropology known as *primatology*, as pioneering Canadian researcher Biruté Galdikas understood.

Primates are intrinsically fascinating animals that serve as illustrations of evolutionary principles of natural selection, adaptive radiation, convergent evolution, and sexual selection. They also inform us about human evolution, offering a window into how early humans may have behaved. In this chapter we will consider how biological anthropologists study nonhuman primates and their social evolution. We will see that evolutionary principles that you learned in Chapter 5, such as natural selection and sexual selection, play key roles in shaping primate behaviour. You'll also examine the diversity of societies in which nonhuman primates may live and explore the reasons these societies evolved the way they did. And you will read about some of the current controversies over the form and function of primate social behaviour.

STUDYING PRIMATES

As we saw in Chapter 7, *sociality* is the most fundamental primate behavioural adaptation (Figure 8.1). It is the hallmark of nearly all the anthropoid primates, and its study is an essential component of nearly all nonhuman primate behaviour research. Primatologists want to learn why nonhuman primates are social. To do this they study the costs and benefits of group living and examine how the same evolutionary processes that promoted sociality in nonhuman primates may have promoted the emergence of humankind.

We can study nonhuman primates in several different settings, each of which strongly influences the sort of research that is possible. A **captive study** allows us to closely observe a nonhuman primate group every day—subjects won't hide in dense trees for hours on end—and to study individuals that have well-recorded life histories. We often study captive populations over many generations and know their kin network. We can also manipulate the study group: The researcher might move a new male into the social group to observe the effect on the rest of the group. This opportunity makes behavioural experiments possible that we cannot usually achieve in the field. The downside of studying nonhuman primates in captivity is obvious: The animals are kept in highly unnatural settings rather than the forests in which their behaviours evolved, and so we cannot expect to see natural patterns of behaviour. Enforced proximity leads to higher levels of aggression, sex, and affiliation than we would see in the same animals in the wild. The artificial food supply also means we cannot conduct ecological studies. A valuable use of captive studies is to confirm and refine the results of studies done in the wild.

captive study Primate behaviour study conducted in a zoo, laboratory, or other enclosed setting.

semi–free-ranging Primate behaviour study conducted in a large area that is enclosed or isolated in some way so the population is captive.

Some nonhuman primate studies are conducted in a more spacious **semi–free-ranging** environment. Very large enclosures, or even small islands, sometimes have nonhuman primate populations. The Arashiyama West population of Japanese macaques in Texas, is one example (Box 8.1). The animals in a semi–free-ranging setting can establish territories, form their own groups, and forage for food, even though they are in captivity. Because they are confined (though in a large area), we can easily study kinship and follow many generations of the animals. This setting is a compromise between the confines of captivity and an entirely natural field study.

FIGURE 8.1 Sociality is the most fundamental behavioural adaptation of the primates.

Box 8.1 The Arashiyama West–East Primate Project

Primatologists began studying a group of Japanese macaques (*Macaca fuscata*) in Arashiyama, near Kyoto, Japan, in 1954. More than a decade later, the group separated along rank and kinship units and formed two groups, one of which began to cause trouble by raiding nearby gardens. So that the animals would not have to be killed, American scientists working at Arashiyama arranged for the group to be translocated to a ranch in Texas in 1972. The Texas group, which numbered approximately 150 monkeys, was given free range over a 42-hectare (104-acre) enclosure of brush land and a number of studies of the monkeys' biology and social relationships began. Professor Linda Fedigan of the University of Calgary was involved in this project from the time of translocation in 1972 until data collection ceased in 1996. She spent over three years living with the macaques. Her research with this population of monkeys has focused since then on analysis of the data that were collected over the 24-year period, especially the data on reproductive and life history patterns in females. For example, Fedigan and Professor Mary Pavelka (University of Calgary) and their students have studied the reproductive biology and behaviour of these macaques, including whether or not menopause is experienced in these monkeys in the same way that it is experienced by human females (O'Neill et al., 2004a, b; Fedigan and Pavelka, 2007). They found that females in the population lost their reproductive ability very late in their life span, at a time when they exhibited outward signs of weakness and deterioration, compared to human females who experience menopause during a healthy middle age. They concluded that the loss of reproductive ability in Japanese macaques is not the same thing as menopause as experienced by human females. They have also studied the roles of "grandmothers" among these monkeys and found that the presence of a living mother was linked to improved reproductive success among female macaques, and the presence of a living grandmother was associated with improved survivorship of infant macaques (Pavelka et al., 2002).

FIGURE A Japanese macaques.

A modern study of primate behaviour called **field study** is conducted in the habitat in which the species evolved. Only in the field can researchers see patterns of behaviour that evolved in response to environmental variables (Figure 8.2). As we saw earlier, the interplay between genes and behaviour depends on a third critical variable: the physical environment. Studies of nonhuman primates in the wild focus on various aspects of ecology, such as diet and its influence on grouping patterns and social behaviour; *positional behaviour*, the relationship between locomotor morphology and the physical environment; and social interactions within and among primate groups.

field study Primate behaviour study conducted in the habitat in which the primate naturally occurs.

The earliest field researchers spent only a few days or weeks watching nonhuman primates in the wild, and little effort was made to collect data systematically. Jane Goodall (1968) was the first researcher to immerse herself in the lives of the animals she was studying. She learned intimate details of their lives and followed her subjects year after year (Figure 8.3). What Goodall did in the early 1960s is now the norm for primatologists; graduate students typically spend 1 to 2 years

FIGURE 8.2 Field research on free-living primates allows primatologists to study patterns of behaviour in the setting where the behaviour evolved.

living in the habitat of the primates for a doctoral thesis project. Many field studies of more than 10 years' duration have been carried out. In extended studies, multiple primate generations can be followed and individuals' lives more fully understood. Studies of nonhuman primate demography have revealed aspects of the evolution of life histories and the ways in which long-term patterns of mating success are related to reproductive success. Primatologists have also added new research tools to their arsenal: paternity tests using DNA from hair follicles, feces, or urine; studies of endocrine influences on behaviour using hormones extracted from feces or urine; and studies of nonhuman primate communication using sophisticated sound recording equipment (Figure 8.4).

There are significant difficulties in studying nonhuman primates in the wild. First, the primatologist must accustom the animals to his or her presence. This is a slow process that can take months or even years. Only once habituated can the primates be identified as individuals and observed closely. However, habituation may also allow other people, including poachers intending to kill the animals, to approach. Therefore, habituation can be undertaken only in areas where the animals' lives will not be placed in danger should the scientists pack up their projects and go home. And even well-habituated primates are difficult to watch because so much of their behaviour takes place behind dense foliage and rocks or in tall trees. Some nonhuman primates have huge home ranges, and just locating the

FIGURE 8.3 Jane Goodall pioneered the modern approach to studying primates in the wild, involving close-up observation of known individuals over many months.

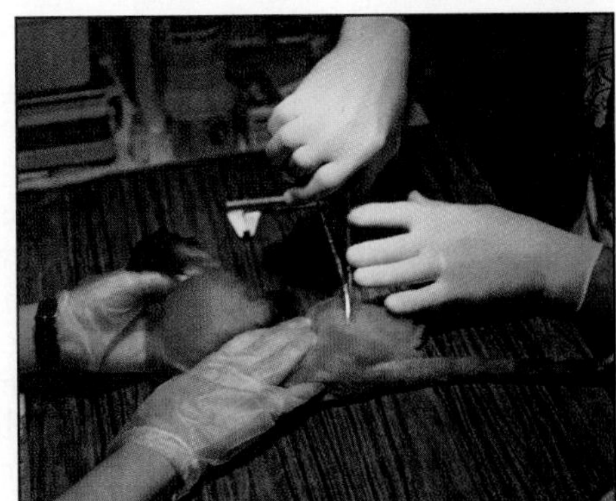

FIGURE 8.4 Modern primate study sometimes involves high-tech methods. This golden lion tamarin is having a battery changed in its radio transmitter collar.

polygynous Mating system consisting of at least one male and more than one female.

group every day can be a challenge. A year spent in the wild watching monkeys may produce a small fraction of the observation hours that a scientist could obtain in a zoo in one month. And the sort of manipulations of the social and physical environment that can be done easily in captivity, such as diet changes, are rare in the wild.

WHY ARE NONHUMAN PRIMATES SOCIAL?

Primatologists choose their study subjects according to the evolutionary principles they intend to investigate. As we saw in Chapter 7, one of the most fundamental primate adaptations is sociality, and the reasons for the diversity of societies among nonhuman primates is a major area of research. A primatologist wanting to understand how monogamy works in nonhuman primates, with an eye toward understanding the origins of monogamy in human societies, might study a monogamous primate such as the gibbon. The gibbon certainly is an animal of great intrinsic beauty and interest, but to a primatologist it is also an illustration of how natural and sexual selection operate in the wild.

THE PARADOX OF SOCIALITY

Nonhuman primates, like all other social mammals, tend to behave in ways that maximize their individual fitness. But this creates a paradox: Why would any animal live in a group if the bottom line, evolutionarily, is individual mating success? Group living is an anthropoid adaptation, and it may provide the individual monkey or ape with access to three basic necessities: mates, food, and protection from predators. Each of these benefits has, however, a significant downside.

Access to Mates Access to multiple potential mates is an obvious benefit of living in a group rather than in pairs or alone. Nonhuman primates exhibit a variety of grouping patterns, but in each mating system male and female goals are the same: enhancing their reproductive success. The behavioural strategies each sex uses to achieve this goal, however, differ markedly.

Group life may provide access to mates, but it also means that males must compete for mating. Among nonhuman primates that live in large social groups, enormous energy and time are consumed in the quest for mating success, and many males lose out. When access to a female is at stake, male baboons are more willing to engage in highly aggressive behaviour toward one another, inflicting injury (Figure 8.5). Males also form alliances when females are ovulating and sexually receptive, and if a male is not in an alliance his ability to obtain matings may suffer.

The intensity of male–male competition, and the importance of female choice of male traits, is also reflected in the level of sexual dimorphism we see among primates. Species in which males compete aggressively for females tend to feature high degrees of sexual dimorphism because male size and strength help to determine mating success. Species exhibiting sexual dimorphism in body size also tend to live in **polygynous** groups, which have multiple females living with either one or multiple males (Figure 8.6). Monogamous and solitary species tend to be less dimorphic. In baboons, for instance, males compete fiercely with other males for mating opportunities and are about 30% larger and heavier than females. Gibbons, on the other hand, live in monogamous pair bonds and are not dimorphic with respect to body size. There are exceptions to this pattern, however, such as the highly dimorphic but largely solitary orangutan.

FIGURE 8.5 Male competition can be fierce. This male baboon has bite wounds suffered in competition with other males.

Feeding Competition Primates live in communities with a host of other animals, both primates and nonprimates. In many tropical forests, when a large tree bears ripe fruit it becomes an arboreal banquet table for a wide variety of animals, both mammals and birds, day and night. Exploiting the food-finding abilities of other

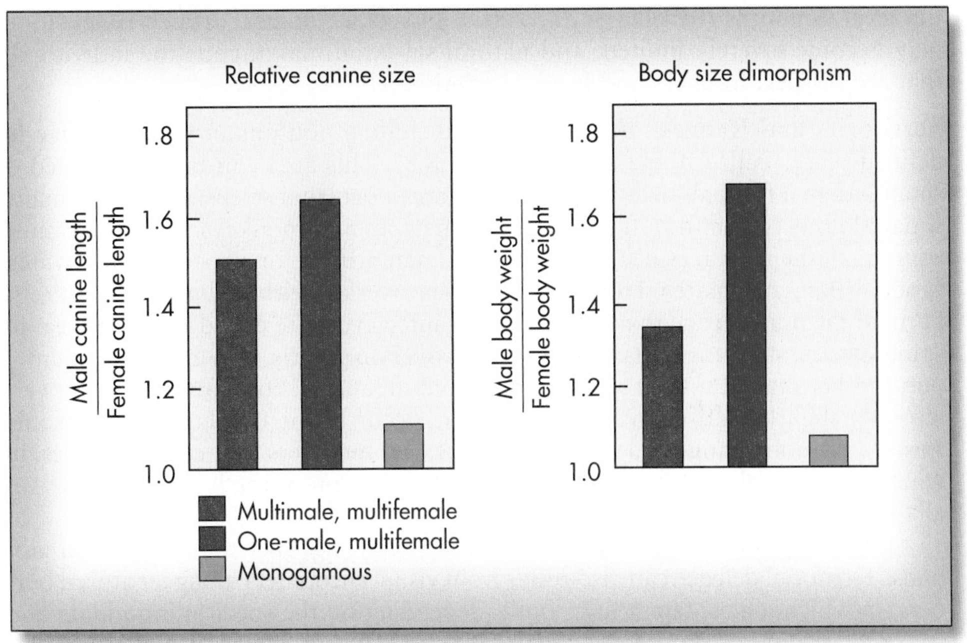

FIGURE 8.6 The most polygynous primates live in groups with many more females than males. In such species the degree of sexual dimorphism tends to be pronounced.

group members to find food oneself is one benefit of group life. But the feeding and foraging benefits of living in a social group are offset by the need to compete for food with group mates once food is found. Much evidence supports the notion that feeding competition strongly affects group life in nonhuman primates. Females are particularly dependent on the availability of food resources in their habitat because they must nourish themselves adequately to bear the costs of reproduction.

Feeding competition is more intense when the quality of the food is high, and especially when the food is distributed in small, scattered parcels that concentrate feeding at a few spots. When a group of monkeys enters a fruit tree, they all want to eat the ripest fruit. But inevitably, higher-ranking animals, older animals, and males tend to control and monopolize the food at the expense of smaller, weaker, lower-ranking animals and females. This direct squabbling over food is called *contest feeding competition* and is very common among frugivorous group-living primates. Although contest competition usually is considered an aspect of intragroup competition, it can also occur between groups.

When feeding competition occurs but enough food exists so that every animal nevertheless gets some food, *scramble feeding competition* has occurred. Folivorous primates are often scramble competitors: Leaves are everywhere, and everybody will find some, even if some animals find more than others. Primate species that practise scramble competition often lack rigid dominance hierarchies, perhaps because there is less pressure to compete intensely when food is evenly distributed. Scramble competition often characterizes intragroup competition in folivorous primate groups.

Some primate ecologists believe that feeding competition matters mainly when the environment takes a turn for the worse. Natural food shortages have a severe effect on wild primate populations. A long-term study of ring-tailed lemurs in Beza Mahafaly Reserve, Madagascar, by Lisa Gould of the University of Victoria (Figure 8.7) and her colleagues showed that infant mortality reached 80% during a particularly harsh two-year drought (Gould et al., 1999, 2003). Similarly, University of Calgary primatologist Mary Pavelka found that when Hurricane Iris levelled much of the forest, a population of black howler monkeys in Belize was reduced in size by 42% and experienced widespread social disorganization

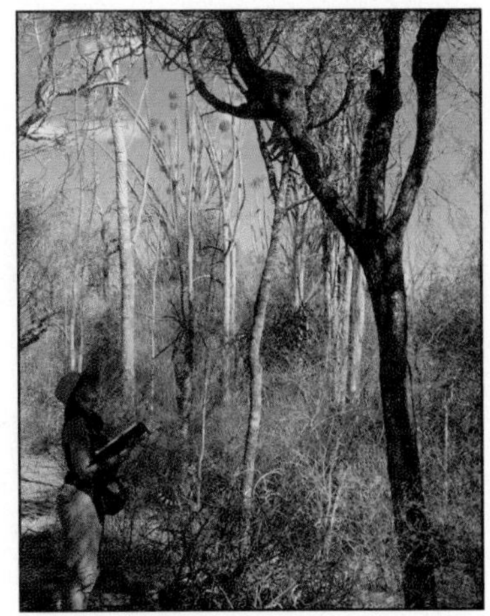

FIGURE 8.7 Lisa Gould studies ring-tailed lemurs in their natural habitat on the island of Madagascar.

home range The spatial area used by a primate group.

core area The part of a home range that is most intensively used.

territory The part of a home range that is defended against other members of the same species.

for several months (Pavelka et al., 2003). In such ecological crunch times, food may become severely limited, and natural selection may favour the individuals that are the best foragers and food competitors.

Territories and Ranges All mammals, including nonhuman primates, live in defined places called **home ranges** (Figure 8.8). This area can be very limited—smaller than a football field in the case of some nocturnal strepsirhines—or many square kilometres (miles) in the case of some apes and monkeys. The range must contain all the resources needed by a nonhuman primate or a social group: water, food, shelter, and mates. Home ranges often overlap, either slightly or entirely. Parts of the home range that are used most intensively are called the **core area.** In some species, such as gorillas, home ranges overlap greatly, and groups encounter one another often. In other species, such as chimpanzees, community ranges overlap only slightly, and aggressive encounters occur in the overlap zone. In some species, the home range is defended against other members of the same species, in which case we call it a **territory**. The defended portion of the home range is usually the part in which critical resources are located.

Territorial defence can take the form of vocalizing, such as the songs of gibbons. Territorial defence can also result from visual encounters along territorial borders, in which males, females, or both (depending on the species) intimidate and chase the potential intruders. Among many Old World monkeys, females rather than males engage in territorial disputes. In some species, territorial disputes may be settled through physical contact. Male chimpanzees, for example, band together to patrol the territorial boundaries on a regular basis and may attack and attempt to kill any chimpanzee, male or female, that is found encroaching on their land.

Why are primates so territorial? Primatologists have spent years trying to understand the key resources nonhuman primate groups are willing to protect. We believe that nonhuman primates defend their home ranges when food resources are worth defending because of their high nutritional value or when males can control females through their defence of territory. But territories typically are defended only when it is energetically possible and worthwhile to do so.

Mate defence territoriality is a different equation. Females in many nonhuman primate species use their habitat to maximize their intake of food for themselves and their offspring. Since males are concerned mainly with where females are, what might appear to be male defence of a territory for the sake of protecting a relished

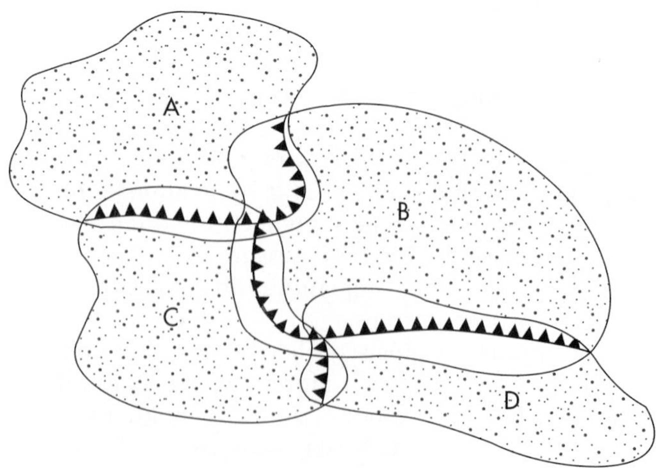

FIGURE 8.8 Primates use their space in a variety of ways: home ranges, core areas, and territories.

fruit tree may in fact be territorial defence aimed at keeping males from other groups away from their females.

Predation Nonhuman primates in the wild face the difficult challenge of finding food while avoiding attacks by predators. Failing to find food on a given afternoon will leave a monkey hungry the next day, but failing to avoid an attack by an eagle or leopard will leave it dead or injured. So we should expect that nonhuman primates have evolved behavioural defences against predators. Actually observing predation is difficult because the predators are stealthy and usually nocturnal and solitary (Figure 8.9). Most often a member of a nonhuman primate group being studied disappears one day, and the researcher has no idea whether disease, accidental death, or a predator was responsible.

Despite a lack of field observations, we can make a few generalizations about predation. For example, small-bodied nonhuman primates are more vulnerable to predation than are larger species. In Madagascar, owls have been reported to kill up to one-quarter of the mouse lemur population each year (Goodman et al., 1993). Even a much lower predation rate could be a major source of mortality in a population of monkeys. Also, many nonhuman primate species exhibit behaviours that appear to have evolved in response to the threat of predation. Alarm calls are often given when a predator approaches, and experimental studies using loudspeakers to play the calls of leopards and eagles have shown that monkeys respond in a variety of ways. Vervet monkeys studied in Amboseli National Park, Kenya, by Dorothy Cheney and Robert Seyfarth (1991) give alarm calls that vary depending on the type of predator spotted; different calls are given for eagles, leopards, and pythons.

Nonhuman primates also tend to be very vigilant, scanning the ground and trees around them continually while feeding. Many studies of primates and other mammals have shown that animals of many species spend less time scanning their surroundings when they live in larger groups, which suggests a greater margin of safety when more eyes are present to look for danger.

In some nonhuman primate species, social groups actually mob predators, counterattacking in the hope of persuading the predator that hunting them is not worth the trouble or risk of injury. Among the small South American white-faced saki, smaller predators (small hawks, cats, and snakes) evoked a mobbing response. Faced with larger, more dangerous predators such as eagles, the monkeys retreated quickly into dense thickets and froze to avoid detection (Gleason and Norconk, 2002).

FIGURE 8.9 Primates face a wide variety of predators in the wild, including birds of prey.

One of the few cases in which we can directly observe predation on nonhuman primates is in African forests in which chimpanzees prey on other nonhuman primates. In Gombe National Park, Tanzania, chimpanzees kill up to 18% of the red colobus population living in their home range in some years (Stanford, 1998a). Red colobuses living in large groups have a lower individual risk of being captured by a chimpanzee, and groups containing many adult males are at less risk than groups with only a few males, because adult male colobuses mount a fierce counterattack when chimpanzees attack them.

The pattern of predation on colobuses also depended on where the colobuses lived relative to the border of the territory of the chimpanzee community: in the chimpanzees' core area, predation on colobus monkeys was intense, whereas hunting was much less common toward the periphery of the chimpanzees' community territory. Chimpanzee predation was overall such a major source of colobus mortality that the colobus population would have been in serious decline at Gombe were it not for the fact that some years predation was infrequent.

PRIMATE COMMUNITIES

If you were to walk through some tropical forests, you would see not one but many species of primates. In the Congo Basin of central Africa or the Amazon Basin of Peru, it's possible to see more than a dozen primate species in 0.4 hectare (1 acre) of forest. If you were to take a walk through the same forest at night, you would see a different, nocturnal community of primates. With so many closely related and often morphologically similar primates sharing the same forest, why isn't there more intense competition among them for food and other resources? The answer is that there is or was competition in the evolutionary past of the species. Ecological theory predicts that when two or more organisms with very similar needs are sympatric, sharing the same space, they will diverge from one another in some critical aspect of their *niche*, or ecological role. For example, two monkeys that seem to eat the same foods will be found to eat different diets when food is scarce. One species might forage high in trees, whereas the other finds its food on the ground. Without such *niche separation*, species would drive one another into extinction far more often than they are observed to (Figure 8.10).

FIGURE 8.10 Ranomafana National Park, Madagascar, home to multiple species of lemurs that divide up their forest resources.

Niche divergence occurs among all primates that are sympatric, and such divergence often is evident only during ecological crunch times. What's more, it can be very difficult to demonstrate feeding competition in the wild—simply overlapping strongly with another species' ecology is not evidence that the two species compete—so field studies more often record the nature of ecological overlap than the occurrence of ecological competition. Gorillas and chimpanzees share forests across central Africa, and both species prefer a diet heavy in ripe fruit. But during lean seasons, gorillas fall back on fibrous plants as their staple, while chimpanzees continue to forage widely for fruit. Although the diets of the two ape species overlap extensively, direct contest competition over food is rare (Stanford and Nkurunungi, 2003).

Some primates form *polyspecific groups*, made up of two, three, or more species that travel and feed together for part or all of each day. The antipredator benefits of foraging in such a group are obvious; more eyes on the lookout mean safer and better foraging. Feeding competition is lessened by the fact that the participating species usually have key differences in some aspect of their diet or feeding strategies. The interactions between primate species can be as diverse as the primate species themselves, depending once again on the habitat and its ecology.

social system The grouping pattern in which a primate species lives, including its size and composition, evolved in response to natural and sexual selection pressures.

Types of Nonhuman Primate Societies

Nonhuman primates number only 250 species but exhibit great diversity in grouping patterns. We call the type of group in which nonhuman primates live their **social system** (Figure 8.11). Earlier generations of primatologists viewed social groups as male-centred; they believed that females wanted to live with or near males, and so males determined the form that social systems took; however, the consensus today is that females have evolved strategies, behavioural and ecological, to cope with the need to balance limited food supplies while avoiding predators with the demands of mating and rearing offspring. Males then use their habitats in such a way as to maximize their access to females. This section outlines the types of nonhuman primate social systems.

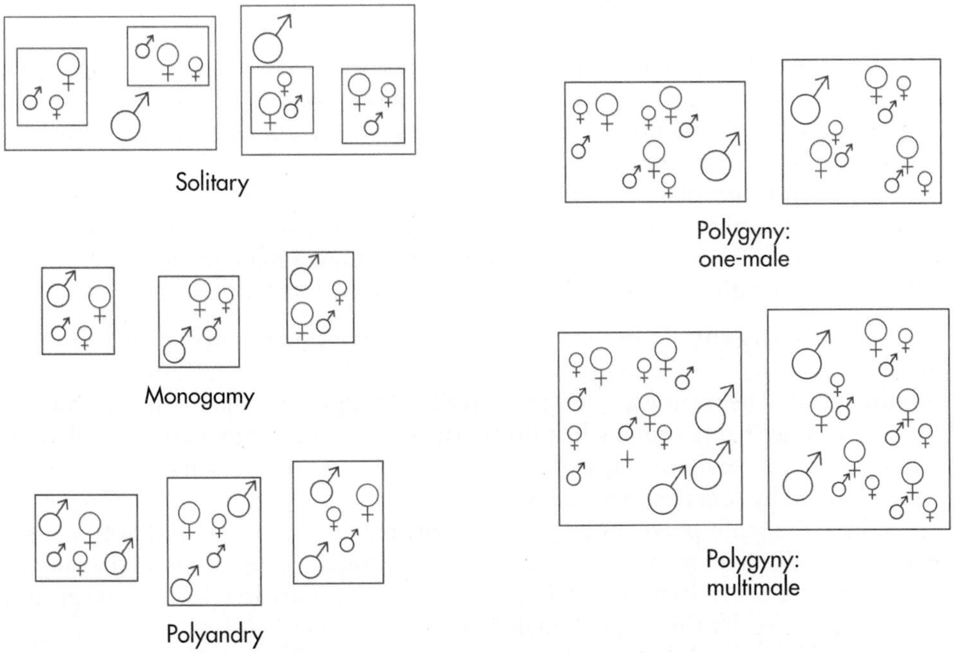

Figure 8.11 A taxonomy of primate social systems. Larger symbols indicate adults.

Solitary Most prosimians live in much the same social system that we believe the earliest primates did. They are largely solitary. Females occupy individual territories along with their dependent offspring, which they defend by scent-marking objects. Of course, no mammal is truly solitary; it must locate mates during the breeding season. Males occupy territories that overlap a number of female territories; they attempt to maintain exclusive mating access to all these females and keep transient males away. Males use scent-marking and a variety of calls to communicate with one another and to warn intruders to stay out. This social system characterizes many of the strepsirhines, especially the nocturnal galagos and lorises.

Monogamy **Monogamy** describes the relationship between a male and female living in a pair bond for an extended period of time, perhaps years. Recent studies have shown that our notion of monogamy needs some adjusting because members of pair bonds sometimes mate secretly outside the pair bond as well. In some cases, a pair of gibbons may live as a socially monogamous pair bond, but both male and female secretively mate with other gibbons. Social monogamy thus is not necessarily strict reproductive monogamy.

Monogamy is best understood as a female reproductive strategy. Monogamous female primates establish and hold territories, and on each territory a single male attaches himself to the resident female. The female therefore tolerates the presence of a male. The male may provide some essential services to the female, such as aiding in territorial and food defence or protecting the female's offspring from marauding males. In a few species, males actually aid in the rearing of infants by carrying young and shielding them from harm. In exchange for this service, they receive a high degree of certainty, although not absolute certainty that they fathered the offspring.

Because males in monogamous pairs don't appear to compete as directly with other males as those in social groups need to, we expect that sexually selected aspects of male competition, such as large canines or big body size, would be deemphasized. And we find this to be the case. For instance, gibbons exhibit little sexual dimorphism except in hair colour.

Polygyny The majority of anthropoid nonhuman primate species are *polygynous;* they live in groups composed of one or more males and more than one female. Groups composed of multiple males and multiple females often are called **polygynandrous** (literally, "many males and many females"). What characterizes nonhuman primate polygyny is the complexity of social interactions. In a few species, sociality has accompanied the evolution of brains capable of remembering a long history of interactions with group mates—the debts and favours an animal owes and is owed by others—and of strategizing accordingly.

The complexity of social interactions in nonhuman primate groups is influenced by the social system. A male in a multiple-male group must by necessity use a far more complex set of tactics to obtain mates than a male living in a group in which he is the only male or lives monogamously with just one female.

One-Male Polygyny *One-male polygynous groups* are what primatologists used to call harems. One male lives with as many females as he can monopolize (Figure 8.12). The term *harem* implies male control over females and is obsolete because it dates from a time when primatologists did not appreciate the role that females play in the mating system. In some cases one-male groups are driven by choices made by females, not males.

When one-male polygynous groups exist, males who are not able to obtain females usually live as extragroup males, either alone or in all-male "bachelor" groups (Figure 8.13). In some species, these all-male groups attack one-male groups and attempt to evict the resident male from his females.

monogamy A mating bond; primates can be socially monogamous but still mate occasionally outside the pair bond.

polygynandrous Primate social system consisting of multiple males and multiple females.

FIGURE 8.12 A polygynous group of capped langurs.

In some one-male group species, there are occasional influxes of males from outside the group, particularly if the species has a well-defined breeding season. The resident male then finds it impossible to restrict access to the group's females, and the females may have an active interest in seeking matings with the extragroup males. These events may contribute to the formation of multimale groups.

Multimale Polygyny A male nonhuman primate would like to have as many females to himself as he can monopolize. The downside of this is that he may have to constantly fend off intruding males who want to mate with his females. As the number of females in a one-male group increases, it becomes impossible for a male to prevent other males from joining the group. A better option for him may be to allow other males to enter the group but continue to obtain the majority of matings with the females by being socially dominant. So in many species, we see multimale, multifemale polygynous groups.

Instead of competing for sole access to females, males in multimale groups may compete for priority of access. Priority often takes the form of a **dominance hierarchy**, in which a top-ranking, *alpha male* allows other males access to the females in the group but may attempt to exclude his rivals when females are in estrus and may conceive. In this way he strikes a balance between the goal of maximizing mating success and the burden of spending all his time and energy fending off other males. In species living in multimale groups, females are not typically all in estrus at the same time. When one female enters estrus, she becomes a focus of competition among the group males. That such competition is far more intense than among monogamous primates is reflected in polygynous primates' canine tooth size and body size sexual dimorphism, both of which contribute to male success in mate competition. It is also reflected in the size of the males' testes, which may allow him to produce more sperm than other males.

dominance hierarchy Ranking of individual primates in a group that reflects their ability to displace, intimidate, or defeat group mates in contests.

In some multimale groups, intense mating competition occurs when the species breeds seasonally. This is because the high-ranking males are unable to restrict

FIGURE 8.13 In one-male group species, extra males typically reside in all-male "bachelor" groups. These are Hanuman langurs.

infanticide The killing of infants, either by members of the infant's group or by a member of a rival group.

fission–fusion (polygyny) Type of primate polygyny in which animals travel in foraging parties of varying sizes instead of a cohesive group.

access to all the females at the same time. In squirrel monkeys (*Saimiri* spp.), for example, males undergo dramatic physiological changes during the mating season, bulking up in order to compete successfully with other males in the group. The largest male tends to be the most dominant for that mating season and also has the highest reproductive success (Boinski, 1987).

Some nonhuman primate species maintain both one-male and multimale groups in the same population. Why this variation occurs is unclear. Primatologists have tried to explain it as a response to the local physical environment, local demographic trends, or the number of females and the overall population density (Newton, 1987; Sommer, 1994). In any case, populations featuring a preponderance of one-male groups also tend to exhibit higher levels of intergroup aggression and especially a tendency for strange males to attempt group takeovers of existing groups, with accompanying **infanticide** of the group's infants.

A few polygynous species organize themselves in multitiered social systems. In northeastern Africa, both hamadryas baboons and gelada baboons live in small one-male groups. But these one-male units join other one-male units to form larger bands, and these bands sometimes merge to form troops. In both species, enormous herds sometimes form, especially at sleeping sites in the evening, made up of many one-male groups (Kummer, 1968; Dunbar, 1983). This unusual social system probably results in part from phylogeny—inherited patterns of social behaviour—and in part from local ecology (sleeping in large groups may help protect individuals from attacks by predators such as leopards). A parallel to this social system may be found among the Asian snub-nosed monkeys, which forage in groups of up to 300 animals, but within this group there are well-defined smaller units, each controlled by only one or a few males (Kirkpatrick, 1998). The groups forage in pine forests and on the ground, feeding heavily on lichens and mosses, which are abundant and evenly distributed. Such a widespread resource may enable the formation of such enormous groups, within which individual males compete for access to smaller numbers of females.

Fission–Fusion Polygyny One additional form of polygyny is perhaps the most complex social system found in nonhuman primates. A few species do not live in cohesive groups; instead, temporary associations of individuals come together and split up repeatedly (Figure 8.14). This is called **fission–fusion polygyny.** Instead of forming a well-defined stable group, populations divide into communities. These communities have distinct home ranges and community membership, within which the community members join and part with one another unpredictably in temporary foraging units called parties. The same chimpanzee may be in a party of two

FIGURE 8.14 Bonobo females form close alliances, maintained through sex, that are lacking in chimpanzees.

at dawn, of ten an hour later, and of thirty later in the day. The only stable unit in the social system is a female and her young offspring. Males often travel together, forming coalitions among themselves.

Fission–fusion polygyny is believed to be an evolved response to reliance on ripe fruit in the diet. Because of the patchy and seasonal distribution of fruits in a tropical forest and the daily variation in fruit availability, foraging for food in large cohesive groups would incite intense competition for resources. Females forage on their own to optimize their access to fruit, and males attempt to control access to females by forming bonds with one another.

polyandry Mating system in which one female mates with multiple males.

Polyandry When one female lives in a reproductive or social unit with multiple males, we say the social system is polyandrous. **Polyandry** is quite rare in nonhuman primates; it is better known in birds, where it has demonstrated key rules of sexual selection. Among nonhuman primates, only a few species of marmosets and tamarins in New World tropical forests exhibit this social system, and it remains poorly understood. In some species of these monkeys, males bond together and help females to rear offspring. This is probably a reproductive strategy by males. Marmosets and tamarins are very small (< 1 kg; 2 lb) monkeys and are vulnerable to a wide range of predators. Females boost their reproductive output by producing twins, but these twins weigh an extraordinary 20% of the mother's body weight. Males assist in infant caregiving by carrying babies and may help in antipredator defence as well. Males may opt to assist a female for the opportunity to achieve reproductive success; if two males mate with the same female, each has a 50% chance of being the father of the twins.

The presence of multiple males increases a female's overall reproductive success as well, a compelling argument for males to engage in this sort of cooperative breeding (Garber, 1997). However, among the two or more males in a marmoset group, one tends to be socially dominant and to sire most of the infants (Digby, 1995). Thus, marmosets and tamarins are perhaps best considered to be socially polyandrous but reproductively monogamous.

THE EVOLUTION OF PRIMATE SOCIAL BEHAVIOUR

We can understand and study behaviour at different levels. All behaviours we see in the wild have immediate causes: hunger, fear, sexual urges, and the like. The immediate, or *proximate*, causes involve the hormonal, physiological reasons for the animal to act. At the same time, behaviours reflect deeper, evolved tendencies that have been shaped over millions of years of natural and sexual selection to promote reproductive success. A baboon mates because of immediate impulses that are both hormonal and social. But ultimately, the urge to mate reflects deeper, evolved strategies that arise through natural selection to enhance the baboon's odds of reproduction. In Chapter 5 you saw how these evolutionary forces work on an organism's phenotype. In this chapter you will examine how the same forces shape primate behaviour as a phenotype.

The value of an evolutionary approach to nonhuman primate behaviour and ecology is that it allows us to test hypotheses. Using an evolutionary framework, we can study mating as one of many behaviours that has fitness consequences. The pattern of mating may be related to everything from dominance relationships and coalitionary networks to female physiology, which may in turn reveal something important about the evolution of the social system. In other words, behaviour can be seen as an adaptation, one aspect of the primate's phenotype. Although the genetic basis for a specific trait remains largely unknown, we can study the consequences of the behaviour. For example, if being aggressive promotes reproductive success for a baboon compared with less aggressive baboons in the group, we may infer that aggression is subject to evolutionary forces.

Social Behaviour and Reproductive Asymmetry

The reproductive asymmetry between males and females plays a key role in our understanding of the evolution of nonhuman primate social strategies. Females invest far more energy and time in offspring, during both gestation and offspring-rearing, than males do. In accordance with Darwinian sexual selection theory, females tend to be competed for by males, rather than the other way around. As a result, we expect females of all social mammals to prioritize obtaining adequate food supplies for themselves and their offspring. Females do not need to be very concerned about finding a male; because of their lower reproductive potential, they will always be the sought-out sex, and males will find them. Because the availability of females is the single factor that most limits a male's opportunity to achieve reproductive success, we expect that males will go where females go.

The form the social system takes therefore depends on the way females distribute themselves (Figure 8.15 and Figure 8.16). The social system of nonhuman primate species in which females form the core of the group is called **female philopatry**. This means that females do not migrate at maturity; they stay in the group of their birth to reproduce and rear offspring. In such groups, males typically migrate. Females in female philopatric groups often form tight bonds, based partly on the likelihood of their kinship. Such matrilines of mother, daughters, grandmother, and so on can form the core of the group. In **male philopatry** males remain in their natal home range throughout life, and females migrate. The two types of social systems are closely connected to other important aspects of behaviour, so each bears closer examination.

female philopatry Primate social system in which females remain and breed in the group of their birth, whereas males emigrate.

male philopatry Primate social system in which males remain and breed in the group of their birth, whereas females emigrate.

When female kin live together, they share a strong incentive to cooperate or at least to limit their competition over food resources. Studies have shown that in female philopatric groups, territorial defence is done mainly by females, and the degree of affiliation among females is far greater than among females in male philopatric species. For instance, in Gombe National Park, Tanzania, female baboons, which are female philopatric, spend much time sitting together and grooming one another. In the same forest, female chimpanzees, which are male philopatric, rarely engage in social grooming or contact. Competition among females can be fierce, with nutrients and calories for bearing and rearing offspring at stake. But on the whole, females in female philopatric societies—such as most macaques, baboons, and numerous other Old World monkeys—socialize in ways that females in male philopatric species do not.

(a)

(b)

FIGURE 8.15 (a) Savannah baboons live in female-philopatric groups, among which males migrate. (b) Chimpanzees live in male-philopatric communities, among which females migrate.

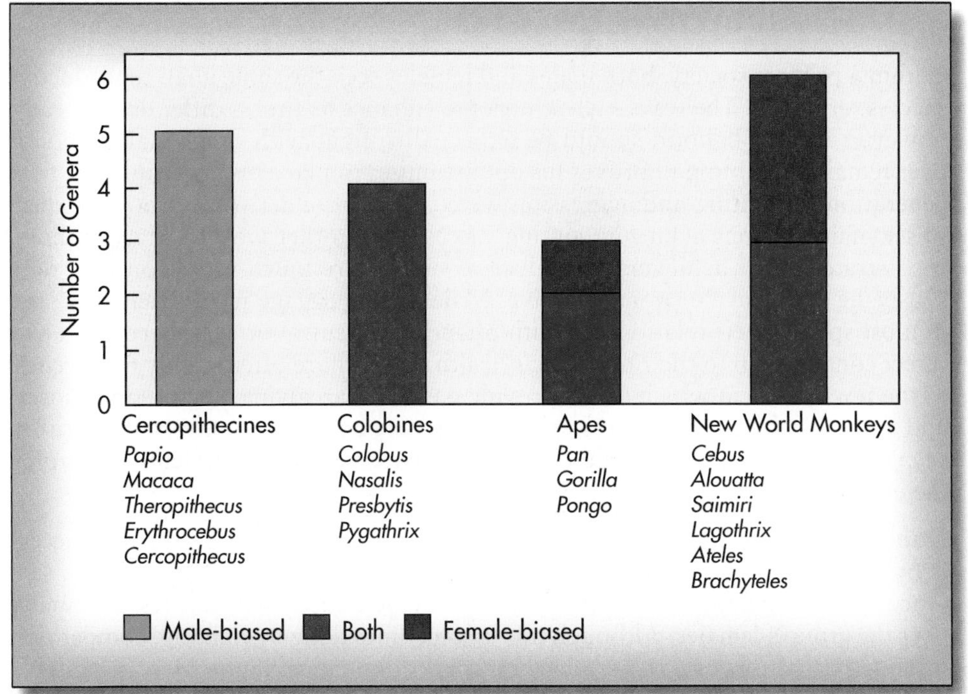

FIGURE 8.16 Male and female philopatry. The internal dynamics of primate societies differ greatly depending on which sex emigrates from the group at sexual maturity.

When females feed on widely scattered resources, as species exhibiting the fission–fusion social system seem to do, males may not be able to maintain access to them. In such a situation, male bonds may be the most effective way of controlling females. This may explain the fact that chimpanzees, bonobos, and a few other species are male-bonded. These bonds are based partly on male kinship because remaining in the natal group means that a male ends up living next to his cousins, brothers, and other male kin. Closely allied males, whether relatives or not, can coerce females for mating purposes, and control access to fruit trees that other male cohorts might want to enter. So male-bonded primate societies offer some major nutritional and reproductive benefits to males and uncertain benefits to females. The benefits to males are believed to be sufficient to keep males on their natal home range. Females tend to be the sex that emigrates.

Females in male philopatric societies, on the other hand, may not show a high degree of affiliation, perhaps because of their lack of kinship. In chimpanzee society, females rarely groom one another, and they often engage in competitive aggression, including infanticidal aggression in which a female may attempt to kill the offspring of another female. Bonobos are an exception to this pattern in that immigrant females in a community, though unrelated, establish close bonds with one another. These bonds are used to protect females from harassment by males.

The form of the social system cannot be entirely explained by the behaviour of females, however. Some researchers have linked the number of males in a primate group to other factors, such as the intensity of the risk of predation. It may be that the number of males in a primate group, though subject to multiple factors, depends most strongly on the number of females and also on the presence of predators in the species' habitat (Mitani et al., 1996; van Schaik and Hörstermann, 1994).

MALE REPRODUCTIVE STRATEGIES

Within a primate society, both males and females seek the same goal: reproductive success, or fitness. The ways each sex tries to enhance its fitness differ dramatically, however. A male baboon should be expected to fight with other male baboons over females if fighting improves his opportunities to place his genes into the next generation. If fighting and aggression were counterproductive, we should expect to see male baboons achieving mating success some other way. In practice, however, strategies for achieving reproductive success are much more complex than just being aggressive or nonaggressive. Males rarely engage in paternal care, and in most species their relationship with offspring is neutral or even harmful. Their direct contribution to their offspring's health and welfare often is only their genes. In the few species in which males provide parental caregiving, such as marmosets and tamarins, the selection pressures on males may be very different from those on, say, a male baboon. The degree of parental investment is a key factor in shaping the evolution of the social system.

Dominance One important way males and females achieve reproductive success is by establishing dominance relationships with other members of the same sex. Once he enters a new group, a male must compete directly with the resident males over the group's females. Although this is sometimes done by fighting, competition often is settled through the establishment of dominance hierarchies, in which a high-ranking and a low-ranking male sort out their relationship through a series of contests that leaves the lower-ranking animal unlikely to challenge the more dominant one.

Dominance relationships among males are established early in life, as males play together and some assert themselves over others. Of course, males that later emigrate from their home group cannot assume high rank in a new group, at least initially. Males growing up in male philopatric groups may face a different dilemma. To achieve high rank they must demonstrate to males that they have grown up and that they are now worthy of respect. In chimpanzee society, all the adult males in the community are dominant to all the females. An adolescent male climbs the dominance hierarchy by first taking on and dominating (fighting with or supplanting at fruit trees) each of the adult females. Once he has risen to the top of the female hierarchy, he will begin to challenge the lowest-ranking males, and so on until he has risen as high as he will go. These challenges illustrate the political nature of life among nonhuman primates.

Males are not the dominant sex in all primate species, however. Among many lemur species, females are dominant to all males, displacing them at food sources

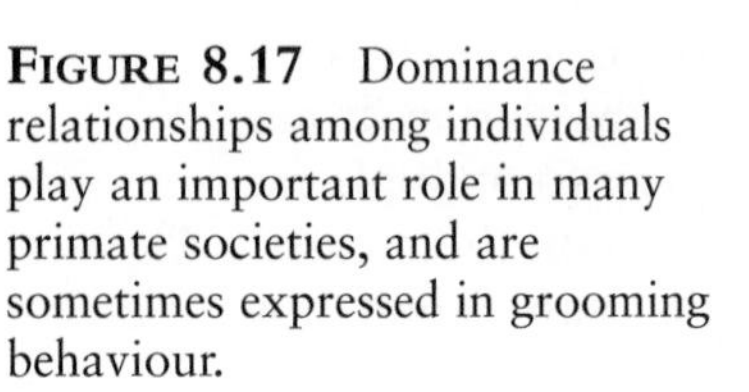

FIGURE 8.17 Dominance relationships among individuals play an important role in many primate societies, and are sometimes expressed in grooming behaviour.

and choosing newly immigrated males with which to mate (Erhardt and Overdorff, 1998). Male lemurs do not engage in the sort of complicated dominance interactions that we see in anthropoid primates, perhaps because much of the social intercourse of the group is strongly controlled by high-ranking females.

Dominance relationships in nonhuman primate males are far more complicated than the image you may have of a pecking order. In fact, rarely do the males of a polygynous group sort themselves into a neatly linear hierarchy. Far more commonly, dominance relationships take a flexible, multifaceted form in which Monkey A is dominant to Monkey B, except when Monkey B is in the company of Monkey C, in which case B and C are dominant to Monkey A. These sorts of fast-paced, often subtle interactions in nonhuman primate groups are challenging for primate researchers to observe but crucial in explaining the role that cognition and social complexity play in nonhuman primate societies (Figure 8.17).

Female Reproductive Strategies

Females invest much more time and energy in reproduction than males do, and their reproductive strategies reflect this. Instead of competing for males, female nonhuman primates typically are competed over. But females do not mate with whichever male is the winner of the competition. Sexual selection theory predicts that females should choose their mates carefully because a given mating may result in years of investment in gestation, lactation, and offspring-rearing (Figure 8.18). A nonhuman primate must undergo years of socialization to learn how to behave successfully as an adult, and this socialization is closely connected to the development and growth of its brain. During the socialization period the maturing offspring is utterly dependent, physically and psychologically, on its mother. And female primates are at greater risk of dying when pregnant or caring for a young infant, presumably because they are less able to escape predators and more likely to suffer nutritional stress, leading to disease.

Role of Dominance Although dominance rank usually is not as important to female primates as it is to males, dominance may nonetheless have important consequences for female reproductive success. A study of the relationship between

FIGURE 8.18 Despite the traditional focus on males, females actively choose mates and are the driving force in the reproductive process.

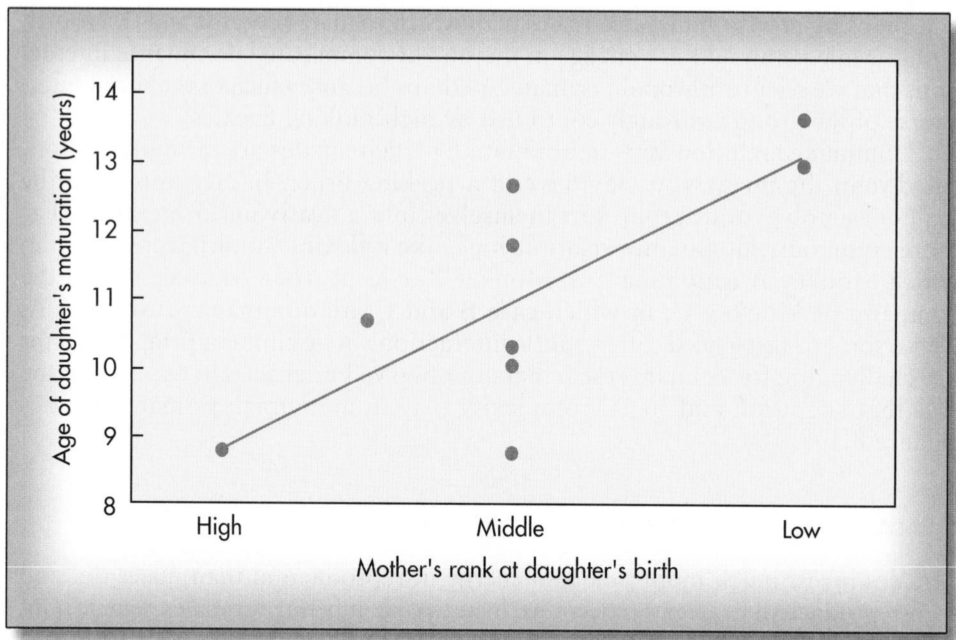

FIGURE 8.19 In some species, dominant females have more surviving offspring that mature earlier indicating an adaptive value for high social status.

dominance and reproductive success among Gombe chimpanzees showed that there was a small but significant influence of rank on the number of surviving offspring a mother bore (Figure 8.19). The daughters of high-ranking females also matured slightly more rapidly than did those of low-ranking females (Pusey et al., 1997). And as we have seen, females form **matrilineal** kin groups in Old World monkeys such as baboons, macaques, and langurs, within which a female's status may influence her reproductive success.

Primatologists think females choose dominant males more often than low-ranking males because dominant animals are so often in better health, with priority of access to food. The offspring of dominant animals also tend to grow up to be high-ranking; we can't say whether this reflects a genetic predisposition to become dominant or whether it is the proximate result of having a mother who is dominant herself and whose alliance network and socialization perpetuate high status.

Sexual Receptivity Signals Female primates use sexual signals to promote their reproductive success. These signals can be behavioural, anatomical, or physiological. Such signals are intended to advertise a female's **sexual receptivity**, or willingness to mate. They also make a female more attractive to males. Some nonhuman primates use body posture to indicate receptivity; female Hanuman langurs arch their tails over their backs and shake their heads side to side to indicate willingness to mate. Females of many other species simply move in front of a male and present their rumps as a solicitation for mating.

Nearly all female mammals are fertile during only a restricted part of each reproductive cycle. The time around ovulation often produces changes in female appearance (Figure 8.20) and behaviour that incite males to compete to mate with them. Only during this time are females likely to conceive, and only then are they willing to mate.

matrilineal Pattern of female kinship in a primate social group.

sexual receptivity Willingness and ability of a female to mate, also defined as fertility.

FIGURE 8.20 Sexual swellings are one way for females to advertise their mating availability, thereby inducing male competition for them.

RECONSTRUCTING THE EVOLUTION OF PRIMATE SOCIETIES

In the early years of modern nonhuman primate behaviour study, many primatologists believed the form a primate social system took followed fairly simple ecological rules. They created taxonomies of social systems in relation to the species' natural habitat. For instance, because a number of distantly related primate species ate a fruit diet and lived in polygynous groups, it was thought that frugivory and polygyny were linked. Monogamy was also thought to be linked to fruit-eating and territoriality because gibbons exhibit both. But as more and more nonhuman primate field studies were carried out, it became clear that such pigeonholes were simplistic.

Today, primatologists use increasingly quantitative models and large numbers of field studies of nonhuman primates and their ecology to understand the workings of primate social systems. However, primate social systems are moulded by the evolutionary history of each species. This makes interpreting the effect of natural selection difficult because for many primates the environment that moulded their evolution may not be the one they currently occupy.

Primate ecologists differ on which influences—feeding competition, mate competition, or predation—are the most important in shaping primate societies.

There are survival advantages and disadvantages in both large and small groups for both obtaining food and avoiding predators. As in many other primate examples, group life is all about costs and benefits and tradeoffs between different behaviour options.

In Chapters 7 and 8, you have seen how the lives of nonhuman primates inform us about ourselves and our ancestry. In this chapter we examined social behaviour, but social behaviour and ecology cannot be fully separated from each other. Primate social behaviour has been moulded by natural selection, with the environment as the filter. These same natural forces shaped human ancestry, human anatomy, and perhaps aspects of human behaviour. Now that you have seen the context for the roots of human evolution, it's time to turn in Chapter 9 to the fossil record and what it tells us.

SUMMARY

1. **What are the three major influences on the evolution of nonhuman primate sociality?**

   All wild primates must find mates, find food, and avoid predators in order to survive and reproduce.

2. **What is the difference between a home range and a territory?**

   A home range is the area that a nonhuman primate or nonhuman primate group uses over a long period of time. A territory is the part of the home range that is defended against members of other groups of the same species. All, part, or none of the home range may be defended as a territory.

3. **What are the major types of nonhuman primate grouping patterns?**

   Nonhuman primates may live solitarily, monogamously, or in polygynous groups that can be one-male, multi-male, or fission–fusion, or they can be polyandrous.

4. **Why are social systems and mating systems not always the same?**

   A primate may live in a particular grouping pattern but mate outside that pattern. For instance, a gibbon may live in a socially monogamous pair bond but mate secretly with gibbons other than his or her mate.

5. **What do we mean by the reproductive asymmetry between males and females?**

   Females have a lower reproductive potential than males, which makes them the object of male competition in most species. Because females invest so much more time and energy in reproduction, they tend to be more discriminating in choosing a mate.

6. **What is the basis of female mate choice in nonhuman primates?**

   We know that female primates are choosy when it comes to selecting a mate. We believe that aspects of this choice are under evolutionary pressure. Females may choose males on the basis of size, strength, or aggressiveness. But they may also choose males for their caregiving behaviour and their lack of aggression toward them. We believe females seek genetic quality in a mate; how they discover this in potential mates is an area of intense research.

CRITICAL THINKING QUESTIONS

1. If primate behaviour tells us much about human origins because primates are big-brained and socially complex, then what other animals unrelated to primates might be informative about the origins of human social behaviour?
2. Why would male primates spend their lives striving to rise in dominance rank if being high-ranking does not guarantee high mating success?
3. Nonhuman primates are but one type of animal living in tropical forests. Do you think that they have had a major impact on the evolution of tropical forests? Why or why not?

KEY TERMS

captive study
semi–free-ranging
field study
polygynous
home range
core area
territory
social system
monogamy
polygynandrous
dominance hierarchy
infanticide
fission–fusion polygyny
polyandry
female philopatry
male philopatry
matrilineal
sexual receptivity

SUGGESTED READING

Boesch, Christophe, Hohmann, Gottfried, and Marchant, Linda F. (editors). (2002). *Behavioural Diversity in Chimpanzees and Bonobos*. Cambridge University Press, Cambridge, UK.

Fedigan, Linda Marie. (1992). *Primate Paradigms: Sex Roles and Social Bonds*. University of Chicago Press, Chicago, IL.

Fossey, Dian. (1983). *Gorillas in the Mist*. Houghton Mifflin Company, Boston, MA.

Galdikas, Birutė M. F. (1995). *Reflections of Eden: My Years with the Orangutans of Borneo*. Little, Brown and Company, Boston, MA.

Goodall, Jane. (1968). *In the Shadow of Man*. National Geographic Society, Washington, DC.

Hohmann, Gottfried, Robbins, Martha, and Boesch, Christophe (editors). (2006). *Feeding Ecology in Apes and Other Primates*. Cambridge Studies in Biological and Evolutionary Anthropology. Cambridge University Press, Cambridge, UK.

Lehman, S.M., and Fleagle, J.G. (editors). (2006). *Primate Biogeography*. Springer, New York, NY.

Russon, A.E., and Begun, D. R. (editors). (2004). *The Evolution of Thought: Evolutionary Origins of Great Ape Intelligence*. Cambridge University Press, Cambridge, UK.

Strier, Karen B. (2007). *Primate Behavioural Ecology*, 3rd edition. Allyn and Bacon, Boston, MA.

PART IV

THE FOSSIL RECORD

Chapter 9
Our Fossil Ancestors in Context

As the sun drops toward the horizon over a remote African badland, a sunburnt geologist sets down his rock hammer, takes a swig of lukewarm water from his canteen, and mops the sweat from his forehead with a bandanna. He has just finished collecting chunks of volcanic ash from layers above and below the place where fossils of a primitive human ancestor had been recovered earlier that field season. Physical exhaustion and the excitement of anticipation make his hand shake slightly as he drops the chunks into plastic bags. He carefully seals the bags and records his location. With the samples stowed safely in his backpack, the scientist scrambles down the slope and makes the long hike back to base camp.

Back in his laboratory a few weeks later, portions of each rock sample are broken up in a mortar and pestle. The scientist peers through a microscope, picking through the sample of volcanic ash with steel forceps, carefully selecting fresh feldspar crystals. He cleans the crystals in an acid solution and then places each into the recess of a sample chamber. The chamber is sealed and sent to a nuclear reactor for irradiation, and the scientist moves on to other projects. A month or so later, the chamber returns marked with a radioactive warning label. After a cooling off

period it will be placed in the way of a laser beam, and each crystal in turn will vaporize slightly, then bubble and melt. A key piece of equipment, a mass spectrometer, begins to analyze the isotopes in the gas released from the melting crystal. The scientist checks the results and sits down to begin his calculations.

AFTER SEVERAL MONTHS OF EXPERIMENTS AND CALCULATIONS, checking and rechecking, the scientist picks up the telephone. As he listens to the ringing on the other end, he smiles wryly. It is always interesting to hear a colleague react to just how ancient a new discovery is.

Chapter Outline

Techniques developed over the last 50 years allow scientists such as this geologist to provide a more accurate context for understanding our evolutionary past. To understand our evolution we study **fossils**. As the preserved remnants of once-living things, fossils provide information about past life. **Palaeontology**, a field that takes its name from the Greek words for "old" (*palaeos*) and "existence" (*ontos*), is devoted to gleaning all the information that can be extracted from fossils. This information includes how ancient the fossil is, what kind of organism it represents, and the ecological adaptations of the organism, such as its diet and locomotion. We must also know about how that fossil came to be preserved where it was and how the preservation process affected the fossil. A fossil without its context is almost useless because we have no way of assessing how old it is, what kind of environment it lived in, or what other animals it might have lived and competed with.

In this chapter we will set the stage for answering these questions by looking closely at the field of **geology**, the study of the Earth, to understand the preservation, age, and environment in which fossils are found. Because the evolutionary history of humans and our primate relatives is a story that unfolds through time, geological principles are fundamentally important to the study of human evolution. We will see how materials fossilize and look at what we can learn from both the fossils themselves and the surroundings in which they are found. We'll introduce and compare some of the most important dating methods in use today and the context in which each is most valuable. Finally, we'll explore conditions on Earth during the Cenozoic Era, the time period in which primates evolved.

HOW TO BECOME A FOSSIL

You might think that fossils are abundant. Natural history museums are filled with fossils of dinosaurs and other prehistoric creatures, and some of the most famous fossil sites in the world are found in Canada, including Dinosaur Provincial Park in Alberta and the Burgess Shale in British Columbia's Yoho National Park. In reality, very few living things become fossils. This is a good thing because it means that the tissues of most plants and animals are instead recycled and used by new organisms in the ongoing carbon cycle of the Earth. The nutrients they contain might be lost forever if every organism that died became a fossil. Not only does a minute fraction of living things become preserved as fossils, but only an exceedingly small proportion of the fossils that are preserved end up being discovered, collected, and studied.

Taphonomy, the study of what happens to remains from death to discovery, reveals some of the factors that determine whether an organism becomes a fossil. These include both biological and geological processes.

Death might come in a number of ways, such as injury, disease, or predation. In many instances, the agent of death may leave marks on the skeleton, such as the bite marks of a predator. After death, the carcass begins to decompose when living tissues are no longer maintained by the organism and as numerous microbes, such as bacteria and mould, and carrion-eating insects accelerate decay. While this is happening, scavengers may ravage the carcass, consuming its soft tissues and perhaps even chomping on the bones of the skeleton, especially the soft articular ends of bones that form our joints. Eventually, only the most durable tissues remain, especially the densely constructed cortical bone at the middle of the long bones, the jaws, and the teeth. Even these durable remains can disappear, recycled into the Earth's carbon system, through various means, including erosion and trampling.

fossils The mineralized or otherwise preserved remnants of once-living things.

palaeontology The study of extinct organisms, based on their fossilized remains.

geology The study of the Earth.

taphonomy The study of what happens to the remains of an animal from the time of death to the time of discovery.

However, to become a fossil, part of the organism must be preserved by burial, a natural process in which the carcass, or part of it, is covered with sediment. Burial interrupts the biological phase of decomposition, protecting the skeleton from further ravaging and trampling by biological organisms. Because sediments such as sand, silt, mud, and gravel usually are carried by water, burial often occurs in the floodplains of rivers, along the shores of lakes, and in swamps where uplift, erosion, and sedimentation are occurring. In other circumstances, sediment such as dust and volcanic ash carried by the wind sweeps over the remains. Once buried, skeletal remains may be preserved in a variety of ways. Usually they absorb minerals from the surrounding soil or ground water that eventually replace the organism's original inorganic tissues. The result is *petrifaction*, the process of being turned stone.

Fossilized remains usually preserve only the most durable tissues of the body, such as teeth and bones, and just as the inorganic component is replaced by minerals in ground water, eventually the organic component of the skeleton (collagen) degrades and is lost (Figure 9.1). On occasion, however, soft parts such as skin or

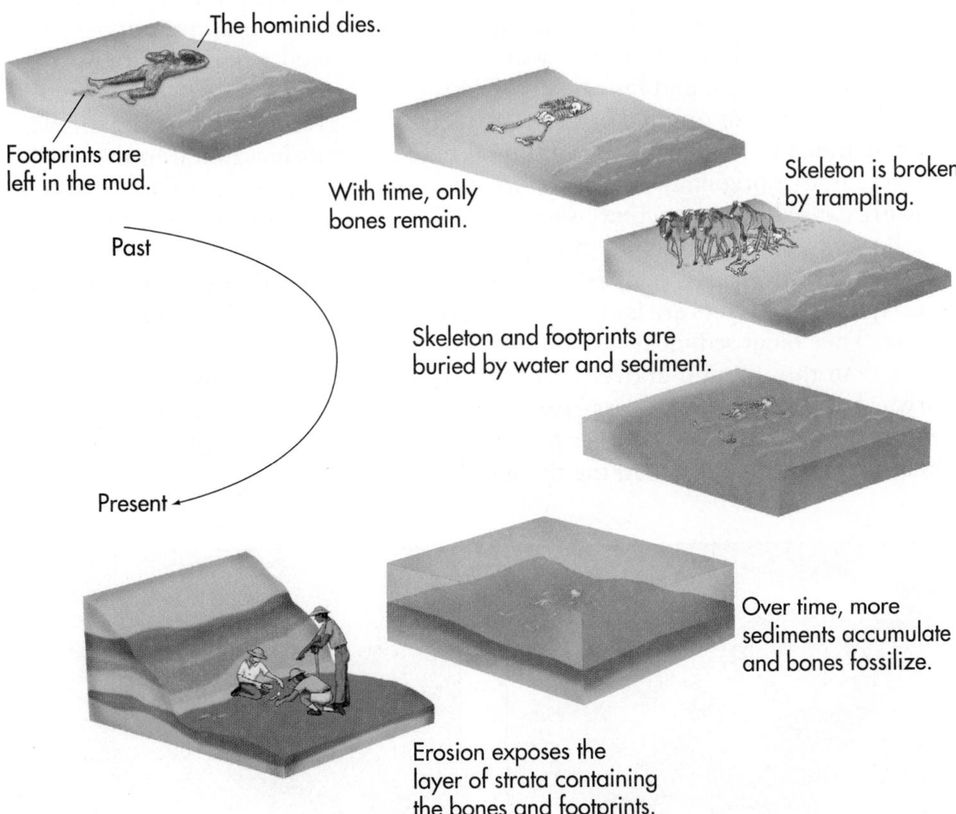
The hominid dies.
Footprints are left in the mud.
With time, only bones remain.
Skeleton is broken by trampling.
Past
Skeleton and footprints are buried by water and sediment.
Present
Over time, more sediments accumulate and bones fossilize.
Erosion exposes the layer of strata containing the bones and footprints.

FIGURE 9.1 Fossils are formed after an animal dies, decomposes, and is covered in sediment. Minerals in ground water replace bone mineral turning bone into stone that may later be discovered if the surrounding rock erodes away.

strata Layers of rock.

stratigraphy The study of the order of rock layers and the sequence of events they reflect.

hair may be preserved. In very exceptional circumstances, the original tissues of an organism are preserved largely intact, as when bodies are naturally mummified in very cold or very dry conditions, or in the absence of oxygen. The preserved remains of sailors from the Franklin Expedition, uncovered by Professor Owen Beattie of the University of Alberta in the permafrost of the Canadian Arctic (Beattie and Geiger, 2005), are excellent examples of natural mummification. Finally, *trace fossils* such as the tracks left by animals may provide impressions of their activities, and *coprolites*, or fossilized feces, also tell us about the presence of past animals (Figure 9.2).

THE IMPORTANCE OF CONTEXT

In this section we review the important principles used in geology to understand the position of a fossil in its rock layers and of different fossil sites relative to one another.

STRATIGRAPHY

Imagine driving through a road cut where you see what looks like layers or bands of rock. These are **strata**, literally "layers" in Latin. In some road cuts these layers are basically horizontal, but in others they may be more vertical or even quite deformed (Figure 9.3). **Stratigraphy** is the study of the distribution of these layers. In 1830, Charles Lyell synthesized a number of accepted geological principles including the principles of stratigraphy. The principles of geology rely in large part on the concept of *uniformitarianism*, which suggests that processes operating today are also those that operated in the past and thus they can explain the fossil and geological record. The principles of stratigraphy include four that are critical to an understanding of the context of a fossil: original horizontality, superposition, cross-cutting relationships, and faunal succession.

The *principle of original horizontality* says that layers of rock (strata) are laid down parallel to the Earth's gravitational field and thus horizontal to the Earth's surface, at least originally. All the deformations and upendings that you see in road cuts are caused by later activity such as earthquakes and volcanic eruptions.

Building on the principle of original horizontality is the principle of superposition. The *principle of superposition* (Figure 9.4) states that with all other factors equal, older layers are laid down first and then covered by younger (overlying) layers. Thus older sediments are on the bottom, and the fossils found in them are older than those found above. However, stratigraphy is not always so straightforward. The *principle of cross-cutting relationships* says simply that a geological feature must exist before another feature can cut across or through it and that the thing that is cut is older than the thing cutting through it.

(a)

(b)

FIGURE 9.2 Past life is preserved in many forms. (a) Soft tissues may be mummified or preserved in amber. (b) Whole skeletons or their parts may be fossilized in rock. From these various clues palaeontologists piece together the evolutionary history of the animals preserved.

FIGURE 9.3 As these images of geological formations in western Canada illustrate, rock layers (strata) usually look like the layers in a cake (a), but processes such as earthquakes and mountain building can deform these once horizontal layers (b). The palaeoanthropologist must understand these deformations in order to figure out which stratum a fossil comes from and how old it is.

Finally, the *principle of faunal succession* addresses the changes or succession of fauna (animals) through layers (Figure 9.5). Certain types of these animals that typify a layer are called index fossils. Once a type of fossil leaves a section, it does not reappear higher in the section: once a type of animal goes extinct, it does not reappear later (and so cannot be fossilized in younger sediments).

Using the principles of stratigraphy we can determine which strata are older and younger. Comparisons between sites can provide a sequence of rocks from

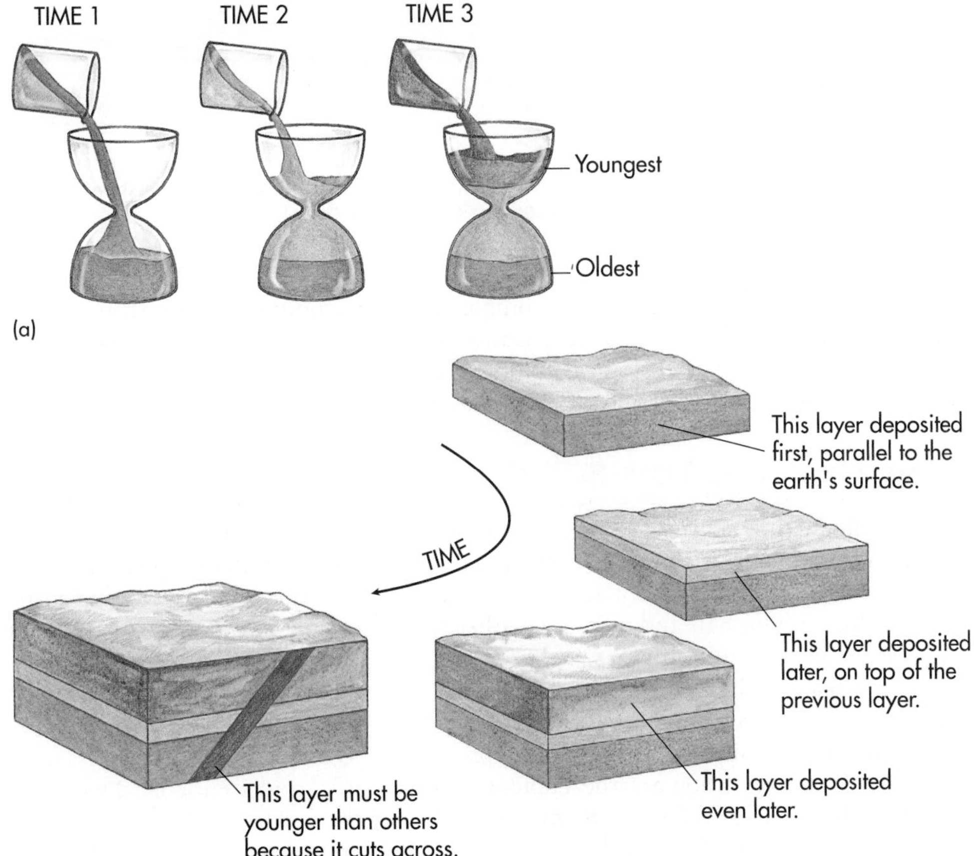

FIGURE 9.4 (a) The principles of stratigraphy help us understand the relative age of rock layers. (b) Layers are deposited parallel to the Earth's surface (horizontality). Younger layers are deposited on top of older layers (superposition). A layer that cuts across others is younger than those it cuts (cross-cutting relationships).

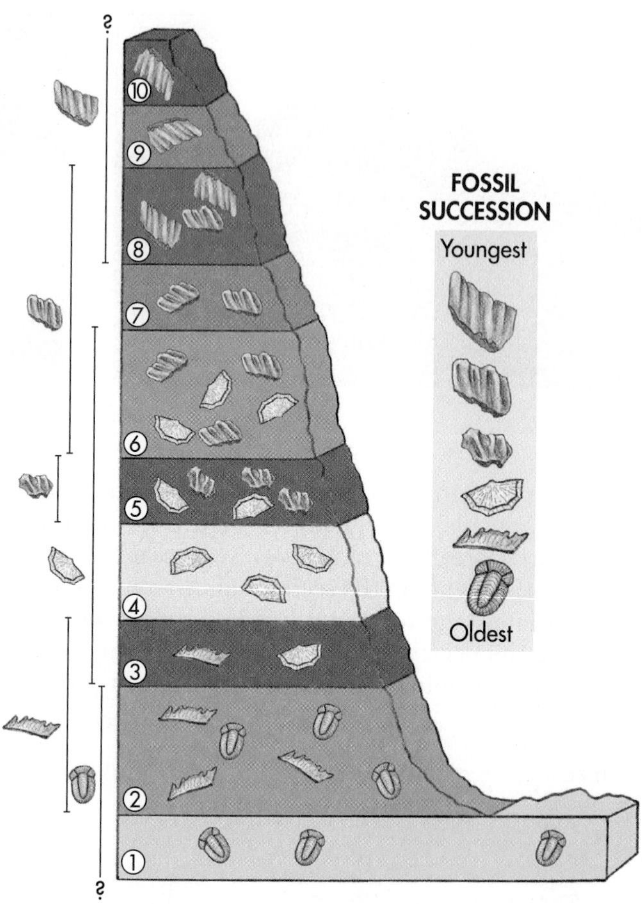

FIGURE 9.5 The principle of faunal succession uses animal fossils to tell relative time.

older to younger for both areas. By comparing the stratigraphy of sites from around the world, especially for marine sediments that are very continuous, geologists have assembled a great geological column from the very oldest to the very youngest rocks on Earth. This geological column is called the geologic time scale.

THE GEOLOGIC TIME SCALE

The **geologic time scale (GTS)** is divided into nested sets of time. From most inclusive to least inclusive these are eons, eras, periods, and epochs (Figure 9.6). The Earth itself is approximately 4.5 billion years old, and the GTS covers this entire time, although human and primate evolution occurs only in the Cenozoic Era, or about the last 65 million years.

The scale is divided into two eons, the Precambrian and Phanerozoic. The Precambrian dates from 4.5 billion to 543 million years ago. The Phanerozoic Eon dates from 543 million years ago to the present and is divided into three eras; from oldest to youngest they are the Palaeozoic, Mesozoic, and Cenozoic. "Zoic" in each of these names refers to the presence of animals.

geologic time scale (GTS) The categories of time into which Earth's history is usually divided by geologists and palaeontologists: eras, periods, epochs.

Although we will spend the next several chapters discussing the fossil record of only the last 65 million years (the Cenozoic Era), take a moment to consider the enormity of time represented by the entire history of the Earth, 4.5 billion years. Primates are present for a little less than 1.5% of that tremendous span, and humans and our closest ancestors are present for only about 0.1% of that time. To put this in perspective, think about the seven days in a week. On this scale, the

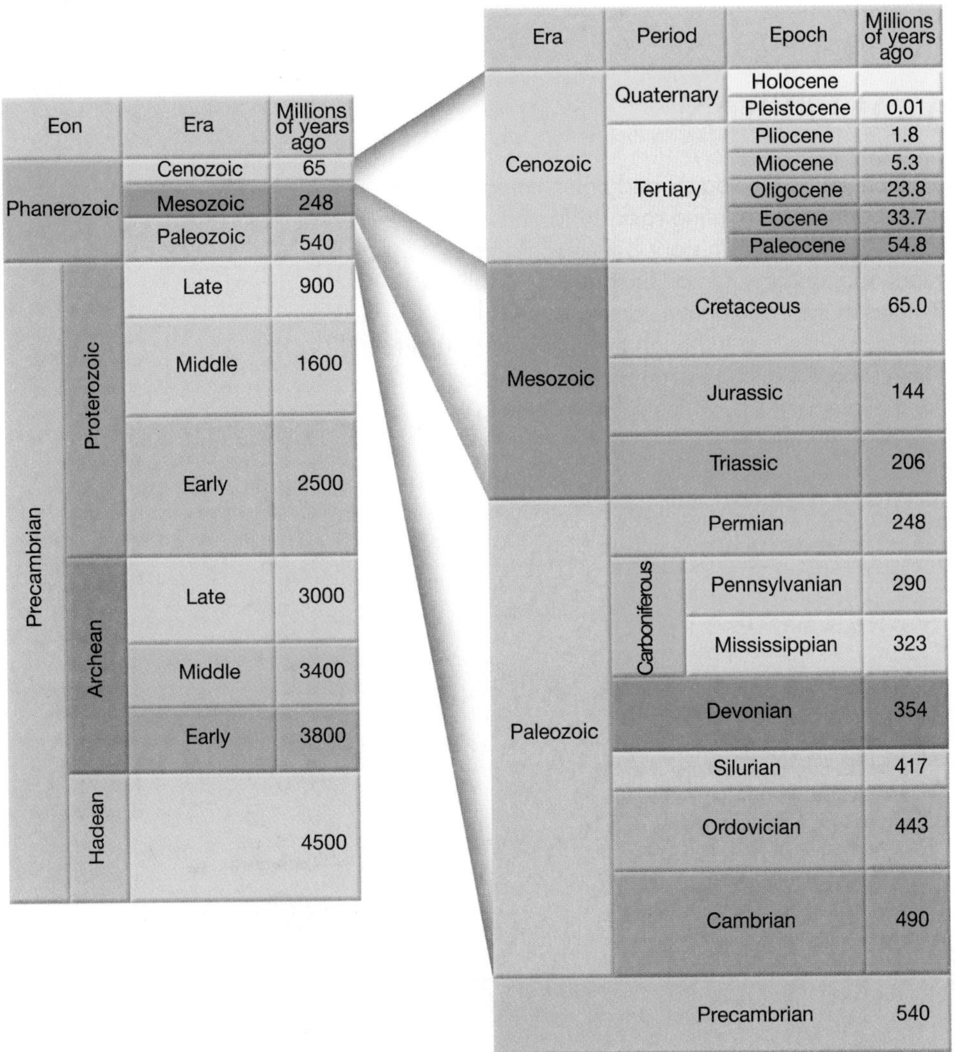

FIGURE 9.6 Earth's history is divided into nested sets of time—eons, eras, periods, and epochs—and called the Geologic Time Scale.

primates have existed for about 2.4 hours, and the human lineage has existed for about 11 minutes and 20 seconds.

The Cenozoic Era spans from 65 million years ago to present and has two periods: the Tertiary and Quaternary. The Tertiary Period, from 65 to 1.8 million years ago spans five epochs: the Palaeocene (65 to 54.8 million years ago), Eocene (54.8 to 33.7 million years ago), Oligocene (33.7 to 23.8 million years ago), Miocene (23.8 to 5.3 million years ago), and Pliocene (5.3 to 1.8 million years ago). The Quaternary period, from 1.8 million years ago to present, spans two epochs: the Pleistocene (1.8 million to 10 thousand years ago) and Holocene (10 thousand years ago to present). We live in the Holocene Epoch of the Quaternary Period of the Cenozoic Era of the Phanerozoic Eon.

The lengths of epochs, periods, and eras are not standard in the GTS. Boundaries are placed at points in the time scale where large shifts are evident in the geological column. The boundary between the Pliocene and Pleistocene Epoch at 1.8 million years ago was originally placed to reflect the onset of more severe glaciation events in the Pleistocene, and some geologists would like to move this boundary earlier in time (to 2.5 million years ago) to reflect evidence for glaciations becoming severe at that time.

Figure 9.7 KEY CHANGES IN EVOLUTION

The Earth's history spans 4.5 billion years. Geologists and paleontologists have pieced together the history of the Earth by correlating rock strata and examining the fossils within those rocks. Most of Earth's history is lifeless. Primates arise only about 65 million years ago, and the human lineage only 6 million years ago. Understanding primates in their geological context is critical to understanding their adaptations and evolution. Although the time line is drawn in equal epochs, vastly more time (about 4 billion years) is represented by the first three epochs than by all of the later periods, which span only the last 540 million years.

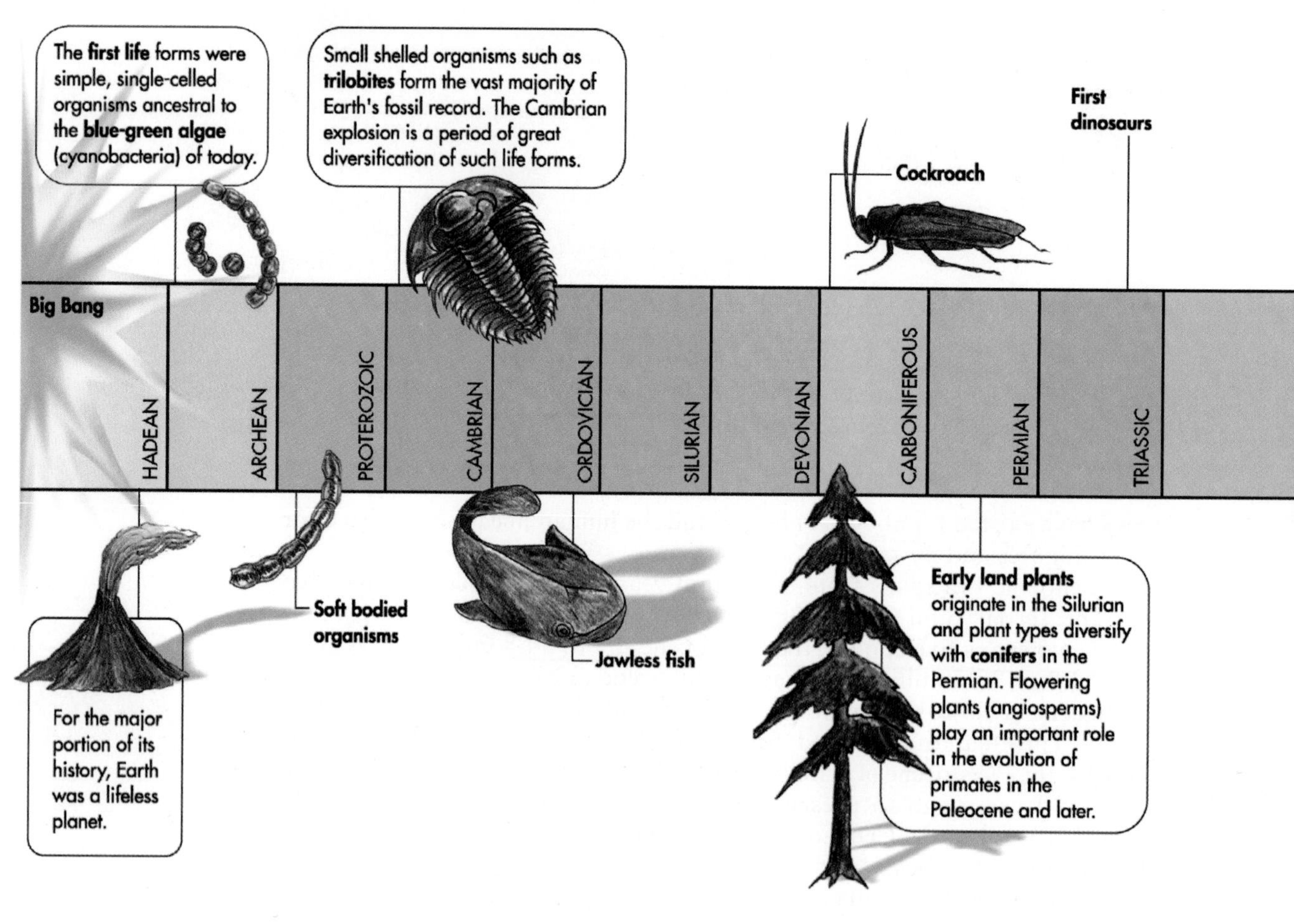

The first life forms were simple, single-celled organisms ancestral to the blue-green algae (cyanobacteria) of today.
Small shelled organisms such as trilobites form the vast majority of Earth's fossil record. The Cambrian explosion is a period of great diversification of such life forms.
First dinosaurs
Cockroach
Big Bang
HADEAN
ARCHEAN
PROTEROZOIC
CAMBRIAN
ORDOVICIAN
SILURIAN
DEVONIAN
CARBONIFEROUS
PERMIAN
TRIASSIC
Soft bodied organisms
Jawless fish
Early land plants originate in the Silurian and plant types diversify with conifers in the Permian. Flowering plants (angiosperms) play an important role in the evolution of primates in the Paleocene and later.
For the major portion of its history, Earth was a lifeless planet.

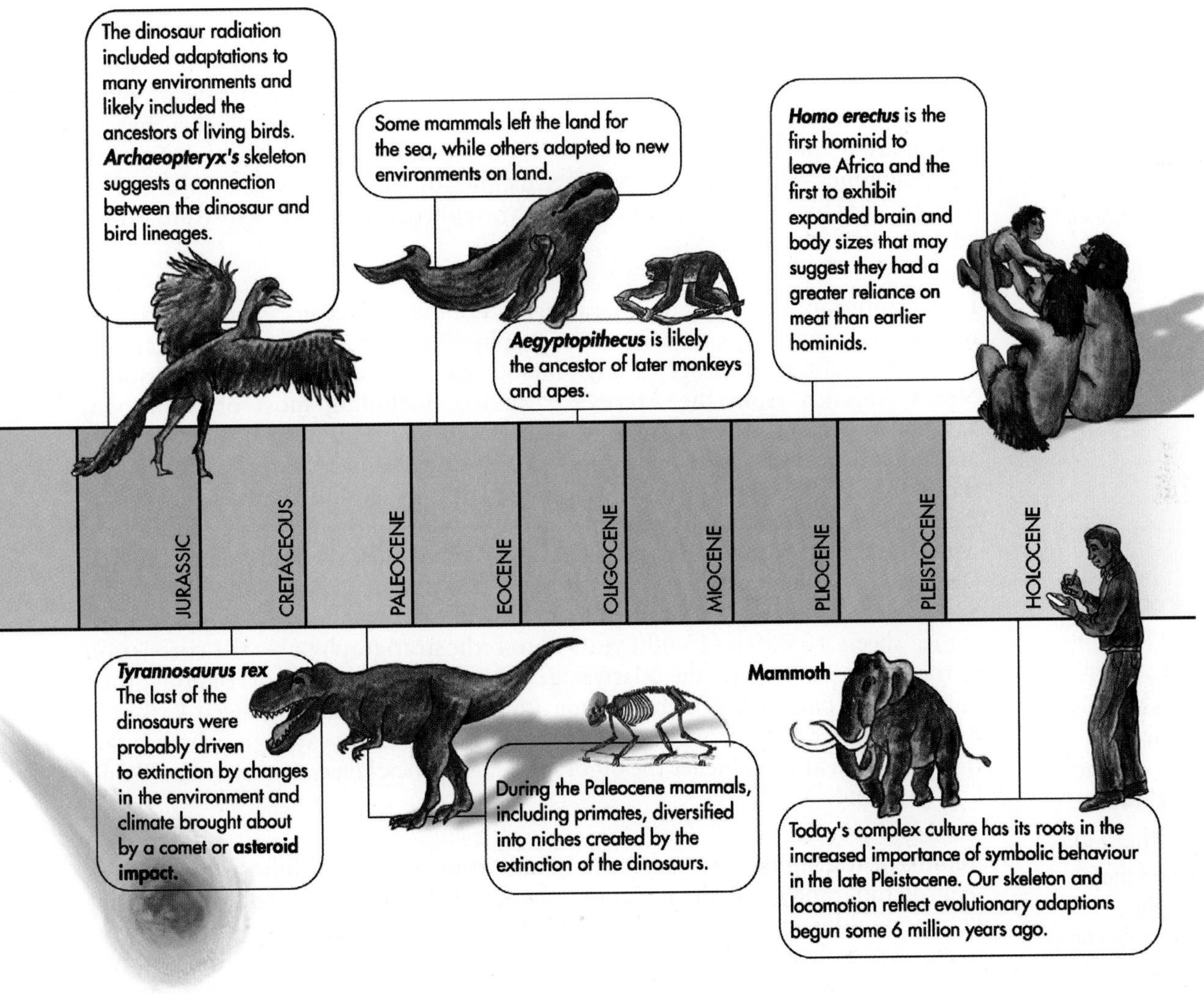
The dinosaur radiation included adaptations to many environments and likely included the ancestors of living birds. Archaeopteryx's skeleton suggests a connection between the dinosaur and bird lineages.
Some mammals left the land for the sea, while others adapted to new environments on land.
Homo erectus is the first hominid to leave Africa and the first to exhibit expanded brain and body sizes that may suggest they had a greater reliance on meat than earlier hominids.
Aegyptopithecus is likely the ancestor of later monkeys and apes.
JURASSIC
CRETACEOUS
PALEOCENE
EOCENE
OLIGOCENE
MIOCENE
PLIOCENE
PLEISTOCENE
HOLOCENE
Tyrannosaurus rex
The last of the dinosaurs were probably driven to extinction by changes in the environment and climate brought about by a comet or asteroid impact.
Mammoth
During the Paleocene mammals, including primates, diversified into niches created by the extinction of the dinosaurs.
Today's complex culture has its roots in the increased importance of symbolic behaviour in the late Pleistocene. Our skeleton and locomotion reflect evolutionary adaptions begun some 6 million years ago.

HOW OLD IS IT?

How do we determine where in the geologic time scale a site and the fossils within it fall? A vital first step in determining the antiquity of fossil remains is learning their **provenience**, the precise location from which the fossils come. After we have established provenience, we can apply a wide variety of techniques to estimating the age of fossil remains. These techniques fall into three main categories depending on the underlying method used. Relative dating techniques use concepts of stratigraphy to establish relative ages between localities and fossils found in these localities. Calibrated relative dating techniques compare a relative technique to an absolute time scale. Chronometric (or "absolute") dating techniques use an absolute clock, such as radioactivity, to produce an age estimate in years before present. Collectively, the field of geology devoted to studying time in the fossil record is *geochronology*. We review some of the major methods of this field in the next section.

RELATIVE DATING TECHNIQUES

Relative dating techniques tell us how old something is in relation to something else without applying an actual chronological age. If you say you have an older brother, we know your relative ages even though we do not know whether the two of you are 6 and 16 years old, 19 and 25, or 60 and 65. Almost all relative dating techniques rely on the geological principles of stratigraphy discussed earlier. These techniques include lithostratigraphy, tephrostratigraphy, biostratigraphy, and chemical methods.

Lithostratigraphy Using the characteristics of the rock layers themselves to correlate across regions is called **lithostratigraphy** (*litho* refers to rock). For example, 100 to 60 million years ago, a large inland sea covered much of the interior of North America from the Arctic to Mexico, including most of Manitoba, Saskatchewan, and Alberta. Sand was deposited on the shore that, over millions and millions of years, slowly compacted to become sandstone rock. Erosion has formed the badlands that can be seen in the Drumheller and Dinosaur Provincial Park regions of Alberta and has exposed the remains of dinosaurs that lived there when the climate was subtropical. The tracts of badlands, extending along the Red Deer River Valley eastward from Red Deer City through Drumheller to the Saskatchewan border, were carved by melt water torrents in the wake of retreating ice sheets 10 000 to 15 000 years ago. Lithostratigraphy uses the correlation of rock units to estimate the relative age of different areas. The overlapping rock units for the badlands of Alberta indicate that at Dinosaur Provincial Park, the Red Deer River cuts through rocks laid down 76 million years ago, whereas farther upstream at Drumheller the dinosaur bearing rock layers are less than 70 million years old.

Tephrostratigraphy An increasingly important variant of lithostratigraphy is **tephrostratigraphy**, the identification of a volcanic ash by its chemical fingerprint of major, minor, and trace elements (Feibel, 1999). Chemical similarities allow us to correlate volcanic ashes (*tephra*) with one another, demonstrating time equivalence even in widely separated sites. This technique has been used with great success in the Turkana Basin of northern Kenya and southern Ethiopia, where researchers have made many important discoveries of ancestral human fossils. Closer to home, archaeological sites in southern British Columbia and Alberta have been dated by their relationship to a layer of volcanic ash: 7700 years ago, the eruption of Mount Mazama in southern Oregon was so large that volcanic ash reached as far as Calgary and Edmonton.

provenience The origin or original source (as of a fossil).

relative dating techniques Dating techniques that establish the age of a fossil only in comparison to other materials found above and below it.

lithostratigraphy The study of geologic deposits and their formation, stratigraphic relationships, and relative time relationships based on their lithologic (rock) properties.

tephrostratigraphy A form of lithostratigraphy in which the chemical fingerprint of a volcanic ash is used to correlate across regions.

Biostratigraphy Making correlations based on biological organisms is called **biostratigraphy**. Organisms that are geographically widespread and vary anatomically through short time periods are the best biostratigraphic markers. Biostratigraphic markers that appear and disappear (go extinct) at roughly the same chronological time in all regions are most useful. Using the principle of faunal succession (Figure 9.5), we can use the biological organisms found in rocks to correlate age between sites and across regions and thus to provide age estimates for fossils found at those sites.

Rodents often are good biostratigraphic indicators of age. For example, the presence of certain rodent taxa that went extinct in the Early Pleistocene have been used to estimate the age of sites of some of the earliest hominids outside Africa. The presence of such taxa tells you only how old the site is relative to other sites with similar or different animals. An absolute age (that is, an age in years, such as 1.6 million years old) can be assigned only because at other sites with these index fossils there are also associated absolute ages.

The Earth's history spans 4.5 billion years. Geologists and palaeontologists have pieced together the history of the Earth by correlating rock strata and examining the fossils within those rocks. Most of Earth's history is lifeless. Primates arise only about 65 million years ago, and the human lineage only 6 million years ago. Understanding primates in their geological context is critical to understanding their adaptations and evolution. Although the time line is drawn in equal epochs, vastly more time (about 4 billions years) is represented by the first three epochs than by all of the later periods, which span only the last 540 million years.

biostratigraphy Relative dating technique using comparison of fossils from different stratigraphic sequences to estimate which layers are older and which are younger.

calibrated relative dating techniques Techniques that can be correlated to an absolute chronology.

geomagnetic polarity time scale (GPTS) Time scale composed of the sequence of palaeomagnetic orientations of sediments through time.

Chemical Techniques within Sites A few chemical techniques are useful for identifying the relative age of different fossils from the same site. These techniques include the analysis of the fluorine, uranium, and nitrogen content of the fossils themselves. Such techniques become important when the association between different fossils or between the fossils and their sediments is in question, as in the Piltdown hoax, in which chemical techniques proved that the human fossils were fakes (Box 9.1). As bones and teeth lie buried in sediment, they take up elements from the soil, roughly in proportion to the amount of time they have been buried (Oakley, 1963). The presence and quantity of these elements depends on the local environment, so the techniques are not useful between sites. Two bones buried in the same sediments for the same amount of time, however, should have similar chemical signatures. Thus these methods test associations within sites.

Calibrated Relative Dating Techniques

Calibrated relative dating techniques include regular or somewhat regular processes that can be calibrated to a chronological scale if certain conditions are known. **Palaeomagnetism** is one such technique that can be applied to the interpretation of fossils. Palaeomagnetists have assembled a **geomagnetic polarity time scale (GPTS)** that is based on a sequence of changes in the magnetism of ancient layers (Figure 9.8).

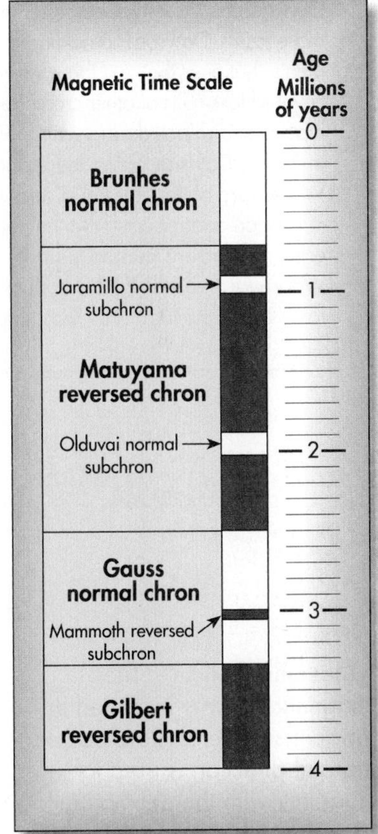

FIGURE 9.8 The geomagnetic polarity time scale shows how the Earth's magnetic pole has changed through geologic time. Red bands indicate periods of reversed polarity and white bands indicate normal polarity.

Although we take for granted the current position of the Earth's north and south magnetic poles, the polarity of the Earth's magnetic field has alternated through geologic time (Brown, 1992). Currents in the Earth's outer core create this magnetism, and as they change, the Earth's polarity may flip. At times in the past, magnetic north has been in the South Pole. Such reversals occur quickly, perhaps over thousands of years, and do not last for set periods of time. As rocks are formed, their magnetic minerals orient themselves toward magnetic north. Rocks

Box 9.1 The Piltdown Hoax

Sometimes in the history of science, preconceptions about the way life should be get in the way of how it really is. The most vivid and embarrassing example of this in the history of palaeoanthropology is Piltdown Man (Figure A). From 1908 to 1913, a number of fossil fragments were uncovered in a gravel pit at Piltdown Common, near the village of Uckfield in southern England, that appeared to show that the cradle of humankind was in the United Kingdom.

A labourer who was quarrying gravel at the site made the first find when his pickaxe struck a human skull fragment. He turned his discovery over to Charles Dawson, a local attorney and amateur geologist, who launched an intensive search at the site for more fossils. Dawson did not find more fragments, but over the next three years he discovered fossil bits of other creatures such as hippos and rhinos during visits to Piltdown. In 1911, Dawson contacted Arthur Smith Woodward of the Natural History Museum in London and reported that he had uncovered an ancient human skull (Figure B). Woodward visited Piltdown and saw the fossils that spring, and was impressed. During ensuing excavations, Dawson and Woodward retrieved more primitive human fossils and fossils of an assortment of long-extinct mammals. The key finds were the original skull, with an estimated cranial capacity smaller than that of a Neandertal but in other respects quite modern looking, and a large mandible with teeth that were decidedly apelike (Spencer, 1990).

The anatomy of "Piltdown Man" might have tipped off experts immediately that it was a fake. Piltdown possessed a large, humanlike braincase, with primitive apelike teeth and jaws. Today, we know that the earliest humans possessed the opposite suite of traits: a small, apelike brain with bipedal lower anatomy.

However, when Piltdown Man was announced to the world in 1912, at the same prehistory conference in which two far better-documented fossil humans, Neandertal and Java Man (*Homo erectus*), were disputed and even dropped from the human family tree by some prominent scientists, the leading scientists of the Western world believed firmly that the first humans lived in Europe and were large brained. European scholars waged nationalistic verbal battles over whether the earliest humans would be found in Britain, France, or Germany. Although a few scientists advocated East Asia as the cradle of

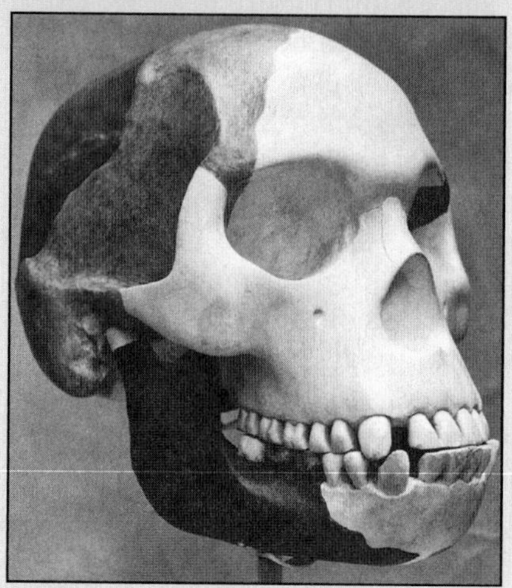

FIGURE A The Piltdown hoax was exposed by fluorine analysis, a relative dating technique that can test whether two bones have come from the same palaeontological site. The mandible and skull fragment were shown to have different fluorine compositions.

laid down today would have a polarity, or orientation, similar to today's magnetic field. Such polarities are called *normal*. Rocks formed under a reversed field have a *reversed polarity*. Geologists use these facts to assist in the dating of stratigraphic units (Figure 9.9 and Figure 9.10).

palaeomagnetism The magnetic polarity recorded in ancient sediments. Reversed or normal direction is used to correlate with the geomagnetic polarity time scale to infer an age for a site.

chronometric dating techniques Techniques that estimate the age of an object in absolute terms through the use of a natural clock such as radioactive decay or tree ring growth.

CHRONOMETRIC DATING TECHNIQUES

Unlike relative dating methods, **chronometric dating techniques** provide a chronological age estimate of the antiquity of an object in years before the present. These methods rely on having a clock of some sort to measure time. Such clocks include annual growth rings on trees and the recording of annual cycles of glacial retreat, which date very recent events. Radioactive clocks date more distant events, depending on the isotope used. The most famous of the radioactive decay clocks is Carbon-14 (^{14}C, or radiocarbon), which is widely used in archaeology. Other important techniques include potassium–argon (K–Ar), argon–argon (^{40}Ar/^{39}Ar), and uranium series (U-series) dating.

Other chronometric methods measure not the amount of radioactivity lost (that is, the amount of radioactive decay) since formation but the amount gained from the environment since deposition. These include the electron trap techniques electron spin resonance (ESR), optical stimulated luminescence (OSL), humankind, no one could imagine big-brained progenitors of our species being Africans. That, together with the abundant other fossil European mammals with which the hominid remains were found, contributed to the acceptance of Piltdown as the first European, something of which the British scientific establishment was quite proud.

Yet as new human fossil finds began to accumulate in the 1920s and 1930s, all presented a view of human prehistory different from that offered by Piltdown's advocates. Instead of a large braincase and apelike jaw, most of the new fossils displayed the opposite. Beginning in 1950, British scientists conducted chemical tests on the fossil and found that the level of fluorine in the skull did not match that of the mandible; Piltdown was indeed a fraud. Piltdown Man was really a nearly modern human skull, artfully stained to appear ancient, with an associated orangutan mandible whose teeth had been filed down to appear more human (the file's scratches were clearly visible under a microscope). The mandible's connecting points with the skull had been carefully broken off to disguise the fact that the two did not belong together.

Once the hoax had been exposed, the question of course became, Who did it? The mystery remained unsolved until the 1980s when a cleaning of the attic of the Natural History Museum in London revealed a trunk with the initials of a former museum clerk named Martin Hinton. Inside the trunk was an assortment of hippo and elephant teeth, all stained to the exact colour of the Piltdown fossils. The trunk also contained human teeth that had been stained in different ways, as though by someone practising the best way to fake an ancient appearance.

Hinton had two possible motives. First, he had a financial dispute with one of the curators of the museum and may have wanted to embarrass the museum officials by luring them into boastful claims about a fake ancestor (Gardiner, 2003). Secondly, Hinton was also an avowed anti-Darwinian, preferring Lamarck's debunked views even at the time of the Piltdown discoveries.

It is not clear how Hinton would have planted the fossils in the quarry for Dawson to find unless Dawson (who had a history of "discovering" historical artifacts that turned out to be frauds) was a co-conspirator. It appears that Hinton and Dawson were the likely perpetrators of one of science's greatest hoaxes.

FIGURE B Anatomists disagreed on the importance of the find.

(a)

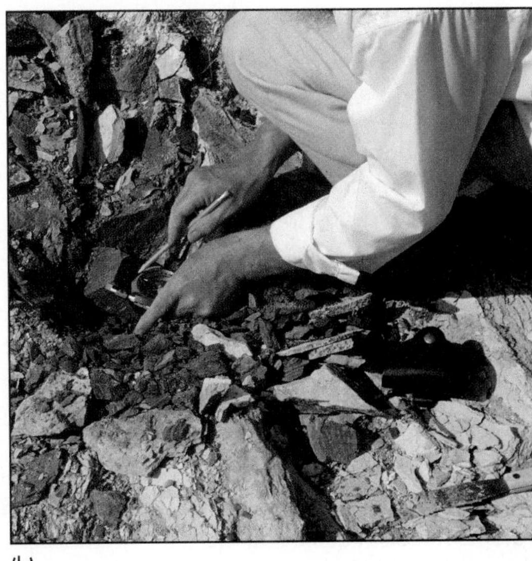

(b)

FIGURE 9.9 (a) At Sangiran, Java, scientists collect rock samples to measure the polarity of the sediments around the time *Homo erectus* fossils were deposited. (b) In the field the scientists use a compass to record the direction of present-day magnetic north that is marked directly on the rock. The polarity of the minerals in the rock itself will be measured later in the lab.

(a)

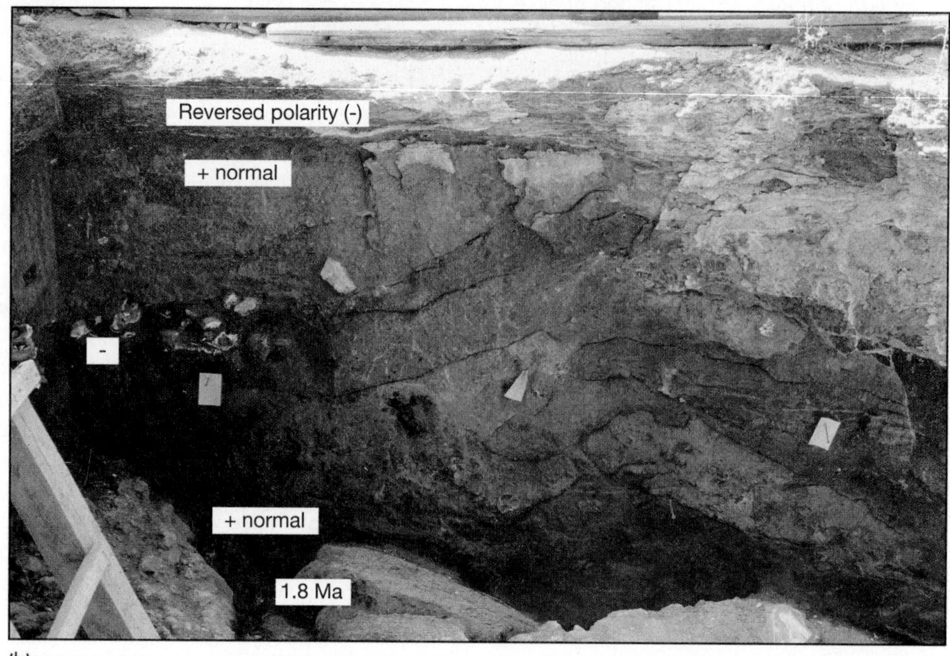

(b)

FIGURE 9.10 (a) The site of Dmanisi, in the Republic of Georgia, has produced some of the earliest *H. erectus* outside of Africa. (b) The basalt below the hominids is dated to 1.8 mya using argon-argon techniques, and the geomagnetic polarity of the sediments is recorded by plusses and minuses on the wall of the excavation. The fossils come from reversed polarity sediments.

and thermoluminescence (TL). Because we are concerned primarily with providing age estimates over the past 65 million years to perhaps as recently as 100 or 50 thousand years ago, we focus here on the clocks appropriate for this time scale. Figure 9.11 illustrates the relative age ranges of the different chronometric techniques discussed in this chapter, and Table 9.1 compares the materials dated.

radiometric dating Chronometric techniques that use radioactive decay of isotopes to estimate age.

isotopes Variant forms of an element that differ based on the number of neutrons in the nucleus. Both stable and unstable (radioactive) isotopes exist in nature.

potassium–argon (K–Ar) dating Radiometric technique using the decay of ^{40}K to ^{40}Ar in potassium-bearing rocks; estimates the age of sediments in which fossils are found.

Radiometric Dating **Radiometric dating** relies on the natural, clocklike decay of unstable isotopes of an element to more stable forms. *Elements* are chemically irreducible categories of matter such as carbon (C), hydrogen (H), and oxygen (O) that form the building blocks of all other matter, such as molecules of water (H_2O) and carbon monoxide (CO). Elements often occur in nature in more than one form, differing in the number of neutrons in the nucleus. These different forms are called **isotopes**.

In this section we review the radiometric techniques most commonly used in palaeoanthropology, beginning with those that measure samples of the oldest geological age.

Potassium–argon (K–Ar) dating measures the decay of a **parent isotope** ^{40}K (potassium) to a **daughter isotope** ^{40}Ar (argon) and requires potassium-bearing minerals,

TABLE 9.1 Comparison of Chronometric Techniques

TECHNIQUE	AGE RANGE	MATERIALS DATED
K–Ar	10 000 to 4.5 billion years	K-bearing minerals and glass
$^{40}Ar/^{39}Ar$	10 000 to 4.5 billion years	K-bearing minerals (can date single grains)
Fission track	Tens of millions of years	Uranium-bearing, noncrystalline minerals, zircon, apatite, and glasses
Uranium series	Thousands to 500 000 years	Uranium-bearing minerals, $CaCo_3$, flowstones, corals, shells, teeth
Radiocarbon	< 40 000 years	Organic materials such as wood, bone, shell
TL	100 000 to 500 000 years depending on material	Quartz, feldspars, pottery, tools
OSL	1 000 to 400 000 years	Quartz, feldspars, pottery, tools
ESR	Typically to 500 000 years and possibly to a few million years depending on material	Uranium-bearing materials and either closed or open systems in which uranium has been taken up from external sources

such as feldspars, to work. The decay from potassium to argon has a **half-life** of 1.3 billion years, making its effective range quite extensive (Deino et al., 1998).

Argon–argon ($^{40}Ar/^{39}Ar$) dating is a refinement of the K–Ar method that allows the use of smaller samples, sometimes even a single crystal, and greater control over the measurements and possible sources of sample error.

K–Ar and the $^{40}Ar/^{39}Ar$ methods have been widely used in palaeoanthropology for dating volcanic sediments associated with hominids in Africa, Georgia, and Indonesia. These methods date the timing of the formation of the volcanic rocks. Fortunately, there are many situations in which fossil hominids are in sediments sandwiched between volcanic sediments, so we can estimate the fossil ages by their association with the age of the volcanics.

Fission track dating provides age estimates for noncrystalline materials such as volcanic glasses. Fission track techniques rely on counting the small tracks produced each time an atom of ^{238}U decays by fission (hence its name). Fission track dating provides a viable age range from about 100 years to the oldest rocks on Earth,

parent isotope The original radioactive isotope in a sample.

daughter isotope (product) The isotope that is produced as the result of radioactive decay of the parent isotope.

half-life The time it takes for half of the original amount of an unstable isotope of an element to decay into more stable forms.

argon–argon ($^{40}Ar/^{39}Ar$) dating Radiometric technique modified from K–Ar that measures ^{40}K by proxy using ^{39}Ar. Allows measurement of smaller samples with less error.

fission track dating Radiometric technique for dating noncrystalline materials using the decay of ^{238}Ur and counting the tracks that are produced by this fission. Estimates the age of sediments in which fossils are found.

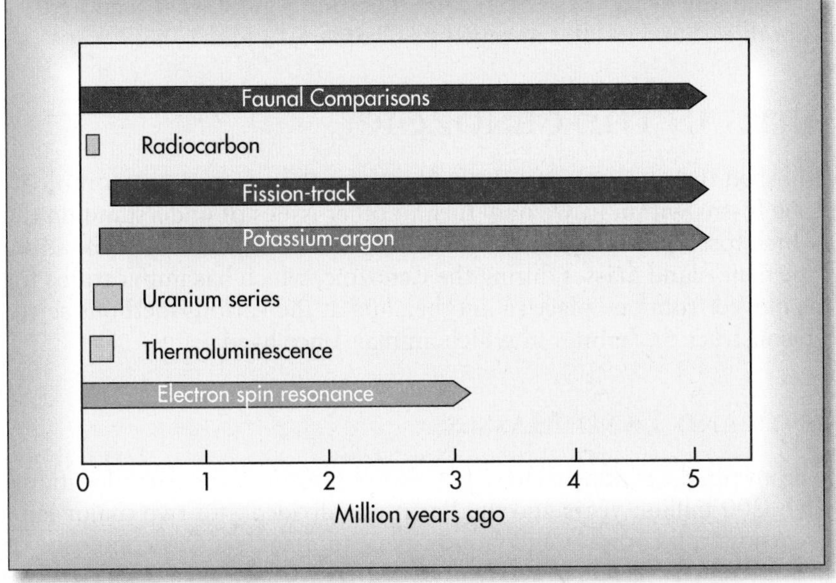

FIGURE 9.11 The relative age ranges of different dating techniques depend upon the half-life of the system used.

uranium series (U-series) techniques Radiometric techniques using the decay of uranium to estimate an age for calcium carbonates including flowstones, shells, and teeth.

radiocarbon dating Radiometric technique that uses the decay of ^{14}C in organic remains such as wood and bone to estimate the time since death of the organism.

electron trap techniques Radiometric techniques that measure the accumulation of electrons in traps in the crystal lattice of a specimen.

thermoluminescence (TL) Electron trap technique that uses heat to measure the amount of radioactivity accumulated by a specimen such as a stone tool since its last heating.

optically stimulated luminescence (OSL) Electron trap technique that uses light to measure the amount of radioactivity accumulated by crystals in sediments (such as sand grains) since burial.

electron spin resonance (ESR) Electron trap technique that measures the total amount of radioactivity accumulated by a specimen such as tooth or bone since burial.

although it is not as reliable for very young (<100 000 years) or very old samples. It often is used as an ancillary to other chronometric techniques. The fission track method has been used to date materials in China that are associated with early evidence of stone tool manufacture.

Uranium series (U-series) techniques use the decay chain of ^{238}U, ^{235}U, and ^{232}Th to provide age estimates for calcium carbonates, such as flowstones precipitated in caves, shells of invertebrates, and sometimes teeth. Uranium series techniques usually date strata associated with a fossil, not the fossil itself. Associations therefore are critical to providing the correct age estimate for a fossil, and because cave stratigraphy is often complex, these associations may not be accurate.

Uranium series techniques have been critical for estimating ages for hominid sites, particularly those outside the range of radiocarbon and those in areas lacking volcanic rocks, such as China. Uranium series techniques on both flowstones and teeth at Chinese hominid sites have established ages for the famous Peking Man site that suggest a time range between about 250 000 and 600 000 years ago (see Chapter 12).

Radiocarbon dating is the primary technique for estimating the antiquity of organic items from the latest Pleistocene through the present, including primate and human fossils as well as artifacts from archaeological sites. Radiocarbon dating can be used only on organic materials such as wood or bone, and is useful for remains from the last 30 000 to 40 000 years. Although the method has been used to date some rare and fascinating artifacts, such as a 9500-year-old stick wrapped in cordage recovered from a waterlogged site in Haida Gwaii (Fedje et al., 2005), the limited age range of the ^{14}C technique limits its palaeoanthropological applications to the latest part of the Neandertal lineage and their overlap with anatomically modern humans.

Electron Trap Techniques, which include electron spin resonance, thermoluminescence, and optical stimulated luminescence, rely not on the decay of radioactive isotopes in a specimen but on the effect that exposure to radioactivity has on the specimen. Only crystalline materials can be dated with these methods.

Thermoluminescence (TL) has been used on archaeological tools made of burnt flint, producing dates that suggest that Neandertals and modern humans alternated their use of the region over time, perhaps in response to climatic conditions in the region (see Chapter 13). **Optically stimulated luminescence** (**OSL**) is another electron trap technique that has been used successfully to investigate the initial colonization of Australia. **Electron spin resonance** (**ESR**) has been most successfully applied to tooth enamel and has been critical in corroborating the early age of fossils in the Near East (Stringer et al., 1989; Grun et al., 1991) (Figure 9.12). In conjunction with uranium series and TL analyses, these data suggest that modern humans occupied the Near East early but that the region was occupied by Neandertals both earlier and later in time (see Chapters 13 and 14).

THE EARTH IN THE CENOZOIC

Having established the various ways we might assess the age of a palaeontological site and the fossils within it, we now turn to other issues of understanding the context in which fossil primates are found. Most importantly we will look at the position of the major land masses during the Cenozoic, which has implications for how animals moved from one place to another, and at the various methods scientists use to reconstruct the habitat in which animals once lived.

CONTINENTS AND LAND MASSES

As you may be aware, the continents have not always been in their current locations. Approximately 200 million years ago the Earth was divided into two major land masses that we now call Laurasia and Gondwanaland. Laurasia was composed of

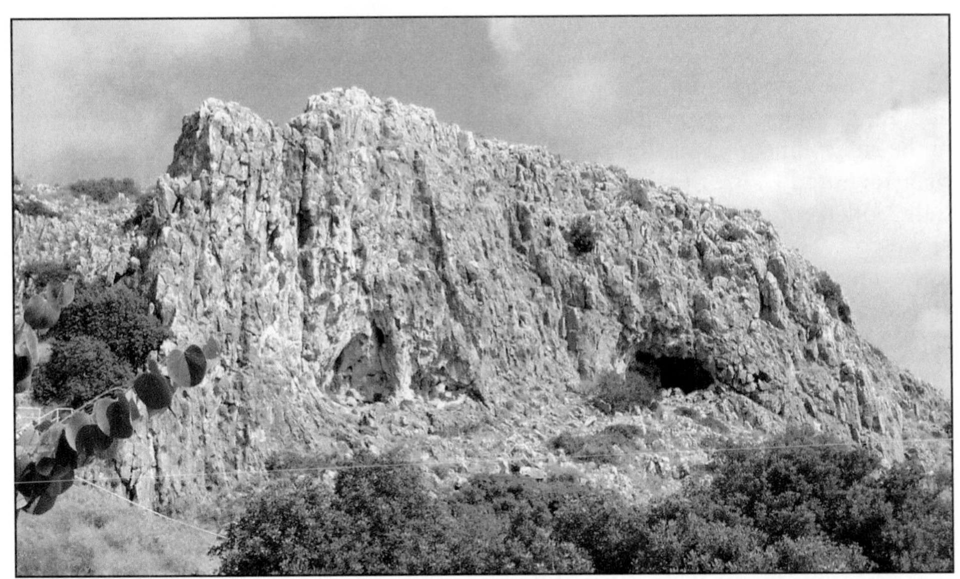

FIGURE 9.12 In the caves of the Mount Carmel region of Israel, electronic spin resonance, uranium series techniques, and thermoluminescence have shown that modern humans and Neandertals alternated their use of the region.

most of present-day North America and Asia, and Gondwanaland included Africa and South America (Figure 9.13). By 50 million years ago North America and Asia were beginning to spread apart, and both South America and Africa had separated from each other and from the other continents. Africa eventually became connected to Asia via the Near East. North America and Asia were separated by a chain of islands (but remained connected during low sea levels). South America was an island continent until well into the Pliocene (~ 3.5 million years ago), when the Central American land bridge connected it to North America. These movements are critical for understanding early primate evolution, particularly the distribution of the Eocene primates and the conundrum of the origin of the South American primates (which appeared while that continent was still an island). Once the continents were in their present positions, the onset of severe glacial events in the Late Pliocene and Pleistocene periodically lowered sea levels, exposing additional land and sometimes resulting, as is the case between continental Asia and Indonesia, in land bridges between otherwise isolated areas (see Chapter 12).

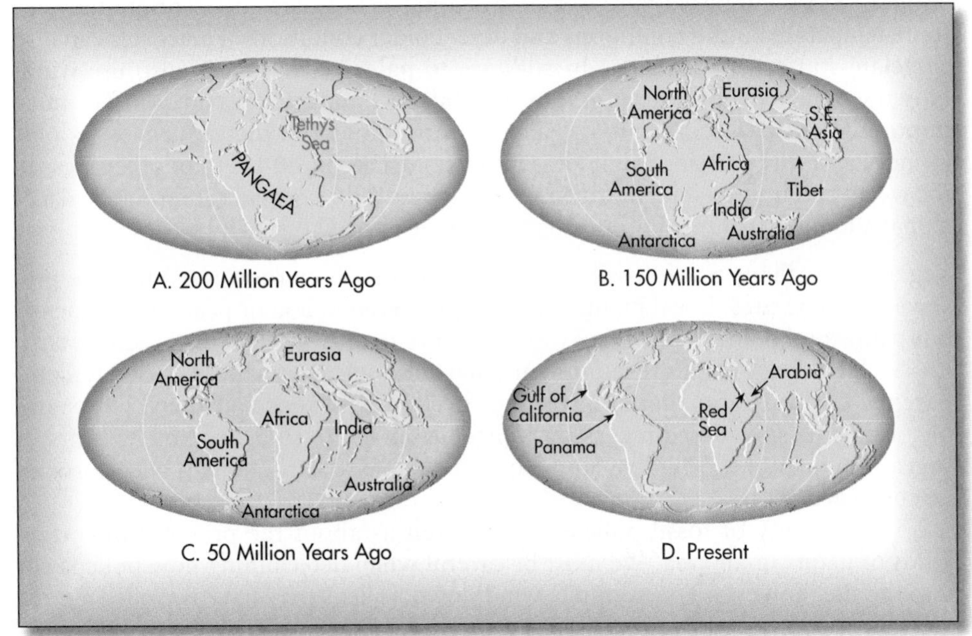

FIGURE 9.13 The continents were not always in their present positions. The position of the continents is important for understanding movements of primates in the past.

How Cold Was It?

Familiarity with an animal's environment is critical to understanding its survival and, in the long run, its evolution or extinction. As we saw in Chapter 2, conditions in the environment naturally select individuals most suited to them, and because of their favoured traits, these individuals reproduce more than others in the population. Understanding past environmental conditions is critical, if complicated. We can reconstruct environmental conditions from several kinds of geological and biological evidence that we refer to here as environmental proxies. For our purposes we consider proxies for reconstruction of temperature, sea levels, and animal and plant communities. Each of these proxies can help us reconstruct local environments from the record at a particular palaeontological or archaeological site. We can aggregate these proxies from different sites over time and across space to infer what the global environment was like and how it changed through time.

Oxygen Isotopes, Temperature, and Sea Level Perhaps the best-known climate proxies are oxygen-isotope curves that rely on the past ratio of stable oxygen isotopes as a proxy for global temperature and sea level. Geologists studying marine cores measure the $^{18}O/^{16}O$ ratio of marine shells through time to develop oxygen isotope curves. Higher ratios indicate colder climates and lower sea levels, whereas lower ratios indicate warmer climates and higher sea levels. We can also use the oxygen isotope ratios in lake sediments to infer local climate, and some scientists have even measured these ratios in human teeth to estimate the temperatures in which those humans lived.

The Plio-Pleistocene is characterized by oscillations in temperature from colder (glacial) to milder (interglacial) periods. Oxygen isotope curves have been important for reconstructing climate patterns in the Middle and Late Pleistocene and correlating the movements of Neandertals and modern humans in relation to climate change (as we'll see in Chapter 13). Microclimates still exist within these patterns—for example, think of the differences in climate between the beach and the mountains—but global climatic proxies can help us understand what kinds of conditions animals lived in during the past.

Palaeosols and Loess Soil formation occurs by weathering of surrounding sediments, and soil structure reflects conditions in the environment at the time the soil was formed. For this reason we can use **palaeosol**, or ancient soil, to understand the environmental conditions that existed for ancient plants and plant-eating animals. For example, differences between palaeosols can differentiate between more temperate humid conditions and dryer colder conditions. Palaeosols can also correlate strata between sites. In addition to palaeosols, we can also use windblown sediments in both stratigraphy and palaeoclimate reconstruction. The most important of these sediments to palaeoanthropology are the sequences of loess (windblown silt) in Asia. Asian loess indicates drier conditions than other loess in the world and is often interstratified with palaeosols that provide additional palaeoclimatic and environmental information (Lowe and Walker, 1997).

Vegetation Plant macrofossils (or other traces such as root casts) may be preserved at some sites. Local plants often are preserved in bog or peat environments, but plants and plant imprints may also fossilize in very fine-grained sediments.

Such evidence of the vegetation at palaeontological sites can be used to compare the environments that animals once lived in with those of today. For example, using fossilized sediments and vegetation data from ancient habitats, a vegetation map of the "edible landscape" available to early human ancestors can be constructed.

The recovery of fossil pollens can also tell us about the presence of certain kinds of plants in an area. We must be careful when determining how pollens got into the site, however. For example, windblown pollens may have travelled a great

palaeosol Ancient soil.

distance, so their presence at a locality may indicate a certain plant within some particular distance of the locality but not precisely at the locality. Mixed pollen samples therefore may be particularly prevalent in patchy environments as well. Also, contamination by modern pollens may be difficult to differentiate.

Another direct means of assessing plant resources is the presence of **phytoliths**, opaline silica bodies secreted by some plants, especially grasses, whose shape is often characteristic of that plant. Fine, wet screening of sediments is needed to retrieve these small items. The presence of phytoliths has been important in the reconstruction of available plants and diet of fossil apes and has been used to interpret the uses of some stone tools.

Stable Carbon Isotope Ratios *Stable carbon isotope ratios* are also useful tools in climatic and environmental reconstructions. They are used to reconstruct the types of vegetation in a region by differentiating between plants using different photosynthetic pathways. Because of their different pathways for photosynthesis, different types of plants retain different ratios of carbon isotopes. By looking at these ratios of stable carbon isotopes in the teeth of fossil animals, we can infer the type of vegetation the animals ate and the type of vegetation present in the area. And by looking at these ratios in various animal taxa in an area or through time, we can begin to build a vegetation map. For example, fossil horse teeth have been used to look at the distribution of grass types throughout the world during the Pleistocene (McFadden et al., 1999). This work suggests that Pleistocene vegetation gradients varied by latitude, as they do today.

We can also look at the stable carbon isotope ratios in palaeosols because the organic carbon found in soils comes from local plants. Analyzing palaeosols in this way has been important in reconstructing environments in Africa during hominid evolution, particularly because the abundance of different grasses varies between open (savannah) environments and shaded or wooded environments.

Animal Communities Although some types of animals seem to be able to live just about anywhere, most have preferred types of habitats. Hippos and crocodiles live near water sources, and the presence of monkeys usually indicates wooded areas. Animals that are adapted to running long distances over open terrain tend to have longer, slighter limbs; those adapted to life in forested areas often tend to have shorter limbs. Based on comparisons with the adaptations in living animals of known habitat preference, palaeontologists infer the climatic and environmental preferences of past animals associated with hominid sites and thus the palaeoenviromental conditions in which hominids lived.

These types of analyses focus on all the animals found at a particular site during a particular time interval, not just on a single species. This is important because the relative abundance of animals can tell you more about an environment than can the presence of a single species. As with pollen analysis, palaeontologists must be careful to consider how the animals were introduced to the site. Does the site represent a single community at a single time or a single community through time? Could the site be sampling animals from different areas? For example, running water might wash in animals from different areas that didn't inhabit the same environmental zone. Therefore, we must carefully assess the taphonomic processes at work on an assemblage.

Once this has been done, the work focuses on trying to reconstruct the ecological community of animals that lived at the site and their diversity. Palaeontologists consider the dietary and locomotor adaptations of the animal. Locomotor categories might include whether the animal in question is terrestrial, arboreal, a combination of the two, aquatic, or a burrower or digger. Trophic level categories describe whether the animal is a browser (eats leaves), grazer (eats grass), frugivore (eats fruit, in combination with other foods), carnivore (eats meat and of what source or in combination with what other foods), or omnivore.

phytoliths Silica bodies produced by some plants, especially grasses, that can be used to indicate the presence of certain types of vegetation at a fossil site.

Combining this information from all the animals of the site gives a good impression of the kind of habitat (trees, water, open areas, and so on) and food (grasses, trees, insects, and so on) that was available. This gives a pretty clear idea of what kind of habitat hominids were living in. For example, based on different species of fossil antelopes found in early hominid sites (Figure 9.14), it appears that the likely habitat in which most early australopithecines lived was wooded regions interspersed with lakes and rivers, and later in the fossil record, again with antelope taxa as markers, the robust australopithecines appeared to prefer habitats that included swamps and marshes (Reed, 1997). These kinds of reconstructions of animal communities have been critical for reconstructing palaeoenvironments of the Plio-Pleistocene hominids in Africa and elsewhere.

Overview of Climatic Changes during the Cenozoic

Based on the kinds of studies just described, scientists have drawn a general picture of the climate during the evolution of the Primate order. In this section we provide an overview of climate changes through the Cenozoic, and in following chapters we will discuss how specific climatic changes affected the evolution of human and nonhuman primates. Recall that climate and environment are the source of important selective pressures that influence the evolution of all animal groups. Figure 9.15 provides a graphic overview of temperature changes throughout the Cenozoic.

Palaeocene to Miocene Climate The story of Cenozoic climate change is generally one of cooling and drying. The Cenozoic began much, much warmer than it is today. Furthermore, there was less difference between temperatures at the equator and the North and South poles than we currently experience. Thus, when primates first arose, not only were they equatorial and subequatorial animals, as they largely are today, but they existed in abundance fairly far north and south. Although it was warmer than today, there was some climatic fluctuation during each epoch. As the era proceeded, the climate cooled and dried but still fluctuated somewhat.

The Palaeocene and Early Eocene were by far the warmest epochs of the Cenozoic. During the Eocene there was a precipitous drop in global temperature until finally, at about the Eocene/Oligocene boundary (around 36 million years ago), there was a decided cold snap that resulted in large-scale extinction and replacement of many species. This "turnover" is often called the *Grande Coupure* (or big cut) because of the large number of taxa that went extinct. The Early Oligocene continued to see decreases in temperature, and then late in the Oligocene temperature rose a bit, returning to the levels at the beginning of the epoch (so it was still quite cold compared with most of the Eocene but warm by modern standards). It is likely that

FIGURE 9.14 Antelope species have specific habitat preferences. These wildebeest prefer more open areas, other species prefer more wooded areas. Identifying the kinds of fossil antelope at hominid sites suggests the kind of environment that existed at that site in the past.

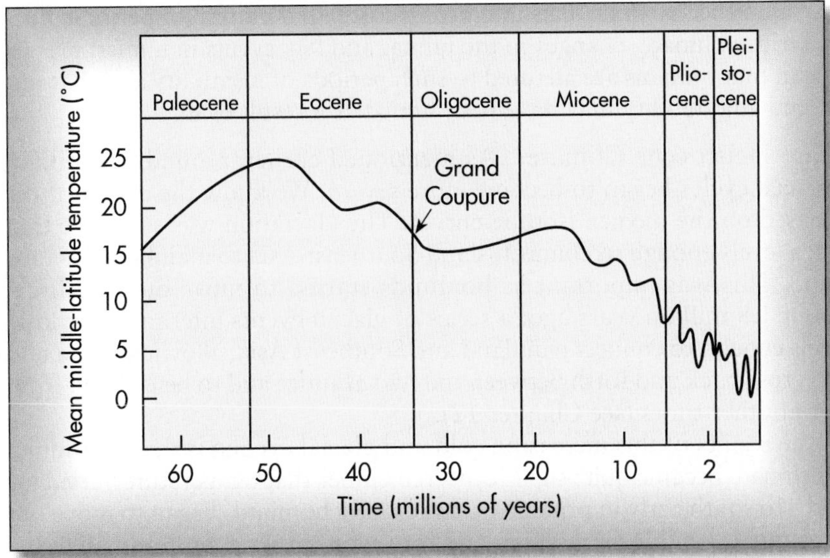

FIGURE 9.15 Climate has cooled substantially during primate evolution.

the lowest temperatures in the Oligocene (at the start, and then again around 31 and 24 million years ago) were associated with short glacial periods. The movement of continents and the resulting changes in ocean and wind currents may have caused these temperature changes.

From the end of the Oligocene to about the middle of the Miocene, temperature rose again gradually, although it remained well below levels of the Eocene. About the middle of the Miocene, perhaps 15 million years ago, another abrupt cooling and drying trend occurred, this time driving temperatures well below any previously experienced in the Cenozoic. This severe cooling probably was related to the appearance of a permanent Antarctic ice sheet at the South Pole. The evolution of the Antarctic ice sheet removed much water from the oceans, resulting in the so-called Messinian event or crisis, in which the Mediterranean ran dry, leaving a great salt lake. These changes in climate often are correlated with the origin, extinction, or diversification of primate groups.

Pliocene to Early Pleistocene Climate During the Early Pliocene temperatures increased and the Mediterranean Sea refilled, but shortly thereafter cooling began again. Ice sheets at both poles became permanent features throughout the Pliocene. Cyclic glaciation set in only about 3 million years ago but did not become more intense until 2.5 million years ago and then became even more intense in the Pleistocene. Most of the palaeoclimatic reconstructions with which we are concerned for human evolution are for the continent of Africa because until a little less than 2 million years ago, our ancestors were entirely restricted to that continent.

It has been argued that there is evidence in the climate data from Earth's history to suggest that physical environmental factors (long-term trends in rainfall and temperature) were more important than biological factors (predators, for example) for mammalian evolution in East Africa. Climate fluctuations over the past 5 to 10 million years occurred as pulses, or punctuated events, that wrought major changes in the community of large animals in East Africa (Vrba, 1996).

In another study, changes in the abundance of various mammalian taxa, from rodents to ungulates, changed over time between 4 and 2 million years ago in the Omo region of Ethiopia (Bobe and Behrensmeyer, 2004). The period of greatest variability in the fossil record (that is, when we see the most shifts in the occurrence of different species of mammals) coincided with the first appearance of the genus *Homo* in the fossil record. A later period of climatic fluctuation that was tied to changes in mammal species diversity was also linked to the appearance of early stone tools, and a still later fluctuation period was linked to the apparent extinction of some australopithecine taxa. This interesting correlated pattern of periodic fluctuations in African climate, changes in the fauna, and key events in human prehistory may mean that humans are adapted to such periods of instability and that our intelligence and adaptability may have been honed as a result of it.

Early to Late Pleistocene Climate As mentioned earlier, around 2.5 million years ago glacial cycles began to become more severe. We know the extent of the glaciation based on the oxygen isotope curves. The glaciation was so severe that it lowered sea levels enough to connect island Southeast Asia to mainland Asia for the first time. This was important as hominids started to move out of Africa. Starting about 1.8 million years ago, a series of glacial events intermittently lowered sea levels enough to connect mainland and Southeast Asia, allowing fauna and hominids to cross back and forth between the two at times and to be isolated from one another at other times (see Chapter 12).

One of the results of this increasing cold and glacial cycling is that latitudinal variation in climate became quite significant (remember that temperature varied little from north to south early in primate evolution). As hominids began to move out of Africa around 1.8 million years ago and into western Asia and ultimately the northerly latitudes of Europe (~800 000), climatic conditions in some instances were quite harsh. This harsh climate appears to have kept hominids from moving too far north permanently until they had sufficient cultural means of mitigating the conditions. Not until Neandertals and their ancestors was there permanent settlement in Europe (see Chapters 13 and 14).

Understanding the context in which fossils are formed and found is critical to identifying their age and the natural selective factors that influence their evolution. Here we have set the foundation for understanding the geological age and environmental context of primate evolution. Next we embark on the evolutionary journey as written in the fossil record.

THE ORIGIN OF PRIMATES

As we have seen, environmental conditions shape the characteristics of a group by favouring individuals who exhibit certain traits and selecting against individuals without those traits (see Chapter 2). So what environmental change or problem favoured the origin of the primate trends? The Palaeocene was warmer than today and was a period of recovery from the giant impact described earlier. In the Palaeocene flowering plants evolved, insects increased in number and diversity as pollinators for these plants, and the plants evolved visual cues to lure these insects. Primate ancestors took advantage of these changing resources by eating insects and possibly fruit from new plants. We know that living primates emphasize vision over olfaction and have tactile pads on their fingers, not hard pads and claws (see Chapter 7). As we move into the Eocene, we see the first true primates and the many ways in which they expand on this early primate adaptation.

EARLY PRIMATES OF THE EOCENE

Climate warmed significantly at the beginning of the Eocene, around 54 million years ago, resulting in the replacement of the archaic mammals of the Palaeocene by the first representatives of a number of modern orders of placental mammals. The fossil record of the Eocene reveals the first true primates, those that possess the bony characters by which we identify living primates. We recognize these fossils as true primates because they possess the full suite of primate trends, including eye sockets positioned on the front of the face (allowing stereoscopic vision and depth perception), a complete postorbital bar for greater protection of the eye, an opposable big toe, and nails (rather than claws) at the ends of their fingers and toes.

At the same time, the reduction of their snouts and whiskers suggests that smell was less important for locating food than was sight (Figure 9.16). The early primates come in two groups, the adapoids and omomyoids. The adapoids are lemurlike and we think they gave rise to the lineages that became the living strepsirhines (lemurs and lorises). The omomyoids are tarsierlike and appear to be ancestral to haplorhines (tarsiers, monkeys, and apes).

adapoids Family of mostly Eocene primates, probably ancestral to all strepsirhines.

omomyoids Family of mostly Eocene primates probably ancestral to all haplorhines.

Adapoids are best considered the most primitive known group of early modern primates. They were mostly small- to medium-sized and weighed approximately 100 grams to 6.9 kilograms (3.5 oz to 15 lb). They were slow-moving arboreal quadrupeds that were active by day and probably ate fruit and leaves. The fossil record of true lemurs is confined to the Holocene of Madagascar. This record of lemur diversity before human occupation of the islands provides a good example of an adaptive radiation.

Omomyoids were even more diverse than the adapoids. They were smaller-bodied primates (30 grams to 2.2 kilograms [1 oz to 5 lbs]) that ate diets of insects

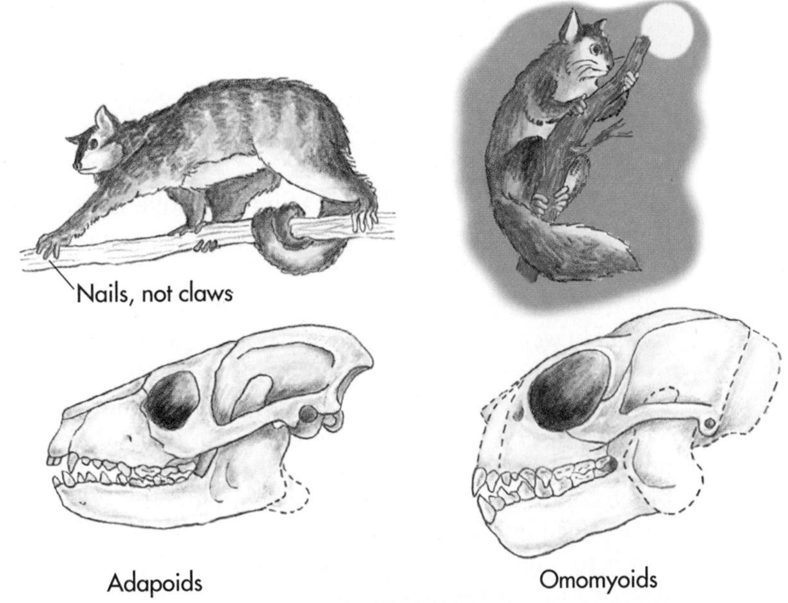

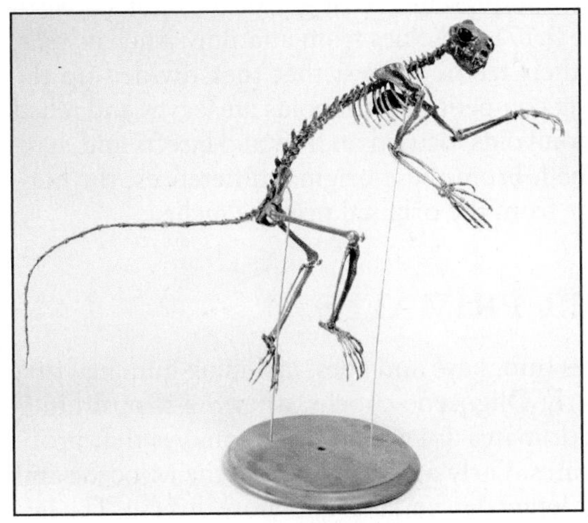

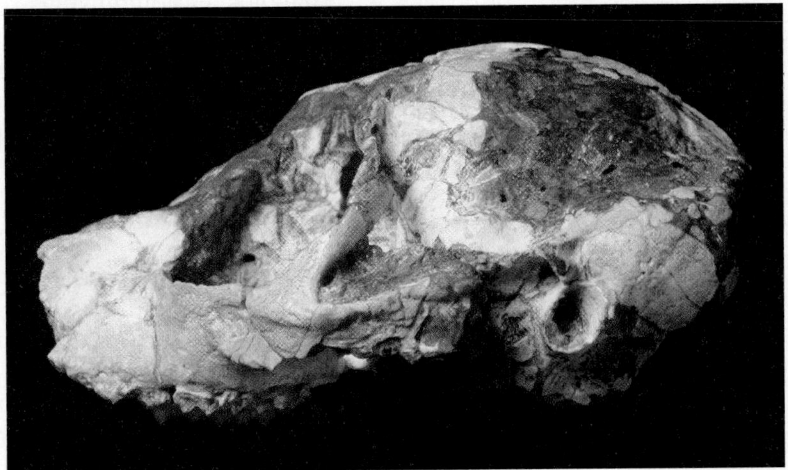

FIGURE 9.16 Adapoids (left) and omomyoids (right) are the first "true" primates. Both have a postorbital bar. Omomyoids have shorter snouts.

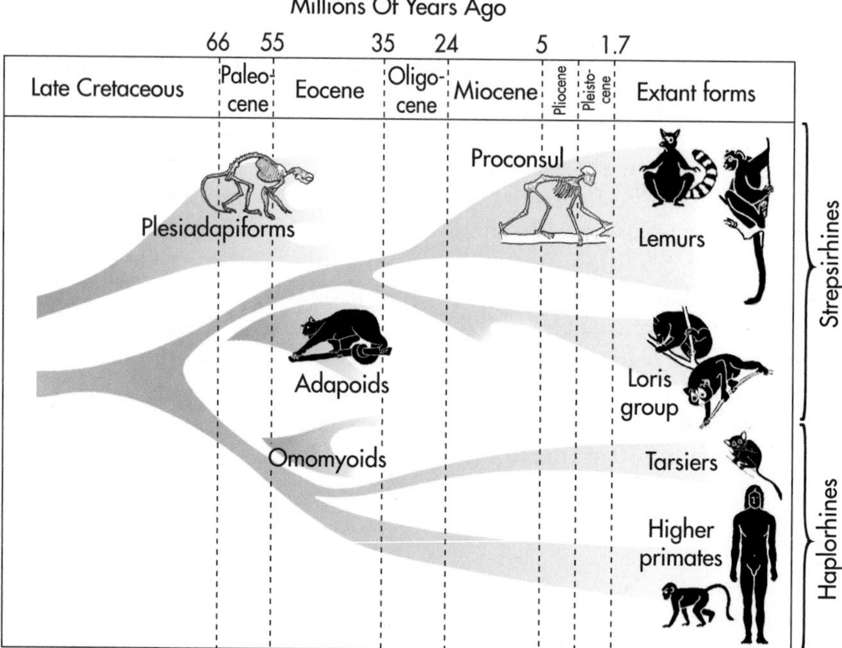

FIGURE 9.17 Possible relationships between fossil and living primates: Plesiadapiforms may or may not be primates. Adapoids are probably ancestral to living strepsirhines, and omomyoids to living haplorhines.

and fruit and had larger orbits, probably for a nocturnal lifestyle. Their limb bones probably were evolved for active arboreal quadrupedalism and leaping, as indicated by the anatomy of their hind limb and ankle bones. Although they occur in both Europe and North America, omomyoids are more abundant in North America. The geographic distribution of the adapoids and omomyoids in North America and Europe is understandable if you recall from earlier in this chapter the position of the continents between 54 and 34 million years ago. Europe and North America were joined by a broad band of land, and there was little difference in climate from north to south or east to west. Thus the distribution of primates from North America to Europe makes sense given that they could have freely moved between the two.

Adapoids and omomyoids seem to represent the origin of the split between strepsirhines and haplorhines (Figure 9.17) and clues from anatomy (such as relative snout length and the shape of their teeth) suggest that they divided up the available food resources, thus avoiding competition. Adapoids ate leaves and relied more on their sense of smell while omomyoids focused on fruit and insects and, having a shorter snout, relied less on smell. From these original differences, the haplorhines eventually diverged quite far from the original primate niche.

EVOLUTION OF HIGHER PRIMATES

Representatives of the higher primates (monkeys and apes, including humans) first appeared in the Late Eocene and Early Oligocene epochs, after the strepsirhine–haplorhine split. The earliest higher primates are generalized monkeys that probably gave rise to all later higher primates. Early apes appeared in the Miocene and were also more generalized than their living descendants and more diverse. The initially diverse apes decreased in abundance through time, while the monkeys became more abundant.

Box 9.2 Questionable Primates: The Plesiadapiforms

During the Palaeocene Epoch, many archaic groups of mammals arose that are not precisely like any living group. Among the new arrivals at the beginning of the Palaeocene are primate-like mammals, the **plesiadapiforms**, either a separate order of mammals or a suborder of the primates, on equal footing with strepsirhines and haplorhines (Figure A). For this reason we call the plesiadapiforms questionable primates. Known mainly from North America, the plesiadapiforms have also been discovered in Europe and in China and range from the Early Palaeocene to the Late Eocene.

Palaeontologists use the form of teeth and bones to decide to which group a fossil belongs, so to be identified as primates fossils must show the primate trends in anatomy. The controversy with the plesiadapiforms arises because in many ways they were more primitive than any living primate. They had small brains, a prognathic face that projected well in front of their braincase, and small eye sockets positioned on the sides rather than the front of their face. They lacked a postorbital bar, a bony ring encircling the eye, a key feature of primates that indicates the importance of vision to the order. Many plesiadapiforms possessed large, rodentlike lower incisors that were separated from the premolars by a large diastema, or gap between their anterior teeth Some had claws (rather than nails) and lacked an opposable big toe. In all these ways plesiadapiforms do not look like primates.

An *adaptive radiation* of plesiadapiforms led to a variety of these mammals, ranging from the very tiny, mouse-sized forms, approximately 20 grams (0.70 lb) to creatures that are about the size of a small monkey at 5 kilograms (11 lb). The plesiadapiform radiation reveals clearly that very early primates (or primatelike mammals) were anatomically more primitive than living primates in almost all respects, although some families were also quite specialized. Some of the more generalized forms may have been ancestors of the primates alone or of primates and other closely related mammals (such as tree shrews and bats). In recent years there has been a tendency to exclude some or all of the plesiadapiforms from the order Primates (Rasmussen, 2002). However, Professor Mary Silcox of the University of Winnipeg has been studying the skeletal remains of several of the plesiadapiforms and argues that there is fossil evidence that indicates that at least some of these archaic forms were true primates that diverged before the last common ancestor (LCA) of living species (Bloch and Silcox, 2001, 2005; Silcox, 2003).

Although some plesiadapiforms persisted into the Eocene, they failed to compete with the first "primates of modern aspect."

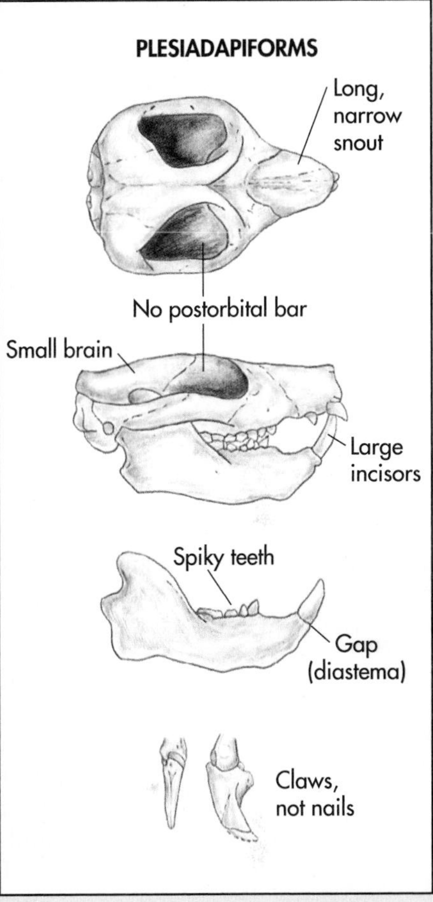

Figure A The plesiadapiforms may have been primates but they lacked certain features, such as a postorbital bar and nails, common to living primates. Note also their small brain and long nose.

The First Monkeys?

The marked cooling and drying of the climate at the end of the Eocene resulted in a large-scale faunal turnover that created both challenges and opportunities for the animal populations alive at the time. In response, the adapoids and omomyoids nearly vanished from North America and Europe, as did many other mammalian taxa. Likewise, animals that we recognize as monkeys first appeared in the Oligocene. Remember from Chapter 7 that all higher primates (monkeys, apes, and humans) share certain anatomical characters, including greater enclosure of the orbits, smaller snouts, fewer teeth, a fused frontal bone and a fused mandible (Figure 9.18), as well as larger body size. These anatomical changes signal alterations in the foraging habits of these primates, probably catalyzed by changing environmental conditions.

plesiadapiforms Fossil mammals of the Palaeocene Epoch that appear primate-like, but lack certain features of the skull that are common to living primates. Thus they are referred to as "questionable" primates.

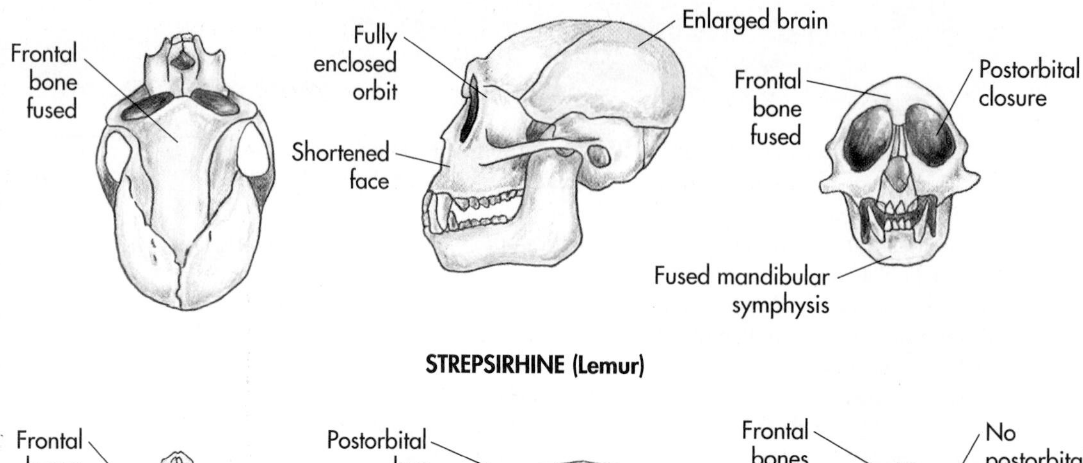

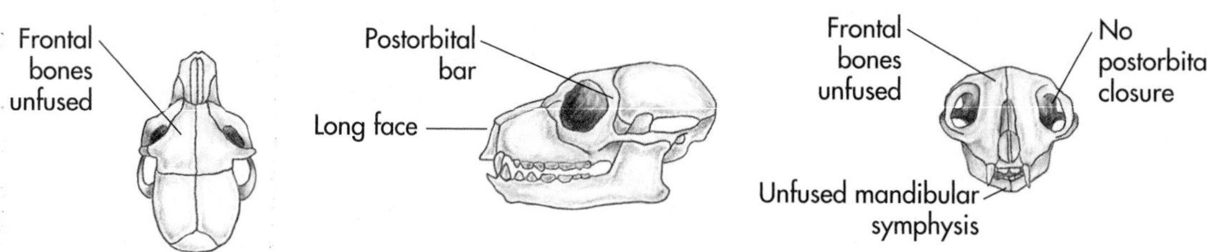

FIGURE 9.18 The skulls of living haplorhines differ from those of strepsirhines by having enlarged brains, an enclosed orbit, and fused frontals and mandibles.

The fossil record provides two windows into the origin of anthropoids. One is in China, the other in North Africa and the Middle East. These fossils combine primitive features and anthropoidlike features. It is not until the end of the Eocene and the Early Oligocene that we find clear anthropoids in the fossil record. Like modern higher primates, these early anthropoids possessed advanced features of the skull and jaws, including a fused frontal bone, a fused lower jaw, and post-orbital closure, that distinguish them from strepsirhines (Figure 9.18). Early anthropoids reveal a radiation of monkeys, some of which may have been ancestral to all later anthropoids, whereas others may have been early representatives of the Old World higher primates, before the divergence of Old World monkeys, apes, and humans.

Much of what we know about the evolution of higher primates in the Late Eocene and Early Oligocene comes from research at the Fayum depression in Egypt, which was at the time a lushly forested area that supported a variety of tropical flora and fauna. Scientists have found several genera of small early anthropoids in the Fayum deposits, including the genus *Apidium*, which possessed three premolars (that is, a dental formula of 2:1:3:3) like living New World monkeys, suggesting that it may have been ancestral to all later anthropoids. Another genus in the Fayum fossil record, *Aegyptopithecus*, had a 2:1:2:3 dental formula and thus may have been an early representative of the Old World higher primates, before the divergence of Old World monkeys, apes, and humans.

NEW WORLD MONKEYS

The earliest fossil record of monkeys in South America comes from Late Oligocene (about 30 to 25 million years ago) deposits in Bolivia (Fleagle and Tejedor, 2002). How monkeys got to South America is still something of a mystery. As we learned earlier in this chapter, South America was an island continent during the early part of the Cenozoic (the connection to Central and North America, via the Panamanian Isthmus, was established less than 5 million years ago by sea level changes), but the

Atlantic Ocean would have been far less of a geographic barrier to dispersal from the Old World because it was not as wide as it is today. Most scientists currently support a model that supposes an ancestor "rafting over" from Africa to South America during the Late Eocene or Early Oligocene (Hartwig, 1994) in the same way that animals get isolated on floating mats (natural or vegetative) during floods and are carried to sea.

However they got there, in the Early and Middle Miocene we see an increasingly rich fossil record of New World monkeys (Rosenberger, 2002).

Old World Monkeys

The fossil record tells us that the common ancestor of Old World monkeys and apes had anatomical features shared by both monkeys and apes, such as a bony ear tube and the presence of two rather than three premolars, but lacked characters unique to each group, such as the bilophodont molars characteristic of modern Old World monkeys and the suspensory shoulder characteristic of modern apes. The earliest fossil evidence of a lineage leading just to Old World monkeys comes from a 19-million-year-old site in Uganda.

The Plio-Pleistocene radiation of African Old World monkeys is based on fossils collected at numerous sites. These monkeys were more diverse in terms of their body size, locomotion, and dietary habits than monkeys are today. They also appear to have formed distinct communities in eastern and southern areas of Africa. For example, there were many medium- and large-sized species in the Plio-Pleistocene of eastern Africa, where some were adapted for life in the trees and others apparently lived on the ground.

The Earliest Apes

Living ape species are few in number and limited to just four genera: *Hylobates* (the gibbons and Siamangs), *Pongo* (the orangutan), *Gorilla* (the gorilla), and *Pan* (the bonobo and the common chimpanzee). However, the fossil record of hominoid primates reveals a surprisingly diverse succession of adaptive radiations. This ape fossil record is characterized first by the appearance of **dental apes**, animals with apelike teeth but monkeylike postcranial skeletons.

Fossil apes first appeared during the Early Miocene, approximately 23 to 16 million years ago. At that time, hominoids were almost totally restricted to Africa (Figure 9.19). Unlike today, the Early Miocene of Africa probably was covered by uninterrupted expanses of forest and moist woodland. The uplifting and rifting that dominate eastern Africa today had not yet occurred, nor had the climatic divisions of arid and wet zones.

On this forested continent lived dozens of genera of early apes with very monkeylike postcranial skeletons but with the characteristic Y-5 molar pattern of apes (Figure 9.20). These primitive apes were small-bodied compared with modern apes, they lacked a suspensory shoulder for brachiating, and they walked on the soles of their feet rather than on their knuckles. But we call them dental apes to show that we recognize them as apes based on their dental anatomy. In contrast to Old World monkeys, which have high-crested molars for shearing leaves, all apes possess molars with five rounded cusps, connected by a pattern of Y-shaped fissures or grooves.

The best known of the early dental apes is the genus *Proconsul* (Figure 9.21), which lived in Africa about 20 to 18 million years ago. Until recently, *Proconsul* was thought to be the LCA of great apes and hominids, but in 1997 a new species of Miocene ape, *Morotopithecus bishopi*, was identified. *Morotopithecus* exhibits primitive conditions of the upper jaws that indicate a basal position within the hominoid radiation, but portions of the backbone and the shoulder girdle suggest

dental apes Early apes exhibiting Y-5 molar patterns but monkeylike postcranial skeletons.

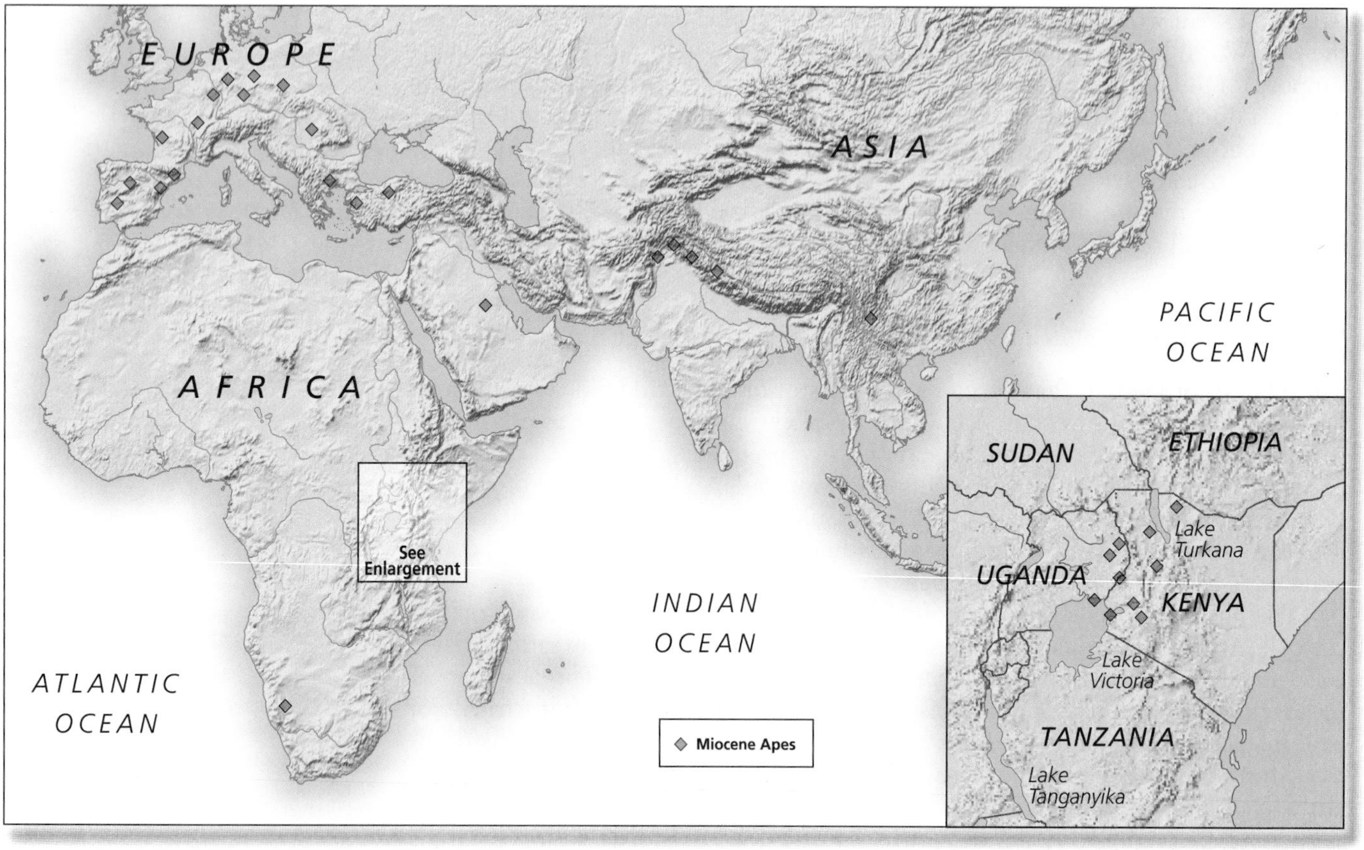

FIGURE 9.19 Miocene apes were found throughout Europe, continental Asia, and Africa. Important East African localities are plotted on the inset map.

that, unlike *Proconsul, Morotopithecus* possessed the short and stiff back and suspensory shoulder anatomy of the modern brachiating (arm-swinging) apes (MacLatchy et al., 2000). *Morotopithecus* was one of the earliest and largest hominoids from this time period (Gebo et al., 1997).

Around 17 million years ago there appeared the first evidence of a land connection between Africa and Eurasia, created mainly by the northern movement of the plate on which Africa rests. This connection allowed hominoid primates to migrate outside Africa for the first time, and small, gibbonlike forms appeared in China (Harrison and Gu, 1999).

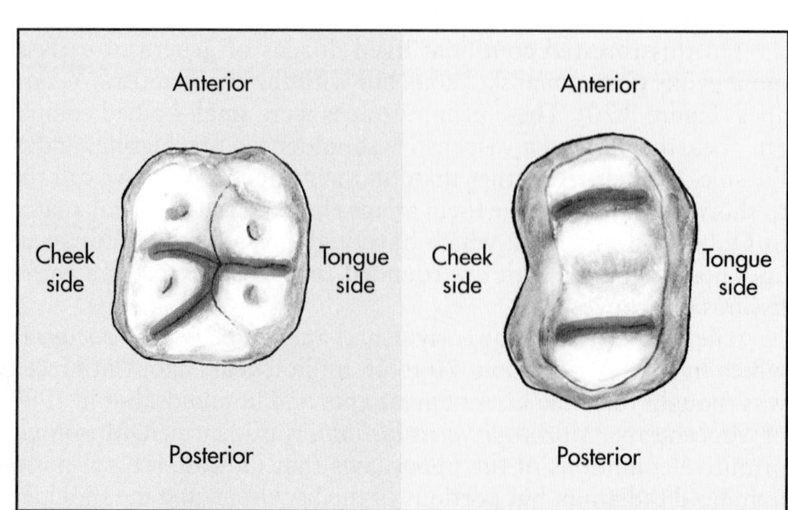

FIGURE 9.20 The Y-5 molar pattern (left) characterizes the ape whereas bilophodont molar (right) characterizes the Old World monkey. Both indicate a 2:1:3:3 dental formula.

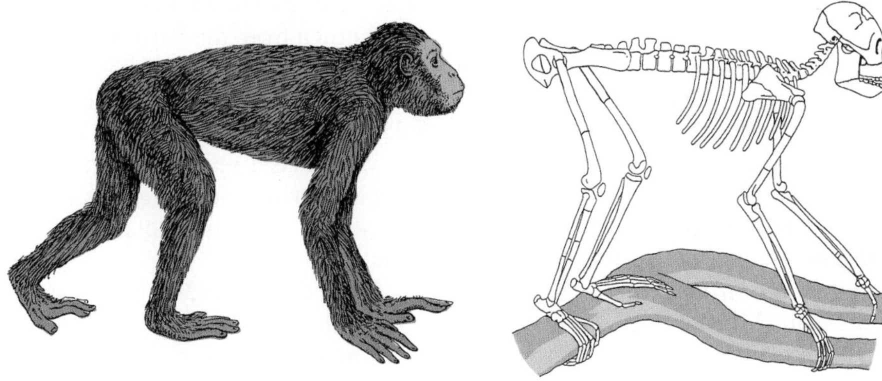

FIGURE 9.21 The dental ape *Proconsul* has an apelike dentition but monkeylike skeleton.

Sweeping environmental changes transformed the world during the Middle Miocene, and the first fossil apes that show both cranial and postcranial characteristics linking them to living African apes appeared in the fossil record. Previously, Africa had been moist and forested, but fauna and flora from Middle Miocene sites in Kenya indicate that these areas were dry and the vegetation was open, with dry woodland and even grassland emerging as the dominant environment. Around this time (14 million years ago) the African great ape and human lineage diverged from the Asian great ape lineage (the orangutans). The skeleton of one Middle Miocene hominoid, *Kenyapithecus* (Leakey, 1962), shows that it practised a primitive form of knuckle-walking, the distinctive pattern of locomotion shared by living gorillas and chimpanzees. This ape was the first to descend from the trees to the ground (McCrossin et al., 1998). One species in particular, *Kenyapithecus wickeri*, may be closely allied with the lineage leading to the hominids.

During the Middle and Late Miocene (approximately 11 to 5 million years ago), large-bodied hominoids diversified and dispersed into Europe and Asia. A primitive apelike hominoid, called *Sivapithecus*, is known from the Late Miocene of the foothills of the Himalaya Mountains (Figure 9.22). Cranial and dental remains of *Sivapithecus* exhibit several similarities to the orangutan but also distinct differences. *Sivapithecus* is thus considered a relative of the modern orangutan but not its unique ancestor.

At about the same time that *Sivapithecus* lived, a huge new ape arose in the same geographic region. In the 1930s, German palaeontologist Ralph von Koenigswald searched for fossils in drugstores as well as the field because bones and teeth often are used in traditional East Asian medicine. In 1935, in drugstores in Hong Kong and the Philippines, he found enormous primate molars. He named the previously unknown creature to which they belonged *Gigantopithecus* (von Koenigswald, 1952).

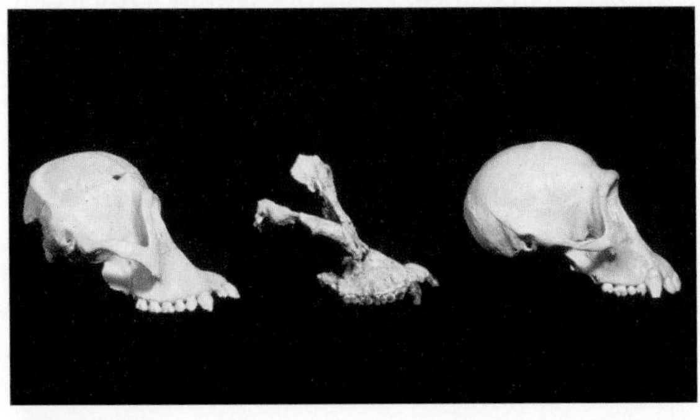

(a)

(b)

FIGURE 9.22 (a) *Sivapithecus* is a Miocene ape (middle) with anatomical similarities to orangutans (left) rather than chimpanzees (right). (b) Siwaliks, Pakistan, where *Sivapithecus* was found.

Gigantopithecus is known mostly from jaws and teeth. Although an early form of this genus occurred in the Late Miocene, it is better known from the Early and Middle Pleistocene of China and Vietnam, where it grew to an enormous size, perhaps as large as 300 kilograms (660 lb), and coexisted with *Homo erectus*. *Gigantopithecus* was thus the largest primate that ever lived (Figure 9.23). Some scholars speculate that legends of the sasquatch in North America and the yeti in Asia may have begun long ago when *Gigantopithecus* walked the Earth. Most authorities view *Gigantopithecus* as a distant relative of *Sivapithecus*. Based on its large size and molar anatomy, *Gigantopithecus* probably ate a tough, fibrous diet.

In Europe, *Ouranopithecus* was a very large 110 kilograms (242 lb) hominoid from the Late Miocene (10 million years ago) of Greece (deBonis and Koufos, 1993). Unlike *Sivapithecus* and orangutans, *Ouranopithecus* possessed a massive browridge and a wide space between the eye sockets, thus superficially resembling a gorilla. Some researchers have argued that *Ouranopithecus* is an ancestor of both African great apes and hominids, but details of its face, jaws, and teeth indicate that it lacks aspects of cranial anatomy that are shared, derived features of both African great apes and humans (Benefit and McCrossin, 1995).

Another Late Miocene ape from Europe is *Dryopithecus*, long known from isolated jaws, teeth, and an upper arm bone and dating to 12 to 8 million years ago. Palaeoanthropologist David Begun of the University of Toronto and his colleagues have been studying the large-bodied (20 to 35 kg; 44 to 77 lb) *Dryopithecus* in Eurasia as a part of their examination of evidence of the origins of the great apes in Europe and western Asia and the spread and diversification of great apes across Eurasia (Kordos and Begun, 2001; Begun, 2003). A *Dryopithecus* skull that they discovered at Rudabánya, Hungary, was the first specimen with a preserved piece of the cranium between the face and the braincase that suggests a close evolutionary relationship to the African apes and humans lineage. This idea is not without controversy, however, and we do not yet know enough about *Dryopithecus* to say whether it represents Asian ape ancestors, African ape ancestors, or dead-end apes.

Although we have identified many ape taxa from the Miocene, we have little or no fossil evidence for the lineages that led directly to gorillas, chimpanzees, and bonobos. One possible exception is *Samburupithecus*, a poorly known fossil ape from the Late Miocene (approximately 9 to 8 million years ago) of Kenya (Ishida and Pickford, 1997). In some respects, the upper molars of *Samburupithecus* are reminiscent of those of a gorilla. The dearth of fossils is related in part to the tropical forests in which apes live: moist places where biological processes often lead to the complete destruction of the skeleton.

The Miocene hominoids provide a picture of the ape and human family tree before it was so drastically pruned back to just the few branches that exist today. Some genera, such as *Proconsul*, were early representatives of the superfamily that diversified before the common ancestor of living forms. One Miocene hominoid, *Sivapithecus*, appears to be allied to the modern Asian great ape lineage, the orangutan. Other Late Miocene Eurasian hominoids appear to be side branches that left no modern descendants. A few genera, including *Kenyapithecus* and *Samburupithecus*, appear to be members of the African ape and human clade that diversified before the LCA of gorillas, chimpanzees, and humans. The environmental conditions that favoured the divergence of this lineage from that of the monkeys and that later so severely reduced its diversity are reviewed in the next two sections.

(a)

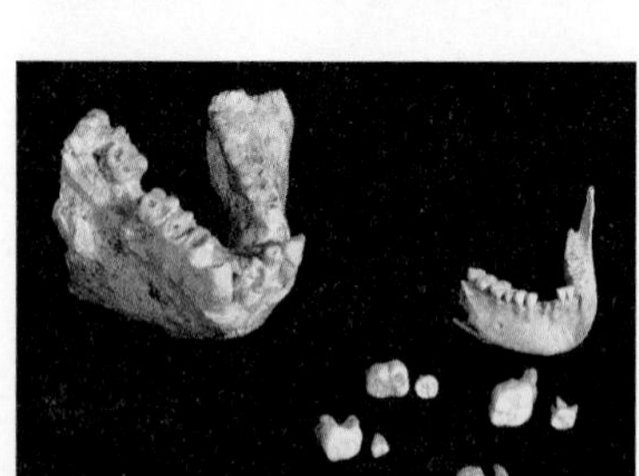

(b)

FIGURE 9.23 (a) Reconstruction of *Gigantopithecus*, a fossil ape, towers over artist Bill Munns. (b) The enormous mandible of *Gigantopithecus* dwarfs a modern human mandible.

SELECTION PRESSURES AND THE DIVERGENCE OF MONKEYS AND APES

Monkeys and apes differ in specific anatomical ways related to their form of locomotion (Figure 9.24), so the origin of hominoids probably is related in part to this shift in locomotor pattern. The apes appear to have evolved their specialized locomotor

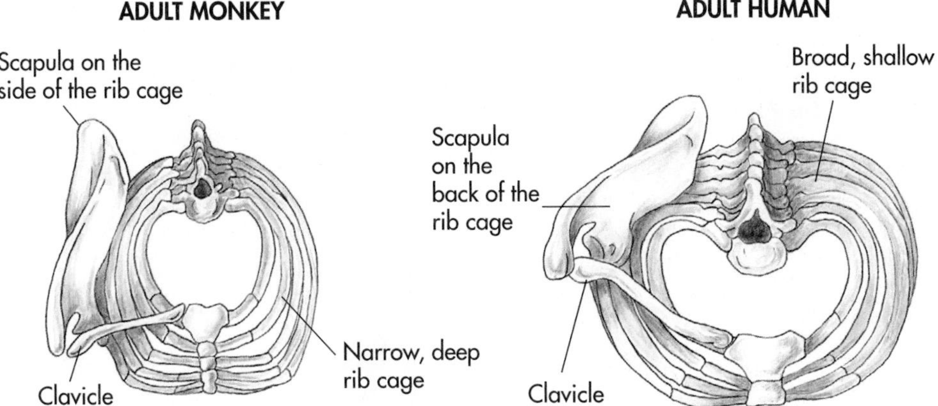

FIGURE 9.24 The thorax of apes and humans reflects our brachiating ancestry and is broad but shallow in contrast to the narrower, deeper chest of the monkey.

capacity early in the Middle Miocene when forests were widespread. Later the African apes modified this brachiating anatomy for knuckle-walking so that in the Middle Miocene, when body size increased and apes became more terrestrial, we see evidence of knuckle-walking anatomy. The Asian apes eventually become quadrumanous (four-handed) after *Sivapithecus*.

Thus, part of the origin of the living hominoid pattern is related to shifts in climate and the relative abundance of forested and unforested areas. However, you will recall that the first distinctive evidence of apes in the fossil record is from the dentition and the groups we called dental apes. The shape of these dentitions suggests that the initial change in the ape lineage was a dietary shift, probably due to eating more fruits. During the Miocene we see the drying and cooling of the environment and the breaking up of habitats into smaller wooded areas and patchy grasslands. And in this changing environment we see a differentiation between monkey and ape lineages, with monkeys focusing increasingly on more leafy diets and early apes focusing more on fruits. Later apes, such as the gorilla, return to a fibrous diet, modifying the original ape niche.

THE MONKEY'S TALE: WHAT HAPPENED TO PRIMATE DIVERSITY IN THE MIOCENE?

From the beginning to about the middle of the Miocene, fossil apes were abundant and monkeys fairly rare. But after the Middle Miocene it was a monkey's world, with apes decreasing in both diversity and number of taxa. Why this shift?

Recall the climatic changes of the Miocene, when the world got drier and colder. Forests dried up, grasslands and wooded grasslands became more abundant, new niches became available. Animals that once lived in the forest had a few possible routes to survive: Stick with the same old pattern but reduce numbers of individuals (after all, the forested areas were smaller) or strike out into a new area with new resources necessitating new adaptations. Animals that reproduce more quickly (that is, those that are **r-selected**, with each female having many offspring during her lifetime at short interbirth intervals and making less maternal investment per offspring) could colonize areas faster and rebound from population declines more quickly and thoroughly. Although monkeys reproduce more slowly than many nonprimates, they reproduce more quickly than apes and so had an advantage in colonizing new areas. (Apes are strongly **k-selected**, exhibiting the opposite reproductive characteristics of r-selected animals.) In addition, the shape of the monkey thorax and limbs is more conducive to evolution of quick terrestrial locomotion. These attributes seem to have favoured the monkeys over the apes during

r-selected Reproductive strategy in which females have many offspring, interbirth intervals are short, and maternal investment per offspring is low.

k-selected Reproductive strategy in which few offspring are produced per female, interbirth intervals are long, and maternal investment is high.

Figure 9.25 **PRIMATE EVOLUTION**

Primates or primate ancestors appear around 63 million years ago and diversify into niches created by the extinction of the dinosaurs but do not show most of the anatomical characters of living primates. Strepsirhine and haplorhine lineages appear in the early Eocene. The first monkeys with postorbital closure appear in the Oligocene. Apes diversify in the Miocene but are rare by the Pliocene.

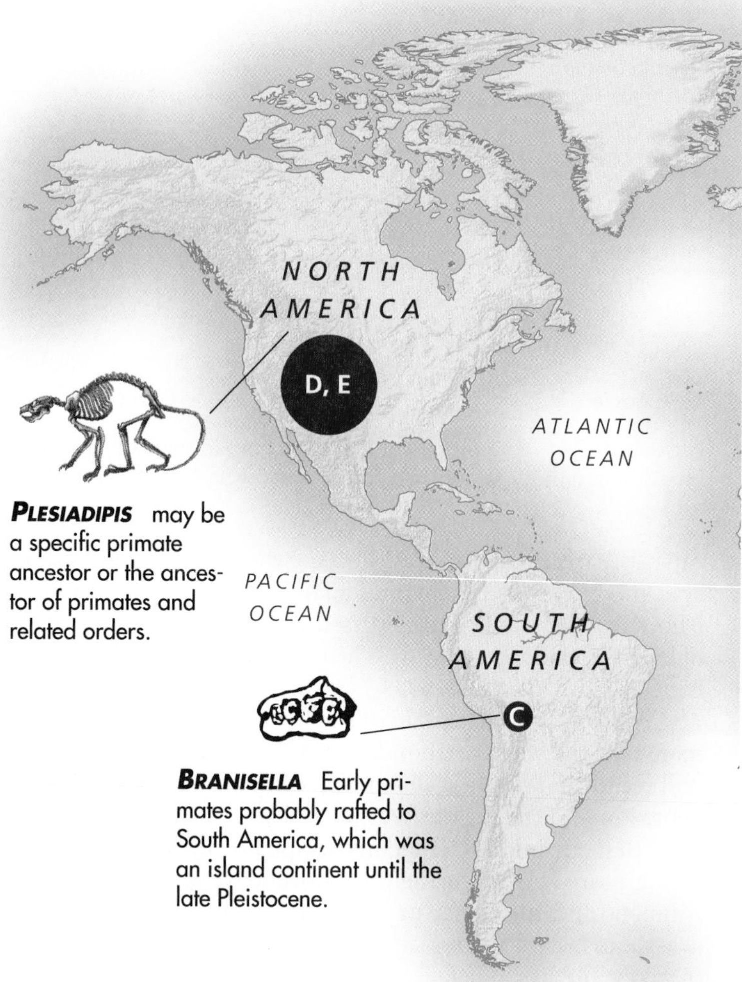

PLESIADIPIS may be a specific primate ancestor or the ancestor of primates and related orders.

BRANISELLA Early primates probably rafted to South America, which was an island continent until the late Pleistocene.

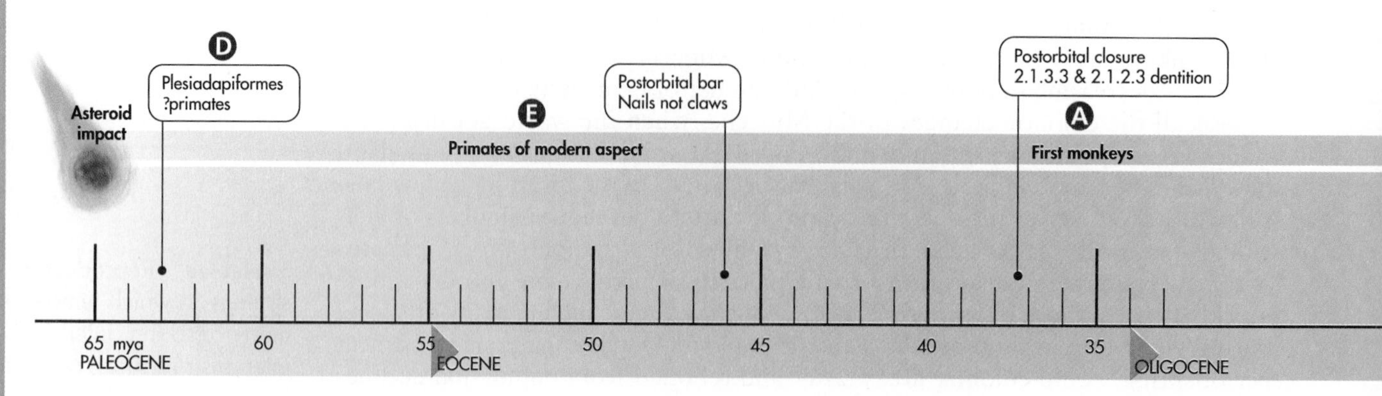

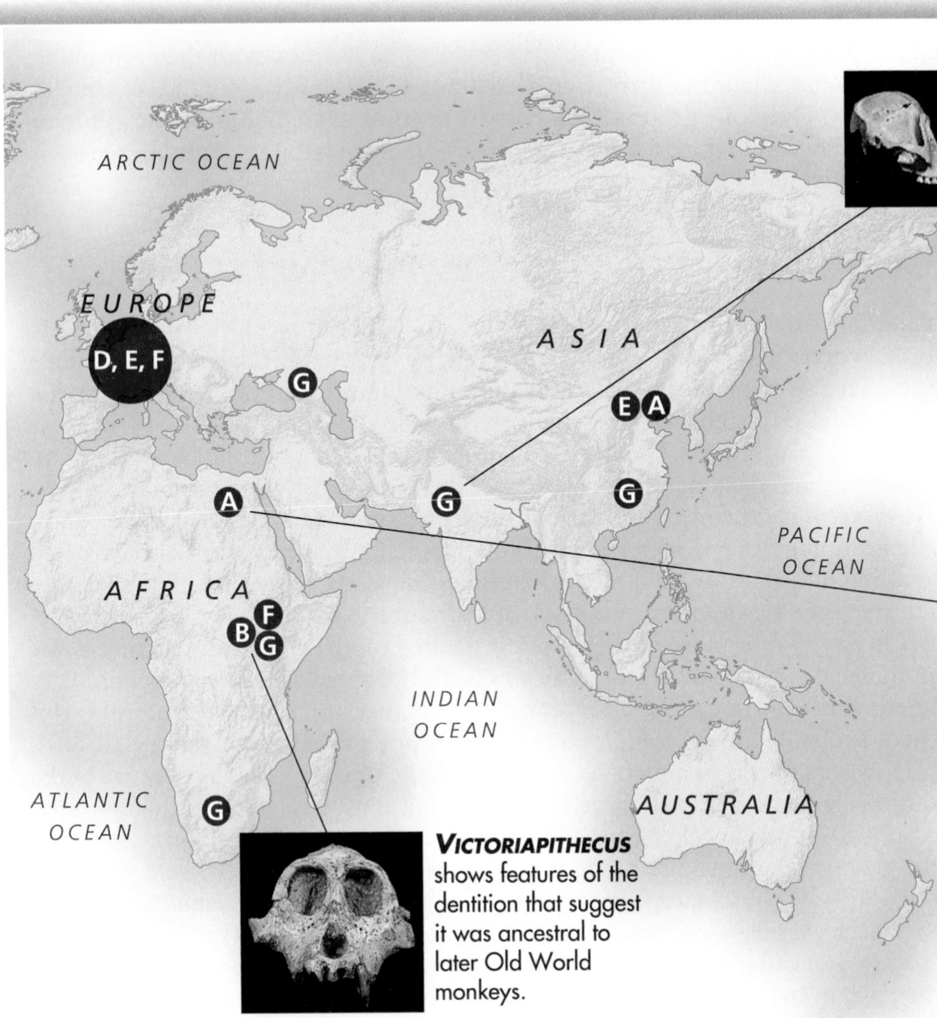

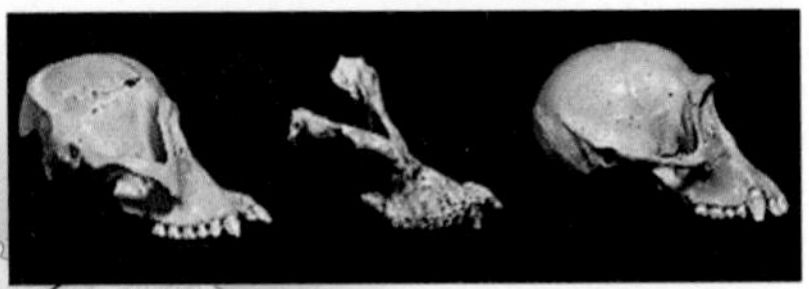

ARCTIC OCEAN

EUROPE

ASIA

AFRICA

PACIFIC OCEAN

INDIAN OCEAN

ATLANTIC OCEAN

AUSTRALIA

D, E, F

SIVAPITHECUS is one of many ape genera in the Miocene. *Sivapithecus* may have been ancestral to *Gigantopithecus* and closely related to orangutans.

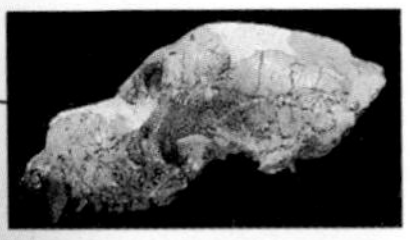

AEGYPTOPITHECUS
The Fayum in Egypt is famous for early anthropoids, such as *Aegyptopithecus* who may be ancestral to Old World monkeys and apes and others of which may be ancestral to New World monkeys.

VICTORIAPITHECUS shows features of the dentition that suggest it was ancestral to later Old World monkeys.

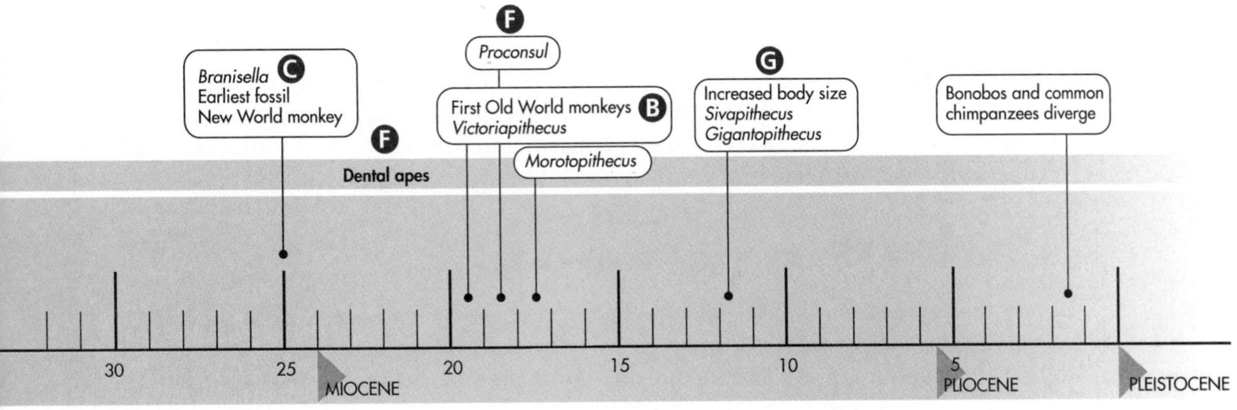

the Late Miocene. In contrast, the apes seem to have stuck with their shrinking, forested homes. Their numbers decreased along with their habitat and continue to do so today. Only one group of apes seems to have overcome the issues of locomotion and reproduction to move into new, more open habitats. This lineage eventually evolved into humans.

MOLECULAR EVOLUTION IN PRIMATES

In Chapter 3 we discussed several methods by which molecules can be used to inform evolutionary studies—to figure out phylogenetic relationships among species. We use some of these methods (immunological method, DNA hybridization) to indirectly compare the structure of molecules, and we use other, direct methods, such as DNA sequencing, to compare differences in the base pair composition of genes or noncoding portions of the genome between different species.

A *molecular phylogeny* is a tree of relatedness among species, or larger taxonomic groupings, based on a gene or protein (such a tree can also be constructed by pooling information from more than one gene (see Chapter 6)). The structure of the tree provides a visual summary of how similar or dissimilar a given molecule is in any two or more of the taxa represented on the tree. Constructing a tree from molecular data can be a statistically complex operation. If the taxa are very different and have not shared a recent common ancestor, then the molecular differences probably are profound, and making a phylogenetic tree is not that difficult. However, scientists are not as interested in the obvious cases as they are in the evolutionary relationships between three or four closely related taxa whose lineages split from one another over a short period of time several million years ago or the genetic relationships among populations within a species.

In 1967, a key advance in molecular phylogenetics occurred when anthropologist Vincent Sarich and biochemist Allan Wilson demonstrated that it was possible to use molecular relationships between species to determine divergence dates in the past; in other words, there existed a **molecular clock**, or a systematic accumulation of genetic differences through time that, if measured, could be used to estimate the amount of time since two groups shared a LCA.

Not all genetic systems can be used as molecular clocks because some systems are influenced by natural selection, lineage-specific rate changes, and other factors that make them inappropriate for timing evolutionary events. On the other hand, several different proteins, genes, and noncoding regions of DNA have proven useful as molecular clocks, and researchers have used them to shed new light on evolutionary relationships between all forms of life on Earth. Molecular phylogenies sometimes have been controversial, especially when they do not agree with phylogenies determined by traditional anatomical and palaeontological methods. However, only one history is being reconstructed and ultimately molecular and palaeontological phylogenies must agree with each other.

A PRIMATE MOLECULAR PHYLOGENY

Over the years, several molecular phylogenies of the primates have been proposed. One of these places the LCA of all primates at 63 million years ago (Goodman et al., 1998; Goodman, 1999). It is at this point that we get the deepest split within primates, that between the strepsirhines and the haplorhines. Subsequent splits are illustrated in Figure 9.26.

molecular clock A systematic accumulation of genetic change that can be used to estimate the time of divergence between two groups if relative rates are constant and a calibration point from the fossil record is available.

In terms of the largest branches and major nodes, this molecular phylogeny, which relies on multiple calibrations from the fossil record, fairly accurately represents current ideas about the major phylogenetic events in primate evolution. However, controversy still remains regarding the synthesis of fossil and molecular data in determining primate phylogenetics of closely related groups of primate

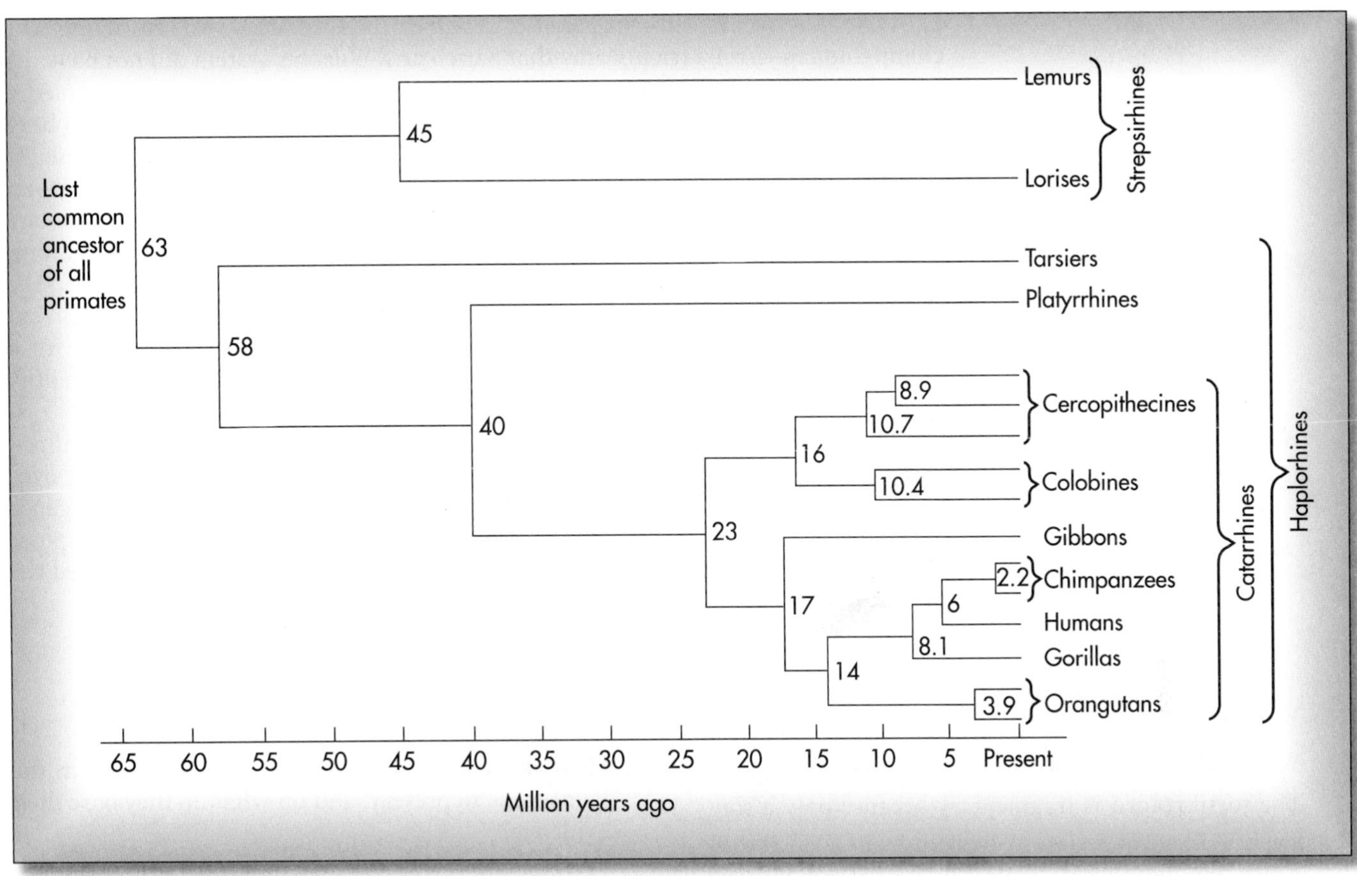

FIGURE 9.26 Relationships and dates of divergence of living primate groups based on molecular and DNA comparisons (Data from Goodman, M., 1999).

species (Stewart and Disotell, 1998). The first major debate involving molecular phylogenetics in understanding primate evolution was focused around the dating of the human split from the great apes and the implications for that date on interpretations of the fossil record and the timing of hominid origins.

Molecular Phylogeny and Human Origins

Prior to Sarich and Wilson's application of the molecular clock, the supposed earliest hominid represented in the fossil record implied that the hominid line originated about 15 million years ago. In addition, specific Miocene ape species were considered the likely direct ancestors of the chimpanzees, gorillas, and gibbons. (Recall from our earlier discussions that the current view recognizes no direct fossil record for the living African apes.)

Using a phylogeny based on the immunological method and calibrating the tree using a date of about 30 million years ago (derived from the fossil record) for the separation of apes from the other catarrhines, Sarich and Wilson determined a date for the origins of hominids of 5 million years ago, some 10 million years younger than previously suggested from the fossil record. At this node in the tree, humans shared a common ancestor with both the African apes, the gorilla and the chimpanzee, and hence were more closely related to the African apes than to the orangutan, which branched off earlier in the Miocene. For several years this claim was hotly debated, but it has been substantiated by later molecular and palaeontological research.

Over the years, much genetic research has focused on resolving the chimp–human–gorilla trichotomy that Sarich and Wilson's system did not have the resolving power to separate. In 1997, Professor Maryellen Ruvolo performed a combined analysis of DNA sequence data from fourteen different loci that had been analyzed in humans, chimpanzees, and gorillas. She concluded, "It is overwhelmingly likely that *Homo* and *Pan* are most closely related, with *Gorilla* as a sister group on the hominoid species tree" (p. 261). In other words, chimps and humans are more closely related to each other than either is to the gorilla, despite strong anatomical similarities between chimps and gorillas. This division is also favoured in the Goodman phylogeny. Given the molecular consensus on this issue and the current understanding of the hominid fossil record, it is safe to say that any claims for a hominid ancestor older than about 6 million years will be regarded with a healthy amount of skepticism by both molecular geneticists and palaeontologists.

The fossil record of primate evolution provides a full view of the history of primate relationships, adaptations, and ecology. In addition to documenting the evolutionary history of nonhuman primates, this record sets the stage for the emergence of the lineage that ultimately led to humans. In the following chapters we explore the fossil record for hominid evolution and the selective pressures that shaped the evolution of our ancestors.

SUMMARY

1. **Why is the fossil record so fragmentary?**

   The fossil record is fragmentary because only a tiny fraction of Earth's creatures die in a circumstance in which they may be fossilized, and then palaeontologists find only a tiny fraction of those fossils.

2. **What is taphonomy?**

   Taphonomy is the study of what happens to remains from the death of the organism until the discovery of the fossils.

3. **What is the difference between relative and chronometric dating techniques?**

   Chronometric dating techniques provide a fairly precise date for a fossil, based on measurement of some natural clock, often the radioactive decay of an element such as potassium (K) or carbon (C) in either the rock in which the fossil is found or in the fossil itself. Relative dating techniques provide only an estimate of whether a fossil is older or younger than other materials found above and below it at the same site or in sediments at other sites.

4. **Why does ^{14}C usually date younger sites than K–Ar?**

   Because of the short half-life of radiocarbon, too little of the radioactive isotope remains after about 30 000 to 40 000 years to be accurately measured. K has a longer half-life and thus can estimate age over longer time periods. In special circumstances we can also use it to determine the age of younger fossils.

5. **How do scientists think climate changed from the Palaeocene to present, and on what do they base their evidence?**

   Past climate reconstructions are based on geological and biological data including oxygen isotope curves, fossil soils, fossil animals, fossil plants, and pollens. These reconstructions suggest that temperatures were warmer and moister in the past and have cooled and dried over the Cenozoic. There were marked cooling events at the Eocene/Oligocene boundary and the onset of severe glaciation in the Late Pliocene and Pleistocene.

6. **Were plesiadapids the first primates?**

   This depends on which authority you ask. After their discovery, plesiadapids were considered to be primates. This view faded after many researchers noted their lack of modern primate anatomical traits. They occur about the right time, according to molecular data to be primate ancestors, but they may be just primatelike mammals. In recent years, however, researchers have begun to reconsider the role of plesiadapiforms in primate evolution.

7. **How are adapoids and omomyoids similar, and how do they differ?**

   Both existed in Europe and North America, although adapoids were more prevalent in Europe and omomyoids in North America. Adapoids had longer snouts and smaller eyes and probably ate leaves. They are the likely ancestors of strepsirhines. Omomyoids had shorter snouts and larger eyes and probably ate fruit and insects. They are the likely ancestors of haplorhines.

8. **What is the significance of the 2:1:3:3 dental formula for reconstructing the primate phylogeny?**

   The significance of the 2:1:3:3 dental formula is that it is the primary link between Old and New World fossil monkeys, supporting the hypothesis that New World monkeys are descendants of fossil Old World monkeys that rafted across the then-smaller Atlantic Ocean in the Late Eocene.

9. **Why were the earliest apes not easily identified as such?**

   The earliest apes did not possess the anatomical features of living apes such as a suspensory shoulder and knuckle-walking hands. They can be identified as apes based on their molar teeth, which feature the same Y-5 configuration of cusps and fissures as those of all living apes. For this reason we call these primitive hominoids the dental apes.

10. **How do molecular phylogenies help us to understand primate evolution?**

    Molecular phylogenies provide an estimate of the relationships and dates of divergence of living primate taxa that we can use to augment information from the fossil record. However, divergence dates are calibrated by the fossil record.

CRITICAL THINKING QUESTIONS

1. Given how few of Earth's creatures end up as fossils, do you think we will continue finding new and important fossils, or have we already found most of those fossils that exist?
2. Given the different techniques to reconstruct climate and environment, if you were leading a palaeontological project, how would you design your research program to figure out the context in which the fossils from your site came?
3. Imagine that you find a fossil hominid with some animal bones. How would you go about determining whether the animals and the hominids were deposited at the same time (were the same age)? Do you think that you could be mistaken, and what factors might make determining the age of the fossils difficult?
4. When we had only anatomical comparisons to rely on, we could not learn whether New World monkeys were descended from Old World monkeys or from Early Eocene primates in North America. Now, with the rise of genetic dating, the answer is still unclear. What do you think this tells us about the limitations of genetic techniques for resolving problems of primate phylogenetics?
5. Discuss the possible selective pressures involved in the origin of primates, strepsirhines, and anthropoids. Can you think of other possible scenarios for the origins of these groups?

KEY TERMS

fossils
palaeontology
geology
taphonomy
strata
stratigraphy
geologic time scale (GTS)
provenience
relative dating techniques
lithostratigraphy
tephrostratigraphy
biostratigraphy
calibrated relative dating techniques
palaeomagnetism
geomagnetic polarity time scale (GPTS)
chronometric dating techniques
radiometric dating
isotope
potassium–argon (K–Ar) dating
parent isotope
daughter isotope (product)
half-life
argon–argon ($^{40}Ar/^{39}Ar$) dating
fission track dating
uranium series (U-series) techniques
radiocarbon dating
electron trap techniques
thermoluminescence (TL)
optical stimulated luminescence (OSL)
electron spin resonance (ESR)
palaeosol
phytoliths
adapoids
omomyoids
plesiadapiforms
dental apes
r-selected
k-selected
molecular clock

SUGGESTED READING

Beard, Christopher K. (2004). *The Hunt for the Dawn Monkey: Unearthing the Origins of Monkeys, Apes, and Humans*. University of California Press, San Francisco, CA.

Cutler, Alan. (2003). *The Seashell on the Mountaintop*. Penguin Group, New York, NY.

Fleagle, John G. (1998). *Primate Adaptation and Evolution*, 2nd edition. Academic Press, San Diego, CA.

Lowe, John J., and Walker, Mike, J. C. (1997). *Reconstructing Quaternary Environments*, 2nd edition. Prentice Hall, Englewood Cliffs, NJ.

Repcheck, Jack. (2003). *The Man Who Found Time: James Hutton and the Discovery of the Earth's Antiquity*. Perseus Publishing, New York, NY.

Shipman, Pat. (1981). *Life History of a Fossil*. Harvard University Press, Cambridge, MA.

Tarbuck, Edward J., Lutgens, Frederick K., and Tsujita, Cameron J. (2005). *Earth: An Introduction to Physical Geology*, Canadian edition. Pearson Prentice Hall, Toronto, ON.

Taylor, R. E., and Aitken, M. J. (1998). *Chronometric Dating in Archaeology*. Kluwer, Dordrecht, The Netherlands.

Chapter 10

Becoming Human: The Ape–Hominid Transition

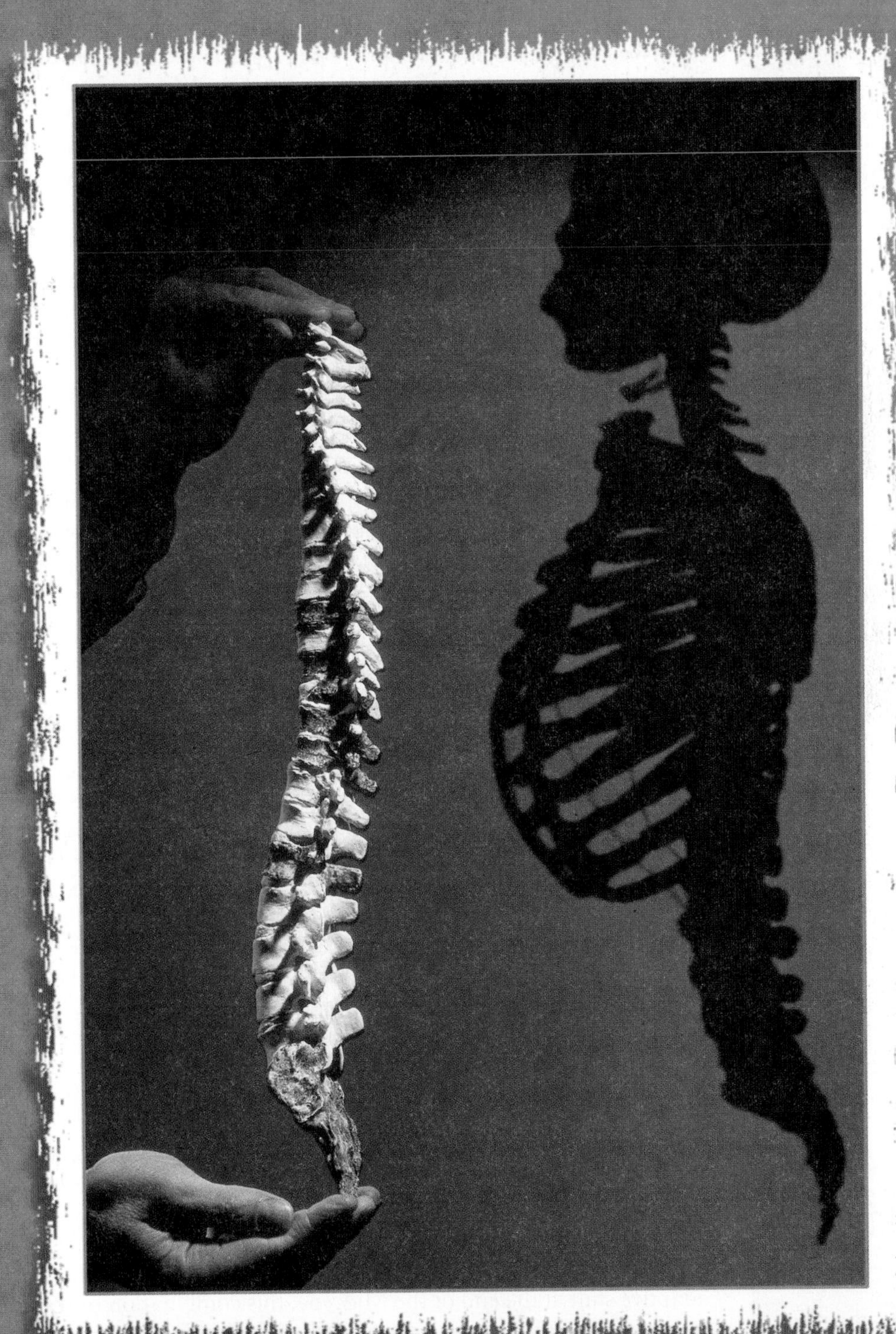

As the sun rose over the treetops, the young australopithecine opened her eyes reluctantly, rolled over in her leafy nest, and yawned. By the time the sun had moved fully above the horizon she was climbing out of the tree and shimmying down the trunk. Watching her do this, you might easily have mistaken her for a chimpanzee. But as she reached the ground and stepped away from the tree, she assumed an upright posture. She walked purposefully on two legs across a clearing to some fruit trees. There she joined a small cluster of others like her, some of them perched in branches, others collecting fruits that had fallen to the ground. She sniffed a fruit for ripeness and popped it in her mouth. She looked over at the alpha male of the group, an imposing creature much bigger than she with large canine teeth, a prominent brow ridge above his eyes, and a muscular body carried about on equally muscular legs.

AS THE DAY WARMED UP, the group headed toward some low, densely forested hills a kilometre away. There were patches of grassland amid the expanse of forest, but they stuck to the comforting safety of the trees. Only last month, in this same spot, a young female had been ambushed by a lion. She had screamed in fear and tried to escape to the safety of the trees. The males came to her aid but too late: The lion had caught and eaten her.

ALTHOUGH PREDATORS WERE A CONSTANT WORRY, so too was the possibility that when they reached their objective a neighbouring group of their own species would have gotten there first. The battles that raged between the two adjacent groups were as terrifying for them as any lion, and many family members and allies had been brutally injured. Today they reached the trees without competition and settled in for a meal of ripe fruits.

Chapter Outline

We will never know exactly how the earliest humans looked or behaved. But biological anthropologists have a number of intellectual tools that help them reconstruct the likeliest path from an ape ancestor to a hominid. Anatomically inclined anthropologists analyze the functional shifts involved in changing a four-legged ape into a two-legged human. After all, the fossil record for human origins is the only direct physical evidence of our ancestry that we will ever have. Behaviour experts attempt to extrapolate likely patterns of behaviour for the earliest humans, or at least define the likely range of behaviours that might have been present in the last common ancestor (LCA) of apes and humans, from comparative studies of living nonhuman primates. And genetic studies have helped unravel the mystery of our divergence from the apes and have become increasingly central to our understanding of our own relationship to extinct species in our lineage.

Recall from Chapter 7 the adaptations that characterize living African apes, our closest relatives. These adaptations include a large brain-to-body size ratio and extended ontogeny compared with monkeys, traits related to knuckle-walking, and traits related to a brachiator ancestor, including thorax shape, a highly mobile shoulder, and the absence of a tail. In a remarkable adaptive shift at the end of the Miocene, this combination of traits gave way to a new suite of traits in a new family, the Hominidae. (Hominids include humans and our extinct ancestors after the split from the LCA with chimps.)

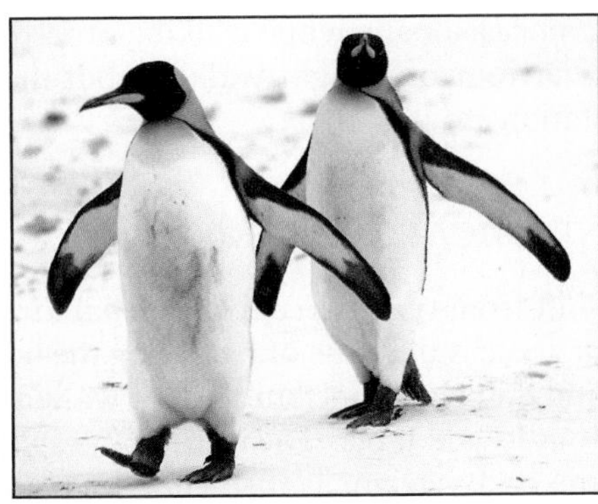

FIGURE 10.1 Habitual bipedality is a relatively rare occurrence and the striding bipedalism of hominids required particular anatomical adaptations not found in quadrupeds.

Initially, the most noticeable anatomical development in the hominids is in locomotion; bipedality was among the earliest adaptations, along with slightly smaller canine teeth. The dramatic expansion of the brain that characterizes living humans came millions of years later. The appearance of cultural traditions such as stone tool use was probably just a difference in degree, rather than kind, from the ape–human common ancestor. Because the fundamental adaptation was the shift to upright postures, this is where we begin to try to understand how and why one lineage of Miocene apes evolved into the earliest hominids.

This chapter is about the quest to understand the origin of the earliest humans. First we review the basic anatomical changes that natural selection produced in the bipedal skeleton. Once we understand how anatomy changed, we explore scenarios for why a bipedal primate might have evolved. Many of the time-honoured assumptions about human origins have been questioned or challenged in recent years, and we review some of the controversy. Then we examine the behavioural changes that mark the transition from an apelike ancestor to a human lineage, specifically those related to the evolution of the brain and intelligence. This focus on the anatomical and behavioural changes that occur at the transition from ape to human sets the stage for the next four chapters, which look in detail at the fossil record for hominid evolution.

BECOMING A BIPED

Walking upright is an extremely rare way to move about (Figure 10.1). In the entire history of life on Earth, truly bipedal posture and walking have appeared in just a few lineages. Only among the dinosaurs—where creatures such as *T. rex* and its two-legged kin proliferated over eons—and in hominids did bipedalism become a widespread adaptation. Of some 4000 living mammals, humans are the only habitual bipedal walkers today.

Although we tend to think that there was a natural progression from four-legged walking to a transitional state to fully upright posture, the example of the dinosaurs shows us that this is not necessarily the case. All dinosaurs evolved from a small bipedal species, which gave rise to the gigantic quadrupeds and bipeds. So among dinosaurs, two-legged posture was simply a primitive adaptation that allowed some forms to exploit new resources. Although we are more efficient bipeds than our earliest hominid ancestors, it is quite possible that early in human evolution, bipedality was an experiment that natural selection favoured in different ways for different ecological reasons (Figure 10.2).

FIGURE 10.2 Some nonhuman primates can walk bipedally for short periods of time but lack key bipedal adaptations.

Bipedalism is extraordinarily different from other ways that primates use for getting around. A number of other primates, from sifakas to chimpanzees, stand

vertebrae of the ... the ribs.

lumbar vertebrae The five vertebrae of the lower back.

sacrum The fused vertebrae that form the back of the pelvis.

coccyx The fused tail vertebrae that are very small in humans and apes.

upright occasionally while walking or feeding. However, hominids not only exhibit the behaviour of upright walking, but they also possess extensive morphological adaptations to it.

Anatomical Changes

The shift from quadrupedal to bipedal locomotion poses several problems. Critical among these is the issue of balancing the body's weight over two limbs (while standing) and often over one limb (while walking) (Figure 10.2). Think of the quadruped as a four-legged table: The centre of gravity falls in the area between the four legs, and the body weight is distributed equally over all four limbs (while standing). Remove one leg and it is still possible to balance the body's weight by shifting it to the area between the three legs. But take away two legs and the task becomes extremely difficult. When an animal that evolved to walk on four legs walks on its two hind limbs instead, it compensates for this lack of support by constantly moving its weight between the remaining limbs. When you stand, your body weight falls naturally between your two feet. And when you walk, your foot naturally falls directly under your centre of gravity without you even having to try (Figure 10.3). This greater efficiency means that while standing at rest, you burn only a few more calories than you would lying down. The reasons for these differences lie in the structural changes in our skeleton that directly affect the skull, spine, pelvis, legs, and feet.

The Vertebral Column and Skull The spine, or **vertebral column**, is made up of a series of vertebrae from the neck (**cervical vertebrae**), thorax (**thoracic vertebrae**), lower back (**lumbar vertebrae**), and pelvic regions (**sacrum** and **coccyx**) (Appendix A). The quadruped has a gently C-shaped curve that makes the thoracic region of the spine slightly convex. The biped has an S-shaped spine made by adding two secondary and opposing curvatures (in the cervical and lumbar regions) to the C-shape curvature of the quadruped (Figure 10.4). If you stand a quadruped up on its back legs, the C-shape of its spine tends to put the centre of gravity in front of its feet, causing the animal to fall forward. The secondary curvatures in the bipedal spine compensate for that C-curve and bring the centre of gravity back closer to the hips, ultimately resting over the biped's two feet.

The weight of the biped is borne down the spine to the sacrum, where it passes to the hips and from there through the two legs. The amount of weight increases as you go down the spine, so the vertebrae of a biped get increasingly large as you

Figure 10.3 Becoming a biped changes the way an animal balances. The quadruped's centre of gravity goes right through its back to the ground, balancing its weight over four legs (a). If the quadruped stands on two legs it either must bend its knees (b) or fall forward (c). A habitual biped has structural changes in the skeleton so that the centre of gravity falls between the two feet when standing with legs extended (d). (After Wolpoff, 1999).

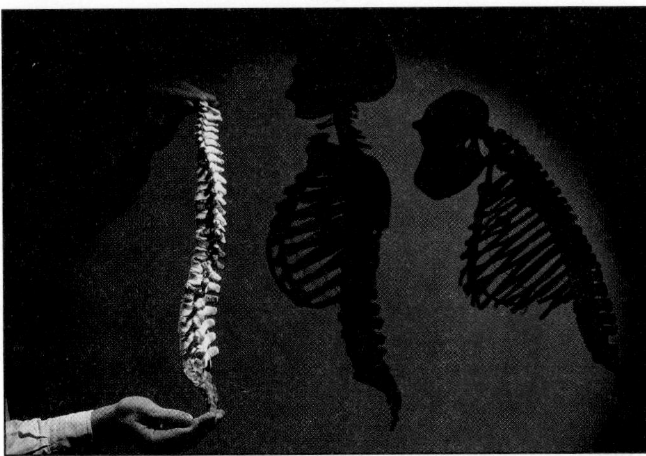

FIGURE 10.4 The spine of a biped has two additional curves in it at the neck and lower back to move the centre of gravity over two feet. The ape (quadruped) had a C-shaped spine.

approach the lumbar region. In contrast, weight bearing doesn't increase along the quadruped's spine, and the vertebral bodies are of nearly equal size in different regions of the spine. These differences can have adverse effects on the biped's body. Lower back problems, especially among pregnant women, are among the most common medical ailments today; these problems are a result of the changes wrought in our ancestral skeleton.

The vertebral column is also oriented differently to the head of the biped, coming out from the bottom rather than the back of the skull. So the junction of the spinal cord and the brain, which occurs through a hole called the **foramen magnum** in the occipital bone, is positioned underneath the skull in bipeds but toward the back of the skull in quadrupeds (Figure 10.5 and Appendix A). In addition to the foramen magnum, another indicator of the angle at which an animal holds its body in life is the form of the **nuchal plane**, the flattened bony area of the occipital to the rear of the foramen magnum that provides surface area for the attachment of neck muscles. In modern humans the nuchal plane is a horizontally flat region on the

foramen magnum Hole in the occipital bone through which the spinal cord connects to the brain.

nuchal plane Flattened bony area of the occipital posterior to the foramen magnum, to which neck muscles attach.

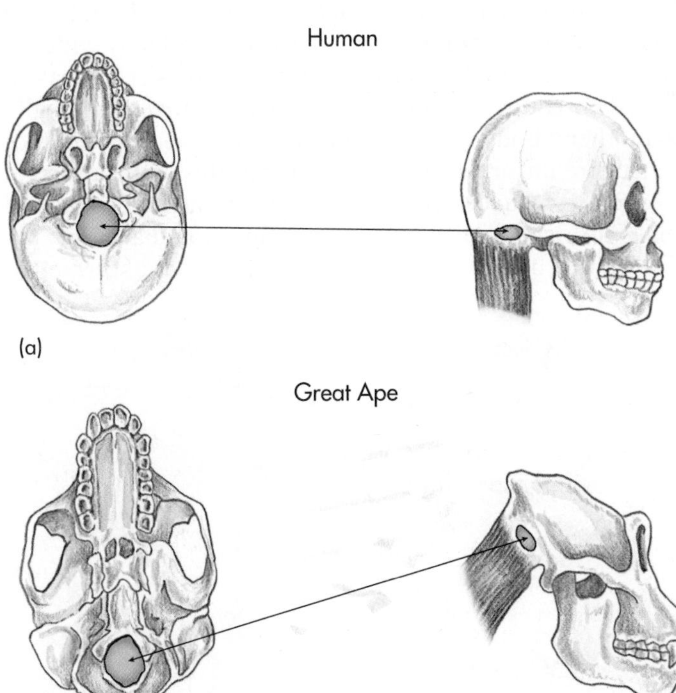

FIGURE 10.5 (a) The spine meets the skull from below in a biped, so the foramen magnum is directly beneath the skull and the neck muscles run down from the skull. (b) In the ape the spine meets the skull from the back so the foramen magnum is positioned posteriorly and the neck muscles also run posteriorly from the skull.

ate bones (os coxae) pair of bones that compose lateral parts of the pelvis; each innominate is made up of 3 bones that fuse during adolescence.

ischium Portion of the innominate bone that forms the bony underpinning of the rump.

ilium The blade of the innominate to which gluteal muscles attach.

pubis Portion of the innominate that forms the anterior part of the birth canal.

gluteal muscles Gluteus maximus, medius, and minimus, the muscles of walking, which have undergone radical realignment in habitual bipeds.

acetabulum The cup-shaped joint formed by the ilium, ischium, and pubis at which the head of the femur attaches to the pelvis.

bottom of the skull, facing directly downward. In a quadruped, however, the nuchal plane faces rearward. In apes the nuchal plane's angle is somewhere between the human and quadruped condition. So the occipital bone is a clue for paleoanthropologists about the way in which an extinct being may have stood and walked.

The Pelvis and Birth Canal When you walk, you spend a significant amount of time on one leg. This entails keeping your centre of gravity over that one support and not falling off to the unsupported side. Quadrupeds such as chimps accomplish this by throwing their weight over the supporting limb when they walk bipedally, resulting in a rocking from side to side that wastes a lot of energy. The skeleton of habitual bipeds such as hominids is rearranged to counter this shift automatically, and many of these changes occur in the pelvis. The bony pelvis consists of two **innominate bones (os coxae)**, each of which is composed of three bones (the **ischium, ilium**, and **pubis**) that fuse during adolescence and the sacrum, part of the vertebral column (Figure 10.6 and Appendix A). The ischium is the bone you sit on. The ilium is the bone you feel when you put your hands on your hips. And the pubis is the bony portion of the pelvis in the pubic region.

The pelvis of a biped is basin-shaped with a short, broad ilium that runs from the posterior to the anterior of the animal. The quadruped ilium is long and flat and situated on the back of the animal. The basin shape supports abdominal organs that tend to be pulled downward by gravity, and it places important locomotor and postural muscles in a better mechanical position. Most important are the anterior **gluteal muscles** (gluteus minimus and medius), which attach to the ilium and are rotated around to the front and side of the biped. In this position they connect the ilium to the top of the femur (thigh bone), and when you stand on one limb they contract, pulling the ilium (and the rest of your trunk) toward the support side, so your centre of gravity balances over the single foot. The gluteus maximus runs from the back of the ilium to the back of the femur, and when it contracts it keeps your pelvis (and you) from tipping forward in front of your feet (Figure 10.7). The shortening and widening of the ilium also results in the hip joint (**acetabulum**) being closer to the sacroiliac joint. This is good for balance but narrows the birth canal, a problem with which later hominids, including ourselves, will have to contend.

Efficient bipedalism requires a narrow pelvis, but that need must be balanced against the need for a birth canal wide enough for the large shoulders of an infant. Early in hominid history selection for birth canal size probably widened the pelvis from side to side by widening the sacrum. Later, as brain size increased, the baby was also required to rotate during delivery. Chimpanzee or gorilla babies emerge from the mother's body face up, but human babies emerge face down. Paleoanthropologists are unsure about exactly when this shift occurred, but its evolution was crucial to successful birthing in later, larger-brained hominids. The evolutionary drawback of this new anatomy was that it left the mother unable to assist in the birth of her own child. The constraints of

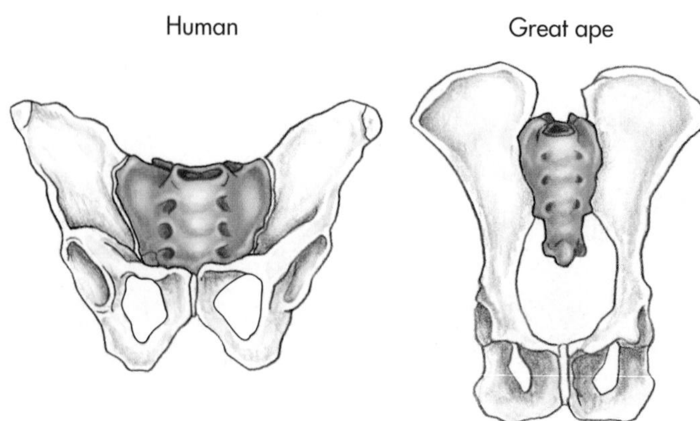

FIGURE 10.6 To maintain balance the bipedal pelvis has a foreshortened ilium and is broader and bowl-shaped. The quadrupedal pelvis has a long ilium positioned on the back, not the side, of the animal.

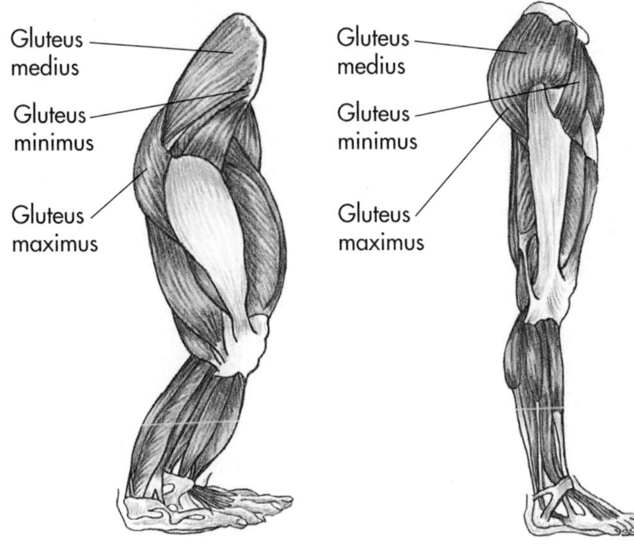

FIGURE 10.7 The gluteal muscles are repositioned in the biped and aid in support.

bipedalism may have served as an evolutionary incentive for the development of socially assisted birthing, in which females aid one another in achieving successful births (Rosenberg and Trevathan, 1996).

The Leg The broad pelvis places the top of the femur far to the side of the biped, but remember that when you walk your foot must fall directly below your centre of gravity. A straight femur, such as that seen in a quadruped, would result in a foot far to the side of the centre of gravity. The solution is to angle the femur from the hip into the knee; this places the foot below the centre of gravity (Figure 10.8). However, it creates problems for the knee because the musculature attached to the femur is also acting at an angle. When the animal flexes its muscles on the front of the femur in an effort to extend the knee, the muscles pull both up and out. The patella (knee cap) sits in the tendon of this muscle and is likewise displaced outward. To avoid dislocating the patella in a biped, the groove on the femur that the patella sits in is deep, and the outside edge or lip is enlarged. In addition, to help support the excess body weight going through each limb, the bottom of the femur (**femoral condyles**) is enlarged. The top of the tibia or shin bone reflects similar changes.

Although relatively short in early hominids, the leg lengthened relative to trunk length during human evolution. This increased stride length and efficiency in walking. Imagine a Great Dane and a Chihuahua walking side by side and the greater number of steps the shorter-legged dog takes compared with the longer strides of the Great Dane. The leg attained modern human proportions with the origin of *Homo erectus*.

femoral condyles The enlarged inferior end of the femur that forms the top of the knee joint.

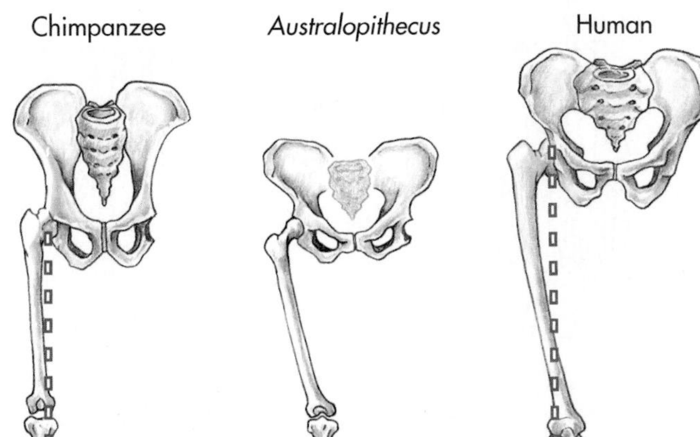

FIGURE 10.8 To keep the foot under the centre of gravity, the biped leg is angled from hip to knee. The quadruped leg is not.

tarsals Foot bones that form the ankle and arches of the foot.

metatarsals Five foot bones that join the tarsals to the toes and form a portion of the longitudinal arch of the foot.

phalanges Bones that form the fingers and toes.

The Foot The foot skeleton is composed of three types of bones: **tarsals**, which form the heel and ankle region; **metatarsals**; and **phalanges** (the toes) (Figure 10.9 and Appendix A). In bipedal walking, the heel strikes first, followed by the rest of the foot. The main propulsive force comes at toe-off, when the big toe pushes off from the ground and the toes bend strongly backward. To accommodate toe-off, the big toe moves in line with the other toes and becomes much, much larger than the other toes, and all the phalanges shorten and change joint orientation. Imagine the advantage to the biped of shorter toes; it is rather like the difference between walking in floppy clown shoes and wearing shoes with regular-sized toes.

A biped's foot is stouter and has arches that accommodate the great weight put through the two feet. The tarsal bones and big toe are robust and bound tightly together by ligaments, providing stability but decreasing overall manipulability of the foot. The foot has two structural arches: a transverse arch running from medial to lateral that is formed by the wedge-shaped tarsals, much like a stone architectural arch, and a longitudinal arch running the length of the foot and formed by the metatarsals and tarsals. The arches are shock absorbers that store and return some of the energy to the walking biped. Arches help to reduce the incidence of fatigue fractures to the lower leg.

The Arm One advantage of walking on two legs is that it frees the arms to do other things. Carrying objects and tool making are two activities often associated with the hominid lineage (although, as we shall see, they are not exclusive associations). Throughout hominid evolution the arm and hand skeleton have changed as a result of their release from locomotor activities and their new use, particularly in tool making. Although early hominids have relatively long arms, through hominid evolution the arms shortened relative to trunk length, and arm strength decreased because the arms were no longer weight bearing. The thumb became opposable and the phalanges shortened. The arm assumed modern human proportions around the time of the origin of *Homo erectus*.

Constructing the Bipedal Body Plan

It is easy to make the mistake of thinking that once the shift from quadrupedalism to bipedalism began, it was somehow preordained that an efficient biped would result. But remember that such master plans do not exist in evolution: All the anatomical changes we've discussed occurred like the construction of a mosaic, with interlocking pieces driven by natural selection in every generation. Natural selection drove the evolution of bipedalism because in each subsequent generation once the shift began, each transitional stage conferred survival and reproductive benefits on individuals. The mental image of a shuffling prehominid that was neither efficient quadruped nor biped is certainly wrong. Instead, in each generation

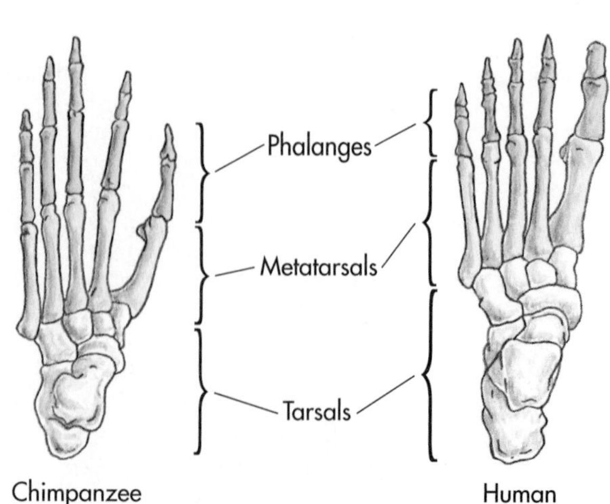

FIGURE 10.9 The biped's foot bears more weight than the quadruped's, therefore the bones are stouter. The big toe is especially big and in line with the others, and the phalanges are shorter and less curved.

the emerging biped must have been very good at surviving and reproducing, or else natural selection would not have pushed the process further. This strongly suggests that bipedalism arose in a variety of forms and functions, some of which may have died out while others succeeded. Ultimately, one lineage of bipeds—our own—succeeded, and we are the product of that lengthy process.

Locomotion of the Last Common Ancestor

Because African apes and humans differ so dramatically in their anatomical adaptations to locomotion, identifying our ancestors in the fossil record is easy. We just look for the anatomical adaptations to bipedalism. However, scientists disagree as to the most logical precursor of bipedalism. Did the LCA of African apes and humans knuckle-walk? Or were they adapted to life in the trees? In this latter view, the LCA of apes and humans was arboreal, not a knuckle-walker (Figure 10.10a). Alternatively, although a deeper arboreal ancestor is accepted, other researchers argue that the LCA of chimps, gorillas, and humans was a knuckle-walker (Gebo, 1996; Figure 10.10b). This would be the most parsimonious explanation since it does not require that knuckle-walking evolved twice, independently, in the anthropoid line.

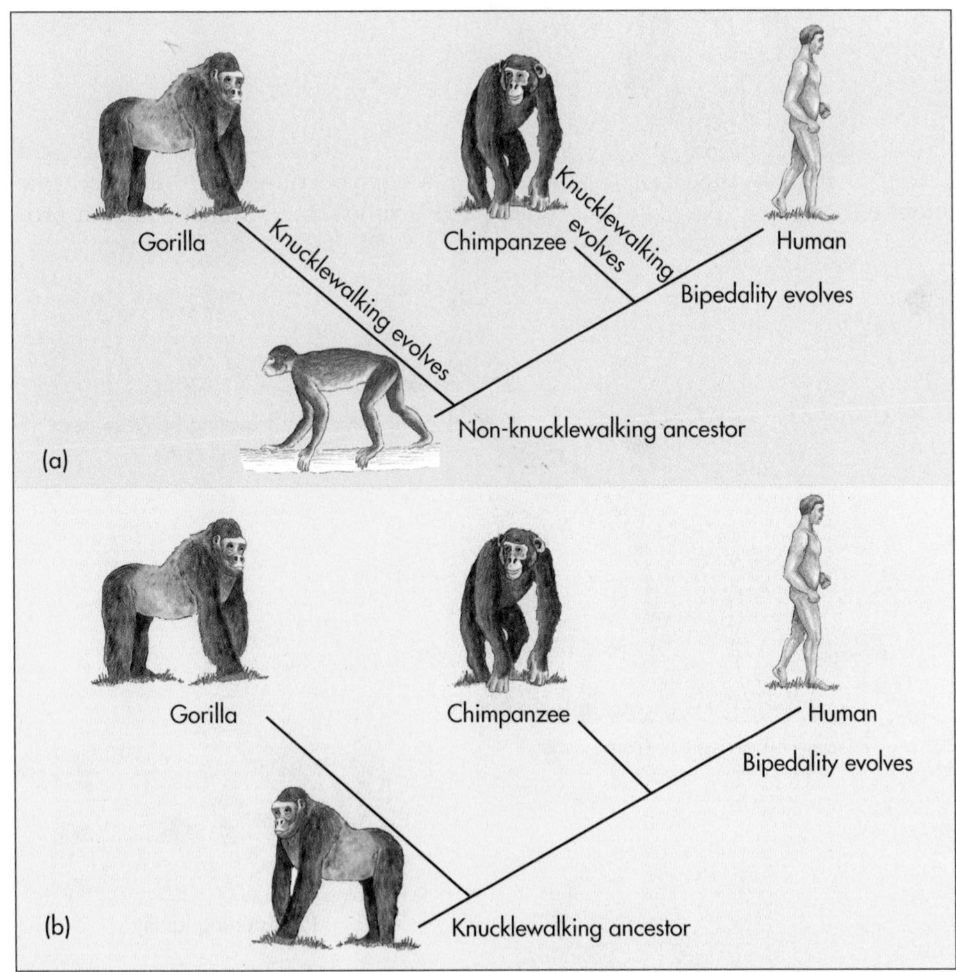

Figure 10.10 (a) If the last common ancestor of gorillas, chimpanzees, and humans was not a knuckle-walker, then knuckle-walking would have to have evolved twice: independently in both the chimpanzee and gorilla lineages. In this view, the ancestral condition for humans is not knuckle-walking. (b) Alternatively, if the last common ancestor of gorillas, chimpanzees, and humans was a knuckle-walker, then the ancestral condition for humans is knuckle-walking.

WHY BIPEDS?

Bipedalism is the basic adaptation of the hominid line, and by now you should be wondering what selective pressures favoured bipeds. Why did bipedalism evolve? Many scenarios have been proposed (Figure 10.11), most of which have a fatal flaw. For purposes of explanation, we can categorize bipedalism scenarios as relating to energetics, ecology, diet, and sexual selection. Some of the scenarios overlap. It is important to remember as you review these scenarios that bipedalism had to already exist in a limited form in some individuals and conferred a reproductive advantage, according to Darwinian theory.

Energetic Efficiency Bipedal walking is a more efficient way of travelling than walking on all fours, at least if we compare human and chimpanzee walking (Rodman and McHenry, 1980). Although humans do not necessarily walk more efficiently than all quadrupeds, they certainly walk more efficiently than knuckle-walking apes. In other words, if hominids evolved from knuckle-walking apes, then the shift to upright posture would have made perfect energetic sense. Although

Carrying tools, food, or infants

Ecological influences: traveling between trees or seeing over tall grass

Feeding on grasses or from bushes

Provisioning family

Energy efficiency

FIGURE 10.11 Several scenarios for what led to the origin of habitual bipedalism.

there is still some argument about the relative efficiency of early hominid walking, most energetic analyses indicate that bipedal walking (but not running) is a more efficient means of locomotion than knuckle-walking (Leonard and Robertson, 1997).

A second way in which the body plan of a biped may have been more efficient than its ape ancestor is in its ability to dissipate heat. Successful hominids in open (unforested) areas apparently had a means of draining blood that also cooled the brain (Falk, 1990; Falk and Conroy, 1983), in what is called the radiator model of bipedal origins (Box 10.1). In addition, bipeds dissipate heat faster than quadrupeds because they stand slightly taller above the ground, and when exposed to midday sun they present less surface area to be heated (Wheeler, 1991). However, although hominids may have been better at dissipating heat from their bodies and brains than was the LCA, it seems unlikely that hominids arose because of these qualities, rather than simply benefiting from them once bipedality was favoured for other reasons.

Ecological Influences Ecological models for the origin of bipedalism focus on the role of the changing environment of East Africa between 8 and 5 million years ago that may have placed a premium on the ability to walk upright. As we learned in Chapter 9, Africa experienced a major drying and cooling trend in the Late Miocene that led to the expansion of grassland and a decrease in the amount of forest. This trend culminated in the widespread savannas we find in East Africa today. Some scientists argue that increased grassland caused a wider scattering of the food trees protohominids needed for their meals, so they had to forage over longer distances across more open country. With increased travel across open country, natural selection may have driven the evolution of a more energy-efficient mode of transport, namely bipedalism.

Many researchers have observed that, particularly in grasslands, standing upright would have offered greater ability to see over tall grass or to scan for potential predators. Gaining a better view of one's surroundings by walking upright has long been advocated as the selective advantage necessary to drive the evolution of bipedalism. But other researchers ask why the enormous changes to the anatomy that allow habitual bipedalism would have taken place, when a brief look over tall grass now and then might have been just as effective without these fundamental anatomical changes.

Dietary Scenarios Most of the models that seek to explain the origins of bipedalism invoke its behavioural advantages. The most persuasive and influential of the dietary models may be the idea that a lineage of fossil apes became bipedal because of the value of standing upright for feeding in fruit trees. Temporary bipedalism while foraging has been observed in gibbons (Tuttle, 1981), baboons (Jolly, 1968), and chimpanzees (Stanford, 2002), so it is possible to envision a protohominid that became increasingly bipedal for the feeding advantages that this posture offered, eventually becoming a habitual biped. Whether such feeding benefits would have made the conversion to full-time bipedalism likely is a question that has not yet been answered.

Others have argued that bipedality, group size, and body size increased in response not only to the greater patchiness of food resources and the need to walk across open areas to access food, but also to the greater risk of being eaten while crossing those areas, as we saw in the vignette. In this case, safety in numbers applies to animals crossing savannas. Therefore, one possible response to the increasing patchiness of forests might have been to increase group size and body size and adopt efficient bipedal locomotion (Isbell and Young, 1996). An alternative response is to stay in forested areas and keep group size small when foraging, but to re-merge groups for mating and other behaviours. This latter response may have been taken by the chimpanzee lineage, leading to their fission–fusion group form (see Chapter 8).

Box 10.1 Overheated Radiator?

Dogs pant when they're hot, slobbering all over your carpet. We sweat, sometimes profusely. People who lose the ability to sweat are in grave danger of lethal overheating. When early humans began to walk upright, their walking no doubt took them out of the forest and into blazing tropical sunshine. Like any other warm-blooded animal, they must have had a way of cooling themselves.

A four-legged animal walking in the hot equatorial sun exposes the expanse of its broad back to the sun, a sure recipe for hyperthermia without some adaptation for rapid, effective heat loss. Many mammals use a complex system of transferring heat from the blood of the arteries being pumped from the heart to the cooler blood of the veins as it returns to the heart.

Humans don't possess this system. But two-legged walkers are in a better position, literally: The sun strikes only the top of their head and shoulders (Figure A). Even the slight height difference between a quadruped's head and that of a biped puts us in significantly cooler air because wind speed is higher and the temperature is cooler than near the ground. Being naked rather than hairy helps too, because hair traps heat.

But standing tall created a new problem: the need to get blood up to the head, counter to the force of gravity. Most animals that constantly shift from horizontal to vertical orientations have evolved circulatory system features that combat the pull of gravity. When snakes climb upward, the pattern of blood flow to the head is radically altered by circulatory adaptations, including a forward-positioned heart, designed to keep blood flowing. When a giraffe leans its elegant neck down to a waterhole and then raises it again, special valves, tissue wraps, and pumps prevent blood from pooling in the lower body and boost it up to the head.

When you lie down, blood flowing to the heart drains away from your skull through your neck's jugular veins. But when you stand up, the blood seeks a different escape route through a vast network of veins surrounding the spinal cord. Called the vertebral plexus, this network extends from the skull down to the base of your spine. It diverts blood into the smallest vessels, boosting the blood's flow rate and its capacity to move about the body.

Anthropologists Dean Falk and Glenn Conroy applied this knowledge to the human fossil record and found two different methods of draining blood in different fossil lineages. They reasoned that the routing of the circulatory system provides keys to the lives and habitats of the earliest humans. When the shift to bipedalism happened, it must have been accompanied by a change in the way blood was moved up and down the now-vertical column of the body.

Brains in particular need to be kept cool; overheating poses a greater risk to the brain than to other parts of the body. Falk (1990) suggested that the vertebral plexus evolved to cool down a rapidly expanding brain as emerging humans moved out onto the open, sun-soaked grassland. The idea is striking: the circulatory system as a radiator designed to keep a growing brain cool, enabling more and more brain expansion in one lineage but not in another. If Falk is right, there were two ways to drain blood from the hominid skull in prehistory. One way led to the early hominids that were direct forerunners of modern people. The other way led to other lineages that went extinct without any descendants.

This hypothesis is not without detractors. Both ways of draining the blood can be found in modern people, suggesting that variation between individuals in prehistory may be more important than species-wide differences. And the correlation between species with "radiator" skulls and open-country habitats is not perfect. But as a working hypothesis, the idea has generated a great deal of valuable discussion. (Adapted from Stanford, 2003).

FIGURE A At midday, the sun strikes only the head and shoulders of this Masai.

Sexual Selection and Mating Strategies Several researchers have proposed that bipedalism arose because it conferred mating benefits on protohominids that were upright. For example, bipedalism would have been beneficial to males engaging in social displays (Jablonski and Chaplin, 1993). Male chimpanzees often stand upright briefly when they assert their dominance over other males during charging displays; upright posture presumably makes a charging male look more impressive. Thus the benefits of walking upright lie in the ability of males to look impressive and therefore mate more often with females by being bipedal. But it is unclear why this benefit would lead to habitual bipedalism and all the accompanying anatomical alterations rather than just a temporary behavioural tactic.

THE TRANSITION TO HUMAN BEHAVIOUR

We have now considered the fundamental anatomical change that marked the rise of the hominids: the appearance of a wholly new posture and mode of travel 5 to 6 million years ago in East Africa. Now we must examine how the behaviour of those emerging hominids changed. This is a much more difficult, speculative task than reconstructing the morphological changes because behaviour does not fossilize in the way that bones do. Or does it?

Although the behaviour of extinct primates is not preserved in their fossilized remains, we can make strong inferences about how they behaved in life because we have every reason to assume that primates living in the past followed the same guiding principles of natural selection and sexual selection that primates follow today. The inference that the present reflects the past allows us to reconstruct diets, modes of locomotion, and other aspects of primate lives that inform us about the ways extinct hominids behaved.

As we saw in Chapter 8, primates possess traits that few other mammals have. Foremost among these are intelligence and social complexity. Any attempt to use the behaviour of living primates to understand the behaviour of extinct primates, including hominids, has these two traits as central features. The most primitive primates, the strepsirhines such as lorises and galagos, resemble ancient primates you saw in Chapter 9 and also resemble lower mammals rather than haplorhine primates in many ways. These nocturnal strepsirhines are generally solitary, lacking in advanced social complexity. Of course, intelligence and social complexity have evolved in nonprimate lineages too, from dolphins to elephants. But given the phylogenetic relationship between humans and nonhuman primates, we look to the higher primates first when we want to reconstruct aspects of the behaviour of our ancestors. We are therefore using the principle of homology, as discussed in Chapter 5, that shared ancestry allows us to infer how we once used to be.

PRIMATE INTELLIGENCE: WHY ARE HUMANS SO SMART?

If the fundamental hominid adaptation was bipedalism, the fundamental primate adaptation that reaches its zenith in humans is intelligence. Although many large mammals, such as elephants and whales, have brains larger in absolute size, no mammalian group rivals the higher primates for the ratio of brain to body size. Because a huge output of caloric energy is needed to grow a large brain, we can be sure there were benefits to the evolution of intelligence that drove brain size and reorganization forward in successive generations. Although we all agree that big brains are a defining feature of humankind and that their existence suggests they must have conferred a survival advantage to hominids, how exactly big brains facilitated survival is still unknown.

Scholars have disagreed for years about how to define intelligence. The term "intelligent" has very little precise meaning when we speak of animal behaviour in particular; does it refer to learning, memory, or some other cognitive factor? Psychologist Richard Byrne (1995), one of the leading researchers in the area of primate intelligence, considers problem-solving capacity to be a measure of intelligence. Problem-solving cognition allows primates to respond effectively to novel situations. Each day, all primates past and present must navigate their way through an environment, both physical and social, that tests their ability to survive and reproduce. Primate intelligence, Byrne and others believe, is the way natural selection chose to promote those skills. We will consider three competing schools of thought for the origins and evolution of primate intelligence: technical, ecological, and social.

technical intelligence Hominid intelligence and brain size increase modelled as a result of tool use and extractive foraging.

Technical Intelligence and Tool Use **Technical intelligence** is the ability of some nonhuman primates to use cognitive skills to extract food and other resources from their natural environment by modifying that environment. Because we regard the advent of tool use to be a major hallmark of the rise of human intellect, anthropologists feel tool use by other primates offers intriguing clues about the evolution of intelligence and of culture. As we will see in Chapter 12, human tool use dates back at least 2.5 million years. Before that time, however, our most primitive ancestors no doubt fashioned and used tools in much the same way that some great apes do today (Figure 10.12).

Consider these two examples:

- A chimpanzee in Tanzania pauses in her daily journeys to pluck a twig from a bush. She strips the leaves from the twig, then inserts it between her lips and walks on. A hundred metres (330 ft) ahead she arrives at an enormous termite mound, standing 2 metres (2.5 ft) high and extending an equal distance underground. Inside, millions of the small insects live in a colony, using tunnels that extend to the surface. The chimp scratches the dirt away from the entrance to one of the tunnels and extends her probe into it. Soldier termites rush to defend their nest, grabbing the twig with their mandibles. Smaller worker termites also swarm onto the stick. The chimpanzee delicately draws the probe from the tunnel and runs it between her lips, crunching the meaty soldiers along with hundreds of workers. In 30 minutes, the chimpanzee eats thousands of termites.
- In another forest, a chimpanzee is climbing in an old tree when he sees a small hole in the trunk. Poking his finger into the hole, he flushes a woodpecker. After repeated attempts to reach some unseen object with his fingers, he descends to the ground and locates a strong stick. Returning to the woodpecker hole, he inserts the stick deep into the cavity several times, each time inspecting the end of the stick as he withdraws it. Finally, the end of the stick emerges from the hole dripping with liquid: runny egg yolk. The chimp licks the egg yolk from the stick and continues to probe the hole with the tool, breaking the eggs inside and lapping the contents from the stick.

These incidents are examples of tool-using behaviour. Not all tool-using primates make their own tools. The actual manufacture of tools seems to be limited to chimpanzees and orangutans, although many other primates manipulate objects in a variety of ways. For example, monkeys have been seen to carefully place a nut on a hard surface and then use a rock or stick to pound the nut time and again until the nut breaks open, revealing a meal rich in protein and fat. In general, a monkey's approach to tool use seems to be one of trial and error, as opposed to the insightful approach of a chimpanzee.

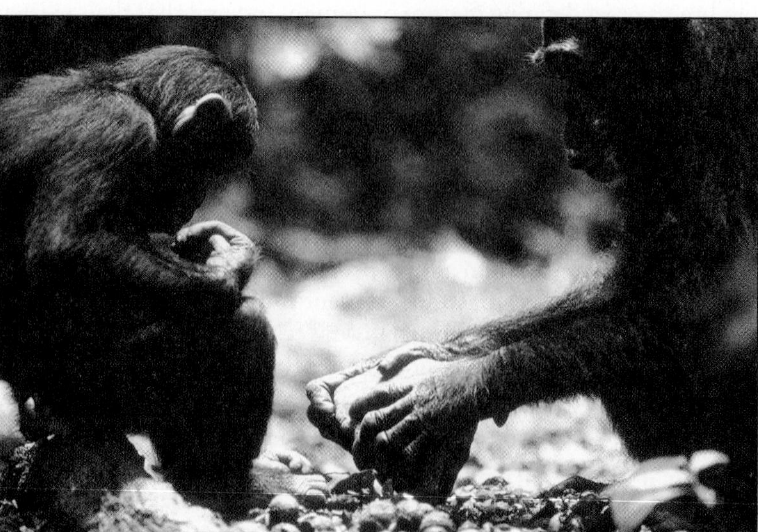

FIGURE 10.12 Technical intelligence, tool use, and culture may have spurred our intellectual development and favoured the origin of our large brains.

Chimpanzees are the most technological of all nonhuman primates by a wide margin. Melissa Panger (2007) notes that chimpanzees are the only primates for which every known wild population has been seen to use tools habitually. Chimpanzee tools fall into four broad categories: probes to extract insects and other food items, hammers to crack open nuts, sponges to soak up liquids, and branches wielded as weapons against prey or other chimpanzees. Tool use varies widely between different chimpanzee populations across Africa.

William McGrew (1992) has done extensive research on this variation in patterns of tool use by wild chimpanzees and what this variation may mean for the advent of human culture. Defining culture as the learned traditions of a group, McGrew considered whether the differences in tool cultures across Africa are the result of genetic differences among chimpanzee populations, environmental differences among the sites, or cultural traditions that differ between sites. He concluded that cultural traditions best explained the diversity of tool cultures. Although there has been genetic differentiation among African chimpanzee populations, there is no reason to expect that individual tool-using behaviours would be under genetic control, just as cultural traits particular to individual human cultures have no basis in genes. The environmental explanation fails because in many cases the same resources are available in different forests, yet chimpanzee cultures differ across those forests. For example, Gombe National Park is a rock-strewn landscape, yet Gombe chimpanzees do not use rocks as tools. By contrast, the lowland rain forests of western Africa, where chimpanzees use stones as tools, have few rocks, and the apes must search for the tools they need. There are also gender differences in chimpanzee tool use. Females at Gombe are more avid termite foragers throughout the year, whereas males tend to fish for termites seasonally (McGrew, 1992). This contrasts with the effort put into acquiring the meat of other mammals, in which males predominate.

Tools are an obvious element of cultural variation among chimpanzees, but they are not the only examples of culture. In a study of the diversity of chimpanzee cultural traditions across several long-term study sites, the researchers documented 38 cultural features—not only tool use but also styles of grooming and other behaviours—that occurred consistently across populations and appeared not to be environmentally determined (Whiten et al., 1999).

Because a primate must be able to think ahead, plan, and be flexible enough to apply the tool to a variety of similar contexts, it has been argued that the ability to use tools entails some sophisticated cognitive skills. Furthermore, offspring in each generation must observe the style and technique of tool use in order to master it. However, research shown that such technical intelligence is not reproduced in other common measures of cognition, such as tactical deception and recognition of oneself in a mirror (Panger, 2007).

As important as the use of tools would have been for early humans, there is at least one good reason that technical intelligence probably was not the impetus for hominid origins. The earliest bipeds arose between 5 and 6 million years ago, but the first stone tools did not appear in the fossil record until 2.5 million years ago. Tool use therefore is unlikely to have played a major role in the origins of bipedal locomotion. And brain size did not expand dramatically until about 300 000 years ago, with the rise of modern people. Until that time brain expansion was incremental, and it may have been scaled to gradual evolutionary increases in body size (see Chapter 15).

Ecological Intelligence Models of **ecological intelligence** suggest that the key impetus for the expansion of the brain was the selective advantage of being able to navigate and find food in a highly complex environment. A tropical forest, with its patchy and temporary availability and distribution of fruit, placed a premium on the evolution of large brains, especially in frugivorous species, which had to

ecological intelligence Hominid intelligence and brain size increase theorized as a result of benefits of navigating and foraging in a complex tropical forest ecosystem.

social intelligence Hominid intelligence and brain size increase theorized as a result of benefits of being politically or socially clever when living with others; sometimes called Machiavellian intelligence.

remember food locations and be able to navigate among them. Although many animals forage in ways that optimize their chances of stumbling onto good food patches—hummingbirds and bumblebees fly optimized routes in fields of wildflowers, for example—primates possess mental maps of the landscape they live in.

Evidence exists that highly frugivorous anthropoid primates may have larger brain-to-body size ratios than folivorous species (Milton, 1981). In African forests, chimpanzees travel from tree to tree, feeding all day long. Many fruit species, such as figs, ripen unpredictably, but a party of chimpanzees usually will be at the tree as soon as ripe fruits appear. This suggests that the apes are monitoring the fruiting status of trees as they forage and remember which trees are worth waiting for (Figure 10.13). Even monkeys have the ability to recall the locations of hundreds of potential food trees (Garber, 1989). We know that nonhuman primates can hold fairly sophisticated information about food items in their heads: rhesus macaques can count up to three food items (Hauser et al., 2001), a skill that might be useful when foraging. Monkeys appear to use a cognitive map that keys on familiar food items to locate food (Menzel, 1991).

If environmental complexity accounted for the increase in brain size that began with the emergence of the hominids, then the expansion of savannah that occurred in the Late Miocene might have been the driving force. As forests became more fragmented, the patchiness of the habitat increased, and emerging hominids with the capacity to navigate through it had a selective advantage.

The ecological intelligence school, which enjoyed much support in the 1980s, has become less accepted in recent years. First, some scholars have pointed out that many small-brained animals navigate and forage in the same highly complex environment in which primates were thought to benefit from their large brains. No evidence exists that other small mammals such as squirrels are less efficient foragers than primates. In addition, the premise of the ecological complexity argument for hominization, that hominids arose in fragmented forest with patches of open grass, has been questioned in recent years. As we shall see in the coming chapters, some of the earliest fossil human discoveries have come from sites that appear to have been forest, not savannah, in the Late Miocene and Pliocene.

Social Intelligence The prevailing view among scientists today is that the brain size increase that occurred in great apes and was extended into hominids resulted from the premium that natural selection placed on individuals that were socially clever. This theory, often called **social intelligence**, argues that the primary evolutionary benefit of large brain size was that it allowed apes and hominids to cope with and even exploit increasingly complex social relations. In large social groups, each individual must remember the network of alliances, rivalries, debts, and credits that exist among group members. This is not so different from the politics of our own day-to-day

FIGURE 10.13 The complexity of a tropical forest may have favoured the evolution of primate intelligence.

lives. Chimpanzees seem to engage in a "service economy" in which they barter alliances and other forms of support with one another (de Waal, 1982).

The individuals best able to exploit this web of social relationships would have reaped more mating success than their group mates. The ability to subtly manipulate others is a fundamental aspect of group life (Byrne and Whiten, 1988a, 1988b). As average group size increased, the cerebrum, or neocortex, of the primate brain may have increased in size to handle the additional input of social information (Dunbar, 1992). This effect holds true even when we take into account the evolved patterns of social grouping. Small-brained primates, such as strepsirhines, typically live alone or in smaller groups than do most monkeys and apes.

Lying in nonhuman primates appears to show an evolutionary trend, one that is more widespread in higher primates (Byrne and Whiten, 1988b). Great apes seem to be skilled at deceiving one another, whereas lemurs rarely if ever engage in tactical deception. Vervet monkeys have been seen to engage in tactical deception: a vervet gave a predator alarm call as the group fed in a desired fruit tree, and as other group members fled from the "predator," the call-giver capitalized on its lie by feeding aggressively in their absence.

Why do primate researchers think that deception is at the heart of understanding the roots of human cognition? The reason lies in the nature of intentional deception. In order to lie to someone, you must possess a **theory of mind**. That is, you must be able to place yourself in the mind of another, to understand the other's mental states. The ability to lie, to imitate, and to teach all rely on the assumption that the object of your actions thinks as you do. Whether nonhuman primates possess a humanlike theory of mind is a subject of intense debate. Small children develop a theory of mind as they grow up, but not until they are past the age of about 2 years. Of course, to some extent the ability to impute mental states to others around you is a fundamental prerequisite to living in a complex social group. Among primates social dynamics are complex enough that a theory of mind becomes a critical issue.

Here's an example of why it is difficult to determine whether primates have a theory of mind. Michael Tomasello and his colleagues set out to determine whether a chimpanzee could imitate the way a person performs a task requiring forethought and planning (Tomasello et al., 1993). They set up an experiment in which one could reach a ball at the end of a table only by inserting a rake through a grate from the opposite end and using the rake to drag the ball. When a small child observed this, it took the child only one trial to learn how to get the ball using the rake, and the child perfectly imitated the researcher's demonstration. The chimpanzee also was able to get the ball after watching a single trial. However, the chimp devised its own method of using the rake to obtain the ball, not the style the researcher had demonstrated. The researchers concluded from this that the chimpanzee failed to imitate the process—even though it could achieve the same result—because it lacked a theory of mind that is necessary for true imitation. This was labelled *emulation:* achieving the goal without understanding the importance of imitating the process. A number of researchers doubt that chimpanzees possess a theory of mind, but their critics point out that the rake–ball test is conducted in a context highly familiar to many children and utterly unnatural to any chimpanzee. This is a persistent problem for laboratory studies of great apes, primates that evolved cognitive abilities in response to the ecological and social pressures of tropical forest environments, not captive settings. Most laboratories provide severely impoverished social learning environments for their study subjects relative to what children growing up in families experience.

The problem with the social intelligence model as an explanation for the evolution of intelligence among apes and humans is twofold. First, if increasing social complexity went hand in hand with increasing brain size, then why is the brain-to-body size ratio of early hominids only modestly larger than that of great apes? Second, other animals with much more modest brain size, such as wolves,

theory of mind Ability to place oneself into the mind of others; necessary for possessing an awareness of the knowledge or cognitive ability of others and for imitating or teaching others.

nevertheless exhibit social dynamics as complex as those seen in nearly all non-human primates. At the same time, one of the biggest-brained primates, the orangutan, does not live in large complex groups. In fact, orangutans don't live in groups at all, casting doubt on the ability of the social intelligence school to fully explain the rise of hominid intelligence.

WHAT MADE HUMANS HUMAN?

Although there is no single explanation for the behavioural shift from apes to humans, we can be sure of a few facts. First, the anatomical shift from quadrupedalism came after a behavioural shift began. Whether for feeding or carrying or any other reason, natural selection favoured individuals possessing slight anatomical differences that made them better bipeds.

Second, the transition to bipedality happened only because at every stage of the process, natural selection favoured the form the evolving prehominid took. At each intermediate stage of the evolution of bipedalism, and of neocortical brain size, the emerging hominid had to be very good at what it did or bipedalism and increasing brain size would not have been the result. We can be sure that the earliest hominids were agile, powerful creatures, combining elements of ape and human behaviour and morphology. Even if they were not as efficient at walking upright as modern people are, they were without doubt highly effective foragers.

Third, although we have focused on both bipedalism and intelligence in this chapter, at the earliest stages of hominid evolution brain neocortex size and intelligence were quite apelike. Paleoanthropologists debate exactly when hominids became more like people than like apes, but certainly the very earliest hominids (and also the australopithecines we will discuss in Chapter 11) were still quite primitive. The notion of linear progression in brain size from the most primitive to the brainiest primates is largely a fiction: research on primate brains showed that a good deal of the variation in brain-to-body size ratio in the Primate order results from body size differences between taxa, with the brain being scaled in size accordingly, rather than from natural selection operating directly on brain size itself (Deacon, 1990). The bigger-is-naturally-better notion may be the product of outdated thinking about the evolution of intelligence: natural selection will select for a bigger brain only if other, less costly solutions are not available.

We have now examined several models that seek to explain why primates are intelligent. Earlier in the chapter we considered some models to explain the origin of bipedalism. From this foundation we turn in the next several chapters to the hard evidence for human evolution, the fossils themselves.

SUMMARY

1. **What effect did the shift to bipedal posture have on human birth?**

   The requirements of habitual bipedal posture select for a narrow pelvis, but this need must be balanced by the need to accommodate wide shoulders and eventually large human brain sizes. The shape of the human pelvis reflects this balance, as does the rotational means of giving birth, in which the baby rotates in the birth canal.

2. **How does the foot skeleton differ between a biped and a knuckle-walker?**

   The foot of a biped has more robust bones for greater weight bearing, which are more tightly bound together by ligaments (less flexible). The big toe is enlarged and in line with the other toes, all of which are shortened. The tarsals form two arches that serve as shock absorbers.

3. **What is the "Radiator" model?**

   This model suggests that hominids evolved a special blood drainage system that facilitated the cooling of their enlarged brains as they walked on the savannah.

4. **What is ecological intelligence?**

   Ecological intelligence models suggest that the key impetus for the expansion of the hominid brain was the selective advantage of being able to navigate and find food in a highly complex environment.

5. **What is a theory of mind?**

   To have a theory of mind is to have the ability to place yourself in the mind of another, to be able to understand the other's mental states. The ability to lie, to imitate, and to teach relies on the assumption that the object of your actions thinks as you do.

CRITICAL THINKING QUESTIONS

1. Evolution by natural selection is all about tradeoffs: One trait is enhanced, but another connected trait is compromised as a result. What were some of the tradeoffs that accompanied the evolution of bipedal posture?
2. Many scenarios have been put forward to explain the origin of bipedalism. Which one do you favour and why? Are there elements to a successful model, apart from the factual evidence, that may explain why it is accepted and others are not?
3. You've read about the three leading schools of thought that explain the rise of intelligence: technical, ecological, and social. But are these schools mutually exclusive? Explain why or why not.
4. Do you think human cognitive abilities are an extension of those of nonhuman primates? Or have humans made an evolutionary break from our primate past in some way? If so, in what way?

KEY TERMS

vertebral column
cervical vertebrae
thoracic vertebrae
lumbar vertebrae
sacrum
coccyx
foramen magnum
nuchal plane
innominate bones (os coxae)
ischium
ilium
pubis
gluteal muscles
acetabulum
femoral condyles
tarsals
metatarsals
phalanges
technical intelligence
ecological intelligence
social intelligence
theory of mind

SUGGESTED READING

Byrne, Richard W. (1995). *The Thinking Ape*. Oxford University Press, Oxford.

Meldrum, Jeff E., and Hilton, Charles E. (2004). *From Biped to Strider: The Emergence of Modern Human Walking, Running, and Resource Transport*. Kluwer, Dordrecht, The Netherlands.

Savage-Rumbaugh, Sue, and Lewin, Roger. (1996). *Kanzi: The Ape at the Brink of the Human Mind*. Wiley-Liss, New York, NY.

Stanford, Craig B. (2003). *Upright*. Houghton Mifflin, Boston, MA.

Chapter 11

Early Hominids

THE SKY WAS HAZY AS THE SUN began to lower in the distance. The small hominids coughed slightly as they breathed the dusty air, the result of a burping volcanic eruption earlier in the day. A light rain began falling, dampening the ash layer that covered the ground like a dusting of snow and leaving small impressions as it did. They looked around furtively for a stand of trees and began moving toward them. Night would fall sooner than usual given the volcanic haze, and predators were sure to be on the move. Two hominids walking side by side were followed by a third, smaller individual as they moved toward the relative safety of the trees. Other animals moved about as well, disturbing the pristine ash fall. Gazing back over her shoulder briefly, a young hominid watched the tracks they made, tracks similar to those you and I would make on a wet sand beach. She worried slightly that this strange new trail would give them away. Little did she know how permanent the trail would be, with the ash drying to a hard cement and future explosions soon covering the lot, protecting her resting place and immortalizing her journey.

MILLIONS OF YEARS LATER IN THE 1970S, a team of palaeontologists led by Mary Leakey was unwinding by playing Frisbee at Laetoli in northern Tanzania, not far from Olduvai Gorge. There, Paul Abell, a geochemist with the group, found the first evidence of the fossilized footprint trail that would ultimately yield the long-buried prints of those early hominids, probably ***Australopithecus afarensis***. The tracks were well preserved and dated to about 3.7 to 3.6 million years ago. They told of a small but capable biped weighing 35 to 40 kilograms (75 to 85 lb) walking toward something.

The footprint trail made at Laetoli by this small group of hominids in the Early Pliocene provides scientists with clues about the anatomy and behaviour of our earliest ancestors. In this chapter we examine the fossil record for early hominids, beginning around 7 million years ago. We explore the adaptations of the very earliest hominids and how we recognize their fossils as such. Then we explore the radiation of the genus *Australopithecus*, whose species exhibit a diverse array of dietary adaptations and favoured habitats. One species of the genus is likely to have given rise to our genus, *Homo*. At the end of the chapter we consider who the likely candidates are for the last common ancestor (LCA) of *Homo* and set the stage for Chapters 12 to 14, in which we explore the evolution of our own genus.

WILL YOU KNOW A HOMINID WHEN YOU SEE ONE?

Hominids are the family of primates that includes humans and our ancestors since diverging from the LCA with chimpanzees, about 6 million years ago. (Currently, there is a debate over the best name for this group; the traditional classification we use calls them hominids, but classifications based on molecular evidence call them *hominins*—Box 11.1.) Recognizing a hominid in the fossil record may not be easy, however, because all we have to work with are fossilized skeletal remains. A fundamental adaptation in

Box 11.1 A Rose by Any Other Name: Hominids versus Hominins

As you learned in Chapter 7, in the traditional classification system of the primates based on morphological characteristics, the superfamily Hominoidea contains three families: the Hominidae, Pongidae, and Hylobatidae (Figure A). In this system the Hominidae, or hominids, are humans and our extinct ancestors, the Pongidae includes the great apes, and the Hylobatidae are the lesser apes. This system reflects how startlingly different we as bipeds are from our closest quadrupedal relatives. However, genetic distances suggest a slightly different classification system. Recall from Chapter 10 that humans and chimpanzees are more closely related to each other genetically than either is to gorillas. Therefore, humans and chimps should be grouped together, despite their morphological differences.

A new classification system that reflects these genetic distances is growing in scientific popularity. In this grouping the superfamily Hominoidea still includes three families, Hominidae, Pongidae, and Hylobatidae; however, two of these families include different animals than in the traditional classification. The Pongidae now includes only the orangutan. The Hominidae now includes humans and our extinct ancestors as well as the African apes and their ancestors, that is, everything since the LCA with orangutans. Within the family Hominidae are two subfamilies that separate gorillas (Gorillinae) from chimpanzees and humans (Homininae). And within the subfamily Homininae, humans and our ancestors are in the tribe Hominini, or hominins for short. In this book we use the more traditional classification system and call humans and our exclusive ancestors hominids because this is the way that most of the current literature is constructed. But you should be aware that the use of hominins is on the rise.

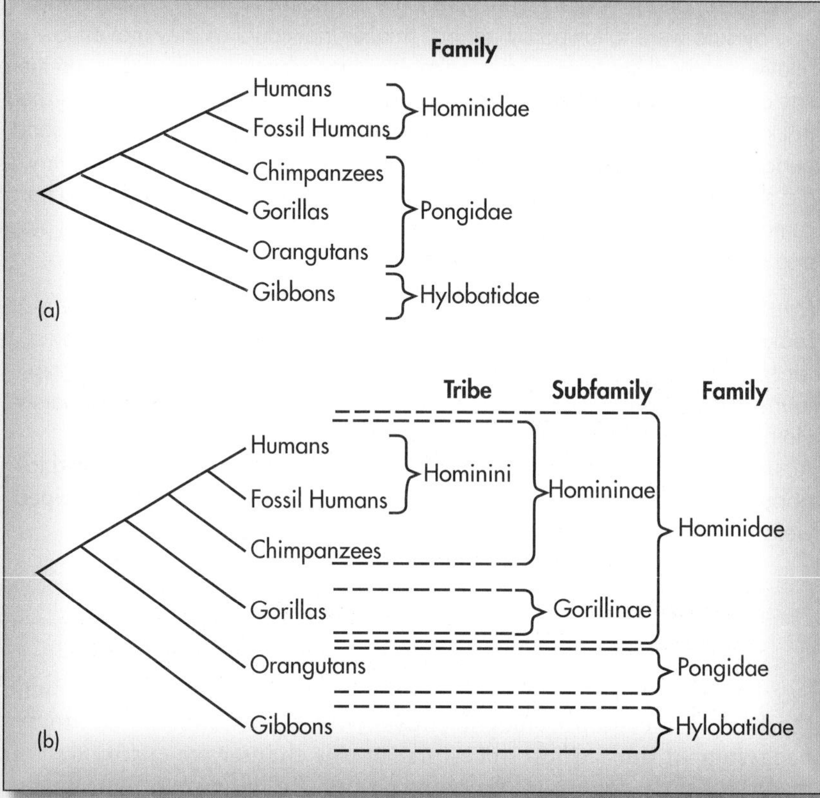

FIGURE A Taxonomic classification of hominins versus hominids. (a) A traditional classification system recognizes only humans and our fossil ancestors in the family Hominidae, which we refer to as hominids. (b) A classification system that reflects molecular relationships groups chimpanzees and humans together at the subfamily level in the Homininae and humans and our ancestors in the tribe Hominini, or hominins.

the hominid lineage is bipedality and in Chapter 10 we discussed the anatomical characters that distinguish bipeds (humans) from quadrupeds (apes). We can use these features to recognize the fossilized remains of bipeds and hence hominids.

Features of the skull and dentition also differ between humans and apes. We infer that a fossil that possesses the human condition of these traits, or an intermediate condition tending toward the human condition, is a hominid. For example, the modern human dental arcade is shaped differently than an ape's. The human tooth row forms a rounded, parabolic arch reflecting the smaller anterior teeth (canines and incisors) and posterior teeth (premolars and molars). The dental arcade of a primate with large canines, such as an ape or baboon, is broader in front (Figure 11.1) and U-shaped, with the teeth behind the canines forming two

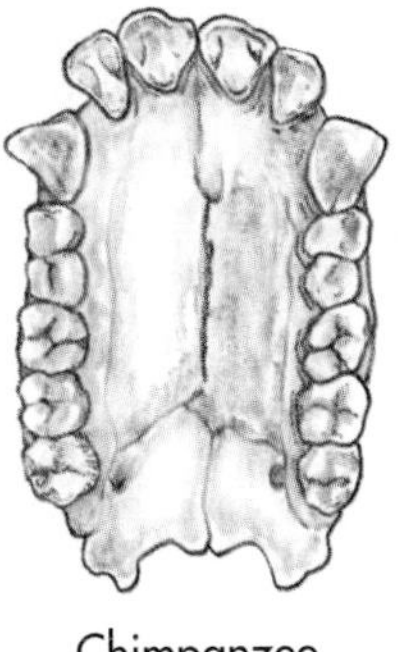

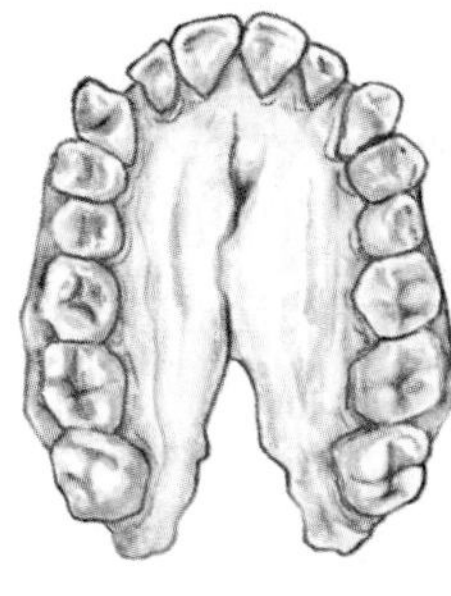

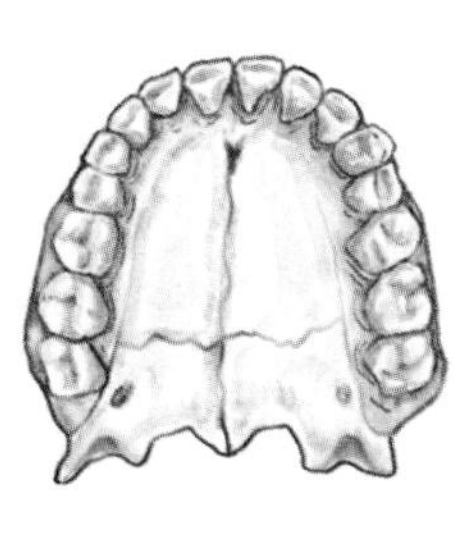

FIGURE 11.1 (a) Chimpanzees and other great apes have large incisors and projecting canines, a diastema, and U-shaped dental arcades caused by parallel rows of cheek teeth. (b) Early hominids have relatively smaller canines, little or no diastema, and a less U-shaped arcade with a still shallow palate. (c) Modern humans have very small canines, no diastema, and a parabolic dental arcade.

parallel rows. Early hominids tend to have somewhat smaller anterior dentition than such primates, but the arcade remains relatively U-shaped. In addition to changing the shape of the dental arcade, large anterior teeth also contribute to greater *facial prognathism*, the degree to which the face projects in front of the braincase. Like that of apes, the face of most early hominids is relatively prognathic.

One aspect of the dental pattern that palaeoanthropologists use to differentiate fossil apes from fossil hominids is the **sectorial premolar complex** (Figure 11.2). In a monkey or ape, the enormous canines of the upper jaw (the maxilla) must fit into a space or *diastema* in the tooth row of the lower jaw (the mandible) where they slide past the premolar. The back of the upper canine is sharpened, or honed, by the bladelike or sectorial premolar. As canines shorten during evolution, the blade on the premolar disappears and the tooth changes from having one cusp to having two. The very earliest **australopithecines** show some reduction of the canine, the absence or reduction of a diastema, and at least partial loss of this honing complex, including the presence of a two-cusped premolar.

Another aspect of the teeth that differs between humans and apes is the thickness of the enamel, the white outer coating of our teeth. Living African ape enamel is thin, but human enamel is thick; thus, thick enamel has often been used to identify hominids. However, thicker enamel probably arose several different times during human evolution as an adaptation to the kinds of foods a group was eating, so just the presence of thick enamel does not guarantee that we are looking at a hominid tooth.

Apes and humans also differ in brain size, cranial proportions, and bony cresting on the cranium. Although early hominids possessed essentially ape-sized brains, throughout hominid evolution brain size increases while facial size decreases. This change in proportions reflects both a de-emphasis of the masticatory (chewing) system and an emphasis on brain size and probably intelligence. In early hominids this deemphasis results in the loss of **cranial crests** in one lineage and as a result a more rounded braincase. The decrease in facial size also reflects the change in the size and shape of the teeth described previously.

sectorial premolar complex Combination of canine and first premolar teeth that form a self-sharpening apparatus.

australopithecines The common name for members of the genus *Australopithecus*.

cranial crests Bony ridges on the skull to which muscles attach.

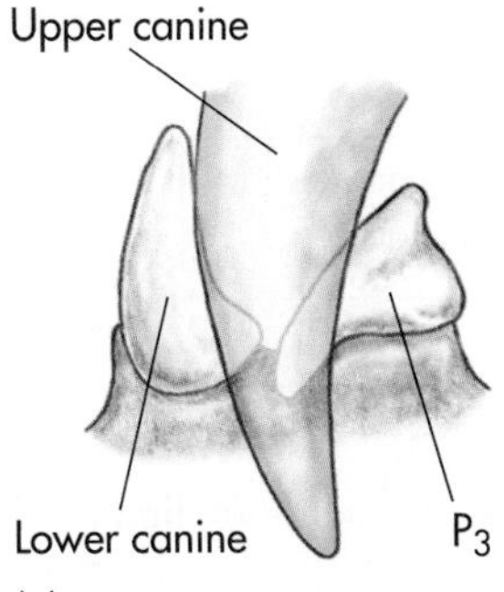

FIGURE 11.2 (a) A canine/premolar or sectorial premolar honing complex consists of a large, projecting upper canine passing across the bladelike edge of the lower premolar. Hominids lose this complex as the anterior teeth decrease in size. (b) Monkeys and apes such as this chimpanzee can be recognized in the fossil record by the anatomy of their teeth.

Thus, fossil hominids, including human ancestors since the split from the chimpanzee lineage, can be recognized by anatomical characters related to bipedality and by reduction of the canine teeth and sectorial premolar complex and changes in palate shape. The very earliest of the hominids show these features to only a very slight degree and therefore are often difficult to differentiate from fossil apes. Other changes that we associate with humans, such as our very large brain and extremely small face and jaws, appear only later in human evolution.

THE FIRST HOMINIDS?

The majority of the fossil evidence of the earliest hominids has come from the Great Rift Valley of East Africa, a broad expanse that runs north to south from the Horn of Africa at the Red Sea southward to Zambia (Figure 11.3). This ancient

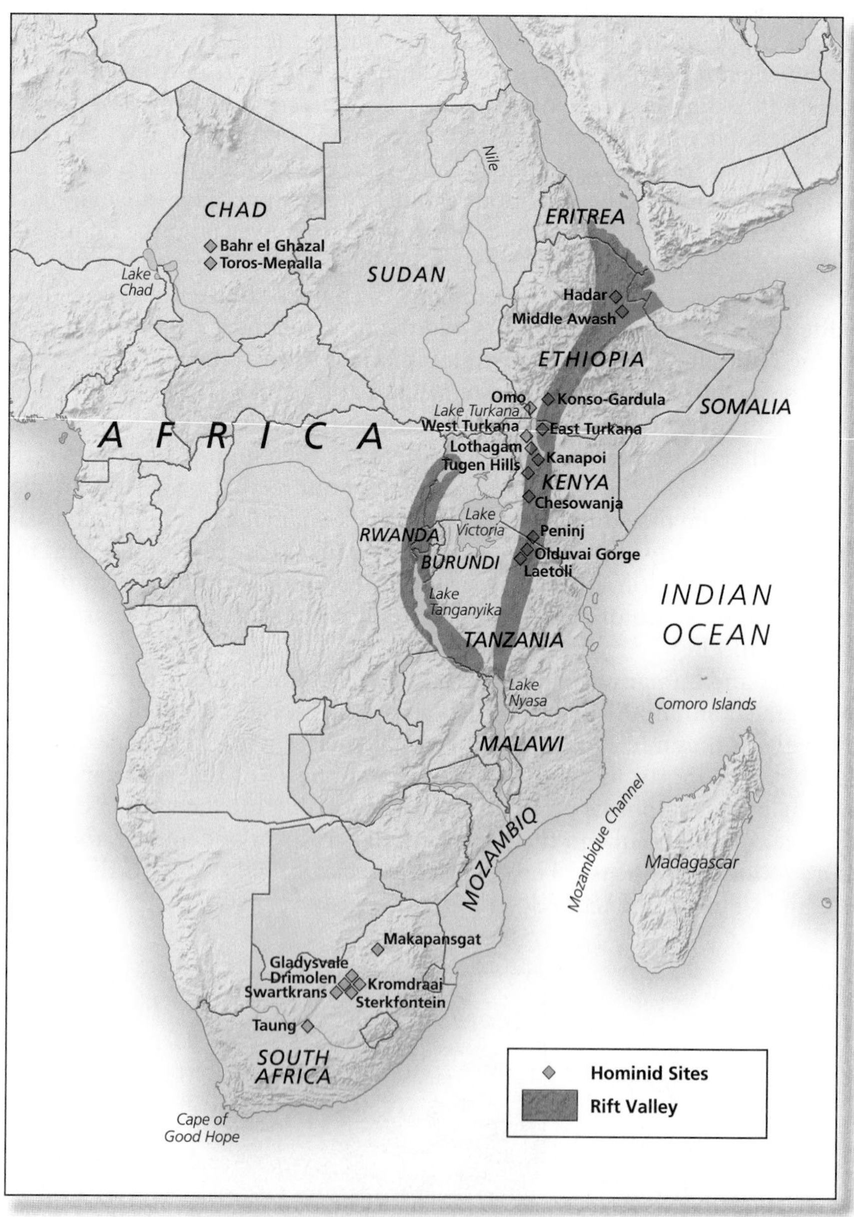

FIGURE 11.3 Geographic distribution of early hominids. Hominids are limited to the continent of Africa until about 1.7 million years ago. Some of the important sites for australopithecine and other early hominid fossils are located on the map.

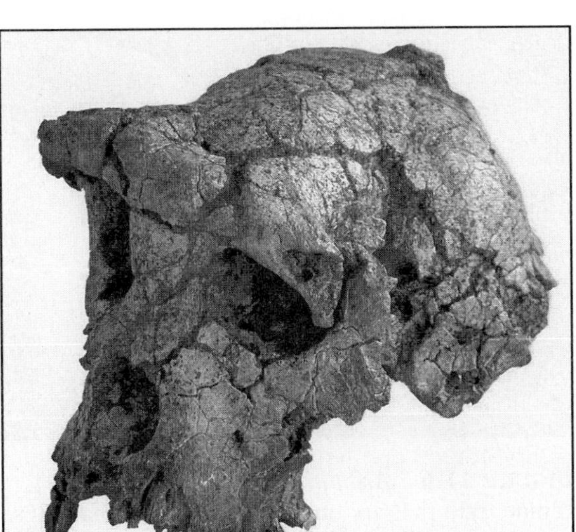

FIGURE 11.4 The skull of *Sahelanthropus tchadensis* is argued to be the earliest of the hominids and one of only two species known from western Africa. Discovered in 2001, the significance of the specimen is still hotly debated, but it may be close to the common ancestor of humans and apes.

rift system is the result of tectonic activity, and the valley contains a string of lakes and a series of ancient volcanoes. The Rift Valley's tectonic history resulted in the creation and disappearance of lakes and streams during hominid evolution. These waterways provided likely habitats for species of early hominids, and the volcanic sediments allow radiometric assessment of fossil ages.

During the Late Miocene from 10 to 5.5 million years ago and Early Pliocene (5.5 to 4 million years ago) at least one lineage of apes made the adaptive shift to a terrestrial niche and became increasingly bipedal. As we learned in Chapters 9 and 10, the shift to bipedality came about partly in response to major climatic changes that were occurring in equatorial Africa in the Late Miocene. This shift was accompanied by anatomical changes to the pelvis, spinal column, and other body systems of hominids.

Molecular evidence suggests that the first signs of hominization should appear in lineages of Late Miocene apes. Unfortunately, between 10 and 6 million years ago, the fossil record for the roots of the Hominidae is poorly represented. Between 7 and 4.4 million years ago, we have several candidates for the site of the earliest hominid remains (Figures 11.4, 11.5, 11.6), but all or some of them may represent

FIGURE 11.5 Brigitte Senut and Martin Pickford with the postcranial remains of *Orrorin tugenensis*, which may be among the oldest of the hominids, although its taxonomic position is still debated.

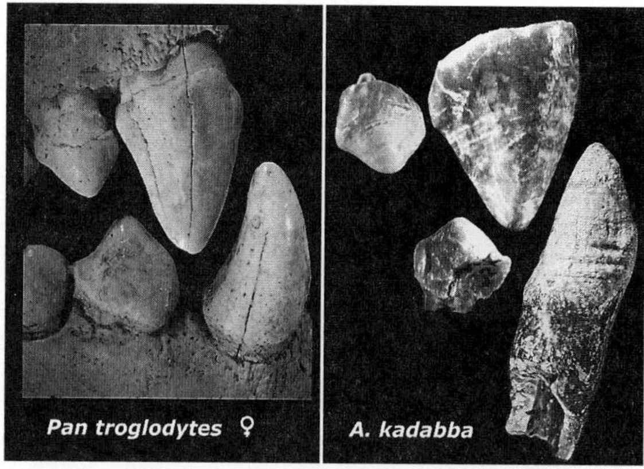

FIGURE 11.6 *Ardipithecus kadabba* has large canine teeth that are only slightly smaller than those of living apes. The oldest of the Ethiopian hominids at 5.7 million years old, *A. kadabba* was ancestral to the 4.4 million-year-old *Ardipithecus ramidus* and perhaps the rest of the hominid lineage.

fossil apes rather than hominids. Some of these sites have produced evidence too fragmentary for an unambiguous answer, while others have produced a plethora of remains but the analysis of the material is still in progress (Table 11.1).

AUSTRALOPITHECUS AND KIN

The identity of the first hominids is as contested as that of the earliest primates. Recognizing the very earliest members of a group is difficult for two reasons: The fossil record is fragmentary, so the evidence is incomplete, and the more ancient the ancestor, the more apelike the fossil. So it will be very hard to differentiate an early hominid from an ape, for example. The first hominids discussed previously fall in this nebulous position.

Most of the early members of the hominidae, however, do not suffer from this ambiguity and are assigned to the genus *Australopithecus*. The name *Australopithecus*, meaning "southern ape," was coined by Raymond Dart in the 1920s since the very first specimen of the genus was discovered in South Africa. Since that time discoveries of australopithecines have revealed an adaptive radiation

TABLE 11.1 Candidates for the Earliest Hominid (all could be fossil apes)

SITE	MYA	SPECIES
Toros-Menalla, Chad	7.0 to 5.2	*Sahelanthropus tchadensis*
Tugen Hills, Kenya	6.0	*Orrorin tugenensis*
Middle Awash, Ethiopia	5.8 to 5.2	*Ardipithecus kadabba*
Lothagam, Kenya	5.8	??
Tabarin, Kenya	5.0	??
Aramis, Ethiopia	4.4	*Ardipithecus ramidus*

*MYA = millions of years ago

of early hominids that filled a variety of habitat types in eastern, southern, and central Africa and are now known to have lived from 4.2 to about 1.0 million years ago. The genus *Australopithecus* can be usefully thought about as several species of bipedal hominids that are characterized by being small bodied (30 to 45 kg; 64 to 100 lbs) and small brained (340 to 500 cc), with moderately prognathic faces, and a mosaic of ancestral and derived craniodental anatomy.

Several species of the genus *Australopithecus* overlapped with one another in time and space, probably avoiding competition by relying on slightly different food resources. In one lineage several species evolved massive jaws, molar teeth, and cranial skeletons optimized for producing large chewing forces; they are referred to as the robust australopithecines. These hominids probably relied on hard chewing to open food items during times of nutritional stress.

As we discover new specimens and new taxa, we will no doubt expand both the geographic distribution and the time span for this group and raise additional questions about their origins and descendants (Figure 11.7).

AUSTRALOPITHECUS ANAMENSIS (4.2 TO 3.9 MYA)

Around 4 million years ago several similar forms appeared roughly simultaneously. The oldest and most primitive of these is *Australopithecus anamensis* (Figure 11.8). *A. anamensis* provides the earliest incontrovertible evidence of bipedality in its postcranial anatomy. The anatomy of its jaws and teeth fall between the earlier hominids such as *Ardipithecus* and later hominids like *A. africanus* (described below).

In many respects, the fossils of *A. anamensis* strongly resemble those of *A. afarensis*, and some researchers think the two species should be considered one and the same; however, in general *A. anamensis* is more primitive than *A. afarensis*, and aspects of the mandible and dentition indicate it is probably ancestral to later australopithecines.

The context in which the hominids lived is critical to our thinking about the selective pressures favouring bipedality. It was once thought that hominids evolved on savannahs, but evidence from some *A. anamensis* sites suggests that at least some early bipeds occupied forested areas.

AUSTRALOPITHECUS AFARENSIS (3.9 TO 2.9 MYA)

The first *Australopithecus afarensis* was discovered in 1974 in the Awash Valley of the Afar triangle of Ethiopia (see Box 11.2). Named Lucy (after the Beatles' song "Lucy in the Sky with Diamonds"), the fossil is extraordinary for two reasons. First, her anatomy is more primitive than that of any hominid discovered up to that time, and it includes a clear mosaic of humanlike and apelike features. She stood a little over a metre (> 3 ft) tall and possessed a cranial vault suggesting a modest brain size about equal to that of an adult chimpanzee. Second, her skeleton is more complete than that of nearly any other fossil human. Although more primitive hominids have been discovered since, none is nearly so well studied, and *A. afarensis* has remained the benchmark by which the anatomy of all other early hominids is interpreted. In addition to Lucy, thousands of finds of *A. afarensis* have been made in the Afar in the past 30 years, as well as at other East African localities.

There are several key anatomical features of *A. afarensis* (Figure 11.9). The cranium and teeth of *A. afarensis* are intermediate in appearance between those of a living ape and a modern human. The cranial capacity is small but slightly larger than that of earlier hominids and living apes (range 350 to 500 cc).

Figure 11.7 EARLY HOMINID EVOLUTION

The earliest hominids appeared around 6 million years ago in western and eastern Africa. About 4 million years ago *Australopithecus*, a bipedal genus characterized by small brains, large jaws, and small body size, arose. *Australopithecus* is probably the first stone tool maker, and one species is likely to have given rise to *Homo*.

Several species of the genus overlapped with one another in time and space, probably avoiding competition by relying on slightly different food resources. In one lineage, the robust australopithecines (*A. aethiopicus, A. robustus,* and *A. boisei*), several species evolved massive jaws, molar teeth, and cranial skeletons optimized for producing large chewing forces. These hominids probably relied on hard chewing to open food items during times of nutritional stress.

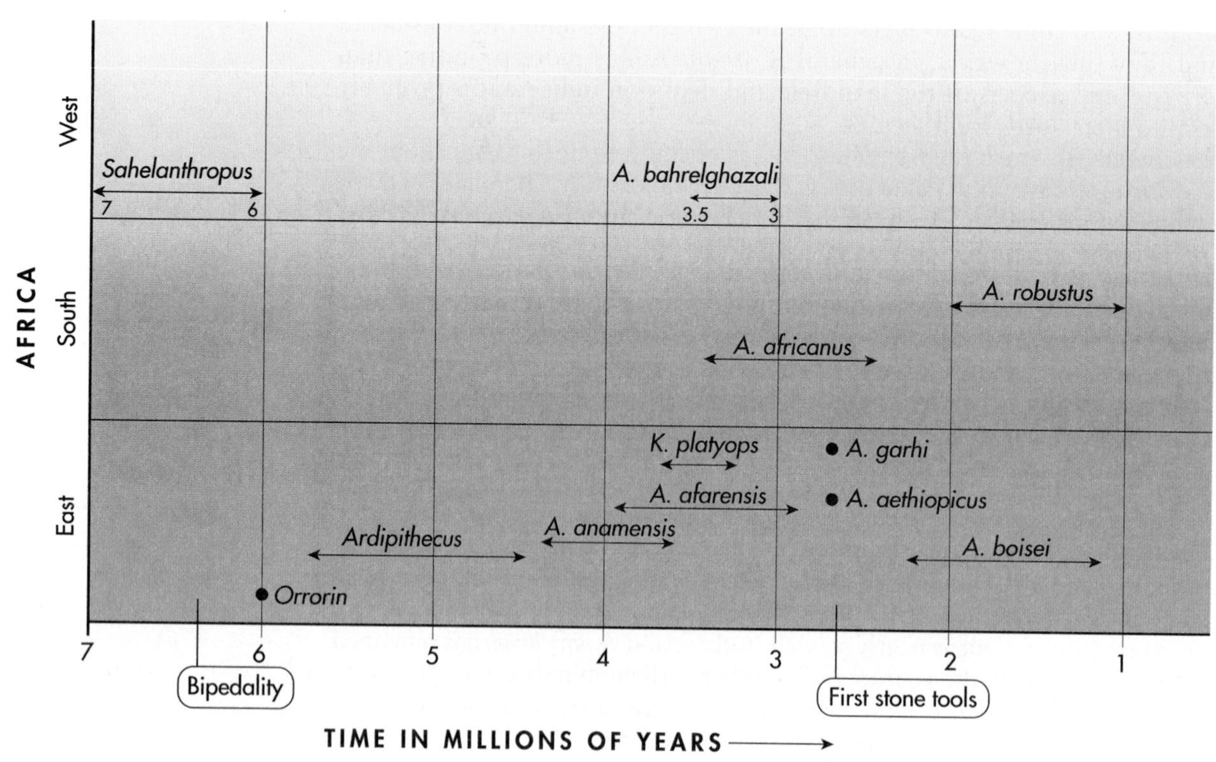

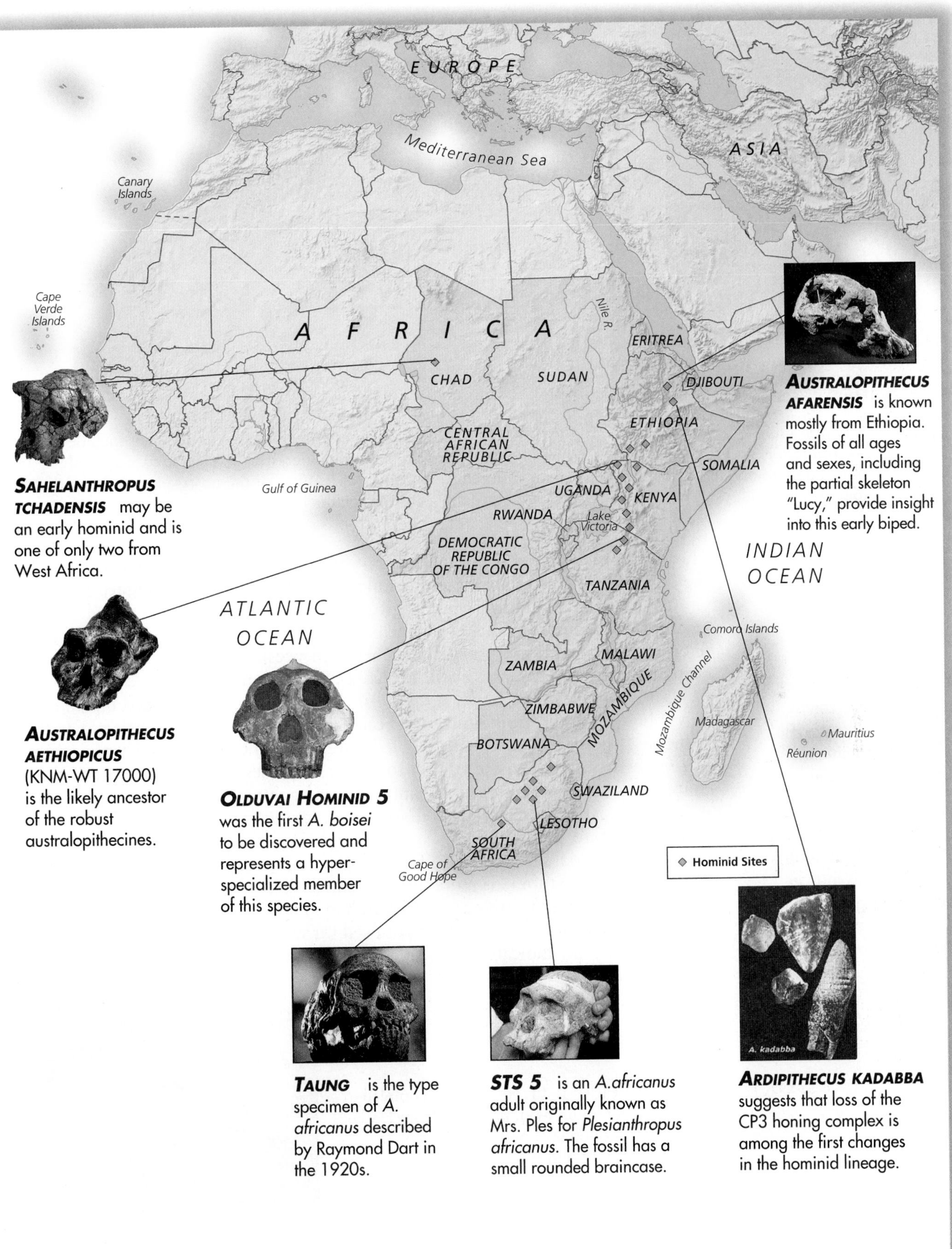

SAHELANTHROPUS TCHADENSIS may be an early hominid and is one of only two from West Africa.

AUSTRALOPITHECUS AFARENSIS is known mostly from Ethiopia. Fossils of all ages and sexes, including the partial skeleton "Lucy," provide insight into this early biped.

AUSTRALOPITHECUS AETHIOPICUS (KNM-WT 17000) is the likely ancestor of the robust australopithecines.

OLDUVAI HOMINID 5 was the first *A. boisei* to be discovered and represents a hyper-specialized member of this species.

TAUNG is the type specimen of *A. africanus* described by Raymond Dart in the 1920s.

STS 5 is an *A.africanus* adult originally known as Mrs. Ples for *Plesianthropus africanus*. The fossil has a small rounded braincase.

ARDIPITHECUS KADABBA suggests that loss of the CP3 honing complex is among the first changes in the hominid lineage.

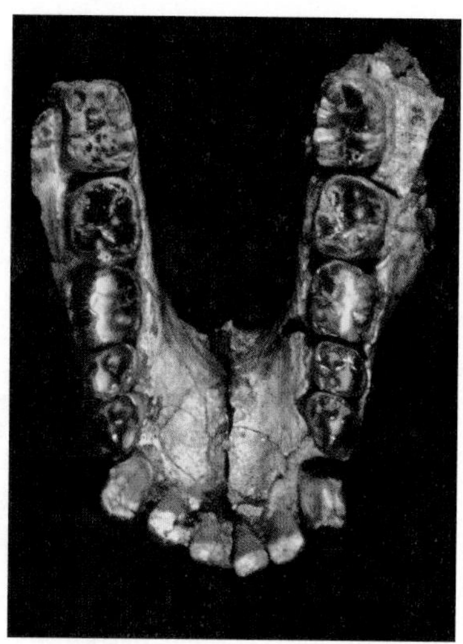

FIGURE 11.8 The remains of *Australopithecus anamensis* from Kenya date to about 3.9 to 4.2 million years old.

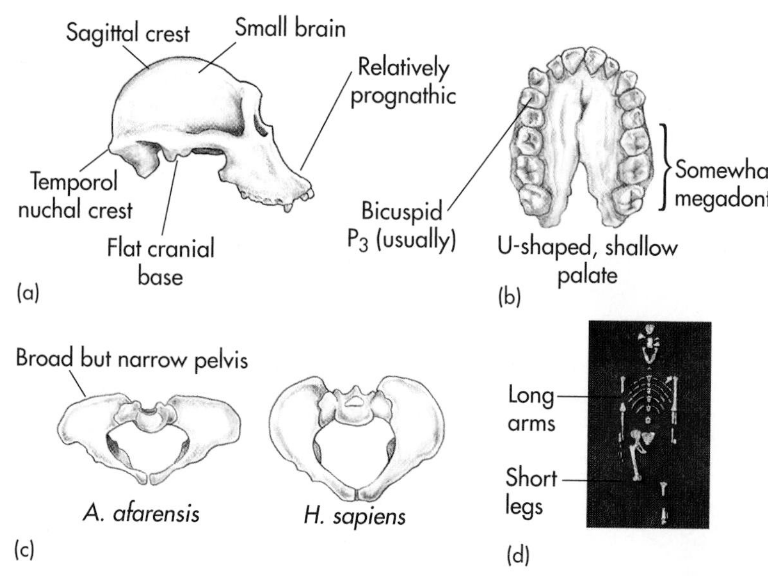

FIGURE 11.9 Key features of *Australopithecus afarensis* include (a) a small cranial capacity and cranial crests, (b) a shallow, U-shaped palate with reduced canine, (c) features of the postcranial skeleton that indicate bipedality, and (d) apelike limb proportions.

The *A. afarensis* face was prognathic, but not as much as in the living apes, and the cranial base was relatively flat, similar to that of living apes (Figure 11.10). Cranial cresting including both a **sagittal crest** (for the temporalis muscle) and a **compound temporonuchal crest** (formed where the neck muscles approach the temporalis muscles) are present, especially in presumed males. These cranial crests tell us that *A. afarensis* still placed a premium on chewing.

sagittal crest Bony crest running lengthwise down the centre of the cranium on the parietal bones; for the attachment of the temporalis muscles.

compound temporonuchal crest Bony crest at the back of the skull formed when an enlarged temporalis muscle approaches enlarged neck (nuchal) muscles, present in apes and *A. afarensis*.

In its postcranial skeleton, *A. afarensis* is clearly an accomplished biped: the pelvic bones, femur, tibia, and foot bones all display features consistent with bipedality (described in Chapter 10). Indirect evidence of bipedal walking in *A. afarensis* comes from the Laetoli footprint track described at the start of this chapter that, on the basis of its age and location, is thought to have been made by *A. afarensis*. All these characters tell us that *A. afarensis* was a striding biped and clearly, therefore, a hominid.

The postcranial skeleton also differs from that of modern humans, however (see Figure 11.11). The thorax is more funnel-shaped, similar to an ape's, and the arms are somewhat longer relative to leg length than in modern humans, although their anatomy tells us that the arms were not used for walking. Aspects of the shoulder and hip joints may indicate some level of arboreality.

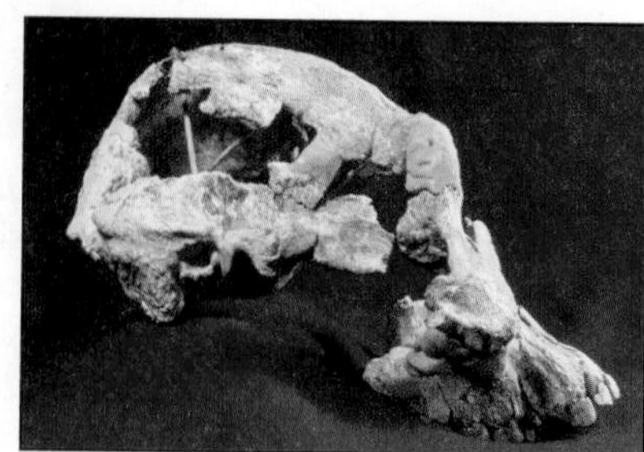

FIGURE 11.10 A near-complete cranium of *A. afarensis* from Hadar, Ethiopia, shows a prognathic face and small braincase.

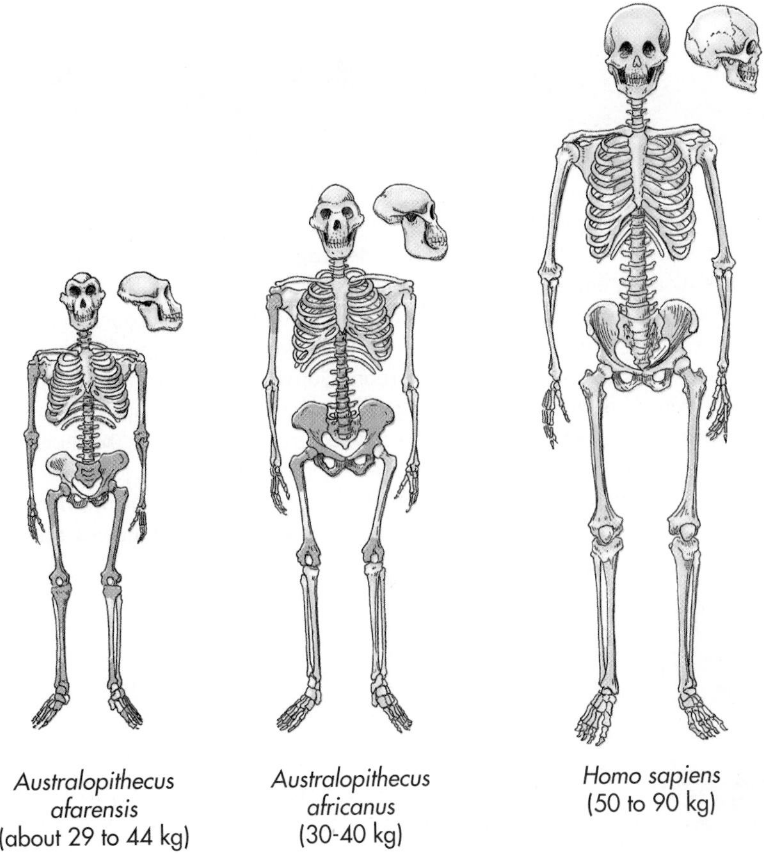

FIGURE 11.11 Comparison of hominid skeletons. The australopithecines (left and centre) were short bipedal hominids with relatively long arms and short legs. Compared to modern humans (right), the australopithecine torso was broad and funnel-shaped.

A marvellous discovery was made in the Awash Valley in late 2000, that of the most complete skeleton of an ancient infant. The Dikika Baby, as it is known, dates to 3.3 million years ago. Although small and incompletely formed, the skeleton shows clear evidence of a small brain, and an upper body like an ape with a lower body consistent with what we would expect in a biped.

This mosaic pattern of postcranial anatomy, indicating a successful biped that probably spent time in the trees as well, has stirred debate about the type of bipedalism practised by *A. afarensis*. It seems likely that on the ground *A. afarensis* moved on two legs. They may have retreated to the trees to escape from predators and to forage for fruits and leaves during the day and to sleep at night. Habitat reconstructions based on antelope remains found at *A. afarensis* sites suggest the hominids were living in woodlands rather than on open savannas (Reed, 1997), which supports the idea that trees served as a refuge from predators or as sleeping areas for these small hominids.

It is likely that *A. afarensis* lived in groups, and because they were very sexually dimorphic, they probably were not monogamous. The largest adults from Hadar are, in some measures, nearly twice the size of the smallest *A. afarensis* (Lucy is one of the very smallest). This extensive range of variation has led some experts to suggest that *A. afarensis* is actually two species, not two sexes; however, the prevailing

BOX 11.2 South African Cave Sites

There are a few key differences between the study of fossils in southern and eastern Africa. Unlike the open-air sites of East Africa, most South African fossil sites are in cave and cliff deposits. Careful taphonomic (decay-process) study of the caves and their included fossils reveals instead that the skeletal remains probably fell into the South African caves, which themselves are the result of dissolution of the bedrock by ground water (see Chapter 9). South African caves often appear as sinkholes in the ground (similar to those seen in Wood Buffalo National Park on the border between Alberta and the Northwest Territories), and often have trees growing along their rims. Animals are thought to have fallen into these caves by accident or in some cases to have been introduced after having been killed by carnivores, such as leopards, which cache their kills in the branches of trees overhanging the sinks to protect them from larger carnivores (Figure A) (Brain, 1981).

South African cave sites were formed by the dissolution and collapse of bedrock that later trapped sediments and animals, including hominids (Figure B): (a) Initially bedrock is dissolved by groundwater, (b) when the water table lowers, there may be roof collapse into the chamber and stalagmite/stalactite formation, (c) with time the chamber may erode further, eventually connecting to the surface, and (d) vegetation, including trees, often grows near these wet openings and sediments and

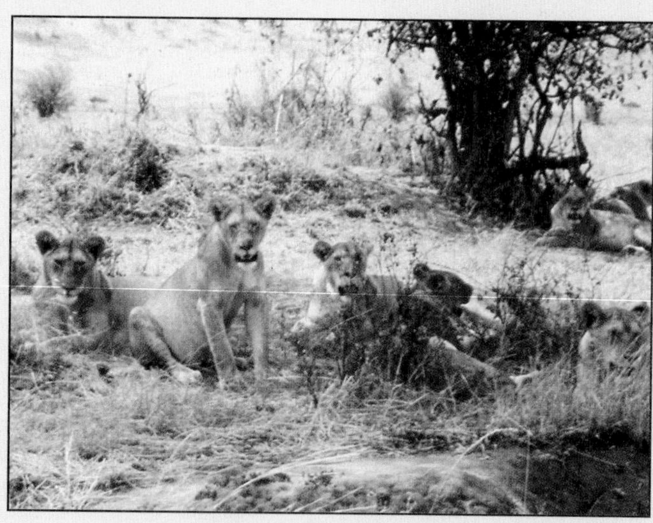

FIGURE A Some fossil remains of early hominids show evidence of carnivore bite marks similar to those made by lions and other carnivores, which suggests that our early ancestors may have been hunted.

opinion is that *A. afarensis* shows an extreme level of sexual dimorphism similar to that of modern orangutans (McHenry, 1991) (Table 11.2). From this we infer that *A. afarensis* had a polygynous mating strategy, because in living primates great sexual dimorphism usually is associated with multiple mates (see Chapter 8).

AUSTRALOPITHECUS BAHRELGHAZALI (3.5 TO 3.0 MYA)

As we have seen, most early fossil hominids have come from eastern Africa, with two exceptions that were found in West Africa: the early hominid *Sahelanthropus tchadensis* and the later-living *Australopithecus bahrelghazali*, both discovered in Chad. *A. bahrelghazali* is known from a single fossil: the front of a mandible with seven teeth (Figure 11.12). Most researchers think that *A. bahrelghazali* is in fact animals may fall into the chambers. (e) Over time other openings to the surface may form, introducing new sediments and bones. (f) Erosion of the surface exposes the stratigraphy of these sediments, the relative ages of which are difficult to interpret because of their complex history.

There is another key difference between the East and South African fossil records. Volcanic ash that forms the matrix in which many East African fossils are embedded can be dated quite precisely (see Chapter 9). However, palaeontologists must rely mostly on geomagnetic polarity data and relative dating methods for South African deposits. They compare the fauna (biostratigraphy) and geology (lithostratigraphy) of rock strata containing human fossils with strata in other regions such as East Africa that contain similar fossil sequences but can be more precisely dated. This provides an estimate of the age of the deposits. However, the stratigraphy of the South African caves is complex, so establishing the sequence of which fossil species lived contemporaneously with others is not always possible.

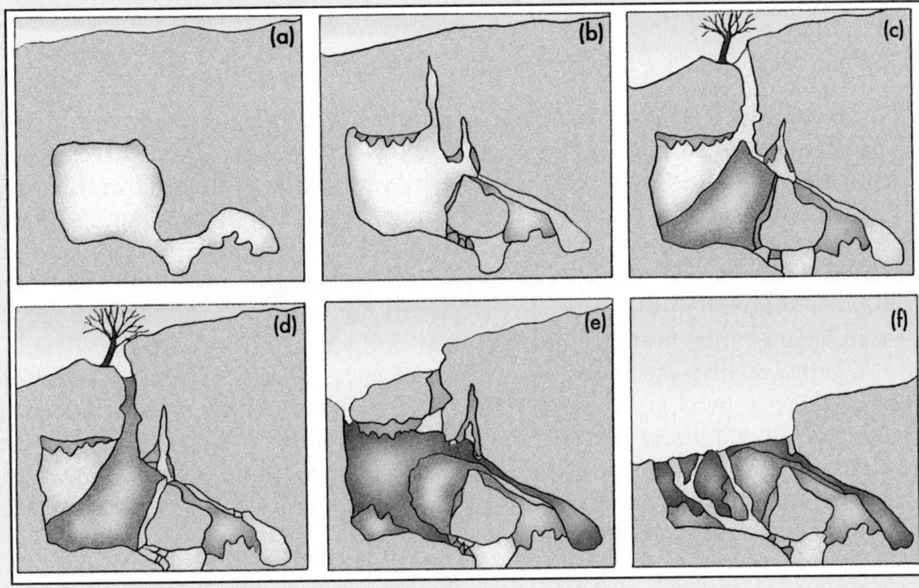

FIGURE B South African cave sites

TABLE 11.2 Comparisons of *A. afarensis*, Great Ape, and Modern Humans

	CRANIAL CAPACITY (CC)	SEXUAL DIMORPHISM (MALES X PERCENT HEAVIER)
A. afarensis	450	56%
Chimpanzee	400	15%
Gorilla	500	50%
Orangutan	400	Nearly 100%
Early genus ***Homo***	600	63%
Modern human	1400	15%

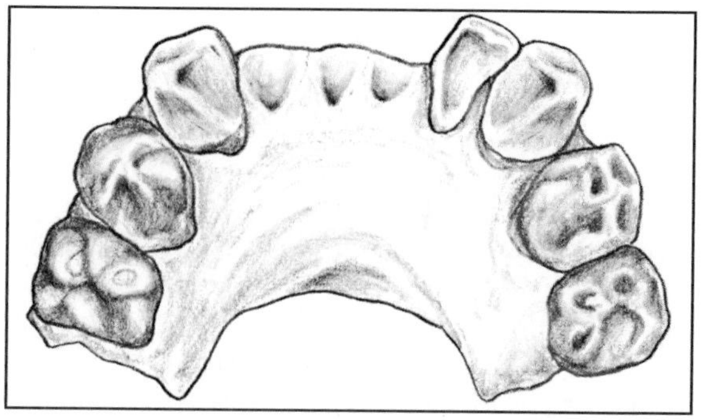

FIGURE 11.12 The mandible of *A. bahrelghazali.* The first hominid found in western Africa, *A. bahrelghazali* dates to about 3.5 million years ago.

a member of *A. afarensis* or at least that it is too fragmentary to define a new species around. Until additional fossils are known, the major importance of this find is its confirmation that hominids lived over much of the African continent, not only in East Africa.

KENYANTHROPUS PLATYOPS (3.5 MYA)

Discovered in 2001, *Kenyanthropus platyops* ("the flat-faced hominid from Kenya") dates to 3.5 million years ago (Leakey et al., 2001). This specimen has a surprisingly flat face (Figure 11.13), a derived trait of later hominids rather than of *A. afarensis* and its kin, and has small molar teeth, a condition more primitive than the other australopithecines. Some researchers think *Kenyanthropus* should be considered just another species of *Australopithecus* or even a member of *A. afarensis*, although it differs from *A. afarensis* not only in facial morphology but also in having other, more primitive cranial characters.

Whether a distinct genus or a separate species, at 3.5 million years old, *Kenyanthropus* lived at the same time as *A. afarensis*, which means that one of these taxa is not a direct ancestor of modern people. It is not possible at this time to determine which is more closely linked to later hominids. But we must now acknowledge that the early days of the bipedal hominid radiation were more complex, and perhaps less linear, than we had realized.

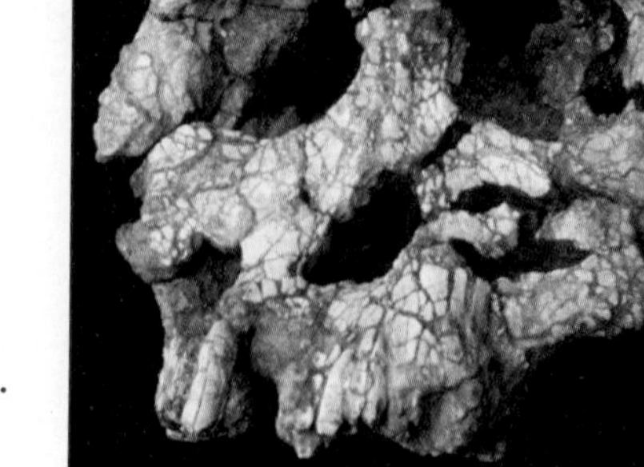

FIGURE 11.13 The cranium of *Kenyanthropus platyops* dates to about 2.5 million years ago in Kenya. The species takes its name from the very flat face.

AUSTRALOPITHECUS AFRICANUS (3.5 TO < 2.0 MYA)

We have thus far discussed in detail only hominids that occurred in East Africa. But southern Africa also saw a major radiation of hominid species during the Pliocene. The oldest of these is *Australopithecus africanus*.

The **type specimen** for *Australopithecus africanus* is a fascinating fossil: a tiny partial skull of a juvenile (Figure 11.14), identified in 1924 from discoveries at the Taung limestone quarry near Johannesburg attached to a fossilized impression of the interior of the skull, a so-called natural **endocast**, which revealed the general appearance and size of the brain of the creature. "The Taung Child" appeared to be a very young apelike hominid who retained some baby teeth. The estimate of Taung's age at death has long been in debate because we can't be sure whether early hominids grew up along the same trajectory as modern people or as the great apes, but most researchers think that the answer is closer to an ape developmental rate and that the Taung child was about two or three years old at the time it died.

Based on a number of specimens from South Africa, we can say that *A. africanus* was a small-bodied hominid that possessed the broad and short iliac blade of the pelvis and structural adaptations in the spine, leg, and foot that characterize habitual bipeds (see Chapter 10). Most of these fossils have been dated to between 3.5 and 2.4 million years ago, with the possibility that some of the material may be much younger, possibly little more than 1 million years old.

An extensive collection of postcranial remains has made it possible to estimate body size at about 29 to 40 kilograms (65 to 90 lbs) for *A. africanus*. *A. africanus* has the same general body plan as *A. afarensis*, with a more funnel-shaped thorax than in humans, although *A. africanus'* arms may be shorter (Figure 11.11).

The other animals found at *A. africanus* sites suggest that these hominids, like those in eastern Africa, were living in woodland and open woodland environments (Reed, 1997). These wooded areas may have provided some protection from predators. There are currently no earlier hominids in South Africa than *A. africanus*, but it is generally assumed that *A. africanus* evolved from a population of East African hominids, probably *A. afarensis*, that migrated to the south.

A. africanus is more derived than *A. afarensis* in several aspects of its cranial skeleton (Figure 11.15). Compared with *A. afarensis*, *A. africanus* has a larger braincase (about 450 to 550 cc, still quite small by modern standards), a rounded vault that lacks cranial crests and has fewer air cells in it, a less prognathic face, and a more flexed cranial base. The teeth of *A. africanus* are generalized and the

type specimen According to the laws of zoological nomenclature, the anatomical reference specimen for the species definition.

endocast A replica (or cast) of the internal surface of the braincase that reflects the impressions made by the brain on the skull walls. Natural endocasts are formed by the filling of the braincase by sediments.

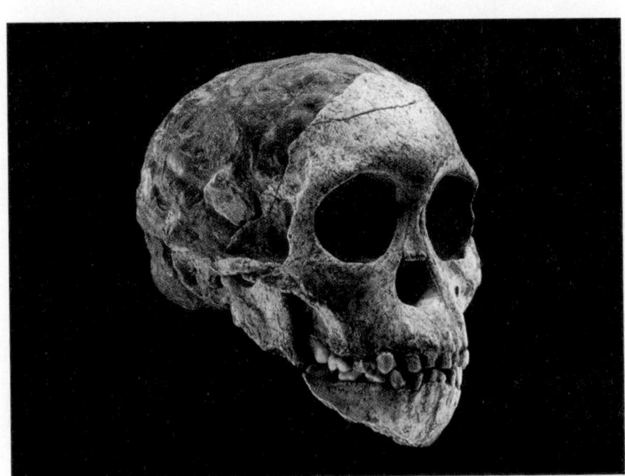

FIGURE 11.14 The Taung child, the first of the australopithecines to be discovered, is the type specimen for *Australopithecus africanus*.

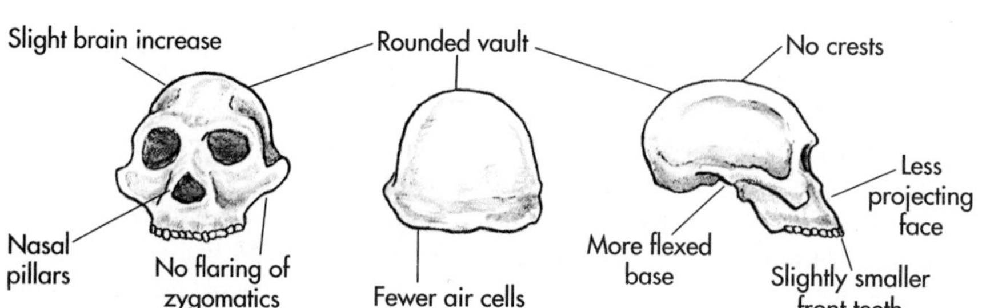

FIGURE 11.15 Key features of *Australopithecus africanus* include a rounded vault without cranial crests, a slightly flexed cranial base, and moderate facial prognathism.

molars more modestly proportioned than in later, more specialized australopithecines such as *A. robustus* and *A. boisei* (described below). This has led to a classification into gracile australopithecines, including *A. africanus*, and robust australopithecines for *A. robustus, A. boisei,* and *A. aethiopicus*. *A. africanus* has small anterior teeth, especially canines, compared with earlier hominids such as *A. afarensis* but larger anterior teeth than most of the later robust australopithecines. The molars of *A. africanus*, however, although clearly larger than in earlier forms, are smaller than the enormous molars of the robust australopithecines.

AUSTRALOPITHECUS GARHI (2.5 MYA)

Found in the Afar region of Ethiopia, *Australopithecus garhi* dates to approximately 2.5 million years ago (Asfaw et al., 1999). It has a small brain (450 cc), a prominent prognathic face, large canines, and a sagittal crest (Figure 11.16). In most respects *A. garhi* is quite primitive anatomically, even for an australopithecine. Some workers argue that *A. garhi* may be better interpreted as a late surviving member of *A. afarensis*; remember that that species existed until about 2.9 million years ago in the same geographic area. Besides its age, *A. garhi* differs from *A. afarensis* only in a few anatomical characters, such as having more robust premolars and molars. If the postcrania from a nearby site belong to this species, then, surprisingly, *A. garhi* has more humanlike proportions between its arms and legs (because of a long femur) but apelike proportions between its upper arm (humerus) and forearm (radius and ulna). These proportions seem to differ from those of *A. afarensis,* which has a shorter lower limb.

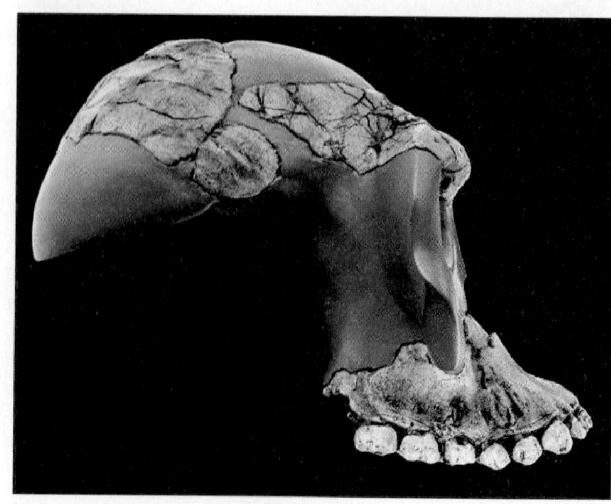

FIGURE 11.16 *Australopithecus garhi* dates to about 2.5 million years ago in Ethiopia and was found in the same beds as early stone tools. It is slightly younger than *A. afarensis*, and its cheek teeth are more robust.

hard object feeding Chewing tough, hard-to-break food items such as nuts or fibrous vegetation.

Regardless of its taxonomic attribution, the proximity of *A. garhi* fossils to the earliest known stone tools is significant. At Bouri, and also at nearby Gona, archaeologists found stone tools in association with the fossilized remains of antelope and other likely prey species. These bones show cut marks and percussion marks, unmistakable evidence that early hominids had been using stone tools to butcher carcasses. We cannot say whether *A. garhi* was the butcher, but no other early hominid fossils have been found in the same strata. If supported by further field research, this would be the earliest evidence of tool use by an australopithecine. Although *A. gahri's* role in later evolution cannot be resolved on the known morphology, the species ultimately could be ancestral to later *Homo*.

The Robust Australopithecines (or Paranthropines)

The robust australopithecines are a group of early hominids that, more clearly than any other group, appears to have been an evolutionary dead end because of their extreme anatomical specializations.

The robust australopithecines are united by a suite of cranial features related to their feeding adaptation that make them extremely efficient at producing a lot of force at their molars (Figure 11.17). These cranial features often are thought of as an adaptation to **hard object feeding**, chewing tough food items such as hard-shelled nuts or fibrous vegetation.

Scientists think that these adaptations allowed robust australopithecines to survive during times when not much food existed because they were specialized for eating a kind of food that other hominids could not eat. Most of the time robusts probably ate a variety of different things, but when food was scarce they relied on their "fallback food." However, their reliance on tough foods during times of resource scarcity seems to become more specialized through time. Eventually, this overspecialization would lead to their demise when food resources changed too dramatically and their fallback foods disappeared.

Some scientists think that the robust australopithecines are so different from other australopithecines that they should have their own genus, *Paranthropus*. The decision to define a new genus in the fossil record rests on the evidence that a sufficiently different adaptive plateau exists for a given group of species, in this case the robusts, than for other closely related species. Proponents of the use of *Paranthropus* argue that the masticatory features of the robusts are evidence of such an adaptive plateau. By using this separate genus name these scientists also are accepting that all the robust species are more closely related to one another than they are to species outside of *Paranthropus* and thus that they descend from a recent common ancestor. As we shall see, other scientists disagree as to how closely related the robust species are to one another, so in this book we take a conservative approach and include them in *Australopithecus*.

Australopithecus aethiopicus There is no evidence that the robust australopithecines left any descendants, but there is some tantalizing evidence about their origin, believed to date to 2.7 to 2.5 mya. The oldest fossil was discovered on the western shore of Lake Turkana, an area famous for many other fossil hominid finds. When unearthed, the fossil was stained black by minerals in the sediment and therefore was dubbed "the Black Skull" (Figure 11.18).

Many palaeoanthropologists think that *A. aethiopicus* is primitive enough to be the evolutionary link between the early trunk of the hominid family tree and the specialized branch that led to the robust australopithecines (Figure 11.19). However, other scholars still consider it possible that the East and South African robusts could represent two more distantly related lineages that have converged on a shared anatomy because of similar dietary adaptation to hard object feeding, at least during fallback periods.

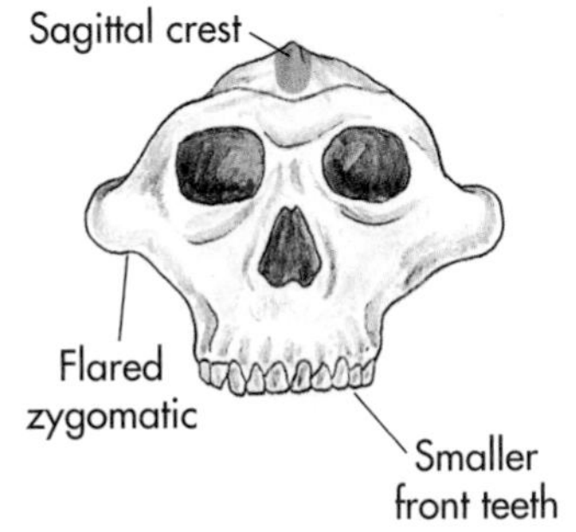

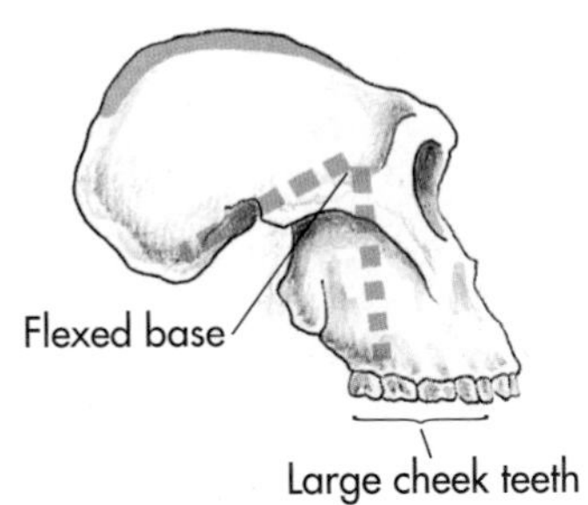

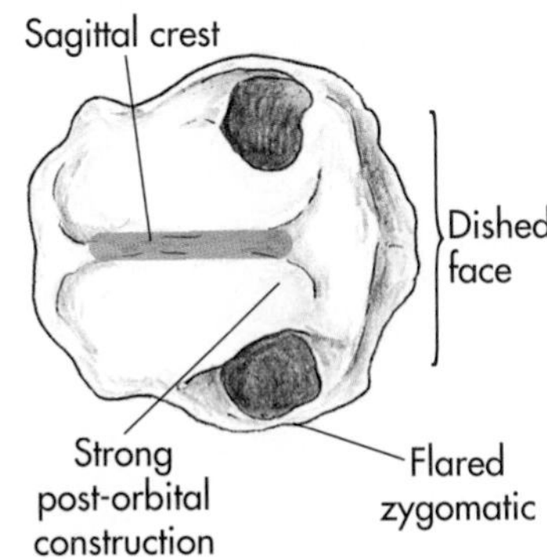

Figure 11.17 Key features of robust australopithecines include adaptations to heavy chewing such as a large sagittal crest and flaring zygomatics, a dished face, and a strongly flexed cranial base.

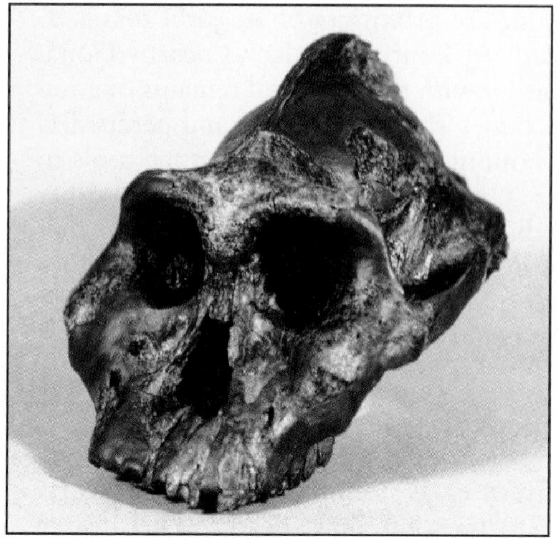

FIGURE 11.18 *Australopithecus aethiopicus,* called the black skull because of its manganese staining, is an early robust form dating to about 2.5 million years ago in Kenya.

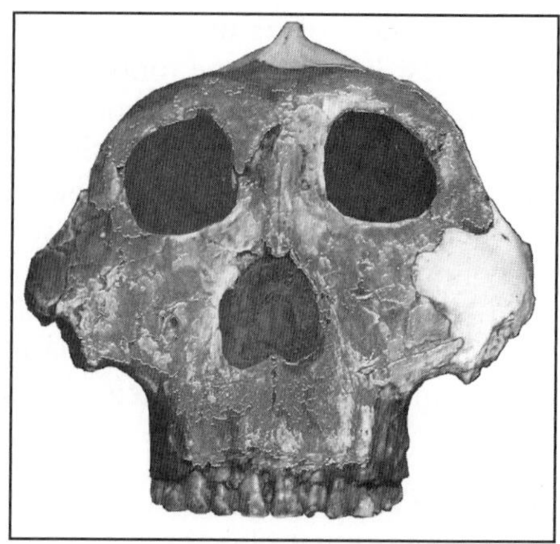

FIGURE 11.19 This hominid from Olduvai Gorge is a hyper-robust member of *Australopithecus boisei.*

A. boisei The culmination of the lineage that started with *A. aethiopicus* is *A. boisei,* dated to 2.3 to 1.2 mya (Figure 11.20). Since 1959, East African sites in Kenya, Tanzania, and Ethiopia have yielded a plethora of *A. boisei* remains, both cranial and postcranial. The brain size is about the same as that of the robusts from South Africa, and the postcranial skeleton is large, with an estimated body size between 34 and 50 kilograms (75 to 110 lb) (McHenry, 1992, 1994).

The cranial skeleton of *A. boisei* reflects the suite of masticatory adaptations discussed previously and some features shared with *A. aethiopicus* but not shared with the South African forms; these include the shape of the nasal bones and browridge, and the absence of nasal pillars. However, an important fossil find from Konso, Ethiopia, shares the South African condition of some of these features, muddying the distinctions.

A. robustus The first robust australopithecine was discovered in 1938 in South Africa (Figure 11.21). Known principally from Kromdraai, Swartkrans, and Drimolen, it dates to about 2.0 to 1.5 million years ago, based on biostratigraphy. Its cranial capacity is between 500 and 550 cc, and the postcranial skeleton indicates a body size of about 30 to 40 kilograms (70 to 90 lb) (McHenry, 1993, 1994).

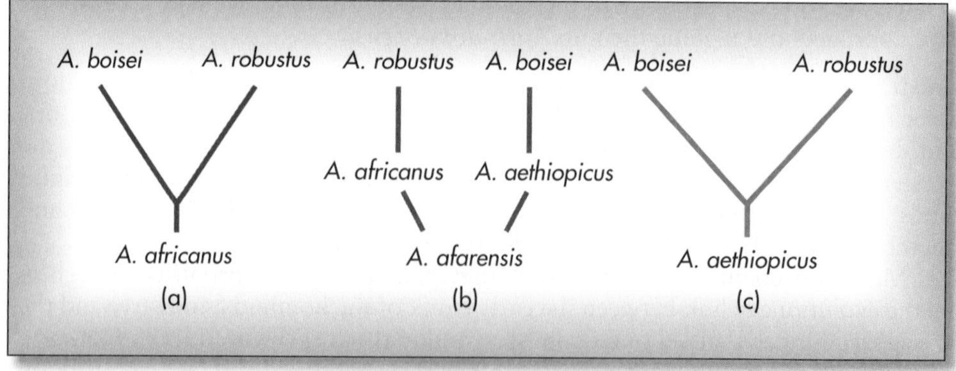

FIGURE 11.20 Some possible phylogenies for the robust australopithecines. (a) *A. africanus* may give rise to both *A. robustus* and *A. boisei.* (b) *A. afarensis* may give rise to two separate robust lineages, one of East African robusts, the other of South African robusts. (c) Or *A. aethiopicus* may give rise to both *A. robustus* and *A. boisei.*

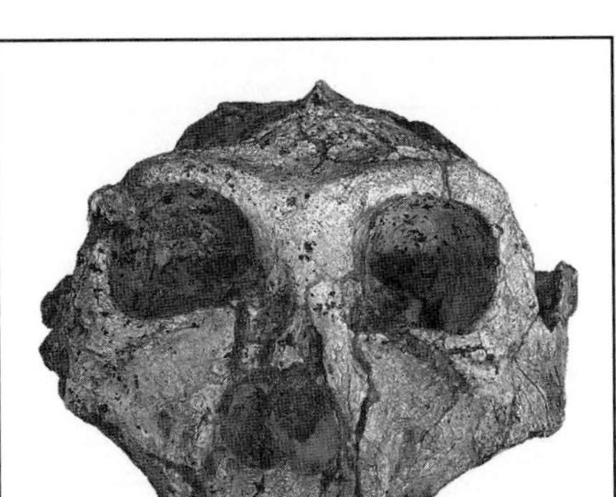

FIGURE 11.21 *Australopithecus robustus* is a South African robust australopithecine that was first discovered in 1938.

A. robustus differ from their East African counterparts in several minor characters, including the shape of the nasals and browridge and the presence of bony pillars next to the nose.

In addition to hard-shelled tough foods, isotopic studies suggest that *A. robustus* also ate substantial quantities of animal protein: probably grass-eating insects such as termites (Lee-Thorp et al., 1994). Supporting this idea are the wear patterns found on the ends of animal bones probably used by *A. robustus* as digging sticks (d'Errico et al., 2001). The researchers think that, unlike chimpanzees, which improvise termite-collecting tools from blades of grass and twigs (see Chapter 10), the robust australopithecines used a more powerful bone tool to open up the massive mounds of hardened soil in which termites live.

UNDERSTANDING THE AUSTRALOPITHECINE RADIATION

Just as the Miocene period was a time of great diversification of the apes, the Pliocene was a time of adaptive radiation and diversification of the early hominids. We still do not know how large this radiation was, but continual discoveries of new taxa suggest that many more species of australopithecines and other hominids remain to be found.

Some of the increase in diversity in the Pliocene results from the "naming game," the splitting into two of species or genera formerly recognized as one. But most of the recently named new species are based on new fossil discoveries. As we have seen, the naming of *Kenyanthropus*, *A. bahrelghazali*, and *A. garhi* drew some criticism from scientists who consider them to be just another species of *Australopithecus* or members of previously named species. Additional finds and comparative studies should resolve these issues.

COHABITATION

It is difficult for us to imagine today that at various times in early prehistory, two or even three hominid species lived in the same regions of the African continent (Table 11.3). In some of these cases, two species occurred contemporaneously in the same habitat. When two or more species with similar diets and behaviours coexist in the same habitat, we predict that some key aspects of their biology will diverge as a result of competition (sympatric speciation). If this did not occur, then one species or the other probably would become rare or extinct in the face of head-to-head food competition with the other.

TABLE 11.3 Examples of Potentially Contemporaneous Hominids by Region			
AGE (MYA)	WEST AFRICA	EAST AFRICA	SOUTH AFRICA
~6	*Sahelanthropus tchadensis*	*Orrorin tugenensis*	
3.9		*Australopithecus afarensis, A. anamensis*	
3.5	*A. bahrelghazali*	*A. afarensis, K. platyops*	*A. africanus*
2.5		*A. garhi, A. aethiopicus*	*A. africanus*
2.5 to 2		*A. boisei, A. garhi*	*A. africanus, A. robustus*
2 to 1.5		*A. boisei, Homo* sp.	*Homo* sp., *A. robustus*

*MYA = millions of years ago

In the case of the australopithecines, taxa that appear to have shared the same habitat at the same time also show striking morphological differences. This suggests that natural selection moulded them to avoid feeding competition.

One good way to understand the likely ecological relationship between sympatric early hominids is to look at how living great apes share a habitat. In Africa, there are many forests in which chimpanzees and gorillas coexist. Both apes travel on the ground to find food, but chimpanzees spend far more time feeding in trees than do gorillas. Both build nests each night, but gorilla nests are usually on the ground, and chimpanzee nests are normally high in trees. And although both species prefer fruit to all other forest foods, gorillas fall back on high-fibre leafy foods in lean seasons, whereas chimpanzees forage far and wide to continue eating fruits. In other words, although these two large-bodied apes are similar in many respects, there are key differences that are probably the result of their ancestors evolving together in African forests and that today allow them to coexist (Stanford, 2008).

In addition to *A. africanus* and *A. robustus* in southern Africa, potential cases of sympatry in the hominid fossil include *A. boisei* (robust) and early genus *Homo* (gracile) in eastern Africa, *A. garhi* and *A. aethiopicus* in eastern Africa, and *A. afarensis* and *K. platyops* in eastern Africa. In all these cases it has been argued that anatomical differences between taxa reflect differences in dietary adaptations that suggest the hominids were partitioning the available resources, which allowed them to coexist.

Tools and Intelligence

We used to think that only members of our own genus *Homo* were clever enough to make tools. Australopithecines were considered dim-witted in comparison and without tools. However, until the 1960s tool making was also unknown in the living great apes. Since tool making is actually common in the great apes and even in some monkeys, we might expect that early hominids including australopithecines fashioned tools, perhaps out of organic materials, but did not necessarily make durable tools.

The archaeological record for australopithecines is quite limited, but there is tantalizing evidence that these hominids were smarter than we think. The earliest evidence of tool use in the genus is the possible association between *A. garhi* and the butchered remains of animals about 2.5 million years ago in Ethiopia. At other sites in East and South Africa stone tools are found in the same beds and even at the same localities as the remains of robust australopithecines. No other hominid genera are known from these particular contexts, so this may indicate the production and use of stone tools by australopithecines.

Hand anatomy also gives us a small clue that the robust australopithecines may have been capable of tool production. The robusts share thumb anatomy that is similar to that of tool-making hominids such as ourselves and other members of the genus *Homo*, but earlier species of *Australopithecus* such as *A. afarensis* lack this anatomy. This may indicate that the robusts could make stone tools, although it does not tell us whether or not they did.

If tool production requires sophisticated cognitive skills, as argued in Chapter 10, then the australopithecines were at least as sophisticated as living great apes. However, it is not until around 2.5 million years ago, well into the australopithecine radiation, that we see the first use of stone tools. Thus, the additional access to resources that these tools provide could not have been among the primary reasons that the genus arose. Indeed, as we discussed in Chapter 10, the benefits of bipedality as a foraging strategy appear to be the primary advantage that early hominids had over their quadrupedal relatives.

Ancestors and Descendants

Based on the anatomy and timing of the known fossil australopithecines, there are several ways to envision the phylogenetic relationships among the early hominids we have examined in this chapter (Figure 11.22). There is no single consensus model, and a number of plausible models exist; however, one thing that almost all scientists agree on is the idea that the robust australopithecines are too specialized to be ancestral to genus *Homo*. The key to a good potential ancestor is that it exists early enough to give rise to the later groups, is not more derived than those groups, and has characters that look as if they could give rise to later groups.

Because the fossil record is sparse, each new fossil discovery throws the tree into brief disarray, after which palaeoanthropologists try to sort out the most likely phylogeny suggested by the sum of the evidence. This may seem as though scientists cannot agree, but disagreement is a healthy feature of evolutionary science. Each new find tests previous hypotheses and produces new interpretations, new research, and new results that push the state of our understanding of human ancestry forward.

QUESTIONS FOR FUTURE PALAEOANTHROPOLOGISTS

Despite all we have learned about the earliest hominids through the eight decades since Raymond Dart's time, the questions still far outnumber the answers.

How Many Species Were There? First and foremost, we don't know how extensive or diverse the early hominid radiation really was. In all likelihood there are more species, perhaps many more, waiting to be found. The rate of discovery of new hominid fossil taxa has increased in recent years; today a new species is described nearly every year.

How Large Was Their Geographic Distribution? So far the fossil record suggests that the earliest divergence of the australopithecines from ancient ape stock occurred in eastern Africa, probably in the Great Rift Valley. But the discovery of *Sahelanthropus* and *A. bahrelghazali* in Chad reminds us that very early hominids, or very hominidlike apes, also lived far outside East Africa. Conditions ideal for bone preservation, fossilization, and later discovery of ancient hominids are present in East Africa. Less ideal conditions and less intensive prospecting have limited the fossil yield from West Africa to date.

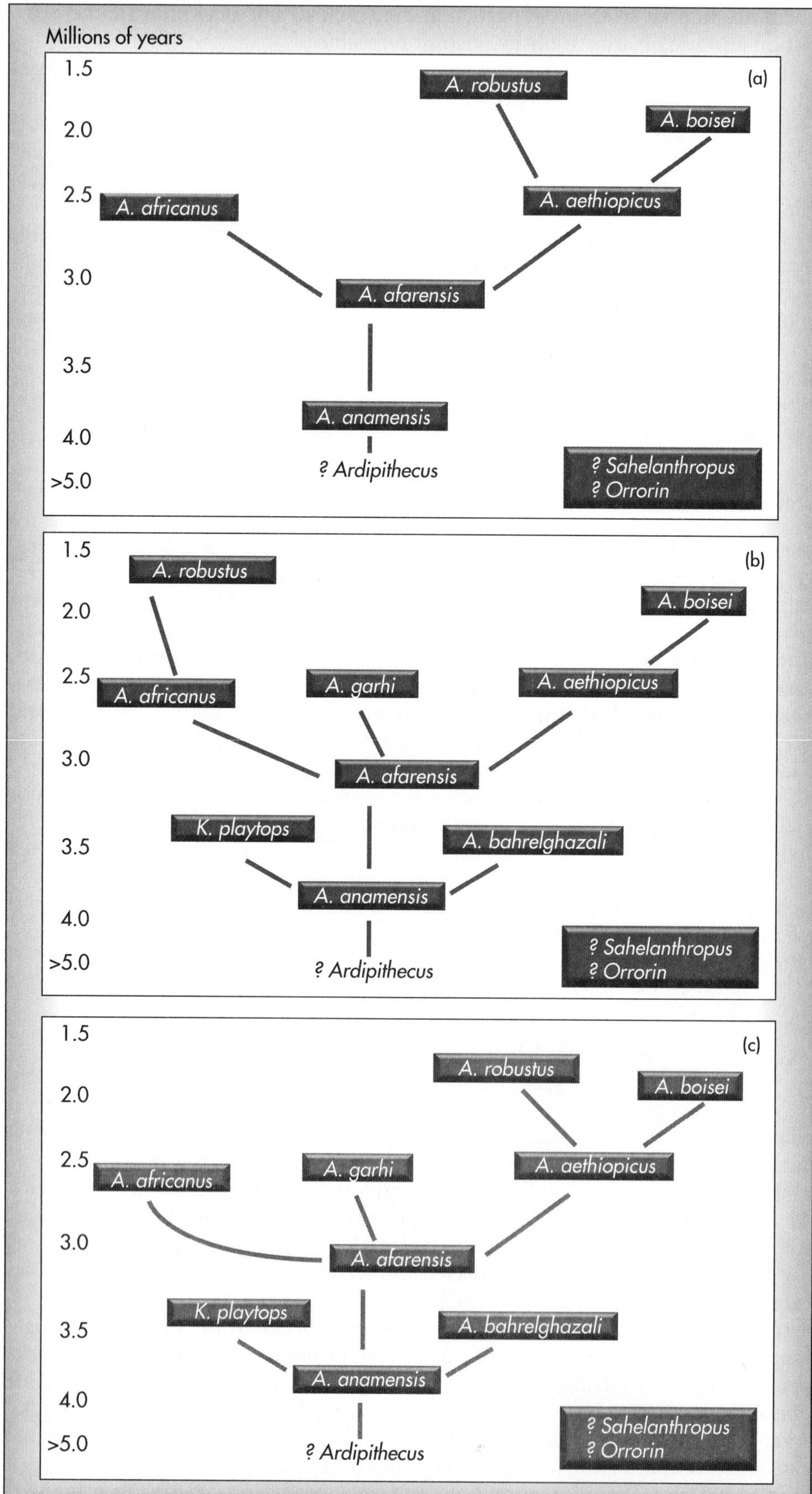

FIGURE 11.22 Three possible phylogenies for the australopithecines with *A. anamensis* as the stem ancestors and recognizing a small number of species and close relationships between (a) *A. robustus* and *A. boisei*, (b) a larger number of species and only distant relationship between *A. robustus* and *A. boisei*, or (c) a large number of species and a close relationship between *A. robustus* and *A. boisei*.

But we must remember the old adage that absence of evidence is not evidence of absence. The African continent is enormous, and there is no reason to believe that early hominids did not inhabit most of it. If early hominids radiated geographically across the warmer regions from east to west, as chimpanzees do today, then there are vast areas and diverse habitats into which they may have radiated. If even a few of the australopithecine taxa were as versatile ecologically as chimpanzees, most of the African continent may have once been populated by early hominids. Their remains are yet to be discovered. There is, however, no evidence that early hominids ever occurred outside the African continent.

Did Only One Lineage Emerge from the Ancestral Ape Stock? There are two ways to interpret the earliest stages of hominid evolution. The first is the traditional view that between 5 and 7 million years ago, a single lineage of primitive apelike anthropoids evolved into hominids, and some species of this lineage eventually evolved into *Homo sapiens*. The alternative view is that early in hominid evolution there were multiple lineages of hominidlike apes in Africa. In this latter view, bipedalism was not the defining hallmark of hominids: more than one bipedal lineage arose, but only one eventually survived to become our direct ancestor. The defining characteristic of the hominids would thus remain unidentified but might include dental changes such as the absence of a functional sectorial premolar honing complex. The degree of taxonomic diversity in the Pliocene will remain an intriguing and important question in decades to come as more and more fossils reinforce some views of the hominid phylogeny and contradict others.

As we have seen, the earliest hominids were a primitive lineage of very apelike creatures that enjoyed a diversification and wide distribution in Africa between about 6 and about 1 million years ago. Sometime around 2.5 million years ago, one lineage of the australopithecines gave rise to a new lineage with a slightly larger brain: genus *Homo*. Initially, *Homo* was not so anatomically different from australopithecines, but shifts in brain size, body shape, and perhaps technology gave it an advantage over *Australopithecus*. As we shall see in Chapters 12 through 14, although the exact point at which we should assign an early hominid to our own genus, *Homo*, is still debated, later shifts in foraging strategy and technology eventually led to modern people.

SUMMARY

1. **Why are the earliest hominids difficult to identify?**

   As you get closer to the LCA, hominid features appear more like the LCA, making it difficult to distinguish early hominids from other apes.

2. **What are the several traits that define the australopithecines? Include both cranial and postcranial traits.**

   The genus *Australopithecus* is defined by being bipedal but of small body size, with a funnel-shaped thorax, small canines but large cheek teeth (premolars and molars), and small brains.

3. **What key anatomical traits define *A. afarensis*?**

   A. afarensis is characterized by a mosaic of ancestral and derived characters. Derived traits include bipedality, reduced canine size, loss of the sectorial premolar honing complex, and large cheek teeth. Ancestral traits include small brain size, compound temporonuchal crest, flat cranial base, shallow, U-shaped palate, large anterior teeth, long arms, and curved phalanges.

4. **Why do we have precise dates on the ages of East African early hominid discoveries and only rough estimates of those in South Africa?**

   East African sites more often have volcanic rocks associated with them that can be dated using radiometric techniques such as argon–argon and potassium–argon. South African sites rely mainly on biostratigraphic age correlations.

5. **What key anatomical traits define the robust australopithecines?**

   The robust australopithecines share a suite of anatomical characters related to mastication. These include enormous postcanine megadontia and increased jaw size, enlarged chewing muscles (as reflected in a large sagittal crest, strong postorbital constriction, and flaring zygomatics), and a dished face and flexed cranial base.

CRITICAL THINKING QUESTIONS

1. How many australopithecine species do you think are waiting to be discovered? How would you go about estimating how many more might exist?
2. If we discover an early hominid that exhibits great sexual dimorphism, such as the Hadar fossils, what are some of the inferences we can make about the social behaviour of those creatures in life?
3. If gracile and robust australopithecines share the same habitat, why don't we see evidence of their hybridizing?
4. As recently as the late 1990s, we believed *A. afarensis* to be the stem of the hominid family. What happened to cast doubt on that view, and what does it tell us about the human family tree?

KEY TERMS

sectorial premolar complex
australopithecines
cranial crests
sagittal crest
compound temporonuchal crest
type specimen
endocast
hard object feeding

SUGGESTED READING

Cameron, David W. (2004). *Hominid Adaptations and Extinctions*. University of New South Wales Press, Australia.

Gibbons, Ann. (2006). *The First Human: The Race to Discover Our Earliest Ancestors*. Doubleday, New York, NY.

Johanson, Donald, and Edey, Maitland. (1981). *Lucy: The Beginnings of Humankind*. Simon & Schuster, New York, NY.

Morell, Virginia (1995). *Ancestral Passions: The Leakey Family and the Quest for Humankind's Beginnings*. Simon & Schuster, New York, NY.

Chapter 12

Rise of the Genus *Homo*

Chapter Outline

"FOR THE FOLLOWING FEW WEEKS, the excavating brought nearly non-stop excitement, but there was some meticulous scientific work behind the celebrations.... The bones kept coming, right up to the last moment, so we knew we would have to come back. Nearly everything we found was part of our skeleton.... When we closed down the site for the season, on September 21, 1984, we had found more of ***Homo erectus***—the classic missing link—than anyone had ever seen. The next four field seasons labouring in the pit, as we came to call the enormous excavation, would see 1500 cubic yards [1150 cubic metres] of rock and earth moved by hand. Our schoolboys, who worked with us faithfully year after year, grew from adolescents to young men while the Nariokotome boy, as we took to calling the specimen, grew from a fragment of skull to the most complete early hominid skeleton ever found."

—from ***The Wisdom of the Bones,*** by A. Walker and P. Shipman

The discovery of the skeleton of the Nariokotome boy, the remains of most of a *Homo erectus* skeleton, dramatically changed our understanding of early *Homo*. It showed us for the first time that the modern human proportions of long lower limbs and large body size existed as early as 1.5 million years ago. This finding suggests that the transition from the apelike body proportions of *Australopithecus* to modern human proportions occurred in the short time interval between 2.3 and 1.7 million years ago. What we know about the transition from *Australopithecus* to earliest *Homo* rests ultimately on the fossil record. And what we know of the fossil record, including the discovery of the Nariokotome boy, rests in equal parts on skill, perseverance, planning, and sheer luck. In fact, the early fossil record of genus *Homo* is remarkably sketchy in comparison to the australopithecine record, making the task of understanding the origin of the genus that much more difficult.

In this chapter we examine the early radiation of the genus *Homo,* from its beginnings in apelike African hominids to the first migrations out of Africa and into other parts of the Old World. First we consider the definition of the genus *Homo* and its earliest species. We discuss the appearance of *Homo erectus,* whose larger brain and body size may signal an adaptive shift in diet, who makes increasingly sophisticated tools, and who may use fire. Then we examine early tool technologies and subsistence. And finally we consider the debate over later stages of *H. erectus,* setting the stage for the discussion of other hominids outside Africa in Chapters 13 and 14.

DEFINING THE GENUS *HOMO*

The most primitive species assigned to genus *Homo* are not all that different from some australopithecines. Recall that the australopithecines were the earliest hominid radiation, featuring cranial capacities below 600 cc and a mosaic of apelike and humanlike features. We used to think that even the earliest genus *Homo* were morphologically much more modern-looking than any australopithecine. However, recent discoveries have shown that some members of genus *Homo* had small brains and perhaps primitive postcranial skeletons. We also used to think that genus *Homo* was the sole maker and user of stone tools. But in South Africa there are associations between stone tools and robust australopithecines, and in East Africa there are similar and perhaps earlier associations between hominids and stone tools. So perhaps we can no longer consider the time-honoured hallmark of genus *Homo*, stone tool making, to be unique to the genus.

Recall also that a genus name implies a certain adaptive strategy, so the switch from *Australopithecus* to *Homo* should tell you to expect to see a suite of adaptive differences between species in the two genera. In general, genus *Homo* differs from australopithecines by having a larger, more rounded braincase, a smaller, less projecting face, smaller teeth (Figure 12.1), and eventually a larger body and more efficient striding bipedalism. These features may be related to an adaptation that includes a shift in foraging strategy to a more animal-based diet, greater ranging, and greater food processing through tool use. However, early members of the genus *Homo* differ less from australopithecines than do later members and therefore are harder to distinguish from them.

There is much taxonomic debate over the application of names to the fossil record for genus *Homo*. Depending on the scientist, earliest *Homo* is conceived of either as a single, variable species (*H. habilis*) or as multiple, less variable species (usually *H. habilis, H. rudolfensis*, or *H. sp. nov.*, referring to an unnamed new species of *Homo*). Similarly, *H. erectus* is seen as either a single species or two species, *H. ergaster* and *H. erectus*, and the presence of any of these taxa in Europe and the transition to modern humans is hotly debated. All this disagreement results in part from the paucity of the fossil record, differences in species concepts (lumpers versus splitters), and the inherent difficulty of applying a static classification system to the dynamic process of evolution.

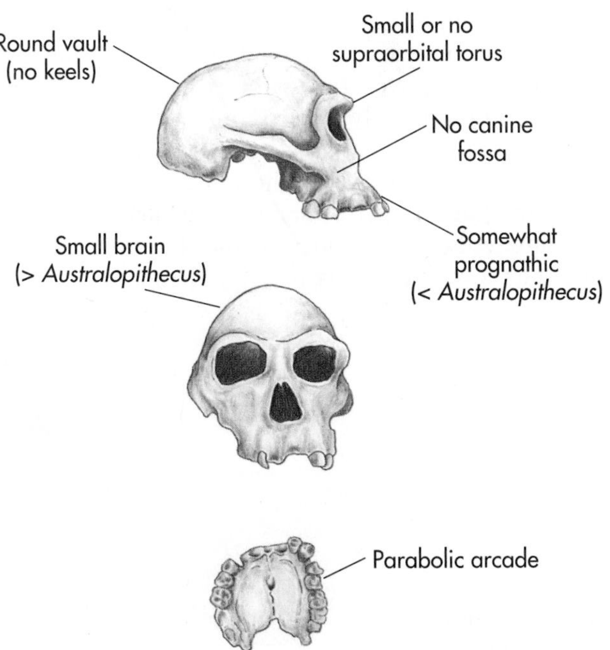

Figure 12.1 Key anatomical features of *Homo habilis* include reduced facial size, a parabolic palate, and some brain enlargement.

EARLIEST GENUS *HOMO*

The great antiquity of the genus *Homo* was established at Olduvai Gorge in the 1960s with the discovery of a nearly 2 million-year-old juvenile partial skull that possessed a brain larger than any known australopithecine. The new species was named *Homo habilis,* or "the skilled human or handy man," referring to the use and manufacture of stone tools.

A number of fossils have since been discovered in Kenya, and range in geological age from about 1.9 to 1.8 million years old. They vary greatly in size and there is some debate as to whether the size differences represent different species, or males and females of the same species. Although some of these specimens are bigger-brained than others, none show the extensive cranial and postcranial enlargement or adaptation for long stride length seen in a later species, *H. erectus.*

EARLY TOOL USE

Whoever the first toolmaker was, stone tools appear in the record starting about 2.5 million years ago. The earliest tools are known as the **Oldowan** industry, so named for their first discovery at Olduvai Gorge in Tanzania. We refer to stone tools made in a particular way or tradition as a **tool industry**. Oldowan tools consist mainly of **cores**, lumps of stone, often river cobbles modified from the original rock by flaking pieces off it, and **flakes**, the small fragments taken from the core (Figure 12.2). Flakes can be extremely sharp and are effective at cutting through tough animal hides and removing meat from bones. Other Oldowan tools called **hammerstones** were used to crack open the bones of large animals to extract marrow and to remove flakes from cores. Oldowan tools are deceptively simple in appearance; if you held one you might not be sure whether it was human-made or naturally created. However, archaeologists, some of whom are proficient stone tool makers, can distinguish human manufacture patterns from natural breakage of stone.

Oldowan The tool industry characterized by simple, usually unifacial core and flake tools.

tool industry A particular style or tradition of making stone tools.

core The raw material source (a river cobble or a large flake) from which flakes are removed.

flake The stone fragment struck from a core, thought to have been the primary tools of the Oldowan.

hammerstone A stone used for striking cores to produce flakes or bones to expose marrow.

Tool making was first and foremost an adaptation to the environment of the Late Pliocene. Through the use of tools hominids could exploit animal resources, which became an increasingly important adaptive strategy for early humans. Based on the archaeological record, early *Homo* probably carried tools with them rather than constantly discarding them and continually making them anew. This signifies the importance of tools in the foraging patterns of these hominids. Being bipedal (and therefore having their hands free) and larger-brained, these early hominids were far more capable than chimpanzees at tool production and use, from acquiring the raw materials, to making the tools, and finally to using them.

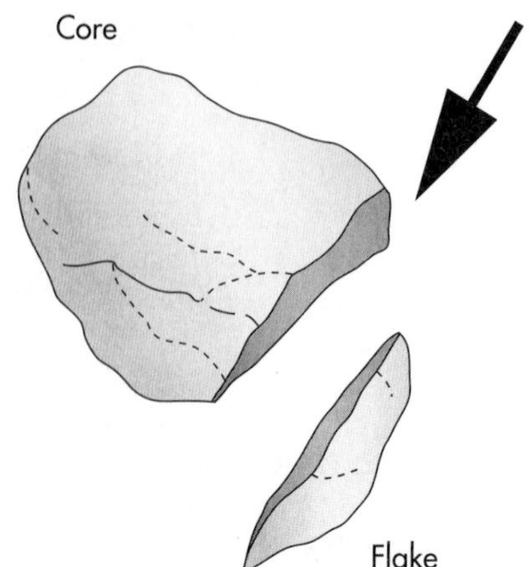

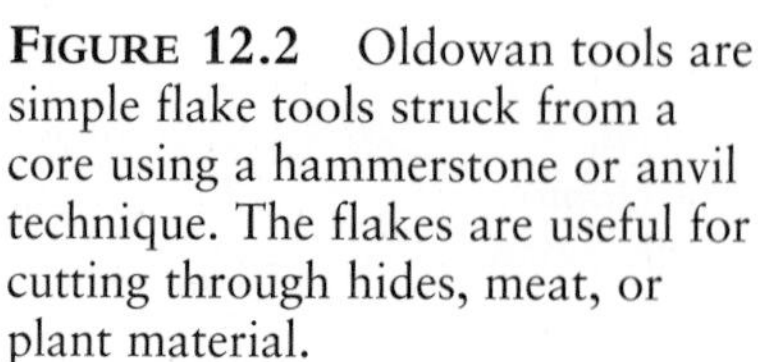

FIGURE 12.2 Oldowan tools are simple flake tools struck from a core using a hammerstone or anvil technique. The flakes are useful for cutting through hides, meat, or plant material.

Archaeologists studying Oldowan tools and the bones associated with them think these tools were used primarily to remove meat from and crack open the bones of animals that were either hunted or scavenged. These butchery tools are sometimes found in association with many fossilized animal bones, such as pigs, ungulates, elephants, carnivores, and even other primates. Taphonomic analysis (see Chapter 9) indicates that some of these accumulations were created by hominids and not simply by natural processes such as erosion, water movement, or the actions of carnivores. A clumped pattern of distribution of the tools on the landscape strongly suggests that these are either sites of intensive food processing by hominids or places where tools were manufactured and then carried somewhere else to be used (Potts, 1988).

We don't know for certain which early hominid made which tools because we don't find hominid fossils actually holding the tools. We can only infer tool use by the association between tools and hominid remains in the same excavations. Despite the enormous amount of evidence of meat eating, in the form of butchered bones, we don't know how often a group of early *Homo* might have actually eaten meat or how important meat (or marrow) was in their diet. Did a group of *H. habilis* butcher and consume one large mammal per week? Per month? Per century? Did all members of the group participate in this butchering activity and in the feast? How much did the incorporation of stone tool manufacture and annual consumption affect other aspects of early hominid behaviour, ecology, physiology, and biology? It seems that after 2.5 million years ago, meat eating took on increasing importance, but the method of measuring that importance has been contentious.

HUNTING AND SCAVENGING

The earliest hominids almost certainly ate most of the same foods that modern apes eat: fruit, leaves, seeds, insects, and some animal prey. The first indisputable evidence of meat eating is stone tool use for carcass butchery (based on cut marks on fossilized bones of antelope), probably by earliest genus *Homo* but possibly also by *A. garhi,* about 2.5 million years ago. Before this time, if emerging humans were making and using tools, they were using materials such as wood or unmodified bone that did not accumulate or preserve in the fossil record. And if they were eating meat or marrow without the assistance of stone tools, we have no visible archaeological record of it.

We would like to know whether our own lineage arose with the help of a hunting or scavenging way of life because each of these entails a different set of behavioural adaptations. There are currently three main models for how early hominids acquired carcasses. Did bands of early humans courageously attack and slaughter large and dangerous game (hunting), did they fight off large predators such as sabre-tooth cats to gain access to significant amounts of meat (confrontational scavenging), or did they creep nervously up to decomposing, nearly stripped carcasses to glean a few scraps of meat and fat (passive scavenging)? Mostly, however, discussion focuses on differences between hunting and scavenging (Box 12.1).

At some fossil sites there was evidence that *H. habilis* had been butchering animal carcasses: Cut marks from their stone tools were visible on the fossilized bones of animals. When palaeoanthropologists studied the bones of animals from Oldowan sites, they found cut marks made by ancient, sharp-edged tools as well as tooth marks made by the gnawing of contemporaneous lions, hyenas, and leopards. When they examined these more closely, they saw that on some of the bones, the human-made cut marks were on top of the carnivore tooth marks, evidence that humans were cutting flesh from the bones *after* they had already been chewed by a predator (Potts, 1988; Shiman, 1986). The implication was clear: On at least some occasions, hominids were scavengers rather than hunters.

Box 12.1 Understanding the Meat-Eating Past through the Present

In the 1970s and 1980s Glynn Isaac, an innovative experimental archaeologist who believed that the past could be better understood through direct analogies with the present, mentored a series of students who turned to the behaviour and ecology of living carnivores to understand how early hominids might have used animal resources. Robert Blumenschine (1987) conducted field studies of lions, hyenas, and other African carnivores on the Serengeti. He found that early hominids would have had an ample supply of resources from carcasses left over after kills by lions and leopards, especially in woodlands located near streams where scavengers such as hyenas are often delayed in finding the kills. In many modern ecosystems, even after a predator is done eating, the carcass provides rich sources of fat and protein in the form of bone marrow and brain that support a community of scavengers, a community that might have once included early hominids.

Blumenschine (1986) also studied how predators and scavengers both follow a customary sequence in which they rapidly devour the hindquarters, then the ribs and forelegs, followed by the bone marrow, and finally the contents of the head. This consumption sequence can be used as a signature in the fossil record to identify hunting and scavenging. Because scavengers eat the remains of what hunters leave behind, they should eat a disproportionate quantity of the last body parts with edible meat. Blumenschine argues these early hominids would not have needed to hunt because scavenging would have been a reliable enough source of calories and nutrients.

Archaeologist Curtis Marean (1989) thinks that early *Homo* could have occupied a scavenging niche simply by cleaning up after sabre-toothed cats. Sabre-tooths were among the top predators in many East African habitats 2 million years ago. Some were powerful, solitary hunters that could kill animals with much more meat than they themselves could hope to eat or store, leaving a potential niche for a scavenging hominid to fill.

Nicholas Toth (Schick and Toth, 1993) was among the first to tackle another old problem in new ways when he learned to make stone tools. By studying stone tools found in archaeological sites such as Koobi Fora, Toth, an expert tool maker, was able to match his own style of tool making with what early hominids were doing. Toth and his assistants carved up the carcass of an elephant (which had died of natural causes in a zoo and was donated as a research subject) to test the cutting power of simple Oldowan tools. They showed that using only the simple core and flake tools of the Oldowan industry, early humans could have sliced through the thick hide of large animals. Because it is unlikely that *H. habilis* and kin would have had the means to kill such large and dangerous animals, Toth's work supports the validity of the scavenging model of early human subsistence.

Perhaps the most sensible view is that *H. habilis* probably would have acquired animal resources in any form they could, through both hunting for small animals and scavenging carcasses. Modern foragers do the same. Cultural diversity in modern chimpanzee populations (see Chapter 10) suggests that some populations of early genus *Homo* could have hunted, whereas others may have preferred scavenging, and both strategies probably were included in a flexible behavioural repertoire. Early views of meat eating tended to emphasize a black-or-white approach, which is rarely the way that living creatures behave. Regardless of whether meat was obtained by hunting or scavenging, the archaeological record shows that hominid stone tool–assisted consumption of large animals began about 2.5 million years ago and gradually increased through time. The two innovations of stone tool manufacture and animal resource exploitation undoubtedly shaped much of subsequent human evolutionary history.

WHO WAS *HOMO ERECTUS*?

Sometime around the Plio-Pleistocene boundary, about 1.8 million years ago, hominids underwent a major adaptive shift. This is reflected in the fossil record by body size increases and changes to the postcranial skeleton (such as lengthening of the femur) that indicate a more efficient gait, similar to that of modern humans. These changes may have been related to environmental and climatic changes during that time period. Remember, however, that while at least one hominid lineage was responding to these climate changes by adaptive shifts, another—the *robust australopithecines*—responded not by changing but by intensifying its previous adaptation to hard object feeding.

H. erectus appeared in Africa about 1.8 million years ago and was the first hominid to leave the continent, probably by at least 1.7 million years ago. Some palaeoanthropologists call these earliest *H. erectus* by another name, *Homo ergaster* (see Figure 12.3) (Wood and Collard, 1999). Whatever you call them, these hominids quickly inhabited areas outside of Africa. Fossils from the site of Dmanisi in the Republic of Georgia look like small-brained versions of early African *H. erectus,* and those from Sangiran in Indonesia look only a bit more

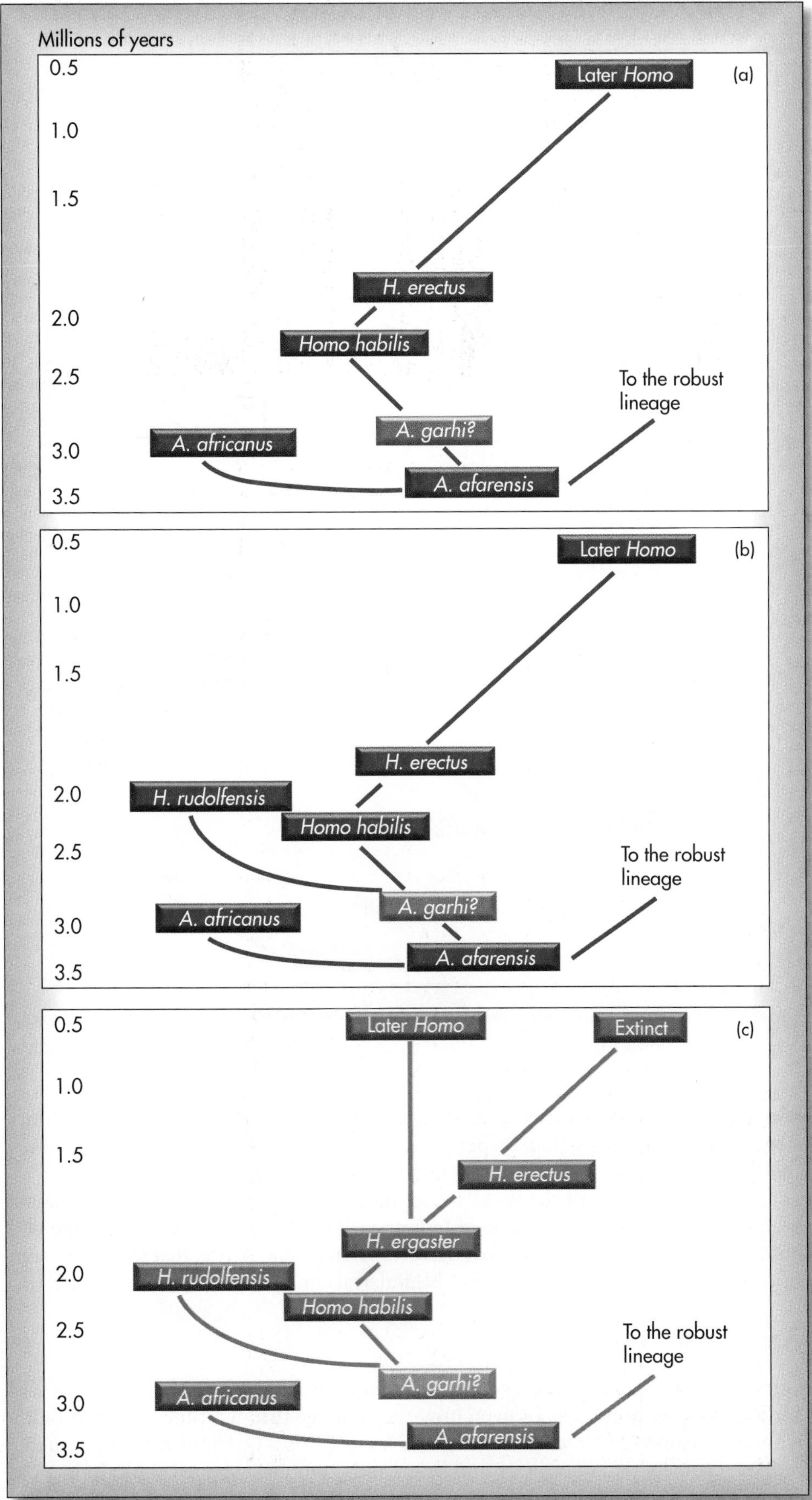

FIGURE 12.3 Possible phylogenies for early *Homo*.

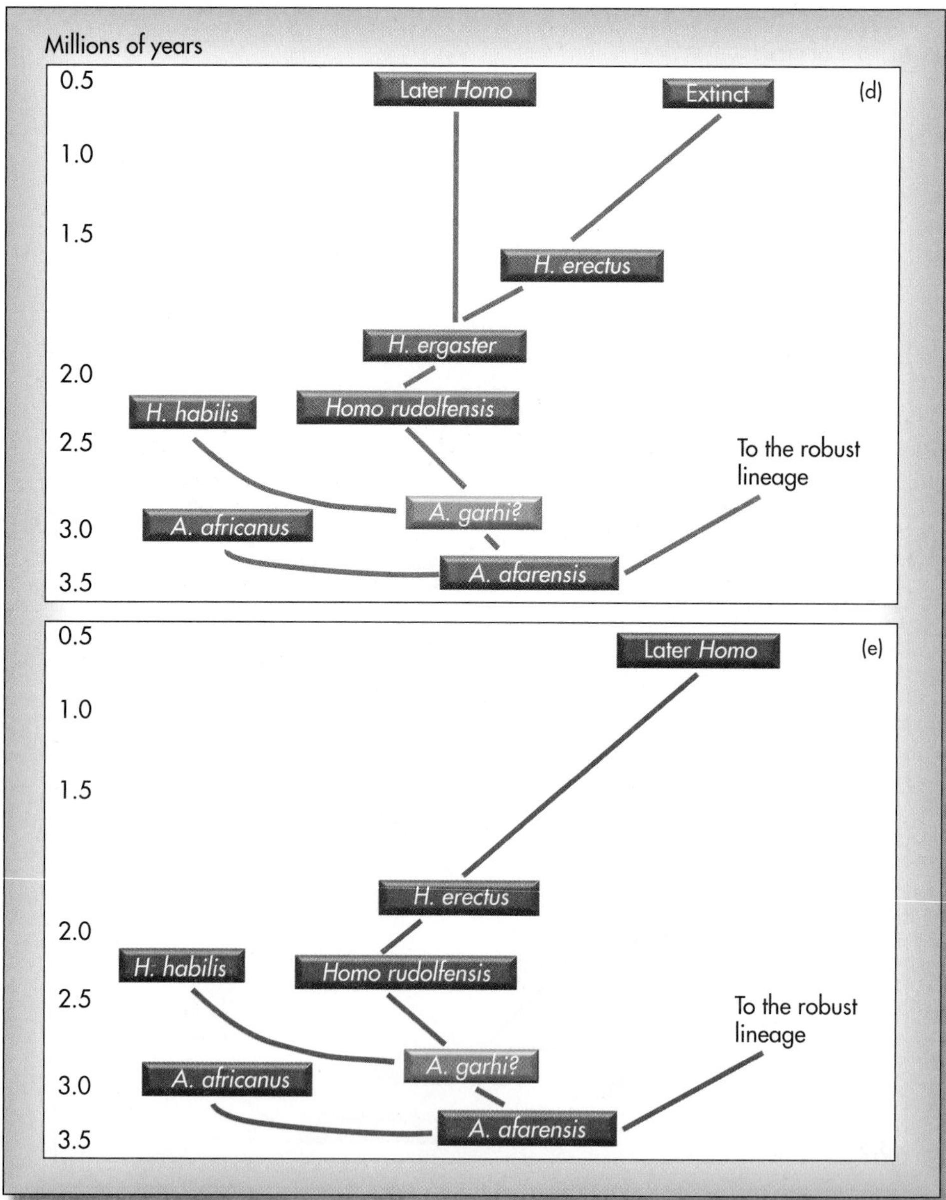

FIGURE 12.3 *(continued)*

derived. Why hominids left Africa when they did is a source of debate. What is largely agreed upon is that dispersal was the result of multiple movements of small groups of hominids into new territories.

The last members of the species exist more than 1.5 million years later, having been found in the Late Pleistocene of Indonesia. These hominids overlap in time with hominids from other parts of the world, such as Europe and Africa, that seem to be transitional between *H. erectus* and either Neandertals or modern humans (Chapter 13).

ANATOMICAL FEATURES

Before we can discuss how they lived, why they left Africa, how they compare with earlier and later hominids, or even how they change through time, we must define what we mean by *H. erectus*. In general, *H. erectus* is a hominid species characterized by a somewhat larger body and brain and a uniquely shaped skull. In its postcranial features *H. erectus* shows the beginnings of a modern human body plan.

The Skull and Teeth *H. erectus* crania are easily identified by their shape (Figure 12.4 and Figure 12.5). The skull is thick-boned and robust, much longer than it is wide, relatively low and angular from the side, and pentagonal in rear view. The angularity of the skull is enhanced by a series of cranial superstructures, regional thickenings of bone along certain sutures and across certain bones. These include thickenings such as the prominent **supraorbital torus** or browridge on the frontal, a thickened **angular torus** on the back of the parietal, and the **occipital torus,** a ridge of bone that runs horizontally across the occipital. In addition, the forehead has a low, sloping or receding appearance and is often separated from the supraorbital torus by a gully or furrow. The pentagonal rear view is formed by other thickenings including those along sutures such as the **sagittal keel** along the sagittal suture that joins the two parietals and the **metopic keel** along the midline frontal at the site once occupied by the metopic suture of the infant. The pentagon is widest at its base; the sides slant inward from there to the lateral part of the parietal and then turn in to meet at the tip of the pentagon, which is formed by the sagittal keel. In addition, *H. erectus* crania do not have a **canine fossa**, a feature seen in modern humans.

supraorbital torus Thickened ridge of bone above the eye orbits of the skull; a browridge.

angular torus A thickened ridge of bone at the posterior angle of the parietal bone.

occipital torus A thickened horizontal ridge of bone on the occipital bone at the rear of the cranium.

sagittal keel Longitudinal ridge or thickening of bone on the sagittal suture not associated with any muscle attachment.

metopic keel Longitudinal ridge or thickening of bone along the midline of the frontal bone.

canine fossa An indentation on the maxilla above the root of the canine tooth, an anatomical feature usually associated with modern humans that may be present in some archaic ***Homo*** species in Europe.

LATERAL VIEW

Enlarged brain in angular vault
Angular torus
Low frontal
Bar-like supraorbital torus
Occipital torus
No chin

FRONTAL VIEW

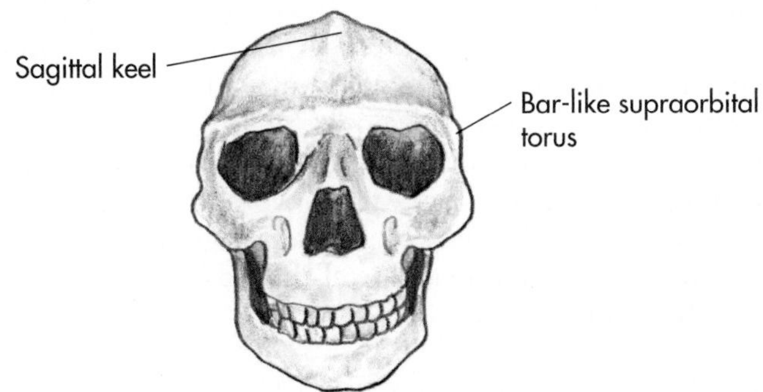

PENTAGONAL REAR VIEW

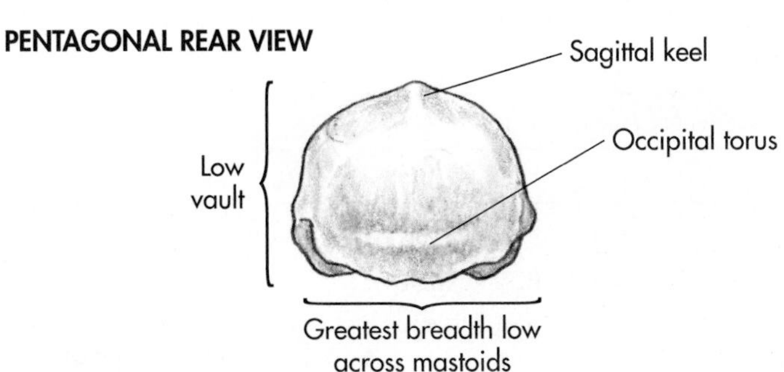

FIGURE 12.4 Major features of *Homo erectus* include increased brain size, an angular vault, and cranial superstructures.

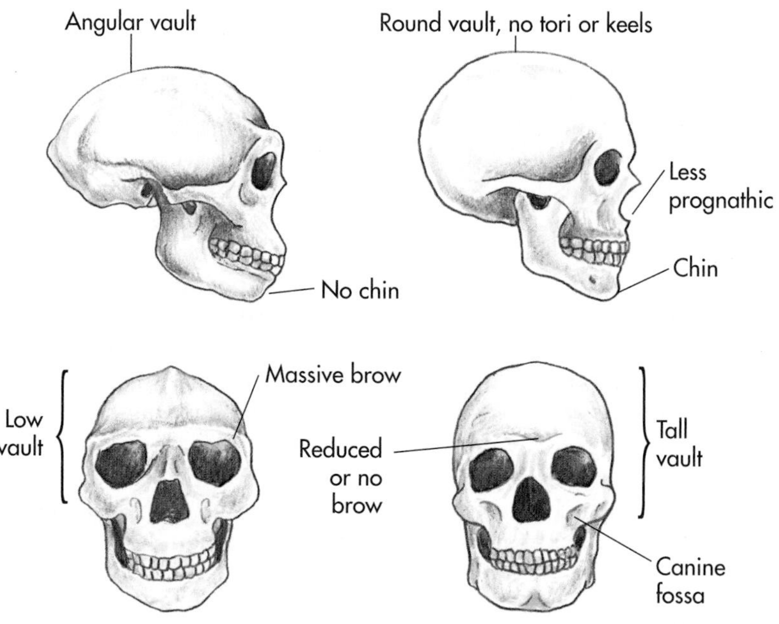

FIGURE 12.5 Compared with modern humans, *Homo erectus* has a larger face, lacks a chin, and has a more angular vault and smaller brain.

H. erectus brain size ranges from approximately 700 cc to 1200 cc, averaging about 900 cc. Partly as a result of this expansion, the degree of *postorbital constriction* is less than in australopithecines but still marked compared with later forms. Early brain size increases in *H. erectus* may occur simply in proportion to body size increases in the species, and real (that is, disproportionately large) brain size evolution may not occur until archaic *H. sapiens,* just a few hundred thousand years ago. Of course, not only sheer volume but also organization of the brain are key factors in determining the cognitive ability of a species. Certainly in absolute brain size, *H. erectus* was less cognitively endowed than modern humans. However, the brain size of *H. erectus* also shows regional and evolutionary variation (Table 12.1), indicating progressive but slow increase in the lineage through time (Antón and Swisher, 2001; Leigh, 1992). Brain size increases by about 160 cc per million years in *H. erectus* but by about 800 cc per million years from archaic *H. Sapiens* to modern humans (Figure 12.6).

The jaw of *H. erectus* was as robust and powerfully built as the rest of the cranial complex. The proportions of the mandible contrast with the small teeth in some of the earlier *H. erectus* specimens from Africa (Wolpoff, 1999). The tongue sides of the incisors are concave, with ridges along their edges forming the shape of a tiny shovel; This feature is referred to as **shovel-shaped incisors** and seems to be an ancestral trait for the genus *Homo*.

shovel-shaped incisors
Anterior teeth that on their lingual (tongue) surface are concave with two raised edges, which makes them look like tiny shovels.

Body Size and Shape Despite the large numbers of *H. erectus* skulls and teeth that have been found over the past century, what we know of the postcranial

TABLE 12.1 Cranial Capacities for *Homo erectus*

REGION	RANGE (CC)
Africa	700 to 1067
Indonesia	800 to 1250
China	855 to 1225

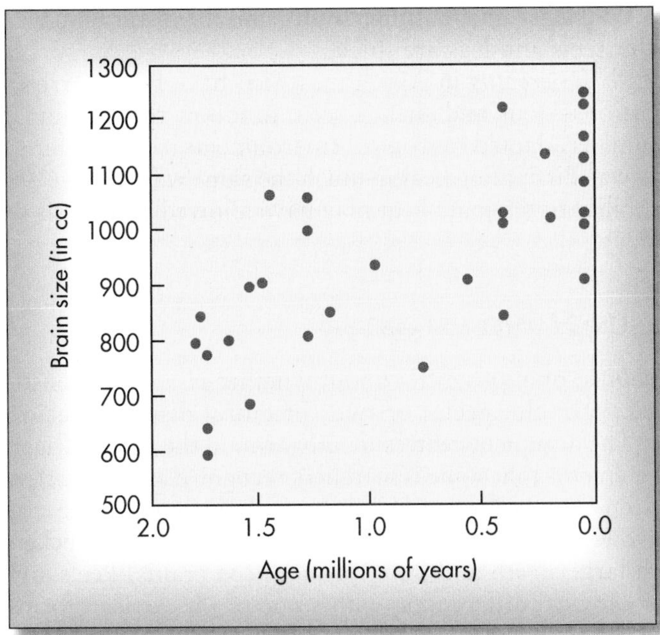

FIGURE 12.6 Although average brain size increases gradually through time in *H. erectus,* individuals with small brains are present even late in time. Dots represent individual fossils.

skeleton comes from just three partial skeletons and some isolated bones, mostly from East Africa. The most important of these is the remarkably complete KNM-WT 15000 skeleton—the Nariokotome boy—found in 1984 on the western side of Lake Turkana in Kenya by Alan Walker and Richard Leakey, whose discovery is described at the beginning of this chapter (Figure 12.7). These specimens suggest not only that *H. erectus* was robustly proportioned (Figure 12.8) but also that some individuals were very tall as adults, between 1.6 and 1.8 metres

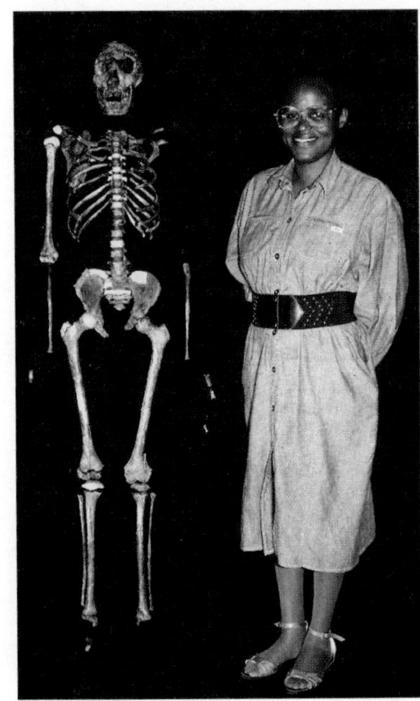

FIGURE 12.7 Dr. Emma Mbua of the National Museum of Kenya stands next to the skeleton of the Nariokotome *H. erectus* boy.

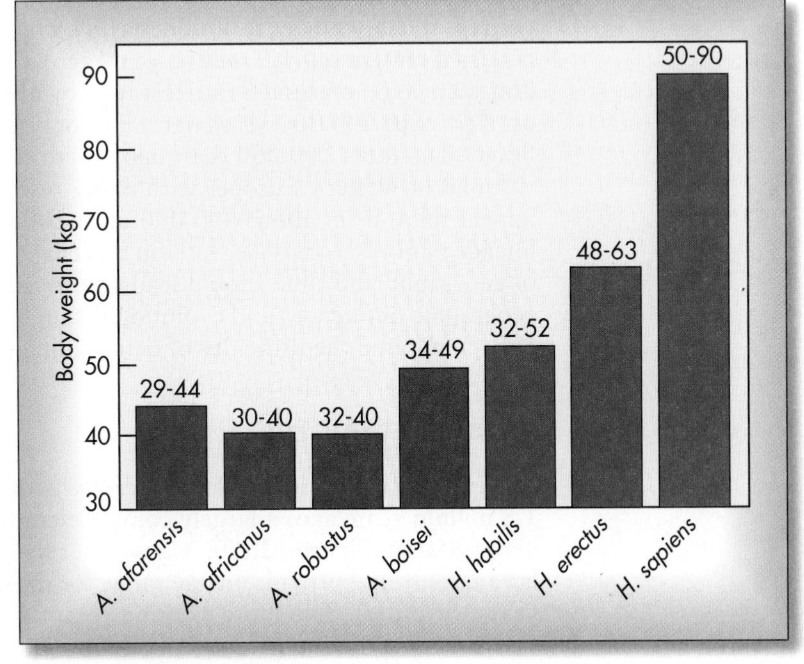

FIGURE 12.8 Body weight estimates from fossil remains show that *H. erectus* had a larger body than earlier hominids.

(5.5 to 6 ft) (Walker, 1993; McHenry and Coffing, 2000), and the lower limb was long. The long bones of the arms and legs are thick.

In addition to being tall, *H. erectus* in Africa may also have been narrow-hipped. These body proportions—long and linear—seem to follow the latitudinal gradient seen in modern humans adapted to tropical environments (see Chapter 6) and suggest that *H. erectus* was dissipating heat in much the same way that we do, that is, by sweating. This ability to dissipate heat may have allowed *H. erectus* to be more active during midday.

HOMO ERECTUS VERSUS *HOMO ERGASTER*

As was the case with *H. habilis,* opinions differ about whether *H. erectus* constitutes one widely dispersed, variable species or two (or more) distinct species, *H. erectus* and *H. ergaster.* The argument centres mainly around the early African (and Georgian) forms of *H. erectus* that some researchers recognize as *H. ergaster*. The main differences between *H. ergaster* and *H. erectus* include more gracile crania with less pronounced browridges in African forms and more robust and thicker-browed Asian forms, with larger teeth and more pronounced cranial keels and tori. There are also archaeological differences, with some of the African forms found in association with somewhat more advanced tools, whereas even later forms of Asian *H. erectus* continue to make Oldowanlike tools (see "The Lifeways of *Homo erectus*"). In practice, *H. ergaster* is used to refer to early African *H. erectus* specimens and is considered by many to be only a slight regional variant of the pan–Old World species *H. erectus* (Rightmire, 1993; Antón, 2003). Here we will consider *H. ergaster* a regional variant or subspecies of *H. erectus.*

HOMO ERECTUS AROUND THE WORLD

If we accept *H. erectus* as a single, widely dispersed species, then it represents more than 1.5 million years of time and a broad geographic range (Figure 12.9). Known *H. erectus* sites range in age from about 1.8 million years to 100 000 years (and perhaps much younger in Indonesia). *H. erectus* is found first in Africa (where it persisted until about 1.0 million years ago), in the Republic of Georgia at 1.7 million years ago, in island Southeast Asia by about 1.8 million years ago (persisting until perhaps 100 000 years ago), and only later in continental Asia from about 800 000 to about 200 000 years ago. There is controversy as to whether *H. erectus* is found in western Europe, with many researchers arguing that the fossils that appear there from about 800 000 until 200 000 years ago belong to a different lineage than *H. erectus* (see later in this chapter and Chapter 13). This broad span of geography and time should lead you to expect that *H. erectus* will show both geographic differences and evolution through time. And these sources of variation only compound the difficulty of determining species definitions.

AFRICAN ORIGINS

The earliest fossil evidence for *H. erectus* comes from the Turkana basin in Kenya 1.8 million years ago: a largely complete cranium with a cranial capacity of only about 850 cc (Figure 12.10). Many other fossils from East Turkana exhibit similar anatomy and provide an age range for the species of about 1.5 to 1.78 million years (or older). The most exciting recent finds are of two early Homo fossils (Spoor et al., 2007). One is the largely complete cranium of a subadult/young adult dated to 1.55 million years ago that has a very small cranial capacity and some characteristics more typically found in Asian *H. erectus*, suggesting that African and Asian *H. erectus* should be included in a single species. The second is the youngest documented *H. habilis* specimen to date: an upper jaw that was found within walking distance of the *H. erectus* fossil and dating from the same general time period (1.44 million years ago). Although this makes it seem unlikely that *H. erectus* evolved from *H. habilis*, the earliest evidence of *Homo* is found outside this region of overlap so it's possible that *H. erectus* evolved from *H. habilis* elsewhere and later moved into the Lake Turkana basin. Although the two species appear to have co-existed for nearly half a million years, they probably didn't interact since each would have had its own ecological niche, much like sympatric chimpanzees and gorillas today.

From the western side of Lake Turkana between 1.6 and 1.5 million years ago comes the nearly complete and quite tall Nariokotome *H. erectus* skeleton of a boy who was between 8 and 11 years old when he died. His age is based on the pattern of tooth eruption (he had just gotten his permanent premolars but still retained his baby canine), and the large range comes from our not knowing if the timing of the boy's development was like ours (if so, he would be about 11 years of age) or more like that of an ape (if so, he would be closer to 8 years of age).

The largest-brained African *H. erectus* has a cranial capacity of a little more than 1000 cc and dates to about 1.47 million years ago (Figure 12.11). Some of the most recent *H. erectus* in Africa are also the smallest, however, with a cranial capacity of only 727 cc, and are dated to perhaps as little as 780 000 years ago. These fossils highlight the differences in size in *H. erectus*.

H. erectus remains from the Bouri Formation of the Middle Awash, Ethiopia (Asfaw et al., 2002), are around 1 million years old (Figure 12.9). Another Ethiopian site, Konso-Gardula, has very ancient (1.8 million years old) fragmentary *H. erectus* fossils and the oldest known *H. erectus*-associated stone tools. The Bouri lineage in particular will prove significant for understanding the evolution of genus *Homo* because it also contains fossils of the earliest *H. sapiens*.

The First African Diaspora: Republic of Georgia

About 80 kilometres (50 mi) southwest of Tbilisi, the capital city of the Republic of Georgia, lies the village of Dmanisi. Nearby, beneath a medieval village built at the confluence of two rivers, a stunning series of finds in the 1990s changed our understanding of when humans left the cradle of Africa. Excavations discovered evidence of early *H. erectus*-like hominids outside Africa at approximately 1.7 million years ago that were associated with Oldowanlike stone tools. Since 1991, at least four crania and some postcranial remains have been found in a small area (16 m^2) beneath the medieval village (Figure 12.12).

The Dmanisi hominids are very similar to early African *H. erectus*, or so-called *H. ergaster* (Table 12.2). They are small-brained (less than 800 cc) but differ in anatomy from more primitive small-brained *H. habilis*. The Dmanisi hominids are linked to *H. erectus* by their premolar and molar tooth structure, the development of browridges, and their high cranial vault. They are markedly more similar to the early African *H. erectus* fossils than they are to contemporary Asian *H. erectus* (Gabunia et al., 2000), but compared with early African *H. erectus*, the Dmanisi hominids are small (Gabunia et al., 2001).

The Dmanisi skulls show conclusively that early humans had migrated out of Africa at nearly the same time that *H. erectus* first appears in Africa. Thus, shortly after the emergence of *H. erectus* in Africa, the species moved out of the African continent and into other regions and other ecosystems.

Figure 12.9 **THE GENUS *HOMO* THROUGH TIME**

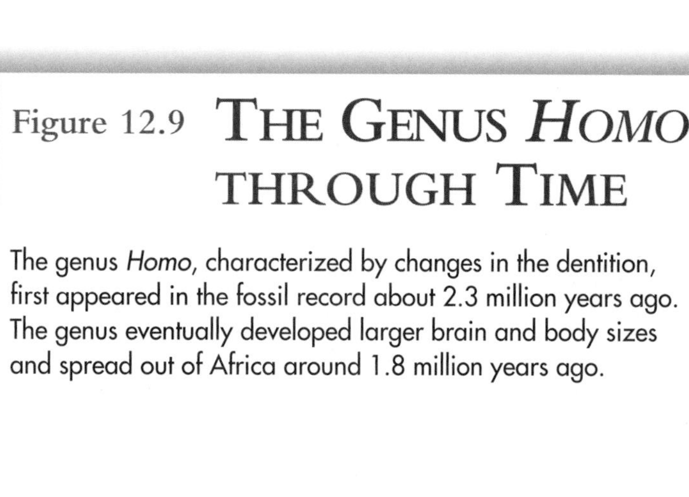

The genus *Homo*, characterized by changes in the dentition, first appeared in the fossil record about 2.3 million years ago. The genus eventually developed larger brain and body sizes and spread out of Africa around 1.8 million years ago.

At 1.7 million years old the Dmanisi fossils are among the oldest hominids outside Africa.

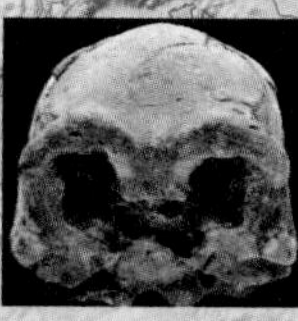

The recently discovered Bouri hominid is one of a long lineage of hominids from the Middle Awash, Ethiopia.

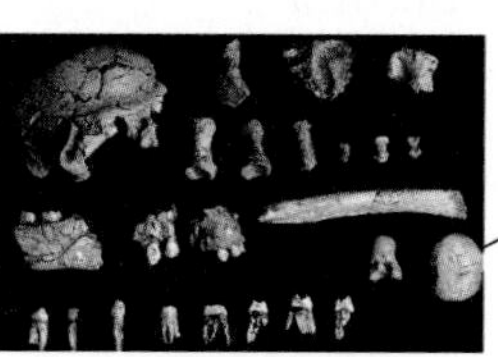

Fragmentary remains of *H. antecessor* are the earliest accepted remains in Europe.

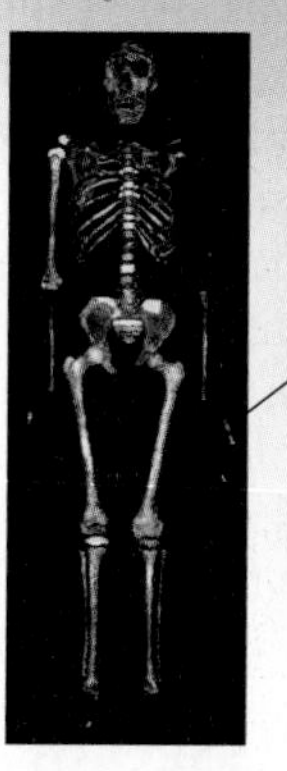

KNM-WT 15000, the Nariokotome boy was a member of *H. erectus* who stood about 5'6" at his death and might have reached 6' tall had he lived to adulthood.

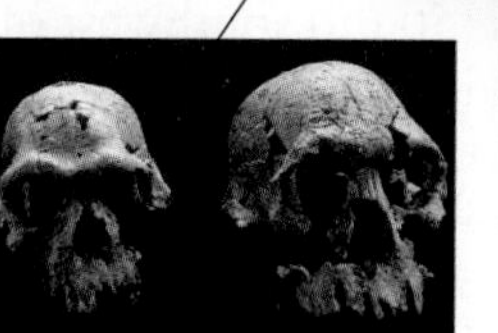

Koobi Fora, Kenya has yielded abundant fossil remains including the largest and smallest skulls of *H. habilis* (KNM-ER1470 and 1813) that some scientists prefer to assign to two separate species.

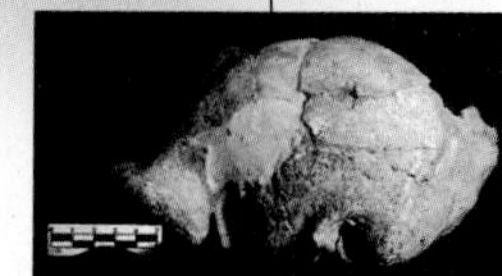

Olduvai Hominid 9 exhibits some characters typical of Asian *H. erectus*.

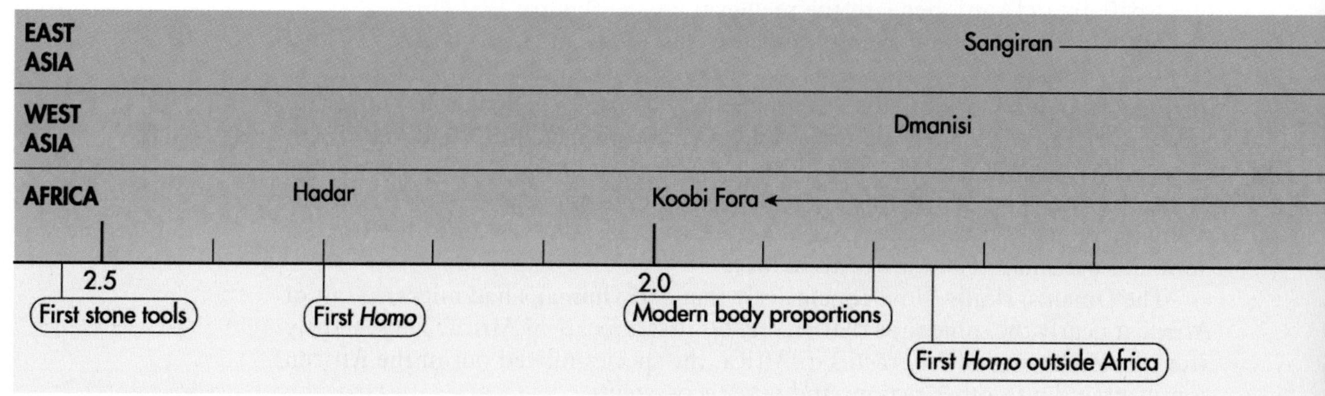

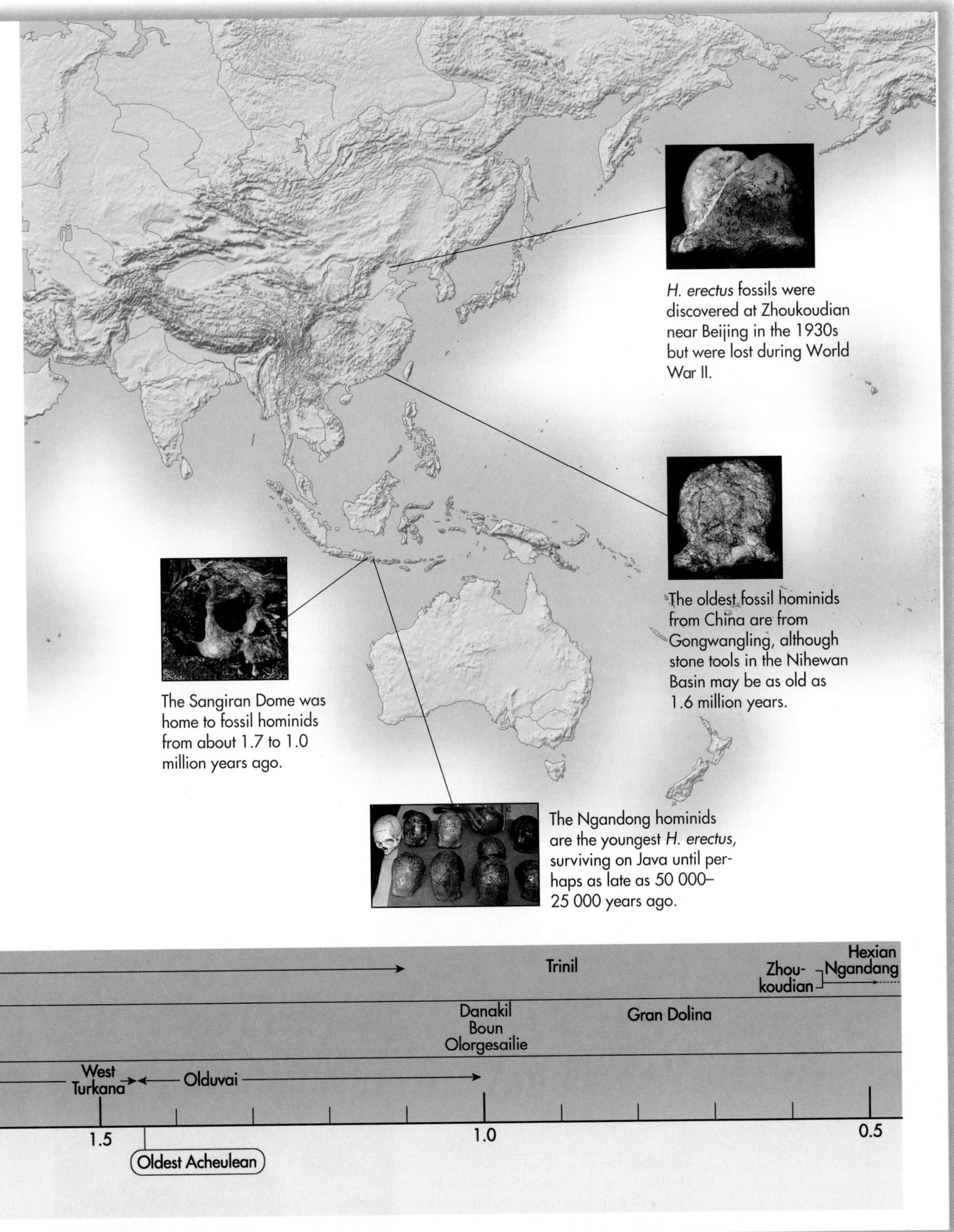
H. erectus fossils were discovered at Zhoukoudian near Beijing in the 1930s but were lost during World War II.
The oldest fossil hominids from China are from Gongwangling, although stone tools in the Nihewan Basin may be as old as 1.6 million years.
The Sangiran Dome was home to fossil hominids from about 1.7 to 1.0 million years ago.
The Ngandong hominids are the youngest H. erectus, surviving on Java until perhaps as late as 50 000–25 000 years ago.
Trinil
Hexian
Zhou-koudian
Ngandang
Danakil
Boun
Olorgesailie
Gran Dolina
West Turkana
Olduvai
1.5
1.0
0.5
Oldest Acheulean

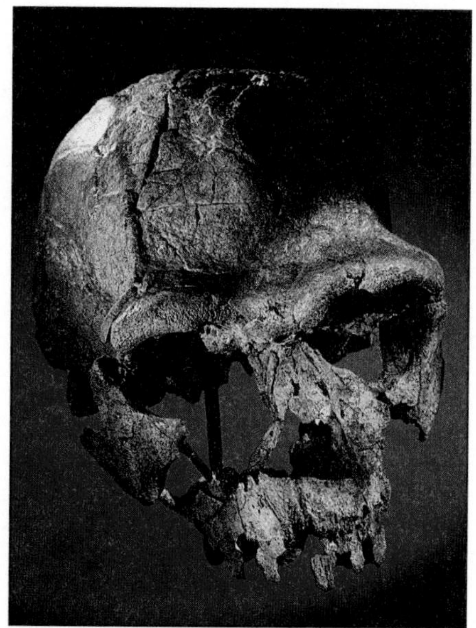

FIGURE 12.10 The cranium of early African *H. erectus* KNM-ER 3733 is nearly 1.8 million years old.

FIGURE 12.11 Olduvai Hominid 9, *H. erectus* from Olduvai Gorge, Tanzania, is nearly 1.5 million years old.

DISPERSAL INTO EAST ASIA

The oldest Asian *H. erectus* are from island Southeast Asia, particularly the island of Java, and date to about 1.8 to 1.6 million years ago. However, 1.8 million years ago sea level was substantially lower than it is today, and Java and nearby islands were part of mainland Asia (Figure 12.13). So colonizing the far reaches of Asia meant only walking a long distance, not crossing water. Although travel through continental Asia is necessary to reach Southeast Asia, so far the earliest evidence of *H. erectus* on the eastern part of the continent is only about 1.5 million years old.

Indonesia The very first *H. erectus* fossil ever found, and thus the type specimen for the species, was discovered in 1891 in Indonesia. A few years earlier, a young doctor named Eugene Dubois left Amsterdam by steam ship in search of human fossils in the Dutch East Indies (now called Indonesia).

calotte The skullcap, or the bones of the skull, excluding those that form the face and the base of the cranium.

In the banks of the Solo River near the village of Trinil, Java, Dubois's team unearthed a large, round fossil (Figure 12.14), the **calotte** or skullcap of an early human. Although only the top of the skull was found, Dubois could see that it was hominid and that in life it possessed a large brain, in a robust cranium more

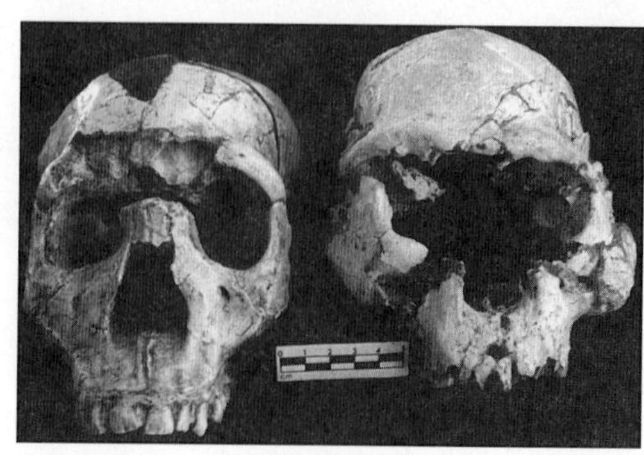

FIGURE 12.12 The Dmanisi cranium (right) shows similarities to early African *H. erectus* including the Nariokotome boy (left).

TABLE 12.2 Dmanisi Hominids Compared with Other Early Hominids

TAXON	BRAIN SIZE (CC)	BODY HEIGHT (IN)	BODY WEIGHT (LB)
Dmanisi	650 to 780	58	105
H. sapiens	1350	63 to 69	108 to 128
African *H. erectus*	700 to 1067	63 to 71	123 to 145
Asian *H. erectus*	800 to 1250	—	—
Earliest *Homo*	500 to 750	39 to 63	70 to 132
A. africanus	448	45 to 54	66 to 90

Source: Gabunia (2001).

primitive than that of any hominid known at that time. He named the species *Pithecanthropus erectus* ("the upright ape-man"), and this specimen, Trinil 2, also nicknamed Java Man, became the type specimen for the species.

The team later found a fossilized femur that Dubois believed to be of the same individual, thereby proving to him that the creature was fully bipedal. By the 1940s *P. erectus* was classified in our own genus as *H. erectus* and recognized as a primitive hominid intermediate between the apes and modern people.

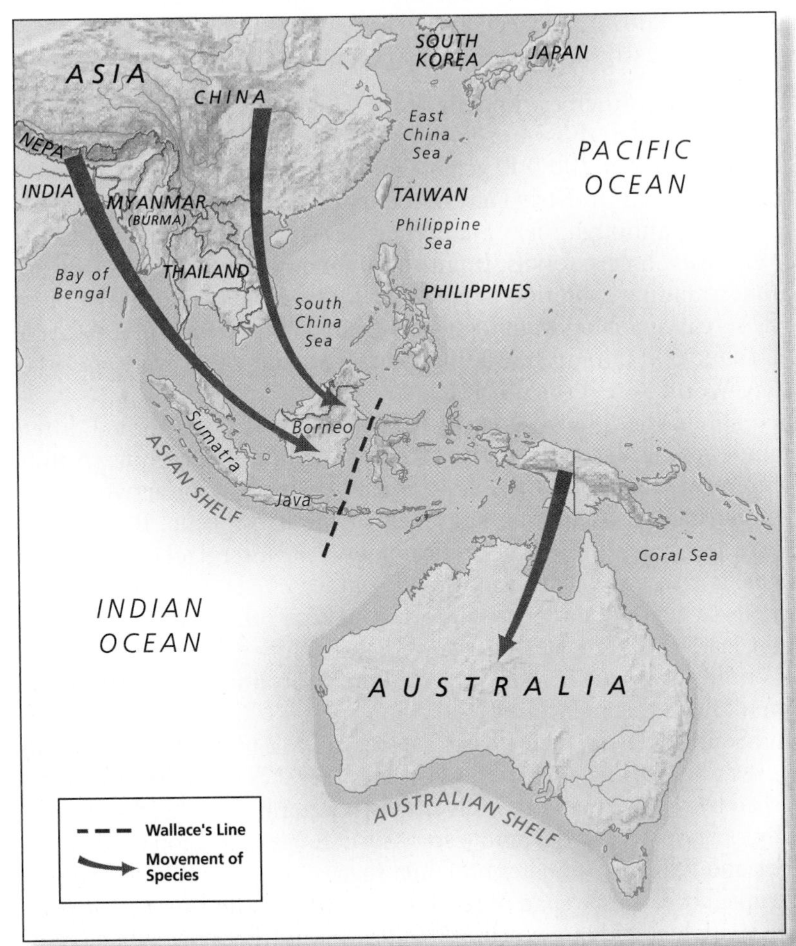

FIGURE 12.13 Landbridge connections between continental Asia and Indonesia during glacial periods (and low sea level) extend as far as Wallace's line.

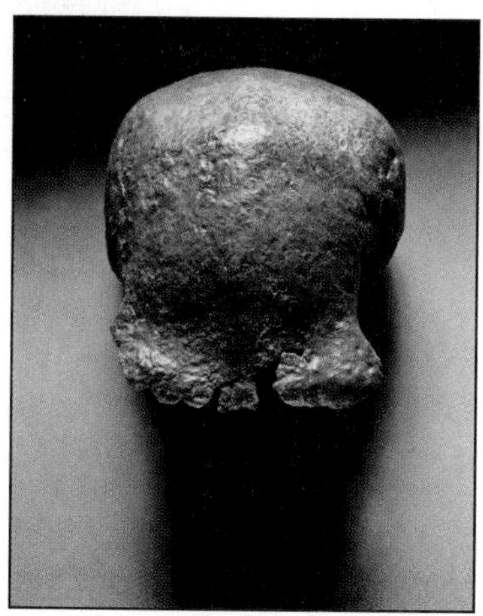

FIGURE 12.14 The skull cap from Trinil, Java, is the type specimen for *H. erectus* and is about 900 000 years old.

The volcanic sediments of Java have yielded a wealth of other *H. erectus* fossils. These include the most ancient specimen from Java, a child's **calvaria** or braincase from the site of Mojokerto dated to about 1.8 million years ago, and a series of fossils from the Sangiran dome region, dated to between 1.7 and 1.0 million years ago. These early Indonesian *H. erectus* have cranial capacities between about 800 and 1000 cc.

Volcanic sediments provide the ideal context for estimating the radiometric age of the fossil hominids using the argon–argon technique (see Chapter 9). A series of samples from more than 80 vertical metres of a geological section at Sangiran conducted by two different research groups have yielded dates ranging from about 1.7 to about 1.0 million years ago for the hominid-bearing parts of the section (Swisher et al., 1994; Larick et al., 2001).

The latest surviving *H. erectus* are also from Java and represent the youngest *H. erectus* anywhere in the world. A series of partial crania and other fossilized remains were excavated in the 1930s at the site of Ngandong in eastern Java. The fauna associated with the Ngandong hominids (but not the hominids themselves) have been dated to a remarkably recent 53 000 to 27 000 years ago (Swisher et al., 1996). Previously thought to have been present at least 500 000 to 250 000 years ago, *H. erectus* may have survived in this island refuge even while going extinct in other parts of the world. However, because the excavations were performed so long ago, the data at hand cannot answer all the criticisms of the ages. Recent finds on Flores dating to 18 000 may also support a young age for *H. erectus* (see Chapter 14).

Since Indonesia achieved independence in 1945, Indonesian scientists have recovered a series of other fossils. These finds have helped us understand the anatomy and evolution of *H. erectus*, but tools are almost entirely lacking in Indonesia. Tools of an Oldowanlike technology have been found, but they are few, and none were found in association with fossil hominids.

China Although perhaps the best known of the *H. erectus* remains, the fossils from China are younger than those in Africa or earliest Indonesia, spanning only from about 800 000 to about 200 000 years ago. However, sites with stone tools also indicate there was likely an Early Pleistocene (approximately 1.6 million years old) hominid presence, although there are no new fossils from these sites (Zhu et al., 2004). The earliest Chinese fossils, fragmentary and crushed remains, are not much help in understanding evolution in *H. erectus*. The most numerous and best preserved are the so-called Peking Man fossils discovered in the 1930s in China and dated between about 600 000 and 300 000 years ago, but these were unfortunately lost during World War II (Box 12.2).

Despite their similarities, Chinese *H. erectus* also show some regional differences from the Indonesian *H. erectus* in their frontal and occipital regions (Antón, 2003). These differences may reflect the intermittent isolation of these two groups from each other during the oscillating sea levels of the Pleistocene. Recall from Chapter 9 that sea level rose and fell periodically with the interglacial and glacial periods. Each time it rose, continental and island Southeast Asia, and the hominids and land mammals living on them, were cut off from each other. These periods of separation might last 10 000 to 50 000 years, that is many generations of fossil hominids, and could have led to some genetic (and morphological) differences between the populations through time.

calvaria The braincase; includes the bones of the calotte and those that form the base of the cranium but excludes the bones of the face.

Unlike island Southeast Asia, China lacks Pleistocene volcanic sediments, posing a problem for the radiometric aging of hominid sites there. Thus Chinese hominid ages are established by relative methods such as biostratigraphy or lithostratigraphy, loess stratigraphy, or, more recently, uranium series or ESR ages. At Zhoukoudian, for example, U-series and ESR age estimates on fauna suggest that the multiple layers at the site were occupied over a time span of several hundred thousand years. The earliest ages associated with hominids are nearly 600 000 years and the youngest a bit more than 200 000 years (Grün et al., 1997). U-series dates suggest that the site represents a long time period, although it may be older than previous estimates, with the youngest hominid layers being perhaps 400 000 years old (Shen and Wang, 2000).

Box 12.2 The Canadian Anatomist and Peking Man

The story of the famed Peking Man fossils is one of discovery and loss. Chinese palaeontologist Pei Wenshong discovered the original skull in December 1929 at a quarry site, Chou Kou Tien (now transliterated as Zhoukoudian), not far from modern Beijing (Figure A). Along with Davidson Black (Figure B), a Canadian anatomist, Wenshong described and initially named the fossil ***Sinanthropus pekinensis*** ("Chinese human from Peking").

Davidson Black was born in Toronto and trained at the University of Toronto as a medical doctor (1906) with a further degree in biology in 1909. He received further training at Manchester University in England in 1914, where he met and studied under some of the most influential anatomists of the time and where he became intrigued by human evolution. In 1919 he was invited to work at the Peking Union Medical College in China, a position he happily accepted because it was then widely thought that humans had originated in central Asia.

From 1926 until 1934 Black was involved in the investigations at Zhoukoudian and performed the major anatomical work on the Peking Man fossils. In 1926 he concluded that some teeth recovered from the site were the remnants of an ancestral hominid dating to perhaps a million years ago.

In 1928 additional cranial and mandibular fragments were found, and in 1929 a well-preserved skull was discovered. Their characteristics vindicated Black's identification and he became highly regarded for his skill and perception.

For the next few years, Black worked hard at publishing descriptions of the Peking Man fossils. Although they were very similar to the Java Man fossils found by Eugene Dubois in Indonesia, they confirmed Black's contention that Peking Man had been a pre-human hominid.

Black had a congenital heart defect that was aggravated by overwork. After supper, he often returned to his office to work through the night, returning home early in the morning to sleep until noon. He had been hospitalized for six weeks in early 1934, but once released he resumed his heavy schedule. In March 1934, he died while working alone during the night, only 49 years of age. Allegedly, he was found at his desk with a fossil in his hand. When von Koenigswald discovered the teeth of an extinct giant ape in China in 1935, he named it ***Gigantopithecus blacki*** in honour of Davidson Black.

After Black's untimely death, Franz Weidenreich, a Jewish anatomist who had fled his native Germany during the early years of the Nazi era, took over anatomical work on Zhoukoudian and produced the primary publications on the fossils.

In the mid-1930s, Japan invaded China before the American entry into World War II, and excavations at Zhoukoudian stopped in 1937. Fear spread that the Zhoukoudian *H. erectus* fossils, objects of great cultural and historical value, would be confiscated, destroyed, or taken as gifts to the Japanese emperor, a noted naturalist. So Weidenreich made extensive measurements, drawings, and plaster casts of the fossils. The fossils were then placed in the care of the United States Marines, who guarded them on a train from Beijing to the coast, where they were to be put on a ship for San Francisco. The train arrived at the Chinese coast on December 7, 1941, the day of the Japanese attack on Pearl Harbor. The Marines were taken prisoner, and the crates of fossils have never been found (Shipman, 2001).

Because of Weidenreich's careful moulding and measuring of the Zhoukoudian fossils, we have replicas of the Peking Man fossils, comprising more than a dozen calvaria and hundreds of associated teeth and bone fragments (Weidenreich, 1943). They represent as many as 40 individuals who lived nearby Zhoukoudian between 600 000 and 250 000 years ago.

Over time, the fossils have attained great symbolic significance in China. In 1998, members of the Chinese Academy of Sciences called for a renewed search for the skullcaps. In 2000, a manifesto, "Searching for Peking Man," was published by Chinese journalists who argued that the only way to prove China's progress was to find the missing skulls of Peking Man, the ancestor of all Chinese. Most recently, a press conference was called in 2005 at the Paleoanthropological Research Center at Dragon Bone Hill in the outskirts of Beijing to announce that a Working Committee to Search for the Lost Skullcaps of Peking Man had been officially established. Although tips continue to come in to the hot line in Beijing, as of this writing there are no new clues as to the fate of the fossils.

FIGURE A The site of Zhoukoudian outside of Beijing, China, spans several hundred thousand years.

FIGURE B Davidson Black.

THE STATUS OF *HOMO ERECTUS* IN EUROPE

The status of *H. erectus* in Europe is a subject of debate among palaeoanthropologists. We know that early humans somewhat resembling *H. erectus* occupied Europe during the same time period that *H. erectus* occurred in Asia. However, most of the fossils discovered so far that are complete enough for us to assess their taxonomy differ from the typical *H. erectus* seen in Africa, Asia, or Southeast Asia. Many of the European fossils resemble *H. sapiens* as well as *H. erectus* and Neandertals, and they may well be transitional, or archaic, forms of *H. sapiens* (see Chapter 13).The later Middle Pleistocene European fossils, those dated between 500 000 and 200 000 years ago, are likely to be ancestral only to Neandertals and are discussed in Chapter 13. The last decade has seen important finds from the Sierra de Atapuerca region of Spain that have been dated to about 800 000 years ago, more than 200 000 years older than any other known hominids in western Europe. Anatomically, however, they cannot be classified as *H. erectus*, suggesting that this taxon may never have made it into Europe.

THE LIFEWAYS OF *HOMO ERECTUS*

From the fossils and stone tools associated with *H. erectus* and from their own anatomy we can begin to piece together how these early *Homo* lived. The species is associated with two different tool technologies that show *H. erectus* possessed advanced cognitive skills. *H. erectus* appears to have undergone a dietary shift to a more heavily meat-based diet than its predecessors, and this shift seems to have fuelled its dispersal from Africa.

HOMO ERECTUS AND THE EARLY STONE AGE

From 1.8 to about 1.5 million years ago in Africa, only Oldowan type tools are found with *H. erectus*. And the earliest tools found outside Africa (at Dmanisi in the Republic of Georgia) are also Oldowanlike assemblages (Gabunia et al., 2001). However, starting at approximately 1.4 million years ago in Africa, some *H. erectus* are found with a different tool technology called the **Acheulean** tradition. Together, the Oldowan and Acheulean are known as the **Early Stone Age** (in Africa) or **Lower Palaeolithic** (outside of Africa).

Acheulean assemblages are characterized by specifically shaped **biface** tools called **hand axes** and **cleavers** (Figure 12.15). For the first time in human prehistory we see hominids making standardized tools that clearly indicate they had a plan or mental template in mind. Hand axes and cleavers were highly uniform in appearance. They were made from stone cobbles or larger flakes that had been carefully selected for size and weight. The tool maker roughed out the axe first, then refined the product to achieve a particular shape.

One of the most extraordinary aspects of the Acheulean industry is its persistence and uniformity over great spans of time and space. We first see hand axes at about 1.5 million years ago, and they persist almost unchanged until about 250 000 years ago. This conservatism is also found across vast geographic areas: Hand axes appear in western and northern Europe, in East and North Africa, and in the Near East, although they are very rare, or absent, in the east Asian *H. erectus* sites.

Hand axes and cleavers might have been specifically developed for the butchery of large animals, but other hypotheses for the use of hand axes cannot be discounted. A recent study found evidence of fossilized *phytoliths,* microscopic mineral particles from plants, on the cutting edge of some hand axes. Their presence suggests that the tool was used to scrape plant material. This could have meant the users of the tools were sharpening a wooden spear, or perhaps stripping bark from wood for building or eating. Alternatively, hand axes might also have been used as digging implements, much as traditional foraging people today use sticks to dig for edible roots and potatolike tubers.

Early Stone Age (or Lower Palaeolithic) The earliest stone tool industries, including the Oldowan and Acheulean industries; called the ESA in Africa and the Lower Palaeolithic outside Africa.

Acheulean Stone tool industry of the Early and Middle Pleistocene characterized by the presence of bifacial hand axes and cleavers. This industry is made by a number of *Homo* species, including ***H. erectus*** and early ***H. sapiens***.

biface A stone tool that has been flaked on two faces or opposing sides forming a cutting edge between the two flake scars.

hand axe Type of Acheulean tool, usually teardrop-shaped, with a long cutting edge.

cleaver Type of Acheulean tool, usually oblong with a broad cutting edge on one end.

FIGURE 12.15 The Acheulean industry is typified by hand axes and cleavers.

A HIGHER-QUALITY DIET: *HOMO ERECTUS* SUBSISTENCE

Although we assume their diet was largely plant foods, as is true for modern foraging people, there is no mistaking the archaeological evidence that *H. erectus* ate meat. About 1.8 million years ago, an important biological shift apparently occurred in the hominid lineage, in which the human form became much more modern, taller, more linear, and with a larger brain. Shortly after this time hominids left Africa and began their worldwide geographic expansion. Both these things tell us that the shift probably was associated with a major increase in the quality of the diet, which was needed to maintain a larger body and brain (Leonard and Robertson, 1997; Antón et al., 2002).

Many scientists think the adaptive shift occurred when hominids became predators (Shipman and Walker, 1989; Antón et al., 2002). Most scientists argue that the adaptive shift happened with the emergence of *H. erectus* about 1.8 million years ago and that *H. erectus* was the first truly predatory human species. They base their assertion on the increasingly sophisticated tools associated with *H. erectus,* which may have been used for butchering prey, and on evidence that as *H. erectus* spread its range across the Old World, they lived at low population densities in the manner of a hunting species. In addition, it seems that human-specific tapeworms share a history with tapeworms that live in hyenas but diverged from them about 1.8 million years ago. This suggests that ancient hyenas and humans were eating the same infected animals about 1.8 million years ago, further suggesting that humans had made the shift from a largely vegetarian to a mostly meat diet.

HOMO ERECTUS LEAVES AFRICA

The most important adaptive shift *H. erectus* made was the first migration out of Africa (Figure 12.16). This emigration meant moving across a variety of ecosystems, climates, and ecological settings. Each of these would have presented *H. erectus* with new challenges never before encountered by a hominid. Most important was the move from tropical and subtropical Africa into the more seasonally cold regions of the Northern Hemisphere in Eurasia and the Far East. This change alone demonstrates the remarkable adaptability and behavioural flexibility our lineage had evolved by just under 2 million years ago. The ability to adapt to a wide range of novel environments is a hallmark of the human species.

One question remains: Why did hominids remain in Africa for more than 3 million years only to disperse rapidly after the first appearance of *H. erectus?* Some of the likely causes form a web of ecological and morphological advantages that facilitated *H. erectus* dispersal. First, recall from Chapter 9 that world climate was beginning to undergo some severe fluctuations at the origin and

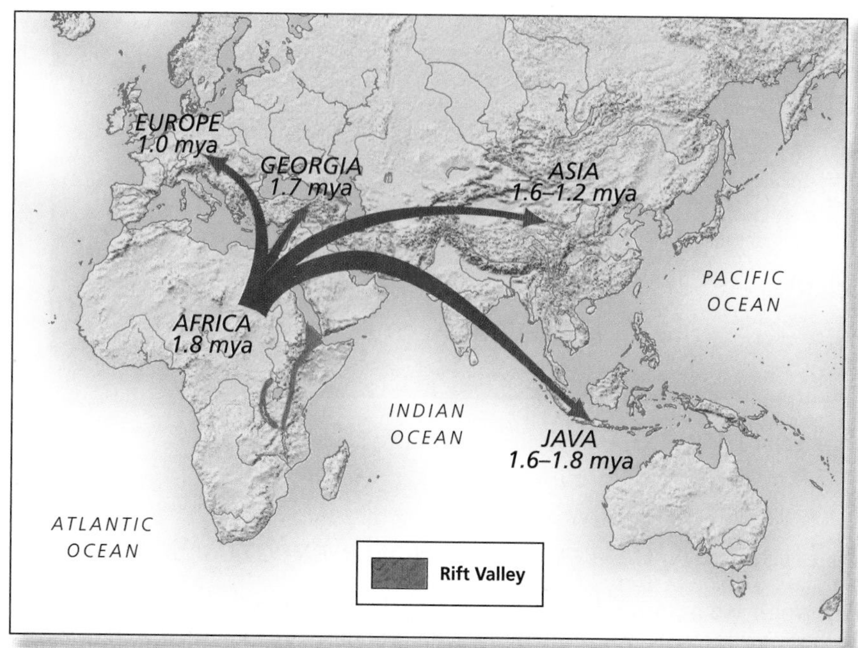

FIGURE 12.16 *H. erectus* migrated out of Africa beginning about 1.8 million years ago and is first known from Georgia and Java.

slightly before the rise of *H. erectus*. The African area was cooling and drying around 2 million years ago, leading to diminished forests with larger grasslands between them. The rise of grasslands saw an increase in the quantities of herbivorous animals and the evolution of a new niche for animals (including hominids) that could eat them.

H. erectus seems to have taken advantage of these opportunities by using Oldowan tools to access animal resources it was not physically adapted to acquire. The higher-quality animal diet that resulted allowed the growth of larger bodies, and their more linear body shape probably allowed greater midday activity because they coped better with the heat. Larger bodies allowed greater ranging (home range, the area an animal traverses over a year, is positively correlated to body size in mammals). As animals such as antelope migrated, hominids may have followed.

In the Late Pliocene, at about the time that we see other African fauna migrating into the Near East and western Asia, we also see *H. erectus* migrating. Were they following this food resource? Earlier hominids had not migrated during earlier faunal migrations out of Africa. They may have remained in place because of their greater reliance on plant foods. So it does seem that at this point *H. erectus* was able to do something that earlier hominids were not capable of doing. It seems reasonable to assume that tool use and the access to previously inaccessible resources it allowed were fundamental to the ability to migrate; however, a complex web of factors is implicated in dispersal.

There is unlikely to have been a single directional dispersal event from Africa to Asia. Rather, random movements of multiple hominid groups over time probably led to the eventual dispersal of the species across the Old World, and some back migrations probably also occurred. Even though the entire dispersal seems a long one (being some 10 000 kilometres [6000 mi] from Kenya to Java), consider that an average change in home range of just 1 kilometre a year (less than a mile), over a period of 10 000 or 15 000 years, would have led to a slow dispersal, yet it would look geologically instantaneous.

Having moved into many parts of the Old World using a combination of technology and physical adaptation, and having made a shift in foraging strategy to a higher-quality diet, early *H. erectus* was poised to begin the brain size expansion and intellectual development characteristic of the genus. Through time, *H. erectus* continued a gradual development of physical and cultural evolution. But more recent species of genus *Homo* exhibited even more dramatic changes. Intelligence is a survival strategy of enormous evolutionary importance to the human lineage. In *H. erectus,* we see the beginning of what intelligence meant for the hominid lineage. Next, we turn to *H. sapiens,* in which cognition and culture take on far more importance.

SUMMARY

1. **How do we define the earliest members of the genus *Homo?***

   Genus *Homo* is defined by brain size greater than 500 cc, a smaller, less prognathic face, and smaller teeth than australopithecines possess.

2. **Why do some researchers consider the earliest genus *Homo* to be *Australopithecus?***

   Some researchers think that the earliest known Homo species, such as *Homo habilis*, are so apelike they should be lumped with *Australopithecus* and that genus *Homo* should be reserved for the larger-brained, longer limbed *H. erectus* and kin that appeared later.

3. **When and where did *H. erectus* appear?**

   The earliest *H. erectus* are often assigned to a separate species, *H. ergaster*, because of their small brain and body size. They appeared in East Africa and also outside Africa in the Republic of Georgia about 1.8 million years ago.

4. **What are the differences between Asian and African *H. erectus?***

   Asian *H. erectus* are different from African *H. erectus* in having thicker-walled crania, more robust facial features, larger teeth, and more cranial superstructures.

5. **What sort of stone tools did *H. erectus* use?**

   H. erectus used both Oldowan and Acheulean tools but may have been the hominid that invented Acheulean tools.

6. **Why do we think that *H. erectus* was the first hominid that ate substantial quantities of meat?**

   H. erectus made stone tools, and there is archaeological evidence that these tools were used to butcher large animals, suggesting substantial meat consumption. In addition, its larger body and brain size and its greater range (across the Old World) suggest that *H. erectus* must have had a higher-quality diet than earlier *Homo* in order to meet its higher energetic needs.

CRITICAL THINKING QUESTIONS

1. Why is the distinction between *Australopithecus* and *Homo* becoming fuzzier as more fossils are discovered?
2. How might we interpret the fact that the earliest *H. erectus* fossils come from East Africa, but that there are other very *H. erectus*-like fossils from outside Africa at about the same time?
3. What was the main survival value of larger brain size to *H. erectus*? What could they do that earlier hominids could not that allowed them to expand the human range beyond Africa?

KEY TERMS

Oldowan
tool industry
core
flake
hammerstone
supraoribital torus
angular torus
occipital torus
sagittal keel
metopic keel
canine fossa
shovel-shaped incisor
calotte
calvaria
Acheulean
Early Stone Age (or Lower Palaeolithic)
biface
hand axe
cleaver

SUGGESTED READING

Lewin, Roger. (1997). *Bones of Contention*, 2nd edition. University of Chicago Press, Chicago, IL.

Schick, Kathy, and Toth, Nicholas. (1993). *Making Silent Stones Speak: Human Evolution and the Dawn of Technology*. Simon & Schuster, New York, NY.

Shipman, Pat. (2001). *The Man Who Found the Missing Link*. Harvard University Press, Cambridge, MA.

Walker, Alan, and Shipman, Pat. (1996). *The Wisdom of the Bones*. Vintage Books, New York, NY.

Wolpoff, Milford. (1999). *Paleoanthropology*, 2nd edition. McGraw-Hill, New York, NY.

Chapter 13

Archaic *Homo sapiens* and Neandertals

IN AN OPEN COAL PIT IN GERMANY, a huge mechanical shovel grinds away at the earth, stripping away not only vast amounts of coal but also Holocene and Pleistocene deposits. Scientists monitor the activity, ready to intervene should something more interesting than coal be exposed. Over the years, archaeologists have identified a number of Lower Palaeolithic sites in the pit, which are located several metres [feet] below the ground. The sites date to about 400 000 years ago: the Middle Pleistocene.

THE MATERIAL FOUND AT THESE SITES is what we might expect given their age and location. The inventory includes flint tools and flakes, combined with the remains of extinct elephants, bovids, deer, and horses. No hominid remains are found, which is unfortunate given the scarcity of fossils from this critical period in human evolution. But after several years of excavation, archaeologist Hartmut Thieme discovered something that was even scarcer, and perhaps more significant, than additional fossil remains: four large wooden spears.

THE SPEARS ARE IMPRESSIVE: Two of them measure more than 2.25 metres (7 ft) in length. Three of them are sharpened at one end. They are carefully shaped and their weight is distributed to make them aerodynamically efficient. It remains possible that they could have been used as lances and thrust at prey rather than thrown. The fourth is smaller (less than 1 metre [3 ft] long) and sharpened at both ends. Thieme classifies it tentatively as a throwing stick or as a small thrusting spear. Three smaller wooden implements, made from the branches of trees, were also found. Although the function of these implements is not clear, they each had a groove cut into one end that could have been used to hold flints, perhaps creating a composite cutting or chopping tool.

THIEME BELIEVES THAT THE DISCOVERY of these wooden spears and the butchered remains of big game provides strong evidence that Middle Pleistocene hominids were capable of organized game hunting and that they could hunt from a distance, increasing their safety. By showing us how these hominids made use of organic materials in their lives, these wooden spears provide us with a window to the past that is typically shuttered. When we look at traditional peoples throughout the world, we see that only a small and biased sample of their material cultures is preserved in the archaeological record. The discovery of these ancient spears from Germany gives us a better idea of just how much we're missing from the material cultures of extinct hominids.

Chapter Outline

In the previous chapters, we reviewed the primate and hominid fossil records primarily by starting in the past and working forward. But it may be useful to consider the past from the perspective of the present and what it can tell us about what may be missing in the fossil and archaeological records. Today, one species of hominid, *Homo sapiens*, is distributed around the globe. As a species, we share a common origin that should be traceable back to a population that existed at a certain time and place. The fossil record makes it quite clear that as hominids and as members of the genus *Homo* we definitely have an African homeland: We do not find hominids outside Africa until after 2 million years ago. But because *Homo erectus*, the presumed ancestor of all later hominid species, lived throughout the Old World in regions that were later occupied by modern humans, it is not immediately clear which *H. erectus* populations, if any, are directly ancestral to us.

Population variability further complicates the matter. Although all modern humans are members of the same species, there is clearly a substantial amount of geographic variability among human populations. Did this variability arise since we last shared a common ancestor as a species? Or is it a reflection of geographic variability that was present in ancestral, pre-*sapiens* populations? Like *H. sapiens*, the widely dispersed *H. erectus* also exhibited substantial geographic variation. A fundamental issue, which we will explore in this chapter and the next, is whether *H. sapiens* evolved from a small localized population that then replaced all other hominids existing at that time or whether the evolution of *H. sapiens* occurred in such a way that variability of ancestral populations was maintained in the transition to modern humans.

Another complicating factor is that as we go back in time, the amount of variability in the hominid fossil record increases. Many palaeoanthropologists would argue that at various points in the past, more than one hominid species lived. The existence of more than one species is obvious in Africa during the period 1 to 2 million years ago, when robust australopithecines and members of the genus *Homo* lived at the same time. No one believes that robust australopithecines can be lumped into a single species with members of *Homo*.

In this chapter, we look at the hominid fossil record of the Middle to Late Pleistocene. Hominid fossils from this evolutionarily dynamic period have been found from throughout much of the Old World, but taxonomic assignments for the fossil specimens during this period in human evolution remain controversial. How many hominid species were present? What constitutes enough variation to differentiate them from one another? How do these species relate to anatomically modern humans? Are the famous Neandertals simply another type of human or something more distinct? As we will see, whether palaeoanthropologists identify more or fewer hominid fossil species during the last 500 000 years is influenced in part by the hypothesis they think best explains the emergence of our own species.

HOMINID EVOLUTION IN THE MIDDLE TO LATE PLEISTOCENE

As we saw in Chapter 9, the Middle Pleistocene dates from about 900 000 years ago (corresponding to the earliest glaciation of continental Europe) to about 125 000 years ago (Conroy, 1997). The period from 125 000 to 10 000 years ago corresponds to the Late Pleistocene. In the latter half of the Middle Pleistocene, the hominid fossil record begins to reveal specimens that are not "classic *H. erectus*" but that exhibit features often interpreted as being more "advanced" or derived in the direction of *H. sapiens*. These specimens often are lumped together and informally labelled "archaic *Homo sapiens*" or "advanced *H. erectus*," designations that distinguish these fossils from anatomically modern *H. sapiens* and classic *H. erectus*. Such informal labels indicate the transitional nature of these specimens between *H. erectus* and *H. sapiens* and the difficulty in achieving consensus among scientists on their phylogenetic placement in hominid evolution. Several anatomically distinguishable hominid groups were present at various times in the latter half of the Middle Pleistocene. In addition to archaic *H. sapiens*, classic *H. erectus* survived in China and Indonesia until at least 250 000 years ago and maybe later (see Chapter 12). In Europe, the earliest representatives of the Neandertals make their first appearance. Finally, although modern *H. sapiens* appear only in the Late Pleistocene, it is possible that the earliest modern humans may have made their first appearance at the very end of the Middle Pleistocene in Africa (see Chapter 14).

Defining Anatomically Modern *Homo sapiens*

Archaic *H. sapiens* are intermediate between classic *H. erectus* and anatomically modern *H. sapiens*. To define what *intermediate* means in this context, we can describe the features that distinguish modern humans from other hominids.

Compared with *H. erectus*, the cranium of anatomically modern *H. sapiens* is distinguished by a larger braincase (mean capacity 1350 cc) and finer bone structure. (Figure 13.1). The jaws and teeth are small. Following jaw size, the face is smaller and retracted under the braincase to a greater degree than in previous hominids. There is marked development of a chin. The limb bones are straight and slightly built, with the lower limbs much longer than the upper.

Intermediate archaic *H. sapiens* typically exhibit a mosaic of *H. erectus* and *H. sapiens* features, in many cases retaining the robustness of classic *H. erectus* but with a larger cranial capacity and a shape more similar to anatomically modern *H. sapiens*. As we will see, the intermediate or transitional nature of archaic *H. sapiens* can pose problems for determining how these specimens should be classified and their precise phylogenetic relationship to later hominid taxa.

ARCHAIC *HOMO SAPIENS*

Palaeontologists have recovered numerous fossil specimens we informally classify as archaic *H. sapiens* from sites across the Old World, although the group is better known from remains found in Europe and Africa. Palaeontological and molecular discoveries over the past two decades, along with improvements in dating techniques, have greatly increased our understanding of the place of archaic *H. sapiens* in the broader context of human evolution.

The specimens reflect an important transitional period during human evolution. Anatomically the group is diverse, but it seems to consistently differ from *H. erectus* by having larger brains (1000 to 1400 cc), more parallel-sided, taller, and less angular cranial vaults, robust but arching rather than straight browridges, and in some instances wide nasal apertures (Figure 13.2). Archaic *H. sapiens* differ from modern humans by retaining robust browridges, large faces, occipital tori, and thicker, lower cranial vaults. As we review the individual fossils, keep in

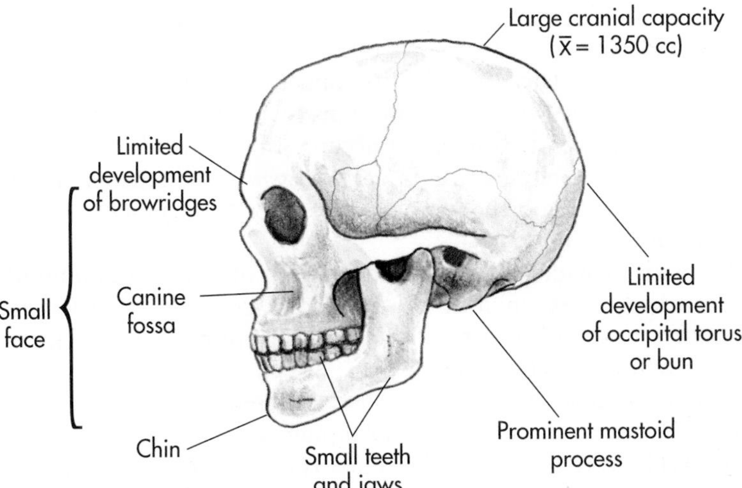

Figure 13.1 Features of the skull of anatomically modern *Homo sapiens*.

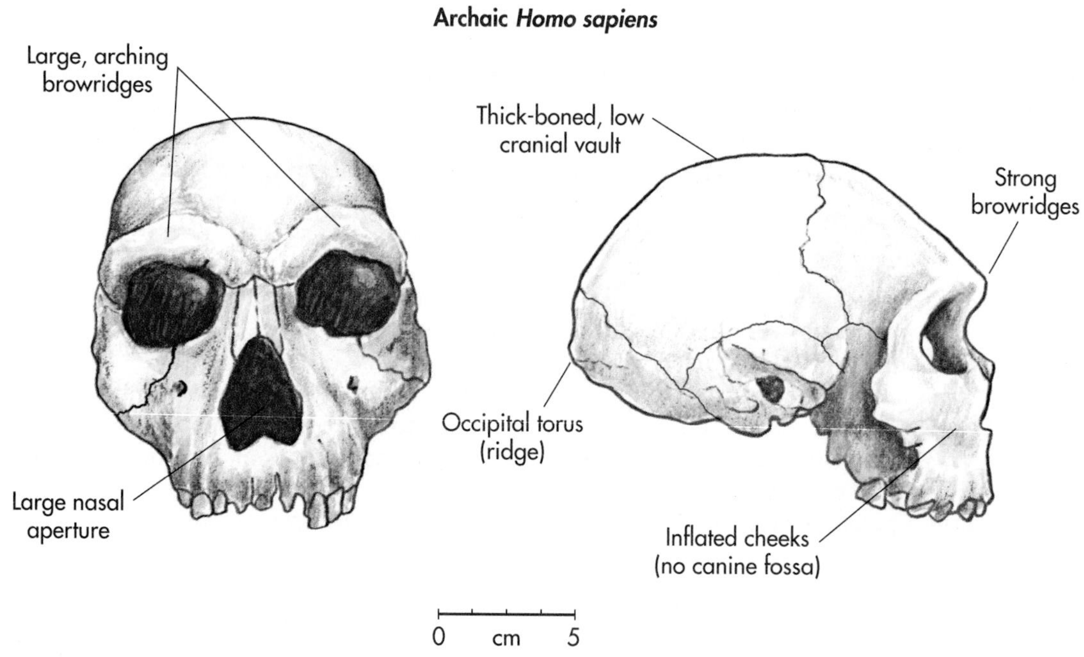

FIGURE 13.2 Features of the skull of archaic *Homo sapiens*.

mind that there are several phylogenetic scenarios into which they can be incorporated. Although we may call them archaic *H. sapiens,* this does not mean we consider them ancestral to later anatomically modern *H. sapiens* (although that may be a reasonable hypothesis), nor do we claim that they necessarily all represent the same species, although many scientists argue that they do.

EUROPEAN ARCHAIC *HOMO SAPIENS*

The earliest hominids in Europe (800 000 years ago) are in Spain, as described in Chapter 12. Most scientists would lump them in the general archaic *H. sapiens* category, although the discoverers have provisionally assigned them to a new taxon, *Homo antecessor.*

The first of the European Middle Pleistocene remains to be discovered was a mandible found in a sandpit in the village of Mauer, near Heidelberg, Germany, in 1907 (Schoetensack, 1908). Based on faunal and stratigraphic dating the mandible was assigned a Middle Pleistocene age of 400 000 to 500 000 years. Because the Mauer mandible is clearly not modern—it is quite robust and lacks a chin—it was identified as a hominid species distinct from our own. But because *Homo (Pithecanthropus) erectus* was not a generally accepted taxon at that time, the Mauer mandible was given the name *Homo heidelbergensis.* Whether it should now keep that species designation or be lumped with other "archaic *H. sapiens*" is discussed at the end of this chapter.

More complete fossils provide a more detailed picture of European hominids in the Middle Pleistocene. These include the Petralona cranium from Greece (300 000 to 150 000 years ago) and the Steinheim cranium from Germany (250 000 to 200 000 years ago) (Figure 13.3).

The greatest trove of archaic *H. sapiens* fossils recovered from a single locality also comes from the cave system in Sierra de Atapuerca, Spain (Arsuaga et al., 1997; Arsuaga, 2002) (Figure 13.4). There the remains of more than 30 individuals, ranging in age from 4 to 35 years, were found in a cave (or pit) known as *Sima de los Huesos* (literally, the "bone pit"). Based on faunal and absolute dating methods, the age of the site is about 300 000 to 400 000 years.

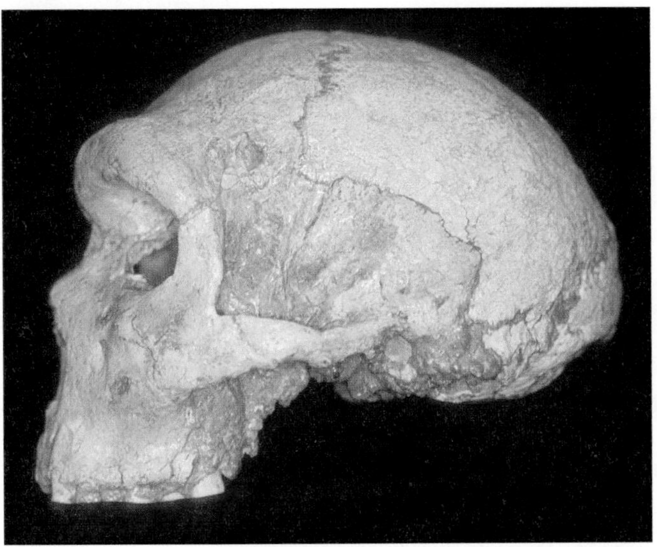

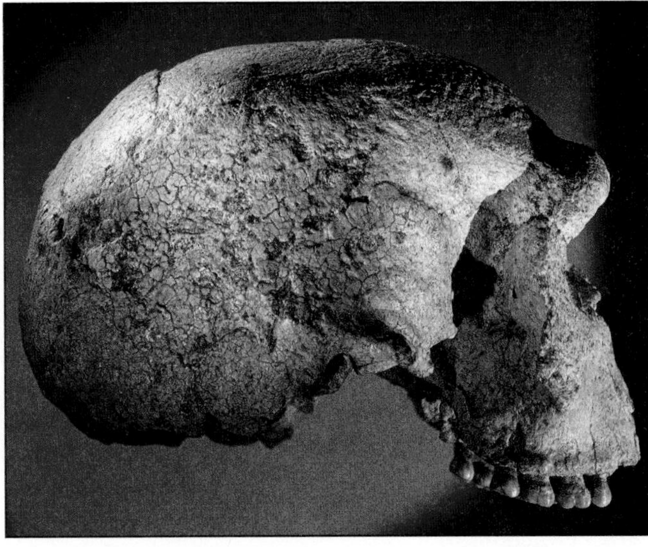

(a) (b)

FIGURE 13.3 (a) The Petralona cranium from Greece. (b) The Steinheim cranium from Germany.

All these archaic *H. sapiens* specimens differ from classic *H. erectus* in vault shape and size, browridge conformation, and facial morphology, although they are similar in having thick cranial bones and less round cranial vaults. Cranial capacities of Mid-Pleistocene European fossils are between 1100 and 1390 cc, making them larger brained than typical *H. erectus* specimens, and they have taller vaults with the greatest cranial breadth high on the parietal. The size range among these fossils suggests that both males and females are present.

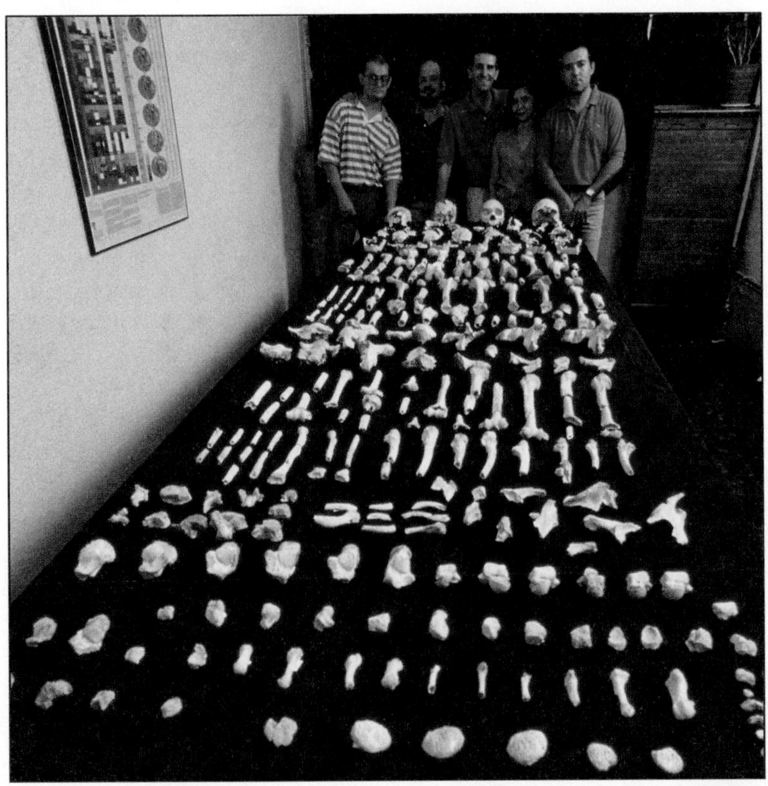

FIGURE 13.4 Skeletal remains from the Sima de los Huesos, Sierra de Atapuerca, Spain.

A 500 000-year-old tibia from Boxgrove in southern England, along with the extensive postcranial remains from Spain, provide information about the size and shape of the postcranial skeleton of archaic *H. sapiens* (Stringer et al., 1998; Arsuaga et al., 1997; Arsuaga, 2002). These postcrania are similar to other pre-modern *Homo* skeletons in being robust with strong muscle markings and thick cortical bone and in having large joint surface areas and strongly buttressed pelvises.

Mid-Pleistocene European hominids are too primitive to be considered Neandertals, but those from the Sima de los Huesos exhibit several cranial features that are very Neandertal-like and seem to indicate that these fossils could be part of a population ancestral to Neandertals and not ancestral to modern humans (Arsuaga et al., 1997, 1999). Facial features that are the most Neandertal-like include a double-arched supraorbital torus and **midfacial prognathism**, the forward projection of the middle facial region, including the nose. The nasal bones actually form a shelf projecting from the face, and the cheekbones gradually recede from these rather than being perpendicular to the nose, as in our face. The nasal aperture is also quite wide. We will discuss this phylogenetic model and others later.

African Archaic *Homo sapiens*

The African continent has yielded at least four crania that are generally regarded as archaic *H. sapiens* because of their large cranial capacities; massive but more arching, non-barlike supraorbital tori; less angular vaults; and a greatest width higher on the cranium. Their geological ages are not fully known. The oldest of these is likely to be the partial cranium from Bodo, Ethiopia, which preserves the face and anterior braincase and dates to as much as 600 000 years ago. The Bodo cranium is large, with a capacity of about 1300 cc (Conroy et al., 1978). Its most extraordinary features are cut marks on the face that appear to be made by stone tools (Figure 13.5) (White, 1986). Smaller archaic *H. sapiens* crania also exist in Africa and may be from small females, with small cranial capacities.

midfacial prognathism The forward projection of the middle facial region, including the nose.

Taken together, the European and African archaic *H. sapiens* specimens share many features and have a similar overall appearance. However, no African archaic *H. sapiens* have been found that possess the specific derived features reminiscent of the Neandertals, whereas in Europe, the Sima de los Huesos hominids and others are claimed by some scientists to share derived features with later Neandertals.

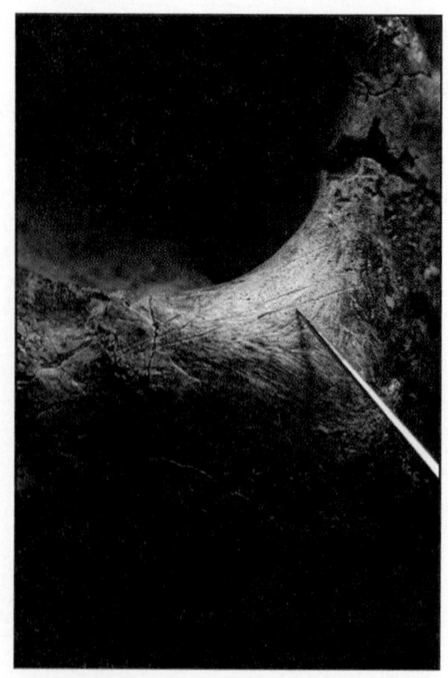

FIGURE 13.5 The Bodo cranium from Ethiopia shows signs of having been defleshed with stone tools.

Asian Archaic *Homo sapiens*

Fossil specimens from several sites in Asia are generally accepted as representing archaic *H. sapiens* based on their enlarged cranial capacities. They also differ from *H. erectus* in vault and supraorbital tori shape. They range in age from 200 000 to 130 000 years ago.

The oldest hominid remains on the Indian sub-continent come from the Narmada Valley, where a partial calvaria dates to the latest part of the Middle Pleistocene (150 000 to 125 000 years ago). The cranium was initially classified as belonging to *H. erectus;* however, later analyses established its transitional character, indicating that it was more similar to archaic *H. sapiens* (Kennedy et al., 1991). It has an estimated cranial capacity of 1150 to 1400 cc, more vertically sided vault walls, and a double-arched browridge.

Although dating is a problem, evidence indicates that archaic *H. sapiens* probably were present in Asia by 200 000 years ago. Given some of the late dates for classic *H. erectus* in Asia (see Chapter 12), if you accept that archaic *H. sapiens* is a different species from *H. erectus,* then two distinct hominid species were present in Asia in the latter part of the Middle Pleistocene.

BEHAVIOUR OF ARCHAIC *HOMO SAPIENS*

Reconstructing the behaviour of archaic *Homo sapiens* poses a somewhat different problem from reconstructing the behaviour of earlier hominids. Given their large brain size and probable close relationship to modern humans, we are compelled to consider archaic *H. sapiens* behaviour from the perspective of what we know about the behaviour of contemporary humans. Unfortunately, the material culture of archaic *H. sapiens* doesn't provide a comprehensive rendering of late Middle Pleistocene behaviour, but archaeological excavations at many sites in the Old World dating from 150 000 to 500 000 years ago indicate this was a period of evolutionary, although perhaps not revolutionary, change in behaviour.

STONE TOOLS

Stone tool types and distributions that characterized the Early Pleistocene were still present in the Middle Pleistocene. In Africa and Europe, where the Acheulean was well represented, Acheulean traditions—including production of bifacial hand axes—continued until about 150 000 years ago. In China, where hand axes were never associated with *H. erectus,* archaic *H. sapiens* are found in association with simple flake tools and cores.

In the Middle Pleistocene, **Middle Palaeolithic (Middle Stone Age)** industries that used *prepared core* technologies developed. Prepared core technologies require that the tool maker modify the original core by a number of flake removal steps in order to prepare it to produce a flake of a prescribed size and shape. Although wasteful of raw material, prepared core technology makes it possible to produce consistently a specific tool type, the so-called *Mousterian* point. Such preparation in pursuit of a particular flake indicates increasing forethought and abstract thinking. In addition to prepared cores, Middle Palaeolithic industries also used other flaking methods, characterized by a greater prevalence of soft hammer techniques (in which materials such as bone, antlers, or limestone were used as hammerstones), more retouched tools, and a larger variety of possibly stylized tool shapes. The advantage of Middle Palaeolithic industries, beyond the predictability of flake size and shape, is that from a given amount of raw material they produce more cutting surface than Early Palaeolithic techniques. Once these tool types appeared in the late Middle Pleistocene, no new tool types were introduced until the Late Pleistocene.

TOOLS FROM ORGANIC MATERIALS

Based on the behaviour of living nonhuman primates and humans, we assume that hominids also used tools made from organic materials that would rarely be preserved in the archaeological record. Chimpanzees fashion tools from twigs and leaves, and it is likely that early hominids did as well. Although modified bone or antler tools are absent from the archaic *H. sapiens* archaeological record, there is indirect evidence, from flake scars on stone, that these items were used as soft hammers to produce stone tools (Stringer et al., 1998).

Until recently, there was no direct evidence of wooden tool use either; however, as described at the beginning of this chapter, in 1997 archaeologist Hartmut Thieme announced the discovery of three javelin-like wooden spears and a throwing stick, along with three other worked branches, recovered from excavations in an open pit coal mine in Schöningen, Germany. They were dated to 400 000 years ago. The spears, made from the trunks of trees, were 1.82 to 2.30 metres (5.9 to 7.5 ft) long and exhibit a high degree of worksmanship. They were found in close association with numerous faunal remains, and Thieme argued that the context of wooden spears with the remains of prey was evidence of large game hunting. The

Middle Palaeolithic (Middle Stone Age) Stone tool industries that used prepared core technologies.

three worked branches may have formed the handles of stone–wood composite tools. These discoveries establish that wooden tools probably were an important part of the toolkit of archaic *H. sapiens*.

BIG GAME HUNTING

In Chapter 12 we discussed the debate about hunting or scavenging in the lives of past hominid species. In the 1960s and early 1970s, several Middle Pleistocene archaeological sites were interpreted as demonstrating that archaic *H. sapiens* were capable of big game hunting (Figure 13.6). There is little doubt that big game hunting would have been advantageous for some archaic *H. sapiens* occupying northern latitudes in Europe or Asia because there would have been a seasonal dependence on animal food and the ability to hunt big game would have made it easier to expand into colder areas.

Excavations at two sites in the 1990s provide increasing evidence in support of the hypothesis that Middle Pleistocene hominids hunted big game. The Schöningen spears were found in direct association with the butchered remains of 10 horses and flake tools that could be used to deflesh the carcasses. Although it is impossible to be certain that 400 000 years ago the spears were used to bring down the horses, it seems reasonable to conclude they were made to be thrown at large, living animals.

Excavations at the Boxgrove site in England provide further evidence of big game hunting in the Middle Pleistocene (Stringer et al., 1998; Roberts and Parfitt, 1999). This site has yielded numerous remains of small and large animals in association with stone tools, mostly hand axes. Big game hunting rather than scavenging explains how these animals and tools came to be deposited together because stone tool cut marks always underlay carnivore teeth marks, and butchering marks indicate that eyes and tongues were removed by hominids ahead of bird scavengers. Furthermore, butchered rhinoceroses at the site were all healthy midlife adults with no apparent disease or defect, and a horse scapula (shoulder blade) recovered from the site has a clear projectile wound, a hole about 50 millimetres (2 in) in diameter; it is the kind of wound that spears like those found at Schöningen would produce.

The hunting versus scavenging debate will go on. But the evidence seems to be mounting that archaic *H. sapiens* were capable of bringing down large game and that they did so in a cooperative manner, using Acheulean technology. At this point, however, it seems that these Middle Pleistocene hominids did not have as great an impact on the populations of large game animals as later modern *H. sapiens* had in some regions of the world in the Late Pleistocene. This may indicate that big game hunting occupied a different role in the subsistence strategies of *H. erectus* and archaic *H. sapiens* than it did for anatomically modern *H. sapiens*.

FIGURE 13.6 These elephant remains at Torralba, Spain, are thought to be evidence of big-game hunting by archaic *H. sapiens*.

Fire, Campsites, and Home Sites

Evidence of the use of fire by archaic *H. sapiens* is similar to that for *H. erectus*. No proper hearths have been discovered, although ash deposits and charred bones recovered from a number of sites indicate that fire may have been used by both *H. erectus* and archaic *H. sapiens*. Archaic *H. sapiens* did not make a particularly strong impact on the landscape. Although it is reasonable to assume that they had campsites and home bases, there are few signs of them in the archaeological record; no Middle Pleistocene postholes or storage pits have been found, for example. The use of caves as shelter was also limited. Although it has been claimed that there is evidence of Acheulean "beach huts" at the site of Terra Amata in the South of France, disruption of the "living floor" of the site and the somewhat random scatter of bone and stone remains make this interpretation difficult to accept (Stringer and Gamble, 1993).

Since there is limited value in continuing to review aspects of archaic *H. sapiens* cultural behaviour for which we do not have evidence, let us now move on to a group of hominids who are sometimes classified as archaic *H. sapiens* but who are more commonly known as the Neandertals.

THE NEANDERTALS

The taxonomically informal term *Neandertals* refers to a group of Late Pleistocene fossil hominids whose remains have been recovered from sites dating between 150 000 and 27 000 years ago in Europe, the Near and Middle East, and western Asia. The complete or partial remains of several hundred Neandertal individuals have been discovered (Stringer and Gamble, 1993; Trinkaus, 1995). As you will recall from Chapter 9, this time period is one of extreme oscillations in temperature caused by strong glacial and interglacial cycles, and thus climate is a particularly important variable for understanding the origin and evolution of this group. At the end of their existence Neandertals and anatomically modern *H. sapiens* overlap in time and space. How they share the landscape, and indeed the relationships between them, are points of some debate.

Scientists disagree as to whether Neandertals should be considered a species within the genus *Homo* (*H. neanderthalensis*) or a subspecies within *H. sapiens* (*H. s. neanderthalensis*). As was the case for archaic *H. sapiens*, choosing a taxonomic name for the Neandertals depends on how we define a species and on the phylogenetic model for the emergence of anatomically modern *H. sapiens* to which we subscribe. At this point, there is no consensus in the field on these issues, so there is no consensus on a formal name for the Neandertals. There is little disagreement, however, that "classic Neandertals" are an anatomically distinct group of hominids that lived during a short period of time and occupied a circumscribed portion of the Old World.

Geographic and Temporal Distribution

The largest number of Neandertal sites, including the oldest (about 150 000 years ago) and the youngest (about 30 000 to 27 000 years ago), are located in western Europe (Figure 13.7), but the Neandertal range extends into central Asia, the Near East (Iraq, Israel, and Syria). In addition to fossil-bearing localities, archaeological sites of the same ages span the entire region, telling us about site distribution and Neandertal movements relative to time and climate.

Most Neandertal fossils are found in caves, indicating extensive use of these areas as living sites. However, most Middle Palaeolithic archaeological sites are open air localities. Cave use results in better preservation of remains and thus a better fossil record for Neandertals than for earlier hominids.

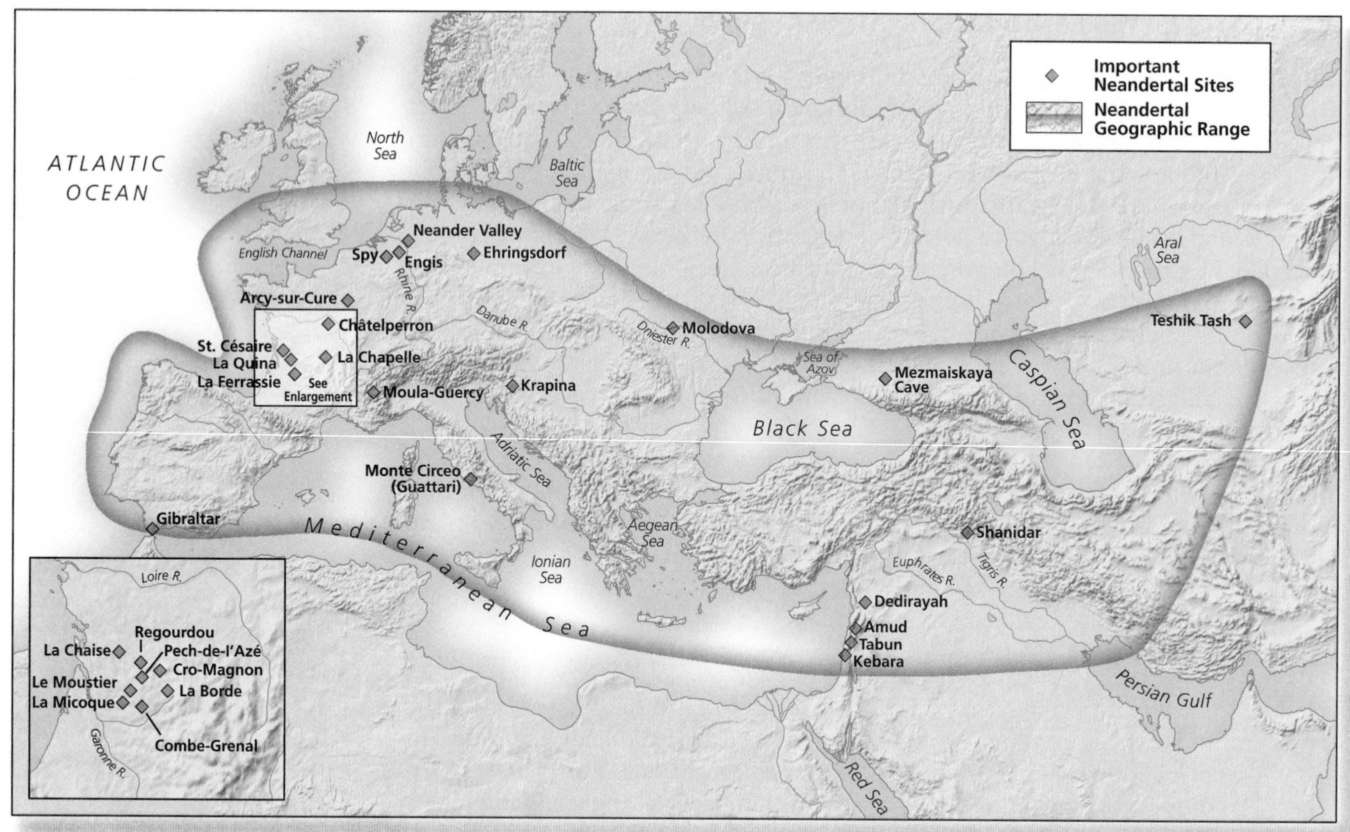

FIGURE 13.7 Distribution of Neandertal sites in Europe and the Near and Middle East.

HISTORY OF NEANDERTAL DISCOVERY

From the mid-1800s until the 1930s Neandertals were the core of the hominid fossil record. In the popular imagination, "Neandertal" and "caveman" have become synonyms, but as the best-known representative of our evolutionary past, Neandertals have also become the focus of negative portrayals and feelings (Box 13.1). Ideas about progress along with anxiety about our animal origins cast the Neandertal in the loser's role in the evolutionary game.

The first Neandertal discovered was found at the Engis cave site in Belgium in 1830 and the second was found in the British territory of Gibraltar on the southern coast of Spain in 1848. The significance of these finds was not appreciated at the time of their discovery, however, and it was not until 1856 that the original Neandertal specimen (for which the group was named) was identified. The Neandertal bones were found in a limestone quarry in the Neander Valley (in German, *Neandertal*—or *Neanderthal* prior to the German spelling reform of 1996) near Düsseldorf. The owner of the quarry saw large bones in the deposit, and thinking that they were from cave bears, contacted a local schoolteacher and natural historian. The teacher identified the remains as human and contacted anatomist Professor Herman Schaafhausen, who led the scientific analysis of the discovery. The Neandertal remains consist of a skullcap and partial skeleton, including several long bones, part of the pelvis, and the right shoulder (Figure 13.8).

Professor Schaafhausen presented his initial analyses of the Neandertal remains in 1857, noting the long and low shape of the skullcap, the large browridges, and the development of an **occipital bun**. All these distinguished this specimen from modern humans. Furthermore, the postcranial bones were very robust and marked with ridges for the attachment of large muscles, and the ribs were rounded,

occipital bun A backward-projecting bulge on the occipital part of the skull.

Box 13.1 Neandertal Image Makeovers

It is definitely not a compliment to be called a Neandertal, and most of us are familiar with the stereotype of the brutish caveman. Although the origins of the stereotype have their roots in early negative portrayals of Neandertals presented by scientists, it is safe to say that the scientific appraisal of Neandertals over the past several decades has been far more positive than negative, despite debates about their status vis-à-vis anatomically modern *H. sapiens*. So why does the negative connotation of Neandertals remain in the popular culture?

Erik Trinkaus and Pat Shipman (1992) have chronicled how popular and scientific images of Neandertals have changed over the years. There seems to be ambivalence about Neandertals, especially as represented in popular media, which emerges from a pervasive unease fuelled by the very existence of Neandertals in our family tree. Trinkaus and Shipman write (pp. 406–407), "They [historical Neandertal images] testify to an ongoing struggle between our willingness to accept Neandertals as close relatives and yet our abhorrence at having anything so potentially inhuman so close at hand. It is the age-old struggle between the godlike and the bestial in humans restated."

The oldest illustration of a Neandertal that Trinkaus and Shipman could track down was from a magazine article published in 1873. This picture of a Neandertal couple—the woman's portrayal constitutes a stereotype of Victorian notions of female passivity—and their dogs has an almost romantic quality. The Neandertal male is portrayed as a kind of "noble savage," ready to meet head-on anything that might appear at the mouth of their cave to challenge them. Clearly, this view of Neandertal men at least is not wholly negative or bestial.

The discovery of the French La Chapelle-aux-Saints Neandertal led to reconstructions of Neandertals in the popular press that were clearly not of the noble savage type. Instead, an image from a popular French publication (1909) reveals a feral and beastly Neandertal who is very unlike a modern human (Figure A). Not long after this, the analysis of the French Neandertal remains by Marcellin Boule led to reconstructions that depicted Neandertals not necessarily as beastly but as stooped and hulking. Their physicality was emphasized over their cognition.

In scientific circles, a different view of Neandertals emerged as early as the 1930s. Anthropologist Carleton Coon produced a drawing of a Neandertal dressed in modern clothing, making the point that a Neandertal could ride on the New York subway with little notice if he were dressed correctly and given a good shave. And yet a 1950s horror movie, *The Neanderthal Man*, indicates that the more beastly view was easier to sell to the movie-going public.

Popular views of Neandertals reflect not only deep-seated tensions about the conflict between humanity and bestiality, as Trinkaus and Shipman suggest, but also feelings about race and racial inferiority and superiority. After all, humans have a long history of considering those who do not come from their own particular group as being something less than human, even when they quite obviously are. In his novel *Dance of the Tiger*, which dramatizes the demise of the Neandertals in northern Europe some 40 000 years ago, noted palaeontologist Björn Kurtèn makes a point of depicting the Neandertals as light-skinned and destined to be replaced by darker-skinned modern humans from the south. Although these skin colour assignments are justifiable based on scientific grounds, from a literary standpoint it is obvious that Kurten was using race as a device to make an ancient species-level conflict more poignant for twentieth-century readers.

FIGURE A Historical reconstruction of Neandertals.

indicating a barrel-chested individual. One of the bones of the lower left arm (the ulna) had clearly been broken and healed awkwardly; it is likely that the arm was not usable in life, and it showed some signs of atrophy due to disuse. However, Schaafhausen concluded that the left arm was the only pathological aspect of the skeleton and that otherwise it reflected the normal development of a race of men who lived in Europe long before the Romans or Celts.

The initial reception of Schaafhausen's analysis was decidedly mixed. Some critics argued that the remains were more apelike, athough the cranial capacity clearly exceeded that of any ape and was in the human range, and the postcranial skeleton, though robust, was essentially human. Others came up with a variety of arguments against the hypothesis that the Neandertal remains represented a

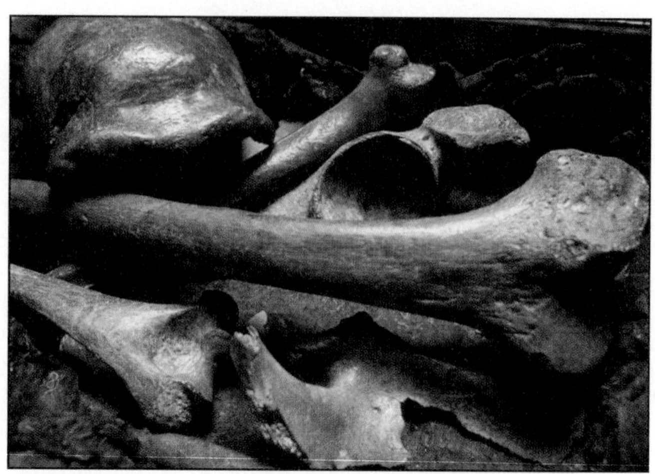

FIGURE 13.8 Skullcap and partial skeleton of the Neandertal remains discovered in 1856.

different and extinct kind of human, some considering the Neandertal specimen to be an unfortunate modern individual who suffered from a variety of pathological conditions, thus explaining his unusual morphology; the obviously injured left arm lent credence to this position.

Arguments that the Neandertal specimen represented only a diseased modern human rather than a distinct fossil ancestor lost force as additional Neandertals were discovered at sites throughout Europe. By 1915, they had been found at sites in Germany, Spain, Belgium, Croatia, and France. In the 1920s and 1930s, they were discovered in sites in the Middle East and as far as Uzbekistan in central Asia. We now have the remains of hundreds of Neandertal individuals recovered from dozens of sites.

Although the original cave where the bones were found no longer exists, the deposits from the cave were found through study of the archives of the mining company, and more than 140 years after they were initially removed (Schmitz et al., 2002), they yielded additional bones and artifacts, which indicate that there were at least three individuals in the cave. Almost unbelievably, additional remains of the original Neandertal specimen were discovered. This re-excavation allowed dating of the finds for the first time, giving them an age of 40 000 years.

Besides modern humans, Neandertals are by far the most thoroughly represented hominids in the fossil record. Given the large number of Neandertal remains available, and a relative abundance of subadult remains, the Neandertals are the only fossil hominid group for which detailed studies on growth and development have been made and Neandertals seem to show, for the first time in hominid evolution, growth patterns similar to our own (Figure 13.9). Other population-level variables that are impossible to realistically examine in earlier hominids can be better assessed in Neandertal remains. But this abundance of information does not mean there is consensus on who exactly the Neandertals were.

NEANDERTAL ANATOMY: BUILT FOR THE COLD

Neandertals possess some derived features that are not present in either anatomically modern humans or archaic *H. sapiens* (Figure 13.10 and Figure 13.11). Therefore, many scientists think that they represent a unique evolutionary trajectory in the context of Middle and Late Pleistocene hominid evolution. Some of their derived features seem to be anticipated by the anatomy of some archaic *H. sapiens,* especially those from Sima de los Huesos, perhaps suggesting that Neandertals descended from these populations.

Although the Neandertal vault is long and low, its size and shape are quite different from that of *H. erectus.* The Neandertal cranium is much larger than that of *H. erectus;* presumed females have an average cranial capacity of 1300 cc and

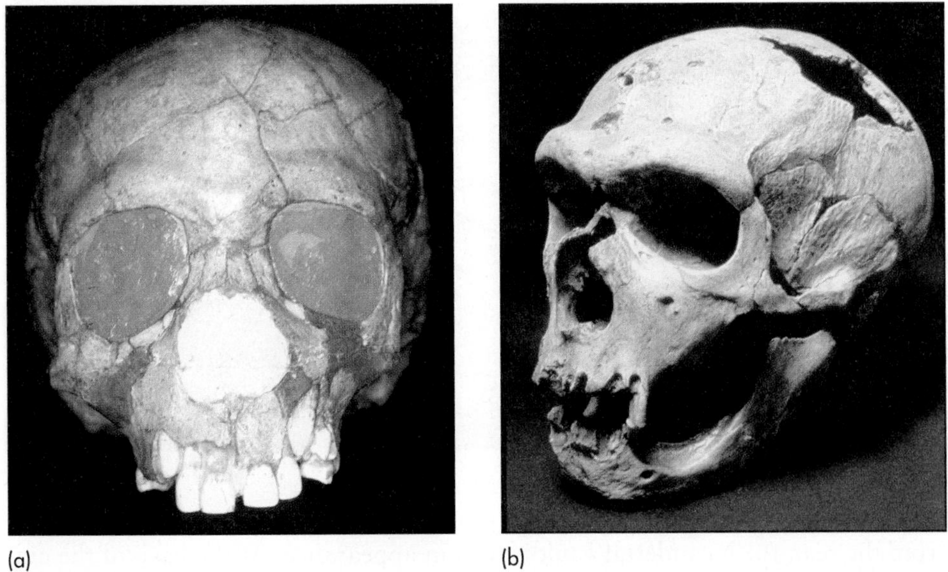

FIGURE 13.9 Neandertal development and aging. (a) Remains of a child from Teshik Tash. (b) The "Old Man" from La Chapelle.

presumed males an average of 1600 cc. Both figures exceed the averages seen in their modern human or *H. erectus* counterparts. Research on Neandertal brains (as studied from the impressions the brain made on the inside of the skull) suggests they were fully modern in their organization and that the large size of the brain was a function of large body size and adaptation to the cold environments in which they evolved (Holloway, 1984).

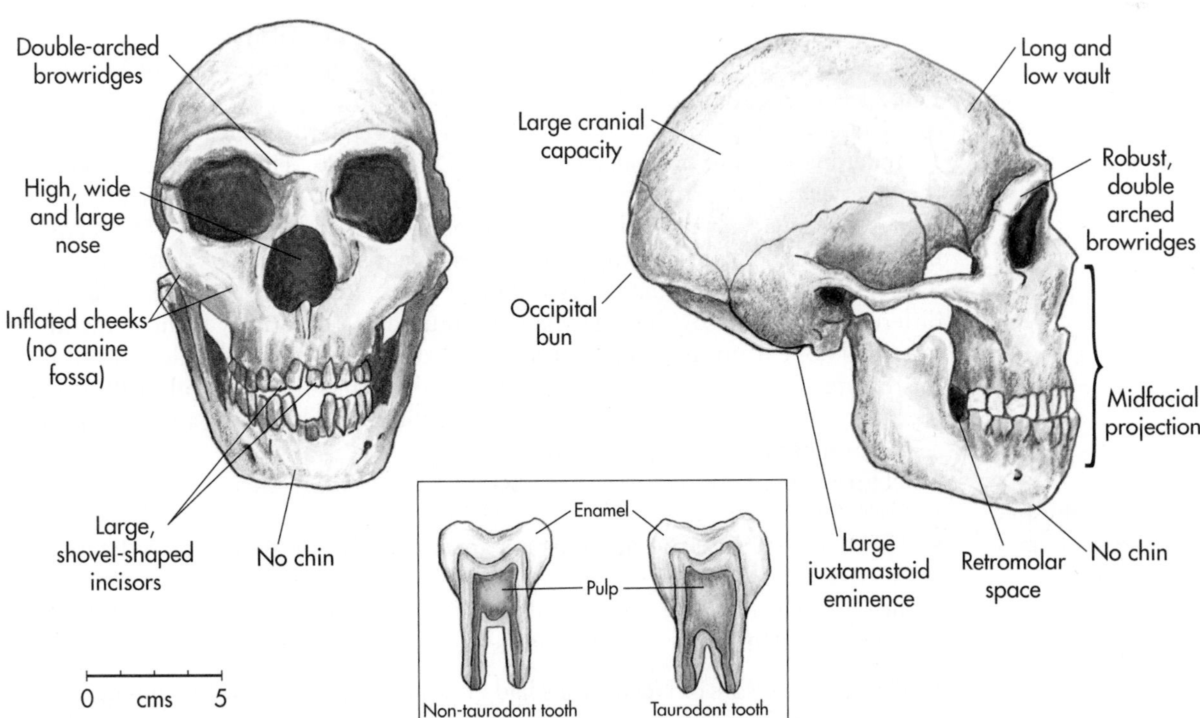

FIGURE 13.10 The Neandertal skull and teeth. Neandertals have taurodont molars.

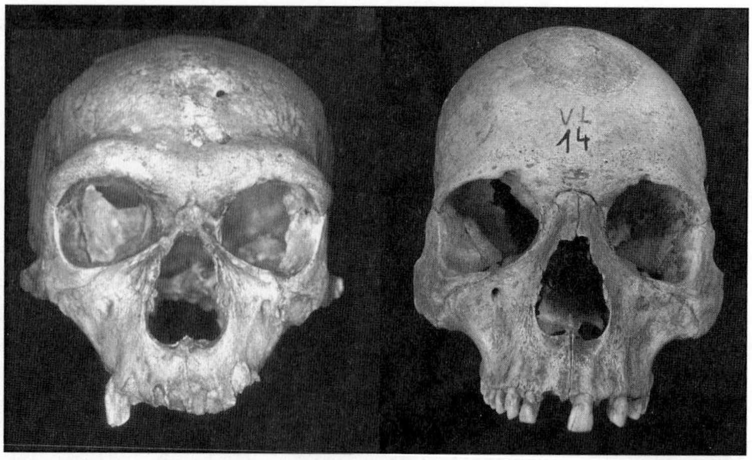

FIGURE 13.11 The faces of Neandertals (left) and anatomically modern *H. sapiens* (right) display anatomical differences including a double-arched brow and absence of a canine fossa in Neandertals.

In contrast to the pentagonal shape of the *H. erectus* cranial vault when viewed from the rear, the Neandertal vault is oval in appearance. At the back of the cranium the occipital bone bulges posteriorly, forming the occipital bun. The **mastoid process** in Neandertals is smaller than in modern humans, but a ridge of bone just next to it, the **juxtamastoid eminence**, is larger than the mastoid process.

The face of the Neandertals also differs from those of *H. erectus* and modern humans. Among the most important of the derived characters of the Neandertals is their midfacial prognathism (Figure 13.11). The middle part of the face, around the nose, projects strongly anteriorly, and the cheek region is placed far posteriorly, with an even grade between the two. It is almost as if someone has grabbed the Neandertal nose and pulled it away from the cheeks, forming a smooth transition from cheek to nose. Therefore, the cheeks of Neandertals are often described as "swept back." Like earlier hominids, Neandertals show no development of a chin.

Although these features are striking compared with modern humans, Erik Trinkaus (2003) points out that the large faces of Neandertals reflect continuation of a trend seen in archaic *H. sapiens;* thus, modern humans should be thought of as having small faces. Similarly, the large nose size of the Neandertals again reflects well-established evolutionary trends observed in a wide range of Middle and Late Pleistocene hominids (Franciscus, 1999, 2003).

There are also important differences between the inner ear anatomy of Neandertals and that of modern humans and *H. erectus.* The semicircular canals of the inner ear assist in maintaining balance, but there is variation in their structure even between closely related species. Although modern humans and *H. erectus* do not differ in inner ear anatomy, three-dimensional imaging shows that Neandertals have a different and probably derived inner ear anatomy (Spoor et al., 2003). The differences are so clear that they have been used to definitively identify the infant temporal bone from Arcy-sur-Cure as a Neandertal, an important identification for this site that had otherwise nondiagnostic fossil remains (Hublin et al., 1996). These clear-cut differences in ear anatomy support the idea that the Neandertals may be a species separate from modern humans.

Three prominent features characterize Neandertal teeth:

- The front teeth show an unusual amount of wear that may indicate that Neandertals used these teeth to hold objects. Cut marks on the teeth further indicate that Neandertals held objects with their front teeth while cutting the objects, perhaps hide or pieces of meat, with stone tools.
- The upper incisors of Neandertals had built-up ridges of enamel on the side nearest the tongue (lingual surface), giving the tooth a *shovel-shaped* appearance. Shovel-shaped incisors generally are considered to provide greater resistance to wear.

mastoid process A protrusion from the temporal bone of the skull located behind the ear.

juxtamastoid eminence A ridge of bone next to the mastoid process; in Neandertals, it is larger than the mastoid process itself.

- The molar teeth of Neandertals had expanded pulp cavities and fused roots, a feature known as **taurodontism**. Taurodont teeth can sustain more wear than non-taurodont teeth because they maintain a broader base for wear after the enamel of the crown has been worn away. Both taurodont molars and shovel-shaped incisors are found in modern human populations at various frequencies.

Many have speculated about why Neandertals had such prognathic faces and large noses. A popular idea is that the nose warmed cold air before it reached the respiratory system and brain. Among modern humans, however, cold-dwelling populations tend to have long and narrow noses to restrict cold airflow to the brain, whereas broad noses are found in more tropical climates and facilitate heat dissipation (Stringer and Gamble, 1993). Others argue that the prognathic midface (and the large nose associated with it) helps dissipate heavy bite loads on the anterior dentition. However, in animals and hominids that produce large bite forces, the face typically is retracted, not prognathic, and Neandertal muscle forces may not have been much greater than in modern human fossils that have very different facial morphologies (Antón, 1996). No convincing argument for an adaptive function for the large Neandertal face and nose has yet to be generally accepted, and it may be that Neandertal facial morphology results from a variety of phylogenetic trends or evolutionary forces. In particular, genetic isolation in glacial environments may have produced the Neandertal face via genetic drift from an already prognathic ancestor, such as the Sima de los Huesos specimens.

The postcranial skeleton of the Neandertals was massive compared with that of modern humans, although Neandertals were on average shorter than Late Pleistocene humans (Figure 13.12). The chest was barrel-shaped and the limbs, especially the forearm and shin, were short. These characteristics are consistent with a body designed to conserve heat in a cold climate (see Bergman's and Allen's rules in Chapter 6), and Neandertals have been described as having "hyper-polar" bodies (Holliday, 1995). The long bones and major joints were all larger and more robust than those found in modern humans, features that Neandertals may have shared with earlier hominids and that indicate a physically demanding lifestyle. Neandertal males are estimated to have been on average 169 centimetres (5 ft 6.5 in) in height, with a weight of 65 kilograms (143 lb), whereas females were 160 centimetres (5 ft 3 in) and 50 kilograms (110 lb) (Stringer and Gamble, 1993).

The Neandertal skeleton shows evidence of very heavy muscle markings, indicating that they had very large, powerful muscles. Erik Trinkaus suggests that this powerful build indicated high levels and possibly even long hours of physically difficult activity. The energetic costs of such activity have been estimated by Mark Sorenson and Bill Leonard (2001), who suggest that physically active Neandertals would have had daily energy needs much higher than those of modern human hunter-gatherers and more similar to those of trained athletes or subsistence farmers.

Health and Disease

The history of Neandertal research has been strongly influenced by the recognition and interpretation of pathological conditions in bone. Recall that the type specimen from the Neander Valley was at the centre of an argument over whether it was a pathological human or a distinct species or subspecies. For many years the common perception of Neandertals as primitive, shuffling creatures came from reconstructions based on a Neandertal skeleton from La Chapelle, France. The "Old Man" of La Chapelle-aux-Saints was found buried in a small cave in the Dordogne region of France and dates to about 40 000 years ago. The skeleton is clearly that of an older male, although in this context *old* could mean about 40 years of age. He suffered from numerous pathological conditions: a deformation in the pelvis, a crushed toe, severe arthritis in several of the vertebrae, and a

taurodontism Molar teeth that have expanded pulp cavities and fused roots.

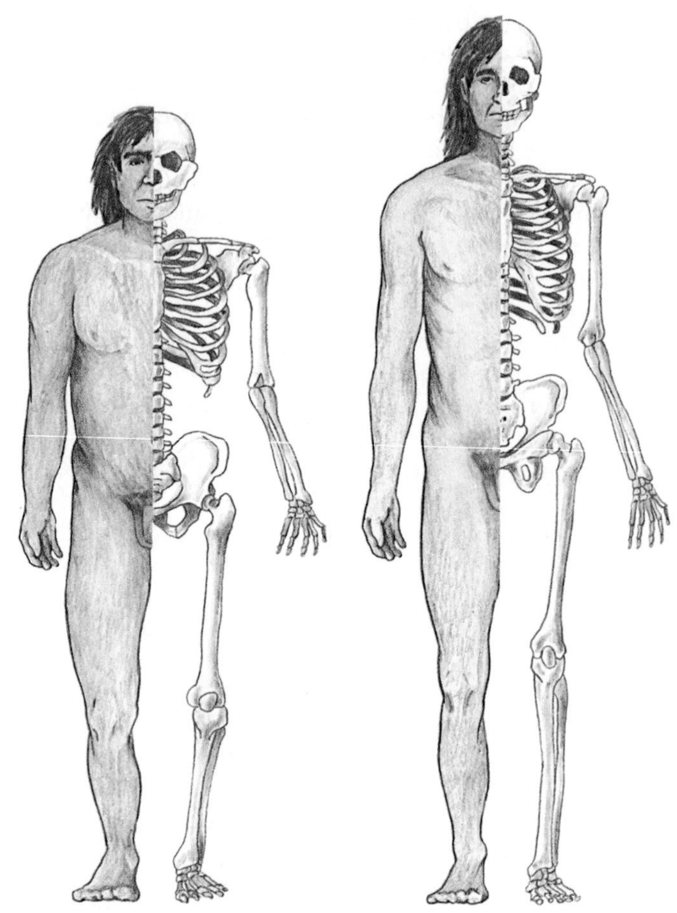

FIGURE 13.12 Neandertals (left) were much more heavily built than anatomically modern humans.

broken rib sustained not long before death. He was missing many teeth, and the mandible and maxilla showed a significant amount of bone loss (Figure 13.9).

The Old Man was portrayed as having a stooped posture and a shuffling gait, far from the upright stride of modern humans, an interpretation of the skeleton that may have been biased by preconceptions about the "primitive" Neandertals. This interpretation of the Old Man of La Chapelle-aux-Saints was very influential and formed the scientific basis for the negative image of Neandertals for decades.

Neandertal skeletons provide abundant evidence of traumatic injuries. In fact, so many Neandertals exhibit healed fractures that their cause has been sought. Some scientists believe the fractures, especially the high incidence of head and neck fractures, indicate that Neandertals were routinely getting close to dangerous prey while hunting (Berger and Trinkaus, 1995). Others see regional differences in fracture frequency and suggest that fracture rates may vary by region according to the difficulty of the substrate, with more rugged terrain and activity leading to greater fracture rates.

NEANDERTAL DNA

In the late 1990s, the original Neandertal remains again came to the attention of the scientific world when it was announced that DNA from this specimen had been successfully extracted, amplified, and sequenced (Krings et al., 1997). DNA from the recently discovered Mesmaiskaya subadult Neandertal specimens has also been extracted and analyzed (Schmitz et al., 2002). Attempts to extract DNA from fossils this old (hominids or other animals) are often unsuccessful, but the cold climate in which the Neandertals lived may have helped to preserve their DNA. Neandertal DNA appears to be quite different from that of living peoples, and we discuss the phylogenetic implications of this difference in the next chapter.

NEANDERTAL BEHAVIOUR

Abundant fossil and archaeological remains the Neandertals left behind should make reconstructing their past life ways and behaviour straightforward. Unfortunately, however, when we reconstruct past human behaviour based on the archaeological record, we can only make inferences based on direct observation of living humans. We can be fairly certain that modern humans do not provide a particularly good model for Neandertal behaviour, but we do not know how bad the fit is. Take something as fundamental to human behaviour as language. It is not unreasonable to assume that the Neandertals possessed some fairly sophisticated form of spoken communication, but how did it compare to language in its ability to transmit ideas and information? The Neandertals' large brains indicate that they were among the most cognitively sophisticated species that have ever lived, but what exactly did they do with these abilities?

MATERIAL CULTURE

Most Neandertal fossils have been found in association with the Middle Palaeolithic tool industry. In general, this tool industry represents an "evolutionary" rather than a "revolutionary" advance on past tool cultures. The prepared core techniques are more fully exploited, and there is a greater reliance on small, flaked tools than in Acheulean industries. However, there is systematic variation in tool complexity. For example, the late Neandertals of Mezmaiskaya Cave possessed a clear Middle Palaeolithic technology, but they made extensive use of bifaces, a feature more commonly associated with the Acheulean. Likewise, both early Neandertals and the contemporaneous anatomically modern humans are associated with Mousterian tools. This indicates that there is no reason to expect that stone tool traditions will correlate with anatomical differences among hominids.

All later anatomically modern humans and a few later Neandertals are found with tools from the **Upper Palaeolithic (Later Stone Age)**. Upper Palaeolithic industries are characterized by the development of blade-based technology (Figure 13.13). **Blades** are flakes that are twice as long as they are wide. In addition, Upper Palaeolithic technologies use more refined flaking techniques, and an increase in the variety of flaked tools has long been considered the exclusive product of anatomically modern *Homo sapiens*.

Late Neandertals from France are associated with tools from an Upper Palaeolithic industry, the **Châtelperronian** (Hublin et al., 1996), which demonstrates that Neandertals were capable of producing Upper Palaeolithic technology, regardless of whether it was a completely Neandertal invention or an adoption of a modern human production technique.

At some archaeological sites we find Châtelperronian and another Upper Palaeolithic industry, the *Aurignacian* (which is associated with modern humans), interstratified through time in the site as if the groups were taking turns using the area. Unfortunately, there are no hominid remains at those sites. Given that most Neandertals produced Middle Palaeolithic tools and only a few, late Neandertals produced Upper Palaeolithic tools, this technology may have been borrowed from contemporaneous anatomically modern human groups.

The development of bone tools is a prominent feature of later Upper Palaeolithic industries, but they are largely absent from Middle Palaeolithic assemblages. Although there have been no wood tool discoveries directly associated with Neandertal remains, small Mousterian points probably were hafted to wooden shafts to form spears or lances.

Upper Palaeolithic (Later Stone Age) Stone tool industries that are characterized by the development of blade-based technology.

blades Flakes that are twice as long as they are wide.

Châtelperronian An Upper Palaeolithic tool industry that has been found in association with later Neandertals.

FIGURE 13.13 Upper Palaeolithic stone tools include blade-based tools as seen here being produced from a blade core.

Coping with Cold

Neandertal bodies are typical of cold-adapted populations, and their archaeological sites also give indications of behavioural adaptations to cold. One way to cope with cold is to avoid it, either by seasonally migrating over long distances or by moving as overall conditions get colder (or warmer) during all parts of the year. Middle Palaeolithic archaeological deposits indicate that Neandertals were a mobile people occupying sites for short periods of time and seasonally; in general, their sites served as temporary camping, hunting, or food processing locales. But their mobility seems to have been limited: Most of the raw materials for stone tools came from within 5 kilometres (3 mi) of where they were found, with a maximum distance of 80 kilometres (Stringer and Gamble, 1993). Thus Neandertal mobility was not of a large enough scale to avoid seasonal cold altogether but rather probably reflected local movements necessary to exploit scarce resources within a small area.

Another way to cope with cold is through the use of fire. Charcoal deposits and ashy dump spots are commonly found in Middle Palaeolithic sites, indicating that Neandertals used fire. True hearths are rare, but they have been identified in a 60 000-year-old Middle Palaeolithic site in Portugal.

It is also very likely that Neandertals used animal skins and hides to protect themselves from the cold. No tools that could be used as sewing implements, such as awls or bone needles, have been found in the Middle Palaeolithic; if they did use hides, it is unlikely that they were sewn. In Molodova in the Ukraine, a Middle Palaeolithic site has yielded a ring of mammoth bones, approximately 5 by 8 metres (15 × 24 ft) in size, which encloses a dense concentration of artifacts, bones, and ash. Although it could be a natural deposition, many scientists believe that this site represents a living space of some kind, a wind-sheltering structure, or perhaps even a tent. It is assumed that the walls of the structure probably were constructed from animal hides. As yet, there is no evidence of more substantial Neandertal structures.

As their cold-adapted bodies attest, Neandertals were able to function in more wintry climates than earlier hominids. On the other hand, the distribution of Neandertal sites through time indicates that they did migrate in and out of areas over longer periods of time depending on whether glacial or interglacial conditions persisted. For example, across the eastern Russian plain Neandertal sites are found far north only during interglacial periods and are located further south during glacial periods, as if the Neandertals were retreating in the face of the harsh glacial climate. And Neandertals never, even during interglacials, occupied as far northerly a latitude as anatomically modern humans eventually did.

Similarly, Neandertals appeared to move south into the Middle East during glacial times, and modern humans occupied the region during warmer interglacials. Five prominent cave sites located in Israel have been the focus of much attention over the years because they possess either Neandertal or anatomically modern fossils. Three of these sites have produced classic Neandertals and two have yielded anatomically modern human fossils. Professor Henry Schwarcz of McMaster University's School of Geography and Earth Sciences applied electron spin resonance (ESR) dating to the question of the ages of the hominid remains and found that a Neandertal burial was younger than the anatomically modern hominids in the area (Schwarcz and Grün, 1992). Many of the dates for the Middle Palaeolithic sites have been obtained by Uranium series and ESR dating: Schwarcz and Professor Jack Rink, also of McMaster, have applied the ESR technique to a variety of materials, including teeth, rock, and flint artifacts.

Neandertals clearly occupied the region for a long time, but the current evidence for occupation by modern-looking humans is more limited. If you accept Neandertals as a separate species, then it is likely that Neandertals and modern humans were alternatively using the region during varying climatic times: Neandertals during cold spells, modern humans during warmer spells. Others argue that Neandertals and modern humans could be representatives of a single, highly variable species. The Middle Eastern hominids as a group would be considered a variant on the classic Neandertal form, and the more modern features seen in some of the specimens would simply reflect local population variation. In a crossroads region (at the intersection of Africa, Europe, and Asia), it might not be surprising that this population would vary more than isolated populations.

HUNTING AND SUBSISTENCE

Chemical analyses of Neandertal bones indicate that they were heavily reliant on meat (Richards et al., 2000). They undoubtedly used all the hunting strategies known by archaic *H. sapiens* and earlier hominids. Different Neandertal sites indicate that they used a variety of subsistence strategies depending on local conditions and the game available in a given area. Although they may have scavenged meat opportunistically, there is little evidence that Neandertals engaged in scavenging on a broad scale (Marean and Assefa, 1999). In general, Neandertals appear to have been competent distance hunters of large game.

It has been argued recently that Neandertals were successful hunters because they engaged in coed hunting, with women's hunting activities closely aligned with those of men, in contrast to the division of labour in subsistence patterns that is seen in modern hunters and foragers and that are thought to characterize the Eurasian Upper Palaeolithic (Kuhn and Stiner, 2006).

CANNIBALISM

Many human cultures have engaged in cannibalism, although it is generally believed that it was typically undertaken in a political or ritualistic context. Because there is little evidence of ritual behaviour in Neandertals, cannibalism has been classified as a kind of specialized subsistence strategy. Evidence of cannibalism can be found in the fragmentary remains from Krapina, Croatia, dated to about 130 000 years ago. Among the thousands of fragmentary hominid bones almost no intact long bones were present at the site, a sign that the bones may have been split open for the marrow within, and many of the bones showed signs of burning. More recent research has definitively established that some of the bones show cut marks as well.

The recently excavated Mousterian cave site of Moula-Guercy in France, dating to about 100 000 years ago, provides an even better case for Neandertal cannibalism (Defleur et al., 1999). Seventy-eight Neandertal bone fragments are mixed in with several hundred animal bone fragments (mostly from red deer) and display numerous cut marks that are consistent with defleshing and butchering patterns (Figure 13.14). All crania and long bones have been broken, presumably to gain access to the brain and marrow. A key piece of evidence indicates that these remains were processed for access to meat rather than for some other purpose: The deer and other faunal remains from the site were treated in the same manner as the hominid remains. Because it is unlikely that the game species were being treated to some sort of mortuary processing that did not involve being eaten, it seems reasonable to conclude that the Neandertals were also being eaten by other Neandertals.

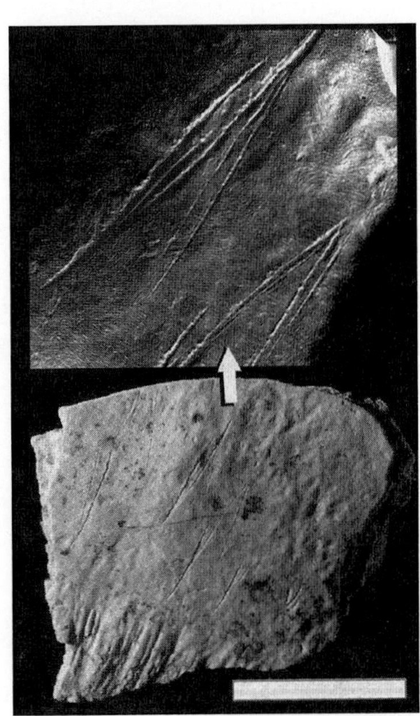

FIGURE 13.14 Cutmarks on Neandertal bone fragments.

BURIALS

Burial of the dead is a traditional practice in many contemporary human cultures. It can be done for different reasons and can be vested with ritual significance. The notion that some Neandertals may have buried their dead goes back to the discovery of the Spy skeletons in Belgium in the 1880s (Stringer et al., 1984).

The two Spy adult skeletons were found complete and fully articulated, suggesting that they may have been intentionally buried in the cave. Further evidence of Neandertal burials came from the site of La Ferrassie in southern France (excavated in the early 1900s), where several adults and subadults, forming a burial complex, were found at a single cave site. Many researchers believe that the assemblage of individuals at the site was not an accidental grouping but indicates deliberate burial or interment.

Later, the idea of Neandertal burial and compassionate Neandertals was further supported by the claim that an individual from the 40 000- to 50 000-year-old Shanidar Cave site in Iraq had been buried and covered in (or on a bed of) wildflowers (Solecki, 1971). A large quantity of wildflower pollen had been found in association with this burial, but there is no certainty that flowers were put there deliberately by Neandertal mourners. The same pollen exists in the region today and could have been blown into the cave.

Since then, numerous Neandertals have been found in caves, and most excavators of these sites believed that they were deliberate burials. A large number of articulated Neandertal skeletons have been recovered *in situ*; many have been found in a flexed position. The sites often are littered with disarticulated animal bones; only the Neandertal bones remain in place, protected from the effects of geology or scavengers.

Although it is not unreasonable to accept that some Neandertals buried their dead, some investigators believe that it is possible to account for the deposition of articulated Neandertal skeletons in caves via natural forces (Gargett, 1989, 1999). One criticism, definitely valid in some cases, is that many Neandertal sites were excavated decades ago, before the development of modern excavation techniques or accurate recordkeeping. Without a clear rendering of the excavation context, it is difficult to assess the status of a claim of deliberate burial. Recent excavators of Neandertal sites, mindful of the need to provide evidence for burial rather than simply assume it, have gone to some effort to prove what was once considered the obvious. Recently excavated Neandertal infants from Amud (Hovers et al., 2000) and Mezmaiskaya Cave (Golovanova et al., 1999) are both claimed to be from deliberate burials, and the context of these discoveries strongly indicates that such small and delicate remains probably were preserved because they were shielded from damage by deliberate burial.

Neandertal burials represent a novel behavioural development of the Middle Palaeolithic. Before that time we may have evidence of mortuary practices in the defleshing of the Bodo cranium and the possibly deliberate deposition of remains in the bone pit of Sima de los Huesos at Atapuereca. But there is no evidence of deliberate burial of archaic *H. sapiens* remains. On the other hand, Neandertal burials are significantly different from the Upper Palaeolithic burials of anatomically modern *H. sapiens* that begin to appear around 40 000 years ago. Neandertals have not been found to be interred with grave goods, objects placed with the corpse at the time of burials. On occasion a stray animal bone or horn has been found in association with a Neandertal burial, but it is very difficult to demonstrate that they were placed there deliberately.

In contrast, grave goods often are found in Upper Palaeolithic burials, sometimes in great abundance. Another difference between Neandertal and Upper Palaeolithic burials is that the Neandertal burials always occur in cave sites, whereas burials at open air sites are common by the late Upper Palaeolithic. Because it is presumed that Neandertals lived and died in open areas as well as in caves, it is apparent that either they did not bury their dead in those regions or, if they did, they did not do so in a way that prevented the disruption of the corpse by other forces.

RITUAL AND SYMBOLIC BEHAVIOUR

Extrapolating from the cultural behaviour of modern humans, it is easy to assume that Neandertal burial indicates some kind of ritualistic belief or significance, but the context of Neandertal burials is equally indicative of "corpse disposal" as it is of ritualized internment (Stringer and Gamble, 1993). It is clear, however, that some Neandertals dedicated a significant amount of time and energy to the burial of the dead, selecting an appropriate site, placing the body in a certain position, and covering the body with a large stone.

If burials cannot be seen as evidence of ritualistic or symbolic behaviour, then there is very little else in the Neandertal archaeological record to indicate such behaviours. A small number of incised bones have been recovered from Mousterian sites, but what these scratches might mean is beyond the scope of scientific inquiry. If Neandertals possessed something like human language, then obviously they were capable of symbolic behaviour because language is reliant on symbolic representation. But there is no direct evidence of this in the archaeological record. The strongest evidence is that of personal adornment items and other engraved or incised items. All these occur late in Neandertal times, with the most secure being 55 000 years old or younger. Even if we accept these intermittent finds as symbolic behaviour in Neandertals, they are qualitatively different from the systematic evidence of such behaviour, including extensive personal adornment, in Upper Palaeolithic sites, as we shall see in Chapter 14.

PHYLOGENETIC AND TAXONOMIC ISSUES: AN OVERVIEW

Our interpretations of taxonomic and phylogenetic relationships between late Middle and Late Pleistocene hominids depend largely on how we view the origins of anatomically modern *H. sapiens*. However, we can have a preliminary discussion based on the archaic *H. sapiens* and Neandertal fossil records.

The labels "archaic *H. sapiens*" and "Neandertal" are not taxonomically formal designations. We use informal labels because there is no consensus as to what the formal labels should be. Archaic *H. sapiens* include a widely distributed group of hominids who lived from about 800 000 to 150 000 years ago (Figure 13.15). *Neandertal* refers to a predominantly European and western Asian group of hominids who lived about 130 000 to 30 000 years ago. Both of these groups possess features that clearly distinguish them from *H. erectus* and anatomically modern *H. sapiens*. Yet many researchers argue either that the differences are not profound enough to warrant species designations or that using such designations would arbitrarily impose separations on a continuous evolutionary lineage and thus be highly misleading (Figure 13.16).

From the "lumper's perspective," the informal, subspecific labels for these groups of hominids provide an acceptable solution to the problem. In the lumper's view, archaic *H. sapiens* and Neandertals were all part of one potentially interbreeding species. Obviously, there was regional variation within the species, and variation across time as well, but lumpers see all the larger-brained hominids of the last half of the Pleistocene as part of a *single evolving species*.

The "splitter's perspective" begins with recognizing the Neandertals as a separate species, *H. neanderthalensis*. Many splitters argue that the distinctive anatomy and limited distribution of the Neandertals indicate a specialized hominid taxon fundamentally different from anatomically modern *H. sapiens*. The species designation means that Neandertals and modern humans did not or could not interbreed or did so very infrequently; it suggests that Neandertals represent an extinct type of hominid, which was ultimately replaced across its entire range by modern humans.

In the splitter's view, archaic *H. sapiens* also gets a species designation, *H. heidelbergensis*. *H. heidelbergensis* is considered a species distinct from *H. erectus* because of anatomical features. In effect, *H. heidelbergensis* becomes the stem species for both Neandertals and anatomically modern *H. sapiens*. In Europe, *H. heidelbergensis* specimens such as Petralona and those from Sima de los Huesos

Figure 13.15 **Hominid Evolution in the Mid-to-Late Pleistocene**

Beginning about 600 000 years ago in Africa, hominids who were somewhat larger-brained than classic *H. erectus* but still cranially robust appeared in Africa, and then later in Europe and Asia. This group is usually referred to as archaic *Homo sapiens* (or by some as *H. heidelbergensis*). In Europe and western Asia, a distinct type of hominid, the Neandertals, appeared about 140 000 years ago. Their antecedents may be represented among the archaic *H. sapiens* specimens of Europe, dating up to 400 000 years ago.

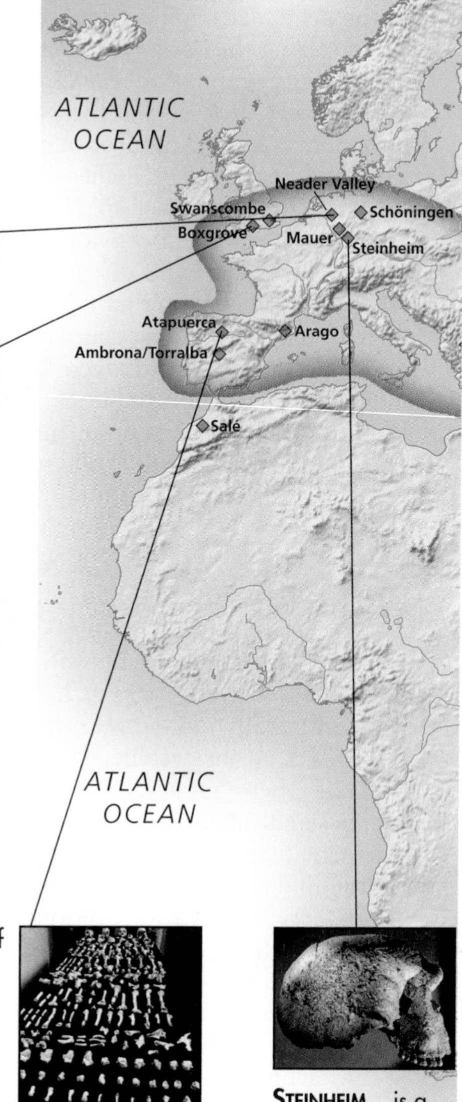

Boxgrove Evidence of big game hunting by archaic *H. sapiens* is hinted by hand axes and deer bones at the Boxgrove site, England.

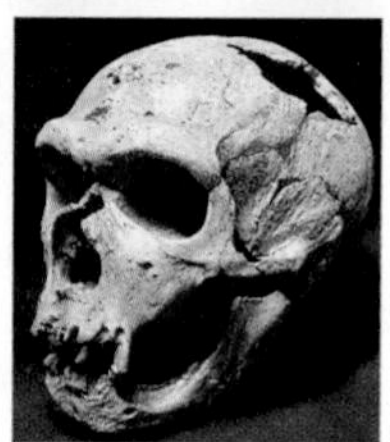

Neandertals Neandertal specimens are numerous enough that we can begin to understand developmental changes across their lifespan.

Atapuerca Remains of more than 30 archaic *H. sapiens* individuals have been found in the *Sima de los Huesos* at Sierra de Atapuerca, Spain.

Steinheim is a possible contemporary of Petralona.

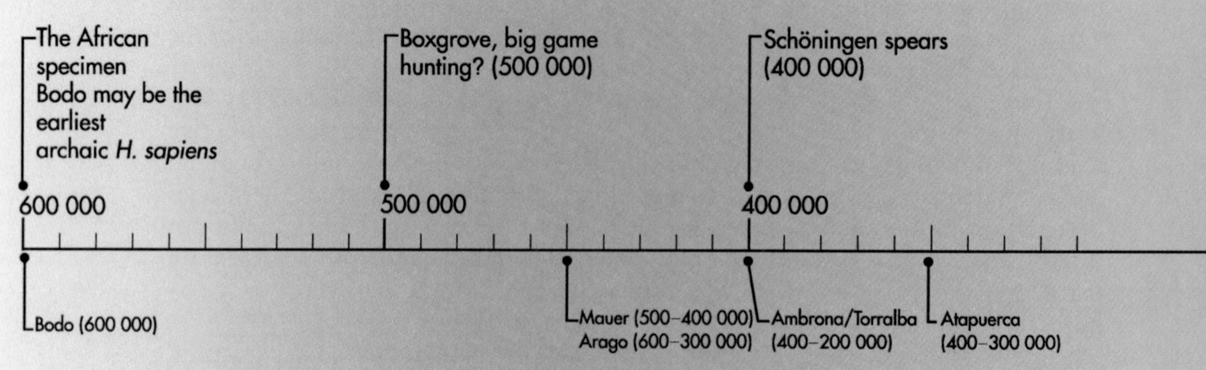

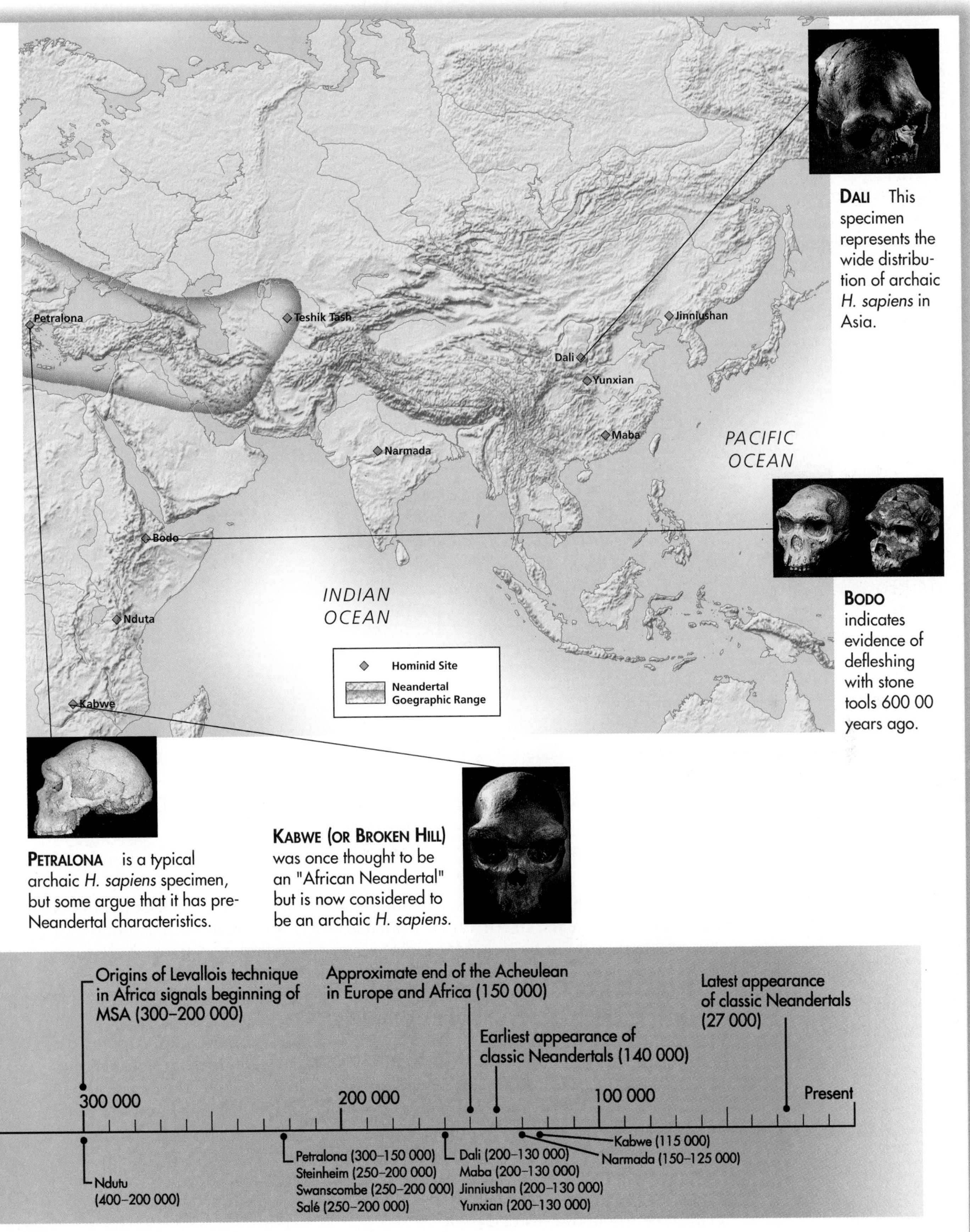

DALI This specimen represents the wide distribution of archaic *H. sapiens* in Asia.

BODO indicates evidence of defleshing with stone tools 600 00 years ago.

PETRALONA is a typical archaic *H. sapiens* specimen, but some argue that it has pre-Neandertal characteristics.

KABWE (OR BROKEN HILL) was once thought to be an "African Neandertal" but is now considered to be an archaic *H. sapiens*.

Origins of Levallois technique in Africa signals beginning of MSA (300–200 000)

Approximate end of the Acheulean in Europe and Africa (150 000)

Earliest appearance of classic Neandertals (140 000)

Latest appearance of classic Neandertals (27 000)

300 000 — 200 000 — 100 000 — Present

Ndutu (400–200 000)

Petralona (300–150 000)
Steinheim (250–200 000)
Swanscombe (250–200 000)
Salé (250–200 000)

Dali (200–130 000)
Maba (200–130 000)
Jinniushan (200–130 000)
Yunxian (200–130 000)

Kabwe (115 000)

Narmada (150–125 000)

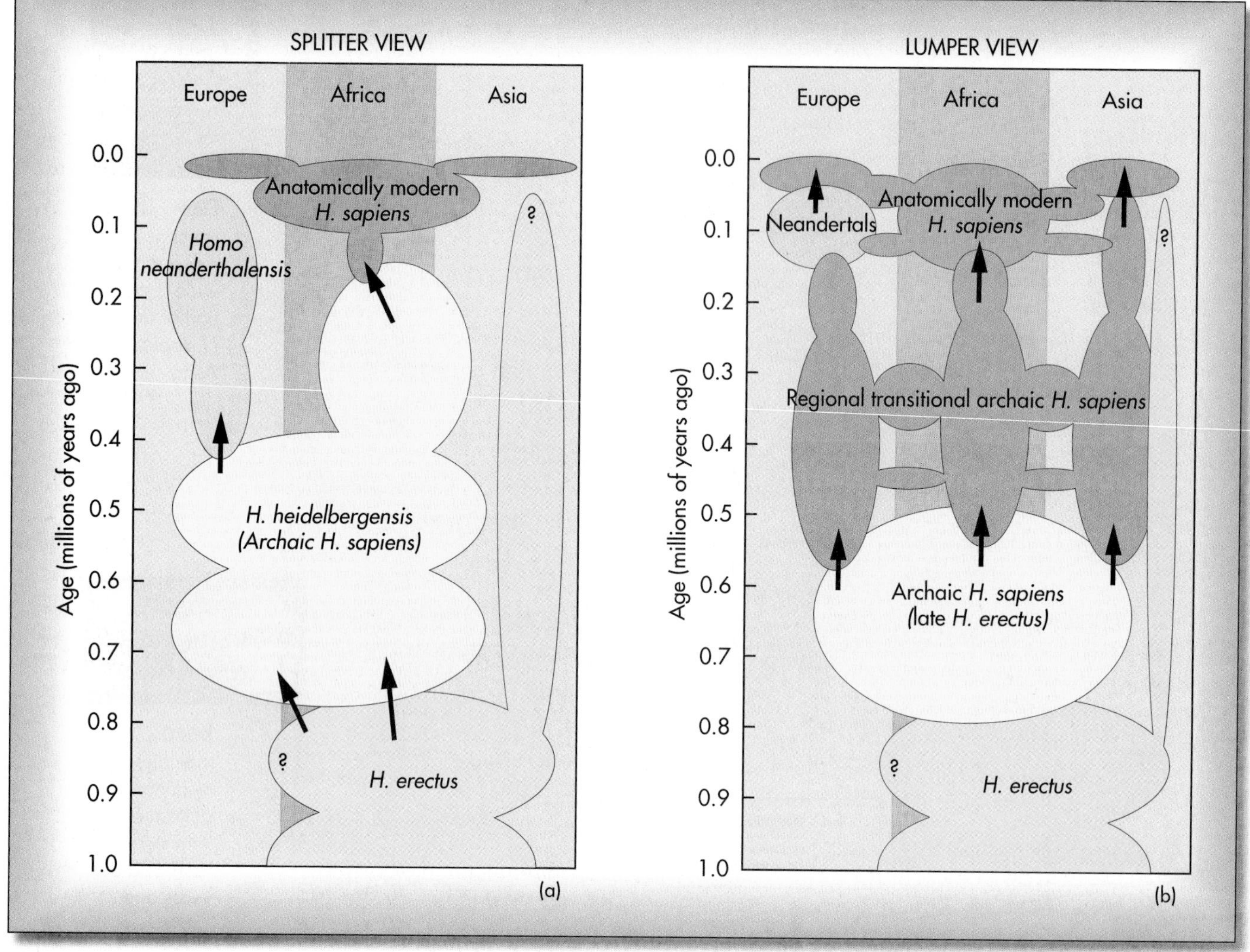

FIGURE 13.16 Two views of the phylogenetic relationship between Neandertals and modern *H. sapiens*. (a) The splitter view. (b) The lumper view.

are seen to be proto-Neandertals, extending the Neandertal lineage back hundreds of thousands of years. In Africa, *H. heidelbergensis* specimens such as Bodo and Kabwe are thought to be early representatives of a population from which anatomically modern *H. sapiens* evolved.

At the same time as Neandertals were living in Europe and western Asia, hominid evolutionary developments were also taking place in other parts of the world, most significantly the evolution of anatomically modern *H. sapiens*. In Chapter 14 we will more fully explore the evolutionary connections between our own species and earlier forms such as Neandertals. As we will see, the debate about the origins of modern humans involves not only palaeontological and archaeological data, but also genetic information derived from contemporary humans and a few fossil specimens. Over the past 20 years, the quest to understand the origins of modern humans has focused on developing a synthesis of sometimes divergent and sometimes convergent molecular and palaeontological perspectives on this critical period in our history.

SUMMARY

1 **What cranial features distinguish archaic *H. sapiens* from anatomically modern *H. sapiens*?**

Archaic *H. sapiens* are much more cranially robust than modern *H. sapiens*, with thicker cranial bones and substantial development of browridges (supraorbital tori). The face, including the jaws and the nasal aperture, tend to be larger in archaic *H. sapiens* than in modern *H. sapiens*. Cranial capacities in archaic H. sapiens range from 1000 to 1400 cc, which places them in the lower half of the modern human range, and the cranial vault is lower and longer.

2 **What cranial features distinguish Neandertals from anatomically modern *H. sapiens*?**

Neandertal crania have double-arched browridges, an occipital bun, and substantial midfacial prognathism. Cranial capacity in Neandertals equals or exceeds that of modern humans, but the shape of the vault is longer and lower, with a maximum cranial width (when viewed from behind) at the midcranium level rather than high on the skull, as it is in modern humans. In rear view the vault is oval shaped. The mastoid eminence is smaller in Neandertals than in modern humans, but the juxtamastoid eminence is larger. The inner ear anatomy of Neandertals is also distinct from that of modern humans. Neandertals were taurodont and had retromolar spaces on their mandibles.

3 **What is the collective significance of sites on Mount Carmel in Israel?**

There are five sites that provide evidence that modern humans and Neandertals lived in the same area but at different times. The earliest site, Tabun (100 000 years ago), was occupied by Neandertals; Skhul and Jebel Qafzeh (90 000 to 110 000 years ago) were occupied by modern humans. Fossils from Kebara (60 000 years ago) and Amud (35 000 to 40 000 years ago) indicate other, later Neandertal occupations. It is possible that Neandertals lived in this area during colder periods, as they were driven southward by glaciers during ice ages, and that anatomically modern humans moved in during warmer interglacials. An alternative explanation is that they are all representatives of a single, highly variable species, located in a region that was subject to a large amount of population movement and gene flow.

4 **Why should we be wary of equating tool industries with specific hominid species or populations, especially during the Middle to Late Pleistocene?**

Although there is some validity to generalizations associating types of hominids with specific tool industries, several counterexamples are available from specific archaeological sites, especially in the later parts of the Pleistocene, to caution us against making too much of these generalizations. For example, at the Mount Carmel sites, modern humans and Neandertals are both found in association with Mousterian tools, and later classic Neandertals are found in association with Upper Palaeolithic tool industries at some sites in Europe (at Saint-Césaire and Arcy-sur-Cure in France). Archaeological associations of Asian hominids cannot be easily fit into tool industry sequences developed for Europe and Africa.

5 **What is *H. heidelbergensis*?**

H. heidelbergensis is a species name used by some researchers to refer to the majority of archaic *H. sapiens* specimens found in Europe and Africa. The type specimen for this species is the Mauer mandible found in Germany in 1907. Many researchers who accept *H. heidelbergensis* as a species also think that Neandertals are a species distinct from anatomically modern humans, *H. neanderthalensis*. *H. heidelbergensis* is seen as the ancestral species to both modern humans (in Africa) and Neandertals (in Europe). Other researchers argue that the archaic *H. sapiens*, Neandertals, and modern humans are all part of a single polytypic species that shows evolutionary change over the course of the later Pleistocene. Thus, they do not accept *H. heidelbergensis* or *H. neanderthalensis* as valid taxa.

CRITICAL THINKING QUESTIONS

1. Besides most wood implements, what other sorts of things do you think are missing in the archaeological record of Middle to Late Pleistocene hominids?
2. Is the label "archaic *H. sapiens*" useful or confusing?
3. What do you think of the "humanity" of Neandertals? In a broader primate context, should they be regarded as just a slightly different kind of human being?

KEY TERMS

midfacial prognathism
Middle Palaeolithic (Middle Stone Age)
occipital bun
mastoid process
juxtamastoid eminence
taurodontism
Upper Palaeolithic (Later Stone Age)
blades
Châtelperronian

SUGGESTED READING

Stringer, Christopher, and Gamble, Clive. (1993). *In Search of the Neanderthals*. Thames and Hudson, New York, NY.

Trinkaus, Erik, and Shipman, Pat. (1993). *The Neandertals: Changing the Image of Mankind*. Knopf, New York, NY.

Wolpoff, Milford, and Caspari, Rachel. (1997). *Race and Human Evolution*. Westview Press, Boulder, CO.

Chapter 14

THE EMERGENCE AND DISPERSAL OF *HOMO SAPIENS*

Chapter Outline

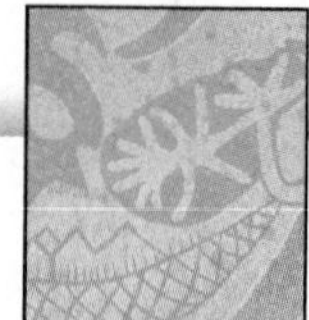

THE YOUNG WOMAN SAT NEXT TO HER MOTHER and a small group of other women near the mouth of the cave. On the other side of the green valley below them rose a distant stretch of mountains. She knew that the pile of soft greenish stone by her side came from those peaks, although she had never been to the spot herself. Her brother and father had brought the stone back from a recent expedition, as they did each year about this time. From the pile she selected one of the oblong pieces of stone that her mother had cut—a blank from which she would fashion a bead—and began rounding one end of it.

AS SHE WORKED SHE LISTENED to the women's stories and watched her mother. Her mother was lovely, she thought, with a high forehead and strong chin, nothing like the women across the valley, with their large faces and forbidding brows. She didn't understand those women when they spoke, although they seemed kind enough.

ONCE THE END OF THE BLANK was rounded, she took another stone and began chipping flakes out of the centre of the blank, first on one side and then on the other. She furrowed her brow as she worked, wrinkling the skin on her high forehead as she noticed that her fingers were stained with the red pigment she had used the previous day, deep in the cave, to spray an outline of her hand on the rock wall. Just as she had only heard about the distant peaks, her brother had only heard about the deepest rooms of the cave where the women undertook their art and ritual.

AN HOUR LATER, the two indentations merged, making a hole through the chunk of stone. Slowly and carefully she enlarged the hole, not wanting to break the piece now that she was so near to finishing. She held the small bead in her palm, rolling it about before she began polishing. Nearly another hour passed before the small bead, lustrous from polishing, was finished and dropped onto a pile of similar beads shaped by the rest of the group. Later the beads would be carefully sewn in rows onto the front of a shirt in the particular sign of their clan. Those signs would represent hundreds of hours of their labour but were critical in signalling their group's membership in a larger network of clans. One day, from one of those clans, would come a mate for her, perhaps food in scarce times, and maybe even other beads, ideas, or information. In the long run, that network would be the difference between their survival and the demise of their heavy-browed neighbours.

Modern human origins are a matter not simply of anatomy but also of behaviour. No matter how cognitively sophisticated our close cousins the Neandertals or archaic *Homo sapiens* were, or how close the size of their brains was to our own, they clearly did not attain a modern human level of technological or intellectual achievement. The bead described in the vignette is not much of an artifact; it is not even a tool. But it provides material evidence of personal decoration and symbolic representation. Such evidence is abundant in the archaeological record of modern humans and all but absent from the records of Neandertals and archaic *H. sapiens*.

In this chapter, we review the three distinct sources of evidence used to reconstruct the critical events surrounding the emergence of modern people. Palaeontological and geological data chart the distribution in time and space of anatomically modern *H. sapiens*. Archaeological data shed light on the changes in behaviour that allowed modern humans to exploit the natural world in a way that would ultimately make us the dominant species on the planet. Genetic data provide information on the web of biological relationships between us and our closest relatives. By synthesizing data from these interrelated realms, biological anthropologists attempt to address the fundamental question of our field: How did human beings evolve?

THE EMERGENCE OF MODERN HUMANS

The emergence of modern humans can be seen anatomically in a combination of cranial features that distinguish us from archaic *H. sapiens* and Neandertals (Chapter 13). To review, these include a gracile skull and postcranial anatomy, limited development of browridges or other cranial superstructures, a rounded cranium with a high maximum cranial breadth and parallel sides, a prominent mastoid process, a retracted face with a canine fossa, small teeth and jaws, and development of an obvious chin (Figure 14.1). Large brain size, however, does not set us apart from archaic *H. sapiens* and the Neandertals. Many Middle and Late Pleistocene hominid specimens possess cranial capacities that are easily within the modern human range (whose average is about 1350 cc), and a number of them exceed the human mean by a substantial amount.

Despite the fact that there is no significant difference in absolute brain size, when we look at the archaeological record associated with modern humans we find evidence of substantial behavioural differences between our close relatives and us. Between 2.5 million and 300 000 years ago the pace of change in stone tool cultures (the Lower Palaeolithic or Early Stone Age) was very slow. With the advent of the Middle Palaeolithic or Middle Stone Age (MSA), many new tool types and techniques were introduced (Ambrose, 2001). However, little change took place during the MSA itself: The same tool types existed at the beginning of the MSA as at the end. In contrast, the Upper Palaeolithic tool assemblages associated with modern humans in some parts of the world are radically different from those of the preceding Middle Palaeolithic, and art and ornamentation, which reflect symbolic thinking, are more heavily represented. The rapid pace of change and the appearance of symbolic behaviour are two of the hallmarks of the Upper

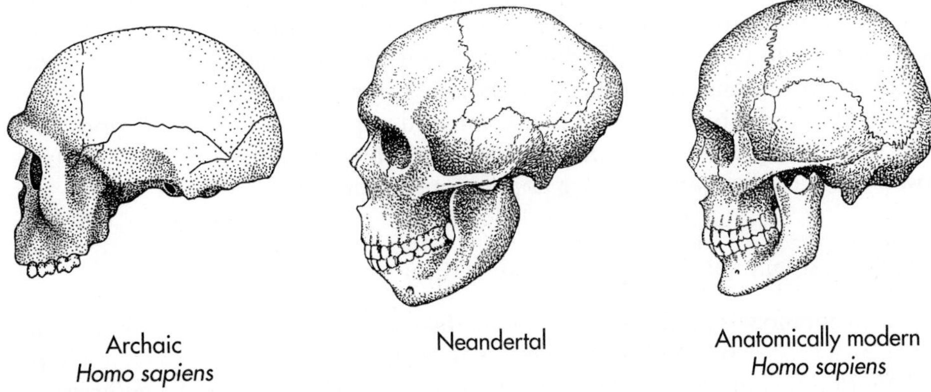

FIGURE 14.1 Variations on a theme: archaic *Homo sapiens*, Neandertal, and anatomically modern *Homo sapiens* skulls.

replacement models
Phylogenetic models that suggest that modern humans evolved in one location and then spread geographically, replacing other earlier hominid populations without or with little admixture.

multiregional models
Phylogenetic models that suggest that modern humans evolved in the context of gene flow among Middle to Late Pleistocene hominid populations from different regions, so there is no single location where modern humans first evolved.

Palaeolithic revolution, which some scientists think occurred with the sudden appearance of anatomically modern humans (Klein and Edgar, 2002). Other scientists think that different aspects of Upper Palaeolithic culture appear at different times during the later MSA, thus indicating a more gradual evolution of behaviourally modern humans (McBrearty and Brooks, 2000).

MODELS OF MODERN HUMAN ORIGINS

Many scientists have attempted to assemble anatomical, behavioural, and genetic data into comprehensive models of the origins of modern humans. In the past two decades, two basic frameworks have been debated: the replacement and multiregional models. Both frameworks agree that there was an initial dispersal of *H. erectus* (or *H. ergaster*) from Africa into the rest of the Old World; however, they disagree as to what happened next.

MULTIREGIONAL AND REPLACEMENT MODELS

The **replacement models** suggest that modern humans had a localized origin—usually thought to be in Africa—and then dispersed into areas already occupied by *H. erectus* and its descendants. Replacement models thus require a second hominid dispersal from Africa. These models often are called "Out of Africa" models or "Out of Africa II," in recognition of the earlier *H. erectus* dispersal. As the word *replacement* implies, these models predict that anatomically modern humans did not interbreed substantially (or at all) with the indigenous hominids that they ultimately replaced. One implication is that all geographic variation seen in modern humans today evolved recently, after the origin of anatomically modern humans.

Multiregional models propose that our origins cannot be pinned down to a single population or area. Instead, gene flow, via repeated population movements and intermixing, is thought to have been extensive among Old World hominid populations. Thus the appearance of anatomically modern humans throughout the Old World resulted not from replacement of many populations by one but from the transmission of alleles underlying the modern human phenotype among populations that were in genetic contact. Therefore, multiregional models do not suggest a second dispersal from Africa. Note that the multiregional models do not call for mutiple separate origins for modern humans; rather, they suggest that modern humans originated in the context of gene flow among multiple regions.

Although it is sometimes stated that multiregional and replacement models are irreconcilable (Wolpoff et al., 2000), this is not entirely true. Certainly, any proof of genetic contributions from regionally dispersed populations means that total replacement could not have happened. But population expansion from a single region could have been the dominant event in recent human evolution, with genetic contributions from other populations being trivial. Conversely, it is very likely that over the past 500 000 years, hominid populations in some regions have been replaced by others without interbreeding, but this does not preclude gene flow from occurring among other populations in the species.

PREDICTIONS OF THE TWO MODELS

Replacement models predict that we should first see modern human fossils in Africa and then at least two anatomically distinct lineages of hominids in each region of the Old World: Neandertals and modern humans in Europe, *Homo heidelbergensis* (archaic *H. sapiens*) and modern humans in mainland Asia, and possibly relict populations of *H. erectus* and modern humans in Southeast Asia. Replacement further predicts that these lineages will overlap for at least a brief period of time in each region. Like the anatomy, the archaeological record would show abrupt changes in technology and behaviour (as modern humans brought their technology with them to new areas), and the genetic record would indicate little overlap between the gene pools of the two lineages.

In contrast, multiregional models predict only a single evolving lineage in each region. We should see anatomical evidence of this evolution in the form of intermediate fossils with characteristics of the ancestors and the descendants. In addition, we should see regional anatomical characters continue from earlier to later populations. Likewise, the archaeological record should show evidence of behavioural continuity. And the genetic evidence should show ancient contributions to the modern gene pool, assuming there has not been a strong genetic bottleneck.

Let us now turn to the fossil, archaeological, and genetic records to see how these predictions fare against the empirical data.

ANATOMY AND DISTRIBUTION OF EARLY HUMANS

Early modern human fossil specimens are rare (Figure 14.2) but are found in Africa, the Near East, Asia and Southeast Asia, Europe, and, for the first time, Australia. In this section we review the anatomy of key fossils in these areas. In many cases early modern human specimens possess both derived features linking them to us and ancestral features they may share with archaic *H. sapiens* or Neandertals (Pearson, 2000). In general, we should not use ancestral features to exclude specimens from modern *H. sapiens* if they also possess derived features justifying their inclusion.

AFRICA

While Neandertals were evolving in Europe, a different kind of hominid was evolving in Africa: anatomically modern *H. sapiens*. As we discussed in Chapter 13, archaic *H. sapiens* fossils have been found in Africa from around 600 000 to about 200 000 years ago. Starting at about 150 000 years ago we begin to see fossils that look more modern from sites in East and South Africa. Typically, their anatomy is intermediate in form, and their ages are often imprecisely known. Slightly later, we find fully anatomically modern humans at other East and South African sites. Although some scientists like to distinguish these two groups by calling them different subspecies, most scholars include both in *H. sapiens sapiens*.

Perhaps the most securely dated of the earlier group of fossils are the recent discoveries from Ethiopia (Figure 14.3), which date to about 160 000 to 154 000 years ago (White et al., 2003). Like other African specimens from this period, these skeletal remains are not yet fully modern. The later group date to about 120 000 to 50 000 years ago (Haile-Selassie et al., 2004; Rightmire and Deacon, 1991). For the most part early *H. sapiens sapiens* are found with typical MSA tool assemblages, but at one South African site the stone tool industry appears to represent an advanced MSA assemblage because it features small, flaked tools called microliths.

This sequence of fossils provides evidence that *H. sapiens sapiens* was well established throughout Africa by 100 000 years ago. Furthermore, a series of specimens dating from 200 000 to 100 000 years ago provide strong evidence of the African transformation of archaic *H. sapiens* to anatomically modern humans.

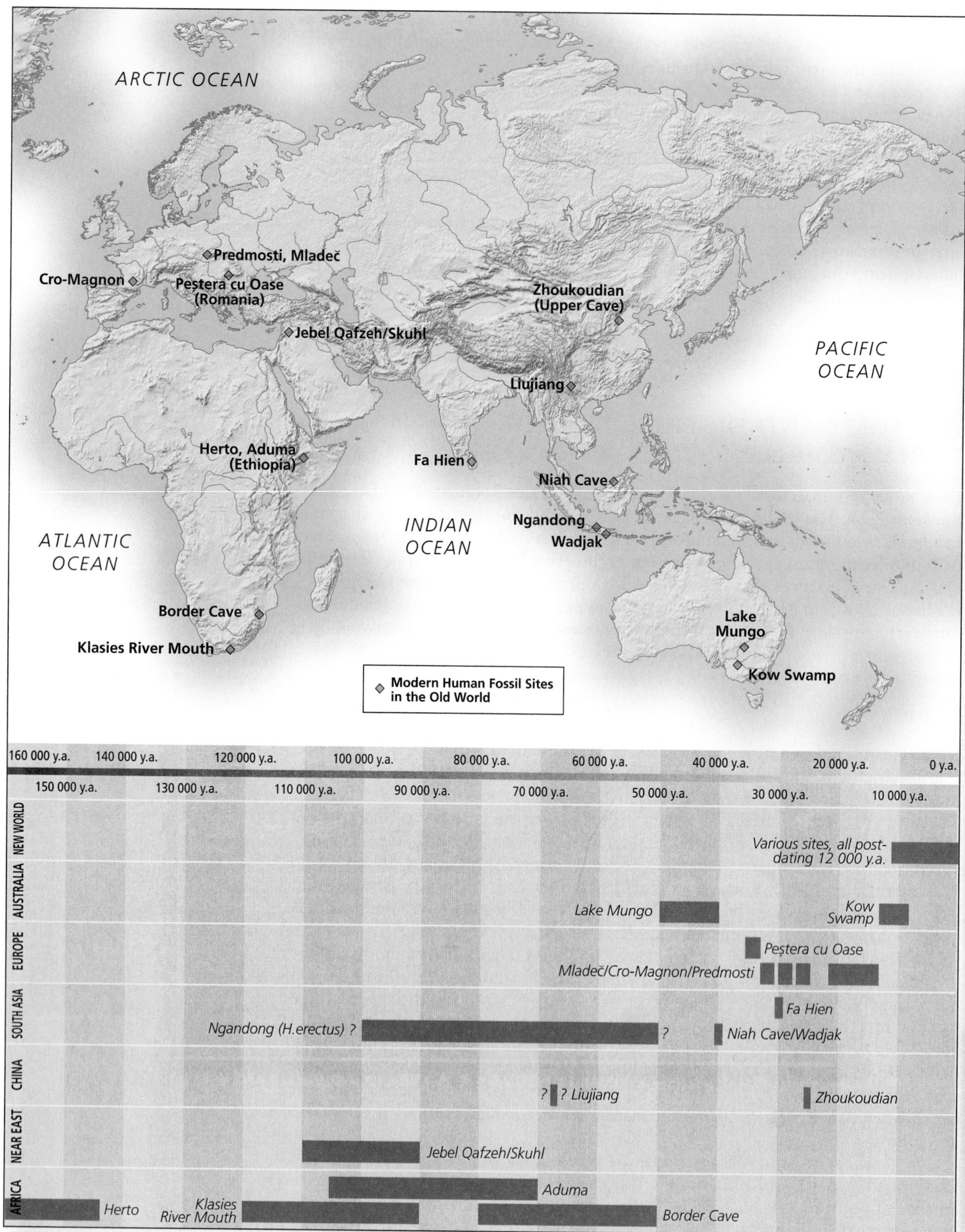

FIGURE 14.2 Modern Human Fossil Sites in the Old World.

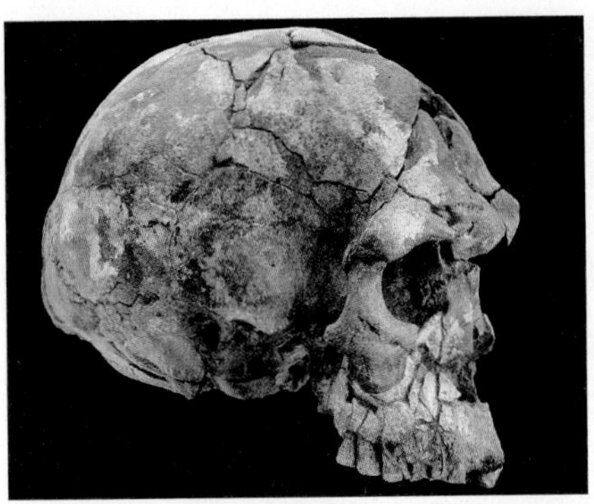

FIGURE 14.3 Hominid remains from Herto, Ethiopia, may be the oldest anatomically modern humans yet discovered.

NEAR EAST

The Near East is the only region outside Africa to have yielded reliable evidence of modern humans earlier than 60 000 years ago. As discussed in Chapter 13, anatomically modern *H. sapiens* dating to 110 000 to 90 000 years ago have been found in Israel. The Near East sits between Africa and the rest of Asia, so if modern humans (or modern human morphology) first evolved in Africa sometime after 150 000 years ago, then these hominids (Figure 14.4) could be considered the first sign of an expansion out of Africa, which only later (60 000 to 40 000 years ago) spread into Asia, Australia, and Europe. Neandertals are known to have occupied the Near East for tens of thousands of years, usually during glacial periods. Many scientists have interpreted the correlation of anatomically modern human specimens with warm (interglacial) periods and of later Neandertals with cold (glacial) periods as a sharing of this area by these two groups through time. Both Neandertals and early *H. sapiens sapiens* in the Near East are associated with MSA tool assemblages.

ASIA AND SOUTHEAST ASIA

In Asia there is a gap in the hominid fossil record between about 100 000 and 40 000 years ago. Archaic or premodern *H. sapiens* are known from a number of sites dating from 250 000 to 100 000 years ago in China (Etler, 1996), but anatomically modern humans do not appear until perhaps as early as 65 000 years ago in China and possibly 40 000 years ago in Indonesia.

Dating is a problem for establishing the earliest human remains in Asia. Well-accepted dates of 25 000 years ago have been obtained for the Upper Cave at Zhoukoudian. Although clearly modern humans, the three Upper Cave skulls differ anatomically from one another and are not similar to skulls of contemporary east Asian peoples. Stringer and Andrews (1988) suggest that the Upper Cave skulls most closely resemble early modern humans from central European sites (Figure 14.5). This indicates that both European and Asian early modern human populations had a common origin (presumably Africa) and that there is little evidence of regional continuity.

The earliest *H. sapiens sapiens* in Southeast Asia are equally problematic. Specimens from the Niah Cave complex in Borneo (Figure 14.6) and from Java have been assigned dates of 40 000 years ago, but complex stratigraphy and provenience issues make such dates highly provisional.

The possible evolutionary relationships of these Asian modern humans exemplify contrasting views of the origin of all modern humans: Some researchers argue

FIGURE 14.4 Anatomically modern humans from the Israeli cave site of Qafzeh may be among the earliest found outside of Africa.

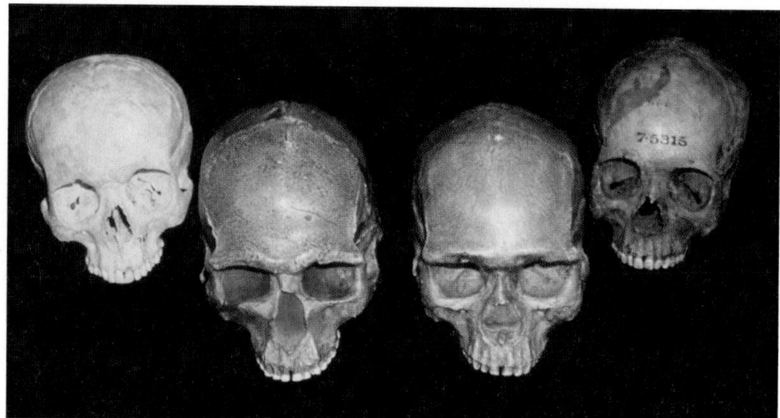

FIGURE 14.5 Fossil remains of anatomically modern humans from the Czech Republic and from China (centre crania) are more robust than recent human crania but are otherwise anatomically identical. All four crania are *Homo sapiens sapiens*.

that they represent the culmination of an unbroken evolutionary trajectory in China and Indonesia that began with variants of *H. erectus* in each area and that extends to contemporary East Asian populations (Wolpoff et al., 1994); other researchers (for example, Stringer and Gamble, 1993) argue that the Upper Cave individuals do not resemble modern Asians in any meaningful way, nor do the early Indonesians represent modern Indonesians, and that both may represent a migration into the region by individuals of an early, geographically undifferentiated modern human group. Filling the Asian fossil gap between 100 000 and 40 000 years ago will be essential in resolving some of these issues.

AUSTRALIA

Although Australia is separated by water from the major Eurasian land mass, evidence suggests that modern humans were in Australia before they were in Europe. To get to Australia modern humans almost certainly had to go through island

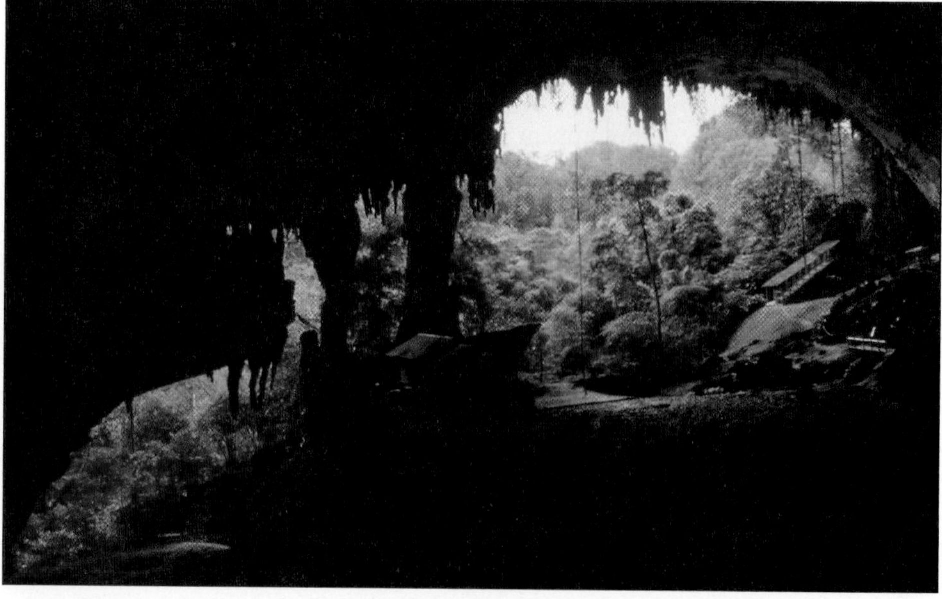

FIGURE 14.6 The Niah Cave complex in Borneo.

Southeast Asia, so the ages of the earliest Australian occupation are also relevant to the peopling of Southeast Asia. During glacial maxima, when sea levels are lowest, Australia and New Guinea form a single land mass which is at all times separated by water from the land mass which forms from some of the islands of Southeast Asia. Although all kinds of primates, including extinct hominids, occupy or occupied Southeast Asia, only modern humans (and apparently another hominid, found recently in Indonesia—see Box 14.1) were able to disperse themselves further. Some scientists argue that the settlement of Australia, New Guinea, and other islands of Melanesia was a fundamental advance in the behaviour of modern humans over earlier hominids (Noble and Davidson, 1996), in part because settlement of these islands could have been accomplished only by using a boat or raft of some kind.

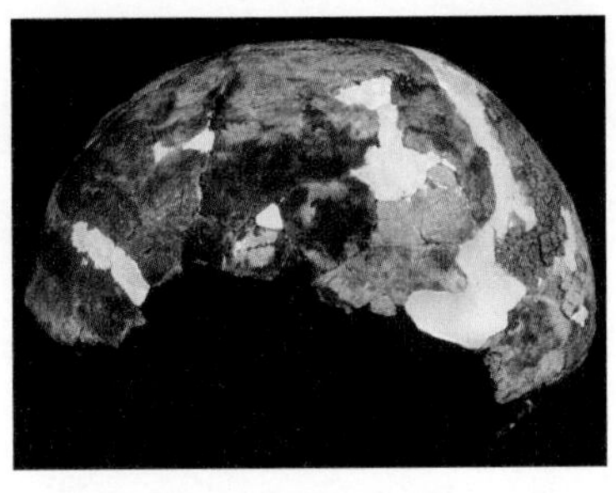

FIGURE 14.7 Partially cremated skull from Lake Mungo, Australia.

The earliest human remains from Australia come from a site in the southeastern part of the continent known as Lake Mungo. Two incomplete skeletons from burials, along with other fragmentary remains and some cremations, have been dated to 40 000 years ago (Figure 14.7), with the earliest archaeological sites dating to 50 000 years ago (Bowler et al., 2003). Mungo I, the buried remains of a young female, shows clear signs of having been cremated; the other burial, Mungo III, is of an old male whose body was covered with red ochre. These are the earliest known examples of such mortuary practices. Both specimens are anatomically modern *H. sapiens*, and they both exhibit a gracile build.

Other Australian sites have yielded a number of reasonably complete crania that are substantially more robust than those of the Lake Mungo people. They are also substantially younger, dating to 13 000 to 9 500 years ago. Some of them are interesting, however, because their thick cranial bones and moderate development of browridges have been argued to demonstrate their close affinities with the latest *H. erectus* found in Indonesia (Wolpoff et al., 1984). We saw in Chapter 13 that a relict population of *H. erectus* may have persisted on Java until less than 100 000 years ago and perhaps as late as 25 000 years ago, although these dates are controversial (Swisher et al., 1996). If true, this finding would support a replacement model of human origins.

However they arose, it seems clear that anatomically modern humans had the ability to cross large bodies of open water and colonize Australia at least 50 000 if not 60 000 years ago.

EUROPE

Scores of Neandertal remains have been recovered in Europe that date 100 000 to 30 000 years ago; however, modern human skeletal remains do not appear in Europe until relatively late. A mandible recently discovered in Romania is so far the oldest modern human in Europe, dating 36 000 to 34 000 years ago (Trinkaus et al., 2003). Like other early modern human specimens, this mandible, Oase 1, is robust and seems to exhibit a mixture of clearly derived features (such as development of the chin) aligning it with anatomically modern *H. sapiens* and ancestral features (such as its robustness and anatomy of the mandibular foramen) linking it to Neandertals (Figure 14.8). The left mandibular foramen (a small hole in the mandible through which nerves and blood vessels pass) of Oase 1 has an anatomy that may be a derived feature of Neandertals and other early modern humans from Europe not seen in human populations today. Although it is an insignificant biological feature, this is the kind of diagnostic trait that can become quite important in debates about phylogenetic relationships among Late Pleistocene hominids.

Central European sites in the Czech Republic have yielded numerous specimens of anatomically modern *H. sapiens*, which also display characters that may align them with Neandertals (Smith, 1984). These sites date to 35 000 to 25 000 years ago. Hominids from these sites show a large degree of sexual dimorphism,

Box 14.1 The Little People of Flores

Homo sapiens never co-existed with *Homo erectus*. Or did they? Conventional wisdom has held that *H. erectus* went extinct in the Middle Pleistocene after giving rise to *Homo sapiens*. But as we saw in Chapter 12, geochronologists estimate that the latest surviving *H. erectus* lived in Java between 50 000 and 25 000 years ago, overlapping in time and space with modern humans who reached the region by as early as 60 000 years ago (Swisher et al., 1996). The recent discovery of the remains of a diminutive hominid, with a cranial capacity of only 380 cc (Figure A), on the island of Flores suggest another group lived just 18 000 years ago (Brown et al., 2004). The postcranial skeleton suggests a female biped that stood just about a metre (3 ft) tall, about the size of the *A. afarensis* skeleton "Lucy." Stone tools at the site may be associated with the hominid.

Although some call it a new species, *H. floresiensis*, it is difficult to distinguish from *H. erectus* except on the basis of its small size. Some argue it is just a small, pathological human, a claim that can be resolved by further study. A common phenomenon for large mammals that colonize small islands (Flores is about 1400 km^2) is to become, over many generations, smaller. In fact the fossil record of Flores yields the remains of a dwarfed elephant as well. This size reduction (called "insular dwarfism") is related to two selective pressures on large island mammals: fewer resources favour smaller individuals who need less food to survive, and fewer predators mean that having a small body doesn't increase the chance of being eaten. The Flores hominid seems to indicate such a process. Perhaps a few members of *H. erectus* were washed onto the island on natural rafts during a storm. Stranded there, they were isolated from other members of their species. Their isolation may explain not only their small size but also their survival. In their island refuge they did not come into competition for resources with, and were not replaced by, modern humans until much later than other archaic hominids. If it is archaic, the hominid from Flores suggests to us that it may have been only a few thousand years since we last shared the Earth with another hominid species.

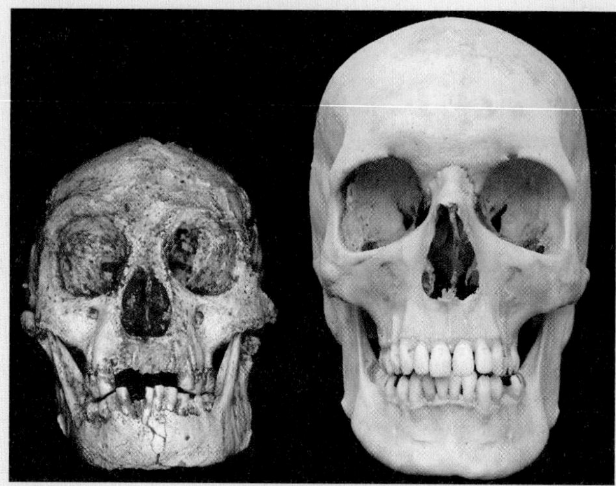

FIGURE A The skull from Flores (left), is less than one-third of the capacity of a modern human skull (right).

with the males displaying a more robust cranial anatomy (such as the presence of browridges). Several crania, probably representing males, show development of an occipital bun or hemi-bun. Though not as fully developed as the Neandertal occipital bun, this feature, in combination with the development of browridges, has been argued by some scholars to show Neandertal ancestry in these early human remains.

A recent review of the anatomy of the earliest modern humans in Europe and later humans remains has argued that, although they have an anatomical pattern consistent with African modern humans, they also exhibit traits (including distinctive Neandertal features) that can be best explained as resulting from modest levels of gene flow between Neandertals and early modern humans (that is, a multiregional model) (Trinkaus, 2007).

Against this, early Upper Palaeolithic human postcranial skeletons appear to be tropically adapted, lacking the cold-adapted proportions we saw in Neandertal skeletons. That is, they have the narrower, more linear proportions of the limbs and thorax associated with humans living in tropical climates who easily dissipate

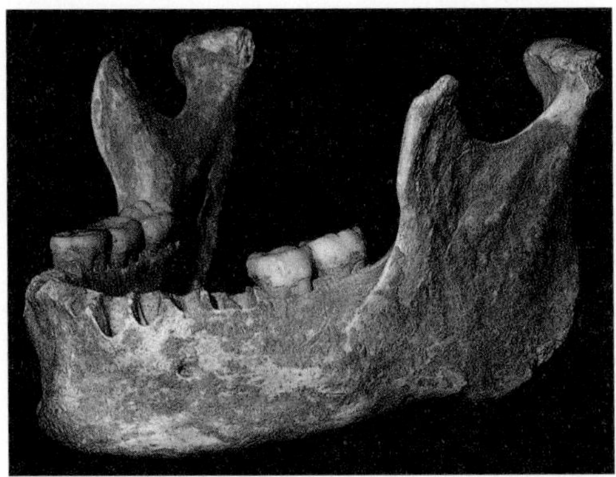

FIGURE 14.8 The Oase 1 mandible, earliest modern human in Europe.

heat. Some scholars interpret this to be evidence that modern humans migrated from tropical Africa to cold Europe more quickly than their skeleton could adapt to the climatic shift. If true, this would support a replacement model.

The best-known early anatomically modern humans from Europe come from the Cro-Magnon rock shelter located in the Dordogne region of France, which includes a number of Neandertal sites as well. The Cro-Magnon remains were discovered in 1868. The site dates to about 27 000 years ago, well after the first appearance of modern humans in Europe.

Cro-Magnon 1 (or the "Old Man" of Cro-Magnon) shows a striking anatomical contrast to Neandertals from the same region (Figure 14.9). Cro-Magnon 1 has a gracile cranium that combines a very small face with a large and bulbous cranial vault. It was not very difficult for archaeologists to develop an evolutionary scenario in western Europe whereby the Middle Palaeolithic Neandertals were replaced over a short period of time by Upper Palaeolithic modern humans sometime between 40 000 to 30 000 years ago. However, according to critics of this scenario, the Cro-Magnon 1 specimen is not particularly representative of early modern humans in Europe (including those from central Europe and even some of the other Cro-Magnon individuals), who generally show a more mosaic pattern of archaic and modern features.

Given their late appearance, it is not surprising that European anatomically modern humans are found only with Upper Palaeolithic tool technologies. In fact, in western Europe there appears to be a one-to-one correlation between *H. sapiens sapiens* and a technology called the Aurignacian, which is characterized by the presence of microliths. As we saw in Chapter 13, a different Upper Palaeolithic technology, the Châtelperronian, is contemporaneous with the Aurignacian but appears to be a Neandertal technology. Whether the Châtelperronian is a Neandertal innovation or the result of Neandertals mimicking *H. sapiens sapiens* remains a point of debate.

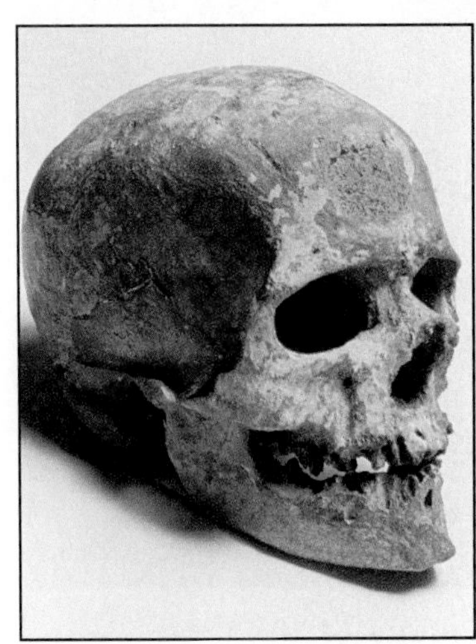

FIGURE 14.9 The "Old Man" of Cro-Magnon, from the Dordogne region of France.

ARCHAEOLOGY OF MODERN HUMAN ORIGINS

The material culture of modern humans extends from simple stone tools to complex mechanical devices. There is no doubt that the archaeological remains of later modern humans reflect cultural and individual behaviours that are substantially more complex than those indicated by the archaeological remains of earlier hominids or even of the earliest *H. sapiens sapiens*. It is important to explore the archaeology of the earliest modern humans if we are to understand the behaviours that allowed them to become the dominant hominid species throughout the world by about 40 000 years ago.

microliths Small, flaked stone tools probably designed to be hafted to wood or bone; common feature of Upper Palaeolithic and Later Stone Age tool industries.

STONE AND OTHER TOOLS

We can look at the changes in tool cultures or industries associated with the emergence of anatomically modern *H. sapiens* as a tale of two continents: Europe and Africa. For many years, the European archaeological record, in conjunction with the rich trove of hominid remains recovered from European sites, stood as the basic model to explain the emergence of modern people. Over the past few decades, however, increasing research into the archaeology of Africa has provided a new context for understanding human origins.

The very earliest modern humans, those dating to 100 000 years ago or earlier in Africa and the Near East, are found with MSA assemblages that are indistinguishable in most ways from those of earlier hominids (or later Neandertals). Thus, there is no one-to-one correlation between the appearance of modern anatomy and Upper Palaeolithic technology.

The European Upper Palaeolithic and the African Later Stone Age are distinguished from the MSA by a greater reliance on the standardized production of blades: long flakes that could be used as blanks to produce a variety of flaked tools. A number of blades could be taken off a prepared stone core in a systematic manner. Refinements in tool flaking techniques also distinguish Upper Palaeolithic and Later Stone Age tool industries from the MSA. For example, long, exquisitely flaked blades from the Solutrean industry of Europe demonstrate the extraordinary level of skill of Upper Palaeolithic tool makers (Figure 14.10).

Microliths are another common feature of Upper Palaeolithic and Later Stone Age tool industries, which appeared after 25 000 years ago in most regions. Microliths are small, flaked tools that probably were designed to be attached to wood or bone (Figure 14.11). Arrowheads are a kind of microlith and appear for the first time around 13 000 to 10 000 years ago. The rate and kind of change in tool types and flaking techniques also increase from the MSA to the Upper Palaeolithic and Later Stone Age.

Another striking feature of the Upper Palaeolithic and Later Stone Age is the vastly greater use of tools made from bone, ivory, antler, and shell. These were ground, polished, and drilled to form objects such as harpoons, spear throwers, awls, needles, and buttons. Upper Palaeolithic Europeans also produced well-known examples of representational cave art and other artistic or ritual objects.

FIGURE 14.10 Upper Palaeolithic refinement in stone tool production, a Solutrean blade.

Because anatomically modern humans first appeared in Africa more than 100 000 years ago, we should assess whether a cultural revolution in the African archaeological record accompanied the appearance of this new biological type. It was long thought that the Middle Palaeolithic of Europe and MSA of Africa were roughly contemporaneous and reflected a similar level of technological development. However, many archaeological elements thought to be uniquely associated with the Upper Palaeolithic and Later Stone Age actually made their first appearance in the MSA of Africa (McBrearty and Brooks, 2000). These innovations did not appear suddenly in a single locality but in different sites at different times. For example, blades are known from several sites, dating from 75 000 years ago to perhaps as early as 280 000 years ago in East Africa. Flake technologies based on the production of points rather than scrapers (a hallmark of the Mousterian in Europe) are also abundant in African MSA sites, some dating to 235 000 years ago.

More surprisingly, microliths, which are typically associated with the late Upper Palaeolithic, were being made in the MSA 65 000 years ago. Tools made from bone have also been found at a variety of African MSA sites.

The transition to the kind of cultural assemblage we associate with modern humans was probably more evolutionary than revolutionary (McBrearty and Brooks, 2000). The European perspective, which may represent the rapid replacement of the Middle Palaeolithic by the Upper Palaeolithic there, may not be representative of what happened in Africa, the region where modern humans first appeared. However, we should pause at this point to reflect on what modernity

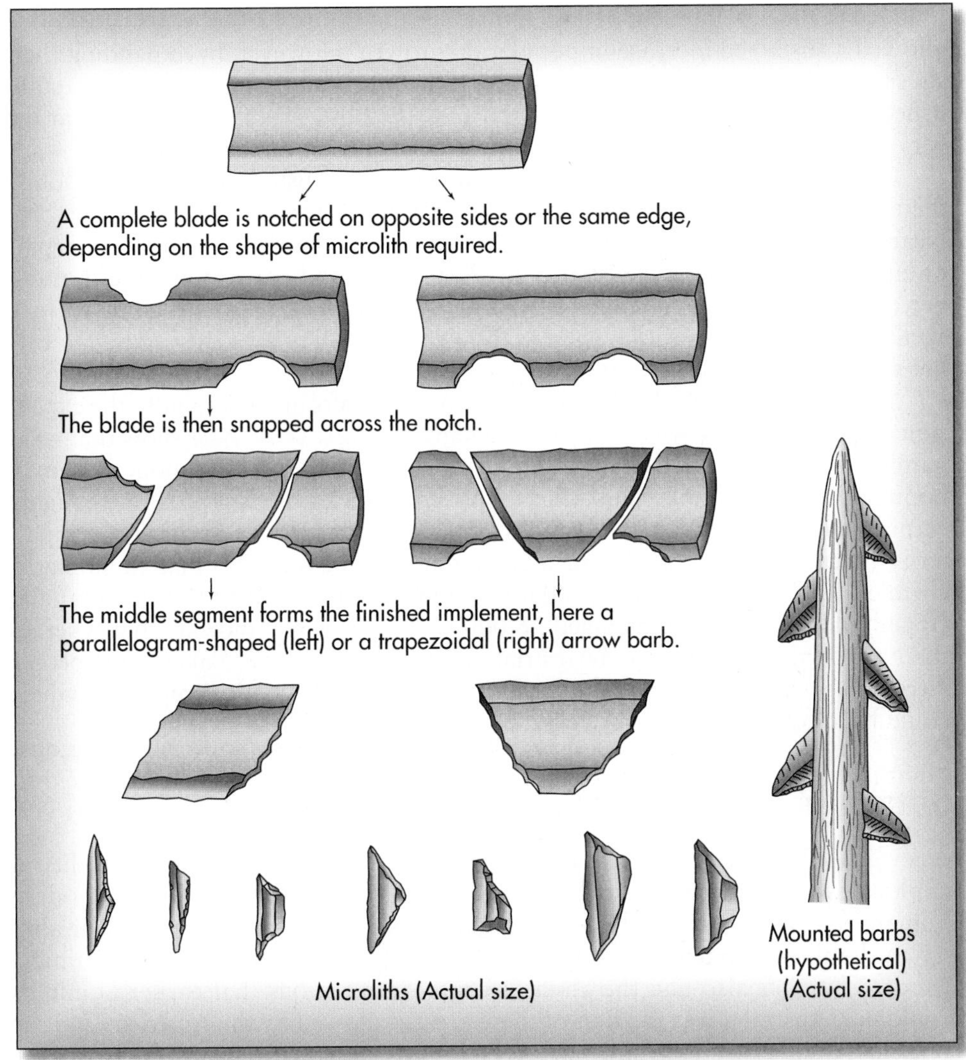

A complete blade is notched on opposite sides or the same edge, depending on the shape of microlith required.
The blade is then snapped across the notch.
The middle segment forms the finished implement, here a parallelogram-shaped (left) or a trapezoidal (right) arrow barb.
Microliths (Actual size)
Mounted barbs (hypothetical) (Actual size)

FIGURE 14.11 Microlith production. Although microliths are typically considered an Upper Palaeolithic technology, their origins can be traced to the Middle Stone Age of Africa.

really means. The appearance of certain tool types often has been the basis for inferring the appearance of modern behaviour. It is not clear, however, that these archaeological signals are good proxies for modernity. Can modern behaviour, like modern anatomy, be signalled by the appearance of a single derived character or the presence of a single tool type, however briefly it appears in the record? Or is it indicated only by the presence of a comprehensive package of behaviours that signifies a different set of interactions with the world? Changes in technological, economic, social, and cognitive behaviours in Africa may have been triggered by rapid environmental changes (Mellars, 2006). The behavioural changes are seen in the archaeological record at approximately the same time as the demographic expansion and ensuing dispersal of modern humans over most regions of Asia, Australasia, and Europe.

SUBSISTENCE

Much evidence supports the idea that modern humans had an advantage in their ability to exploit a wider variety of foodstuffs than those used by Neandertals or archaic *H. sapiens*. Ultimately, the human ability to exploit natural resources for food led to the development of agriculture, starting about 12 000 years ago, which allowed a sustained increase in population growth. However, by expanding their subsistence base in other ways, early anatomically modern humans may have established a pattern of increased population growth relative to other hominids at the very origins of our species, long before the introduction of agriculture.

One example is the use of aquatic resources, such as fish and shellfish. Although there is earlier evidence of the limited use of marine resources, including use by some Neandertal populations, aquatic resources become a widespread and systematic part of human subsistence only in the Upper Palaeolithic and Later Stone Age. A number of MSA coastal sites, however, show exploitation of marine mammals, fish, shellfish, and tortoises earlier than 40 000 years ago. Perhaps they signal an earlier shift to modern behaviour in Africa.

Besides archaeological remains, other sources of information point to the expansion of subsistence patterns in modern humans. *Microwear analyses* show that wear patterns on Neandertal teeth were more similar to those seen in modern human populations (for example, Inuit who follow a traditional lifeway) that have highly carnivorous diets (Lalueza et al., 1996). In contrast, Upper Palaeolithic wear patterns indicate a diet incorporating a greater amount of vegetable matter. Similarly, chemical analyses of Neandertal (dating from 130 000 to 28 000 years ago) and Upper Palaeolithic skeletons (aged 26 000 to 20 000 years) indicate that whereas the Neandertal diet relied on terrestrial herbivores, the Upper Palaeolithic people were eating a more varied diet that included a substantial aquatic component, which could have come from fish, molluscs, or shorebirds (Richards et al., 2001).

SETTLEMENT OF THE NEW WORLD AND PACIFIC ISLANDS

As evidenced by their distribution, modern humans clearly had a greater ability to exploit new environments. Although it is difficult to prove, the ability of modern humans to exploit completely new environments seems to demonstrate their ability to dominate environments that were already occupied by other hominids. Modern humans also had the ability to enter into regions that earlier hominids could not. Australia was the first of these areas, followed by the Americas and the remote islands of the Pacific.

The Americas During ice ages, when sea levels are at their lowest, the Old and New Worlds are connected via the Bering Land Bridge, a broad swath of land (more than 2000 kilometres wide at its maximum) linking eastern Siberia with western Alaska (Figure 14.12). This bridge was open and ice free only periodically, most recently between 75 000 and 45 000 years ago and again 25 000 to 11 000 years ago (Mandryk, 1992). Even when the land bridge was ice free, crossing it seems to have entailed a level of technological or subsistence development not reached by earlier hominids. Alternatively, we know that at least some modern human populations had watercraft by about 40 000 years ago, as demonstrated by the successful over-water colonization of Australia. Colonization of the New World via the coast of Siberia and Alaska or along the Pacific Rim may have been possible (Fagan, 2001).

The date of the peopling of the New World is highly controversial. Although dates as early as 35 000 years ago have been proposed, the most widely accepted archaeological evidence puts Palaeo-Indian occupations in North America at approximately 13 000 years ago. Archaeological sites aside, Palaeo-Indian skeletal remains are rare and the earliest of them exhibit some features that differentiate them from recent North American Aboriginal populations: in a recent study only one of eleven Palaeo-Indian fossils showed a strong resemblance to contemporary Aboriginal populations (Jantz and Owsley, 2001). While there is no universal agreement on the interpretation of genetic data, a recent review of molecular genetic studies of Siberian and North American Aboriginal populations indicates that the initial

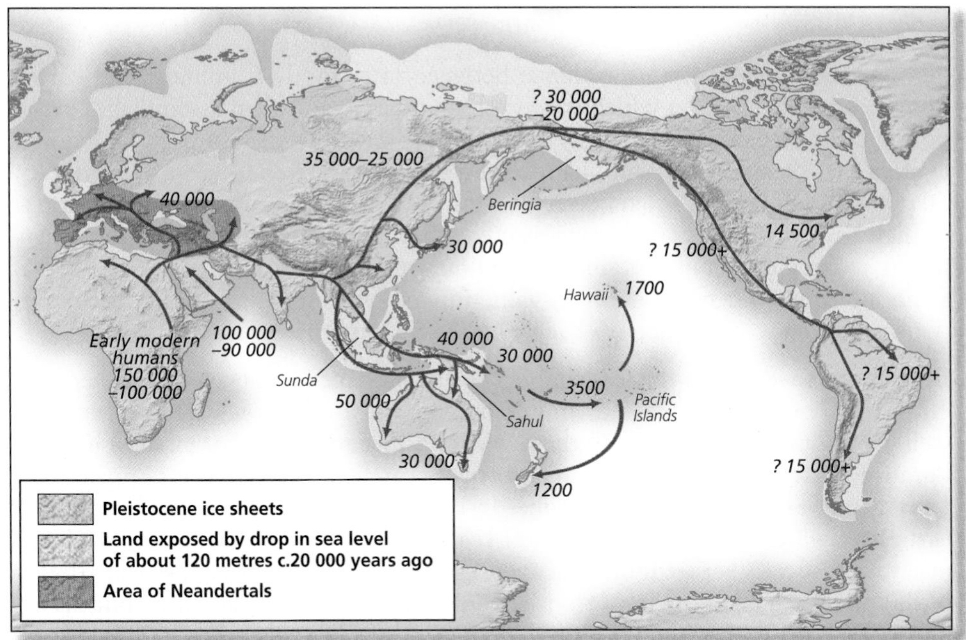

FIGURE 14.12 Routes for the human colonization of the New World and Pacific islands.

migration of ancestral Amerindians metres originated in south-central Siberia and entered the New World between 20 000 to 14 000 years ago (Schurr, 2004). The settlement history of the Americas is clearly complex and will continue to be addressed by genetic, linguistic, archaeological, and palaeontological researchers.

The Pacific The last regions of the world to be colonized by humans are the Pacific Islands. Although people crossed the ocean between Southeast Asia and Australia about 50 000 years ago and inhabited islands off the east coast of Papua New Guinea as early as 28 000 years ago, most of the Pacific was not colonized until 3500 years ago or later. Only the invention of long-distance voyaging technology allowed such crossings, which settlers undertook over vast areas of ocean (Irwin, 1992). Debates continue as to how fast this expansion occurred, how much mixing there was between the expanding Southeast Asia-derived populations and the indigenous New Guinea populations, and thus how purely Asian the source population was.

Genetic, archaeological, and linguistic data seem to indicate that the source people for the peopling of the Pacific came from somewhere in East Asia or island Southeast Asia and moved into New Guinea, fusing with peoples and cultures there, and then into Polynesia (Kirch, 2001). The earliest expansion of these peoples in the Pacific often is traced by their archaeological sites. They appeared earliest in Near Oceania (the Bismarck archipelago) around 3500 years ago and from there spread to Fiji (around 3000 years ago) and then further out to Tonga, Samoa, and Far Oceania. Presumably in outrigger canoes, they brought with them pigs, dogs, rats, agricultural crops, and enough food and water to survive their journey. Once on these remote islands, humans did what we do best. They modified the landscape, took advantage of new natural resources, and interacted with the environment in symbolic ways. The archaeological records of most islands reveal strong impact (extinction of land birds, evidence of forest clearing for agriculture) on the available resources after the arrival of humans.

These settlements mark the end of the initial colonization of the globe by humans. Although the rest of human history on Earth will be marked by both dispersal and migration, no longer is it into ecosystems never before occupied by humans.

SYMBOLISM

Perhaps the most striking difference between later modern humans and earlier hominids is the extent to which modern human archaeological assemblages incorporate clear evidence of symbolic behaviour. Remember the scant and debatable evidence of Neandertal symbolism reviewed in the last chapter. In contrast, by 50 000 to 40 000 years ago modern humans apparently dedicated large percentages of their time to symbolic acts such as creating and presumably wearing ornamentation, making cave and portable art, and burying their dead. All this suggests that symbolic behaviour had a survival value for modern humans and that their relationship to the world may have been ordered by symbols.

Burials As we saw in the last chapter, the significance and even the existence of Neandertal burials are debated, and their symbolic implications are questioned as well. By about 40 000 years ago these questions became moot for modern humans because evidence of new mortuary practices, including cremation, appeared at Lake Mungo in Australia at this time. In Europe, Upper Palaeolithic burials (the earliest of which date to about 28 000 years ago) differ from Mousterian burials in several ways. Whether found in caves or open-air sites, they are associated with burial pits. Perhaps more importantly, a number of Upper Palaeolithic burials are impressively elaborate in terms of the amount of grave goods associated with them and the number and arrangement of bodies they contain (Figure 14.13). For many interpreters of these sites, a ritualistic component in the burial is obvious. Variation in the quality of grave goods or bodily adornment among different burials may also indicate variation in social status. Obviously, not every Upper Palaeolithic burial is an elaborate affair complete with an abundance of finely made grave goods; however, such burials are completely absent in the earlier archaeological record. Interestingly, evidence of deliberate burial of any kind in the later MSA is quite scanty, and Aurignacian burials are also scarce.

Art and Ornamental Objects Unlike the equivocal engravings of Neandertals, the artistic expression of Upper Palaeolithic humans is astounding. Cave art (Figure 14.14) and *petroglyphs* (rock carvings) occur not only in Europe but also in Africa and Australia. The earliest cave art in Europe appeared about 32 000 years ago at Chauvet, France, and is complex in its technique and representation. Rock art appeared in Africa about 26 000 years ago, and somewhat earlier than that in Australia, perhaps as much as 40 000 years ago. The rock art of Australia, which spans thousands of years, provides a particularly rich record of human artistic

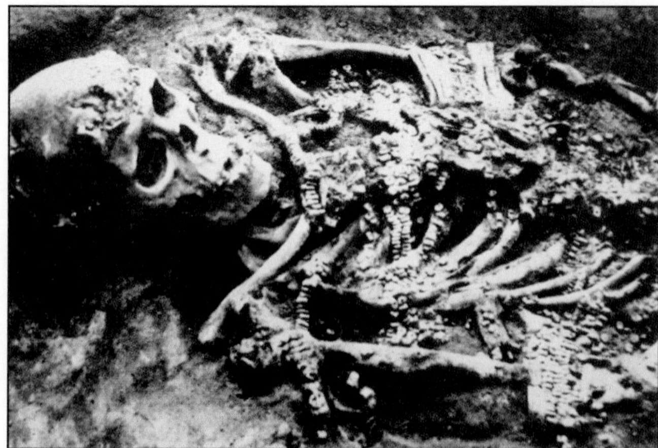

FIGURE 14.13 Anatomically modern humans left archaeological clues, including evidence of burials that indicated ritual and symbolic behaviour were important parts of their culture.

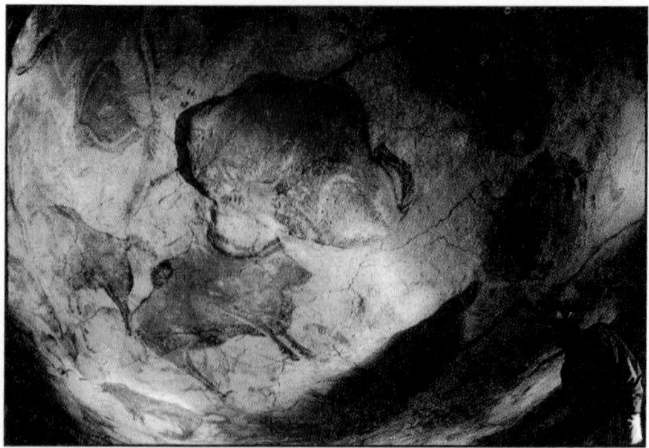

FIGURE 14.14 Abundant cave art after about 30 000 years ago is evidence of the importance of symbolic behaviour for modern human cultures.

expression (Figure 14.15). The animals represented on cave walls such as Chauvet were once interpreted as sympathetic magic to assist in hunting success. But when compared with animals found in faunal assemblages from archaeological sites of the same period, these images suggest that people were mostly drawing animals they did not hunt. Perhaps the animals had some other symbolic or ritual importance for them.

Red ochre (iron oxide) and the colour red were of great significance to Upper Palaeolithic and other modern peoples. One of the bodies from Lake Mungo in Australia may have been covered with red ochre. At the Qafzeh site in Israel, dating to about 92 000 years ago, seventy-one red ochre pieces, including some that were flaked or marked in some way, were found in association with remains of anatomically modern humans, and several stone artifacts were stained with red ochre (Hovers et al., 2003).

FIGURE 14.15 Australian aboriginal art.

Portable art is prevalent in modern human archaeological sites (Figure 14.16). The most famous of these pieces are the Venus figurines that represent various female figures, often interpreted as fertility totems. Other figurines also exist, including many zoomorphic statuettes.

Personal ornamentation is perhaps the most prolific form of symbolic behaviour in the Upper Palaeolithic (Figure 14.17). Upper Palaeolithic European burials often are covered in beads and bear other indications that the dead were buried in elaborately decorated garments (Stringer and Gamble, 1993). Thousands of beads, both isolated and associated with bodies, have been found at Upper Palaeolithic sites and may have been attached to garments. Experimental work indicates that each bead took a few hours to make. Thus, the Upper Palaeolithic peoples invested a huge amount of time in this form of symbolism. Particular materials seem to have been chosen for bead making, mostly representing scarce resources such as ivory, talc, and nonlocal shells. In addition to beads, pendants of animal teeth are also found, but as with the cave paintings they represent animals that were not food staples for Upper Palaeolithic peoples. Especially abundant are perforated fox canines, red deer vestigial canines, and reindeer teeth.

These elaborate displays of human symbolic behaviour occur late in the archaeological record of modern humans, about 40 000 years ago or later, not with the earliest moderns; however, several examples of perforated shell, bone, and stone have been found at MSA African sites earlier in time, and perforated shell beads have recently been argued to be present 73 000 years ago in South Africa (Henshilwood et al., 2004). If these prove on further inspection to be worked beads, they would represent the earliest known ornamentation and would give important support for a gradual accumulation of modern human behaviours.

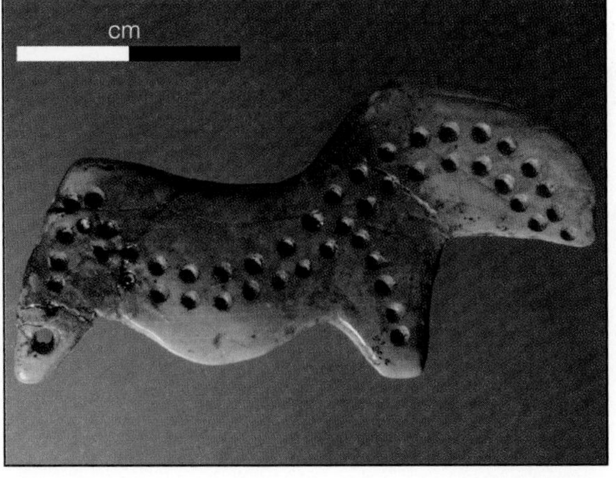

(a)

(b)

(c)

FIGURE 14.16 Portable artwork including (a) zoomorphic figures such as this horse and (b, c) Venus figurines appear frequently in the archaeological sites of anatomically modern humans, suggesting that symbolic behaviour played an important role in their lives.

FIGURE 14.17 Personal ornamentation, including pendants such as this ivory piece from Arcy-sur-Cure in France, are often found with modern humans but rarely with Neandertals.

The extensive evidence of artistic abilities of Late Pleistocene modern humans, expressed in a wide range of media over a large number of populations, stands in stark contrast to the paucity of evidence for such activities in Neandertals and other hominids. Of course, this does not mean that earlier hominids were incapable of symbolic or artistic expression. Indeed, two examples of putative anthropomorphic carvings have been found in Middle Acheulean (approximately 400 000 to 250 000 years ago) deposits from Morocco and Israel (Bednarik, 2003), which may give us a hint of the artistic abilities of archaic *H. sapiens*. Nonetheless, even though modern humans may not have been the only type of hominid capable of inventing art, it is clear that symbolic behaviour took on a whole new significance with the evolution of our species.

MOLECULAR GENETICS AND HUMAN ORIGINS

Since the mid-1980s, molecular geneticists have focused on the issue of modern human origins and the genetic histories of contemporary human populations. In general, geneticists approach these issues by making phylogenetic trees derived from different parts of the genome. These phylogenetic trees are based on the variability in these genetic systems observed in contemporary humans. In most studies, scientists use variability in DNA sequences to make the trees. However, they also use other kinds of genetic information, and trees can be based on, for example, variation in proteins, microsatellites (short, repeating DNA segments), and DNA haplotypes.

In looking at modern human origins, geneticists have used two types of data. The first considers living human genetic variation with the goal of identifying the **most recent common ancestor (MRCA)** of all people living today. The second set of data attempts to isolate DNA sequences from fossil *H. sapiens* and other hominids such as Neandertals. These ancient DNA analyses then consider the difference between the ancient groups and the extent of relatedness between them.

In a phylogenetic tree, the MRCA is indicated by the deepest node from which all contemporary variants can be shown to have evolved. Because all living people are genetically related to one another, the deepest node in a phylogenetic tree corresponds to a basic biological reality: All the variation we observe today evolved from a common ancestor. Identifying the deepest node poses some problems, however. First, in large, complex datasets we can construct a large number of possible phylogenetic trees. Thus, any particular tree represents a statistical model, which incorporates our assumptions about population size, the effects of natural selection, and other factors. Second, after identifying the deepest node in a tree, researchers want to know the date of the node. Putting a date to the node representing the MRCA entails calibration and an accurate determination of rates of genetic change. Finally, we need to remember that the MRCA need not have been an anatomically modern human. Genetic data provide no insights into what the bodies carrying the genes looked like.

At a fundamental level, the biological issue of modern human origins can be addressed only by both genetic and anatomical (palaeontological) data. The molecular identification of the MRCA does not give us any idea about the physical or behavioural changes that led to the establishment of our species; the fossil record has no direct information about whether any past species or populations had any descendants.

most recent common ancestor (MRCA) In a phylogenetic tree, the MRCA is indicated by the deepest node from which all contemporary variants can be shown to have evolved.

MITOCHONDRIAL DNA

Research on the evolution of anatomically modern humans entered a golden age in the mid-1980s with the publication of a pioneering analysis of mitochondrial DNA (mtDNA) variation in living humans (Cann et al., 1987). As we discussed in Chapter 3, mitochondrial DNA is transmitted only through the mother, has a relatively rapid rate of evolution, and does not undergo recombination. A phylogenetic tree was based on sequence differences distributed throughout the mtDNA from a large group of people representing several populations. The tree was quite complex, and there was much overlap among individuals from different populations. There was one exception: At the deepest node (representing the MRCA) on one side of the tree there was a cluster of mtDNA lineages represented exclusively in Africa. Although African mtDNA lineages were also found on the other side of the tree, the exclusive African cluster indicated that the MRCA lived in Africa, between 90 000 and 180 000 years ago. Although an mtDNA phylogeny traces the lineages down to a single mtDNA source, it is important to remember that there was more than one female in the population at the time; we should not think of the mtDNA studies as identifying an African Eve.

More recent analyses of the entire mtDNA genome broadly confirm the findings of the original study (Ingman et al., 2000): three of the deepest branches of the tree are exclusively African, with the next deepest being a mixture of Africans and non-Africans (Figure 14.18a). All non-African mtDNA branches are of a very similar depth, a pattern that would arise if mtDNA lineages evolved initially for some time in Africa, followed by a migration out of Africa of a small number of individuals. This resulted in a population bottleneck, followed by a population expansion, with all later Eurasian mtDNA lineages derived from this initial small population that left Africa. The date of the MRCA for the whole tree is 171 500 (+/– 50 000) years ago, somewhat earlier than that found in the earlier study. The date of the earliest clade that included African and non-African mtDNA was 52 000 (+/– 27 500) years ago.

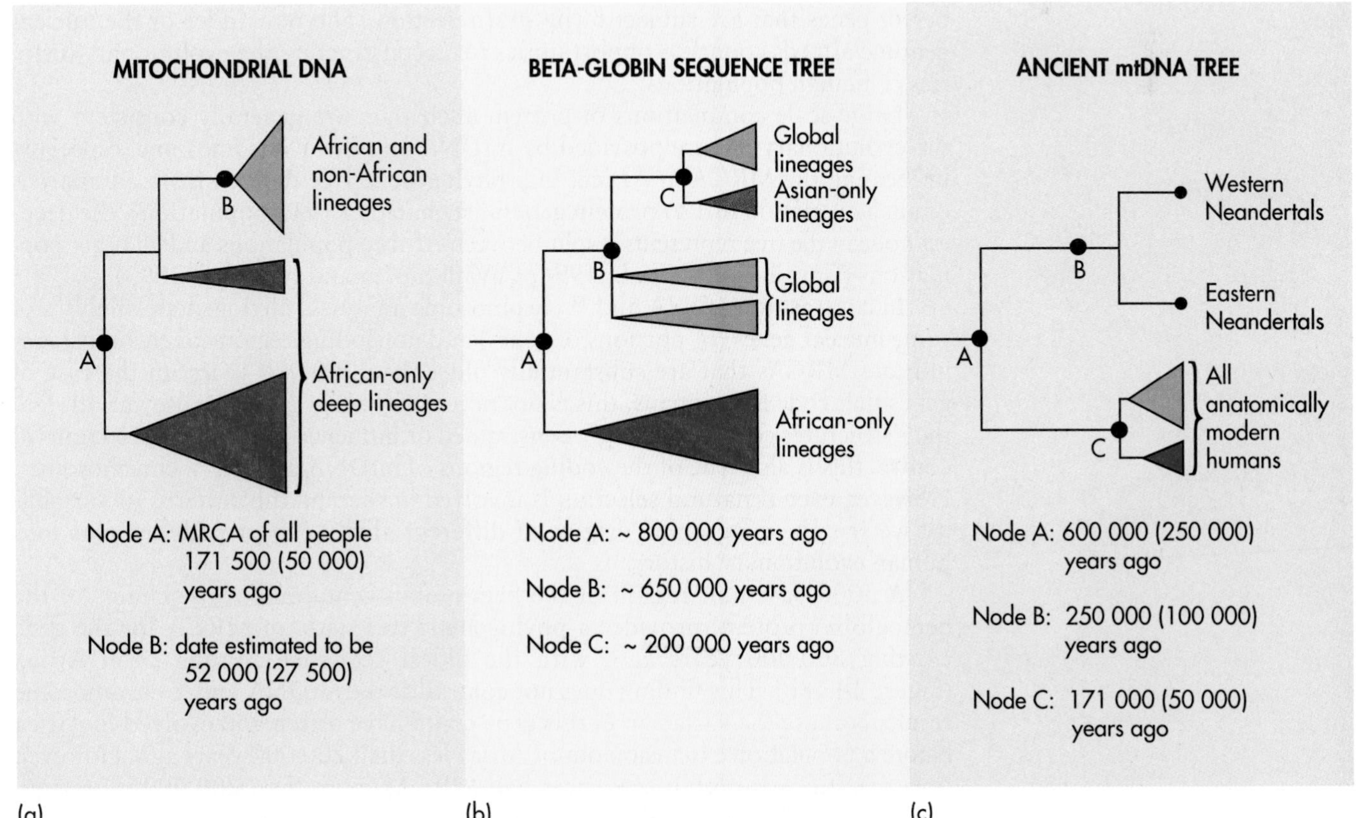

FIGURE 14.18 Three phylogenetic representations of modern human origins: (a) mtDNA, (b) beta-globin gene, and (c) ancient mtDNA.

THE Y CHROMOSOME

The Y chromosome is in some ways the male equivalent of mtDNA. Like mtDNA, it is transmitted across generations in only one sex, in this case males. Although parts of the Y chromosome undergo recombination, a large portion does not, and studies of this portion have been widely used in evolutionary research (Mitchell and Hammer, 1996; Stumpf and Goldstein, 2001; Jobling and Tyler-Smith, 2003). Phylogenetic analyses of the Y chromosome are based on both sequence and haplotype data. Haplotypes are combinations of mutations found together on a single chromosome; we can analyze them phylogenetically or calculate population frequencies for different haplotypes. There are at least eighteen major haplotype groups for the Y chromosome. Haplotypes are useful for tracing population movements and demographic events that have occurred across human history (Box 14.2 discusses a recent event illuminated by the Y chromosome).

The Y chromosome data seem to support the mtDNA story. Several estimates of a date for the Y chromosome MRCA have been suggested; most researchers accept an estimate of 180 000 to 100 000 years ago. Thus, the variation we observe in the Y chromosome and mtDNA of living humans appears to have evolved within similar timeframes. For both, the MRCA is dated with some confidence to less than 200 000 years ago. The Y chromosome and mtDNA data also both place the location of the MRCA in Africa. As was the case for the mtDNA, the deepest Y chromosome lineages are found exclusively in Africa, indicating evolution there first, followed by a population expansion into other parts of the world.

MRCAS FOR NUCLEAR GENES

Although the Y chromosome is part of the nuclear genome, it is a special case because such a large proportion of it is nonrecombining and it has a small number of genes that are subject to natural selection. The remainder of the nuclear genome affords countless opportunities for reconstructing the evolutionary histories of human populations.

Large-scale compilations of protein allele data are generally consistent with the evolutionary picture provided by mtDNA and the Y chromosome, especially in locating the MRCA in Africa. In a phylogenetic tree derived from an analysis of allelic variation in 120 protein genes distributed in 1915 populations, the deepest node in the tree represents a split between African populations and all other populations (Cavalli-Sforza et al., 1994; Cavalli-Sforza and Feldman, 2003).

In contrast to mtDNA and Y chromosome analyses, phylogenetic analyses of some nuclear genes (or portions of genes) and noncoding regions of chromosomes indicate MRCAs that are substantially older than 200 000 years. In the case of genes that code for proteins, this is not necessarily surprising because variation in their structures could be strongly constrained or influenced by natural selection (of course, this is also true of the coding regions of mtDNA and the Y chromosome). However, even if natural selection is involved in shaping the patterns of variability we see, the geographic origins of different alleles can provide insights into human evolutionary history.

A 3000-base pair region of the beta-globin gene (one of the chains of the hemoglobin protein) provides a phylogenetic tree with an MRCA for the gene existing 800 000 years ago, with the oldest sequence coming from Africa (Figure 14.18b). This finding does not contradict the mtDNA and Y chromosome results because the variation in this gene could have arisen and evolved in Africa before a population expansion out of Africa less than 200 000 years ago. However, Asia-specific beta-globin sequences had MRCAs more than 200 000 years ago. This would indicate that Asian populations that existed before 200 000 years ago made unique genetic contributions to the contemporary human genome, a finding that is difficult to reconcile with the mtDNA and Y chromosome results.

Box 14.2 The Genghis Khan Effect

Y chromosome haplotypes can be an important tool in understanding the genetic histories of human populations. In a survey of more than 2000 men from Asia using more than thirty-two genetic markers, Tatiana Zerjal and her colleagues (2003) found a Y chromosome lineage that exhibited an unusual pattern. Given the large number of markers used, most men in the survey had a unique haplotype; if two men shared a haplotype, they were always from the same population. However, one group consisted of very similar haplotypes clearly derived from a single Y chromosome ancestral haplotype. Zerjal and colleagues called this haplotype the star cluster (reflecting the emergence of these similar variants from a common source). The interesting thing about the star cluster lineage is that it is found in sixteen different populations, distributed across Asia from the Pacific Ocean to the Caspian Sea. What could explain this wide distribution?

The MRCA for this cluster was dated to about 1000 years ago. Zerjal and her colleagues point out that the distribution of populations in which the lineage is found corresponds roughly to the maximum extent of the Mongol Empire, which reached its peak under Genghis Khan (c. 1162–1227) (Figure A). Khan and his close male relatives are known to have fathered many children (thousands, according to some historical sources). The lineage appears to have originated in Mongolia, where populations today have some of the highest frequencies of star cluster haplotypes.

The Mongols were notoriously brutal and efficient conquerors, and as they expanded their empire across Asia, they killed many thousands of people. In many areas, relatives of Genghis Khan established dynastic lineages that ruled for centuries after the Mongol Empire proper fell apart (as a unified entity, it did not last long after the death of Genghis Khan). One additional population outside the Mongol Empire also has a high frequency of the star cluster Y chromosome: the Hazaras of Pakistan and Afghanistan. This is puzzling at first glance, but the Hazaras may have a Mongol origin; in fact, many Hazaras consider themselves to be direct male-line descendants of Genghis Khan. The star cluster pattern is absent from other populations in this area.

The star cluster lineage clearly has its roots in Mongolia, and its spread across Asia seems to be linked to the expansion of the Mongol Empire. This distribution could have resulted from the migration of a group of Mongols carrying the haplotype or may even reflect the Y chromosome carried specifically by Genghis Khan and his relatives. Zerjal and her colleagues favour the latter explanation. They point out that there is still a substantial amount of haplotype diversity in Mongolian populations; therefore, it is more likely that the star cluster represents the Y chromosome found in a group of closely related individuals, namely Genghis Khan and his male relatives. Zerjal and colleagues state that the wide distribution of the star cluster lineage is evidence of "a novel form of selection in human populations on the basis of social prestige" (p. 720). With that social prestige and political power, Genghis Khan and his male descendants obviously took advantage of the many reproductive opportunities that came their way. Centuries later, we see the effects of this extraordinary history written in the structure of the Y chromosome, even though the Mongol rulers themselves disappeared long ago, physically and culturally assimilated into the populations they ruled.

FIGURE A Genghis Khan spread more than fear across Eurasia.

Evidence of gene flow between Asian and African populations during the last several hundred thousand years was also found.

Results broadly similar to those for the beta-globin gene have been obtained in other studies of the nuclear genome (Zhao et al., 2000). These findings support the beta-globin results in that an ancient MRCA (>400 000 years old) is identified, with the deepest root of the tree indicating an African origin, and the MRCA for regional variation outside Africa is found to be more than 200 000 years old. Again, these kinds of results indicate a more complex picture of the genetic origins of our species than those suggested by mtDNA and Y chromosome analyses.

ANCIENT DNA

Ancient DNA (aDNA) recovered from fossils can provide a direct window into the genetics of past populations. Unfortunately, only a small percentage of fossil remains actually preserve any DNA. Several factors influence whether DNA will be intact enough for phylogenetic analysis. Age is a critical factor. Although in the early days of ancient DNA research (the late 1980s and early 1990s) many claims were made for the recovery of DNA from very ancient samples (more than 1 million years old), many subsequent research studies indicate that recovering usable DNA from fossils older than 100 000 years is extremely unlikely (Wayne et al., 1999). Temperature and humidity are also critical to whether DNA will be preserved: Cold and dry is better than warm and wet. In terms of hominid fossils, this suggests those from northern Europe and northern Asia are the most likely to provide intact DNA, whereas hominids in the tropics such as portions of Africa and Southeast Asia are least likely.

Ancient DNA from eight Neandertal individuals and seven fossil modern humans, all from Europe, has been recovered and analyzed (more than 25 Neandertals and 40 fossil humans were sampled to achieve these few results). All of the studies agree that the Neandertal samples all fall outside the range of variation that has been observed in modern humans (Carmelli et al., 2003; Krings et al., 1997, 2000; Ovchinikov et al., 2000; Schmitz et al., 2002; Serre et al., 2004) (Figure 14.18c). Furthermore, Neandertal samples cluster together as a clade separate from living humans on a phylogenetic tree. Sequence variation in the Neandertal sample is approximately equivalent to the level of variation observed in living modern human groups. Researchers estimate that the MRCA for modern humans and Neandertals lived between 853 000 and 365 000 years ago. An MRCA date for the western and eastern Neandertal samples has been estimated to be between 352 000 and 151 000 years ago. More importantly, ancient DNA from Neandertals also falls outside the range of variation found in ancient DNA from fossil modern humans. And all fossil humans fail to show any Neandertal DNA or any intermediate sequences and are much closer to living human DNA, despite being closer in age to the Neandertal remains.

Many researchers think that the Neandertal ancient DNA data strongly support the replacement model of modern human origins. However, some analysts (for example, Nordborg, 1998; Relethford, 2001) argue that a small number of divergent mtDNA sequences from Neandertals does not rule out the possibility that they may have interbred with anatomically modern humans; it is not that difficult to construct mathematical population models that can account for the mtDNA data in the context of modern human–Neandertal admixture. At this time, the Neandertal genetic data do not support including Neandertals in *H. sapiens*, but, by the same token, they cannot be used to definitely rule out such a possibility.

INTERPRETING MODELS OF HUMAN ORIGINS

Let us now look at how our three sets of data, palaeontology, archaeology, and genetics, are interpreted with respect to the origin of modern humans.

As originally developed, the multiregional model proposed that *local regional anatomical continuity* provides strong evidence of the multiregional origins of modern humans (Wolpoff et al., 1984, 1994; Wolpoff and Caspari, 1997). *Local regional continuity* means we can trace a particular evolutionary trajectory through a suite of anatomical features shared by fossil specimens in a particular region; we can identify this regional anatomical pattern despite the fact that there has been a substantial amount of morphological evolution between *H. erectus* and anatomically modern *H. sapiens*. For example, widely dispersed populations of *H. erectus* exhibited regional anatomical variation (see Chapter 12), and that regional variation may have been retained in later hominid populations living in the same area.

In contrast to the multiregional model, the replacement model suggests that the earliest modern humans should look very different from the local populations they replaced and should exhibit regional continuity in only one source region, Africa (Bräuer, 1984; Stringer and Andrews, 1988). Anatomically modern humans first appeared in Africa between 200 000 and 100 000 years ago, and fossil lineages from archaic *H. sapiens* provide evidence of an African origin of *H. sapiens sapiens* that predates such a lineage elsewhere in the world. At the same time as anatomically modern humans appear in Africa, archaic *H. sapiens* populations in Europe seem to be evolving into classic Neandertals. Because of their physical distinctiveness, Neandertals are seen to reflect a separate evolutionary trajectory, and thus are likely to have ultimately constituted a separate species. From about 40 000 to 30 000 years ago, Neandertals and anatomically modern humans appear to overlap in time and space in Europe, although they are physically and culturally distinct. By about 30 000 years ago modern humans have replaced Neandertals in Europe.

It is probably safe to say that there is more support for the replacement viewpoint than for the multiregional model of evolution within the palaeoanthropological community. It is equally safe to say, however, that the field is far from consensus on the issue and that many palaeoanthropologists think that the fossil record provides at least some support in some regions for multiregional evolution.

Similarly, genetic data from both living humans and fossil remains provide some clear, but not unequivocal support for a replacement model of human origins. Although the molecular data can say nothing about the anatomy of the MRCA, the picture presented by mtDNA and the Y chromosome is easy to reconcile with the palaeontological replacement model, which places the origins of anatomically modern humans in Africa during roughly the same time period of the MRCA for these molecular phylogenies. The divergent mtDNA sequences of the Neandertals provide further support for a replacement event in Europe, especially in light of the fact that early modern humans in Europe have mtDNA that is well within the range of variation seen in contemporary humans.

Data primarily from nuclear genes appear to indicate MRCAs that significantly predate the MRCAs suggested by mtDNA and the Y chromosome. The most ancient lineages of these nuclear genes tend to come from Africa, but not all do, and some of the lineages outside Africa predate 200 000 years ago (Harding et al., 1997; Takahata et al., 2001). Furthermore, a combined analysis of haplotype trees derived from mtDNA, the Y chromosome, two regions of the X chromosome, and six autosomal nuclear sequences indicates the existence of extensive gene flow between populations throughout the Old World, dating to at least 500 000 years ago and probably longer, including several population expansions out of Africa between the original dispersal 1.7 million years ago and the expansion indicated by mtDNA and the Y chromosome of approximately 100 000 years ago (Templeton, 2002). This may mean that the expansion of cranial capacity that begins to appear about 500 000 to 400 000 years ago in archaic *H. sapiens* coincides with genetic evidence for another out-of-Africa expansion (in the context of gene flow).

There is no simple answer to the question, Where did modern humans come from? Genetic, palaeontological, and archaeological data can be woven together to produce several different scenarios to explain our complex origins (Table 14.1). Some of the controversy surrounding the issue derives from scientific success, as new dating methods, new archaeological and fossil discoveries, and innovative genetic approaches have all provided an unprecedented amount of information devoted to a single evolutionary event. The controversy over which particular model of human origins is correct should not blind us to the fact that we know far more about the biological and cultural evolution of our own species than ever before.

TABLE 14.1 Comparing Replacement and Multiregional Models of Human Origins

	FACT	REPLACEMENT INTERPRETATION	MULTIREGIONAL INTERPRETATION
Palaeontological Record, Middle Pleistocene	Between about 500 000 and 200 000 years ago, archaic *H. sapiens* lived in Africa, Europe, and Asia. Fully modern humans and classic Neandertals appeared by 125 000 years ago.	Archaic *H. sapiens* in Europe evolved into Neandertals. African archaic populations evolved into anatomically modern *Homo sapiens*.	Neandertals and modern humans are not separate evolutionary lineages. Neandertals are transitional to European modern humans.
Palaeontological Record, Late Pleistocene	The anatomically modern human phenotype first appeared outside Africa 100 000 to 90 000 years ago in the Middle East.	Anatomically modern humans replaced pre-existing hominids throughout the Old World without or with little genetic mixings. Similarities between early anatomically modern humans from widely dispersed populations are best explained by evolution from a common source population in Africa.	Anatomically modern humans arose from extensive gene flow among Middle and Late Pleistocene hominid populations throughout the Old World. Some fossils show transitional anatomy.
Recent DNA Studies	mtDNA and the Y chromosome phylogenies indicate greatest variability in Africa, suggesting that the most recent common ancestor (MRCA) of modern humans lived in Africa 200 000 to 150 000 years ago. Nuclear gene sequences indicate MRCAs that significantly predate 200 000 years ago. Furthermore, deep lineages of these trees have been traced to variants that appear to have originated outside Africa.	mtDNA and the Y chromosome support an African origin for modern humans and indicate a population expansion out of Africa starting about 100 000 years ago. Nuclear gene sequences reflect the age of the first dispersal (*H. erectus*) from Africa and do not preclude another dispersal by modern *H. sapiens* about 100 000 years ago. They are inconsistent with a complete replacement event.	Nuclear gene sequences indicate extensive gene flow between Old World populations over the last 500 000 years and perhaps longer. Diverse ancient Old World populations contributed to the modern human gene pool.
Ancient DNA	Ancient DNA from Neandertal and modern human fossils of the same age differ more from one another than does the DNA of living human groups. Differences between Neandertal and modern human DNA are not as great as those between chimp species. Even some fossils considered transitional in anatomy do not have transitional DNA.	Neandertals are a separate species that did not make a substantial genetic contribution to modern humans. Neandertals were replaced across their range 40 000 to 30 000 years ago.	Differences between Neandertals and humans are less than those between chimp species and do not support a separate species for Neandertals.

SUMMARY

1. **How do modern humans differ anatomically from earlier hominids?**

   The emergence of modern humans can be seen anatomically in a combination of cranial features that distinguish us from archaic *H. sapiens* and Neandertals. These include a gracile skull and postcranial anatomy, limited development of browridges or other cranial superstructures, a rounded cranium with a high maximum cranial breadth and parallel sides, a prominent mastoid process, a retracted face with a canine fossa, small teeth and jaws, and development of an obvious chin.

2. **How do replacement models explain the origin of modern humans?**

   Replacement models of modern human origins argue that our species initially evolved in one location (Africa) and then spread out from that location, replacing all other hominid populations without interbreeding with them. All regional variation—genetic or anatomical—that we now observe in contemporary human populations has arisen since that replacement event occurred.

3. **How do multiregional models explain the origin of modern humans?**

   Multiregional models suggest that *H. erectus* hominids distributed throughout the Old World have formed one widely distributed species with substantial gene flow between its diverse populations. Genetic innovations that arose in one population of the species were passed by gene flow to other populations in different regions. Regional variation in *H. erectus* and other Middle to Late Pleistocene taxa is considered to have been maintained even as local *H. erectus* populations made the transition to anatomically modern human form.

4. **How do Upper Palaeolithic and Middle Palaeolithic tools differ?**

   Although they may occur sporadically in the Middle Palaeolithic, the main distinguishing feature of Upper Palaeolithic stone tools is a reliance on blades and microliths. In addition, Upper Palaeolithic industries show a greater reliance on tools made from material other than stone, such as bone, antler, and shell.

5. **What is an MRCA?**

   In a phylogenetic tree, the most recent common ancestor (MRCA) is indicated by the deepest node from which all contemporary variants can be shown to have evolved. Because all living people are genetically related to one another, the deepest node in a phylogenetic tree corresponds to a basic biological reality: All the variation we observe today evolved from a common ancestor.

CRITICAL THINKING QUESTIONS

1. What do you think is the significance of early signals of modern behaviour in the archaeological record of Africa? How would you define modern behaviour?
2. What might be the importance of modern humans using symbolic behaviour to interact with their environment? What advantages and disadvantages would this have for them?
3. Why do you think humans kept expanding into new territories? Do you think we will continue to do so, and where will those areas be?

KEY TERMS

replacement models
multiregional models
microliths
most recent common ancestor (MRCA)

SUGGESTED READING

Klein, Richard G., and Edgar, Blake. (2002). *The Dawn of Human Culture*. Wiley, New York, NY.

Wells, Spencer. (2003). *The Journey of Man: A Genetic Odyssey*. Princeton University Press, Princeton, NJ.

Willoughby, Pamela R. (2007) *The Evolution of Modern Humans in Africa: A comprehensive guide*. AltaMira Press, Lanham, MD.

Part V

BIOLOGY AND BEHAVIOUR OF MODERN HUMANS

Chapter 15
Evolution of the Brain and Language

On the morning of April 12, 1861, Professor Paul Broca walked through the surgical ward of the Bicêtre hospital in Paris. An eminent scientist and surgeon and later a member of the French Senate, Broca was there that morning to meet a gravely ill patient, named Leborgne, who had a long history of abnormal behaviour.

At the time of Broca's meeting with Leborgne, scientists interested in the human brain were embroiled in a fundamental debate about the nature of brain function. Some argued that the functions of the brain were evenly distributed throughout the brain; they believed that there were no regions of the brain that were specialized for any particular behaviour or function. Others, such as Broca, believed that at least some of the functions of the brain were based in, or localized to, certain specific areas. Unfortunately for the advocates of localization, the pseudoscience of phrenology held a similar viewpoint, although the phrenologists believed they could define localized, functional areas of the brain based on the external morphology not of the brain but of the skull. That the phrenologists' claims were not based on empirical studies did not prevent phrenology from becoming a popular fad, famous throughout the world.

When Broca examined Leborgne, he found a 50-year-old man who was very weak and could no longer walk. His vision was poor, but his

Chapter Outline

hearing was still good. He clearly understood what was being said to him, but he had only one response to any question asked of him: "Tan." As Broca talked to his caregivers (Leborgne had been under care for more than 20 years), his parents, and other patients on the ward, he learned that Leborgne had suffered from seizures as a child but had recovered from them. At age 30, however, Leborgne lost the ability to speak, at which time he was first admitted to the Bicêtre hospital. Starting 10 years after losing his speech, Leborgne had slowly developed a paralysis in his right arm and then his right leg, which eventually confined him to his bed.

LEBORGNE WAS NOT SENILE OR INSANE, although the other patients generally considered him to be egotistical and rude. Because almost the only word he could say was *tan*, he became known as Tan to the rest of the hospital. The other word he could say was an expletive that he uttered when agitated or angry.

LEBORGNE DIED ONLY 5 DAYS AFTER MEETING BROCA, on the morning of April 17. Within 24 hours, Broca had performed an autopsy on the patient, and on that same day, obviously with some sense of urgency, he discussed Leborgne's case at a meeting of the Society of Anthropology, an organization he had founded in 1859 (which was the first anthropological organization in the world). Broca described in careful detail the damage he had found on the outer (lateral) surface of the left hemisphere of Leborgne's brain, a region that he concluded must have a specialized function involving the articulation of speech.

BROCA HAD IDENTIFIED A LANGUAGE AREA of the brain. Later neuroscientists called this part of the brain Broca's area in honour of his demonstration of the localization of language function in the human brain.

Although the human species possesses many features that help to make us unique, it is our complex behaviour and extraordinary traditional and material cultures that set us apart from all other animals. Our behaviour is ultimately the product of an anatomical feature: the human brain. Complex cultural behaviour is made possible by a specific behavioural adaptation—**language**—that has evolved since the hominid lineage split from the great apes. The study of the evolution of brain and language highlights the relationship between our behaviour and our biology.

In this chapter, we will review the evolution of the human brain and language. The human brain is a structure of great complexity, and it produces behaviours that are of unparalleled sophistication in the animal world. Yet we need to keep in mind that the human brain is assembled from the same basic cellular parts as found in most other animals, and its basic structural organization is reflected in the brains of both closely and distantly related species. At some point in hominid evolution, changes in the brain led to the appearance of a species that behaved more like us and less like our ape cousins. Compared with the brains of our closest relatives, the human brain is larger, and it exhibits important differences in its functional organization.

Some of these organizational differences in the human brain reflect the evolution of language. When we consider the fundamental importance of language to human social existence, it is not surprising that it is a behaviour that is well represented in the functional organization of the brain. Language has also help shaped the anatomy of the throat, leading to the development of an organ of speech capable of producing an extraordinary range of sounds.

We will never know exactly when our hominid ancestors started to communicate with one another using a system of communication that was more like language and less like the forms of communication used by other primates. Language, and the soft tissues that produce it, do not fossilize. But with a greater understanding of brain function and of the natural history of language, anthropologists, linguists, psychologists, and other scientists have turned to the problem of language origins with increasing enthusiasm in recent years.

OVERVIEW OF THE BRAIN

Before addressing the evolution of the hominid brain and language, it is necessary to briefly review some neuroanatomy. The central nervous system consists of two main parts: the spinal cord and the brain. The spinal cord is a thick bundle of nerve fibres that runs through the bony canal formed by the vertebrae of the spine. It is the structure through which all the nerves of the body connect to the brain. The spinal cord passes through the foramen magnum of the skull (which you read about in Chapter 10 in connection with the evolution of bipedality), where it connects to the brain.

The brain consists of three major parts: the **brain stem**, the **cerebellum**, and the **cerebrum** (Figure 15.1). As its name suggests, the brain stem sits at the base of the brain and connects directly to the spinal cord. The brain stem is important in the regulation and control of complex motor patterns, in breathing, and in the regulation of sleep and consciousness. The cerebellum, or "little brain," sits tucked under the rest of the brain, behind the brain stem. It is densely packed with nerve cells, or neurons. The cerebellum is important in the control of balance, posture, and voluntary movements.

The cerebrum is the part of the brain that has undergone the most obvious changes over the course of human evolution. It is divided almost evenly along the sagittal midline into *left* and *right hemispheres*. The hemispheres can differ subtly in morphology and more substantially in function. The outer surface of the cerebrum is crisscrossed by a complex arrangement of grooves known as **sulci**, which gives the human cerebrum its characteristic wrinkled appearance. The sulci divide the surface of the brain into a series of thick bands or ridges, which are called **gyri**. Although there is individual variation, several basic sulci divide the brain into functional regions that are common to almost everyone.

If we look at a cross-section through the cerebrum (Figure 15.2), we notice that its outer surface is actually formed by a rim of tissue (4 to 6 millimetres [0.16 to 0.24 in] thick) that follows the surface down into the valleys formed by the sulci; this is the cerebral cortex.

language The unique system of communication used by members of the human species.

brain stem The part of the brain that controls basal metabolic rates, respiration, pulse, and other basic body functions.

cerebellum The "little brain" tucked under the cerebrum, which is important in the control of balance, posture, and voluntary movement.

cerebrum The largest part of the human brain, which is split into left and right hemispheres. Seat of all "higher" brain functions.

sulci (sing., sulcus) Grooves on the surface of the brain that divide the hemispheres into gyri.

gyri (sing., gyrus) Ridges on the surface of the brain that are formed by sulci.

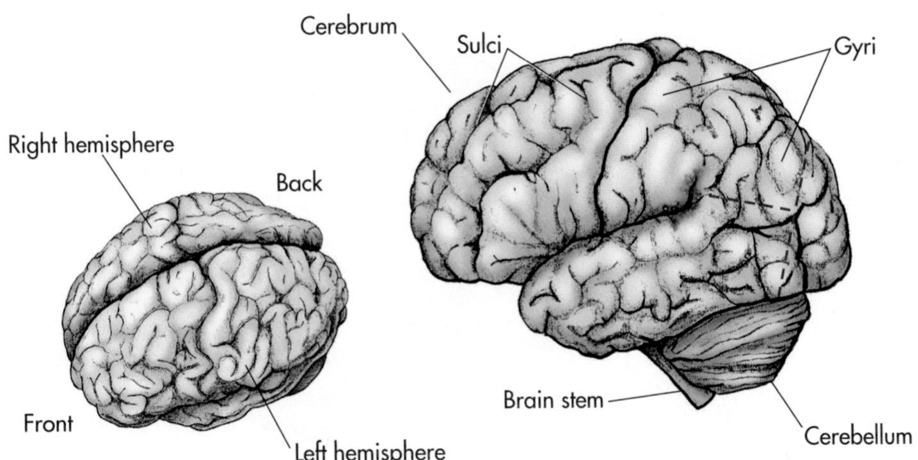

FIGURE 15.1 The human cerebrum is divided into two hemispheres, which are themselves divided by sulci into gyri.

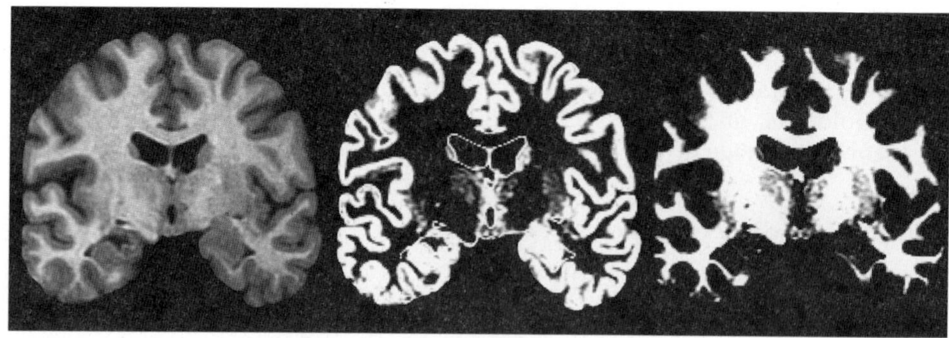

FIGURE 15.2 A cross-section through the cerebral cortex.

Major Divisions of the Cerebrum

Each of the hemispheres is divided into four major sectors, or *lobes* (Figure 15.3). Two of the major boundaries of the lobes are formed by the *Sylvian fissure* and the *central sulcus*. The *frontal lobe*, which makes up about 38% of the hemisphere (Allen et al., 2002), is the part of the brain located just behind your forehead. The *parietal lobe* (about 25% of the hemisphere) is just behind the frontal lobe on the other side of the central sulcus. Below the Sylvian fissure, the *temporal lobe* (22%) forms the "thumb" of the hemisphere, as it appears in a side view. The *occipital lobe* (9 to 10%) forms the "knob" at the back of the hemisphere. In chimpanzees and other primates, the occipital lobe is clearly separated from the other lobes by the *lunate sulcus*, a semicircular sulcus running in an arc along the posterior (back) lateral surface of the hemisphere. In humans, the lunate sulcus often is missing or present only as a minor sulcus that does not indicate a functional boundary for the occipital lobe.

Another significant part of the cerebrum—considered major because of its function—is the *limbic system*. The limbic system is buried within the hemispheres in the midline region of the brain and is composed of several interrelated structures. The limbic system is most notable for being the seat of emotion (Ledoux, 1996).

Primary and Association Areas of the Cerebral Cortex

primary cortex Regions of the cerebral cortex that are involved directly with motor control or sensory input.

Different regions of the cerebrum have different functions. The cerebral cortex is divided into two kinds of functional areas. **Primary cortex** is involved directly with either motor control or input from the senses. Most of the human cerebral cortex

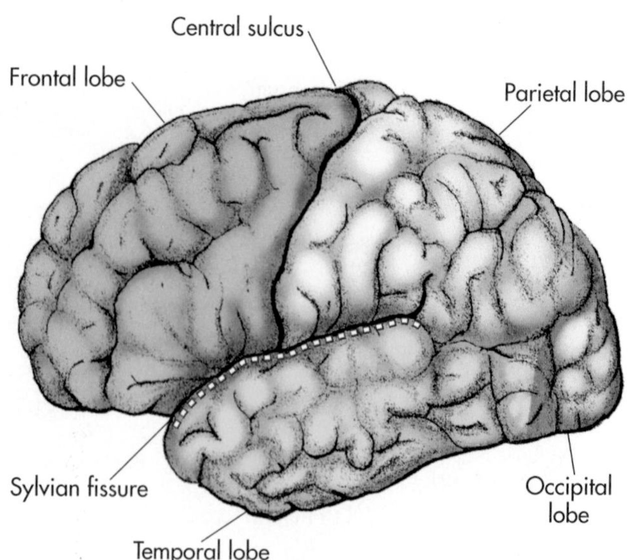

FIGURE 15.3 The major lobes of the cerebrum.

is not primary cortex but rather **association cortex**. We can think of the association cortex as the regions where the processing of primary inputs or information occurs. It is generally believed that in mammals, as brain size increases, the proportion of the brain devoted to association rather than primary regions also increases. Some association areas receive inputs from only one primary area, and other regions receive inputs from multiple primary regions. Anything that we think of as a higher-level function, such as thought, decision making, art, or music, originates in association cortices.

FIGURE 15.4 Pierre Paul Broca, a pioneer neuroscientist and anthropologist.

METHODS FOR STUDYING BRAIN STRUCTURE AND FUNCTION

Several different methods for studying brain structure and function have developed over the past 150 years. Broca's study of his patient Tan included two methods. One was the *autopsy*, for many years the only way scientists had of studying brain structure, in which the brain is examined and described after a person's death. Broca (Figure 15.4) combined the autopsy with the *lesion method*, which correlates a behavioural abnormality in a living person with a brain abnormality observed at autopsy. Broca observed a lesion in the left lateral frontal lobe in a man with impoverished speech production, thus allowing him to make the inference that this region is important in speech. The lesion method relies on "natural experiments": observations of people who have sustained a brain injury (for example, via stroke or infection) and who also exhibit a behavioural deficit. It has also been used widely as an experimental tool using animals as subjects; much of what we know about mammalian brain function comes from such studies.

Over the past 20 years, the development of a field called *neuroimaging* has revolutionized the study of the brain. Noninvasive methods allow us to observe the structure and function of the brain in living, healthy people under controlled experimental conditions. **Magnetic resonance imaging (MRI)** is the most commonly used method to study brain structure in living individuals (Figure 15.5). A magnetic resonance image of the brain is essentially a high-resolution map of water concentration in the brain. For the study of brain function and activity, scientists use techniques such as *positron emission tomography* (PET) scanning and *functional MRI*. These methods show which parts of the brain are activated during a cognitive act (thinking of a word, listening to a sound, remembering an emotion) by identifying areas where metabolism or blood flow has increased.

Although recent technological advances have provided us with some extraordinary tools for examining the brain, the study of the evolution of brain structure and function, or **palaeoneurology**, remains for the most part dependent on the study of endocasts. *Endocasts* are impressions of the interior part of the cranium, from which we can make inferences about the size and structure of the brain (see Tobias, 1971, for an overview) (Figure 15.6). Scientists make endocasts from fossil skulls, or in rare cases endocasts form naturally during fossilization. Unfortunately, the brain is separated from the inside of the cranium by several protective tissue layers and cerebrospinal fluid; therefore, endocasts

association cortex Parts of the cerebral cortex where inputs from primary motor and sensory cortex are processed.

magnetic resonance imaging (MRI) A technique for visualizing body tissues (including the nervous system). It works essentially as a map of water concentration in different tissues of the body.

palaeoneurology The study of the evolution of brain structure and function.

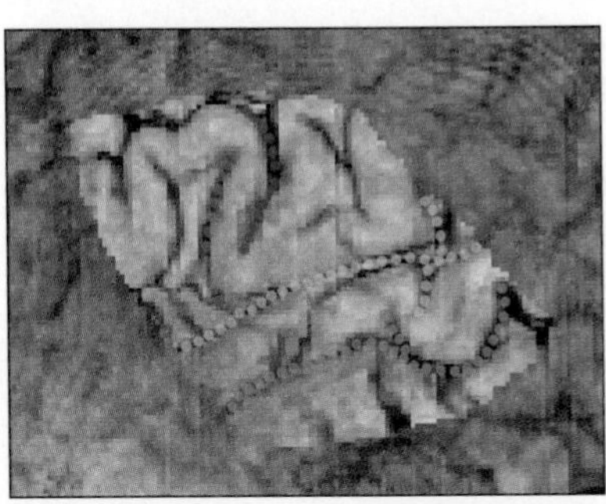

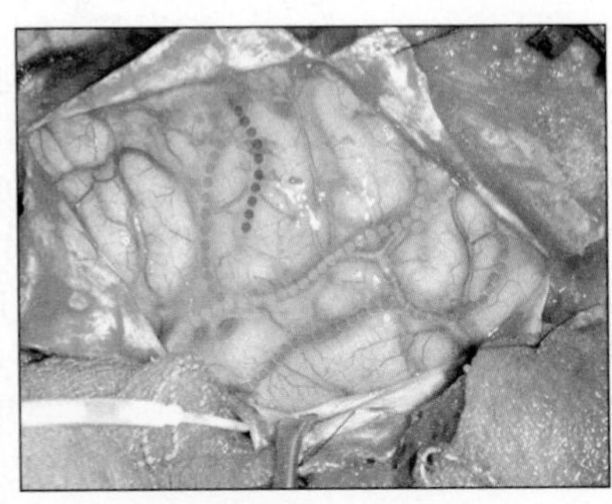

FIGURE 15.5 On the left, a portion of the surface of the brain as seen in an MRI. On the right, the same portion of the brain shown during surgery.

FIGURE 15.6 Endocasts from South African australopithecines.

are inevitably a poor reflection of the brain's anatomy. Nonetheless, they provide us with the only source of direct information we have about the brain structure of extinct species.

ISSUES IN HOMINID BRAIN EVOLUTION

Now we are ready to tackle some specific issues in hominid brain evolution. Understandably, most of the important questions examine ways in which the human brain is different from the brains of other primates and mammals.

BRAIN SIZE AND ENCEPHALIZATION

One of the defining features of the genus *Homo*, and especially our own species, is large brain size. But what do we mean by "large"? In absolute terms, the human brain weighs in at about 1300 grams (46 oz), and human cranial capacities usually are reported to be in the region of 1300 to 1400 cc. These are average figures, and there is much variation in brain size; however, for purposes of cross-species comparisons, the 1350-cc estimate for the volume of the typical human brain is good enough.

Look at the cranial capacities of various primates listed in Table 15.1. As you can see, humans have the largest brains among primates. The second largest brains belong to the gorillas. Among the Old World monkeys, baboons appear to have relatively large brains. As discussed in Chapter 7, among the New World monkeys, spider monkeys have substantially larger brains than their close relatives, howler monkeys. To put these data in a broader zoological context, horses have brains of about 609 cc—somewhat larger than that seen in a great ape (Figure 15.7).

Encephalization Quotients Many scientists find absolute brain size values to be of limited usefulness in understanding brain evolution or the relationship between brain size and behaviour. After all, it comes as no surprise that bigger animals have

TABLE 15.1 Cranial Capacity, Body Weight, and Encephalization Quotient (EQ) of Several Primate Species

SPECIES	CRANIAL CAPACITY (CC)	BODY WEIGHT (KG)	EQ
APES			
Homo sapiens, male	1424.5	71.9	4.32
Homo sapiens, female	1285.2	57.2	4.64
Gorilla gorilla (gorilla), male	537.4	169.5	0.85
Gorilla gorilla (gorilla), female	441.4	71.5	1.34
Pan troglodytes (chimpanzee)	388.6	83.7	1.48
Pongo pygmaeus (orangutan), male	393.1	87.7	1.08
Pongo pygmaeus (orangutan), female	341.2	37.8	1.69
Hylobates lar (gibbon)	98.3	5.5	2.10
OLD WORLD MONKEYS			
Papio anubis (baboon), male	166.4	23.5	1.18
Papio anubis (baboon), female	141.4	11.9	1.69
Cercocebus albigena (grey-cheeked mangabey)	97.3	7.69	1.63
Colobus guerza (black and white colobus)	75.4	9.05	1.11
NEW WORLD MONKEYS			
Ateles geoffroyi (spider monkey)	126.4	6.00	2.55
Alouatta palliata (howler monkey)	62.8	6.55	1.18
Saimiri sciureus (squirrel monkey)	24.4	0.68	2.58

Note: Values from Kappelman (1996), using Martin's (1983) formula for EQ. New World monkey values calculated from Harvey et al. (1987). If male and female values are not shown, midpoint values between male and female averages are shown.

HORSE: weight, 400kg; cranial capacity 600cc
CHIMPANZEE: weight, 80kg; cranial capacity, 400cc

FIGURE 15.7 Chimpanzees and horses have brains that are similar in size.

bigger brains than smaller animals, but just because a big animal has a big brain that does not mean that the animal is more intelligent. Scientists try to deal with this issue by measuring the **encephalization** of a species, which is a measure of brain size relative to body size. The relationship between brain size and body size is somewhat more complicated than a simple linear relationship, but calculations have been developed that allow us to calculate the expected brain size for a mammal of any size (Jerison, 1991; Martin, 1983). The **encephalization quotient (EQ)** is a ratio of the actual brain size to the expected size. Thus mammals that have EQs greater than 1.00 have brains that are larger than expected for a mammal of their size; an EQ less than 1.00 means that it is smaller than expected.

Returning to Table 15.1, we see that humans have the largest brains not only in absolute but also in relative terms, as measured by the EQ. In general, anthropoid primates have EQs greater than 1.00, indicating that their brains are larger than would be expected for mammals of their size. So even though horses have brains that are ape-sized in absolute terms, their EQs are smaller than those of apes because of their larger body sizes. It is generally assumed that the larger brain size in anthropoid primates has evolved in conjunction with the evolution of complex social behaviour and adaptation to the arboreal environment.

Can we say that mammals with higher EQs are in some sense "smarter" than those with lower EQs? Yes and no. The encephalization quotient is derived from both brain size *and* body size and there is a tendency to overlook the fact that animals face strong selection pressures that shape body size as well as brain size (Deacon, 1997). Among dog breeds, for example, chihuahuas are more encephalized than German shepherds; artificial selection on chihuahuas has driven body size down at a faster rate than brain size (Figure 15.8). But no one would argue that a chihuahua is smarter than a German shepherd. In anthropoids, small or even dwarfed species, such as the squirrel monkey in the New World or the talapoin monkey in the Old World, have high EQs. Again, rather than interpreting this as a sign of large brain size, we could also see it as an example of selection for small body size (which is probably more correct).

encephalization A measure relating brain size to body size in a species.

encephalization quotient (EQ) The ratio of the actual brain size of a species to its expected brain size based on a statistical regression of brain to body size based on a large number of species.

Colobine monkeys tend to have lower EQs than cercopithecine monkeys (see the mangabey versus the colobus in Table 15.1). There is no evidence that colobine behaviour is in some sense less sophisticated than cercopithecine behaviour. Colobine monkeys are adapted to a leafy diet; this digestive requirement has driven selection for greater gut and body size, resulting in lower EQs. Colobines are still more encephalized than a typical mammal. Gorillas, who have large brains in absolute size, also have low EQs. Again, their low-quality, leafy diet (as well as other factors, such as protection from predation) may have driven selection for larger body size, leaving them with EQs lower than their closest relatives, the other apes. On the other hand, in a comparison of two closely related species sharing a particular environment, such as the spider and howler monkeys, it is reasonable to hypothesize that larger brain size in the spider monkey may have evolved as a result of the greater cognitive demands of frugivory. In summary, the EQ is a potentially valuable indicator of cognitive ability but we need to remember that it is a function of both brain and body size.

Sex Differences in Primate Brain Size In almost all primate species, males have larger brains than females. In the three highly sexually dimorphic species listed in Table 15.1 (orangutans, gorillas, and baboons), the absolute brain size differences are large, as are the body size differences. In each case, EQs for the females are substantially larger than for males. The EQ for male gorillas is below 1.0, indicating that their brains are smaller than

FIGURE 15.8 Encephalization is a function of both brain size and body size.

we would expect for a mammal their size. There is strong selection for male body size in highly sexually dimorphic primate species, but there is no reason to suppose that there are profound differences in the level of behavioural sophistication between the sexes.

Even in less sexually dimorphic primate species, such as rhesus macaques and humans, males have larger brains than females. This is true after we correct for body size (Holloway, 1980; Falk et al., 1999). Although we could speculate on the selection forces on behaviour or other biological processes that might drive such a sex difference, one conclusion is that the sex difference in brain size observed in humans is not a function of recent evolution for higher cognitive function in hominids but seems to reflect a general primate trend (Falk et al., 1999).

Brain Size and the Fossil Record

In the previous chapters, you read that increasing brain size is a characteristic of genus *Homo*. A compilation of average cranial capacities of different hominid fossil taxa is presented in Table 15.2. (Please note that the *H. sapiens* values in Tables 15.1 and 15.2 differ because they are based on different samples.) As you can see, the different groups can be sorted to some extent according to their cranial capacities and EQs. Of course, this comes as no surprise because cranial capacity is one of the morphological features we use to classify specimens into different taxonomic groups.

Early Hominids and Robust *Australopithecus* Brain size increases from the early australopithecines (*A. afarensis* and *A. africanus*) to the robust australopithecines. The early australopithecines have cranial capacities similar in size to those seen in chimpanzees, orangutans, and female gorillas, whereas the cranial capacities of the robust forms are more similar to those seen in male gorillas.

Are the robust australopithecines species more encephalized than the earlier australopithecines? Are graciles and robusts more encephalized than the contemporary great apes? Answers to these questions depend on estimates of body mass and brain size. It seems that australopithecines were smaller than contemporary great apes; given that their cranial capacities were at least as large, we can conclude that gracile and robust australopithecines were indeed more encephalized than the great apes. In addition, the brain size increase seen in the robust forms relative to the earlier forms is also likely to reflect an increase in encephalization.

Table 15.2 Average Cranial Capacities for Fossil Hominids (adult specimens only)

TAXON	NUMBER OF SPECIMENS	AVERAGE CRANIAL CAPACITY (CC)	RANGE (CC)	ESTIMATED EQ
A. afarensis	2	450	400 to 500	1.87
A. africanus	7	445	405 to 500	2.16
A. robustus and *A. boisei*	7	507	475 to 530	2.50
H. habilis	7	631	509 to 775	2.73 to 3.38
H. erectus	22	1003	650 to 1251	3.27
Archaic *H. sapiens*	18	1330	1100 to 1586	3.52
H. neanderthalensis	19	1445	1200 to 1750	4.04
Modern *H. sapiens* (older than 8000 years)	11	1490	1290 to 1600	5.27

Sources: Aiello and Dean (1990), Kappelman (1996), and Holloway (1999).

Note: Estimated EQs are not derived using all the specimens included in the second column.

Early *Homo* and *Homo erectus* Hominid fossils assigned to *Homo habilis* or early *Homo* have cranial capacities substantially larger on average (by 25 to 30%) than those seen in *Australopithecus* or the great apes, and with the relatively small habiline body size this represents an increase in encephalization over earlier hominids. As you read earlier, the appearance of *H. habilis* roughly coincides with the appearance of stone tools in the archaeological record, providing evidence of at least one kind of cognitive evolution.

The average cranial capacity of fossils assigned to *H. erectus* shows an even more profound jump than *H. habilis* in both relative and absolute size compared with earlier hominid taxa. Although both brain and body size increased in *H. erectus*, brain size may have increased relatively more quickly, leading to an increase in encephalization (Kappelman 1996). *H. erectus* was widely distributed geographically and exhibited gradual change over its more than 1 million years in existence. On average, the earliest *H. erectus* specimens have smaller cranial capacities than later specimens.

Archaic *Homo sapiens*, Neandertals, and Modern *Homo sapiens* Cranial capacities in the modern range are found in both archaic *H. sapiens* and Neandertal specimens. Indeed, one of the apparent paradoxes of the later hominid fossil record is that Neandertal cranial capacities often exceed the average cranial capacity of modern humans. Even the archaic *H. sapiens* mean is within the range of modern *H. sapiens*. The increase in average cranial capacity from *H. erectus* to the later *Homo* species is quite profound and undoubtedly exceeds any increase in body size. Thus the hominid trend for increasing brain size and encephalization continues through the appearance of archaic *H. sapiens* and Neandertals.

What about the apparent decline in brain size in modern humans compared with Neandertals and even with earlier modern humans? In fact, modern humans are more encephalized than Neandertals because their bodies are much smaller but their brains are almost as large as Neandertal brains (Kappelman, 1996) (Figure 15.9).

Brain size increase and increased encephalization have characterized hominid evolution over the past 3 to 4 million years (Figure 15.10). These trends have become more marked over the past 2 million years, as absolute brain size has nearly tripled. During the past 2 million years, increases in brain size have outpaced increases in body size, thus leading to increasingly encephalized hominids. Although brain size and encephalization are not everything, expanding brain size in the hominid lineage clearly reflects an adaptation.

Brain Reorganization

As the brain has expanded, its functional organization has also changed. We know this by comparing our brains with those of our closest relatives, such as the chimpanzee, or of the rhesus macaque, an animal often used as the primate standard in experimental neurological research. For example, there are parts of the brains that are essential for normal language production. Because other primates do not have language, obviously some reorganization of the brain has accompanied the evolution of language ability. Although scientists debate the relative importance of reorganization and expansion in hominid brain evolution, it is quite reasonable to assume that both processes have been crucial.

Several studies have shown that when we look at large numbers of mammal species, the anatomical organizations of their brains are remarkably uniform in terms of the relative size of one structure compared with another or with the whole brain (Jerison, 1991; Finlay and Darlington, 1995). Of course, as with any statistical generalization, there are exceptions. We want to know what exceptions are present in the human brain and when they evolved.

olfactory bulbs Knoblike structures located on the underside of the frontal lobes that form the termination of olfactory nerves running from the nasal region to the brain.

Olfactory Bulbs Compared with other mammals, anthropoids have **olfactory bulbs** (which control our sense of smell) that are small for their overall brain size

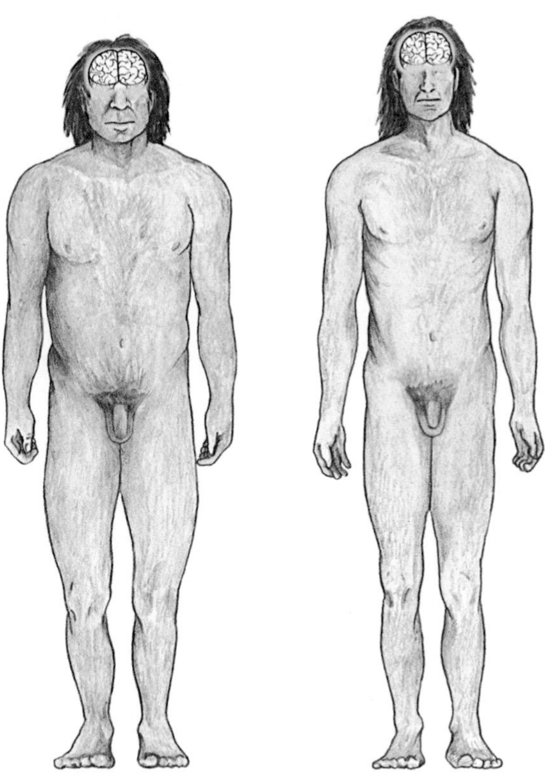

FIGURE 15.9 Although Neandertal brain sizes fall well within (or exceed) the modern human range, their EQ is lower than modern humans because they had larger bodies.

(Jerison, 1991). In contrast, wolves have olfactory bulbs that are about 6 cc in volume, a 60-fold advantage over the human-sized olfactory bulb. Humans have olfactory bulbs that are about the same size as those found in strepsirhine species whose brains are only 1 to 2% the size of human brains.

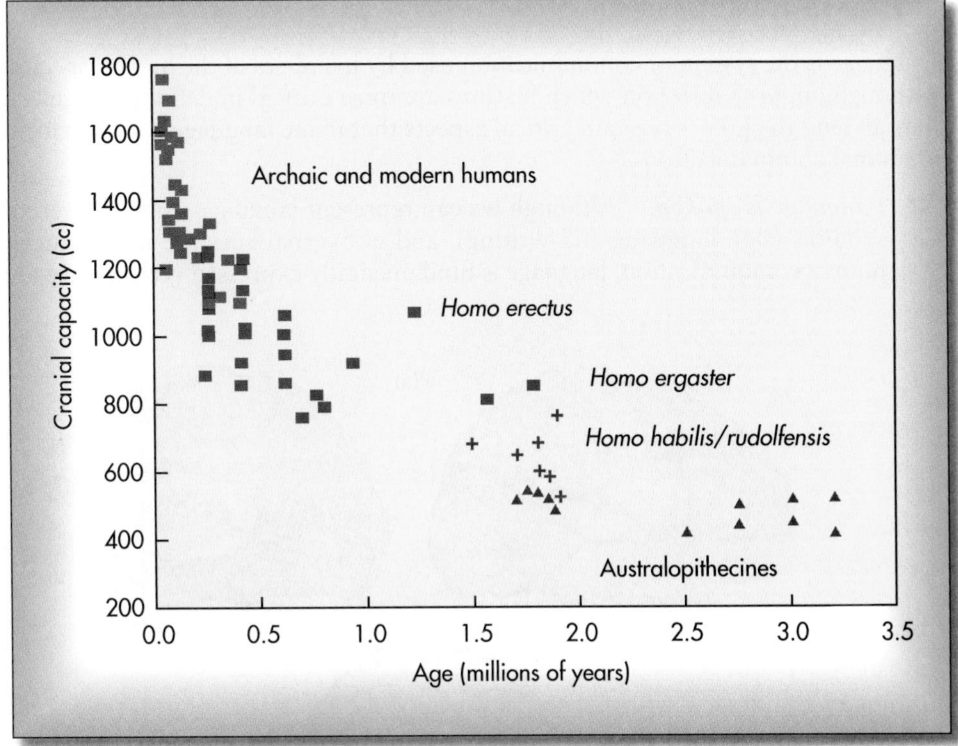

FIGURE 15.10 Cranial capacity has increased approximately fourfold over the last 3.5 million years of hominid evolution.

Humans reflect (in more extreme form) a basic trend in olfactory bulb reduction that we can see in all living anthropoids. We presume that this reduction occurred as other sensory domains (such as vision) and higher-level cognition became more important, reducing reliance on the sense of smell.

Primary Visual Regions The *primary visual region* is the part of the brain where visual information from the eyes is initially processed, and it has been reorganized in humans over the course of hominid evolution. Although it is present in the occipital lobes in both humans and other primates, it is located in different places in the occipital lobe, and it is also smaller in humans than we would expect (Figure 15.11). The reduction and shift of the visual region in primates presumably has allowed the expansion of the parietal association cortex, a region where sensory information from different sources is processed and synthesized.

LANGUAGE: BIOLOGY AND EVOLUTION

Much of what makes human behaviour more complex and more sophisticated than the behaviour of other animals depends on our possession of spoken language. It is one matter to possess sophisticated cognitive abilities—to make plans, to draw complex cause-and-effect relationships between the objects you see in the environment, and to think in terms of the past, present, and future—but without the ability to convey these thoughts to other members of the social group, their usefulness for enhancing survival and reproductive success would be limited.

Language is an adaptation. It is easy to imagine that a social group of hominids who possess language would have an advantage over a social group of hominids who did not. But language ability is as much an anatomical as a behavioural adaptation. As we will see, modern humans are designed by natural selection—in the anatomy of their throats and respiratory system and in various aspects of the structure and function of their brains—to produce language.

WHAT IS LANGUAGE?

Language is the system of communication used by members of the human species. Although linguists differ on which features are most critical in defining language, they all tend to agree on certain critical aspects that make language a unique form of animal communication.

1. ***Language is spoken.*** Although we can represent language using nonverbal symbols (sign language and writing), and nonverbal cues are important in human communication, language is fundamentally expressed verbally. We are

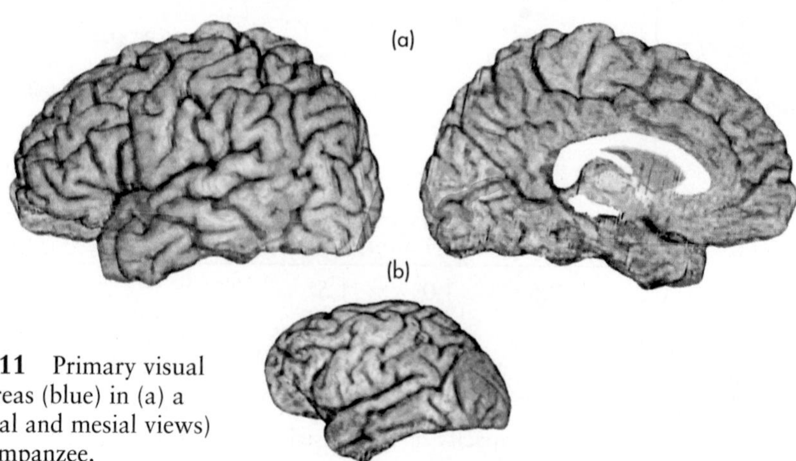

FIGURE 15.11 Primary visual processing areas (blue) in (a) a human (lateral and mesial views) and (b) a chimpanzee.

anatomically specialized both to produce language and to process language-oriented sounds.

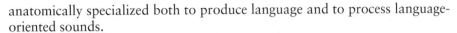

2. ***Language is semantic.*** The words we use in language have meanings; they are linked to real-world objects, events, or actions. Although other animals may have some semantic elements in their communication systems (for example, honeybees convey the position of food sources via their "dance"), the human semantic universe is orders of magnitude larger than that found in any other species. Each speaker of a human language knows the meaning of thousands of words. Obviously, different languages use different words, which can be learned only via *traditional transmission* in a cultural context.
3. ***Language is phonemic.*** Words are assembled from small sound elements known as *phonemes*. Phonemes are the building blocks of words. They have no intrinsic meaning. There is no biological limit to the combinations of phonemes that we can use to produce words. The association between a word and the object or action it represents is arbitrary. For example, *mosquito* is a large word for a small thing, and *whale* is a small word for a big thing. Onomatopoeic words (such as *buzz*) are an exception, but they form only a small percentage of the words in any language.
4. ***Language is grammatical.*** Although there is a limit to the number of words a person can know, there is no limit to the numbers of ways these words can be strung together to produces phrases or sentences. All languages have a *grammar*, an implicit system governing how word classes are defined and used; the rules of sentence structure (syntax) also form an important part of a grammar. Native speakers of a language are grammatical experts, adept at identifying violations of syntax and word classes. For example, a native speaker of English would have no trouble identifying this phrase as nongrammatical: "Through I midterm slept my." As a child first acquires language, he or she assimilates the grammatical rules of language subconsciously.

The Evolution of Grammar

The place of grammar in defining language and studying its evolution has been a point of controversy over the years. One school of linguistic thought, led by Noam Chomsky (1967), placed grammar at the centre of the linguistic universe. Chomsky and his followers argued that by studying the general grammatical rules of language, we can find a "deep structure," which in turn is a reflection of a "mental grammar" found in the brains of all people. Evidence of the existence of mental grammar comes from language acquisition in children. With little apparent effort, children master the rules of grammar (some of them extraordinarily complex) of any language to which they are exposed. Linguist Steven Pinker (1994) has called this ability the language instinct: children appear to be genetically specialized to learn language.

An interesting piece of evidence of the relationship between children and a possible deep structure of language comes from the study of *pidgins* and *creoles*. Pidgins are simplified, nongrammatical communication systems that have arisen in areas where speakers of different languages need to communicate with one another but do not spend enough time around one another to learn one another's languages (new colonial situations, fishers from different countries meeting on the seas). In contrast, creoles are grammatical languages that have arisen and developed, typically in colonial situations (such as in Hawaii or New Guinea), in the context of an ongoing situation of linguistic change or instability (Figure 15.12). It has long been noticed that Creole languages around the world converge on a similar grammatical structure. Linguist Derek Bickerton (1983, 1990) suggests that the source of this convergence is not a common language of origin but the fact that creoles

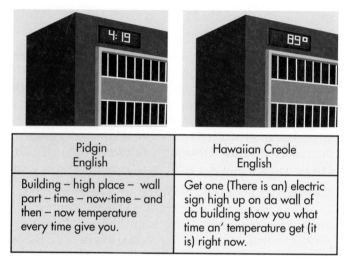

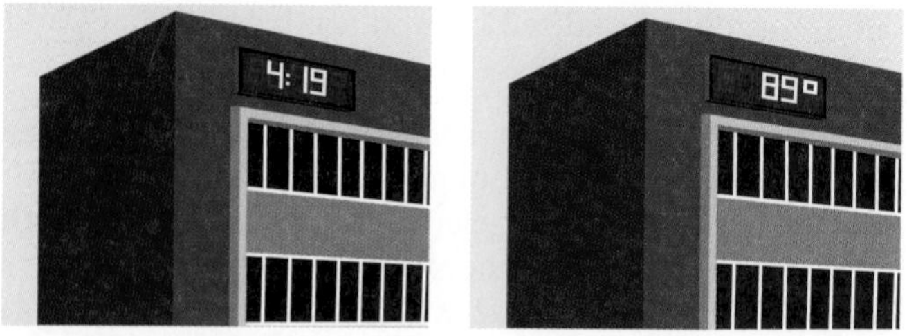

Pidgin English	Hawaiian Creole English
Building – high place – wall part – time – now-time – and then – now temperature every time give you.	Get one (There is an) electric sign high up on da wall of da building show you what time an' temperature get (it is) right now.

FIGURE 15.12 A comparison of pidgin and Hawaiian Creole.

are invented by children who share a common, biologically based, deep structure for language. The first generation of children growing up in these disrupted linguistic environments will not tolerate a nongrammatical system of communication, and they impose a linguistic structure on the language around them, thus leading to the development of creoles.

Many advocates of the deep grammar point of view believe that language represents a cognitive process that is fundamentally different from that underlying any other form of animal communication; however, several recent evolutionary theorists of language have argued against the existence of a universal mental grammar (Savage-Rumbaugh and Rumbaugh, 1993; Hurford, 1991; Schoenemann, 1999). Savage-Rumbaugh and Rumbaugh believe that syntax and grammar must develop once anyone tries to go beyond a two-word utterance; rules have to exist to let the listener know what the speaker is talking about. Thus grammars inevitably emerge, but there is no universal grammar. Such a position is consistent with the view that human language exhibits evolutionary continuity with other forms of animal communication, because it does not posit a zoologically unique cognitive mechanism, such as a deep mental grammar, for the evolution of language (Figure 15.13).

LANGUAGE IN THE BRAIN

We can define a *language area* of the brain as any part of the brain that is activated during the production or comprehension of speech. The classical language regions are found around the left Sylvian fissure, or *perisylvian language area* (Figure 15.14). In the frontal lobe, there is *Broca's area*. As we learned earlier, a lesion in Broca's area causes a disruption in speech production (an *aphasia*), yet comprehension remains intact. At the posterior end of the Sylvian fissure, spanning the top of the temporal lobe and the bottom of the parietal lobe, another language area was identified by German physician Carl Wernicke in 1874. *Wernicke's area* lesions cause a person to have difficulties in speech comprehension. People with Wernicke's area aphasia produce fluent but nonsensical speech, substituting one word for another or producing incomprehensible strings of words. Wernicke predicted that because it is likely that his area and Broca's area are in communication, different lesions in the area joining the two should produce aphasias with different symptoms. These *conduction aphasias* have been observed; for example, a lesion in the projection from Wernicke's area to Broca's area causes someone to produce fluent, nonsensical speech while retaining comprehension (Damasio and Damasio, 1989).

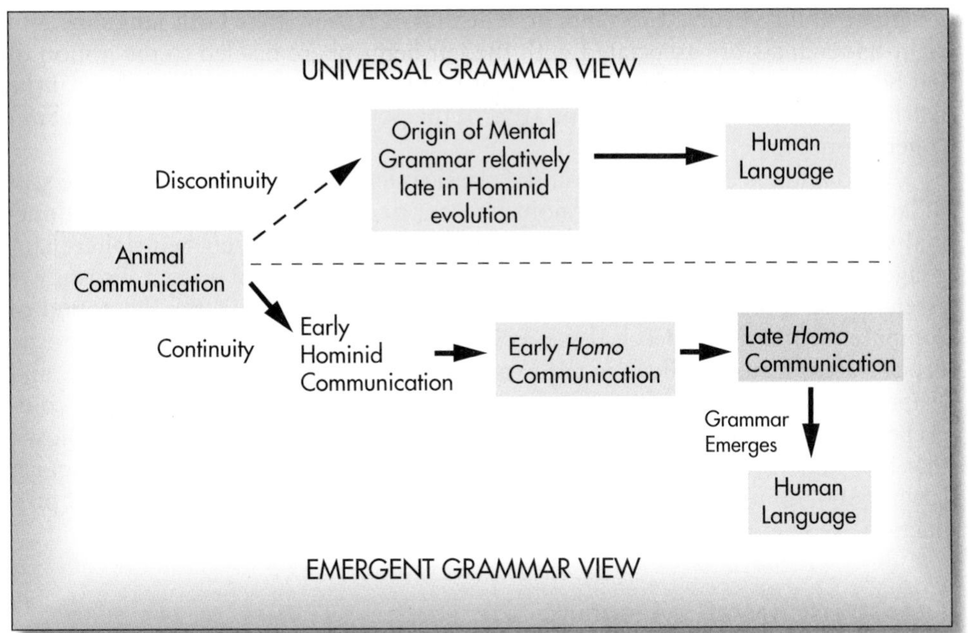

FIGURE 15.13 The Universal Grammar and Emergent Grammar viewpoints lead to very different scenarios of the evolution of language.

Wernicke's insights about conduction aphasias taught us to think about language as the product of interactive networks in the brain rather than of just one or two areas. In addition to Broca's and Wernicke's areas, the perisylvian language areas include several other regions important for speech. In the frontal lobe, Broca's area sits just in front of the motor strip controlling the tongue and mouth, which are obviously involved in speech production. Along the top of the temporal lobe lies the primary auditory cortex, which is essential for speech perception. The angular gyrus in the parietal lobe is important for the comprehension of written language. This is not surprising because projections from the primary visual cortex in the occipital lobe pass through the angular gyrus on the way to Wernicke's area.

Language Lateralization When a function of the brain typically and consistently occurs in only one of the hemispheres, we say that function is *lateralized*. In 95% of people, the perisylvian language area is in the left hemisphere. Most people are also right-handed, and because motor control of one side of the body is housed in the opposite side of the brain, it is very likely that right-handedness and

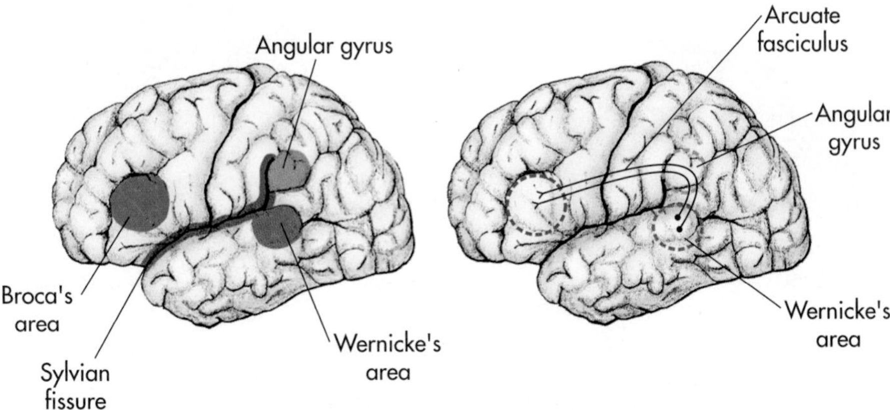

FIGURE 15.14 The major language areas of the left hemisphere of the brain. The connection between Wernicke's and Broca's areas passes through the angular gyrus.

language ability evolved in tandem. The classical view that both language and right-handedness are associated with the left hemisphere has led to the notion of left hemisphere dominance over the right hemisphere (except in about half of the left-handers—who make up about 10% of the population—who have right hemisphere dominance).

Although it is easy to focus on the classical left perisylvian regions as the seat of language, keep in mind that lesions in other parts of the brain also disrupt normal speech. Lesions in the right hemisphere of people with left hemisphere language dominance disrupt the musical or *prosodic* elements of speech. Prosody is essential for speech to sound normal; otherwise, it would have the flat sound of computer-synthesized speech. Lesions in the right inferior frontal lobe (opposite Broca's area) lead to deficits in the production of normal prosody in speech, and lesions in the right hemisphere opposite Wernicke's area lead to deficits in the comprehension of prosody in speech (Nolte, 2002). Neuroimaging studies have shown that the numerous parts of the brain dedicated to the control of the lips, tongue, larynx, and voluntary control of the diaphragm are all active during speech production (Wise et al., 1999).

LANGUAGE IN THE THROAT

Although there is little evidence that evolving language capabilities has cost us anything in terms of brain function—just the opposite, in fact—it is quite clear that the rearrangement of the anatomy of our throats for language purposes has introduced new risks in everyday life that our ancestors did not have to worry about (Laitman, 1984; Lieberman, 1991). To offset these risks, there must have been a strong selective advantage for the development of language abilities over the course of hominid evolution.

The *supralaryngeal airway* is a more precise way to describe the parts of the throat and head that have undergone changes during hominid evolution. As the name suggests, it is that part of the airway that is above the *larynx*, or voice box. The larynx sits at the top of the *trachea* and has vocal folds (vocal cords), which can modulate the passage of air through the trachea to produce different sounds. The cavity above the larynx, at the back of the mouth, is known as the *pharynx*. The posterior part of the tongue, the epiglottis, and the soft palate form the boundaries of the pharynx.

When we compare the supralaryngeal airway of a human with that of a more typical mammal, such as a chimpanzee, we can see several differences that have profound functional implications (Figure 15.15). First, the larynx in humans is much

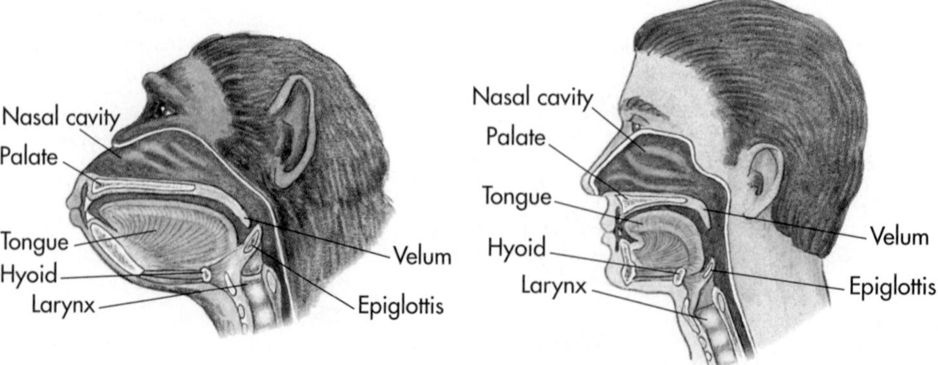

FIGURE 15.15 The supralaryngeal airway in a chimpanzee and a human. Note the relatively low position of the larynx in the human and how the back of the thickened and shortened tongue forms the front part of the pharynx.

lower than in other mammals. The new position of the larynx leads to an expansion of the pharynx. This expanded pharynx, whose anterior wall is formed uniquely in humans by a shortened and rounded tongue, is much more efficient for modifying the stream of air passing through the larynx to generate a greater variety of sounds, leading to fully articulate speech. In other mammals, the small pharynx has very little capacity for modifying the sounds produced by the larynx; supralaryngeal modification of sound can be done only by alteration of the shape of the oral cavity and lips (Laitman, 1984) (Box 15.1).

These changes in anatomy have a profound cost, however: they greatly increase the risk of choking on food or liquid. There is too much distance between the human larynx and nasal cavity for a sealed connection to form between the two, as it does in the typical mammal. The epiglottis and soft palate are separated by the rear part of the tongue. Everything we swallow must pass over the incompletely sealed opening of the larynx, which greatly increases the risk of choking and suffocation. Interestingly, human babies less than 1 year old have a supralaryngeal anatomy that more closely resembles the mammalian norm. This allows them to drink, swallow, and breathe at the same time, which greatly enhances their suckling ability. During the second year, the larynx begins the shift to the adult position, which increases children's risk of choking while increasing their ability to produce articulate speech.

Language Ability and the Fossil Record

The brain and supralaryngeal tract—anatomical structures that demonstrate most clearly our adaptations associated with the production of spoken language—are composed primarily of soft tissues that do not fossilize. However, we do have endocasts, which might preserve information about gross changes in the brain that might be associated with the development of language. In addition, the supralaryngeal tract is connected by muscles and ligaments to bony structures at the base of the cranium and in the neck. It is possible that some insights into the evolution of the soft tissues of the throat may be gained by examining these bony structures.

Endocasts and the Evolution of Brain Asymmetries Because language in the brain is associated with a leftward lateralization of function, it is possible that asymmetries in gross brain structure may be pronounced enough that they could be seen in endocasts. In most modern humans, the left occipital lobe protrudes further back than the right occipital, and the right frontal lobe protrudes more forward than the left. Other primates also show this pattern, but the left occipital and right frontal pattern is found most often in contemporary humans and in hominids. Although this asymmetry may not be directly related to language or handedness, it does reflect an asymmetric pattern that may be unique to hominids.

Another region of the brain that might also show evidence of asymmetry in an endocast is Broca's area. Anthropologists interested in hominid endocasts tend to agree that *H. habilis* resembles humans more than pongids in the anatomical complexity in the region corresponding to Broca's area (Holloway, 1976, 1999; Falk, 1983b; Tobias, 1987). A similar claim has been made for a recently discovered Indonesian *H. erectus* specimen (Broadfield et al., 2001).

Base of the Cranium and Hyoid Bone According to some investigators, the bony remains of fossil hominids yield real clues to the form and position of the supralaryngeal tract, offering insights into the vocal abilities of these earlier hominids. However, most of these claims are somewhat controversial and reflect the inherent difficulty of reconstructing complex soft tissue structures from fossil remains.

Jeffrey Laitman (1984; Laitman and Heimbuch, 1982; Laitman and Reidenberg, 1988) has argued that the degree of *flexion* of the *basicranium* is an

Box 15.1 Ape Language Studies

Few scientific developments in the twentieth century captured the public's imagination as much as the extraordinary spectacle of great apes communicating with their handlers and others via sign language (see Lieberman, 1984, and Ristau, 1999, for historical overviews). Although there had been several attempts to teach apes raised in close contact with humans to talk, these all failed miserably. Humans are adapted to produce the sounds of spoken language, and apes are not. In 1965, a husband-and-wife team of psychologists named Allen and Beatrix Gardner had the idea to train a 10-month-old chimpanzee named Washoe to communicate using American Sign Language, thereby bypassing the inherent vocal limitations of chimpanzees. Although Washoe was disadvantaged in starting her language training at an advanced age and her handlers were not expert ASL signers, she still managed to obtain a substantial number of signs (at least 132) in her initial 4 years of training, used them appropriately, and even coined novel two-word combinations, such as *water bird* for swan and *metal hot* for cigarette lighter. Washoe was also observed signing to herself and to other chimpanzees. In overall language skill, Washoe reached the level of a 2- or 3-year-old human child. Using ALS, she had no trouble making her wishes known to her handlers: "You go car gimme orange. Hurry" (quoted from Lieberman, 1984, p. 248).

Other investigators taught sign language to other apes, such as a gorilla and an orangutan. In some "ape language" studies, hand sign language was not used; rather, chimpanzees were taught to communicate via symbols they could point to or via a kind of keyboard. But even as some investigators were initiating and expanding research into the language skills of great apes, a backlash against such research started to grow. Many scientists were critical of the idea that the word *language* could be used in association with the communication skills displayed by Washoe and the other signing apes. Critics claimed that the signing apes were exhibiting nothing more than a response to unintentional cues from their trainers. Although it was easy to refute the criticisms by using substitute handlers, setting up situations where cuing would have been impossible, or secretly videotaping, funding dried up for further ape language studies (Gibbons, 1991).

Despite the critics, in the 1980s Sue Savage-Rumbaugh and Duane Rumbaugh initiated a sign language research project with bonobos, using symbols (lexigrams) that could be pointed to in sequence to generate phrases. One of their subjects, a young male named Kanzi, picked up the language without being taught; he simply observed his mother as she was being taught (Figure A). He has since become the most proficient sign language ape yet studied, mastering hundreds of symbols and generating thousands of novel combinations of symbols, often referring to objects and situations not in his immediate vicinity (Savage-Rumbaugh and Rumbaugh, 1993). His ability to comprehend simple and complex sentences in spoken English, even though he had never been explicitly taught to do so, is also striking. At 5 years of age, his grasp of spoken English exceeded that of a 2-year-old child. For a fascinating account of Kanzi's life, training, and personality, see Savage-Rumbaugh, Shanker, and Taylor (1998).

No one would argue that Kanzi and the other signing apes have human language, but they do provide us with several insights into the evolution of human language. First, a certain level of linguistic competence is present as part of the general cognitive abilities of great apes and presumably of the common ancestor we shared with them. Second, the research with Kanzi indicates that comprehension exceeds production in the apes. This means that the "speaker–receiver" issue probably was not a problem in the evolution of language: The evolution of speech production skills would not have been limited by the ability of listeners to understand that speech. Third, the learning situation (exposure at a young age to a rich linguistic environment) is critical for language acquisition. We did not know about the language abilities of apes until they were placed in an environment where they could be expressed. Critics of the studies have questioned why apes would have such capacity and never use it. But, all reasonably complex, behaviourally sophisticated animals have new skills they can develop given the proper environmental stimuli. Language abilities in hominids did not evolve from nothing, but reflect an enhancement and elaboration of abilities found in their pongid ancestors and cousins.

FIGURE A Kanzi talks using his keyboard language.

anatomical marker of larynx position (Figure 15.16). His studies show that among living mammals, human adults are unique in that they have a pronounced degree of basicranial flexion; the more flexed the base of the cranium, the lower the larynx and the wider the range of sounds that can be produced. The degree of flexion seen in the base of *H. erectus* crania is greater than that seen in pongids and australopithecines and may signal the beginning of the lowering of the larynx to a more humanlike position (Laitman and Reidenberg, 1988). These claims are controversial, and other investigators (Arensburg et al., 1990) believe that the basic premise of a correlation between variation in the cranial base and vocal abilities has yet to be proven.

Reconstructions of the Neandertal vocal tract have been equally controversial. Because of their long palate and other factors, the shape of the Neandertal tongue should be different from a modern human's, the pharynx would not be as large, and the larynx would be higher up in the throat, with the result that Neandertals would be missing phonetic elements present in human spoken language (Lieberman, 1984, 1991). Like claims about the basicranium and language ability, these claims have also been the subject of much criticism.

A potentially more direct source of evidence about the speech abilities of Neandertals has come with the discovery of a Neandertal **hyoid bone** (a small bone that sits in the throat in front of the larynx) from Kebara Cave, Israel, dating to about 60 000 years ago (Arensburg et al., 1990). The Kebara hyoid is essentially humanlike in its size and shape and very distinct from that of a chimpanzee, for example (Figure 15.17), and its position relative to the mandible and neck vertebrae is humanlike. Thus, Neandertals may have been fully capable of producing speech.

The absence of direct evidence concerning the evolution of language ability means that there are many theories or models for how it might have occurred (Hewes, 1999). Most are untestable, although it is possible to assess the plausibility of some of the claims based on contemporary data. Since the 1980s, scenarios about the evolution of language have proliferated as new kinds of information have become available to researchers.

BRAIN SIZE, LANGUAGE, AND INTELLIGENCE

If there is a fundamental issue in understanding the evolution of human behaviour, it is interpreting the relationships of brain size, language, and intelligence. We have not been too concerned with defining what intelligence is. People interested in material culture, such as archaeologists, have tended to look for clues of intelligence in stone tool remains, attempting to define the level of technical intelligence our ancestors may have had (Wynn, 1999) while acknowledging that these tools may represent only a biased sample of the total material culture repertoire of

hyoid bone A small "floating bone" in the front part of the throat, which is held in place by muscles and ligaments.

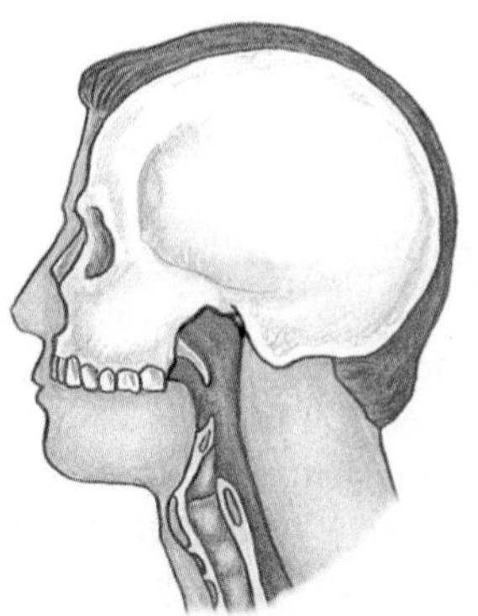

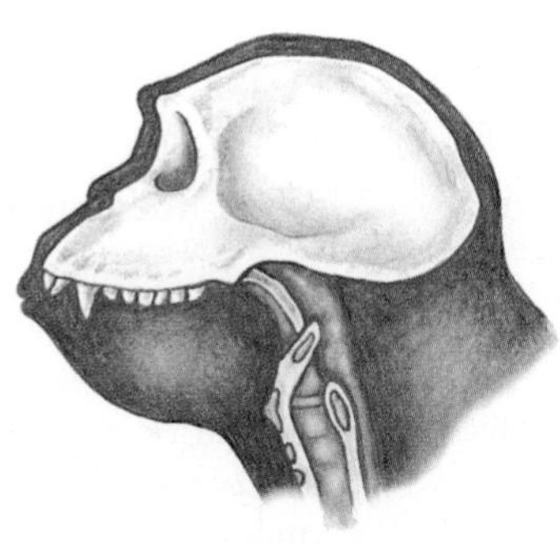

FIGURE 15.16 The base of the human cranium is more flexed than the base of the chimpanzee cranium.

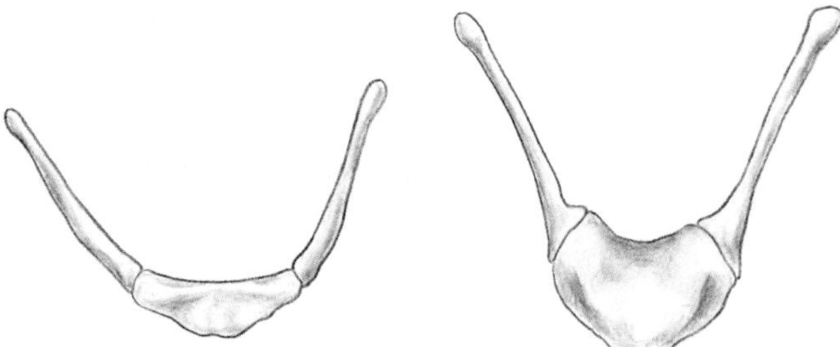

FIGURE 15.17 The hyoid bone from a Neandertal (left) and a chimpanzee. The Neandertal hyoid is much more similar to those found in modern humans.

past hominids. But if language ability is closely tied to level of intelligence, tools give us little to go on. It is also quite clear that the level of sophistication we observe in stone tool production does not correlate very much or at all with changes in brain size over hominid evolution. This does not mean that no insights into human cognition are to be gained from the archaeological record; but stone tools must be considered in a broader investigatory context (Mithen, 1996).

In contrast to archaeologists, scientists more interested in the behaviour of living animals and humans have emphasized the importance of social behaviour in the lives of past hominids as the driving force behind the increase in intelligence (Byrne and Whiten, 1988; Dunbar, 1993, 1997). They argue that technical aspects of intelligence have been emphasized over the social aspects. That may be true, but a reasonable view is that both technical and social intelligences were critical in human evolution. Theorists of intelligence have emphasized the multifaceted nature of intelligence in the real world (Gardner, 1993; Sternberg, 1990), which goes beyond things such as IQ test scores. As we discussed earlier, increases in brain size tend to be distributed throughout the structure rather than localized to specific regions (with some exceptions, of course). Thus selection for an aspect of intelligence that is localized to one part of the brain will lead to size increases in other parts of the brain. This might in turn lead to the appearances of new capabilities that may themselves be selected for in turn.

Although we lack direct information about the evolution of brain functional organization, intelligence, and language, we are developing a clearer and more sophisticated understanding of what happened in human evolution over the past several million years. Increases in knowledge about brain structure and function, the nature of language as an evolving system, the communicatory behaviour of humans and other animals, and the hominid fossil and archaeological record mean that our speculations are both informed and constrained by a growing scientific database.

SUMMARY

1. What are the primary and association areas of the cerebral cortex?

The cerebral cortex is the grey matter (mostly neuron cell bodies) that lines the surface of the brain. The primary cortex is involved directly with motor control or with the initial processing of sensory input. The association cortex is the region of the cortex where the processing of information from one or more primary (or other association) areas occurs.

2. What does encephalization mean?

Encephalization is a measure of brain size relative to body size. Because larger brain size correlates with larger body size, it is often useful to look at brain size in relation to body size to gain an impression of overall cognitive ability. We can derive an encephalization quotient by looking at many species and determining the typical brain–body size relationship. Species with larger than expected brains given their body sizes have

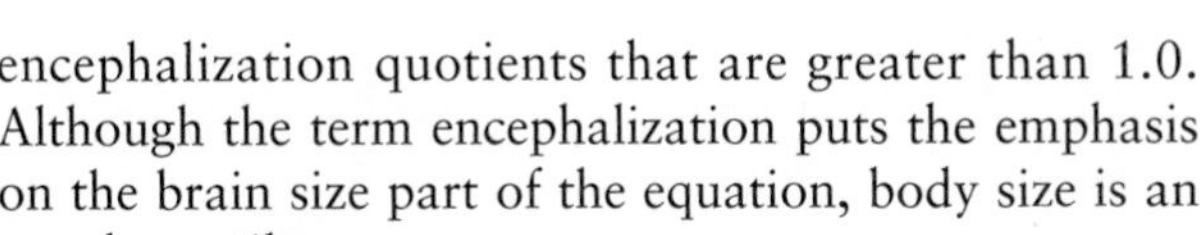

encephalization quotients that are greater than 1.0. Although the term encephalization puts the emphasis on the brain size part of the equation, body size is an equal contributor.

3. **How does the cranial capacity of modern humans compare with that seen in Neandertals and some archaic *Homo sapiens*?**

   Cranial capacities in Neandertals tend on average to be larger than those seen in modern *Homo sapiens*, and some archaic specimens have cranial capacities that are well within the human range. The (estimated) lean body mass of Neandertals and archaic *Homo sapiens* probably was substantially greater than that for modern humans; thus encephalization is greater in modern humans than in these recently extinct hominids.

4. **What are four hallmarks of human language?**

   First, language is spoken. An evolutionary trade-off indicates the importance of language as a biological adaptation: anatomical changes in the throat that allow humans to produce the large variety of sounds in spoken language make us uniquely susceptible to choking. Second, language is semantic. Words have meanings that correspond to real-world objects, events, or actions. Third, language is phonemic. The words used in language are composed of small sound elements known as phonemes. There are no semantic constraints on how these elements can be combined. Finally, language is grammatical. The ways in which words are combined in language are governed by implicit rules relating to word classes and proper word ordering in phrases or sentences. All native speakers of a language can easily detect violations of basic grammatical rules.

5. **What are two areas of the brain that are part of the network that underlies the production of spoken language?**

   Broca's area is in the frontal lobe; Wernicke's area spans the top of the temporal lobe and bottom of the parietal lobe at the end of the Sylvian fissure. In 95% of people these language areas are located in the left hemisphere. In people who are left hemisphere dominant for language, the right hemisphere region corresponding to Broca's area controls the prosodic (musical) aspects of speech.

6. **Why is the Kebara Neandertal hyoid bone important in debates about the evolution of language?**

   The hyoid is a small bone that sits at the front of the throat. Reconstructions of the soft tissue of the throat—specifically of the supralaryngeal airway—are controversial because they were based on the anatomy of the base of the cranium, mandible, and other structures, without the hyoid, until the discovery of the Kebara hyoid. This bone appears to be very humanlike and indicates that Neandertals may have been capable of producing all the sounds that modern humans are capable of producing. Given the inherent uncertainties in soft tissue reconstruction, this claim has not gone unchallenged.

CRITICAL THINKING QUESTIONS

1. Which is more important: increases in brain size over hominid evolution or reorganization of brain function?
2. From an evolutionary perspective, what is intelligence? Defend or refute the statement "Human beings are smarter than chimpanzees."

KEY TERMS

language
brain stem
cerebellum
cerebrum
sulci (sing., sulcus)
gyri (sing., gyrus)
primary cortex
association cortex
magnetic resonance imaging (MRI)
palaeoneurology
encephalization
encephalization quotient (EQ)
olfactory bulbs
hyoid bone

SUGGESTED READING

Calvin, William H. and Ojemann, George A. (1994). *Conversations with Neil's Brain*. Perseus Books, Reading, MA.

Deacon, Terrence W. (1997). *The Symbolic Species*. Norton, New York, NY.

Lieberman, Philip. (1991). *Uniquely Human*. Harvard University Press, Cambridge, MA.

Pinker, Steven. (1994). *The Language Instinct*. HarperPerennial, New York, NY.

Chapter 16

Biomedical Anthropology

LUNCHTIME ON A LATE SUMMER DAY 20 000 years ago in the southwestern part of what is now France: A small group of boys have been playing since midmorning, exploring the caves that are common in their region, looking for old stone tools that have been left behind by hunting parties. They are starting to get hungry. They know not to head back to their village for food: The morning and evening meals will be provided by their parents and other adults in the tribe, but they are on their own between those two meals.

AT THIS TIME OF YEAR, the boys do not mind foraging on their own. It has been a rainy and warm summer, and a large variety of nuts, berries, and seeds are beginning to ripen. Because the summer growing season has been a good one, small game such as rabbits and squirrels are well fed and will make a good meal if the boys can manage to catch one. They spend an hour or two moving from site to site where food can be found, covering a couple of kilometres in the process. They see a rabbit and spend 20 minutes very quietly trying to sneak up on it before realizing that it is no longer in the area. Even without the rabbit, they are all happy with the amount of food they managed to find during their midday forage. In mid-afternoon, they stop by a stream for a rest, and then one by one they fall asleep.

LUNCHTIME ON A LATE SUMMER DAY in the early twenty-first century, at an elementary school in Canada: A large group of children line up in the cafeteria to get their lunch. They have spent the morning behind desks doing their school work. As the children pass through the cafeteria line, most of them ignore the fruit, vegetables, and whole-wheat breads. Instead, they choose foods high in fat, salt, and sugar: chicken nuggets, fries, and cake. The children do not drink the low-fat milk provided but instead favour sweet sodas and fruit-flavoured drinks. Most of them would say that they really like the food the cafeteria gives them. When they are finished, they return to their classrooms for more instruction.

Chapter Outline

At first glance, children in Canada in the early twenty-first century are much healthier than their counterparts who lived 20 000 years ago. They are bigger and more physically mature for their age, and unlike their Palaeolithic ancestors they can reasonably expect to live well into their seventies. They have been vaccinated against several potentially life-threatening viral illnesses, and they need not worry that a small cut, a minor broken bone, or a toothache will turn into a fatal infection. They are blissfully free of parasites.

Nevertheless, Canada has one of the highest childhood obesity rates in the developed world (ranking fifth out of 34 countries); Roughly one in four young Canadians aged 2 through 17 is overweight or obese (McMillan, 2006). A March 2007 report of the House of Commons Standing Committee on Health said that most Canadian children spend too much time in front of TV and computer screens; don't get the expert-recommended 90 minutes a day of exercise; eat too much fat and junk food; consume too many sugary drinks, and don't eat the recommended five daily servings of fruit and vegetables (Merrifield, 2007).

The situation is worst among First Nations children, both on and off reserves, of whom nearly 50% are overweight or obese. The report stated that there is so much poverty among First Nations communities that many people cannot afford nutritious food, especially in remote northern communities. And of more than 500 First Nations schools, only half have a gym.

Children from 20 000 years ago might have grown up more slowly than contemporary children, but upon reaching adulthood they would have had strong, lean bodies, with much more muscle than fat. They would not have spent a lifetime consuming more calories than they expended. If they were lucky enough to avoid infectious disease, injury, and famine, in middle and old age they would have been less likely to suffer from heart disease, high blood pressure, diabetes, and even some kinds of cancer than adults living today.

Health and illness are fundamental parts of the human experience. The individual experience of illness is produced by many factors. Illness is a product of our genes and culture, our environment and evolution, the economic and educational systems we live under, and the things we eat. When we compare how people live now and how they lived 20 000 years ago, it is apparent that it is difficult to define a healthful environment. Is it the quantity of life (years lived) or the quality that matters most? Are we healthier living as our ancestors did, even though we cannot recreate those past environments, or should we rejoice in the abundance and comfort that a steady food supply and modern technology provide us?

Biomedical anthropology is the subfield of biological anthropology concerned with issues of health and illness. Biomedical anthropologists bring the traditional interests of biological anthropology—evolution, human variation, genetics—to the study of medically related phenomena. Like medicine, biomedical anthropology is a biological science, which relies on empiricism and hypothesis testing and, when possible, experimental research to further the understanding of human disease and illness. Biomedical anthropology is also like cultural medical anthropology in its comparative outlook and its attempt to understand illness in the context of specific cultural environments.

In this chapter, we will look at many aspects of human health from both biocultural and evolutionary perspectives. We will see how health relates to growth, development, and aging, and we will look at an aspect of human variation—skin colour—that provides an informative example of the way health factors shape human variation. We will then consider infectious diseases and the problems associated with evolving biological solutions to infectious agents that can also evolve. Finally, we will examine the interaction between diet and disease and the enormous changes in diet that our species has gone through since the advent of modern agriculture.

EPIDEMIOLOGY

Biomedical anthropology is particularly concerned with understanding the expression of disease at the population level. Another health science with a population-level outlook is **epidemiology**. Epidemiology is the quantitative study of the occurrence and cause of disease in populations, and epidemiologists look for broad-scale statistical associations between ill health and the factors that produce it in specific populations (Figure 16.1).

biomedical anthropology The subfield of biological anthropology concerned with issues of health and illness.

epidemiology The quantitative study of the occurrence and cause of disease in populations.

EPIDEMIOLOGICAL TRANSITIONS

In 1971 the term *epidemiological transition* was coined to describe changes in the patterns of disease and mortality from infectious diseases to degenerative diseases (Omran, 1971). In less-developed societies, most deaths are caused by infectious diseases. In developed countries, infectious disease rates dropped dramatically in the

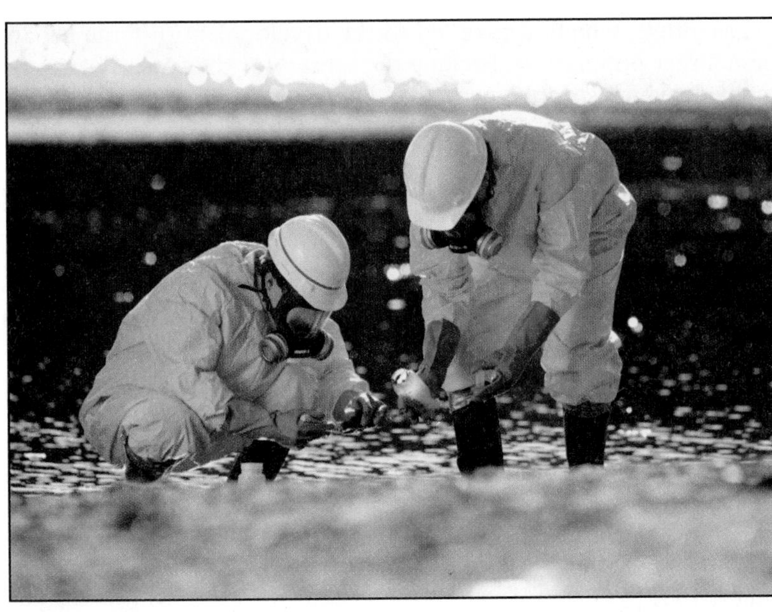

FIGURE 16.1 Epidemiologists look for the causes of disease, such as toxic waste and industrial pollution, at the population level.

second half of the nineteenth century, thanks to better nutrition and hygiene, a better understanding of how infectious agents cause illness, and widespread use of antibiotics and vaccinations. In developed countries now, the most common causes of death are chronic diseases of old age, such as cardiovascular disease and cancer.

Table 16.1 lists the top six causes of death in Canada in 1926 and 1990. The main causes of death in 1990—cardiovascular diseases and cancer—are primarily diseases of old age, accounting for nearly 70% of all deaths. In 1926, they accounted for only about 25% of deaths. In 1926, people were at risk from a variety of infectious diseases, including tuberculosis and other respiratory diseases. In 1990, all infectious diseases, including those of the respiratory system, were much less prevalent.

The concept of an epidemiological transition, which is based on an evolutionary and comparative view of diseases in populations, fits in well with much biomedical anthropological research, and it has been argued that there were two epidemiological transitions (Armelagos et al., 1997), the first occurring with the

TABLE 16.1 Top Causes of Death in Canada, 1926 and 1990 (data compiled from Statistics Canada – Health Sciences Division 2005)

RANK	CAUSE OF DEATH	PERCENTAGE OF ALL DEATHS
	1926	
1	Cardiovascular diseases	19
2	Respiratory diseases	15
3	Infectious diseases	12
4	Diseases of early infancy	9
5	Cancer	7
6	Accidents/violence	5
	1990	
1	Cardiovascular diseases	39
2	Cancer	27
3	Respiratory diseases	9
4	Accidents/violence	7
5	Diseases of early infancy	1
6	Infectious diseases	1

introduction of agriculture, which in turn led to the development of large urban populations. These larger populations became the setting for the spread of infectious diseases, many of which still plagued large cities in 1926 (Figure 16.2).

BIOCULTURAL AND EVOLUTIONARY APPROACHES TO DISEASE

Epidemiology provides the quantitative foundation for biomedical anthropology's mission to understand the evolutionary and cultural factors underlying human disease. Although these factors are interrelated, within biomedical anthropology the biocultural and evolutionary approaches provide insight into the population-level expression of disease from somewhat different perspectives.

The *biocultural approach* recognizes that when we are looking at something as complex as human illness, both biological and cultural variables offer important insights. The biocultural view recognizes that human behaviour is shaped by both our evolutionary and our cultural histories and that, just as human biology does, our behaviour influences the expression of disease at both the individual and population levels (Wiley, 1992, 2004).

Biological anthropologists have long looked at disease from an evolutionary perspective. The term *evolutionary medicine* describes a Darwinian approach to understanding disease, which provides several insights into the expression of disease (Nesse and Williams, 1994).

- *Defences versus defects.* Every disease produces certain signs and symptoms. A *defect* results from the disease process itself, whereas a *defence* is a part of the body's attempt to fight the disease. For example, a fair-skinned person with pneumonia may present with a cough and darkening skin colour. The darkening skin colour is a defect, caused by the fact that the person's haemoglobin is not carrying sufficient oxygen. The cough is a defence—an adaptation—that evolved as a mechanism to eject infectious material from the throat and lungs.
- *Infection and "arms races."* The environment is filled with infectious agents or **pathogens**, such as bacteria and viruses. As our bodies evolve defences to fight them, they too are evolving to combat our defences. A familiar example is the evolution of *antibiotic resistance* in bacteria. Antibiotics were first introduced in the 1930s. By 1944, some strains of staphylococcal bacteria were showing signs of resistance to penicillin, and today 95% are penicillin resistant. As a result we have to use other antibiotics to fight them.

pathogens Organisms and entities that can cause disease.

FIGURE 16.2 Before the advent of vaccination and antibiotics, infectious diseases such as cholera were the scourge of human populations.

- *Environmental mismatch.* Human bodies did not evolve to deal with most aspects of modern life, including fatty diets, low reproductive rates, and noise. Thus certain diseases may be considered to be the result, in whole or part, of the mismatch between our bodies, adapted for life in a hunter-gatherer environment, and contemporary environments. We will discuss examples of these diseases later in the chapter.
- *Pleiotropic gene effects.* We have many genes or alleles that probably did not lead to adaptations in past environments but were simply harmless; however, in modern environments these genes may be expressed in new ways. For example, because we now live longer, we have to deal with genes that cause diseases such as Alzheimer's disease and cancer, which are typically expressed only in old age.
- *Design compromises.* A classic example of an evolutionary design compromise leading to human suffering is back pain. The S-shaped spine we evolved in order to walk upright clearly predisposes us to developing back pain (Figure 16.3). This shape, combined with a sedentary lifestyle, causes 50 to 80% of all people in industrialized societies to suffer from lower back pain at some point in their lives (Anderson, 1999).

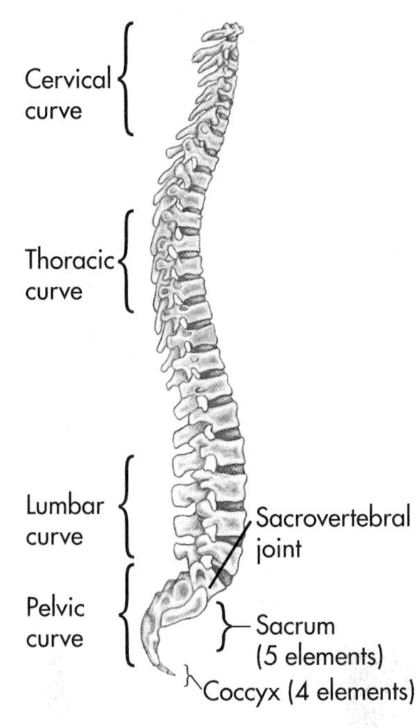

FIGURE 16.3 The S-curve in the human vertebral column—a result of the evolution of bipedality—makes humans highly susceptible to back injury and pain.

Biomedical anthropology sits at the intersection of evolutionary and biocultural approaches to health and illness. A central concept of biomedical anthropology is adaptation. As we have discussed in previous chapters, an adaptation is a feature or behaviour that serves over the long term to enhance fitness in an evolutionary sense. But we can also look at adaptation in the short term; this is known as *adaptability* (Chapter 6). A basic question biomedical anthropologists try to answer is the extent to which adaptability is itself an adaptation. For example, the life history stages that all people go through have been shaped by natural selection, but our biology must be flexible enough to cope with the different environmental challenges we will face over a lifetime.

BIRTH, GROWTH, AND AGING

All animals go through the processes of birth, growth, and aging. Normal growth and development are not medical problems per se, but the process of growth is a sensitive overall indicator of health status (Tanner, 1978). Therefore, studies of growth and development in children provide useful insights into the nutritional or environmental health of populations.

HUMAN CHILDBIRTH

With the expansion of the human brain over the course of hominid evolution, human females give birth to infants whose heads are very large compared with the size of the mother's pelvis. The shape as well as the size of the pelvis is a critical factor in the delivery of a child. Not only is there a tight fit between the size of the newborn's head and the mother's pelvis, but the baby's head and body must rotate or twist as they pass through the birth canal, which is a process that introduces other dangers (such as the umbilical cord wrapping around the baby's neck). The easiest evolutionary solution to this problem would be for women to have evolved larger pelvises, but too large a pelvis would reduce bipedal efficiency. In contrast to humans, birth is easy in the great apes. Their pelvises are substantially larger relative to neonatal brain size, and the shape of their quadrupedal pelvis allows a more direct passage of the newborn through the birth canal (Figure 16.4).

In traditional cultures, women usually give birth with the assistance from a midwife (almost always a woman). Although women vary across cultures in their reactions to the onset of labour, in almost all cases the reaction is emotionally charged

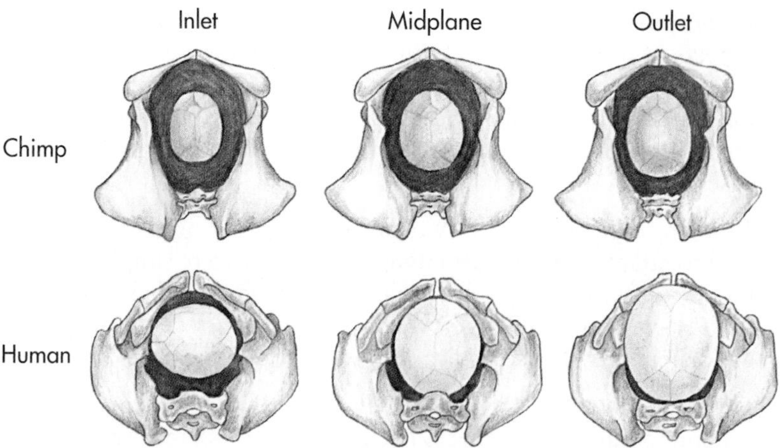

FIGURE 16.4 Compared to a chimpanzee, the human newborn has relatively little room to spare as it passes through the birth canal.

and results in the mother seeking assistance from others. This behaviour may be a biocultural adaptation (Trevathan, 1999). A human birth is much more likely to be successful if someone is present to assist the mother in delivery. Part of the assistance is in actually supporting the newborn through multiple contractions as it passes through the birth canal, but much recent research has shown that the emotional support of mothers provided by birth assistants is also of critical importance (Klaus and Kennell, 1997) (Figure 16.5).

PATTERNS OF HUMAN GROWTH

All animals go through stages of growth that are under some degree of genetic control; however, the processes of growth and development can be acutely sensitive to environmental conditions. Thus, patterns of growth that emerge under different environmental conditions can provide us with clear examples of *biological plasticity* (Mascie-Taylor and Bogin, 1995).

Looking at human growth, we can imagine an optimal environment in which an individual will reach his or her genetic potential; however, most environments are not optimal. We can view growth responses to nonoptimal environments in two different ways (Schell, 1995). The anthropological model views the way

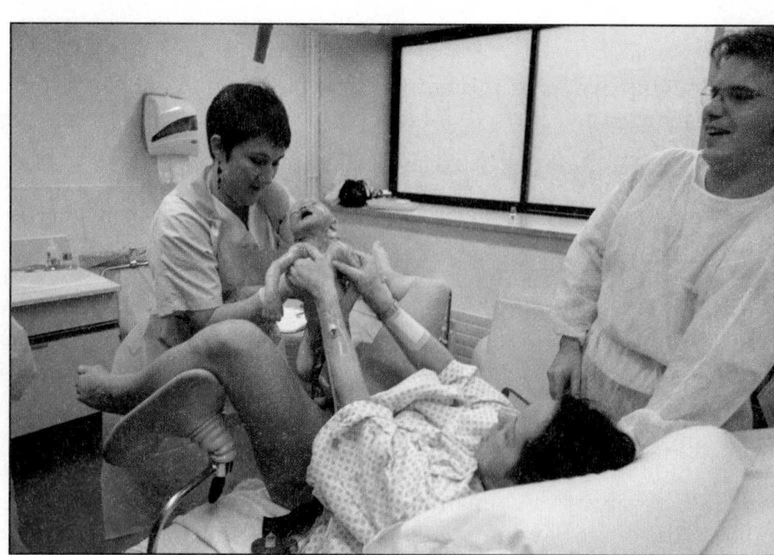

FIGURE 16.5 Women giving birth in traditional cultures usually receive help from other women, or midwives. Midwife-assisted births are increasingly common in hospital settings.

humans grow in high-stress environments (with a lack of food, heavy infectious disease load, and pollution) in the context of nongenetic adaptation, or adaptability. Growth patterns are responses to environmental conditions, which may actually enhance survival. On the other hand, the medical approach assumes that any deviation from optimal growth patterns is evidence of ill health. The biomedical anthropological approach incorporates both of these perspectives.

We chart growth and development using several different measures including height, weight, and head circumference. Cognitive skills, such as those governing the development of language, also appear in a typical sequence as the child matures. We can also assess age by looking at dentition or sexual reproductive capacity. Different parts of the body mature at different rates (Figure 16.6). For example, a nearly adult brain size is achieved very early, whereas physical and reproductive maturation all come later in childhood and adolescence.

Stages of Human Growth

In the 1960s, Adolph Schultz (1969) proposed a model of growth in primates that incorporated four stages shared by all primates. This model is presented in Figure 16.7. In general, as life span increases across primate species, each stage of growth increases in length as well.

The Prenatal or Gestational Stage The first stage of growth is the prenatal or gestational stage. This begins with conception and ends with the birth of the newborn. As indicated in Figure 16.7, gestational length increases across primates with increasing life span but is not simply a function of larger body size. Gibbons have a 30-week gestation, compared with the approximately 25-week gestation of baboons, even though they are much smaller. Growth during the prenatal period is extraordinarily rapid. In humans, during the *embryonic stage* (first 8 weeks after conception), the fertilized ovum (0.005 milligrams) increases in size 275 000 times. During the remainder of the pregnancy (the *foetal period*), growth continues at a rate of about 90 times the initial weight (the weight at the

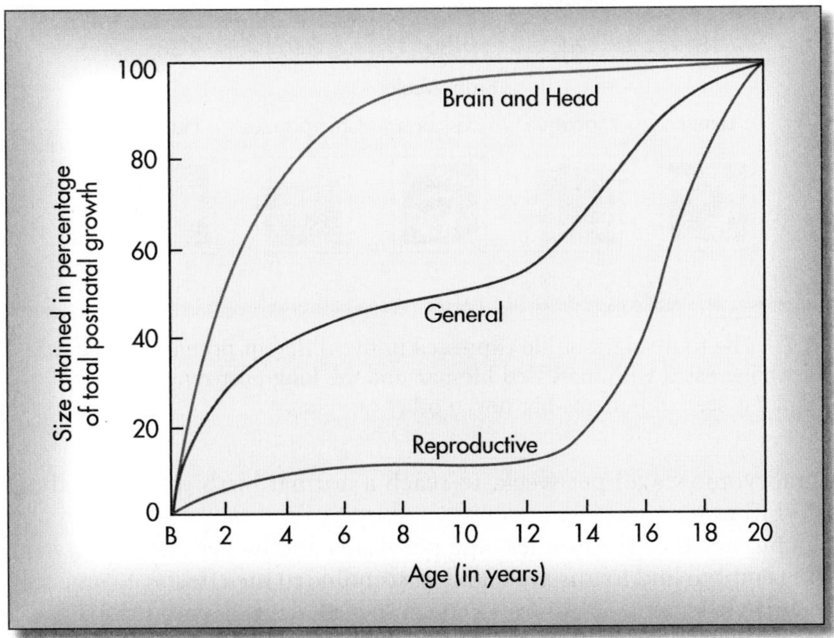

Figure 16.6 Different parts of the body mature at different rates. "General" refers to the body as a whole, the major organ systems (nonreproductive), musculature, and blood volume.

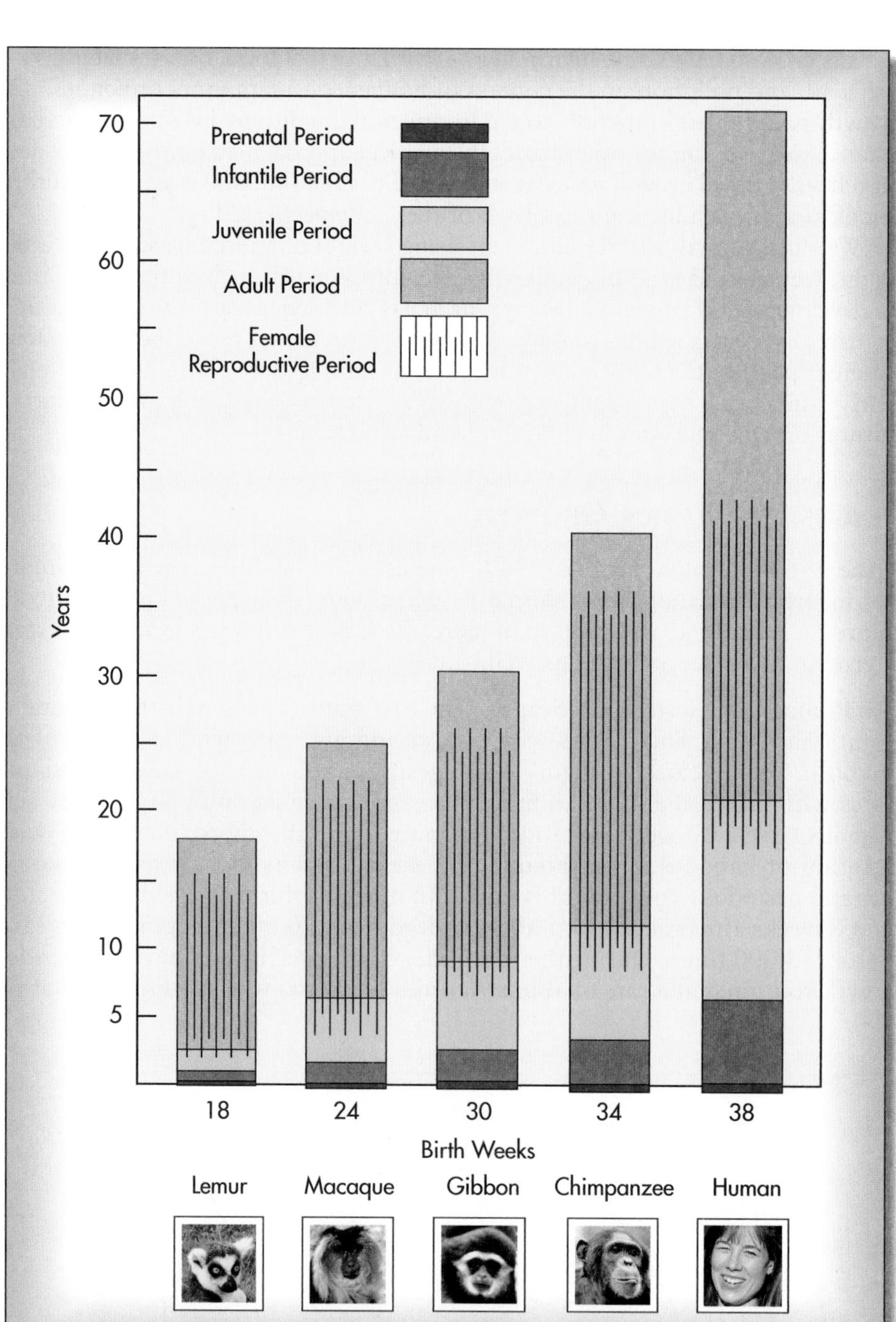

FIGURE 16.7 The four stages of life expressed in five different primates. Note that gestation length increases with increased lifespan and the long post-reproductive (female) lifespan is seen in humans but not in other primates.

end of the embryonic stage) per week, to reach a normal birth weight of about 3200 grams (113 oz).

teratogens Substances that cause birth defects or other abnormalities in the developing embryo or foetus during pregnancy.

Although protected by the mother both physically and by her immune system, the developing embryo and foetus are highly susceptible to the effects of some substances in their environment. Substances that cause birth defects or abnormal development of the foetus are known as **teratogens**. The most common human teratogen is alcohol. *Foetal alcohol spectrum disorder* (formerly referred to as foetal alcohol syndrome) is a condition seen in children that results from "excessive" drinking of alcohol by the mother during pregnancy. At this point, it is not exactly clear what the threshold for excessive drinking is or whether binge drinking or a prolonged low level of drinking is worse for the foetus (Thackray and Tifft, 2001). Nonetheless, it is clear that heavy maternal drinking can lead to the development of characteristic facial abnormalities and behavioural problems in children. It is estimated that up to 5 in 1000 children have some form of alcohol-related birth defect.

Although they are not teratogens, other substances in the environment may affect the developing foetus. Pollutants such as lead and polychlorinated biphenyls (PCBs) may cause low birth weight and other abnormalities. Excessive noise in the environment has been conclusively linked to reduced prenatal growth (Schell, 1991).

Infancy, Juvenile Stage, Adolescence, and Adulthood Schultz defined the three stages of growth following birth—infancy, juvenile stage, and adulthood—with reference to the appearance of permanent teeth. Infancy lasts from birth until the appearance of the first permanent tooth. In humans, this tooth usually is the lower first molar, and it appears at 5 to 6 years of age. The juvenile stage begins at this point and lasts until the eruption of the last permanent tooth, the third molar. Eruption of the third molars (your "wisdom teeth") is highly variable (they never erupt in some people) but usually occurs between the ages of 16 and 30.

Tooth eruption patterns provide useful landmarks for looking at stages of growth across different species of primates, but they do not tell the whole story. Besides the length of stages, there is much variation in the patterns of growth and development in primate species. The four-stage model of primate growth may be too simple, as it does not reflect patterns of growth that may be unique to humans. In particular, during *adolescence* humans have a growth spurt that may reflect a species-specific adaptation (Bogin, 1999).

The end of the juvenile period is marked by the onset of *puberty*. The word *puberty* literally refers to the appearance of pubic hair, but as a marker of growth it refers more comprehensively to the period during which there is rapid growth and maturation of the body (Tanner, 1978). The age at which puberty occurs is tremendously variable both within and between populations, and even within an individual, different parts of the body may mature at different rates and times. Puberty tends to occur earlier in girls than boys. In industrialized societies, almost all children go through puberty among the ages of 10 and 14 years (Figure 16.8).

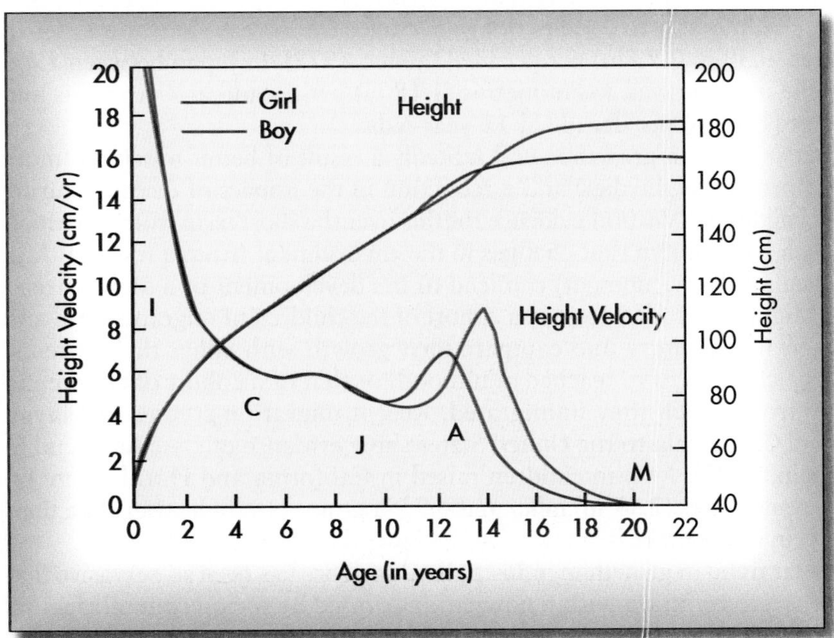

Figure 16.8 The adolescent growth spurt in humans is seen as a "bump" in the height curve and a "spike" in the height velocity curve.

Adolescence begins with puberty. During adolescence, maturation of the primary and secondary sexual characteristics continues. In addition, there is an *adolescent growth spurt*. The expanding database on primate maturation patterns indicates that the adolescent growth spurt—and therefore adolescence—is most pronounced in humans (Bogin, 1993, 1999). Why do we need adolescence? From an evolutionary standpoint, the early stages of mammalian growth are fairly self-explanatory. There must be a gestational stage and period of dependence on the mother for nutrition (infancy). The length of the juvenile stage, most of which occurs after brain size has reached adult proportions, varies widely among mammal species. There is a cost to a prolonged juvenile stage because it delays the onset of full sexual maturity and the ability to reproduce. But the juvenile stage is also necessary as a training period during which younger animals can learn their adult roles and the social behaviours necessary to survive and reproduce within their own species. The evolutionary costs of delaying maturation are offset by the benefits of social life. Among mammals, the juvenile stage is longest in highly social animals, such as wolves and primates.

Humans are the ultimate social animal. The complex social and cultural life of humans, mediated by language, requires an extended period of social learning and development: adolescence. In support of the view that adolescence is a period necessary for social learning, recent research on human brain growth has demonstrated that although approximate adult brain size is reached around 6 to 7 years of age, there is also an adolescent period of growth in some parts of the brain, including the frontal and parietal lobes (Giedd et al., 1999; Sowell et al., 1999). These are both areas substantially devoted to higher brain functions (such as decision making). Thus, the uniquely human adolescent growth spurt includes the brain.

The Secular Trend in Growth

One of the most striking changes in patterns of growth the *secular trend in growth*. Based on data collected as long ago as the eighteenth century, children in industrialized countries have been growing larger and maturing more rapidly with each passing decade, starting in the late nineteenth century in Europe and North America (Figure 16.9). The secular trend started in Japan after World War II, and it is just being initiated now in parts of the developing world. In Europe and North America, since 1900, children at 5 to 7 years of age averaged an increase in stature of 1 to 2 centimetres (0.39 to 0.79 in) per decade (Tanner, 1978). In Japan between 1950 and 1970, the increase was 3 centimetres (1.18 in) per decade in 7-year-olds and 5 centimetres (1.97 in) per decade in 12-year-olds.

The secular trend in growth is undoubtedly a result of better nutrition (more calories and protein in the diet) and a reduction in the impact of diseases during infancy and childhood. We find evidence for this over the short term from *migration studies*, which have shown that changes in the environment (from a less healthful to a more healthful environment) can lead to the development of a secular trend in growth. Migration studies look at a cohort of the children of migrants born and raised in their new country and compare their growth with either their parents' growth (if the children have reached adulthood) or that of a cohort of children in the country from which they immigrated. Recent migration studies of Mayan refugees from Guatemala to the United States show evidence of a secular trend in growth (Bogin, 1995): Mayan children raised in California and Florida were on average 5.5 centimetres (2.17 in) taller and 4.7 kilograms (10 lb) heavier than their counterparts in Guatemala.

The secular trend in growth in industrialized societies has been so pervasive that it tends to obscure variation within populations caused by socio-economic factors (Tanner, 1978). However, where children live below the poverty level, mild but persistent patterns of short stature have been observed (Crooks, 1999). Professor Tina Moffat of McMaster University and her colleagues compared stature and

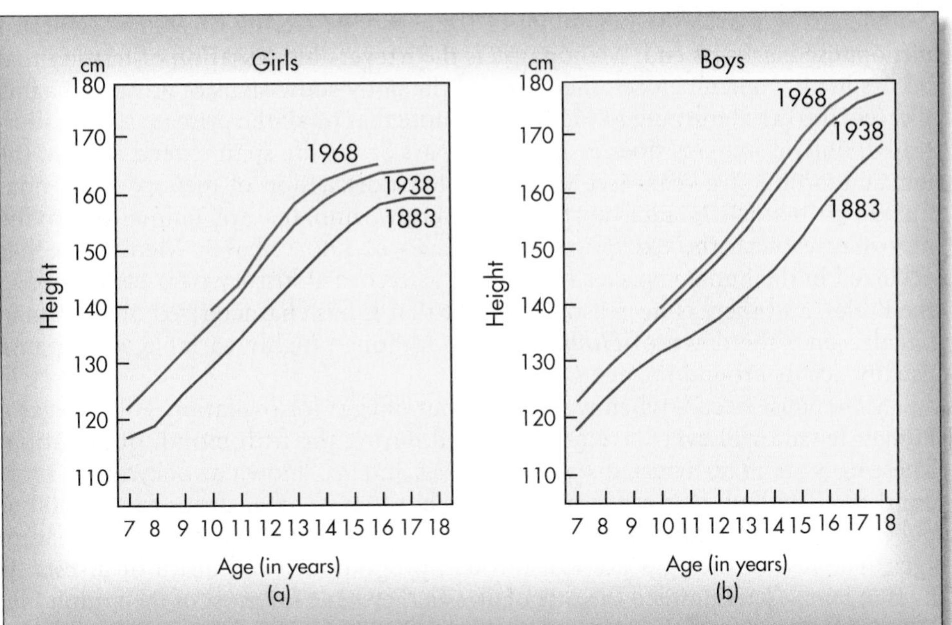

FIGURE 16.9 The secular trend in growth as measured in Swedish (a) girls and (b) boys between 1883 and 1968.

adiposity (fat levels) among children attending elementary schools in three neighbourhoods in Hamilton, Ontario, which differed by socio-economic status and recent immigrant status (Moffat et al., 2005). Results revealed that there were approximately twice as many children in the overweight/obese category in the two low-socio-economic status schools compared to the high-socio-economic school, and that children in the school in the poorest neighbourhoods had significantly lower statures for their age compared to children in the most affluent school.

Although the secular trend in growth appears to be a simple relationship between increased stature and industrialization, at the individual level the interplay of causative factors (genetics, economic status, and nutritional availability) is highly complex. "Modernization," for example, may have negative effects on growth. Professor Eric Roth of the University of Victoria and his colleagues have observed growth stunting among children in sedentary villages in northern Kenya compared to pastoralist groups (Fratkin et al., 2004). Pastoral sedentarization is promoted by international development and government agencies for its benefits (for example, food security, access to health care), but it reduces children's access to milk (an important nutrient for growth) and is linked to poverty.

MENARCHE AND MENOPAUSE

Another hallmark of the secular trend in growth is a decrease in the age of **menarche**—a girl's first menstrual period—seen throughout the industrialized world. From the 1850s until the 1970s, the average age of menarche in European and North American populations dropped from around 16 to 17 years to 12 to 13 years (Tanner, 1978; Coleman and Coleman, 2002).

In cultures undergoing rapid development, changes in the age of menarche have been measured over short periods of time. Among the Bundi of highland Papua New Guinea, age of menarche dropped from 18.0 years in the mid-1960s to 15.8 years for urban Bundi girls in the mid-1980s (Worthman, 1999). Over the long term, the rate of decrease in age of menarche in most of the population was in the range 0.3 to 0.6 years per decade. For urban Bundi girls, the rate is 1.29 years per decade, which may be a measure of the rapid pace of modernization in their society.

menarche The onset of a girl's first menstrual period.

Menarche marks the beginning of the reproductive life of women, whereas **menopause** marks its end. Menopause is the irreversible cessation of fertility that occurs in all women before other parts of the body show signs of advanced aging (Peccei, 2001a). Returning to Figure 16.7, note that of all the primate species illustrated, only in humans does a significant part of the life span extend beyond the female reproductive years (see Chapter 8 for a discussion of menopause in nonhuman primates). In fact, as far as we know, humans are unique in having menopause (with the exception of a species of pilot whale). Menopause has occurred in the human species for as long as recorded history (it is mentioned in the Bible), and there is no reason to doubt that it has characterized older human females since the dawn of *Homo sapiens*. Although highly variable, menopause usually occurs around the age of 50 years.

Menopause occurs when women run out of eggs for ovulation. All the eggs a human female will ever have are produced during the fifth month of gestation. These eggs are in an arrested stage of meiosis and are known as *oocytes*. At birth a girl has 2 million oocytes in her ovaries, but that number drops to 400 000 at puberty. Over the course of her lifetime, a woman ovulates only about 400 mature eggs. The rest of the eggs are lost through programmed cell death or *atresia*. If human females maintained the rate of atresia they have for most of their adult life, they would have enough oocytes to last until they were 70 years old; however, the rate of atresia increases starting at age 40, with menopause resulting by about the age of 50. There is no strong evidence that the secular trend in growth has influenced the age of menopause in any way (Peccei, 2001b).

At first glance, menopause looks to be a well-defined, programmed life history stage. Why does it occur? Jocelyn Peccei (1995) suggests a combination of factors, including adaptation, physiological tradeoff, and an artifact of the extended human life span. Some adaptive models focus on the potential fitness benefits of having older woman around to help their daughters raise their children, or the grandmothering hypothesis (Hill and Hurtado, 1991). Kristen Hawkes (2003) proposes that menopause is the most prominent aspect of a unique human pattern of longevity and that this pattern has been shaped largely by the inclusive fitness benefits derived by postmenopausal grandmothers who contribute to the care of their grandchildren. In support of this idea, a recent study of Finnish and Canadian historical records indicates that women who had long postreproductive lives had greater lifetime reproductive success (Lahdenpera et al., 2004). Peccei suggest that an alternative to the grandmothering hypothesis may be more plausible: the mothering hypothesis. She argues that the postreproductive life span of women allows them to devote greater resources to the (slowly maturing) children they already have and that this factor alone could account for the evolution of menopause.

AGING

Compared with almost all other animal species, humans live a long time, at least as measured by maximum life span potential (approximately 120 years). But the body begins to age, or undergo **senescence**, starting at a much younger age. Many bodily processes actually start to decline in function starting at age 20, although the decline becomes much steeper starting between the ages of 40 and 50 (Figure 16.10). The physical and mental changes associated with aging are numerous and well known, either directly or indirectly, to most of us (Schulz and Salthouse, 1999).

Why do we age? We can answer from both the physiological and the evolutionary standpoints (Figure 16.11). From a physiological perspective, several theories or models of aging have been offered (Nesse and Williams, 1994; Schulz and Salthouse, 1999). Some have focused on DNA, with the idea that over the lifetime, the accumulated damage to DNA, in the form of mutations caused by radiation and other forces, leads to poor cell function and ultimately cell death. Higher levels of DNA repair enzymes are found in longer-lived species, so there may be

menopause The postreproductive period in the lives of women, after the cessation of ovulation and menses.

senescence Age-related decline in physiological or behavioural function in adult organisms.

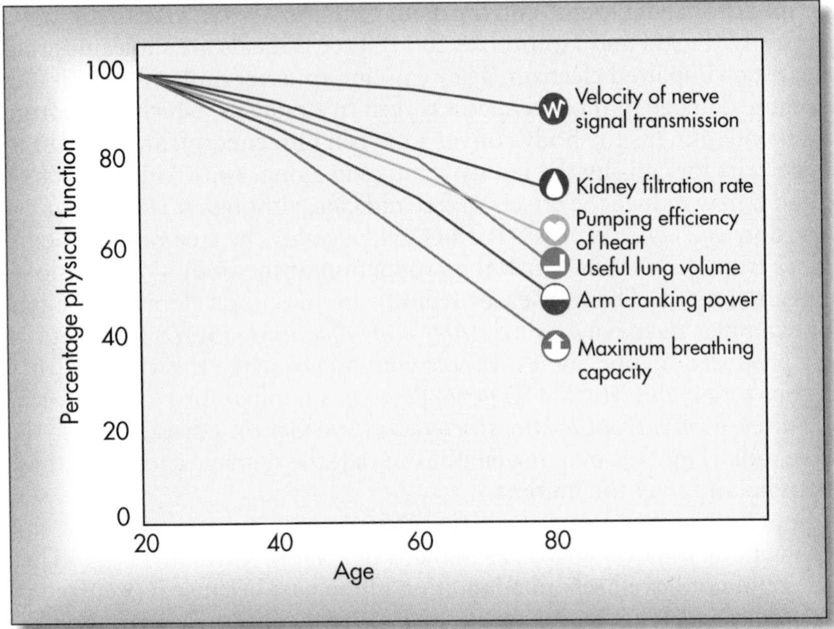

FIGURE 16.10 The effects of aging can be seen in the decline in function of many physiological systems.

some validity to this hypothesis, although in general the DNA molecule is quite stable. Support for the DNA damage theory of aging comes from a rare (1 in 10 million people) autosomal recessive disorder known as *Werner syndrome* (Kirkwood, 2002). When they are young, people with this condition suffer from a variety of ailments that are common in the elderly (such as cataracts and osteoporosis). Werner syndrome is caused by an abnormal form of the enzyme *helicase*, which unwinds DNA during replication, repair, and gene expression. This disease provides evidence that accumulating DNA errors can cause aging.

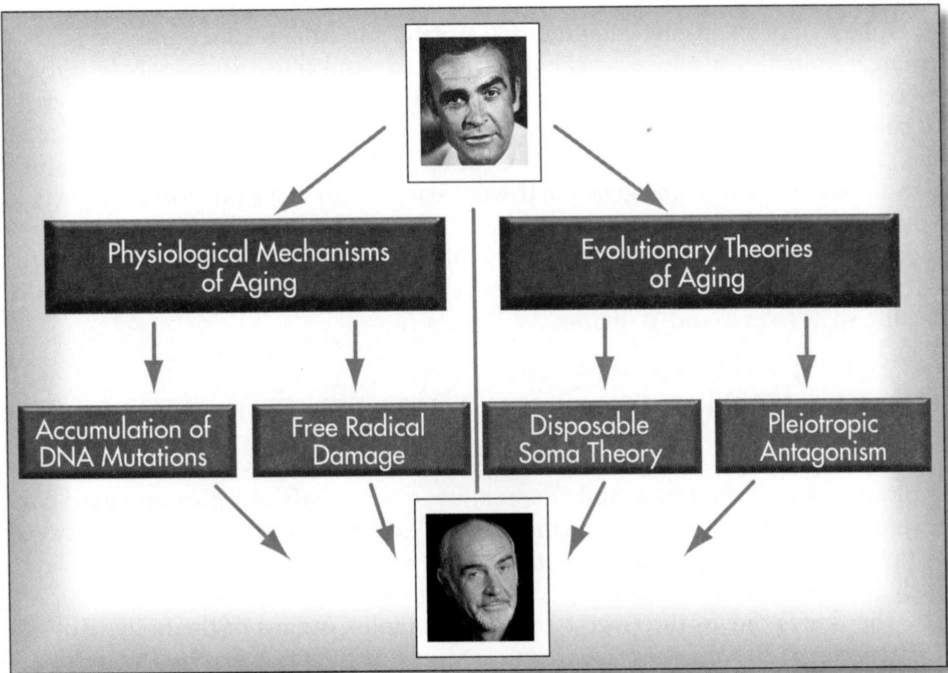

FIGURE 16.11 Physiological and evolutionary theories of aging.

Another model of aging focuses on the damage that *free radicals* can do to the tissues of the body (Finkel and Holbrook, 2000). Free radicals are molecules that contain at least one unpaired electron. They can link to other molecules in tissues and thereby cause damage to those tissues. Oxygen free radicals, which result from the process of oxidation (as the body converts oxygen into energy), are thought to be the main culprits for causing the bodily changes in aging. Antioxidants such as vitamins C and E may reduce the effects of free radicals, although it is not clear yet whether they slow the aging process. Further evidence for the free radical theory of aging comes from diseases in which the production of the body's own antioxidants is severely limited. These diseases seem to mimic or accelerate the aging process. For example, an enzyme called *superoxide dismutase* (SOD) is an antioxidant usually produced by our bodies. People who do not make this enzyme (they are homozygous for an abnormal SOD gene) develop a familial form of the degenerative nerve disease *amyotrophic lateral sclerosis* (Lou Gehrig's disease). Both the DNA and free radical models of aging emphasize that the damage caused by these processes accumulates over the lifetime.

In wild populations, aging is not a major contributor to mortality: Most animals die of something besides old age, as humans did before the modern age. Thus aging per se, could not have been an adaptation in the past because it occurred so rarely in the natural world (Kirkwood, 2002). Two nonadaptive evolutionary theories of aging take the position that old organisms are not as evolutionarily important as young organisms. The *disposable soma theory* posits that it is more efficient for an organism to devote resources to reproduction rather than maintenance of a body (Kirkwood and Austad, 2000). After all, even a body in perfect shape can still be killed by an accident, predator, or disease; therefore, organisms are better off devoting resources to getting their genes into the next generation rather than fighting the physiological tide of aging.

The *pleiotropic gene theory* has a similar logic, although it comes at the problem from a different angle. As you recall, *pleiotropy* refers to the fact that most genes have multiple phenotypic effects. For all organisms, the effects of natural selection are more pronounced based on the phenotypic effects of the genes during the earliest rather than later phases of reproductive life. The simple reason for this is that a much higher proportion of organisms live long enough to reach the early reproductive phase than the proportion that make it until the late reproductive phase. For example, imagine that a gene for calcium metabolism helps a younger animal heal more quickly from wounds and thus increase its fertility. A pleiotropic effect of that same gene in an older animal might be the development of calcium deposits and heart disease, but this "aged" effect has little influence on the reproductive fitness of the animal. Aging itself may be caused by the cumulative actions of pleiotropic genes that were selected for their phenotypic effects in younger bodies but have negative effects as the body ages. A key point of the pleiotropic model of aging is that you cannot select against senescence because the effects of natural selection are always more pronounced earlier rather than later in the life span (Nesse and Williams, 1994).

HUMAN VARIATION AND HEALTH: SKIN COLOUR

Like human growth and development, skin colour provides us with a means to explore issues of adaptation and adaptability in a biomedical anthropological context. Skin colour offers us one the most visible examples of the interaction between the phenotype and the environment and the importance of evolutionary forces such as natural selection and migration in the expression of disease.

The skin is one of the largest and most complex organs of the body (Robins, 1991; Molnar, 2002). It has two main components: the thick *dermis* and the much thinner *epidermis*, which covers it (Figure 16.12). The dermis is a connective tissue layer consisting of collagen and other fibres, sweat and sebaceous glands, hair

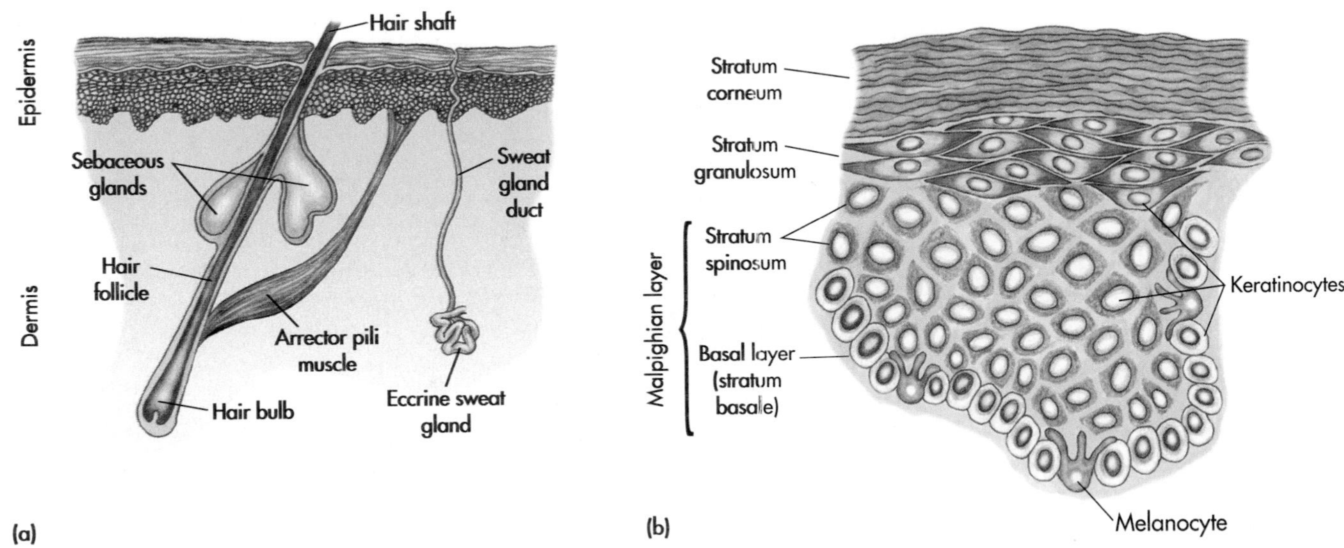

FIGURE 16.12 The structure of (a) skin and (b) epidermis, at the microscopic level.

follicles, and hair. The epidermis is a thin layer of tissue consisting mostly (95%) of epithelial cells called *keratinocytes*, with pigment cells, or **melanocytes**, making up the remainder (5%). Keratinocytes are synthesized at the base of the epidermis and migrate over the course of 4 to 6 weeks to the surface, where they are shed. Thus the epidermis is a continually renewing tissue layer.

Skin has several important functions. It is a fluid barrier, keeping the body protected from most of the chemicals in the environment. It is extremely important in *thermoregulation* (maintaining body temperature in the normal range) thanks to blood vessels located in the dermis and the cooling effects of the evaporation of sweat on the surface of the body. Skin also plays a critical function in the metabolism of various vitamins. As we will see, this function may be critical to our understanding of the evolution of skin colour in human populations.

The colour of skin is produced by a combination of three substances. *Oxidized haemoglobin* in red blood cells contributes red, and *carotene* (which is derived from the diet) makes a small contribution in the yellow range to overall skin colour. By far the most important component of skin colour is **melanin**, a dark pigment produced by the melanocytes of the epidermis. People with darker skin have more melanin in their epidermis than people with lighter skin.

The distribution of skin colour in the populations of the world follows a fairly orderly pattern, especially in the Old World. People with the darkest skin live at the equator or in the tropics (Figure 16.13). As you go north or south to higher latitudes, skin colour becomes progressively lighter. In the New World, skin colour does not follow such an orderly distribution, probably because of the relatively recent migration of peoples to the New World from temperate Asia. Migration patterns over the past few hundred years have further disrupted this orderly picture, with people from higher latitudes moving to places with an abundance of sun (for example, people of northern European ancestry living in Australia) and people from equatorial regions moving to places where there is not so much sun (for example, people of west African ancestry living in Atlantic Canada). Such migrations and mixings are nothing new. For example, Khoisan peoples have lived in the temperate climate of South Africa for thousands of years and have substantially lighter skin colour than Bantu-speaking Zulu people, who came to the area from equatorial Africa only 1000 years ago (Jablonski and Chaplin, 2002). Of course, the lightest South Africans are the descendants of northern Europeans who immigrated to the region over the past few hundred years.

melanocytes Cells in the epidermis that produce melanin.

melanin A dark pigment produced by the melanocytes of the epidermis, which is the most important component of skin colour.

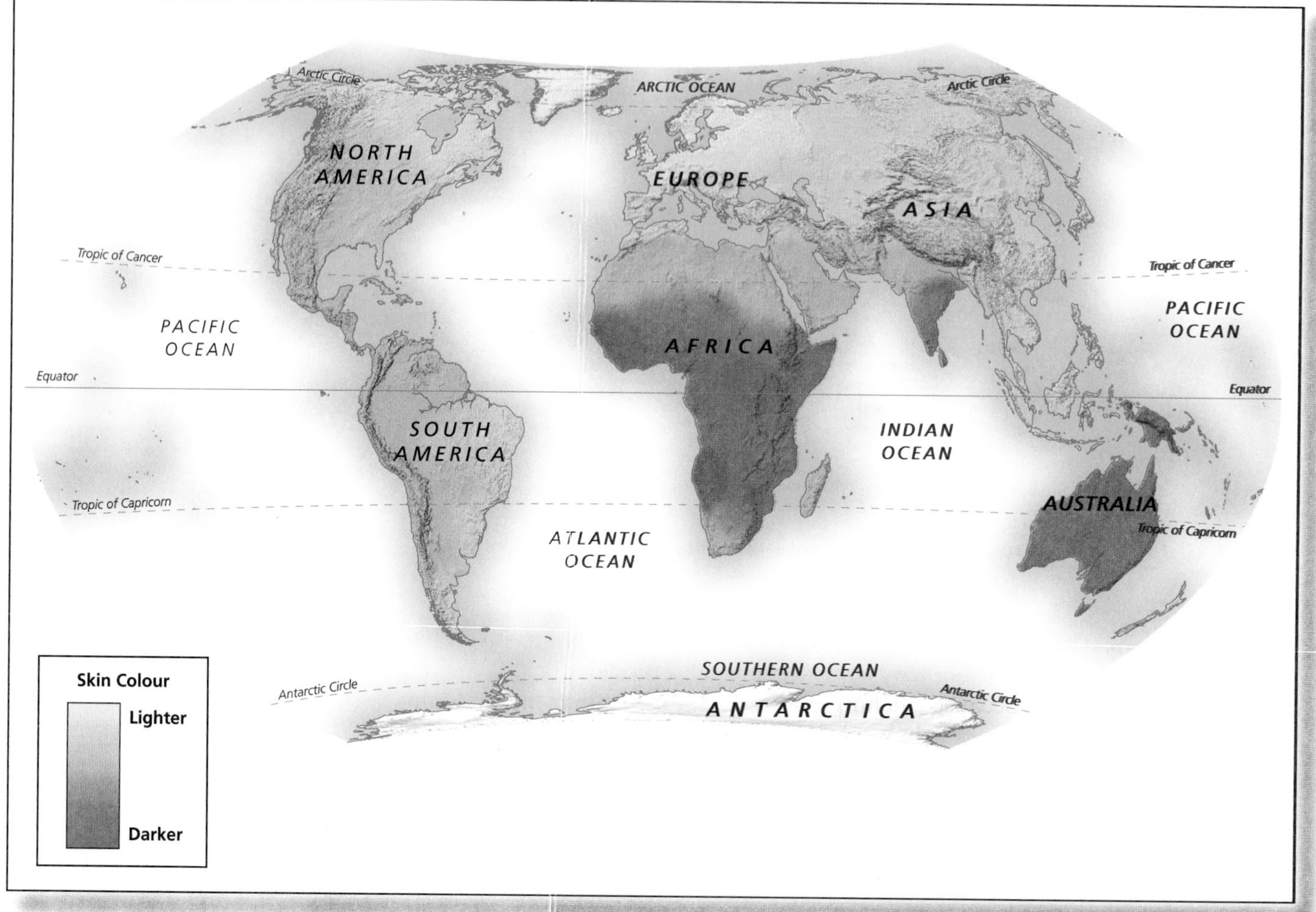

FIGURE 16.13 World map of the distribution of skin colour, prior to 1500 CE. Note that darker skin colours are found near the equator, especially in the Old World.

Reconstructing the evolution of skin colour depends on explaining the advantages of dark skin in more abundant sunlight and of light skin in less abundant sunlight. Many attempts to explain this pattern have been based on diseases or conditions associated with having the "wrong" skin colour for the environment.

ADVANTAGES AND DISADVANTAGES OF LIGHT AND DARK SKIN COLOUR

Electromagnetic energy from the sun comes to the Earth not only in the form of visible light but also in the form of *ultraviolet radiation* (UVR), which is below the wavelength for visible light. Although much of the UVR is absorbed by the ozone layer, enough reaches the Earth to profoundly affect the biology of many organisms, including human beings.

Sunburn and Skin Cancer In humans, the two most visible effects of UVR are sunburn and skin cancer. Sunburn causes congestion of subcutaneous capillaries, destruction of skin cells, and oedema (collection of fluids under the skin), and it can permanently damage skin. Besides being uncomfortable, sunburn can be very serious because it may interfere with the body's ability to cool itself and lead to the development of wounds that are highly vulnerable to infection. Ultraviolet radiation also damages DNA, which in turn leads to the development of skin cancer. Most skin cancers, though unsightly, are benign. However, cancer of the melanocytes, *malignant melanoma*, spreads easily throughout the body and must be treated early.

Melanin blocks or filters out incoming UV waves. Thus people with more melanin or the ability to temporarily produce more melanin in response to light (that is, *tanning*) are less susceptible to the effects of UVR than people who have less melanin. As most of us know, very light-skinned people who cannot tan are very susceptible to sunburn. They are also more susceptible to skin cancer. People from the British Isles who have migrated to sunnier climates provide an example of the effects of increased UVR on light skin. In Britain, the skin cancer rate is 28 per 100 000 in males and 15 per 100 000 in females. In Queensland, Australia, much of which is tropical, the rates are 265 and 156 per 100 000. Despite the health risks of skin cancer in light-skinned peoples today, for most of human history it was probably protection against sunburn that provided the greater fitness benefit because cancer typically takes its toll later in life, after the prime years for reproduction.

Vitamin D Synthesis Vitamin D is an essential compound in calcium metabolism and is necessary for the normal development of bones and teeth. Dietary sources of vitamin D are not common, although it is present in large quantities in some fish oils and to a much lesser degree in eggs and butter. Most people get their vitamin D from the sun, or, more accurately, UVR in the sun causes a photochemical reaction in the epidermis, converting *7-dehydrocholesterol* (7-DHC) into a precursor of vitamin D, which is transformed in the kidney into vitamin D over a period of 2 to 3 days. Vitamin D deficiency leads to the development of a serious medical condition known as *rickets*. Because calcium metabolism is disrupted, children with rickets have bones that are severely weakened. The bones can become deformed or are prone to breakage. Rickets can range from very mild to quite severe and can even result in death. On the other side of the coin, vitamin D toxicity can also have important health consequences, but it is almost impossible to get enough vitamin D via exposure to sunlight to cause toxicity (Robins, 1991).

Because melanin blocks the effects of UVR, people with darker skin cannot synthesize vitamin D as efficiently as people with lighter skin. Dark skin takes six times longer to make vitamin D as light skin (Holick et al., 1981). In the tropics, this is not an issue because intense sunlight is readily available and seasonality is minimal. At the higher latitudes, however, the sunlight is less intense, and seasonality means that access to sunlight is nearly cut off during certain times of the year. Cold weather necessitates covering the skin, further limiting the skin's exposure to direct sunlight. Vitamin D synthesis in the skin is very efficient, however, so even the exposure of a limited amount of skin (as little as 20 cm^2) to sunlight can provide sufficient vitamin D.

Rickets was first recognized to be a major health problem in the industrialized cities of northern Europe and North America at the beginning of the twentieth century. The cities' northern locations and smoky pollution limited exposure to sunlight, and it was very dark in the dingy, overcrowded tenements where factory workers and their children lived. Up to 90% of children in these cities suffered from some degree of rickets (Robins, 1991). In the 1920s, rates for rickets in African American children in the United States were two to three times higher than for European American children. Recognition of this pattern led to the development of the *vitamin D hypothesis* for the evolution of skin colour (Murray, 1934; Loomis, 1967). In a nutshell, this hypothesis proposes that the evolution of lighter skin colour—starting from darker-skinned ancestry—occurred in areas with less sunlight as a direct result of selection for more efficient vitamin D synthesis. Impaired movement or childbearing ability (if the pelvis is affected) in rickets would provide the negative consequences of vitamin D deficiency that would drive the selection for light skin colour.

Folate (Folic Acid) Folate is a B vitamin essential for DNA synthesis and cell replication, and exposure to UVR in the dermis causes the breakdown of folate in the bloodstream. This effect is particularly pronounced in people with light skin, who do not filter out UVR as efficiently as people with dark skin (Branda and Eaton, 1978). Deficiencies in folate during pregnancy can cause neural tube birth defects in the developing embryo. Thus, retention of folate may be a critical factor in the evolution of dark skin colour in places with strong sunlight (Jablonski and Chaplin, 2000, 2002).

Skin Colour and Health: Evolutionary Synthesis

Diseases associated with skin and skin colour provide several potential insights into the evolution of skin colour. In one model, the distribution of skin colour in human populations is maintained by a balance between the contrasting effects of UVR on vitamin D synthesis and on folate degradation. In another, factors such as resistance to sunburn and skin cancer, and even protection from cold injury (light-skinned Europeans are less likely to suffer from frostbite than people of African descent) may have also contributed to the evolution of the distribution of skin colour. Although there may have been some primary driving force in the evolution of skin colour, these different evolutionary models are not mutually exclusive.

INFECTIOUS DISEASE AND BIOCULTURAL EVOLUTION

Our bodies provide the living and reproductive environment for a wide variety of viruses, bacteria, single-celled eukaryotic parasites, and more biologically complex parasites, such as worms. As we develop defences to combat these disease-causing organisms, they in turn are evolving ways to get around our defences. Understanding the nature of this arms race and the environments in which it is played out may be critical to developing more effective treatments in the future.

Infectious diseases are those in which a biological agent, or pathogen, parasitizes or infects a *host*. Human health is affected by a vast array of pathogens. These pathogens usually are classified taxonomically (such as bacteria or viruses), by their *mode of transmission* (such as sexually transmitted, airborne, or waterborne), or by the organ systems they affect (such as respiratory infections, encephalitis, or "food poisoning" for the digestive tract). Pathogens vary tremendously in their survival strategies. Some pathogens can survive only when they are in a host, whereas others can persist for long periods of time outside a host. Some pathogens live exclusively within a single host species, whereas others can infect multiple species or may even depend on different species at different points in their life cycle.

Human Behaviour and the Spread of Infectious Disease

Human behaviour is one of the critical factors in the spread of infectious disease. Actions we take every day influence our exposure to infectious agents and determine which of them may or may not be able to enter our bodies and cause an illness. Food preparation practices, toiletry habits, sex practices, whether one spends time in proximity to large numbers of adults or children—all of these can influence a person's chances of contracting an infectious disease. Another critical factor that influences susceptibility to infectious disease is overall nutritional health and well-being. People weakened by food shortage, starvation, or another disease (such as cancer) are especially vulnerable to infectious illness. Of course, it works both ways. Some studies indicate that children in areas where the parasitic worm *Ascaris* is common show improved nutritional status after receiving medication to treat the infection, even without changes in diet (Mascie-Taylor, 1993; Brown and Gilman, 1986).

Just as individual habits play an important role in the spread of infectious disease, so can widespread cultural practices. Sharing a communion cup has been linked to the spread of bacterial infection, as has the sharing of a water source for ritual washing before prayer in poor Muslim countries (Mascie-Taylor, 1993). Cultural biases against homosexuality and the open discussion of sexuality gave shape to the entire AIDS epidemic, from its initial appearance in gay communities to delays by leaders in acknowledging the disease as a serious public health problem.

Agriculture Agricultural populations are not necessarily more vulnerable to infectious disease than hunter-gatherer populations; however, by virtue of their larger population size, agricultural populations are likely to play host to all the diseases that affect hunter-gatherer populations and others that can be maintained only in larger populations. This is the basis of the first epidemiological transition discussed earlier. For example, when a child is exposed to measles, his or her immune system takes about 2 weeks to develop effective antibodies to fight the disease. This means that in order to be maintained in a population, the measles virus needs to find a new host every 2 weeks; in other words, there must be a pool of 26 new children available over the course of a year to host the measles virus. This is possible in a large agricultural population, but almost impossible in a much smaller hunter-gatherer population (Figure 16.14).

Another difference between agricultural and nonagricultural populations is that the former tend to be sedentary, whereas the latter tend to be nomadic. Large, sedentary agricultural populations are therefore more susceptible to diseases that are transmitted by contact with human waste products; these diseases include a variety of bacterial infections and parasitic worms. In addition, many diseases are carried by water, and agricultural populations are far more dependent on a limited number of water sources than nonagricultural populations. Finally, agricultural populations generally have domestic animals and also play host to a variety of commensal animals, such as rats, each of which is a potential carrier of diseases that may affect humans.

As mentioned in Chapter 6, specific agricultural practices may change the environment and encourage the spread of such infectious diseases as sickle cell and malaria. Slash-and-burn agriculture leads to more open forests and standing pools of stagnant water. Such pools are an ideal breeding ground for the mosquitoes that carry the protozoa that cause malaria. Agriculture that makes extensive use of irrigation and water damming brings people into contact with large flatworms of the genus *Schistoma*. These flatworms cause a disease known as *schistosomiasis*, which is often characterized by blood in the urine. *Schistoma* species have an extraordinary life cycle that

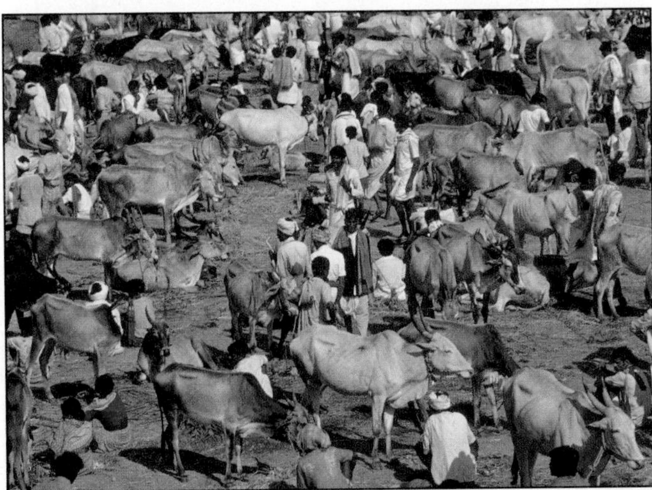

FIGURE 16.14 Risks of infectious disease increase in (left) high-density agricultural populations compared to (right) low-density, dispersed hunter-gatherer populations.

involves several distinct stages lived both inside and outside its two hosts: humans and a particular snail species. Schistosomiasis can damage the bladder, kidney, liver, spleen, and intestines. The World Health Organization estimates that 200 million people may be infected with the parasite and that 200 000 die annually from its effects.

Mobility and Migration The human species is characterized by its mobility. One price of this mobility has been the transmission of infectious agents from one population to another, leading to uncontrolled outbreaks of disease in the populations that have never been exposed to the newly introduced diseases.

The Black Death in Europe (1348–1350) is one example of just such an outbreak (Figure 16.15). The Black Death was bubonic plague, a disease caused by the bacterium *Yersinia pestis*. The bacterium is transmitted by the rat flea, which lives on rats. When the fleas run out of rodent hosts, they move to other mammals, such as humans. The bacteria can quickly overwhelm the body, causing swollen lymph nodes (or buboes, hence the name) and in more severe cases leading to infection of the respiratory system and blood. It can kill very quickly. An outbreak of bubonic plague was recorded in China in the 1330s, and by the late 1340s it had reached Europe. In a single Italian city a contemporary report placed the number dying between March and October 1348 at 96 000. By the end of the epidemic, a third of Europeans (25 to 40 million) had been killed, and the economic and cultural life of Europe was forever changed.

Similar devastation awaited the Aboriginal peoples of the New World upon the arrival of European explorers and colonists after 1492. Measles, smallpox, influenza, whooping cough, and sexually transmitted diseases exacted a huge toll on native populations throughout North and South America, the Island Pacific, and Australia. Some populations were completely wiped out, and others had such severe and rapid population depletion that their cultures were destroyed. In North

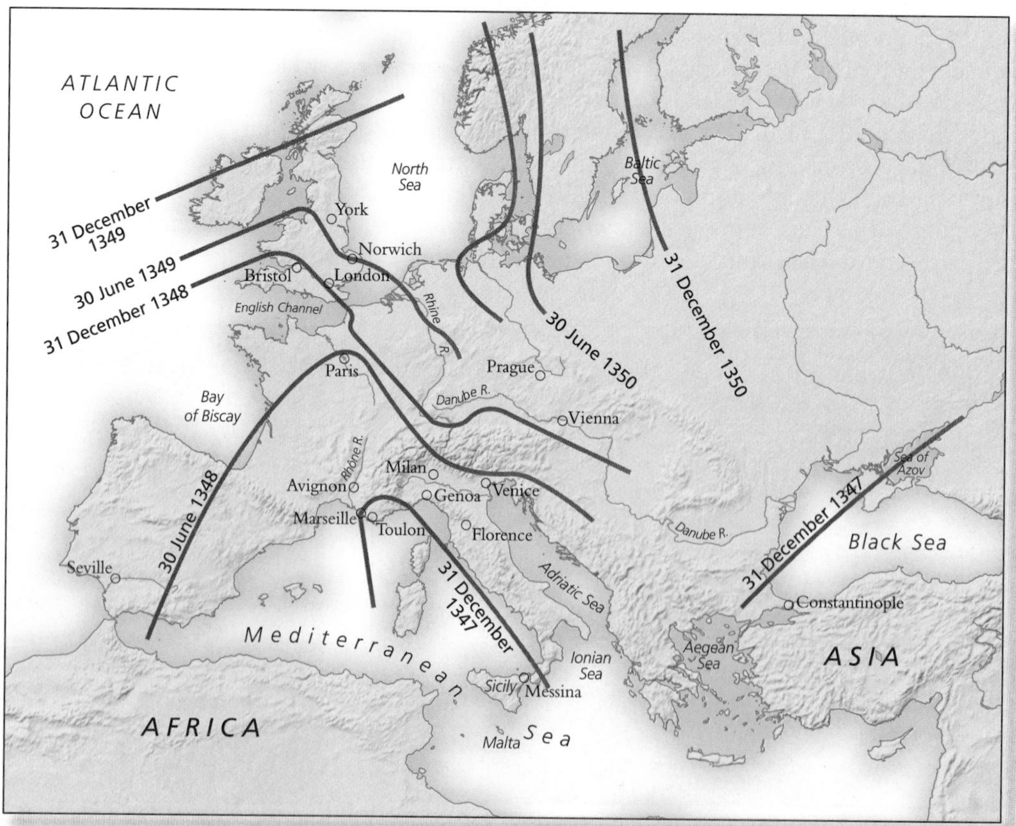

FIGURE 16.15 The Black Death spread over much of Europe in a three year period in the middle of the fourteenth century.

America, for example, many communities of First Nations peoples lost up to 90% of their population through the introduction of European diseases (Pritzker, 2000). Infectious diseases often reached Aboriginal communities before the explorers or colonizers did, giving the impression that North America was an open and pristine land waiting to be filled.

Professor Ann Herring of McMaster University and her colleagues have examined the impact of more recent epidemics (for example, influenza and tuberculosis in the nineteenth and twentieth centuries) on Aboriginal health in Canada, as well as the biosocial circumstances that favour epidemics and the biosocial processes that result from the experience of epidemics (Herring and Sattenspiel, 2007; Sattenspiel et al., 2000). They have noted that although discussion of health problems facing northern First Nations peoples in Canada emphasizes obesity and related conditions such as diabetes, until the last half of the twentieth century infectious diseases dominated the health profile of northern communities. Their research has focused on understanding the underlying reasons for variation in the frequencies of influenza and tuberculosis among communities and within households, and has determined that travel from one community to another was not a primary factor in the height of epidemic peaks and the length of epidemics within communities. Rather, the social structure and social interactions within a community had major roles in determining the impact of an epidemic on a community, and these factors were grounded in the history, geography, and political economy of northern Canada.

Infectious Disease and the Evolutionary Arms Race

As a species, we fight infectious diseases in many ways; however, no matter what we do, parasites and pathogens continuously evolve to overcome our defences. Over the last 50 years, it appeared that medical science was gaining the upper hand on infectious disease, at least in developed countries. Despite real advances, however, infectious diseases such as the virus that causes AIDS and antibiotic-resistant bacteria remind us that this struggle will continue.

The Immune System One of the most extraordinary biological systems that has ever evolved is the vertebrate immune system, the main line of defence in the fight against infectious disease. At its heart is the ability to distinguish self from nonself. The immune system identifies foreign substances, or **antigens**, in the body and synthesizes **antibodies**, which comprise a class of proteins known as **immunoglobulins** that are specifically designed to bind to and destroy specific antigens.

One of the most extraordinary qualities of the immune system is its ability to remember previous exposures to an antigen, thus priming the system in case later exposures to the antigen occur. This is the immunological basis of *vaccination* (discussed in more detail in the next section), whereby exposure to a killed or inactivated form of an antigen such as a virus protects an individual from developing an illness upon later exposure to the active form of the antigen. The immune system is a complex mechanism that has evolved to deal with the countless number of potential antigens in the environment.

Cultural and Behavioural Interventions Although the immune system does a remarkable job fighting infectious disease, it is obviously not always enough. Even before the basis of infectious diseases was understood, humans took steps to limit their transmission. Throughout the Old World, people with leprosy were shunned and forced to live apart from the bulk of the population. This isolation amounted to *quarantine*, in recognition of the contagious nature of their condition.

One of the most effective biocultural measures developed to fight infectious diseases is vaccination. The elimination of *smallpox* as a scourge of humanity is one of the great triumphs of widespread vaccination. Smallpox is a viral illness that originated in Africa some 12 000 years ago and subsequently spread throughout the Old World (Barquet and Domingo, 1997). It was a disfiguring illness, causing pus-filled lesions

antigens Whole or part of an invading organism that prompts a response (such as production of antibodies) from the body's immune system.

antibodies Proteins (immunoglobulins) formed by the immune system that are specifically structured to bind to and neutralize invading antigens.

immunoglobulins Proteins that function as antibodies.

on the skin, and it was often fatal. Smallpox killed millions of people upon its introduction to the New World; in the Old World, smallpox epidemics periodically decimated entire populations. In 180 a.d., a smallpox epidemic killed 3.5 to 7 million people in the Roman Empire, precipitating the first period of its decline.

Numerous remedies were used to combat the spread of smallpox. In some cultures, children were exposed to people with mild cases of smallpox in the hopes that it would strengthen their resistance to the disease. In China, powdered scabs of smallpox sores were blown into the nostrils of healthy people. The Turkish method was to make four or five small scratches on the skin and introduce some pus from an infected person into them. This method was introduced to England (and Western medicine) in the early eighteenth century, and early medical statisticians verified its success at preventing the development of serious forms of the illness (although 2 to 3% of the people vaccinated by this method died). We now have much safer forms of vaccination against smallpox, which have led to the total eradication of this horrible disease.

The most recently developed forms of intervention against infectious disease are drug based. The long-term success of these drugs will depend on the inability of the infectious agents to evolve resistance to their effects. Overuse of anti-infectious drugs may actually hasten the evolution of resistant forms by intensifying the selection pressures on pathogens.

Evolutionary Adaptations The immune system is the supreme evolutionary adaptation in the fight against infectious disease; however, specific adaptations to disease that do not involve the immune system are also quite common (Jackson, 2000).

The sickle-cell allele has spread in some populations because it functions as an adaptation against malaria (described in Chapter 6). Another adaptation to malaria is the Duffy blood group. In Duffy-positive individuals, the proteins Fya and Fyb are found on the surface of red blood cells. These proteins facilitate entry of the malaria-causing protozoan *Plasmodium vivax*. Duffy-negative individuals do not have Fya and Fyb on the surface of their red blood cells, so people with this phenotype are resistant to vivax malaria. Many Duffy-negative people are found in parts of Africa where malaria is common, while others who live elsewhere have African ancestry.

DIET AND DISEASE

It seems that there are always conflicting reports on what particular parts of our diet are good or bad for us. Carbohydrates are good one year and bad the next. Fats go in and out of fashion. From a biocultural anthropological perspective, North American attitudes toward diet and health at the turn of the twenty-first century provide a rich source of material for analysis. For example, what do you think when you hear the word *cholesterol?* On one hand, cholesterol is essential for the synthesis of many steroid hormones in the body, and its consumption is normal and necessary. On the other, high blood serum levels of cholesterol increase the risk of heart disease. Some people feel as if having high cholesterol is a sign of moral failure or weakness. Thus cholesterol has gone from being just a molecule to being a nutritional evil, to be avoided via the consumption of low-cholesterol and cholesterol-free foods.

Despite all the confusion about diet, we all have the same basic nutritional needs. We need energy (often measured in calories) for body maintenance, growth, and metabolism. Carbohydrates, fat, and proteins are all sources of energy. We especially need protein for tissue growth and repair. In addition to energy, fat provides us with essential fatty acids important for building and supporting nerve tissue. We need vitamins, which are basically organic molecules that our bodies cannot synthesize but that we need in small quantities for a variety of metabolic processes. We also need a certain quantity of inorganic elements, such as iron and zinc. For example, with insufficient iron, the ability of red blood cells to transport oxygen is compromised, leading to anaemia. Finally, we all need water to survive.

In this section, we will look at reconstructions of the typical *Palaeolithic diet*, which theoretically reflects the kinds of foods people ate during the pre-agricultural part of human history. Many researchers believe that our bodies are evolved for functioning in this kind of nutritional environment. We will then consider how agriculture changed everything, at least in terms of the human diet. New foods were introduced, but variety was lost, and problems associated with specific dietary deficiencies (other than total calories) became common in some agricultural populations. Ultimately, however, the legacy of modern agriculture is not scarcity but abundance, and we will see how we as a species are not particularly well adapted to living in an environment of continuous nutritional abundance.

THE PALAEOLITHIC DIET

For most of human history, people lived in small groups and subsisted on wild foods that they could collect by hunting or gathering. Obviously, diets varied in different areas: Sub-Saharan Africans were not eating the same thing as First Nations peoples on the northwest Pacific Coast. Nonetheless, it has been argued that we can reconstruct an *average* Palaeolithic diet from a wide range of information derived from palaeoanthropology, epidemiology, and nutritional studies (Eaton and Konner, 1985; Eaton et al., 1999). A comparison of the average Palaeolithic and contemporary diets is presented in Table 16.2 (Eaton et al., 1999).

TABLE 16.2 Comparison of Palaeolithic and Contemporary Diets

DIETARY COMPONENT	PALAEOLITHIC DIET	CONTEMPORARY DIET
Energy (calories)	High caloric intake and expenditure to support active lifestyle and large body size.	More sedentary lifestyle uses fewer calories, yet caloric consumption often exceeds expenditure.
Micronutrients (vitamins, antioxidants, folic acid, iron, zinc)	High consumption (65 to 70% of diet) of foods rich in micronutrients, such as fruits, roots, nuts, and other noncereals.	Low consumption of foods rich in micronutrients.
Electrolytes (sodium, calcium, and potassium, needed for a variety of physiological processes)	High consumption of potassium relative to sodium (10 500 mg/day vs. 770 mg/day). High blood pressure is rare in contemporary hunter-gatherers with high potassium/sodium ratios.	Low consumption of potassium relative to sodium (3000 mg/day vs. 4000 mg/day). High sodium intake from processed foods is associated with high blood pressure.
Carbohydrates	Provide about 45 to 50% of daily calories, mostly from vegetables and fruits, which are rich in amino acids, fatty acids, and micronutrients.	Provide about 45 to 50% of daily calories, mostly from processed cereal grains, sugars, and sweeteners, which are low in amino acids, fatty acids, and micronutrients.
Fat	Provides about 20 to 25% of daily calories, mostly from lean game animals, which have less fat and saturated fat than domestic animals, leading to lower serum cholesterol levels.	Provides about 40% of calories, mostly from meat and dairy products. Some contemporary diets, such as from Japan and the Mediterranean region, are low in total or saturated fat and are associated with lower heart disease rates.
Protein	High consumption, providing about 30% of daily calorie intake, mostly from wild game that is low in fat.	Recommended daily allowance about 12% of total calories. High protein intake has been associated with higher heart disease rates, probably because contemporary high-protein diets also tend to be high in fat.
Fibre	50 to 100 g [1.76 to 3.53 oz]/day. High-fibre diets sometimes are considered risky because of loss of micronutrients, but this would be less of a worry in a Palaeolithic diet rich in micronutrients.	20 g [0.71 oz]/day.

AGRICULTURE AND NUTRITIONAL DEFICIENCY

The essential paradox of the development of agriculture is that although it allowed the establishment of large population centres—which in turn led to the development of large-scale, stratified civilizations with role specialization—from a nutritional standpoint, most people led lives that were inferior to the lives of hunter-gatherers. Agricultural peoples often suffered from *nutritional stress* as dependence on a few crops made their large populations vulnerable to both chronic nutritional shortages and occasional famines. The "success" of agricultural peoples relative to hunter-gatherers came about not because agriculturalists lived longer, but because there were more of them.

An example of the decline in health associated with the intensification of agriculture comes from palaeopathological research in the Illinois Valley (Cook, 1979; Cook and Buikstra, 1979). Over the period 600 to 1200 CE, the people there went from lives that were characterized predominantly by subsistence based on hunting and gathering (with some trade for agricultural products) to an agricultural economy with significant maize production. Population centres increased in size. At the same time, however, signs of malnutrition also increased. Enamel defects in tooth development became more common, and we can associate them with higher death rates during the weaning years (Figure 16.16). Skeletal growth rates slowed. Specific skeletal lesions associated with malnutrition also increased in frequency.

With their dependence on a single staple cereal food, agricultural populations throughout the world have been plagued by diseases associated with specific nutritional deficiencies. As in the Illinois Valley, many populations of the New World were dependent on maize as a staple food crop. One of the negative health outcomes of a dependence on maize is associated with the development of *pellagra*, a disease caused by a deficiency of the B vitamin *niacin* in the diet. Pellagra causes a distinctive rash, diarrhoea, and mental disturbances, including dementia. Ground corn is low in niacin and in the amino acid tryptophan, which the body can use to synthesize niacin. Even into the twentieth century, poor sharecroppers in the southern United States and poor farmers in southern Europe, both groups that consumed large quantities of cornmeal in their diets, were commonly afflicted with pellagra. Some maize-dependent groups in Central and South America were not so strongly affected by pellagra because they processed the corn with an alkali (lye, lime, or ash) that released niacin from the hull of the corn.

In Asia, rice has been the staple food crop for at least the last 6000 years. In China, a disease we now call *beriberi* was first described in 2697 BCE. We now know that beriberi is caused by a deficiency in vitamin B1 or *thiamine*. Beriberi is characterized by fatigue, drowsiness, and nausea, leading to a variety of more serious complications related to problems with the nervous system (especially tingling, burning, and numbness in the extremities) and ultimately heart failure. Rice is not lacking in vitamins; however, white rice, which has been polished and milled to remove the hull, has been stripped of most of its vitamin content, including thiamine. Recognition of an association between rice overdependence and beriberi began to develop in the late nineteenth century, when the Japanese navy reported that beriberi could be eliminated among its sailors (half of whom contracted the disease) by increasing the meat, vegetables, and fish in their diets.

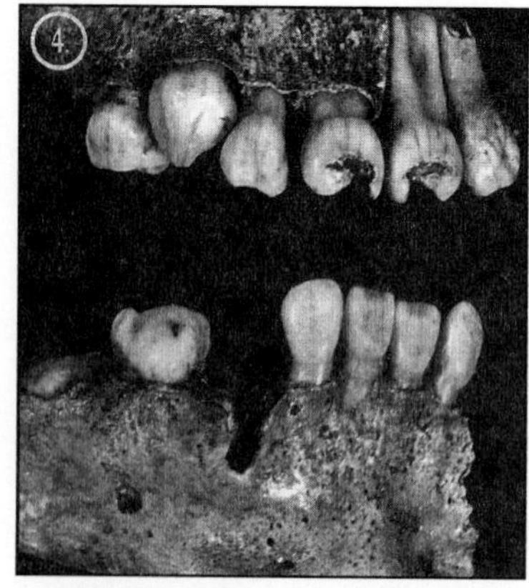

FIGURE 16.16 Enamel defects due to malnutrition in a prehistoric child.

AGRICULTURE AND ABUNDANCE: THRIFTY, NONTHRIFTY, AND THRIFTY-PLEIOTROPIC GENOTYPES

The advent of agriculture ushered in a long era of nutritional deficiency for most people. However, the recent agricultural period, as exemplified in the developed nations of the early twenty-first century, is one of nutritional excess, especially in terms of the consumption of fat and carbohydrates of little nutritional value other than calories. The amount and variety of foods available to people in contemporary societies are unparalleled in human history.

In 1962, geneticist James Neel introduced the idea of a *thrifty genotype*, a genotype that is very efficient at storing food in the body in the form of fat, after observing that many non-Western populations that had recently adopted a Western or modern diet were much more likely than Western populations to have high rates of obesity, diabetes (especially Type 2 or non–insulin-dependent diabetes), and all the health problems associated with those conditions (see also Neel, 1982).

According to Neel, hunter-gatherers needed a thrifty genotype to adapt to their nonabundant nutritional environments; in contrast, the thrifty genotype had been selected against in the supposedly abundant European environment through the negative consequences of diabetes and obesity. Diabetes among First Nations and Métis peoples is at least three times as common in the rest of the Canadian population, and has been attributed to a genetic predisposition to store caloric energy as fat that is related to their ancestors' hunting-foraging-fishing lifestyles (Health Canada, 2000). A move from traditional foods to a diet high in calories and fat is, of course, part of the problem. At the heart of the notion of a thrifty genotype is the idea that we are adapted to a past lifestyle and nutritional environment far different from what we experience today.

A refinement and expansion of the thrifty genotype model called the *thrifty-pleiotropic genotype* model proposes that, whereas Neel concentrated primarily on energy intake, the thrifty genotype should apply to any nutrient in the environment that is (or was) potentially scarce (Gerber and Crews, 1999). Thus we should expect negative health consequences for the overconsumption of a variety of nutrients: Excess cholesterol consumption leads to heart disease, excess salt consumption leads to high blood pressure, and so on. The deficiency syndromes of agriculture are part of this adaptive balance: Too little of a nutrient can also lead to disease. The pleiotropic aspect of the model is based on the observation that most of the diseases associated with overconsumption are chronic illnesses that have their effects late in life; they are to some extent a consequence of aging. If the efficiency of the thrifty genotype increases reproductive fitness early in life, the negative pleiotropic consequences in middle and old age will not be selected against, even in an environment of nutritional abundance.

We have seen how growth patterns, infectious disease exposure, nutritional status, and a host of other health-related issues are fundamentally changed by the adoption of new cultural practices and technologies. Conditions such as rickets and diabetes have been called diseases of civilization because they seem to be a direct result of the development of the industrialized urban landscape and contemporary food production. But this label is misleading. Rickets could also be called a disease of migration and maladaptation to a specific environment. Diabetes could be characterized as a disease of nutritional abundance, which was certainly *not* a characteristic of civilization for most of human history.

Biomedical anthropology is interested in understanding the patterns of human variation, adaptation, and evolution as they relate to health issues. This entails an investigation of the relationship between our biologies and the environments we live in. Understanding environmental transitions helps us understand not only the development of disease, but also the mechanisms of adaptation that have evolved over thousands of years of evolution. Change is the norm in the modern world. In the future, we should expect human health to continue to be affected by these changes. By their training and interests, biological anthropologists will be in an ideal position to make an important contribution to understanding the dynamic biocultural factors that influence human health and illness.

SUMMARY

1. **Why are both biocultural and evolutionary approaches important in biomedical anthropology?**

   Biomedical anthropology is concerned with the processes of adaptation and adaptability with reference to health and human variation. In evolutionary terms, this encompasses how human biology adapts to stressful environments by evolving adaptations to overcome them; in addition, understanding the mismatch between biological adaptations and current environments can also provide insight into human health. Humans must also respond to environment stress in the short term. Human adaptability studies show that biological plasticity and biocultural traditions can have a profound effect on health status.

2. **What are the four stages of growth seen across primates? Why is adolescence possibly a fifth stage of growth, unique to humans?**

   The four stages of growth are prenatal or gestational, infancy, juvenile stage, and adulthood. Barry Bogin argues that humans have a unique stage of growth, adolescence, which begins with puberty and is marked by a growth spurt not seen in other mammals. Adolescence may also provide an extended time period for human children to better learn their adult behavioural roles.

3. **What is the secular trend in growth?**

   It has been demonstrated in several populations at different times that stature and weight increase with the advent of economic development, industrialization, and improved nutrition. This trend plateaus when the population reaches its genetic potential. Migration studies provide further evidence of the secular trend in growth by comparing growth between migrant populations living in nutrition-rich environments and nonmigrant populations in nutrition-poor environments.

4. **What are some of the selection pressures influencing the distribution of skin colour around the world?**

   The main selection pressure is exposure to UVR; however, exposure to UVR can influence the evolution of skin colour in several ways. In areas of high UVR (high sunlight), selection for dark skin as a protection from sunburn and skin cancer may have occurred; dark skin colour may also prevent the breakdown of folic acid. In northern latitudes with less direct sunlight exposure, light skin colour may have been selected in order to facilitate vitamin D synthesis. Low vitamin D levels can cause the disease known as rickets.

5. **Why are agricultural populations more susceptible to infectious disease than hunter-gatherer populations?**

   Agricultural populations are larger than hunter-gatherer populations, providing a larger pool of potential hosts who have not developed antibodies to the pathogen. They are more sedentary, which makes them more susceptible to diseases transmitted in human waste. Agricultural populations are also more dependent on only a few water sources, making them more susceptible to waterborne diseases. Finally, they live in close proximity to both domestic animals and commensals (such as rats) and therefore are susceptible to diseases these animals carry or transmit.

6. **What are pellagra and beriberi?**

   Both are vitamin-deficiency diseases. Pellagra is caused by niacin deficiency and is seen in populations that have corn or maize as a staple cereal. Ground corn is low in niacin and the amino acid tryptophan, which the body uses to synthesize niacin. Beriberi is a disease common in populations where polished white rice is a staple cereal. It is caused by a deficiency in thiamine, which is present in the rice hull but is removed during processing to make white rice.

CRITICAL THINKING QUESTIONS

1. Is aging an adaptation or an indirect by-product of natural selection acting on other biological, physiological, and genetic factors?
2. What do we mean when we say there is an evolutionary arms race between pathogens and hosts?
3. Should everyone adopt the Palaeolithic diet? Why or why not?

KEY TERMS

biomedical anthropology
epidemiology
pathogens
teratogens
menarche
menopause
senescence
melanocytes
melanin
antigens
antibodies
immunoglobulins

SUGGESTED READING

Bogin, Barry. (2001). *The Growth of Humanity*. Wiley-Liss, New York, NY.

Nesse, Randolph M., and Williams, George C. (1994). *Why We Get Sick: The New Science of Darwinian Medicine*. Times Books, New York, NY.

Tanner, J. M. (1978). *Foetus into Man*. Harvard University Press, Cambridge, MA.

Trevathan, Wenda, Smith, E. O., and McKenna, J. J. (editors). (1999). *Evolutionary Medicine*. Oxford University Press, New York, NY.

Waldram, J. B., Herring, D. A., and Young, T. Kue. (2006). *Aboriginal Health in Canada: Historical, Cultural, and Epidemiological Perspectives*, 2nd edition. University of Toronto Press, Toronto, ON.

Steckel, Richard H., and Rose, Jerome C. (editors). (2005). *The Backbone of History: Health and Nutrition in the Western Hemisphere*, Volume I. Cambridge University Press, Cambridge, UK.

Chapter 17

The Evolution of Human Behaviour

DEBATES ABOUT THE RELEVANCE of biological and evolutionary approaches to understanding human behaviour have a long history. One of the liveliest periods was the mid-1970s, when new evolutionary and ecological approaches to understanding animal behaviour were starting to be applied to human behaviour. Increasing knowledge about the sophisticated social behaviour of other primates further fueled the effort to place human behaviour in a broader evolutionary and zoological context.

IN 1978, A MEETING of the American Association for the Advancement of Science brought together a number of prominent scientists who had different views about the relevance of these approaches for the study of human behaviour. One of these scientists was Edward O. Wilson, a Harvard biology professor, who argued that all animal behaviour, including that of humans, is influenced by genes. An opposing view was voiced by Stephen Jay Gould, also a Harvard biology professor, who cautioned that arguments about the biological basis of human behaviour had been used in the past to justify racist and sexist ideologies. Many supporters of the evolutionary study of human behaviour (then called sociobiology) and their opponents alike were caught up in a volatile combination of emotions.

WHAT HAPPENED AT THAT MEETING is now legend: just before Wilson was to speak, protesters stormed the podium and poured a pitcher of water over his head. They took over the microphone and denounced sociobiology, then quickly disappeared. Understandably, great commotion ensued until the meeting organizer regained control. Wilson then gave his talk, which was, by all accounts, rather anticlimactic.

Chapter Outline

We are fortunate that most debates about the evolution of human behaviour do not end with someone being doused with water. But the incident provides an indication of just how heated these debates can become.

The basic conflict is over whether human behaviour is "in the genes" or is a product of our culture and upbringing: that is, nature versus nurture. The nurture, or cultural, side accuses the nature, or evolutionary, side of being *genetic determinists*, people who believe that all observed behavioural differences between individuals, the sexes, or populations can be ascribed only to differences in genetics. The genetic side accuses the cultural side of embracing the logic of creationism: that once culture evolved, the rules of the game changed, and we were no longer subject (at the behavioural level) to the forces of evolution, which are so readily apparent in the animal world.

As you might expect, neither of these two extreme views reflects the views of most biological anthropologists. Biological anthropologists, with their appreciation for the biology and behaviour of our closest primate relatives, understand that human bodies and human behaviour evolved. Although behaviours do not fossilize, we can draw inferences about how they may have evolved by examining contemporary human and nonhuman primate behaviour and biology.

Biological anthropologists also understand the importance of culture and experience in shaping human behaviour. **Behavioural plasticity** is one of the critical adaptations that accompanied the evolution of a large brain. But many behavioural scientists today believe that although a large brain does confer on humans the ability to adopt a wide range of behaviours, some patterns of behaviour we observe across cultures and populations are most directly explained by evolution and natural selection. The behaviours are not purely genetically determined but reflect the interactions of genes and environments that yield patterns of behaviour we can analyze statistically.

To understand the evolutionary foundations of contemporary human behaviour, we need to apply the same logic and inferences that we use when studying other evolutionary phenomena. We can use the vast amount of information we have about human behaviour and look for patterns that are consistent with evolutionary models. We can also take advantage of "natural experiments" that provide unusual combinations of variables and allow us to gain new perspectives on human behaviour. The same principles that we use to make inferences about the phylogenetic relationships of the Old World monkeys, the adaptive value of the trunk of an elephant, the plumage of the male peacock, or the social behaviour of prairie dogs can also guide our inferences about the evolution of human behaviour. However, human behaviour occurs in a cultural context. Like the biomedical anthropology approach to health and illness (discussed in Chapter 16), a comprehensive understanding of the evolution of human behaviour entails a biocultural perspective.

In this chapter, we will address several aspects of human behaviour from an evolutionary perspective. These include the ecology and demography of traditional human societies, patterns of human behaviour that have been shaped by sexual selection, the interaction between culture and biology in the expression of language, and the emergence of behavioural disease in an evolutionary context. We recognize, of course, that each of these topics can be productively analyzed from a cultural or nonevolutionary perspective; these other perspectives may provide alternative or complementary analyses to those provided here. However, as we have emphasized throughout this text, the biological anthropological approach is defined both by evolutionary theory and by the quest to understand the human species—including human behaviour—in a biocultural context. Therefore, this chapter focuses on these evolutionary and biocultural explanations of human behaviour.

STUDYING THE EVOLUTION OF HUMAN BEHAVIOUR

Evolutionary approaches to understanding behaviour did not make much of an impact through the first half of the twentieth century. A major development in the study of the evolution of behaviour was the publication of G. C. Williams's book *Adaptation and Natural Selection* (1966). Williams saw the evolution of social behaviour in terms of benefits not to the group as a whole but to the individuals who made up the group (and their genes). Following on this work and others, in 1975 zoologist Edward O. Wilson published a book called *Sociobiology: The New Synthesis*. For a variety of social and political reasons, which are beyond the scope of this text (see Segerstråle, 2000; Alcock, 2001), Wilson's book became a lightning rod for critics of evolutionary interpretations of human behaviour. Wilson defined **sociobiology** simply as the science of the biological basis of social behaviour. Only a small part of his book was dedicated to humans, with most of it focusing on examples and discussions drawn from the animal world, especially the insects that were the main focus of his research. Although a classic work, *Sociobiology* was not *The Origin of Species*: it emerged from an intellectual climate that was, at least in part, already in tune with the message.

behavioural plasticity Changing a response to a particular circumstance after an experience alters the meaning of that circumstance; associated with memory and learning.

sociobiology Name popularized by E.O. Wilson for the evolutionary study of animal social behaviour.

Critics of sociobiology, such as palaeontologist and writer Stephen Jay Gould, claimed that sociobiology in general was not good science and was susceptible to political misapplication. Mindful of these criticisms, the field of the evolution of human behaviour has moved away from Wilson's grand vision of human sociobiology (that it would subsume all the social sciences) and embraced several different, sometimes competing approaches to human behaviour, which are seen to be complementary to or a part of traditional human behavioural sciences.

The Evolution of Human Behaviour: Four Approaches

Anthropologists and other scientists interested in the evolution of human behaviour use quite different approaches to the subject depending on their particular research interests and training. Four of the most common approaches are palaeontological reconstructions of behaviour, biocultural approaches, evolutionary psychology, and human evolutionary (or behavioural) ecology (Figure 17.1). The examples covered in this chapter make use of the latter three approaches.

Palaeontological Reconstructions of Behaviour In previous chapters we discussed several reconstructions of the behaviour of earlier hominids. These reconstructions were based on the anatomy of extinct hominids and, when present, the archaeological remains with which they were associated. They were also based on correlations among behaviour, anatomy, and ecology we have observed in nonhuman primate species and in contemporary humans, especially those living under traditional hunter-gatherer conditions. Any reconstruction of the behaviour of our hominid ancestors is a synthesis of both palaeontological and contemporary data. Although there are limits to how much we can learn from such reconstructions, they are the only source of information we have to understand the *sequence* of events in human behavioural evolution.

Biocultural Approaches It is clear that human cultural behaviour has influenced human evolution. For example, the adoption of slash-and-burn agriculture had an indirect effect on the evolution of the sickle-cell polymorphism, and the development of dairying in some populations was a direct selective factor in the evolution of lactose tolerance. As we will see in this chapter, our biological and evolutionary heritage may have shaped several patterns of behaviour that are expressed in a cultural context. One aspect of human behaviour that we have already discussed in detail—language—is a prime example.

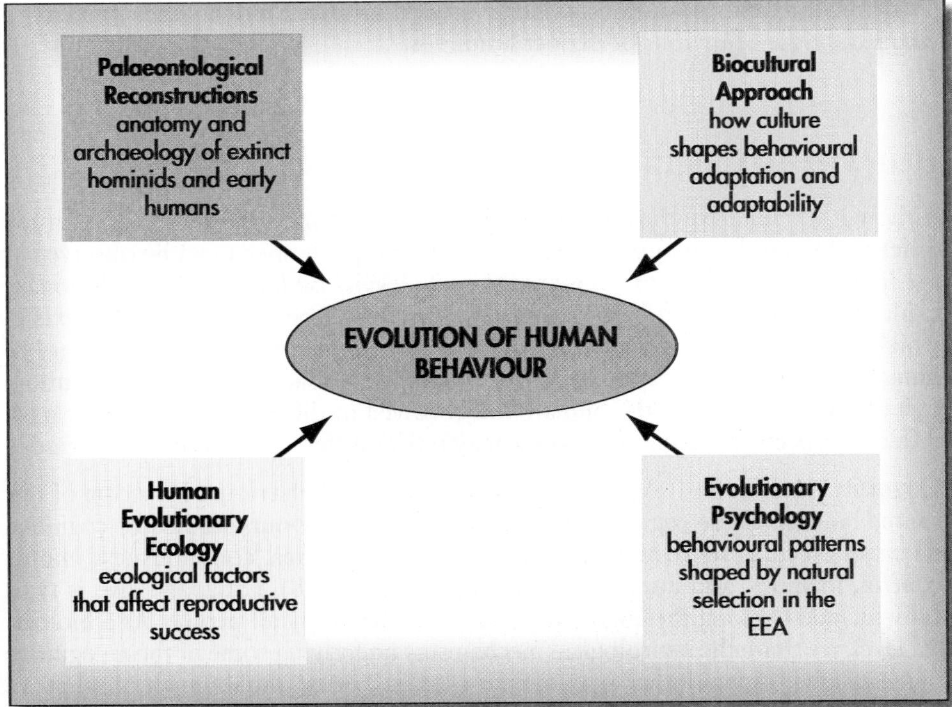

Figure 17.1 Four approaches to studying the evolution of human behaviour.

Evolutionary Psychology Evolutionary psychology is characterized by an adherence to three main principles. First, human and animal behaviour is not produced by minds that are general-purpose devices. Rather, the mind is composed of cognitive modules—which are assumed to have an underlying neuroanatomical basis—that express specific behaviours in specific situations. Second, cognitive modules are complex design features of organisms. Because natural selection is the only way to evolve complex design features, evolutionary psychology focuses on understanding behaviours or cognitive modules as adaptations. Third, for most of our history, humans and hominids have lived in small groups as hunter-gatherers. Evolutionary psychologists believe that our evolved behaviour may reflect or should be interpreted in terms of this hypothetical **environment of evolutionary adaptedness (EEA)**.

Evolutionary psychologists acknowledge that some behaviours, such as some physical features, are the by-products of other evolutionary forces and therefore should not be considered adaptations (musical ability is such a behaviour, for example). Furthermore, although the EEA figures prominently in their interpretation of behavioural data, most evolutionary psychologists study the behaviour of contemporary humans living in developed countries, via surveys, psychological experiments, and observations of people in day-to-day settings. They use such data to uncover the adaptations that characterized life in the EEA, whatever that may have been. Over the past decade the principles of evolutionary psychology have been elucidated by two of its main proponents, anthropologist John Tooby and psychologist Leda Cosmides (Barkow et al., 1992; Tooby and Cosmides, 2000).

evolutionary psychology Approach to understanding the evolution of human behaviour that emphasizes the selection of specific behavioural patterns in the context of the environment of evolutionary adaptedness.

environment of evolutionary adaptedness (EEA) According to evolutionary psychologists, the critical period for understanding the selective forces that shape human behaviour; exemplified by hunter-gatherer lifestyles of hominids before the advent of agriculture.

human evolutionary ecology Approach to understanding the evolution of human behaviour that attempts to explore ecological and demographic factors important in determining individual reproductive success and fitness in a cultural context.

cognitive universals Cognitive phenomena such as sensory processing, the basic emotions, consciousness, motor control, memory, and attention that are expressed by all normal individuals.

Human Evolutionary (or Behavioural) Ecology In contrast to evolutionary psychology, which focuses more on psychological experiments and surveys of people living in developed countries, **human evolutionary ecology** focuses on the ecological factors that influence reproductive success in the few remaining hunter-gatherer populations. Among the groups studied most intensely have been the Yanomamö of Amazonia (Chagnon, 1988, 1997), the Aché of Paraguay (Hill and Hurtado, 1996), and the Hadza of Tanzania (Hawkes et al., 2001). Topics of interest to human evolutionary ecologists include the relationship between status and reproductive success, demographic effects of tribal warfare and aggression, and the underlying social impact of hunting and food sharing. Researchers use data on contemporary hunter-gatherer groups to refine models that purport to reconstruct the behaviour of extinct hominids.

Behavioural Patterns and Evolution

Although we talk about investigating human *behaviour*, in reality scientists study different human *behaviours*. Human behavioural phenomena can be observed at the individual, cultural, or even species-wide levels. Biological and evolutionary explanations of different behavioural patterns vary depending on the contexts in which those behaviours are expressed. But to understand the natural history of human behaviour, it is important to remember the mosaic nature of its evolution. Just as different parts of the human body evolved at different points in our past, different aspects of human behaviour may reflect different evolutionary periods.

Cognitive Universals As a species we share many behaviours by virtue of our shared biology. These **cognitive universals** include behaviours studied by cognitive scientists, such as sensory processing, the basic emotions, consciousness, motor control, memory, and attention (Gazzaniga et al., 1998). Language also is typically included among the cognitive behaviours shared by all people. At a biological level, we share the neurological mechanisms underlying some of these cognitive universals with many other mammalian species. For example, much of what we know about the specifics of visual processing comes from experimental work on cats and monkeys. Other universals, such as language, clearly have emerged fully only in the hominid lineage (although we may study its biological antecedents by looking at other species).

Given the universal, and in many cases cross-species, expression of these cognitive processes, it is reasonable to assume they are biological adaptations that have been shaped by natural selection. Although cognitive universals have a basic common expression in all people, we often see variation in the way they are expressed. It is likely that this variation results from both environmental and genetic factors.

Cross-Cultural Universals When we look across the diverse cultures of the world, it is easy to notice that many commonalities emerge, which can be called **cross-cultural universals** (Brown, 1991). For example, all cultures have a language. We also find that each culture develops rituals and traditions to mark and recognize status. They develop systems for identifying and naming kin. They organize social and occupational roles along sex and gender lines. Standards of sexual attractiveness and beauty may show common patterns across cultures. Many biological anthropologists argue that common cultural practices did not develop independently over and over again but rather reflect underlying genetic factors that are widely distributed in our species. If we cannot find a common cultural origin for a widespread behavioural pattern observed across cultures, then it is reasonable to hypothesize that the pattern may reflect a common biological origin. This is especially true if we find the behaviour in a majority of human cultures or if we can show it to be associated with a common ecological variable. One way to look at this is that we are not "hardwired" to develop these behaviours but rather are "prewired" to express them given a proper ecological or cultural environment (Marcus, 2004).

Remember that cross-cultural universals are not individual universals. For example, we could say that singing and dancing are cross-cultural universals, but that does not mean that all members of every culture sing and dance. Similar forms of behavioural disease are found in different cultures, so in one sense we can say that mental illnesses are a cross-cultural universal, even if only a small proportion of the population develops these conditions.

Within-Culture Variation Male and female mammals may adopt different sexual and reproductive strategies because of their differential investment in time and energy in each offspring. How has this mammalian pattern been rendered in a human cultural context? Do we see evidence that humans have evolved away from typical primate patterns? If so, how and why has this *within-culture variation* happened? Variation in behaviour correlated with age may also have been shaped by evolutionary pressures. Is the young, risk-taking male a Western cultural construct or a cross-cultural phenomenon amenable to evolutionary theorizing? Although age and sex are the primary biological variables that figure into studies of the evolution of within-culture variation, we can study other aspects of within-culture variation from an evolutionary perspective.

Biological Constraints on Human Behaviour People are capable of doing just about anything, and any number of behaviours shaped by culture are not easily explained in a bioevolutionary context. On the other hand, when we look across cultures, there seem to be some *constraints* on what people do, which in turn lead to behavioural convergences across cultures. Unlike cross-cultural universals, behavioural convergences that arise from biological constraints are not the primary result of biological processes. A nonbehavioural example of a behavioural convergence is footwear. Footwear tends to converge on a similar basic shape, which is functionally constrained by the shape and action of the human foot. In a similar fashion, human behaviour may be channelled into similar patterns by constraints imposed by our neurobiology. A basic issue in the evolution of behaviour is determining whether any given behaviour is an adaptation or simply the result of a biological constraint on behaviour. Of course, similar debates arise about anatomical features as well.

cross-cultural universals Behavioural phenomena, such as singing, dancing, and mental illness, that are found in almost all human cultures, but are not necessarily exhibited by each member of a cultural group.

TRADITIONAL LIVES IN EVOLUTIONARY ECOLOGICAL PERSPECTIVE

Over the past three decades human evolutionary ecologists have undertaken intensive study of several traditional cultures to better understand the interplay between biological and cultural factors in human behaviour and human behavioural evolution. Studies of traditional hunter-gatherers and traditional agricultural cultures are important because their lifestyles reflect more closely the selective environments (the EEA) that shaped hominid evolution, until the advent of agriculture and large-scale societies starting about 10 000 years ago.

Evolutionary ecology represents a profound theoretical departure from traditional cultural anthropology. Investigating the complex interplay between behaviour, culture, and ecology, evolutionary ecologists typically live for extended periods of time with the groups they are studying (as cultural anthropologists do) (Figure 17.2); however, they differ from other cultural anthropologists in their reliance on quantitative research methods, which are necessary to test evolutionary hypotheses.

QUANTIFICATION IN EVOLUTIONARY ECOLOGY RESEARCH

To rigorously test evolutionary hypotheses and to discover how ecological factors affect human behaviour, evolutionary ecologists must collect quantifiable data. These data include birth, death, and marriage statistics (that is, demographic variables), nutritional data, and calculations of daily energy expenditure. Some evolutionary ecologists use sophisticated mathematical models to try to understand human cultural behaviour in an evolutionary context (Boyd and Richerson, 1988). Let's look at a couple of examples of quantitative research in human evolutionary ecology.

Wealth, Reproductive Success, and Survival One of the basic tenets of human evolutionary ecology is that cultural success should be related to increased fitness (Irons, 1979). William Irons tested this hypothesis in a study of fertility and mortality among the tribal Turkmen of Iran. In this culture, wealth (in terms of money, jewellery, and consumable goods) is a primary measure of cultural success. Irons found that for men, fertility and survivorship were higher for the wealthier half of the population than for the poorer half (Figure 17.3); survivorship was significantly higher for the wealthier women, but there was no difference in fertility. He also

FIGURE 17.2 Evolutionary ecologists live and do research in contemporary cultures that maintain all or some aspects of their traditional life ways, such as these tribespeople from New Guinea.

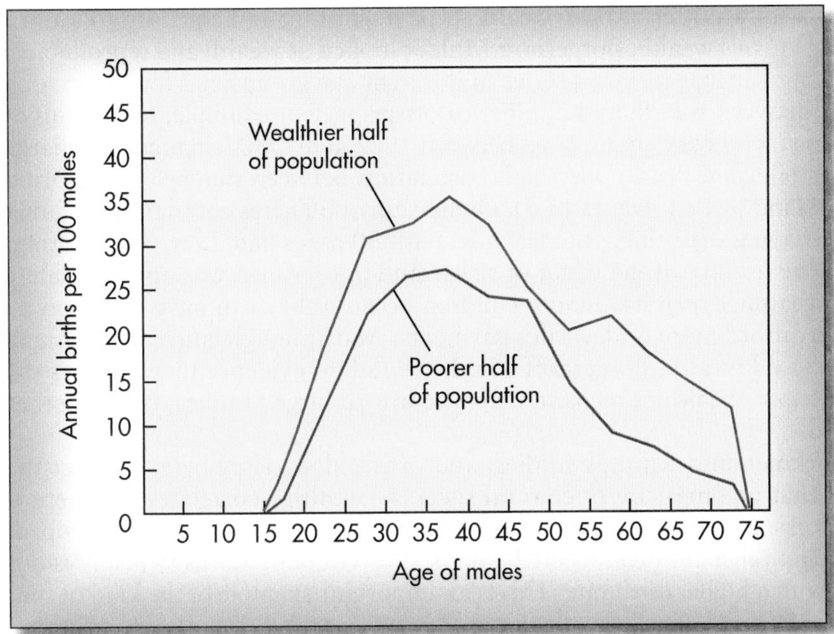

FIGURE 17.3 Male Turkmen in the wealthier half of the population had higher fertility rates than those in the poorer half.

found that male reproductive success was more variable among men than among women (that is, the difference between the richer and poorer halves was more pronounced for men than for women), as predicted by sexual selection theory.

Monique Borgerhoff Mulder (1987, 1990) looked at the relationship between wealth and reproductive success in a different population, the Kipsigis of Kenya (Figure 17.4). The Kipsigis are a pastoral people who moved into Kenya from northeastern Africa in the late eighteenth century. The wealth of a Kipsigis man is defined in terms of his land holdings, the number of animals he has, and his household possessions. Borgerhoff Mulder found that all these measures correlate strongly to amount of land owned, so she used that as her primary statistic of wealth.

The Kipsigis practise polygyny, which means that a man can have more than one wife at a time. When a man wants to marry a young woman, he approaches

FIGURE 17.4 The Kipsigis of Kenya.

her parents with an offer of **bridewealth**, a payment that can equal up to a third of an average man's wealth. Borgerhoff Mulder looked at wealth and reproductive success among Kipsigis men in a series of different age groups and found a strong correlation between wealth and number of offspring. For example, in a group of forty-four men who were circumcised between 1922 and 1930 (circumcision marks coming of age), there was a very high correlation between number of offspring and acres of land owned (Figure 17.5). Ownership of 30 acres correlated to having 15 to 20 surviving offspring, whereas men with 90 acres had 25 to 30 offspring. In general, the fertility of the wives of richer and poorer men was approximately the same. Wealthier men have more children because they can have more wives, being able to afford more bridewealth payments. And although larger families may lead to increased wealth, Borgerhoff Mulder found no evidence that this was the causal direction: Wealthier men were able to afford large families, not the other way around.

The Turkmen and Kipsigis studies, and others done elsewhere, support the hypothesis that one measure of cultural success—wealth—correlates with reproductive success. However, this correlation does not generally hold for developed, urbanized, capitalist cultures, where higher socio-economic status typically is not associated with a higher birth rate. This is an important example of the kind of fundamental biocultural change that can occur in a society when it transforms from an undeveloped to a developed economy.

bridewealth Payment offered by a man to the parents of a woman he wants to marry.

progesterone A steroid hormone produced by the corpus luteum and the placenta, which prepares the uterus for pregnancy and helps maintain pregnancy once fertilization has occurred.

Physiology and Ecology Another method for quantifying the relationship between cultural and ecological factors in human behaviour is to look at the way physiological measures vary across ecological contexts. For example, Peter Ellison (1990, 1994) developed a method of measuring levels of reproductive hormones in saliva as a noninvasive means to assess reproductive function in women living in diverse environments.

Progesterone is a steroid hormone produced by the corpus luteum and the placenta that prepares the uterus for pregnancy and helps maintain pregnancy once fertilization has occurred. Progesterone levels measured in saliva correlate with ovarian function. Salivary progesterone levels are strongly correlated with age over

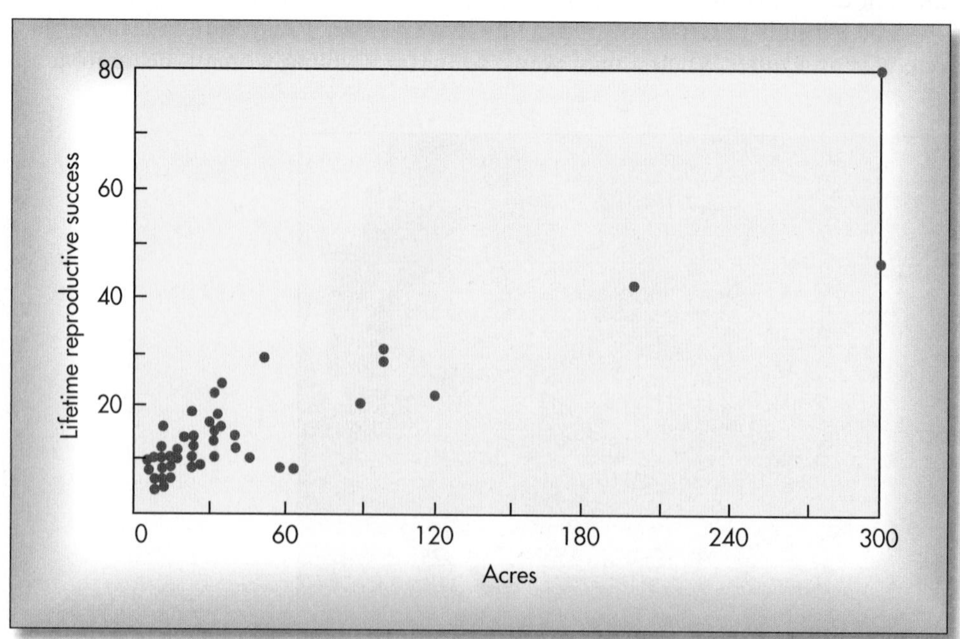

FIGURE 17.5 The relationship between number of acres a Kipsigis man owns and the number of offspring he has during his lifetime.

the course of a woman's reproductive life (between about ages 15 and 50 years). Progesterone levels increase from a baseline level at the end of puberty, peaking between 25 and 30 years of age and dropping off thereafter. Thus it seems that ovarian function matures at approximately the same age as the pelvis becomes structurally mature (Ellison, 1990, 1994).

Studies among two traditional agricultural groups, the Lese of Zaire and the Tamang of Nepal, and women from the Boston area showed that the basic age-dependent curve of salivary progesterone production was the same in all three populations (Figure 17.6). Ellison believes that this pattern probably represents a fundamental feature of human reproductive physiology. This discovery refines our view of the female reproductive years as an evolved life-history stage (beginning at menarche and ending at menopause).

Although the shapes of the progesterone-versus-age curves were the same in Boston, Lese, and Tamang women, the amount of progesterone produced varied among the groups. Boston women, who presumably had the most nutritionally rich environment with few infectious diseases, had higher progesterone levels at every age than the other two populations. It may be that chronic stress that delays growth and maturation, such as nutritional deficiencies, leads to lower levels of ovarian function throughout the lifetime. Such a stress-response relationship could be adaptive because in a stressful environment it may be better to devote more effort and energy to body maintenance and survival rather than reproduction.

Hunting, Gathering, and the Sexual Division of Labour

Recent research on contemporary hunter-gatherer groups has revolutionized our knowledge of how people without agriculture acquire the food they eat and how hunting and gathering patterns in hominids may have evolved. It has become increasingly clear that earlier speculations (Lee and DeVore, 1968) were based on inadequate understanding of hunter-gatherer life ways. The concept of "man the hunter, woman the gatherer" reflects a division of labour between the sexes in all

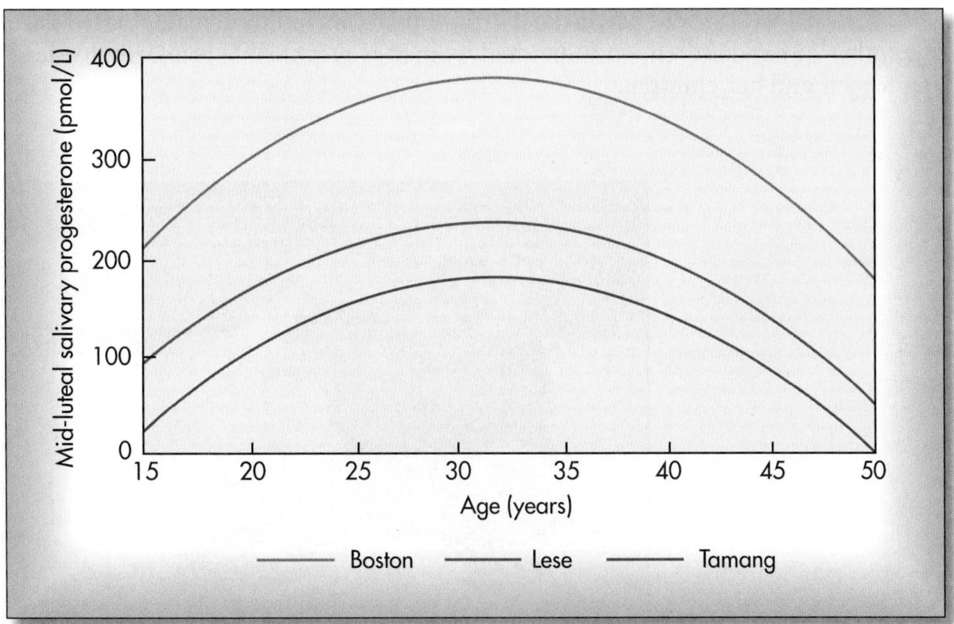

Figure 17.6 The age-dependent curve of salivary progesterone levels in three populations.

human cultures, but it is all too easy to turn it into a simplistic, stereotypical picture of evolved, hardwired gender roles (Figure 17.7) (Bird, 1999; Panter-Brick, 2002). Furthermore, observing sex differences in food acquisition practices is not the same as explaining why they exist.

In almost every traditional foraging culture, both men and women devote a substantial portion of their time and energy to the search for and acquisition of food. And in almost every culture, despite the fact that they live in the same environment, men and women exploit different aspects of that environment when acquiring food, leading to a pronounced sexual division of labour. For example, among the aboriginal peoples of Mer Island in the Coral Sea, both men and women forage for food on the coral reef. Men concentrate on using large spears to kill large fish swimming around the edges of the reef while women walk the dry part of the reef, collecting shellfish or catching small fish or octopus with small spears. Women almost always succeed in bringing home a reasonable amount of food, whereas the men have much more variable success (Bird, 1999). Among the Hadza of Tanzania, men concentrate on large game hunting while women focus almost exclusively on foraging for berries, nuts, fruits, and roots (O'Connell et al., 1992; Hawkes et al., 1997).

There are several models for the origins of the sexual division of labour. The *co-operative provisioning model*, based on the study of monogamous birds, predicts that the sexual division of labour occurred as a result of the evolution of monogamous relationships, because it would allow the pair to more fully exploit the environment if they did not compete with each other for resources. An alternative model, the *conflict model*, suggests that hominid males and females were already exploiting the environment in fundamentally different ways before males began contributing energy and resources to females and their young (Bird, 1999). The "sexual division of labour" is not really a division but reflects the fact that males and females have different problems to overcome (conflicts) in the course of mating, reproduction, and parenting.

It is nonsensical to ask whether hunting or gathering is more important. Neither provides more energy than the other on a regular basis. The productivity of hunting and gathering varies by season, environment, and a host of other factors (Kaplan et al., 2000). Women and men do vary in the package size of the food they focus on acquiring. Women concentrate on small foodstuffs that tend to be predictable, immobile, and obtainable while caring for infants and young children. Even though she almost always receives assistance from others, including female relatives and the father of her children, an individual woman is responsible primarily for feeding herself and her children.

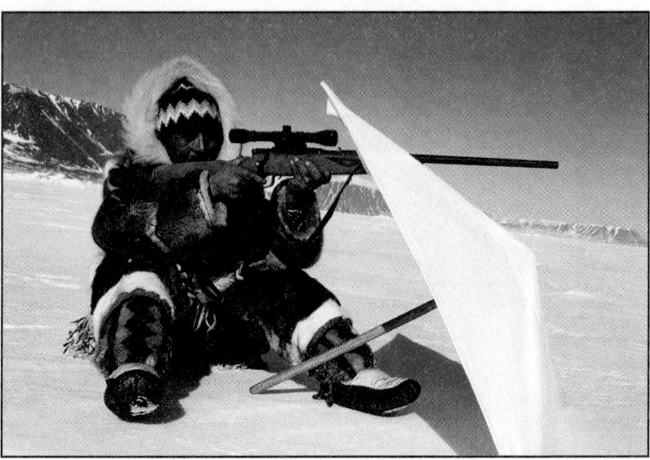

FIGURE 17.7 The evolutionary significance of "man the hunter" has been debated for decades.

Men concentrate on obtaining foods in large sizes that they cannot consume at once by themselves and that they redistribute to families or the larger social group. These foods almost always come in the form of dead animals, which may be obtained by hunting, trapping, fishing, or even scavenging. In some Melanesian societies, however, men compete to grow the largest yams, which, although they are too fibrous to eat, can be distributed and used for propagation of new plants (Weiner, 1988). Big yams aside, animals provide protein and fat in quantities not available from any other source, and animal food is almost always highly prized in human cultures. But why do males provide nutrients for others?

Why Do Men Hunt and Share Meat? Male cooperative hunting and meat sharing, which we see in chimpanzees, may have a long history in hominid evolution. As hominids became more adept at hunting larger game that could not be butchered, transported, or consumed by a single individual, meat sharing could become a central component of human culture. A fascinating aspect of big game hunting in many cultures is that the hunter or hunters most responsible for the catch may have little to say about how the meat is distributed. Research among the Hadza in Tanzania shows that a successful hunter may not even be able to recoup his losses via reciprocal altruism later (Hawkes et al., 2001).

The *tolerated theft model* of hunting and meat sharing explains meat sharing in part by suggesting that defending a large kill takes more energy than it is worth; in other words, it may pay off in the long run to tolerate the "theft" of meat (that is, sharing) rather than to work hard to defend a kill (which may be too large for a single individual to consume). The reward for hunting would come not from the meat itself but from the increase in social status and prestige, which reflects on family members as well (Figure 17.8). In effect then, large-animal hunting becomes a form of *costly signalling* (Bird, 1999), which ultimately increases the opportunities for males to acquire new mates. In the tolerated theft model, large-game hunting did not evolve primarily as a means of paternal provisioning, although females and their young definitely benefit from males' hunting activity.

Critics of the tolerated theft or costly signalling model argue that because most of the food that is shared after a hunt goes to close kin or reproductive partners, sharing enhances the fitness of the male hunter and therefore should be considered an adaptation (Hill and Kaplan, 1993); they suggest that the provisioning itself, not

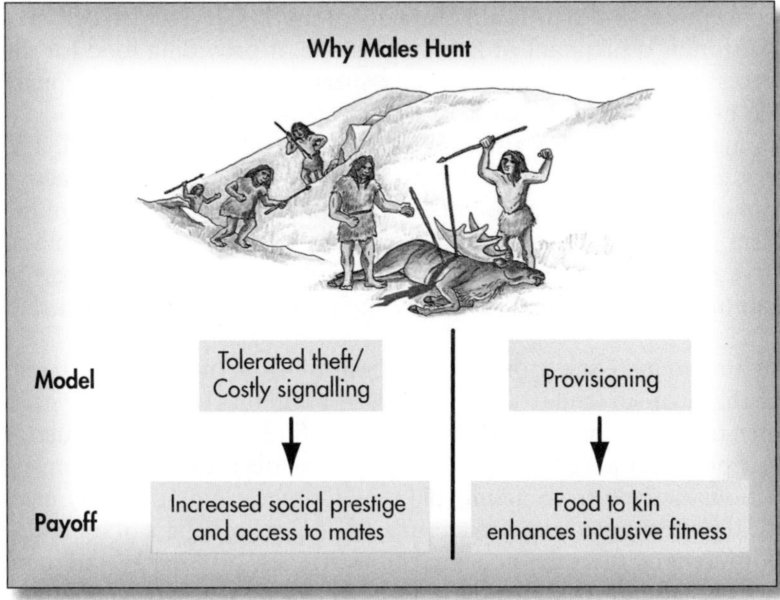

FIGURE 17.8 Models for the evolution of hunting by males.

the costly signalling, is the fitness-enhancing aspect of the behaviour. Hunting and meat sharing intensified in hominid evolution in the context of a pair bond and paternal investment in the young (Kaplan et al., 2000). Part of their evidence for this hypothesis is that reproductive-age women in hunter-gatherer populations almost always receive nutritional support from men. Because most of that support comes in the form of animals that have been hunted, and such altruistic behaviour is much more likely to have evolved in the context of provisioning kin, paternal investment via hunting may be an adaptation, not simply a secondary result of hunting for social prestige.

In the costly signalling model, hunting by men and meat sharing evolved in the context of sexual selection. Hunting itself is not seen as a critical behaviour in hominid evolution, and nutritional benefits to children may be an incidental outcome of the process (Bird, 1999). In contrast, advocates of the provisioning model give hunting and meat sharing a central role in hominid evolution: They argue that it was a prime impetus in the evolution of a larger brain and increased longevity (Kaplan et al., 2000). Studies of the Aché in Paraguay show that hunters do not achieve peak hunting proficiency until they are in their forties (Walker et al., 2002).

Resolution of the debate about why men hunt—for mates and prestige or to provision—will require further study. Unfortunately, the limited number of cultures that still practise a hunter-gather lifestyle (mostly in marginal environments) may make obtaining new data on the issue difficult. Obviously there is merit to both views, but they cannot both be correct because they posit divergent views on the importance of hunting in hominid evolution.

SEXUAL SELECTION AND HUMAN BEHAVIOUR

The study of human sexual behaviour has been revolutionized over the past 25 years by the development of an evolutionary perspective on human reproductive strategies, sex and gender differences in behaviour, and cross-cultural patterns of attractiveness and mate selection (Symons, 1979; Fisher, 1992; Buss, 2003). This evolutionary perspective is based in large part on the fact that humans are mammals. Male and female mammals vary profoundly in their energetic investment in producing offspring. Female mammals provide not only eggs but also a body in which foetal growth takes place. After birth, they are obligated to provide milk and care for offspring until the age of weaning. Males are obligated to provide sperm at the time of conception, and that is all. Subsequent investment, which can take the form of provisioning a pregnant or lactating female or providing food for the young, is not necessarily required, and in many species, including most primate species, males do not directly participate or invest in rearing of young.

Mammalian males and females also vary in their reproductive potential. The energetic costs of gestation and lactation limit a female mammal's reproductive potential; she can only have a limited number of offspring in her lifetime. On the other hand, sperm production does not impose much of a limit on a male mammal's reproductive potential. In general, mammalian males compete for access to females, and mammalian females should choose high-quality males, however that is defined.

Research on human mate selection and standards of attractiveness in different cultures indicate that women tend to value resource-providing ability in their partners, whereas men tend to value youth and appearance (indicators of reproductive potential) in their potential partners (Buss, 2003). These observations are consistent with predictions derived from mammalian evolutionary biology. Of course, these are statistical patterns generated from surveys of large numbers of individuals. Obviously, different cultures define sexual attractiveness differently, and there is much individual variation in sexual preferences. Nonetheless, according to many evolutionary researchers, the statistical patterns of sexual behaviour that are observed across cultures are not easily explained by cultural convergence. Instead, they may reflect underlying behavioural trends that have been shaped by natural selection.

FIGURE 17.9 Risk-taking behaviour is illustrated by this snowboarder.

RISK-TAKING BEHAVIOUR

When we look across human cultures, we find that as a group young adult males have the highest death rates from accidents or violence. For example, data from 2000 to 2004 shows that death rates in motor vehicle accidents for Canadian males are two to three times higher than in females (Statistics Canada, 2007). Young males do not die from accidents more often because they are unlucky, but because they are more likely to put themselves in risky situations (Figure 17.9). Proclivity toward risk-taking behaviour in males may reflect a significant sex difference in human behaviour, which may have a long evolutionary history (Low, 2000).

Why should males engage in risk-taking behaviour more than females? The reason may go back to general sex differences in mammalian biology (Low, 2001). For a female mammal, the costs associated with risk-taking behaviour are unlikely to outweigh the benefits. She is likely to be able to find mates and fulfil her reproductive potential throughout her lifetime, so she has no particular need to engage in risk-taking behaviour to acquire mates. On the other hand, male mammals vary much more in reproductive success. A male mammal may engage in high-risk, potentially very costly (even life-threatening) activities because such behaviours could have a potentially high reproductive benefit. For example, aggressive behaviour between male mammals over access to females is very common; it has clearly been selected for in the context of sexual access to mates. Females may also find risk-taking in males to be attractive because they may consider it a manifestation of ambition or "good genes" or a proxy for the ability to provide resources for the female and her offspring.

Some researchers are attempting to understand risky or binge drinking in the context of sexual selection for risk-taking behaviour. Binge drinking (defined as consuming at least five alcoholic drinks at one sitting) is almost twice as common among Canadian university-aged men than women: at ages 18 to 24, fully 44% of men binged at least once a month, compared with 23% of women. Males are also more likely to drive after drinking. These aspects of risky drinking in young men suggest that it may be another manifestation of the evolved pattern of risk-taking behaviour (Hill and Chow, 2002). It has been argued that risk-taking behaviours are not deviant but that we should recognize them as an evolved response to environmental instability. At an individual level, the environmental instability may be related to the person's family or work life.

INBREEDING AVOIDANCE AND INCEST TABOOS

Evolutionary factors may have played an important role in shaping not only mate choice preferences but also mate choice aversions. Inbreeding is defined as reproduction between close relatives. Close inbreeding has two major biological costs. First, a highly inbred population or species loses genetic variability over time. This means that when environments or other selective forces change, the population does not have the variability to respond to these changes via natural selection. Second, when close relatives interbreed, it increases the likelihood that lethal or debilitating recessive alleles will be expressed. Studies of a wide range of mammal species have demonstrated that inbred individuals suffer from greater mortality or loss of fitness, a phenomenon known as **inbreeding depression**, relative to less inbred individuals in the same species (Mettler et al., 1988). Studies of inbreeding in humans clearly demonstrate the potentially harmful effects of reproduction between first-degree relatives (such as father and daughter or sister and brother).

inbreeding depression Lesser fitness of offspring of closely related individuals compared with the fitness of the offspring of less closely related individuals, caused largely by the expression of lethal or debilitating recessive alleles.

Offspring of first-degree relatives (who share 50% of alleles) are far more likely than other children to be stillborn or to die within the first year of life, and physical and mental abnormalities are much more common among them.

Only a very small proportion of all human births are the result of matings between first-degree relatives. Sexual contact between close relatives is rare, and the proportion of those contacts in which pregnancy could occur (in which both parties are sexually mature and sexual intercourse takes place) is also very small (Van den Berghe, 1983). Across the world's cultures, 2 to 3% allow matings between close relatives, but this is usually only among elites, and it has the primary goal of consolidating resources or political power.

Inbreeding Avoidance and Incest Rules All human cultures have rules and traditions that regulate sexual contact and reproductive relationships. **Incest** is any violation of such rules by members of a kin group. *Incest rules* are sometimes explicit (stated in legal or customary form) and sometimes implicit (followed but not overtly stated or codified). Definitions of kin vary from culture to culture and do not always closely follow biological patterns of relatedness. For example, in North American culture, sexual contact between stepparents and stepchildren is generally regarded as being incestuous, although from a biological standpoint a pregnancy that resulted from such a mating would not constitute inbreeding.

Both cultural and biological scientists agree on the universality of cultural rules governing sexual relations between close kin—the *incest taboo*—but they differ on why it exists. Biological theories of inbreeding avoidance have focused on the fact that mechanisms that encourage outbreeding should be selected for; the cross-cultural universality of the incest taboo (which is essentially a mechanism for outbreeding) is taken to be evidence that such an adaptive mechanism may be present in the human species as a whole.

A basic social science criticism of the biological evolutionary view of inbreeding avoidance asks why cultures make laws against incest. If its basis is biological, the argument goes, then there should be no need to have cultural laws or institutions to prevent it. An analysis of incest rules suggests that most of them are more concerned with regulating sexual (and economic and power) relationships between more distantly related kin; incest taboos among close relatives are more likely to be implicit than explicit (Thornhill, 1991).

LANGUAGE-RELATED CROSS-CULTURAL BEHAVIOURS

In Chapter 15 we discussed the evolution of language, a behaviour (in a very large sense) that almost all scientists agree is a biological universal in our species. It is not surprising that something as pervasive and essential as language has multiple effects on several aspects of human behaviour (Box 17.1). Many anthropologists believe that language is what makes human culture possible. Indeed, when we look at the central place of language in defining a specific culture, we could argue that cultural diversity is inevitable given that languages themselves evolve and diverge. And yet, even beyond the basic biology and structure of language, cross-cultural patterns emerge that we can best explain from a broader evolutionary perspective.

BASIC COLOUR TERMS

A trip to the paint store or a glance at a large box of crayons could lead you to believe that there is an almost unlimited number of colour names. But if we look beyond the "peach parfaits" and "iceberg whites" of the decorative arts, we see that we can limit the number of *basic colour terms* to a much smaller number. Anthropological linguists Brent Berlin and Paul Kay published a groundbreaking study in 1969 in

incest A violation of cultural rules regulating mating behaviour.

Box 17.1 Reading, Writing, and Evolution

Reading and writing are *not* human cross-cultural universals. After all, most traditional cultures do not or did not have writing systems. The invention of writing, which has occurred several times in diverse locations, is recent; even the oldest writing systems are only a few thousand years old. We did not evolve to read and write, although it is quite clear that almost all people, no matter what their particular cultural or biological heritage, are capable of learning these skills.

The ability to learn to read is clearly part of our shared biological heritage, even if it is not a biologically evolved behaviour. Neuroscientist Stanislas Dehaene (2003) believes that although our brains have not been shaped by evolution specifically to read, our brains have shaped the writing systems that cultures develop: "I suggest that writing systems themselves were subjected to selective pressure and had to evolve within constraints fixed by our primate visual system" (p. 33).

Dehaene points out that our brains are truly adept at reading. For example, we recognize that EVOLUTION, ***evolution***, eVoLuTiOn, and evolution are all the same word, despite their varied appearances. On the other hand, we also recognize that subtle differences, such as that between "but" and "butt," can signal profound differences in meaning. Of course, reading piggybacks on spoken language, whose neural basis has been shaped by natural selection. Neuroimaging research indicates that many parts of our brain are activated by reading (Dehaene et al., 1997; Dehaene, 2003). However, a part of the cortex of the left temporal lobe, located near the boundary of the occipital lobe, is invariably activated during reading in all individuals. Furthermore, no matter what the language, whether it uses an alphabet-based writing system, as in English, or a character-based system, such as Japanese Kanji, activation in this region occurs not only during the reading of actual words but also during the recognition of wordlike sequences of letters. As children learn to read, activation in this region increases, whereas adults with *dyslexia* show reduced levels of activation.

In primates, this "reading region" is devoted almost exclusively to visual recognition, especially of complex visual forms. Although part of the temporal lobe, the region is located close to the occipital lobe, which is concerned primarily with visual processing. In humans, the reading region seems to be adapted primarily to identifying objects based on their shape, no matter what their size or orientation (Dehaene, 2003). For example, even without specific training, it is not hard to recognize letters that are upside down. Children often have difficulty distinguishing the letters ***p***, ***q***, ***d***, and ***b***. Given that the reading region may be concerned primarily with shape, this is not too surprising. All these letters have the same shape, varying only in their orientation in space. The development of reading behaviour specifically entails training and refining the shape recognition ability associated with this small part of the temporal lobe. It is interesting that this region is not a classic spoken language area, although the left lateralization of activation follows the spoken language pattern.

Dehaene proposes that our brain biology constrains the cultural expression of human writing systems and that it should be possible to identify features common to all writing systems. Although written Chinese and English are profoundly different in some ways (Figure A), from a neurobiological perspective they obviously share some basic similarities as well.

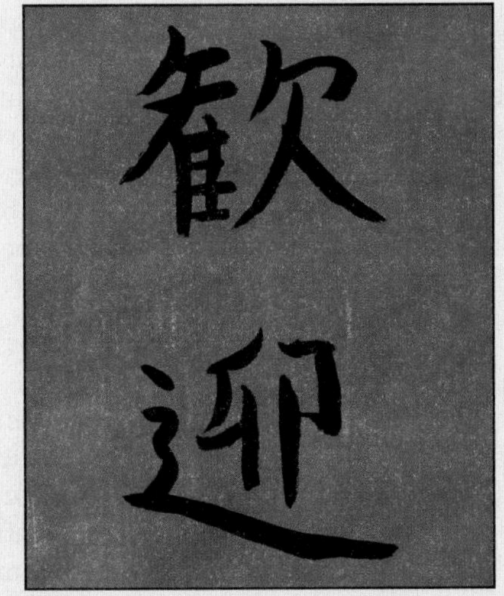

FIGURE A Chinese characters.

which they analyzed colour terms used by native informants speaking a wide range of languages and found significant constraints on the ways in which languages identify colour (colour term data on more than 100 languages are now available [Kay and Berlin, 1997]).

Basic colour terms are defined as single words used to describe colours that can be applied to a wide range of objects, which are widely known within a culture, and that are not subsumed into a more inclusive colour category (for example, *green* is a basic colour term but *lime* is not). The actual words used to describe colours are not similar cross-culturally; rather, the naming of colours appears to follow a systematic and perhaps evolved pattern. In cultures that identify only two *focal colours*, or colours that exemplify the basic colour categories, these always correspond to black and white (light and dark). In cultures that have three colour terms, the named colours are always black, white, and red. In cultures with four

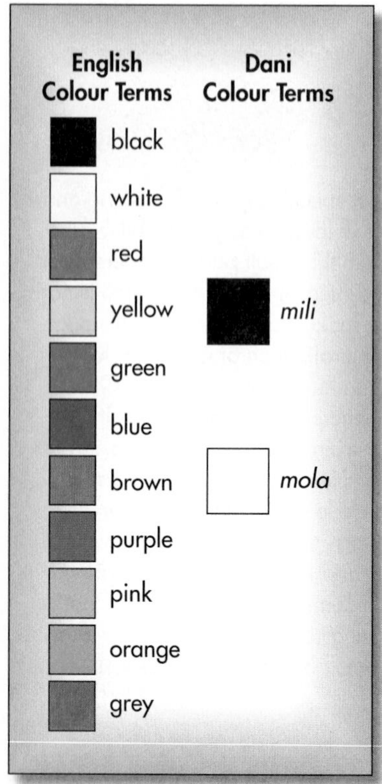

FIGURE 17.10 English and Dani basic colour terms.

terms, the colours are black, white, red, and blue/green/yellow. Above four colour terms, patterns are still evident, although they are more variable and complex. The cross-cultural distribution of colour terms suggests a cultural evolutionary scenario for developing colour terms: The black versus white distinction came first, followed by the addition of red and then other colours.

English has eleven focal colours: black, white, red, yellow, green, blue, brown, purple, pink, orange, and grey. In contrast, the Dani of New Guinea recognize only two colours: *mola* for bright, warm colours and *mili* for dark colours (Figure 17.10). Although these are the only two colour terms that the Dani use, the colour terms themselves do not constrain the Dani perception of the variety of colours in the world. Dani people have no trouble remembering or differentiating between colours or hues for which they have no name (Heider, 1972). Interestingly, the Pirahã of Amazonia have no simple terms for colours at all, and they do not talk about colours except when describing objects in their own experience (Everett, 2005). They do use descriptive phrases to distinguish colours, and the pattern of Pirahã language related to colour has been interpreted as reflecting cultural constraints on communication (Everett, 2005).

Colour naming patterns are probably constrained by factors related to the physiology of colour vision and perception, although there is much debate about how the physiology of colour vision is converted into the psychology of colour naming (Dedrick, 1996). Colour vision is extremely important to anthropoid primates, including human beings, and our colour vision system reflects a long evolutionary history; it comes as no surprise that cultural colour naming behaviours might be strongly influenced by this adaptation to the environment. Since 1969, a vast amount of research has been done on colour naming, and the cross-cultural sequence of acquiring colour terms probably is more complicated than outlined above, especially as we get beyond four colour terms. Nonetheless, given the infinite number of colours and names that human perception and language could generate, there can be little doubt that this cultural behaviour is constrained by some aspect of our perceptual biology.

BEHAVIOURAL DISEASE

Many behavioural diseases are expressed in much the same way in different cultures (Allen, 1997; Murphy, 1976). In modern biological psychiatry, we consider mental illnesses to result primarily from the interaction of genetic predispositions and environmental factors. Because many genetically influenced behavioural disorders are common, and we cannot explain their prevalence by mutation rate or environmental factors alone, it is reasonable to explore the evolutionary factors that may underlie their distribution. Note that this does *not* mean we should necessarily consider the behavioural diseases themselves to be adaptive, but rather that we may better understand them in the context of behavioural phenotypes shaped by natural selection.

DEPRESSION AND NATURAL SELECTION

Psychiatrists define *mood* as a persistent emotional state. Over the course of a lifetime, all people go through periods of high or low mood. Changes in mood in response to the environment or particular events are only natural. For example, low mood, or *minor depression*, is a perfectly reasonable response to an unhappy event, such as the death of a loved one (Figure 17.11). On the other hand, when depression gets out of hand and strongly affects a person's ability to function or care for himself or herself, then it is clearly not an adaptive behavioural phenotype. Psychiatrists say that a person has *major depression* if he or she suffers from two or more weeks of depressed mood or impaired enjoyment, disturbed sleep and appetite, psychomotor changes (such as restlessness or feeling slowed down),

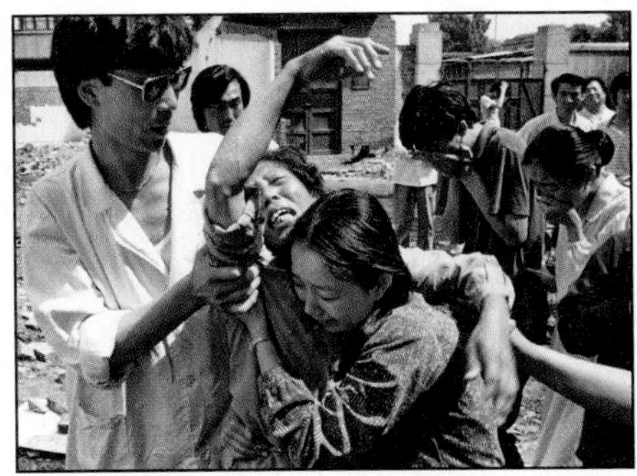
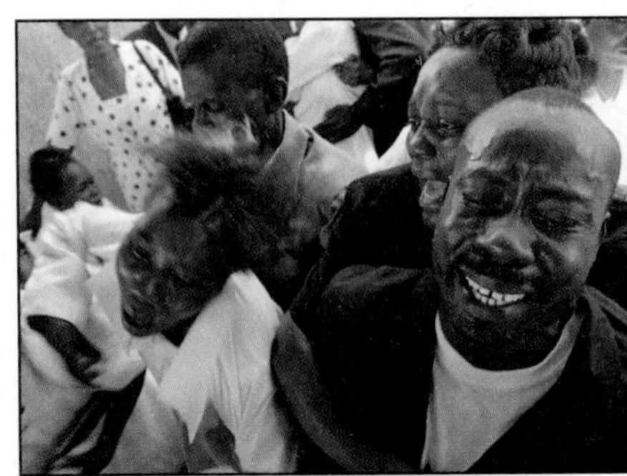

FIGURE 17.11 Grieving behaviour can have common expressions in different cultures.

reduced concentration, excessive guilt, or suicidal thoughts or actions (Health Canada, 2002). Major depression is surprisingly common, with about 8% of adult Canadians suffering from it at some point in their lives; the onset of mood disorders usually occurs during adolescence (Health Canada, 2002).

Why is major depression so common? In its severe form, depression is clearly not adaptive because it not only leads to increased mortality via suicide but also diminishes a person's ability to respond to all kinds of environmental and social stimuli. The genetics underlying mood are undoubtedly complex, but many studies have shown that there is a genetic component to developing major depression, and two specific alleles have been identified (Caspi et al., 2003; Zubenko et al., 2002). The alleles that cause some people to become clinically depressed have an additive effect, exacerbating a normal tendency toward developing (minor) depression that all people share. It is likely that, as with other phenotypes influenced by multiple genes (such as stature), there is a normal distribution in the expression of mood, with people at one extreme suffering from major depression.

Minor Depression as an Adaptation In general, minor depression, or low mood, is a psychological and physiological mechanism that regulates our behaviour when we are placed in any situation that might constitute an adaptive challenge (Nesse, 2000). Minor depression is common because decreased motivation or activity is beneficial in many situations. For example, over the course of hominid evolution, the loss of a loved one probably signalled a number of things: a dangerous situation, loss of information, loss of a contributing member to the community or family, and loss of future contributors to the community (in the case of children). Whatever the particular situation, temporary low mood would encourage the surviving individuals to disengage from activity in the short term, allowing them to establish new goals and directions.

Major depression is increasing in developed countries and becoming a larger health problem. Why? Another possible adaptive function of low mood is to dissuade people from wasting energy in the pursuit of unreachable goals (Nesse, 2000). Most people living in hierarchical societies (in which resources and power are not distributed equally) face an ongoing conflict between their knowledge of a more prosperous life and their inability to achieve it. The contemporary media culture may exacerbate this conflict by presenting a range of unachievable goals while promoting the pursuit of such goals as a cultural ideal.

In the environments in which it evolved, low mood is a short-term adaptation to a transient challenge; once the challenge or event is over, mood improves. In contemporary urbanized societies, however, people live in an environment in which challenges to status or goal achievement are ongoing, encouraging the development of persistent low mood. This persistent low mood can slip into major depression in genetically susceptible individuals.

Of course, the hypothesis on the adaptive nature of depression is speculative. However, we know that mood is important in all social primates: Whether or not we want to say they are "happy" or "sad," it is clear that we can see social primates exhibiting high or low mood. Mood has been shaped by millions of years of evolution in a social context. Thus socio-cultural factors, such as the development of a media culture, may indeed be playing a role in the expression of mood and the increased development of major depression.

SCHIZOPHRENIA

Schizophrenia is the chronic brain disease most typically associated with cultural notions of "crazy" behaviour or "insanity." It is found in almost all human cultures, with a lifetime prevalence typically estimated to be somewhere between 0.2 and 2.0%, with 1% being the usual best estimate (Health Canada, 2002). Although that percentage seems low, it translates into more than 300 000 people with schizophrenia in Canada alone. Schizophrenia is characterized by several symptoms, including delusions (often of a paranoid nature), auditory hallucinations, disorganized speech, grossly disorganized or catatonic behaviour, and negative symptoms, which are characterized by emotional flattening, not talking, or not moving (Health Canada, 2002). Age of onset typically is between the late teens and mid-30s (usually a bit later in females than males), and the course of illness is highly variable.

Schizophrenia is clearly a genetic disease. Evidence of its origin comes from a variety of sources; among them is the fact that a family history of schizophrenia is associated with a much higher risk of developing the disease. However, concordance rates for identical twins tend to be no higher than 50% (Gottesman and Shields, 1982), indicating that some people carry the alleles that predispose development of schizophrenia but do not develop the illness.

Why Is Schizophrenia So Common? The basic evolutionary question about schizophrenia is why it is so common. The estimated prevalence rate of 1% is much higher than can be maintained via mutation rate alone, whether schizophrenia is caused by the effect of a single major allele or of multiple alleles. In addition, numerous studies conducted over the past century have shown that people with schizophrenia, particularly males, have reduced fertility and fitness (Nimgaonkar et al., 1997). This is not surprising because the disease strikes at an age when people are entering their reproductive years.

Because schizophrenia is associated with reduced fertility and is a genetic condition, the alleles underlying the condition eventually should be eliminated from the population by negative selection. This does not seem to be happening. If anything, over the past 200 years schizophrenia seems to be getting more rather than less common, and it may be more common in large, developed societies than in traditional ones (Allen, 1997). The clinical schizophrenia phenotype itself obviously is not adaptive because it leads to demonstrably reduced fitness. Thus, individuals who carry schizophrenia-causing alleles but who do not develop the disease may have some characteristics that help them to reproductively compensate for the loss of alleles in individuals who have full-blown schizophrenia.

PSYCHOACTIVE SUBSTANCE USE AND ABUSE

The consumption of *psychoactive substances* (drugs) seems to be a cross-cultural human universal, and its history dates back tens of thousands of years. The most commonly consumed psychoactive substances are alcohol, tobacco, betel nut (used throughout South and Southeast Asia and Oceania), opium and its derivatives, coca and cocaine (coca leaves are a mild stimulant when chewed; cocaine is a concentrated form of the active ingredient), cannabis (marijuana), caffeine, and khat (chewed in East Africa) (Smith, 1999; Sullivan and Hagen, 2002) (Figure 17.12). Contemporary psychoactive drugs for the most part appeared with the development

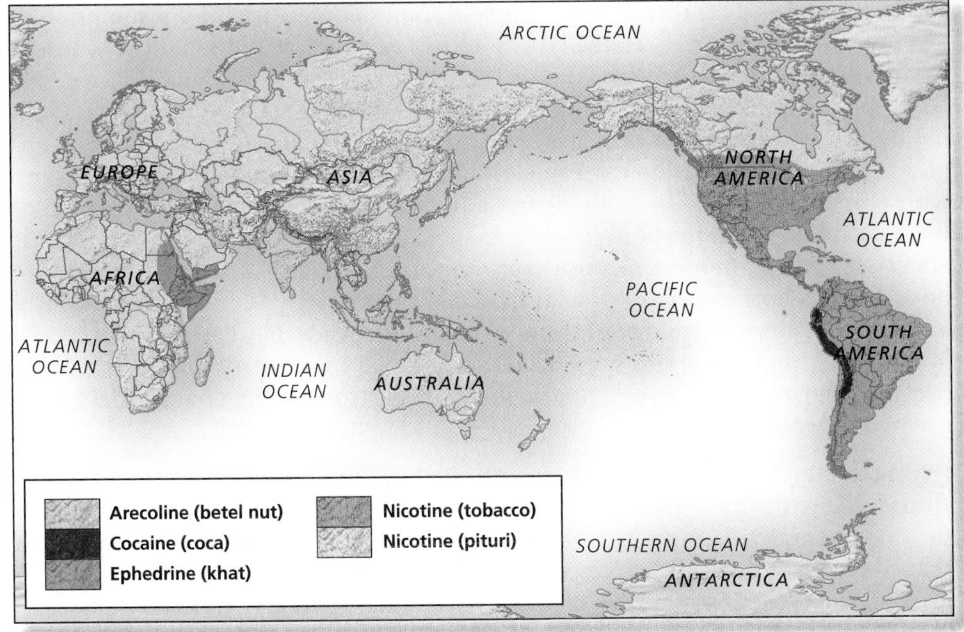

FIGURE 17.12 Worldwide map of traditional psychoactive substance use.

of agriculture, starting 10 000 to 15 000 years ago. Preagricultural peoples undoubtedly used available psychoactive substances in plants, but large and steady quantities of such substances did not become available until the development of agriculture (Smith, 1999).

Psychoactive drugs generally work by mimicking the effects of neurotransmitters found in the nervous system or by stimulating the production of neurotransmitters that influence behaviour or mood. Biological research on *drug addiction*, or *substance dependence*, indicates that both genetic and environmental factors play key roles in the development of drug dependence. A person with a substance dependence problem exhibits the following: tolerance to the effects of a drug, leading to the use of increasing amounts; psychological or physiological withdrawal if the drug is removed, making giving up the drug difficult; and use of the drug despite knowledge of the negative consequences of continued usage.

Genetic Polymorphisms Associated with Psychoactive Substance Dependence Much biological research on drug dependence has focused on the neurotransmitter *dopamine*. Dopamine is an important component of the pleasure and reward system in the brain. Stimulants, opiates, nicotine, and THC (the active ingredient in marijuana) all affect this neurotransmitter system (Enoch and Goldman, 1999). Kenneth Blum and colleagues (1996) suggest that a whole range of addictive behaviours (including drug addiction, gambling addiction, and so on) may be related to polymorphisms in dopamine receptor genes. Specifically, individuals with severe addiction problems may be much more likely to carry an allele associated with a reduction in the total number of dopamine receptors. These individuals appear to need more of a stimulus (drug or activity) to derive a sense of reward or pleasure. Therefore, they are at higher risk for increased drug usage and ultimately substance dependence. Blum and colleagues call this constellation of behaviours *reward deficiency syndrome*.

In contrast to reward deficiency syndrome, a different polymorphism may make addiction to a specific drug—alcohol—less likely than usual (Enoch and Goldman, 1999). *Ethanol* (the "alcohol" we consume) is metabolized first to acetaldehyde by the enzyme *alcohol dehydrogenase* (ADH) and then to acetate by *aldehyde dehydrogenase* (ALDH). Acetaldehyde is the chemical that produces facial flushing, increased heart rate, and nausea in some people after the consumption of alcohol. In most people acetaldehyde does not accumulate in the body because it is quickly converted to acetate (Figure 17.13); however, alleles found in some East Asian populations lead to a build-up of acetaldehyde in the body, either increasing its rate of synthesis or decreasing its rate of conversion to acetate. For example, an allele *ALDH2*2* (due to a single amino acid substitution in ALDH) is found with a frequency of 35% in the Japanese population. This allele leads to a build-up of acetaldehyde in the body, leading to facial flushing and other unpleasant side effects after even modest alcohol consumption. *ALDH2*2* heterozygotes and homozygotes both experience facial flushing; their risk of developing alcoholism is one-tenth to one-fourth that of those who do not possess the allele. No *ALDH2*2* homozygote individual has ever been observed to be an alcoholic, presumably because their physiology prevents them from ever consuming enough alcohol to become dependent on it.

Evolutionary Psychology Theories about Psychoactive Substance Use and Abuse One theory is that psychoactive drug use cannot be adaptive because it so fundamentally disrupts longstanding emotional mechanisms that have been shaped by natural selection (Nesse and Berridge, 1997). Drugs that simulate positive emotions (heroin, cocaine, alcohol, marijuana, and amphetamine) send false signals of fitness benefit, which in turn have the potential to disrupt a person's entire biological system of "wants" and "likes." Drugs that block negative emotions or reduce anxiety are potentially even more disruptive because they remove the body's signals to take action or to avoid potential threats.

A different evolutionary analysis of human psychoactive substance use argues that hominids have probably had a long-term evolutionary relationship with psychoactive substances (Sullivan and Hagen, 2002). With the exception of alcohol, most of the active ingredients of commonly used psychoactive drugs are formed naturally in plants and are similar to neurotransmitters found in the brain. Thus, we

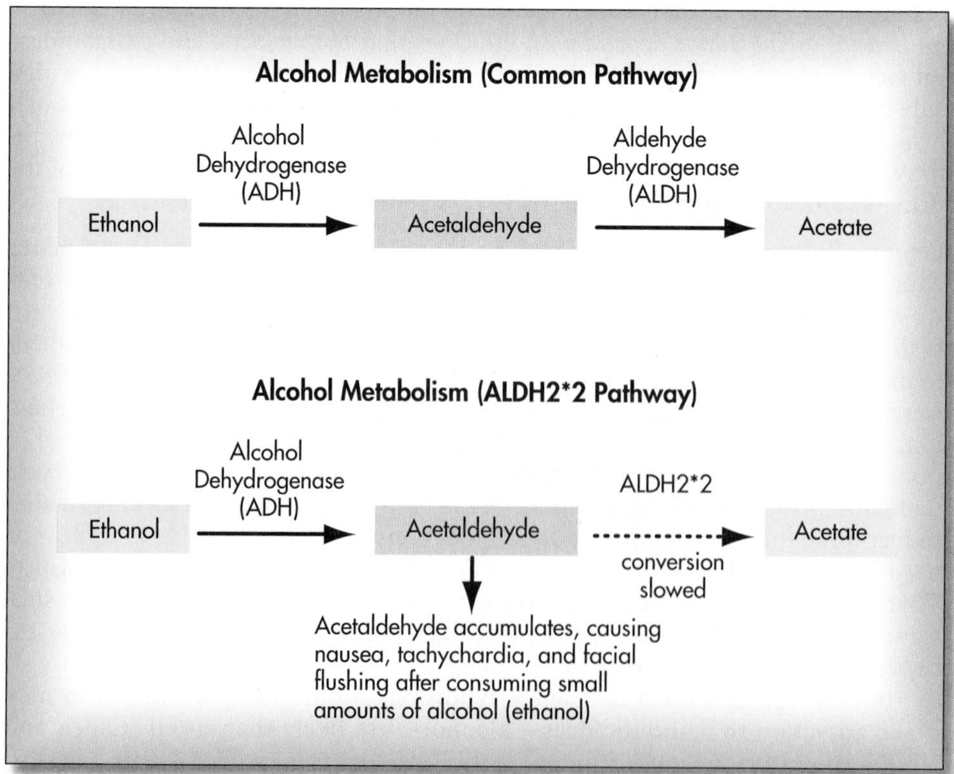

FIGURE 17.13 Genetic variation in the metabolism of alcohol.

benefit from consuming small quantities of these neurotransmitter-like chemicals in the same way that we need to consume small quantities of essential vitamins and minerals. In many traditional cultures no distinction is made between drugs and food (Sullivan and Hagen, 2002). People consume "food" for sustenance and to have more energy; for example, some traditional cultures classify tobacco as a "food." Much psychoactive substance use in traditional cultures is associated not with developing a hedonic rush ("getting high") but with gaining increased stamina in a marginal environment (such as the Australian desert or Andean mountains). Even today, nonhedonic substances constitute most drug consumption (caffeine, nicotine, arecoline in betel nuts). Psychoactive drug use in past environments could have been adaptive (providing increased stamina and neurotransmitters), although it may not be so in contemporary environments, which are characterized by easy access to both food and psychoactive substances.

SUMMARY

1. **What are four approaches to understanding the evolution of human behaviour?**

   The four approaches are palaeontological reconstructions of behaviour, evolutionary psychology, biocultural anthropology, and human evolutionary (or behaviour) ecology. All approaches are interested in understanding human behaviour in an evolutionary context, although they differ in the kinds of data they use and the methods they use to collect those data.

2. **How are human evolutionary ecologists similar and dissimilar to traditional cultural anthropologists?**

   Traditional cultural anthropologists and human evolutionary ecologists both typically engage in intensive fieldwork conducted in traditional and nontraditional communities. Human evolutionary ecologists tend to be more quantitative than cultural anthropologists and focus on collecting data on population structure, reproductive factors, energetic expenditure, and nutrition, which can be used to test evolutionary and ecological hypotheses.

3. **What is the sexual division of labour? In what ways is it manifest in traditional cultures around the world?**

   In the older anthropological literature, the sexual division of labour is characterized by men being hunters and women being gatherers. More recent formulations suggest that men focus on collecting "large package" foodstuffs (such as big game) and women on "small package" items (which include plant material or small game). These differences are manifest in different cultural and ecological environments.

4. **Why are young males deemed risk-takers by researchers interested in the evolution of behaviour?**

   Young males (15 to 30 years of age) have higher accident rates and engage in more apparently antisocial and aggressive behaviour than any other sex–age group. This can be understood in terms of sexual selection theory, in which young males who take large risks may ultimately derive from them large reproductive advantages. Although this is not true in contemporary societies, the risk-taking behaviours are still manifest in young males trying to establish themselves in society as a whole.

5. **What is the empirical evidence underlying the claim that there are biological constraints on naming colour terms?**

   Across a wide range of cultures, if a culture has only two basic colour terms, they correspond to black and white. If there are three colour terms, then they are black, white, and red. The fourth colour term added is blue/green/yellow. The cultural convergence in basic colour terms may result from the physiology of colour perception in humans.

6. **In what ways might minor depression be considered an adaptation? How are major and minor depression different?**

   Minor depression, or low mood, is a normal response to a variety of events that occur in the lives of individuals. It may be adaptive in that it causes an individual to inhibit his or her actions at a time when low activity may be temporarily beneficial. Low mood prevents individuals from pursuing unrealistic goals and wasting energy. Persistent low mood, or major depression, is not adaptive because it leads not only to increased rates of suicide but also to other behavioural patterns that increase mortality.

7. **Give two examples that illustrate how people vary biologically in their responses to psychoactive substances. How do these relate to the tendency to develop substance dependence?**

   Some individuals have alleles that cause them to have fewer receptors for the neurotransmitter dopamine, which is important in the brain's reward system. These individuals appear to need a greater amount of a stimulant (such as drugs or gambling) before they derive a sense of reward from the substance or activity. This predisposes them to developing addictive behaviours and substance dependence. In contrast, individuals who possess the ALDH2*2 allele for alcohol metabolism rarely develop alcoholism. The reason is that this allele leads to the build-up of acetaldehyde in the body after the consumption of even limited amounts of alcohol. Acetaldehyde is a toxic substance that can cause facial flushing, rapid heart rate, and nausea. Individuals with the ALDH2*2 allele do not become alcoholics because they cannot consume enough alcohol to become dependent on it.

CRITICAL THINKING QUESTIONS

1. Why is it necessary to approach the evolution of human behaviour from diverse viewpoints?
2. Defend or critique the following statement: Human psychoactive substance use is an adaptive behaviour in many environments.
3. Human evolutionary ecologists uncover many cultural patterns of behaviour that make sense in light of evolutionary theory. What does this say about the motivations of individuals living in human societies? Should we regard people in general as operating as "fitness maximizers" no matter what they are doing?
4. How should society deal with young male risk-takers? Does the evolutionary perspective help us understand and deal with the antisocial or unduly aggressive behaviour of some young adult males? Can increases in the aggressive or antisocial behaviour of young females be explained in an evolutionary context?
5. Drawing on what you have learned while reading this textbook, can you think of any areas in which understanding the evolutionary history of our species could directly lead to a betterment of the contemporary human condition?

KEY TERMS

behavioural plasticity
sociobiology
evolutionary psychology
environment of evolutionary adaptedness (EEA)
human evolutionary ecology
cognitive universals
cross-cultural universals
bridewealth
progesterone
inbreeding depression
incest

SUGGESTED READING

Alcock, J. (2001). *The Triumph of Sociobiology*. Oxford University Press, New York, NY.

Allman, W. F. (1995). *The Stone Age Present*. Touchstone, New York, NY.

Barkow, J. H., Tooby J., and Cosmides, L. (1992). *The Adapted Mind*. Oxford University Press, New York, NY.

Barrett, L., Dunbar, R., and Lycett, J. (2002). *Human Evolutionary Psychology*. Princeton University Press, Princeton, NJ.

Betzig, L. (editor). (1997). *Human Nature: A Critical Reader*. Oxford University Press, New York, NY.

Low, Bobbi S. (1999). *Why Sex Matters*. Princeton University Press, Princeton, NJ.

Chapter 18

Human Osteology and Skeletal Biology

A BIOLOGICAL ANTHROPOLOGIST IN TORONTO lays out a partial skeleton on a table in her lab and begins the painstaking task of cleaning the remains and identifying each bone, tooth, and skeletal fragment. The skeleton was found along a stream bed in one of the many ravines that run through the city, and the Toronto regional coroner has requested a biological profile. This profile will provide the estimated age of the individual at the time of death, the sex, and other pertinent features of the skeleton and will help officials identify the deceased. As she removes scraps of decomposing flesh from the bones she sees gnaw marks that probably came from carnivores, perhaps coyotes, that scavenged the remains. This observation goes a long way to explaining why the skeleton is not complete, since scavengers will often remove body parts from a carcass and take them back to a den or nest. But she makes a more disturbing discovery when she cleans the skull of dirt and bits of scalp and hair: the bone at the back of the head is marred by a small circular hole and fracture lines, probably caused by a small calibre bullet. This is not the body of a lost hiker but that of a murder victim.

ACROSS THE COUNTRY IN EDMONTON, a biological anthropologist examines ancient skeletons from Egypt for evidence of infections, fractures, and malnutrition. These skeletons date to the Pyramid Age and are the remains of the social elite of Pharaoh's court and members of the extended royal family. The anthropologist has already studied the skeletons of many of the workers who built one of the pyramids and has recorded high frequencies of fractures and pronounced bony growths where the muscles attached to the bone. These findings are consistent with a life of hard labour and high risk of injury on the job. But the bones and teeth of the upper-class ancient Egyptians are revealing a different picture. While these people appear to have been well fed and protected from the rigours of manual labour, their teeth show many cavities and their jaw bones are riddled with holes caused by pus draining from dental abscesses. Apparently, their high status also provided them with easy access to cavity-causing dates, figs, and honey, luxury food items documented in the ancient papyri that were not readily available to other segments of Egyptian society.

What these two biological anthropologists have in common is their expertise in the human musculoskeletal system: its structure, function, growth and development, and variability. Human osteologists, also known as skeletal biologists, study **osteology**, the branch of anatomy that deals with the structure and function of bones. They are able to construct a biological profile, or **osteobiography**, of aspects of a person's life history that are recorded in the individual's skeleton. When applied in a medico-legal context, this branch of skeletal biology is called **forensic anthropology** (described in more detail later in this chapter).

BIOLOGICAL PROFILES

Life history data that are used to construct a biological profile include age at death, sex, indicators of biological ancestry, and estimation of living stature, as well as individualizing features such as evidence of injury or illness, indicators of diet, markers of habitual activities, and cultural modifications to the body. The objective is to shed some light on the person's way of life and what happened over the course of his or her life. Data obtained from individual skeletons are of interest in themselves, but when retrieved from a number of skeletons that represent a past population, the information can be applied to questions of archaeological or culture-historical interest, such as the size and age structure of a past population, the biological relatedness of ancient populations, or the impact on health of subsistence change. Biological and medical historical applications are also the subject of much osteoarchaeological study, including estimation of life expectancy in the past, the geographic and sociocultural correlates of disease, and the problem of infant mortality.

osteology The branch of anatomy that deals with the structure and function of bones.

osteobiography A biological profile of aspects of a person's life history that are recorded in the individual's skeleton.

forensic anthropology The study of human remains applied in a medico-legal context.

Age

As the human body develops from foetus to old age, dramatic changes occur in the skeleton and teeth (Figure 18.1). Humans have two sets of teeth of different shapes and sizes that erupt at fairly predictable ages, so teeth that are visible in the jaws (or that can be seen with x-rays) can help distinguish between children of different ages and between older juveniles and adults of the same size. The long bones of the arms and legs acquire characteristic bony growths at their ends (the epiphyses), which are composed of cartilage at birth and which become bone during the years between birth and puberty. The lengths and proportions of bones change in predictable ways as children grow, and in small children the degree of closure of the cranial bones (covering the fontanelles or "soft spots" of the skull) also changes with age. Thus a number of features can be used to assess the age of a person before his or her skeleton reaches maturity (Figure 18.2 and Figure 18.3). Age is harder to determine in adults because the growth and maturation of the bones and teeth is essentially complete. Several methods have been developed, however, to assess degenerative and structural changes in the skeleton that have been documented to occur with increasing age.

When osteologists determine age, they report it as a range rather than as a single number. In children the age estimate may be fairly precise, such as within a few months. Adult age estimates are less precise, however, and may reflect a range of plus or minus several years. This range reflects the variation in growth and aging in the human population and denotes the person's biological age, which should encompass the person's chronological age at the time of his or her death.

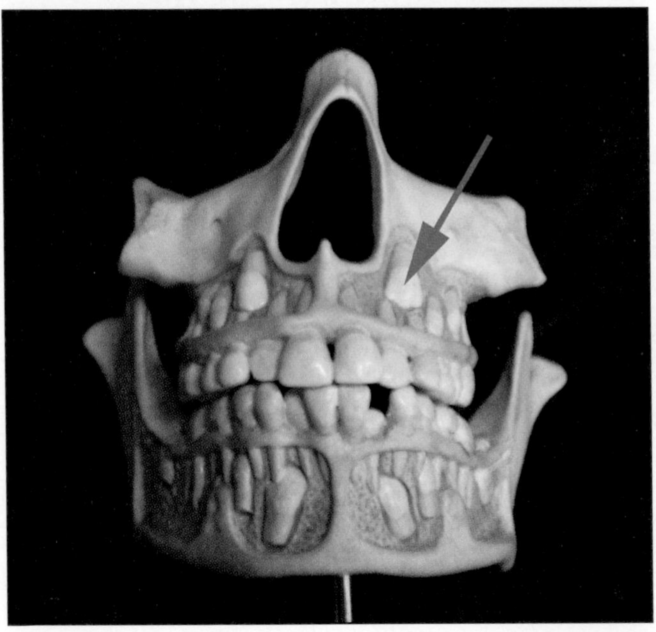

Figure 18.1 This replica of a child's jaws shows how the "baby" teeth would be visible in the mouth, while the adult, or permanent, teeth are forming within the bone of the jaw (arrow). The teeth begin as small tooth buds, which grow into the complete crown (the part that is visible in a person's mouth). The permanent tooth crowns break through the gums as their roots develop, while at the same time the roots of the baby teeth dissolve and the teeth eventually "fall out."

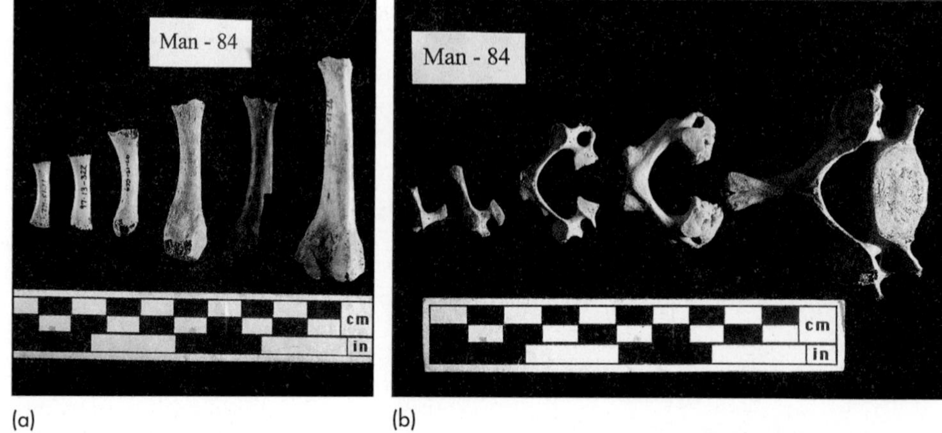

(a) (b)

FIGURE 18.2 Since bones change in size and shape as an individual grows, bone anatomy helps to provide an age estimate, particularly in children. Foot bones (a) and vertebrae (b) from an archaeological site are shown from younger (left) to older (right).

SEX

The sex of the living person also can be determined from the skeleton, although sex characteristics are more prominent in an adult skeleton than in a child's skeleton because they are influenced by hormonal activity during puberty. The two parts of the skeleton that most readily reveal sex are the pelvis and the skull (Figure 18.4). Because of selective pressures for bipedality and childbirth, human females have evolved a pelvis that provides a large birth canal (see Chapter 10). This affects the shape of the innominate (hip bone) and sacrum. Osteologists can usually determine sex with 95 to 98% accuracy using the human pelvis.

The skull is also a useful indicator of sex, at least in adults. Male skulls and teeth (and other bones of the skeleton) are usually larger and more robust than female skulls of the same population. However, these differences are relative and population dependent: some human populations are more fine-boned than others. Typical features scored in sex estimation are the mastoid process of the temporal bone and the muscle markings of the occipital bone, which are larger in males; the

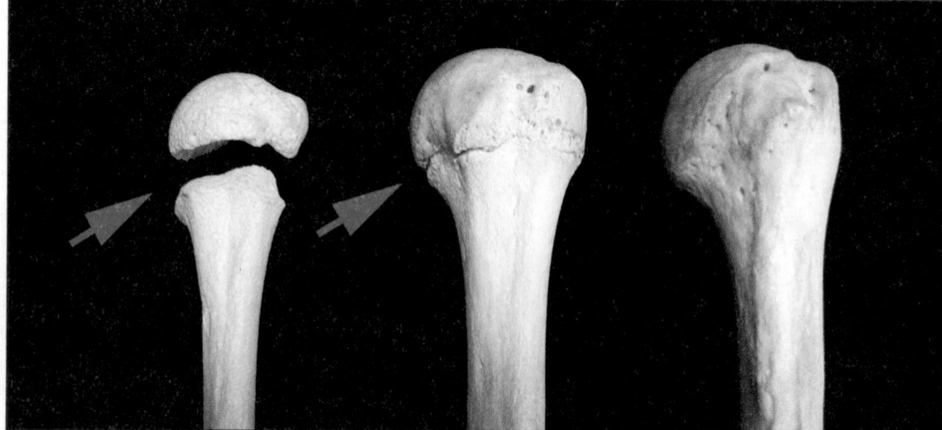

FIGURE 18.3 These upper arm bones show the maturation process. The bone on the left is a child's; the image shows a piece of bone, the epiphysis, which in life is separated from the rest of the bone by a growth plate of cartilage (arrow). The middle bone is an adolescent's; the image shows a line (arrow) where the epiphysis is fusing to the rest of the bone as growth stops. The bone on the right is an adult's; the epiphyseal line is no longer visible.

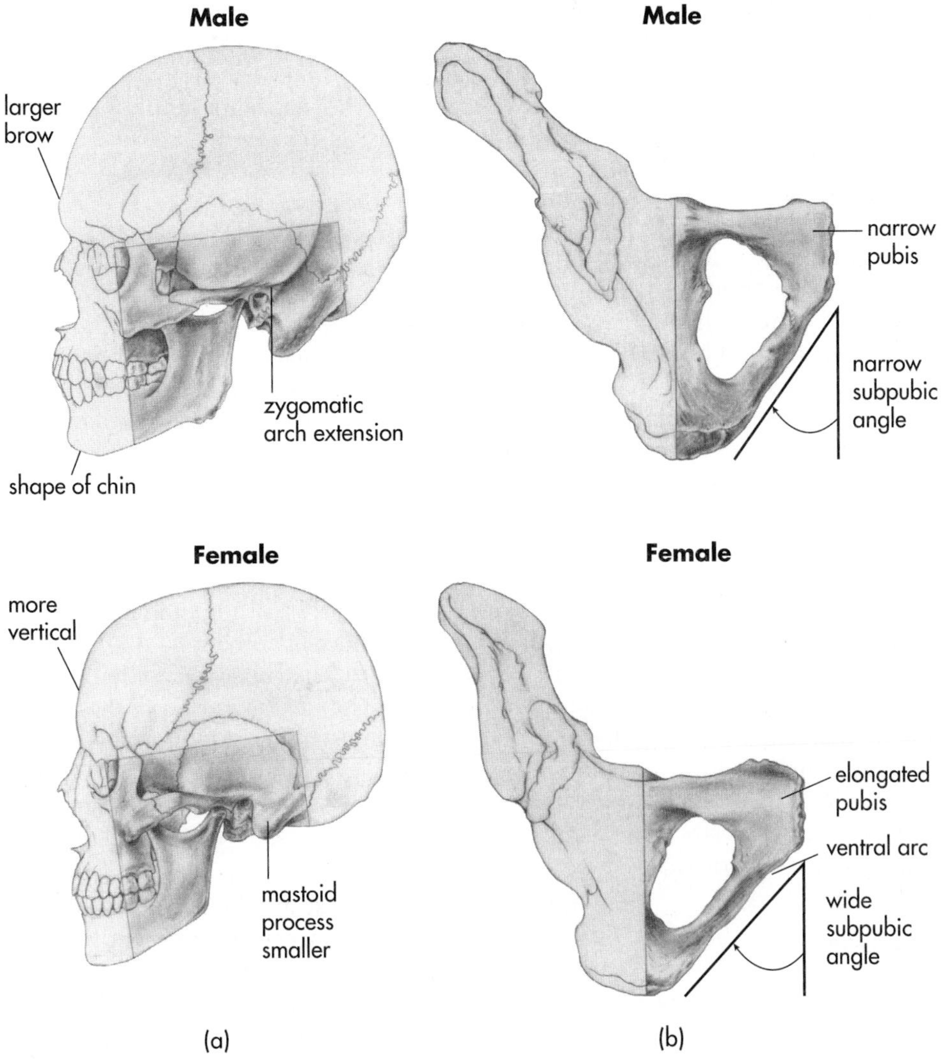

FIGURE 18.4 Comparison of (a) male and female skulls and (b) male and female pelvises.

shape and size of the browridge and orbital rim, which are less developed and sharper in females; the chin, which is squarer in males; and the frontal bone, which is more vertical in females (Figure 18.4). These differences form a continuum and provide successful sex estimates in perhaps 80 to 85% of cases when the population is known.

STATURE

Physical stature is reflected in the length of the bones that contribute to a person's height. Biological anthropologists have developed formulas for estimating stature based on leg bone lengths, using skeletal remains of individuals of known stature. These formulas also allow an estimate of the height of a victim based on partially preserved bones, although the formulas vary by population, partly because different body shapes result from ecological rules such as Bergmann's and Allen's rules (described in Chapter 6). Like age, stature is estimated as a range (for example, 1.79 metres to 1.83 metres [5 ft 10 in to 6 ft 0 in]) that captures the person's true height at the time of death. Stature estimates obtained from skeletal remains in forensic investigations are often inconsistent with the stature reported for the living individual, apparently due to the fact that living stature is either anecdotal or self-reported (such as on a driver's license) and men tend to overestimate their stature by an average of 2.5 centimetres (1 in), while women overestimate by about 1 cm (0.39 in) (Giles and Hutchinson, 1991).

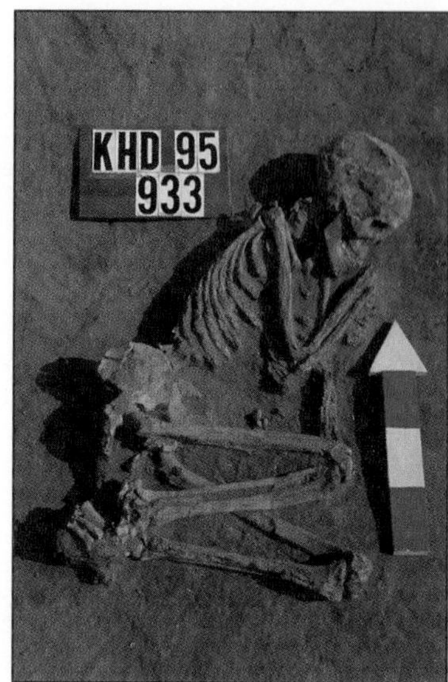

FIGURE 18.5 Information about age at death, sex, and other biological features, as well as cultural information, can be determined from ancient skeletons, such as this 5000-year-old skeleton from an archaeological site in Egypt.

BIOLOGICAL PATTERNS IN ARCHAELOGICAL POPULATIONS

Bioarchaeology is the field of study that deals with the excavation and analysis of human skeletal remains from archaeological contexts (Figure 18.5). Whether prehistoric or historic, human remains are the source of a variety of biological and cultural data that can be applied to questions of archaeological or cultural-historical interest, such as the size and age structure of a past population, the biological relatedness of ancient populations, or the impact on health of subsistence change. In addition, biological and medical historical applications are the subject of much bioarchaeological study, including estimation of life expectancy in the past, the geographic and socio-cultural correlates of disease, and the problem of infant mortality. Cultural data such as the modification of bones and teeth for aesthetic purposes or during medical practices may be obtained from skeletal remains themselves. **Palaeodemography** takes the osteobiographical data for all the individuals in an archaeological sample and analyzes those data to learn something about a past population. Key features of palaeodemographic reconstruction include determination of the age and sex structure of the population, examination of the rate of infant and childhood mortality, and detection of unusual peaks in mortality, which may indicate cultural practices such as war. The principal aims of palaeodemographic investigations include the determination of trends in human life span and mortality and the size and structure of past populations, particularly those that left no written records.

HEALTH

The analysis of evidence of ancient disease is called **palaeopathology**. The underlying principle of palaeopathology is that many kinds of illness and injury leave their mark on bone. As a discipline, palaeopathology is approximately 200 years old. Currently, its objectives include the reconstruction of the history and geography of certain diseases (such as tuberculosis or syphilis) and a better understanding of the interaction of disease and cultural processes, of how diseases have evolved over time, and of how disease processes affect bone growth and development.

Skeletal evidence of healed fractures (Figure 18.6), chronic infectious disease, and malnutrition provide important details of an osteobiography and can be examined in terms of similarities and differences within and among sexes, age groups, status groups, and subsistence practices, and across space and time. Trauma, arthritis, and dental disease are the most commonly seen pathological conditions in skeletons.

Palaeopathology has a time span of interest that covers many millions of years. Evidence of fractures and arthritis in dinosaurs as well as of injury and illness in fossilized plants is a reminder that trauma and disease are not solely afflictions of contemporary human society. In the study of archaeological human skeletons, palaeopathology is particularly important in prehistoric contexts from which no written records of health or medical practices remain.

It is one of the unfortunate paradoxes of palaeopathology that we are rarely able to determine how an individual died. Many diseases, especially those that are leading causes of death today, such as heart attacks and acute gastrointestinal and respiratory infections, do not leave evidence on the skeleton. Thus, palaeopathological investigation is generally confined to trauma and chronic conditions (those of slow progress and long duration). As such, pathological lesions in the skeleton may tell us much about morbidity but tend to tell us little about mortality patterns in the past,

Bioarchaeology Field of study that deals with the excavation and analysis of human skeletal remains from archaeological contexts.

Palaeodemography Analyzes the osteobiographical data for all the individuals in an archaeological sample to learn something about a past population.

palaeopathology The study of disease and injury in antiquity.

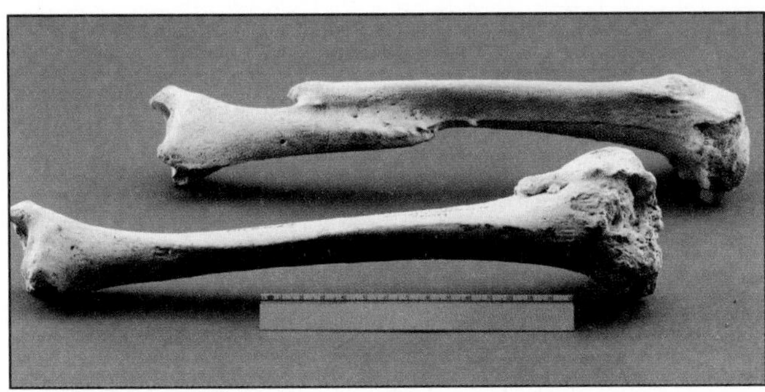

FIGURE 18.6 Bone fractures that occur before death show signs of healing. Note the shortened tibia (top) due to a massive healed fracture and the less severe fracture on the proximal (right) end of the lower tibia.

such as those caused by epidemic diseases that had such a devastating impact historically (for example, influenza and smallpox). Furthermore, it is likely that the frequency in antiquity of some conditions, such as infectious disease, is underestimated since the disease doesn't always spread to the skeleton or the individual may die before the skeleton becomes involved. Recent advances in ancient DNA studies, however, now make it possible to identify some infections from the DNA of the pathogen, as has been done for tuberculosis by the Paleo-DNA Laboratory at Lakehead University in Thunder Bay (Spigelman et al., 2002).

Palaeopathological investigation has obvious osteobiographic value, but is also of importance in establishing populational patterns of illness and injury, in what is called the palaeoepidemiological approach. Research questions in anthropologically based palaeopathology are usually related to socio-cultural contexts and are population specific. Examples include the examination of the effects on health of the transition from a nomadic hunting-fishing-foraging life way to a sedentary agricultural one; the effects of social stratification on the health and nutritional status of different segments of a population; and the health consequences of a sexual division of labour. A comprehensive review of the health and nutritional status of prehistoric hunters and foragers compared to agriculturalists living in settled communities found that despite the preconception that modernization (that is, agriculture), was "better," health status in many ways declined. The decline occurred because an over-reliance on one or two staple crops meant that crop failure could easily lead to malnutrition, and because a diet primarily based on grain-based carbohydrates didn't provide adequate nutrition, especially in the form of protein, and tended to increase the frequency of dental diseases such as cavities (Cohen and Armelagos, 1984).

The most ambitious project of this type is the Global History of Health Project, based at Ohio State University, which involves collaborators from around the world. This project seeks to examine how human health and welfare were transformed by the transition from foraging to farming, the rise of cities and complex forms of social and political organization, European colonization, and industrialization. A precursor to this project has been completed, in which skeletal indicators of health were examined for populations living in the western hemisphere from 5000 BC until the late nineteenth century. Researchers found a long-term decline in the skeletal health of First Nations peoples in North America prior to the arrival of Columbus. In particular, First Nations peoples underwent increased biological stress during childhood, as populations moved into less healthy ecological environments (Steckel and Rose, 2002).

Other research has examined biological and socio-cultural impacts of and adaptations to political and military conquests and territorial incursions (Larsen, 2002; Larsen and Milner, 1993). Evidence indicates that not all populations responded in the same way. For example, after the political expansion of Egypt into neighbouring Nubia (modern Sudan) to the south, Egypt appears to have used diplomacy and cooperation, not violence, to reach its colonial goals, and some communities were able to ensure a relatively peaceful co-existence with their conquerors by adopting introduced cultural practices (Buzon, 2006; Buzon and Richman, 2007).

Besides the obvious risk of violence between conqueror and conquered, interpersonal violence within communities has also been documented and is linked to likely increases in psychological stress and socio-cultural tensions wrought by competition over access to resources, environmental deterioration, or social change (Judd, 2004, 2006; Paine et al., 2006; Torres-Rouff and Costa Junqueira, 2006).

ANCESTRY

In days long past, biological anthropologists tried to assign people to racial categories, which amounted to little more than pigeonholes that reinforced racist stereotypes. According to this approach, a certain set of traits identifies a "type" and all individuals possessing these traits belong to the same type, or race. Racial characteristics are different things to people who are interested in the social aspects of race and to those who are concerned with the genetics of inheritance and biological ancestry over thousands of years. Throughout most of human history the movement of genes throughout different populations and the sharing of genes through interbreeding ensures that different populations around the world have been becoming more alike, and thus distinctive types do not adequately describe human diversity.

Although biological anthropologists are in general agreement that fixed morphological types, or races, of people are incompatible with the biological diversity that has been documented for the human species (see Chapter 6), the concept of race has widely held social and historical applications and may be a useful guide in forensic assessment of ancestry by narrowing the range of potential identifications. For example, officials in western Canada seeking to relate unidentified skeletal remains to someone on a missing persons list can do so more easily if they know whether the deceased was likely recognized as being of European or of Aboriginal ancestry, and officials in many parts of the United States find the distinction between African Americans and Americans of European ancestry to be useful. The North American social classification system (White, Black, Native, and Hispanic) has little value in other geographic areas, however, especially for prehistoric contexts. Thus, except for applications in forensic anthropology, it is neither valid nor meaningful to assign a typological racial designation to an individual.

The racial typological approach has been replaced by the populational approach in contemporary biological anthropology. The populational approach recognizes that all levels of biological difference incorporate a normal range of variation, and no single individual or set of individuals can be identified by a specified trait or traits. For example, as described in Chapter 6, morphological traits of the tooth crown exhibit such significant differences in frequency among populations of East and Southeast Asia and North America that Turner (1989, 1990) has proposed that the dental patterns sinodonty and sundadonty reflect migrational links and gene flow, a model that is consistent with historical, archaeological, and other genetic data. Degrees of biological affinity, or relatedness, are expressed as patterns of similarity or difference among skeletal samples that are believed to be representative of ancient populations. An underlying assumption is that the degree of similarity in a set of biological characteristics, such as morphological variants of the teeth, is proportional to the degree of genetic relatedness. Similarity may also be due to evolutionary convergence, parallelism, or chance, however, and thus the selection of comparisons must be informed by archaeological, linguistic, documentary, or other biological data. Biological affinity is a continuum that reflects genetic mixing from different local and regional areas in antiquity in addition to the influences of other evolutionary factors, such as natural selection and genetic drift.

The relatedness of human populations is therefore useful for evaluating biological hypotheses generated from cultural data, such as continuity from prehistoric to historic groups or social practices such as within-group marriage rules. To resolve this kind of problem, the biological data are analyzed in the context of archaeological, documentary, and other data (for example, geophysical). Investigations of biological affinities may discern, for example, that females in a skeletal sample have sufficiently different frequencies of some skeletal and/or dental traits when compared to males that the cultural practice of females marrying out of their natal group can be identified. This type of distinction would not be possible were the osteologist to simply describe each individual as belonging to one or another race. Professor Nancy Lovell and her students at the University of Alberta identified evidence of endogamy (marriage within a social group) among high status ancient Egyptians during the Predynastic period, a practice that was well documented in later periods of Egyptian history. Lovell's evidence resulted from her comparison of dental and cranial morphology patterns in skeletal populations buried in different cemeteries with different types of grave goods (Johnson and Lovell, 1994; Prowse and Lovell, 1996).

Ancient DNA, preserved in bones and teeth, is increasingly used to investigate questions of biological relationships. For example, researchers at the Ancient DNA Centre at McMaster University, in collaboration with colleagues at the Memorial University of Newfoundland, have examined mitochondrial and nuclear DNA from two individuals in an Aboriginal population from Newfoundland, the Beothuk, that became extinct approximately 180 years ago. They found that the two individuals carried mtDNA haplotypes that are consistent with those of modern First Nations populations of the northeastern portion of North America, which, when combined with nuclear Y data, indicate biological relationships between the Beothuk and present-day Mikmaq (Kuch et al., 2007). Similarly, researchers at the Human Identification Laboratory for Archaeology at the University of Alberta, using maternally inherited mtDNA, have discovered that matrilineal affinities did not overtly influence the spatial organization of an early cemetery in the Lake Baikal region of Siberia; however, these affinities may have influenced an individual's type of grave and the nature of an individual's burial, in turn reflecting the power structure within a community (Mooder et al., 2005).

Ancient Diets

An important aspect of bioarchaeology is the reconstruction of what people ate in the past. Plant and animal remains recovered from archaeological sites provide information about the food items available, but because these remains have been discarded rather than ingested, they are only indirect indicators of food consumption. Therefore, bioarchaeologists often incorporate data obtained directly from human bones and teeth in their studies of ancient diets.

Dietary questions of archaeological interest often concern subsistence transitions and choices, such as the origins and intensification of agriculture, the consumption of marine versus terrestrial foods, and the differential access to some foods by age, sex, and/or status. The data obtained from bones and teeth can't identify every individual food item in the diet but have been used to identify the relative contributions of different food groups to human diets.

Since the teeth are usually involved in the first stages of food processing by the body, it follows that they may provide clues to the types of foods eaten and the ways in which those foods were prepared for consumption. Two dental features, enamel wear and cavities, have proven to be most informative in this regard. The degree of tooth wear is generally considered to be a function of the coarseness of the diet—although nondietary factors such as the age of the individual, the use of teeth as tools, and tooth-grinding due to stress may confound interpretations of diet based on wear (while providing fascinating insights into individual or culturally patterned behaviours).

Tooth wear is correlated with abrasives in food but the source of the abrasives is not always clear. Tough and fibrous foods, such as unrefined cereals and uncooked or lightly cooked meats and vegetables, cause tooth wear, but so does the grit adhering to root crops and leafy vegetables because of poor cleaning or the mechanics of food storage or processing. For example, the use of stone implements to grind grain has been linked to severe tooth wear.

Cavities in teeth are the result of dental caries, a disease process in which the tooth is progressively demineralized by acids produced by the fermentation of food sugars in the mouth. The bacteria in plaque, an invisible film that coats tooth surfaces, cause this fermentation. Bacteria consume simple sugars most rapidly because they diffuse quickly through the plaque. The consumption of sugary beverages and foods such as honey and sugar cane is strongly linked to the presence of cavities. Soft and sticky foods, such as potato, rice, corn, and fruits such as figs, dates, and raisins are also implicated and are the most likely causes of cavities in pre-modern populations. Dietary studies generally have found that high frequencies of cavities are linked to the consumption of processed carbohydrates. This is the case among settled agriculturalists, whereas the severe tooth wear hunting-foraging peoples are more likely to suffer has been linked to the consumption of raw or lightly cooked meats, tubers, and fruits.

Bone chemistry studies also provide extensive information about ancient diets. Researchers can measure the presence of carbon and nitrogen in collagen (the organic fraction of bone) and of carbonate in the inorganic fraction of bone. Using these measurements, researchers can identify components of ancient diets because the elements serve as biochemical tracers for the movement of isotopes and elements through food webs. The use of stable isotopic measurements to study maize consumption in North America began in the late 1970s. Because the carbon in maize follows a particular photosynthetic pathway, its introduction and increased utilization in a temperate grass environment (in which carbon follows a different photosynthetic pathway) was readily detected through stable carbon isotope analysis of human bone collagen. The results demonstrated that large-scale dependence on maize agriculture in much of North America began several hundred years later than scientists had supposed previously.

More recently, differences in isotopic ratios patterned within a population by age or sex have been found to indicate, for example, status differences in diet, sex-based residence patterns linked to exogamous marriage rules, and shifts in food consumption at the time of weaning. Weaning, for example, is a physiological process in which semi-solid and eventually solid foods replace mother's milk in an infant's diet. Weaning is of interest in bioarchaeological studies for two reasons: because of the possible links between weaning and the risk of sickness and death when the child no longer receives passive immunity to disease from its mother, and because of the alleged contraceptive effects of nursing, which has an influence on birth spacing and population growth. The age at which weaning occurs varies culturally, and may also be influenced by the family's socio-economic status and size. An early study of weaning was based on infant skeletons from St. Thomas' Anglican Church in Belleville, Ontario. These skeletons were recovered when the graveyard, dating 1821–1874, was relocated due to construction development. Parish records of burials and stable isotope analyses were used to reconstruct the pattern of weaning, in which foods other than breast milk were introduced beginning at about 5 months of age, although variation in the time and duration of weaning was noted (Herring et al., 1998). Further studies elsewhere have identified not only likely weaning ages but also the nature of nutrient consumption during weaning, differences in childhood diet over time, and the possibility of sex differences in the consumption of animal or fish protein (Fuller et al., 2006; Richards et al., 2002; Williams et al., 2005).

The collagen from teeth, skin, and hair can also be sampled for stable isotope analysis. Soft tissue analysis provides evidence on diet that is complementary to, and independent of, that obtained from bone collagen and carbonate, since the carbon turnover rate for soft tissues is much faster than for bone and thus the period of time for which the diet is determined amounts to the last weeks or months of the individual's life. This principle was applied by Professor Christine White of the University of Western Ontario to the interpretation of carbon isotope data from the hair of naturally preserved mummies from ancient Nubia in order to identify ingestion of a seasonally restricted food item. Because a majority of the individuals from the cemetery sample apparently consumed this food in the months just prior to death, the season in which more people died is evident, which also implies that the season was one of relative hardship (White, 1993).

Residence and Mobility Studies

Recent research in skeletal biogeochemistry has focused on chemical signatures that derive from the geology of the place of habitation and enter the diet through water and nutrients in foodstuffs, allowing researchers to trace the place of birth, residence, and mobility of individuals and populations in the past. These studies, using oxygen and strontium isotopes in bones and teeth, have illustrated that locals can be differentiated from nonlocals in communities in ancient Mesoamerica, the Nile Valley, and elsewhere, which has implications for our understanding of who wields power in ancient empires and who populates the local labour force (Buzon et al., 2007; White et al., 1998, 2002, 2004). As well, it has been shown that population movements in ancient empires often involved families with children, contrary to the assumption that single men were the typical immigrants (Prowse et al., 2007).

Cultural Modification of Bones and Teeth

Archaeological human remains often exhibit evidence of cultural modification. Intentional modification of the body may occur either before or after death. Examples of antemortem modification include skeletal or dental alteration for status or aesthetic purposes, such as by head- or foot-binding or the filing or inlaying of teeth. The practices of tattooing and piercings are examples of such modifications in contemporary Canadian society. Alteration of the skeleton may also result from medical practices such as surgery or from punishment or ritual practices, including amputation and scalping. Postmortem modifications include cremation, defleshing, or disarticulation activities (recognized by cut marks) that may be due to mortuary practices or warfare, and ceremonial alteration such as the decorating or mounting on poles of ancestral or trophy skulls.

One of the earliest known medical practices is trepanation (or trephination), the surgical removal of a portion of the cranial vault without damage to the underlying soft tissues. Most archaeological examples of this practice come from Peru. The majority show some evidence of healing, and there are examples of multiple healed trepanations in the same individual. Four methods of trepanation appear to have been developed in prehistory: drilling, rectangular cutting, circular grooving, and scraping. The use of a surgical burr or trepanning instrument was developed in medieval times and is still common today. Modern ethnographic accounts of trepanation, in conjunction with ancient literary accounts, suggest that prehistoric trepanations were likely performed to relieve pressure or bone fragmentation after head injury; to cure headaches, epilepsy, or mental illness; or for magical or ritual purposes.

Amputations can be readily classified into one of four categories: surgical removal, blade injuries, punishment, and ritual. Regardless of the reason for the amputation, the procedure generally involves the complete or partial removal of a limb or digit, usually with a sharp-edged instrument. If the individual survives the amputation, the affected bone will usually remodel and produce a smooth, rounded end. It may be impossible to differentiate medical amputation from that due to punishment or ritual; however, the bone involved may provide some clue in this regard, since the hand is commonly amputated as punishment for stealing and decapitation would hardly be ascribed to therapeutic practice! Finger amputation appears to be commonly associated with ritual: some First Nations peoples were observed historically to amputate a finger or part of a finger during initiation rites, and in many cultures the amputation of a finger is a symbol of mourning. Hands may be removed after battle as trophies or as a means of recording the number killed. Accidental amputation as a result of blade injuries did not likely occur until the Middle Ages, when the metal used in sword blades, for example, became hard and sharp enough to slice through bone. Battlefield burials in Europe often provide evidence of blade injuries to the head or other parts of the body that would lend support to apparent blade-induced amputations.

HABITUAL ACTIVITY INDICATORS

Activity-related features of the skeleton range from exaggerated developments of bony features in the arms of baseball pitchers to arthritic knees in runners. These indicators are also referred to as *musculoskeletal stress markers* and *markers of occupational stress*. Some skeletal biologists have examined populational and group patterns of habitual activity indicators in an attempt to reconstruct past behaviours related to subsistence or occupation, such as spear-throwing, archery, and kayak paddling. The skeletal remains of sailors and soldiers who drowned when the *Mary Rose*, one of Henry VIII's warships, sank in 1545 were recovered in 1982, and subsequent osteological analysis identified some of the soldiers as longbow archers, based on recognizable deformities that included fractured shoulder bones, enlarged left arms, and pronounced bone spurs on the bones of the left wrists and shoulders and right fingers (Stirland, 2005). Archers in the Tudor military were capable of 10 to 20 aimed shots per minute, but the force required to draw the bow was considerable: the long bow had a length of over 2 metres (6 ft) and draw forces 3 times that of typical modern longbows (Strickland and Hardy, 2005).

Unusual patterns of tooth wear are interesting incidental cultural modifications. In addition to the attrition caused by normal tooth-to-tooth contact during chewing and the abrasion caused by food, habitual activities such as leather chewing can lead to tooth wear. Grooves or unusual wear on teeth may indicate habitual pipe-smoking, the use of toothpicks, or the processing of sinew, thread, or other fibres. Chips in the front teeth may indicate use of the teeth to retouch the edges of stone tools.

Some osteologists have studied activity indicators in the context of adaptation and evolution. Professor Susan Pfeiffer and her students at the University of Toronto have examined the biomechanical remodelling of bone at the macro- and microscopic levels by focusing on skeletal material from prehistoric southern Africa, a region with a rich archaeological record and evidence of a long history of successful hunting and foraging behaviours among past populations (Stock and Pfeiffer, 2001, 2004). The remodelling of bone and its microarchitectural characteristics are also the focus of research by Professor Richard Lazenby at the University of Northern British Columbia. Lazenby is studying geometric morphological variation in the hand skeleton of humans and other primates in an attempt to understand when and why humans became predominantly right-handed. Handedness may be related to the development of language, since fine motor control and speech function both gradually evolved in the left side of the brain. Handedness appears to be identifiable in the skeleton by virtue of asymmetry in the size of hand bones as well as in the volume of bone per unit of mass.

ETHICAL ISSUES IN BIOARCHAEOLOGY

Ethical issues in bioarchaeology revolve around treatment of and respect for the dead. Skeletal collections in Canada, the United States, Australia, and New Zealand were amassed mainly in the nineteenth century, largely from the remains of Aboriginal peoples in these colonial countries and often under appalling conditions. Post-colonial socio-political issues, particularly in the past 25 years, have had a large impact on these collections and on the way bioarchaeologists conduct research. Since 1990, the *Native American Graves Protection and Repatriation Act* (NAGPRA), a U.S. federal law, has allowed Native Americans to regain control over the skeletal remains of their ancestors and the associated artifacts, in order to reassert their cultural identities. Canada has no sweeping legislation of this type, but archaeological practice in Canada follows the protocol established by the Canadian Archaeological Association in its Principles for Ethical Conduct Pertaining to Aboriginal Peoples. The repatriation and reburial of human remains and artifacts is done on a small scale, between the institution (usually a university or museum) that holds the remains and the First Nations and Métis Nation representatives who claim these remains as ancestral. Similarly, movements in New Zealand and Australia have ensured that the remains of ancestral Maori and Australian Aboriginal people have been given traditional burial when requested.

These issues have not affected the United Kingdom and most countries in Europe and other parts of the world to the same degree because the archaeologists and biological anthropologists in those countries are typically descendants of the population being studied, rather than being descendants of a colonizing people. In England, for example, English bioarchaeologists excavate and study English skeletons, and Egyptian bioarchaeologists excavate and study their Egyptian ancestors in Egypt. The discovery of archaeological sites during construction of new buildings and transportation routes has become so commonplace in Britain that the Museum of London operates an archaeological service devoted to the excavation, analysis, storage, and display of human and other remains. Ethical issues may arise, however, when skeletal remains are excavated at now-forgotten historic Christian cemeteries, which are often located in churchyards, or at pre-Christian burial grounds. In the latter case, British pagan groups are increasingly asking for human remains and grave goods to be returned to them, which poses problems related to identifying affiliations between the dead and the living that are religious and cultural, not biological (Randerson, 2007). In order to address issues such as these, the British government developed a policy for England, Wales, and Northern Ireland for handling claims and evaluating inquiries from claimant communities by considering whether genealogical, religious, or cultural affiliations would justify the return of human remains, and whether scientific or other public interests justify retention (Department for Culture, Media, and Sport, 2005).

FORENSIC ANTHROPOLOGY

Human osteologists and bioarchaeologists are well prepared to contribute to forensic anthropology, an applied branch of human skeletal biology in which the principles of skeletal analysis are used in legal or criminal investigations. Forensic anthropologists bring a broad perspective of human variation and natural selection to their work, as well as a focus on hard tissue (bones, teeth, and sometimes cartilage). Usually the forensic anthropologist is involved when the body is badly or completely decomposed or burned and cannot be identified by the more usual methods of documentary identification found on the body, intact facial features, or fingerprints. Many aspects of research in forensic anthropology deal with improving our understanding of the skeleton and its adaptations during life and reactions after death. Knowledge of the effects of burning on bone, for example, is not only applicable in cases of forensic interest; this knowledge also has relevance in bioarchaeology.

The reconstruction of an individual's osteobiography is important in forensic anthropology, where the purpose is the identification of a decedent in a medico-legal context. Crucial to identification is the determination of the age, sex, stature, and ancestry of the person, but individualizing characteristics such as evidence of healed fractures can make identification easier. Forensic anthropology was recognized as a specialization within the American Academy of Forensic Sciences (AAFS) in 1972, although anatomists and biological anthropologists had been assisting law enforcement agencies with personal identification since the late 1800s. The number of forensic anthropologists who belong to the AAFS is a very small proportion (less than 1 percent) of the total membership of forensic professionals. In 2007 biological anthropologists as a whole composed about 6% of total membership.

There are a number of other forensic specialists, including forensic geneticists, forensic odontologists (dentists), and forensic entomologists (bug experts). Crime analysts (such as the criminalists on television's three popular *CSI* programs) examine the physical evidence of a crime. Although this is often the responsibility of law enforcement officers, several programs in Canada (such as the Centre for Forensic and Security Technology Studies at the British Columbia Institute of Technology, the Forensic Science Program at the University of Toronto, Mississauga, and the Department of Forensic Science at Laurentian University) train students for civilian jobs working as crime analysts or as forensic scientists in police laboratories.

There are no full-time forensic anthropologists in Canada, so when unidentifiable remains are found, law enforcement agencies, medical examiners, or coroners will consult a biological anthropologist who is a specialist in the field of human osteology. Almost all forensic anthropologists in Canada teach at universities and colleges; others work in museums. In the United States, the employment situation is similar although there is one full-time forensic anthropologist for the city of New York, and several forensic anthropologists work for the U.S. military's Central Identification Laboratory. As of 2000 there were only 15 full-time forensic anthropologists working in the United States, a country with a population of more than 280 000 000 that year.

Forensic anthropologists must work in accordance with the rules not only of science but also of the courts. They must be able to convince their colleagues of their findings, and their findings must withstand the scrutiny of lawyers, juries, and judges. In the medico-legal community each province has medical examiners or coroners who are legally responsible for signing death certificates and determining the cause and manner of death of people who did not die of a condition for which they were under a doctor's care.

Sometimes bones are brought to the forensic anthropologist's lab, or the anthropologist is asked to examine remains at the morgue. But in other cases the forensic anthropologist's involvement begins at the scene of recovery, with the most immediate work being done where the body is found or is thought to be buried (Figure 18.7). Occasionally, the task is over almost as soon as it begins, when the osteologist determines that the bones are those of a deer or a dog, not a human. Archaeological techniques are used to retrieve remains and plot their position and that of associated items such as bullets, clothing, and jewellery. Once recovered, the remains are taken to the lab for more detailed examination.

FIGURE 18.7 Forensic anthropologists use archaeological techniques to recover remains, including detailed mapping of the locations of bones and objects during exposure and excavation.

Back in the lab the remains may be cleaned of adhering soft tissue and dirt, then laid out in anatomical position, the way they would have looked in the skeleton in life. An osteological inventory is made of each bone present. Most adult humans have 206 bones, many of which are extremely small (see Appendix A). The bodies of foetuses and children contain many more bones because many bones develop separately and fuse together only later in life. Often, a long-deceased and hidden body consists of no more than a few fragments. The forensic anthropologist therefore must be a skilled osteologist very familiar with patterns of interpopulational and intrapopulational human variation.

How Biological Profiles Can Work

Once the inventory has been completed, the osteologist determines age, sex, and ancestry. He or she examines the skeleton for signs of premortem disease or trauma, which occurred while the person was alive; perimortem changes, which occurred around the time of death; and postmortem changes, which occurred after death. The forensic anthropologist also notes any other potential identifying features, such as clothing or soft tissue that remained on the corpse. From these combined data the forensic anthropologist puts together a written report that documents his or her methods and conclusions. This report goes to the person or agency for which the forensic anthropologist is working.

When skeletal material has been fragmented during a disaster (as in the World Trade Center crime scene), forensic anthropologists may be very limited in what they can determine with certainty and so other forensic scientists, such as forensic geneticists, may be involved. To use DNA for identification, the scientist needs to find living relatives to whom DNA can be matched and thus must have some idea of the identity of the victim (see Chapter 3 for more detail on DNA fingerprinting and ancient DNA analysis).

An isolated skull can be measured and compared using multivariate statistics from the University of Tennessee Forensic Data Bank of measurements from crania of known ancestry. This process provides a likely assignment of ancestry and a range of possible error, although human variation is such that many people exist in every population whose skulls do not match well with most other skulls of similar geographic origin. The ability to even partially assign ancestry can be useful in several forensic contexts, however. Missing person reports often indicate ancestry (for example, Asian), and a skeletal determination of ancestry may suggest a match that can then be confirmed by other, more time-consuming and expensive means, such as dental record comparisons or DNA analysis. In another context, forensic anthropologists are still working to identify the remains of soldiers killed in the Vietnam War, 30 years after that conflict ended. If a local contact leads a forensic team to a field where an American soldier was reportedly buried, the team will begin to search and excavate. Upon finding human remains, the forensic anthropologist can confirm whether the skeleton is likely that of an American of European or African ancestry, rather than that of a Vietnamese person.

Injuries and sickness suffered by a victim in life can leave lasting marks on the skeleton that serve as key identifiers for forensic anthropologists. Old injuries and dental work can be matched to X-rays taken when the victim was living. Orthopaedic implants and pins often resolve issues of identity. In addition, lifestyle may leave an indelible mark on the skeleton: an athlete who uses one side of the body for intense activity (such as a baseball pitcher or tennis player) will have a more robustly developed arm on that side. Surfers tend to develop one big toe that is larger than the other. Such individualizing characteristics provide helpful information but require a documented context before they can serve as confirmatory evidence in identification.

EXAMINING THE CIRCUMSTANCES OF DEATH

One of the most critical tasks a forensic anthropologist undertakes is amassing evidence that may help investigators understand the cause and manner of death. In forensic investigations the cause of death is a determination that must be left to the medical examiner or coroner. Similarly, the manner of death (accident, suicide, homicide, natural, unknown) is a legal determination. But forensic anthropologists can be helpful in reconstructing the death event (Box 18.1).

For example, features that may indicate activities associated with death include unhealed fractures, premortem fractures in different stages of healing (such as in battered infant syndrome), burning, and projectiles found embedded in a bone or within a body cavity. The presence of telltale fractures of the hyoid, a small bone in the neck, suggests strangulation, for example. **Perimortem trauma** may also indicate a perpetrator's intent to hide or dispose of a body. For example, circular saws and reciprocating saws leave different marks on bone and sometimes leave portions of themselves embedded in bone. Experts can identify types of blades and sometimes make direct matches to tools owned by a suspect.

A **coroner** is responsible for overseeing the investigation of deaths, particularly those occurring unexpectedly, violently, or under unusual circumstances. Some provinces in Canada have a coroner system while others rely on **medical examiners**. Although many coroners are physicians, a medical examiner must be a licensed pathologist, a specialist in disease, who is usually the specialist that performs autopsies.

One of the more difficult tasks for a forensic anthropologist is determining how long the victim has been dead. This assessment is so complicated that a research program in forensic anthropology at the University of Tennessee maintains an outdoor morgue in which human bodies are left to decompose under a variety of conditions so researchers can learn how natural processes affect the rate of decay. A similar program at the University of Alberta maintains a facility outside of Edmonton in which the decomposition of pig carcasses (excellent proxies for human bodies because of similarities in tissue composition) can be studied in a cold climate region. In general, bodies left on the surface of the ground decompose most quickly and those buried in the ground most slowly; however, temperature and humidity are the primary factors affecting decay rate because they, in turn, influence insect activity and other physiological rates of decay. The timing of insect life cycles is well-known and their preferences for tissue types and extent of decay are also well studied, so insect evidence is the most accurate method for determining elapsed time since death when death has occurred days or weeks previously. Gail Anderson, a forensic entomologist at Simon Fraser University, has been involved in studies of decomposition in different biogeoclimatic zones, including grassland regions around Edmonton and Saskatoon, forested areas in Manitoba, and glacial freshwater lakes in Ontario, and has worked with police on dozens of criminal investigations.

Taphonomists study the ways in which natural processes affect the body from death to decomposition and discovery (see also Chapter 9). They attempt to distinguish naturally caused bone changes from those that appear to be human-created. For forensic investigations, taphonomic analysis may help to determine the length of time the victim was dead and the nature of perimortem trauma. But forensic anthropologists must be careful to distinguish postmortem events from perimortem events because postmortem events do not suggest cause or manner of death. Although neither perimortem nor postmortem trauma shows healing, they can be differentiated from each other because bones broken in the perimortem interval retain an organic component and therefore break differently from those that dry out after death; think of the difference between how a small living tree branch bends when you try to break it compared to how a dried stick on the ground snaps.

Postmortem events may also rule out a crime if they suggest that marks on bone are made by natural causes, such as rodent chewing or coyote scavenging,

perimortem trauma Perimortem trauma is the physical evidence of activity that happened around the time of death, either slightly before or slightly after. We can differentiate it from premortem injury because in perimortem trauma no healing is evident at the trauma site.

coroner Responsible for overseeing the investigation of deaths, particularly those occurring unexpectedly, violently, or under unusual circumstances.

medical examiner A licensed pathologist, a specialist in disease, who specializes in performing autopsies.

rather than knives, guns, or chainsaws, or if they show that the skeleton is of ancient rather than forensic interest.

Although forensic anthropologists most often work on cases of lone victims of homicide, suicide, or accidental death, they may also be called to the scene of disasters and may be involved in the identification of soldiers killed in combat, the documentation of human rights abuses, and the identification of victims in hidden or mass graves.

Mass Fatalities

Forensic anthropologists play key roles in the attempt to identify victims of disasters such as earthquakes, plane crashes, floods, and other natural and human-wrought disasters. A head-on collision between an eastbound Via Rail passenger train and a westbound Canadian National Railway freight train near Hinton, Alberta, in 1986 left 23 people dead and dozens more injured. A fireball of ignited fuel destroyed parts of both trains. Forensic anthropologists from the University of Alberta were involved in the analysis of the bodies, many of which were burned beyond recognition.

The United States has regional emergency response teams called Disaster Mortuary Teams (DMORT) that include pathologists, forensic anthropologists, and forensic odontologists who are mobilized in response to national mass disasters such as the World Trade Center fire and collapse. In 1994 a DMORT team responded to an unusual mass disaster. Flooding of historic proportions caused the remains from a cemetery in Albany, Georgia, to surface. The lids of the concrete vaults in which coffins were placed during burial were removed by the floodwaters, causing coffins to float to the surface and into the town of Albany. Some remains

Box 18.1 Forensic Anthropology and Crime Scene Investigation

Canada's largest crime scene investigation took place in Port Coquitlam, a suburb of greater Vancouver, and involved dozens of forensic anthropology students working as civilian contractors for the RCMP. Robert William Pickton was charged with the murders of 26 women, and in early 2007 his trial began for the murders of 6 women who disappeared from Vancouver's downtown eastside.

Professor Tracy Rogers of the University of Toronto began the forensic anthropological work at the Pickton farm in 2002 as the Chief Forensic Anthropologist, and for the better part of two summers she helped uncover and analyze thousands of bone and tooth fragments, and organized and trained teams of students.

The forensic anthropology students represented universities from across Canada, in particular the University of Toronto, the University of Manitoba, the University of Saskatchewan, the University of Alberta, and Simon Fraser University. All had experience identifying human bone from fragments as small as a fingernail to complete skeletal elements. Because the bodies were disposed of at Pickton's pig farm, the students had to be able to differentiate between human and animal bones and had to identify pieces of bone that had been intentionally fragmented and damaged by fire, water, and mud.

The job involved careful attention to detail and intense concentration. For most of the farm, soil was dug up by heavy equipment and team members stood over conveyor belts, examining soil that came through a sifter, looking for bone and other material with potential forensic value. Some areas, however, required painstaking examination of the ground with the investigators working on their hands and knees. Recovered bones and teeth were taken to a special processing area, where procedures to protect the possible DNA viability of each item was carefully followed.

For some, the job didn't end with the work at the farm, as they were later called to testify in Pickton's trial.

Rogers has served as a consultant to law enforcement agencies on murder and missing persons cases since 1996. She teaches for the Forensic Sciences Program at the University of Toronto, Mississauga and conducts research into new means of personal identification, such as using the sinuses of the skull, the spinal vertebrae, and X-rays of the chest and abdomen as unique identifiers.

were separated entirely from their coffins. The DMORT team recovered the remains and established a morgue to process them, to attempt to forensically identify them, and to reconnect them to their place of interment (Figure 18.8). Of the 415 disinterred remains, the DMORT team was able to positively identify 320 people.

Although Canada doesn't have DMORT teams, BC-FORT is a team of forensic odontologists in British Columbia that is trained and prepared to respond to mass fatality incidents to identify victims.

Mass fatalities may involve war dead. U.S. forensic anthropologists first became involved in the identification of those who died in war when the Central Identification Laboratory (CIL) in Hawaii was formed to aid in the identification of those missing in action during World War II. Since then the skeletal remains of U.S. soldiers and civilians from World War II, the Korean War, the Vietnam War, and other military actions have been recovered and identified by this group of anthropologists. The remains are brought back to the CIL, thoroughly examined, and identified. In addition to standard forensic anthropological techniques, forensic DNA techniques are used to reach a positive identification so that remains may be returned to the next of kin. Some of the most important forensic anthropological research—such as methods for determining stature, which were developed from the skeletal remains of soldiers who died in the Korean War—has been conducted at the CIL. This large body of work remains a standard in forensic analyses today and would not have been possible without the detailed medical histories of these military personnel.

Canadian war dead have also been identified through forensic anthropology. Professor Carney Matheson and his team at the Palaeo-DNA Lab at Lakehead University recently confirmed the identity of the body of a 22-year-old soldier who died at Vimy Ridge in World War I. The remains of Pte. Herbert Peterson, originally from rural Alberta, were identified in 2003 by analyses that matched his DNA with the DNA of his nephew.

Other wars also leave military and other victims who may not be identified and returned home for burial at the time of their death. The 1974 Turkish invasion and occupation of the northern part of the island of Cyprus resulted in the deaths of several thousand Greek and Turkish Cypriots and Greek soldiers due to military and paramilitary actions from both sides in the conflict. The International Forensic Program of the organization Physicians for Human Rights, including forensic anthropologist Owen Beattie and his students at the University of Alberta, have been exhuming and analyzing Greek Cypriot and Greek war dead from cemeteries in Cyprus since 1999. Genetic material from the skeletons is compared to a comparative bank of genetic material from relatives of missing and war dead in order to establish the identity of the remains.

Perhaps the most important contributions made by Canadian forensic anthropologists have been in the area of human rights investigations. Owen Beattie (University of Alberta), Mark Skinner (Simon Fraser University), and others have participated in the excavation of mass graves and identification of bodies in

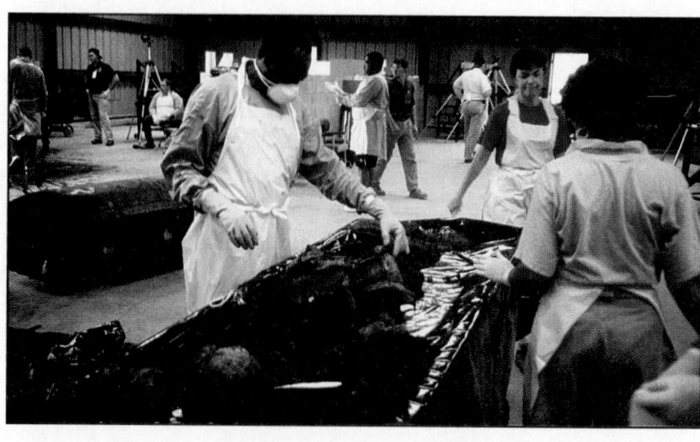

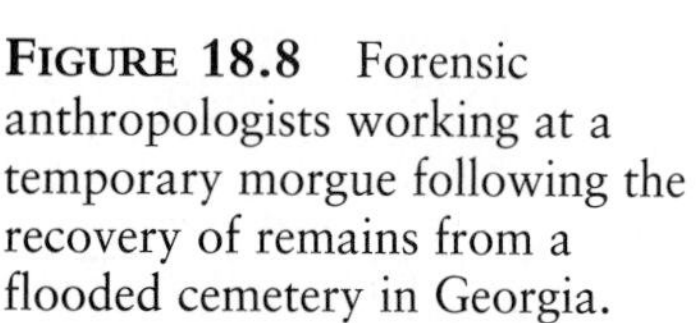

FIGURE 18.8 Forensic anthropologists working at a temporary morgue following the recovery of remains from a flooded cemetery in Georgia.

them, and their investigations have served as important evidence in the prosecution of war crimes in Rwanda, Somalia, Afghanistan, Bosnia-Herzegovina, East Timor, and Serbia. Repressive regimes may attempt to intimidate the population through mass murder or may undertake **genocide**, the deliberate and systematic killing of members of a particular religious, political, or cultural group. The mass graves that are left contain the bodies of hundreds or even thousands of victims, whose loved ones spend lifetimes attempting to locate them and determine their fate. Forensic anthropologists help to identify the victims for the sake of surviving family members and may provide key evidence in documenting atrocities in an effort to bring those responsible to justice. Forensic anthropologists in these areas work for both government and private groups such as Physicians for Human Rights, the International Commission for Missing Persons, and the United Nations.

genocide The deliberate and systematic killing of a particular religious, political, or cultural group.

For example, under the auspices of the United Nations (UN) and in particular the International Criminal Tribunal for the former Yugoslavia (ICTY), in partnership with Physicians for Human Rights, mass graves in the former Yugoslavia were exhumed beginning in 1996. Some of these exhumations concentrated in eastern Croatia on a grave site known as Ovcara, which contained victims from a massacre in Vukovar. The Vukovar massacre occurred in November 1991, and the mass grave site was located in 1992 based on information from a person who had escaped the massacre. Excavation waited until 1996 because of continuing hostilities in the region (although the site was guarded by the UN for the entire time).

The forensic teams consisted of scientists from around the world and included forensic anthropologists and archaeologists, pathologists, evidence technicians, radiologists, odontologists, autopsy technicians, and computer scientists. The teams exhumed about 200 bodies from Ovcara, nearly all of them males. Mapping the grave site took more than a month. The remains were autopsied in Zagreb with the goals of constructing a biological profile that would help in identification and interpreting perimortem trauma to understand the cause of death. Many of the victims had multiple gunshot wounds and other forms of trauma. Biological profiles were compared with the medical and dental records of missing people, a task hampered by the destruction of hospitals and other medical facilities during the war, and lists of identifying characteristics (including tattoos) provided by family members of missing people. Through these comparisons about half of the 200 were positively identified. This evidence has been used in the prosecution of war crimes by the UN-ICTY, including the case against the region's former leader, Slobodan Milosevic.

The study of the skeletal remains of modern humans is one that incorporates the principles of biological anthropology that we have examined in this text. The modern human skeleton reveals evidence of evolutionary processes, adaptation to physical and social-cultural environments, and the expression of biological variation that is at the heart of our species. Like the other specializations within biological anthropology, it generates new knowledge that contributes to our understanding of human biology and behaviour, and brings the results of research to applications that have a profound impact on the human condition.

EPILOGUE

The place of humans in the natural world has been the major theme of this book. We have explored this topic from a wide variety of perspectives, including the fossil record, the behaviour of living nonhuman primates, the lives of people in traditional societies, the workings of the brain, and the biology of modern people; however, our explorations of these diverse topics have been linked by a single common thread, evolutionary theory.

You've now completed a comprehensive look at your own evolutionary past, and at the place of humankind in the history of the world. As you have seen, the evidence of our past is present in us today. It is visible in our DNA, our hominid anatomy, our physiological adaptations, and even in aspects of our behaviour.

Many people live in denial or in ignorance of this evolutionary past. In contrast, we feel that embracing and understanding it is critical to being an enlightened citizen of the twenty-first century.

It is important to keep in mind, however, that to embrace an evolutionary perspective of humankind is not to deny the importance of culture in our lives. We have seen that culture may be the most fundamental of human traits. Many aspects of the biology of modern people are influenced in some way by culture, while at the same time our cultural nature is a direct outgrowth of our biology.

This book has been concerned with our evolutionary past, but the most pressing question for humankind in the early twenty-first century is whether our species will survive long enough to experience further significant evolutionary change. Environmental degradation, overpopulation, warfare, and a host of other problems plague our species. It is safe to say that no species in Earth's history has contended with so many self-induced problems and survived. But of course no other species has had the capability to solve problems and change its world for the better the way that we humans have.

SUMMARY

1. **What is an osteobiography?**

   An osteobiography is essentially a person's life history as recorded in his or her skeleton, and includes information about his or her age at the time of death, biological sex, height (stature), and individualizing characteristics such as evidence for disease and injury or for cultural modifications to the body. Information from a group of individuals can be used to examine populational patterns, such as the rate of infant mortality or the frequency of infectious diseases.

2. **What types of cultural information can be obtained from the human skeleton?**

   The skeleton can reveal evidence of medical practices such as amputation and trepanation, dietary strategies, and population movements and interactions. These are all important aspects of understanding how modern humans have interacted with their physical and social environments.

3. **What does forensic anthropology have to do with biological anthropology?**

   Forensic anthropologists apply the method and theory of biological anthropology to the investigation of recent deaths. They may rely on a diverse range of studies that are also used in other aspects of biological anthropology during their investigations. These other aspects include, for example, human growth and development, anthropological genetics, and taphonomy.

CRITICAL THINKING QUESTIONS

1. How can the demands of scientific research, such as in palaeopathology, be reconciled with ethical issues regarding human remains?
2. Why would it be difficult to apply methods for estimating age and determining sex of modern human skeletons to the remains of early hominids?

KEY TERMS

osteology
osteobiography
forensic anthropology
bioarchaeology
palaeodemography
palaeopathology
perimortem trauma
coroner
medical examiner
genocide

SUGGESTED READING

Bass, B., and Jefferson, J. (2004). *Death's Acre: Inside the Legendary Forensics Lab – The Body Farm – Where the Dead Do Tell Tales*. Berkley Books (Penguin Group), New York, NY.

Roberts, C., and Manchester, K. (2005). *The Archaeology of Disease*, 3rd edition. Cornell University Press, Ithaca, NY.

Stirland, A. L. (2005). *The Men of the Mary Rose: Raising the Dead*. Sutton Publishing, Stroud, UK.

White, T. D., and Folkens, P. A. (2005). *The Human Bone Manual*. Elsevier Academic, Boston, MA.

PRIMATE AND HUMAN SKELETAL ANATOMY

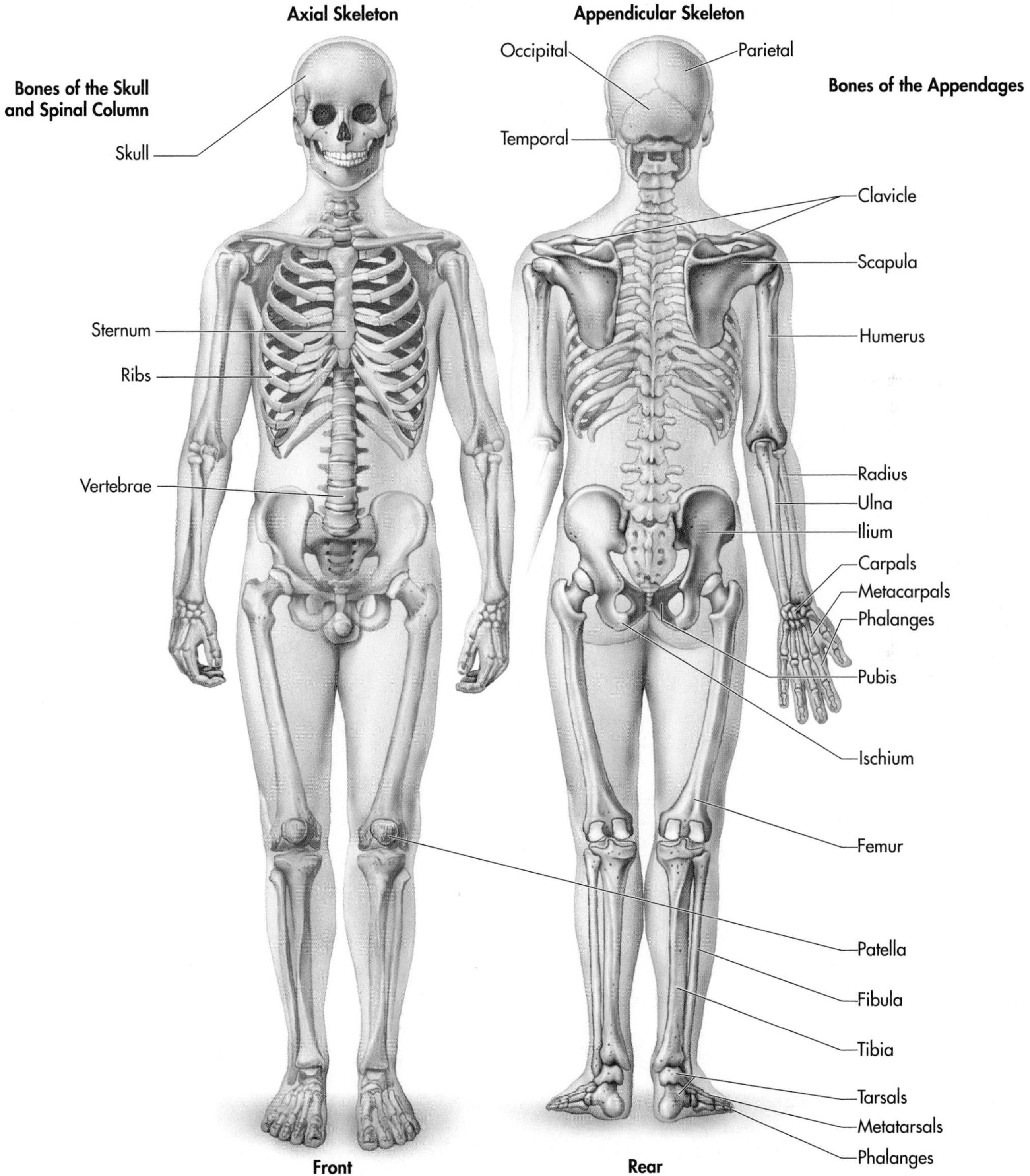

FIGURE A.1 The Human Axial and Appendicular Skeletons.

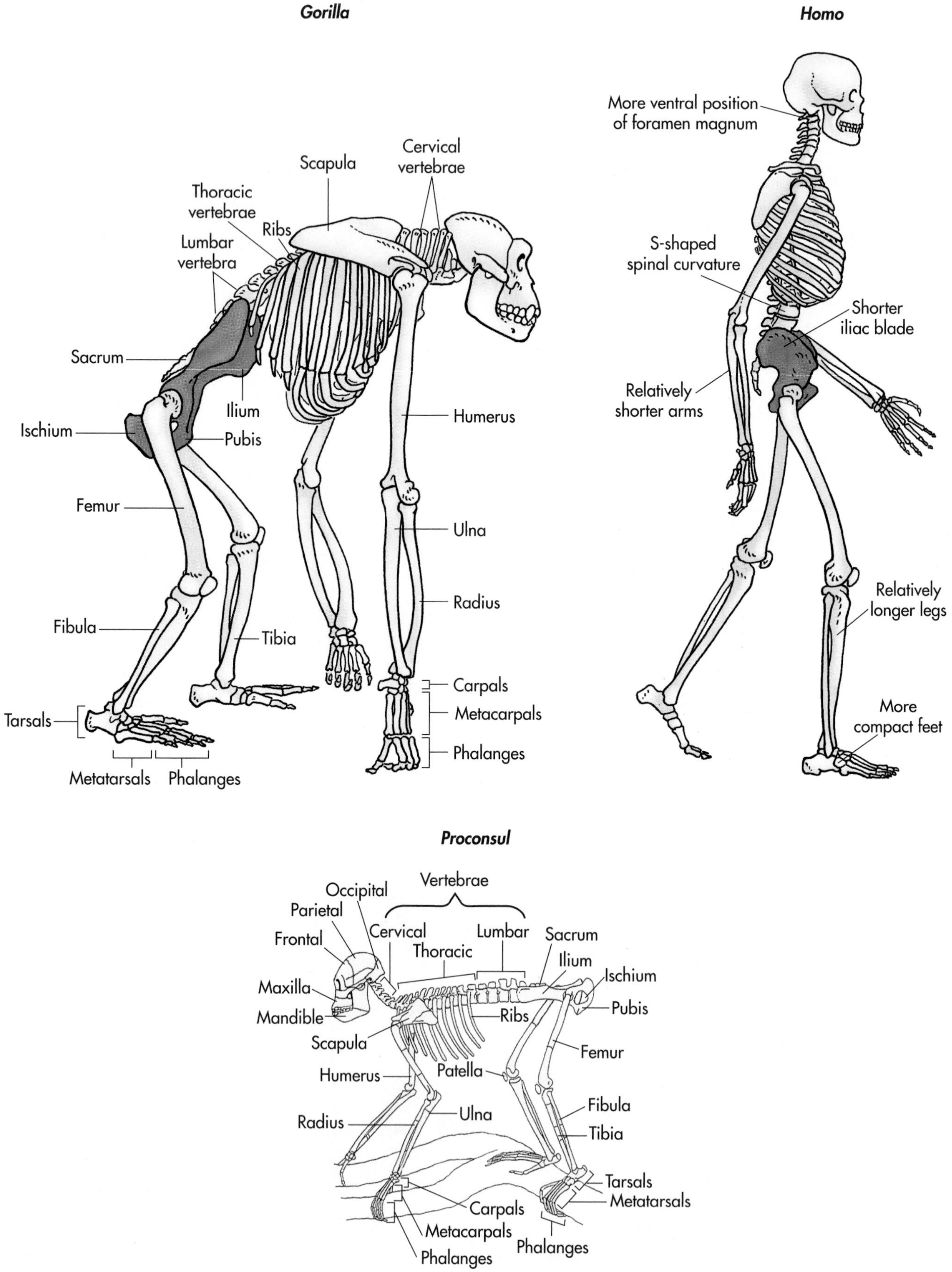

Gorilla
Homo
Cervical vertebrae
Scapula
Thoracic vertebrae
Ribs
Lumbar vertebra
Sacrum
Ilium
Ischium
Pubis
Humerus
Femur
Ulna
Radius
Fibula
Tibia
Carpals
Metacarpals
Tarsals
Phalanges
Metatarsals
Phalanges
More ventral position of foramen magnum
S-shaped spinal curvature
Shorter iliac blade
Relatively shorter arms
Relatively longer legs
More compact feet
Proconsul
Vertebrae
Occipital
Parietal
Frontal
Cervical
Thoracic
Lumbar
Sacrum
Ilium
Ischium
Maxilla
Mandible
Pubis
Ribs
Scapula
Femur
Humerus
Patella
Radius
Ulna
Fibula
Tibia
Tarsals
Metatarsals
Carpals
Metacarpals
Phalanges
Phalanges

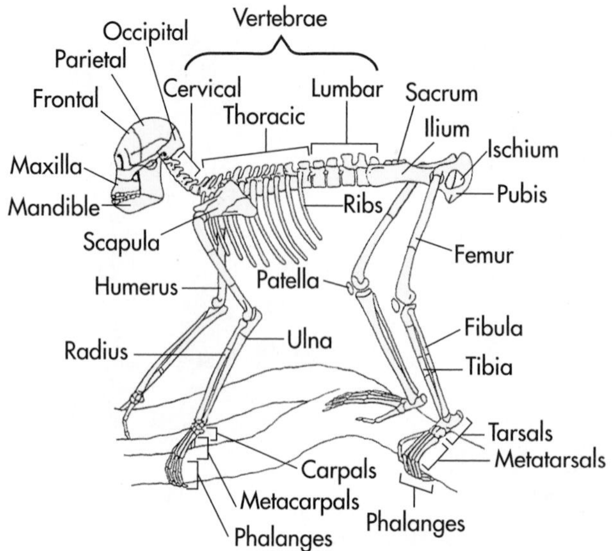

FIGURE A.2 Comparisons of *Gorilla*, *Homo*, and *Proconsul* skeletons.

Human Skull

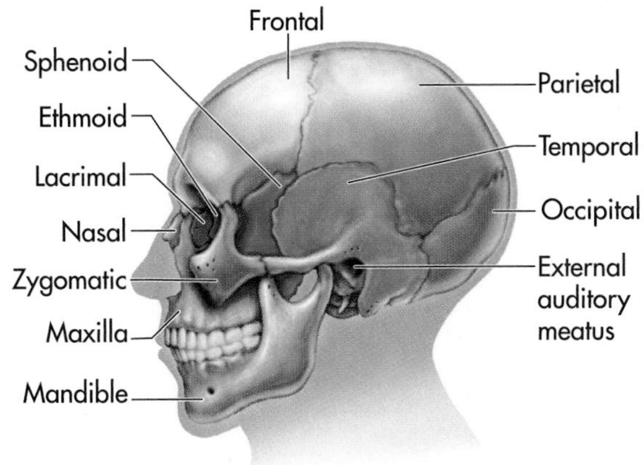

(a) The major bones of the skull and face

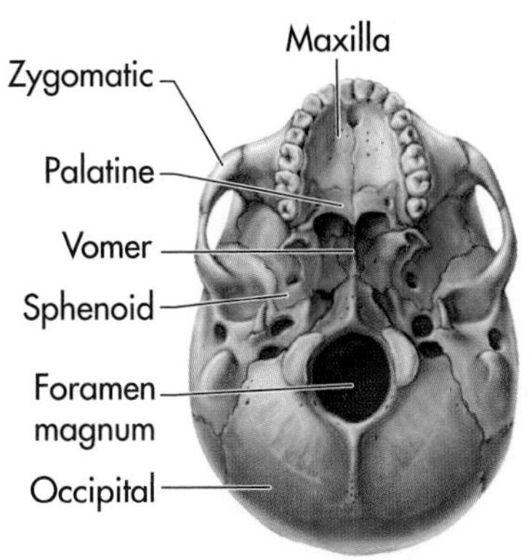

(b) Base of the skull

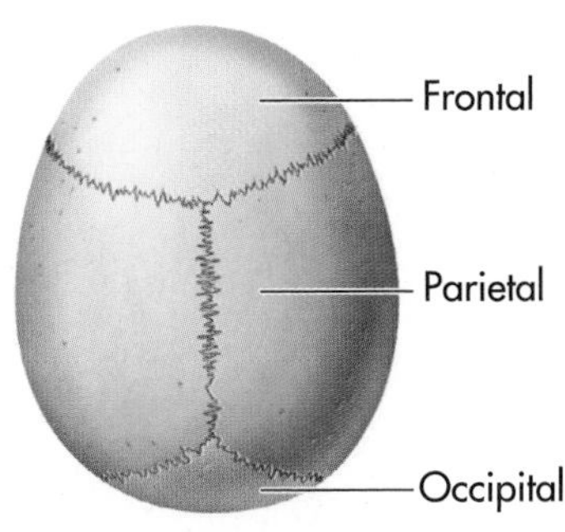

(c) Top view of skull

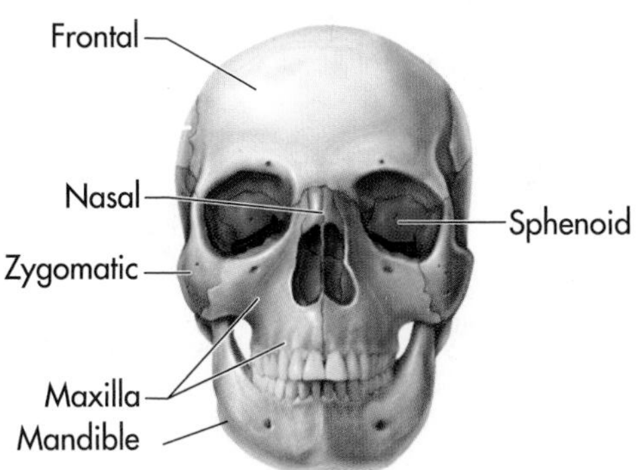

(d) Front view of skull showing facial bones

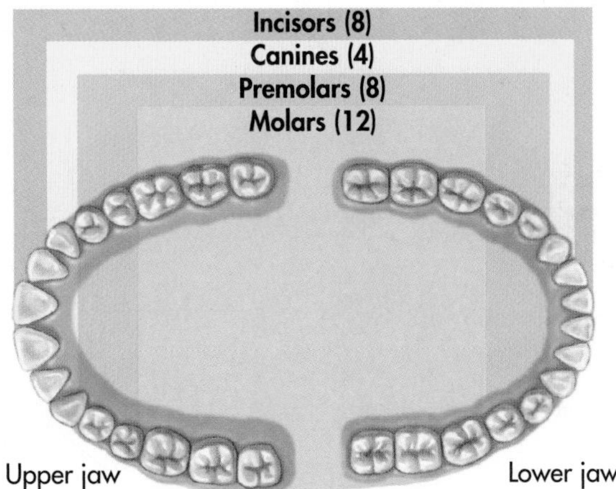

(e) Upper and lower jaws

FIGURE A.3 (a, b, c, d) The major bones of the skull and face, and (e) the teeth in the upper and lower jaws.

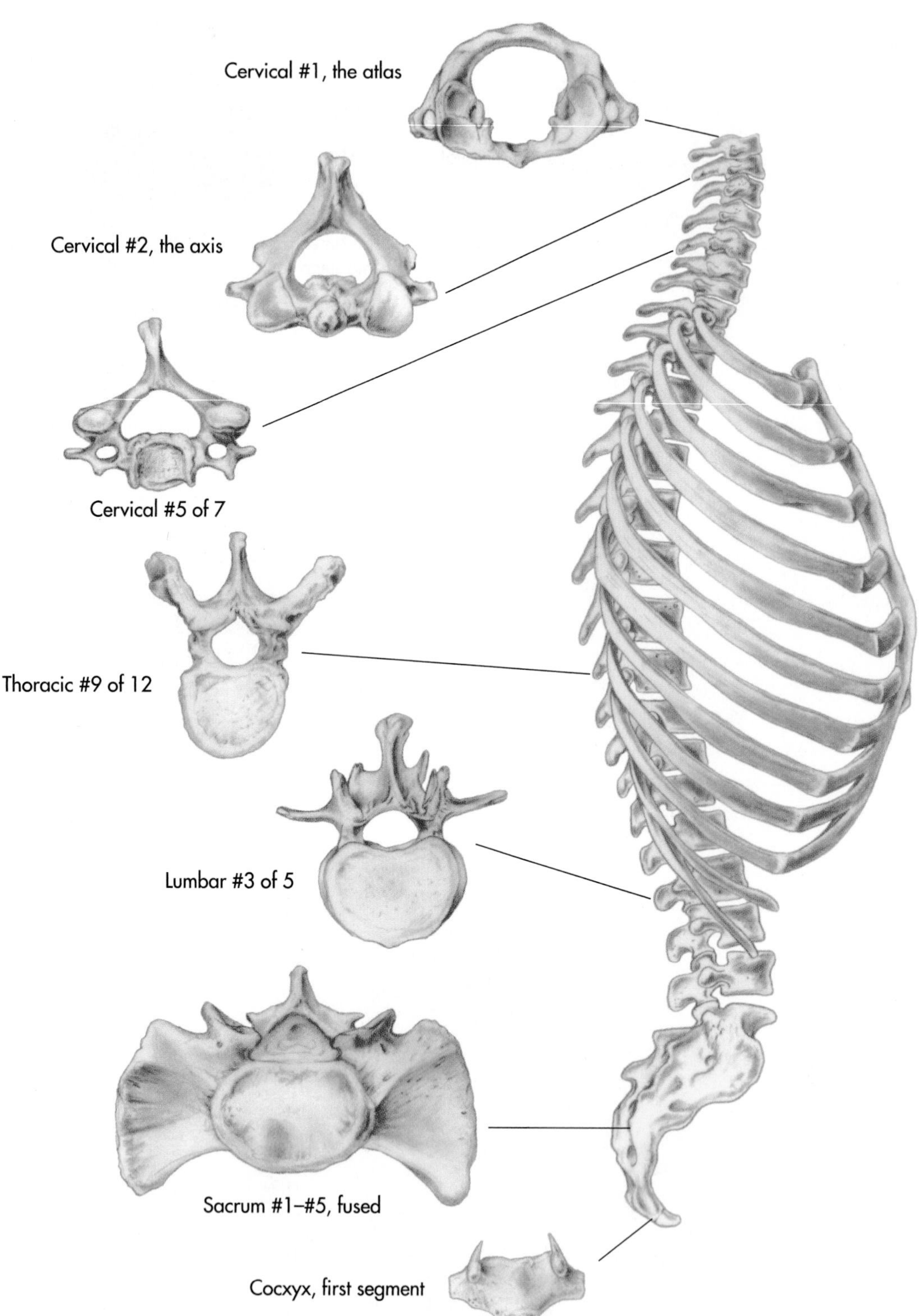

FIGURE A.4 The Vertebral Column. The human vertebral column consists of 7 cervical, 12 thoracic, 5 lumbar, 5 fused sacral, and 4 or 5 diminutive coccygeal vertebrae.

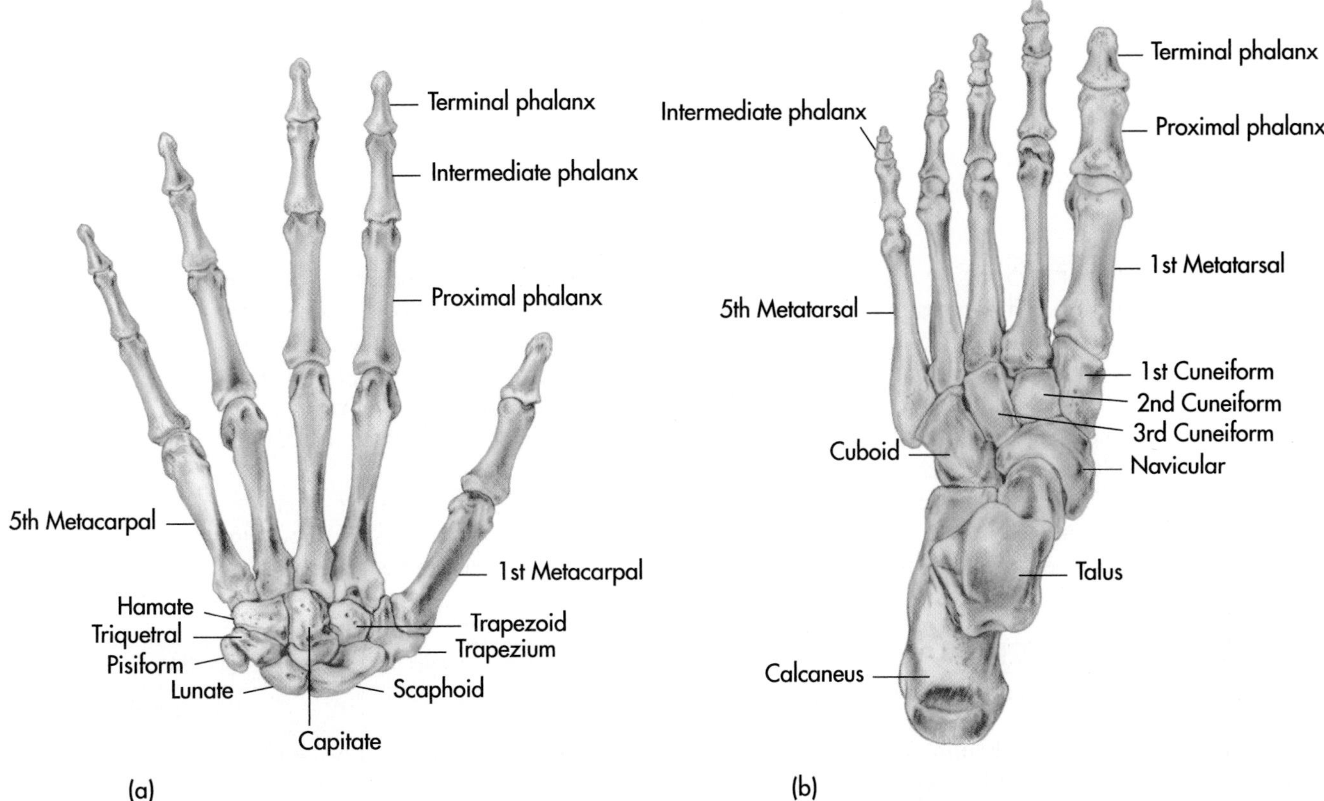

FIGURE A.5 (a) Left hand and wrist bones and (b) left foot and ankle bones.

Appendix B

The Hardy–Weinberg Equilibrium

In Chapter 5, we introduced the Hardy–Weinberg equilibrium in the context of our discussion of the forces of evolutionary change. Population genetics provides the mathematical underpinnings of evolutionary theory, and the Hardy–Weinberg equilibrium is at the heart of mathematical and quantitative approaches to understanding evolutionary change in diploid organisms. In this appendix, we will briefly go over a derivation of the Hardy–Weinberg equilibrium and show some applications of the equilibrium in evolutionary research.

Throughout the discussion, we will use the simplest case to illustrate our examples: a single gene (or locus) with two alleles, A and *a*. The frequency of A in the population is represented by *p*; the frequency of *a* is represented by *q*. By definition, $p + q = 1$.

Derivation of the Hardy–Weinberg Equilibrium

The Hardy–Weinberg equilibrium states that, given known allele frequencies p and q, we can represent the genotype frequencies by $AA = p^2$, $Aa = 2pq$, and $aa = q^2$. Furthermore, these allele frequencies remain constant from generation to generation if the following conditions are met:

- Large population size (or theoretically infinite population size), which minimizes the influence of genetic drift on allele frequencies
- Random mating (no inbreeding or assortative or disassortative mating)
- No mutation
- No gene flow
- No natural selection

Let us begin by considering a specific example, where the allele frequency of A is 0.6 ($p = 0.6$) and that of a is 0.4 ($q = 0.4$). To look at this another way, the probability that any given sperm or egg will carry A is 0.6, and the probability that it will carry a is 0.4. Thus, under equilibrium conditions (totally random mating with no other evolutionary forces in effect), the probability of producing a zygote with a homozygous AA genotype is $(0.6)(0.6) = 0.36$. We can represent the probabilities of all the genotypes occurring in a modified Punnett square:

		SPERM	
		FREQ(A) = p = 0.6	FREQ(a) = q = 0.4
EGGS	**freq(A) = p = 0.6**	freq(AA) = p^2 = (0.6)(0.6) = 0.36	freq(Aa) = pq = (0.6)(0.4) = 0.24
	freq(a) = q = 0.4	freq(Aa) = pq = (0.6)(0.4) = 0.24	freq(aa) = q^2 = (0.4)(0.4) = 0.16

This gives us a population with genotype frequencies of 0.36 (for AA), 0.48 (for Aa), and 0.16 (for aa). What are the allele frequencies for this population? For A, it is $0.36 + (0.5)(0.48) = 0.36 + 0.24 = 0.6$, which is what the frequency of A was originally. The allele frequency of a is $0.16 + (0.5)(0.48) = 0.16 + 0.24 = 0.40$, which is the original frequency of a. This demonstrates that allele frequencies are maintained in equilibrium under conditions of random mating and in the absence of other evolutionary forces.

The general equation for the distribution of genotypes for a population in Hardy–Weinberg equilibrium is given by the equation

$$p^2 + 2pq + q^2 = 1$$

We can derive this equation directly from the modified Punnett square.

The constancy of allele frequencies over generations is shown by the following equations. Let p' equal the allele frequency of A in the first generation. From the preceding example we see that

$$p' = (\text{frequency of } AA) + (0.5)(\text{frequency of } Aa)$$

We want to count only half the alleles for A in the heterozygotes. Substituting the allele frequency values from the Hardy–Weinberg equation, we get

$$p' = p^2 + (0.5)(2pq)$$

Because $(0.5)(2pq) = pq$, we now have

$$p' = p^2 + pq$$

Which, factoring out p, is the same thing as

$$p' = p(p + q)$$

As you recall, $p + q = 1$; therefore,

$$p' = p$$

This demonstrates that allele frequencies remain constant in a population in Hardy–Weinberg equilibrium.

One of the main uses of the Hardy–Weinberg equation is to determine if a population is *not* in equilibrium. We do this by comparing observed allele frequencies with observed genotype frequencies. If the observed genotype frequencies are significantly different from those expected based on the allele frequencies (which we usually check by using a chi-square statistical test), then we can say the population is not in equilibrium. This result indicates that one of the assumptions of the Hardy–Weinberg equilibrium is being violated and that an evolutionary force may be acting on the population or acted on the population in the past to produce the nonequilibrium distribution of alleles.

Another application of the Hardy–Weinberg equation is to estimate the frequency of heterozygotes in a population. It is particularly useful for estimating the frequency in a population of carriers of a recessive autosomal illnesses, such as sickle cell anemia. The recessive allele frequency is simply

$$q = \sqrt{\text{frequency of autosomal recessive condition}}$$

and the dominant allele frequency is

$$p = 1 - q$$

Thus the frequency of heterozygous carriers $= 2pq$.

HARDY–WEINBERG AND NATURAL SELECTION

The Hardy–Weinberg equilibrium can help us mathematically model the effects of any of the forces of evolution (mutation, genetic drift, gene flow, and natural selection). Let us consider how to use the Hardy– Weinberg equation to understand how natural selection may affect the distribution of allele frequencies in a population. In these equations, we assume that natural selection is the only force of evolution acting on the population.

In the simple case of one gene with two alleles, we have three possible genotypes that are subject to natural selection. To model the change in allele frequencies, we need to know not the absolute fitness of each genotype (which we could measure as its likelihood of survival) but rather the genotypes' fitness relative to one another. Relative fitness usually is represented by the letter w; thus we have

$$w_{AA} = \text{relative fitness of } AA$$
$$w_{Aa} = \text{relative fitness of } Aa$$
$$w_{aa} = \text{relative fitness of } aa$$

Let's say that the homozygous genotype AA has the highest fitness; its relative fitness w_{AA} would therefore be equal to 1. The relative fitnesses of Aa and aa are lower, such that

$$w_{AA} = 1.0$$
$$w_{Aa} = 0.8$$
$$w_{aa} = 0.4$$

Let's also assume starting allele frequencies of $p = 0.7$ and $q = 0.3$.

If the population were in Hardy–Weinberg equilibrium, the expected genotype frequencies after one generation would be

$$p^2 = (0.7)(0.7) = 0.49 \text{ for } AA$$
$$2pq = 2(0.7)(0.3) = 0.42 \text{ for } Aa$$
$$q^2 = (0.3)(0.3) = 0.09 \text{ for } aa$$

However, natural selection is working on this population and affecting the survival of the different genotypes. So the genotype frequencies after selection are

$$wAA\ p^2 = 1.0(0.7)(0.7) = 0.49 \text{ for } AA$$
$$w_{Aa}\ 2pq = 0.8(2)(0.7)(0.3) = 0.336 \text{ for } Aa$$
$$w_{aa}\ q^2 = 0.4(0.3)(0.3) = 0.036 \text{ for } aa$$

The frequency of p after natural selection has acted on the population is

$$p' = [(0.49) + (0.5)(0.336)]/(0.49 + 0.336 + 0.036)$$
$$= 0.658/0.862$$
$$= 0.763$$

The frequency of q is

$$q' = 1 - p' = 1 - 0.763 = 0.237$$

So after only one generation of natural selection operating at these levels, there is a substantial change in allele frequencies, with A going from 0.7 to 0.763 and a decreasing from 0.3 to 0.237. Following this through five generations, the allele frequencies would be:

GENERATION	1	2	3	4	5
p	0.763	0.813	0.852	0.883	0.907
q	0.237	0.187	0.148	0.117	0.093

In the case of a lethal autosomal recessive condition (such as Tay–Sachs disease), in which the relative fitness of the recessive homozygote is 0 and for the other two genotypes it is 1, we can represent the change in allele frequency of the recessive allele by a simple equation (which is derived from the Hardy–Weinberg equation):

$$q_g = q_0/(1 + gq_0)$$

where g is the number of generations passed, q_g is the frequency of a in generation g, and q_0 is the starting frequency of a. Consider a founding population in which the allele frequency of a lethal recessive is 0.20. Over ten generations, the frequency of this allele will decrease to

$$\begin{aligned} q_{10} &= 0.2/[1 + (10)(0.2)] \\ &= 0.2/3 \\ &= 0.067 \end{aligned}$$

Of course, a small founding population violates one of the conditions of the Hardy–Weinberg equilibrium (infinite population size), but we can ignore that for the sake of this example.

METRIC–IMPERIAL CONVERSIONS

METRIC UNIT	IMPERIAL EQUIVALENT
1 centimetre	0.39 inches
1 metre	3.28 feet
1 kilometre	0.62 miles
1 kilogram	2.20 pounds
454 grams	1 pound
1 gram	0.035 ounces
1 litre	0.88 quarts
400 cubic centimetres	24.4 cubic inches
1 square kilometre	0.39 square miles
1 square kilometre	247 acres
0 degrees Celsius	32 degrees Fahrenheit

Glossary

ABO blood type system Refers to the genetic system for one of the proteins found on the surface of red blood cells. Consists of one gene with three alleles: A, B, and O.

acclimatization Short-term changes in physiology that occur in an organism in response to changes in environmental conditions.

acetabulum The cup-shaped joint formed by the ilium, ischium, and pubis at which the head of the femur attaches to the pelvis.

Acheulean Stone tool industry of the Early and Middle Pleistocene characterized by the presence of bifacial hand axes and cleavers. This industry is made by a number of *Homo* species, including *H. erectus* and early *H. sapiens*.

activity budget The pattern of waking, eating, moving, socializing, and sleeping that all nonhuman primates engage in each day.

adapoids Family of mostly Eocene primates, probably ancestral to all strepsirhines.

adaptability The ability of an individual organism to make positive anatomical or physiological changes after short- or long-term exposure to stressful environmental conditions.

adaptation A trait that increases the reproductive success of an organism, produced by natural selection in the context of a particular environment.

adaptationism A premise that all aspects of an organism have been moulded by natural selection to a form optimal for enhancing reproductive success.

adaptive radiation The diversification of one founding species into multiple species and niches.

alleles Alternative versions of a gene. Different alleles are distinguished from one another by their different affects on the phenotypic expression of the same gene.

Allen's rule Stipulates that in warmer climates, the limbs of the body are longer relative to body size to dissipate body heat.

allopatric speciation Speciation occurring via geographic isolation.

amino acids Molecules that form the basic building blocks of protein.

anagenesis Evolution of a trait or a species into another over a period of time.

analogous Having similar traits due to similar use, not due to shared ancestry.

angular torus A thickened ridge of bone at the posterior angle of the parietal bone.

anthropoid Members of the primate suborder Anthropoidea that includes the monkeys, apes, and hominids.

antibodies Proteins (immunoglobulins) formed by the immune system that are specifically structured to bind to and neutralize invading antigens.

antigens Whole or part of an invading organism that prompts a response (such as production of antibodies) from the body's immune system.

arboreal hypothesis Hypothesis for the origin of primate adaptation that focuses on the value of grasping hands and stereoscopic vision for life in the trees.

argon–argon (^{40}Ar/^{39}Ar) dating Radiometric technique modified from K–Ar that measures ^{40}K by proxy using ^{39}Ar. Allows measurement of smaller samples with less error.

association cortex Parts of the cerebral cortex where inputs from primary motor and sensory cortex are processed.

australopithecines The common name for members of the genus Australopithecus.

autoimmune diseases Occur when a body's immune system attacks its own tissues.

autosomal dominant disease A disease that is caused by a dominant allele: Only one copy needs to be inherited from either parent for the disease to develop.

autosomal recessive disease A disease caused by a recessive allele; one copy of the allele must be inherited from each parent for the disease to develop.

autosomes Any of the chromosomes other than the sex chromosomes.

balanced polymorphism A stable polymorphism in a population in which natural selection prevents any of the alternative phenotypes (or underlying alleles) from becoming fixed or being lost.

base Variable component of the nucleotides that form nucleic acids DNA and RNA. In DNA, the bases are adenine, guanine, thymine, and cytosine. In RNA, uracil replaces thymine.

behavioural plasticity Changing a response to a particular circumstance after an experience alters the meaning of that circumstance; associated with memory and learning.

Bergmann's rule Stipulates that body size is larger in colder climates to conserve body temperature.

biface A stone tool that has been flaked on two faces or opposing sides forming a cutting edge between the two flake scars.

binomial nomenclature Linnaean naming system for all organisms, consisting of a genus and species label.

Bioarchaeology Field of study that deals with the excavation and analysis of human skeletal remains from archaeological contexts.

biocultural anthropology The study of the interaction between biology and culture, which plays a role in most human traits.

biological anthropology The study of humans as biological organisms, considered in an evolutionary framework; sometimes called physical anthropology.

biological species concept Defines species as interbreeding populations reproductively isolated from other such populations.

biomedical anthropology The subfield of biological anthropology concerned with issues of health and illness.

biostratigraphy Relative dating technique using comparison of fossils from different stratigraphic sequences to estimate which layers are older and which are younger.
blades Flakes that are twice as long as they are wide.
blending inheritance A discredited nineteenth-century idea that genetic factors from the parents averaged-out or blended together when they were passed on to offspring.
brachiation Mode of arm-hanging and arm-swinging that uses a rotating shoulder to suspend the body of an ape or hominid beneath a branch or to travel between branches.
brain stem The part of the brain that controls basal metabolic rates, respiration, pulse, and other basic body functions.
bridewealth Payment offered by a man to the parents of a woman he wants to marry.
calibrated relative dating techniques Techniques that can be correlated to an absolute chronology.
calotte The skullcap, or the bones of the skull, excluding those that form the face and the base of the cranium.
calvaria The braincase; includes the bones of the calotte and those that form the base of the cranium but excludes the bones of the face.
canine fossa An indentation on the maxilla above the root of the canine tooth, an anatomical feature usually associated with modern humans that may be present in some archaic *Homo* species in Europe.
captive study Primate behaviour study conducted in a zoo, laboratory, or other enclosed setting.
Catarrhini Infraorder of the order Primates that includes the Old World monkeys, apes, and hominids.
catastrophism Theory that there have been multiple creations interspersed by great natural disasters such as Noah's flood.
centromere Condensed and constricted region of a chromosome. During mitosis and meiosis, this is the location where sister chromatids attach to one another.
cerebellum The "little brain" tucked under the cerebrum, which is important in the control of balance, posture, and voluntary movement.
cerebrum The largest part of the human brain, which is split into left and right hemispheres. Seat of all "higher" brain functions.
cervical vertebrae The seven neck vertebrae.
Châtelperronian An Upper Palaeolithic tool industry that has been found in association with later Neandertals.
chromatin The diffuse form of DNA as it exists during the interphase of the cell cycle.
chromosome Discrete structures composed of condensed DNA and supporting proteins.
chronometric dating techniques Techniques that estimate the age of an object in absolute terms through the use of a natural clock such as radioactive decay or tree ring growth.
cladistics Method of classification using ancestral and derived traits to distinguish patterns of evolution within lineages.
cladogenesis Evolution through the branching of a species or a lineage.
cladogram Branching diagram showing evolved relationships among members of a lineage.
cleaver Type of Acheulean tool, usually oblong with a broad cutting edge on one end.
cline The distribution of a trait or allele across geographical space.
co-dominant In a diploid organism, two different alleles of a gene that are both expressed in a heterozygous individual.
coccyx The fused tail vertebrae that are very small in humans and apes.
codon A triplet of nucleotide bases in messenger RNA that specifies an amino acid or the initiation or termination of a polypeptide sequence.
cognitive universals Cognitive phenomena such as sensory processing, the basic emotions, consciousness, motor control, memory, and attention that are expressed by all normal individuals.
compound temporonuchal crest Bony crest at the back of the skull formed when an enlarged temporalis muscle approaches enlarged neck (nuchal) muscles, present in apes and *A. afarensis*.
convergent evolution Similar form or function brought about by natural selection under similar environments rather than shared ancestry.
core The raw material source (a river cobble or a large flake) from which flakes are removed.
core area The part of a home range that is most intensively used.
coroner Responsible for overseeing the investigation of deaths, particularly those occurring unexpectedly, violently, or under unusual circumstances.
cranial crests Bony ridges on the skull to which muscles attach.
creation science A creationist attempt to refute the evidence of evolution.
cross-cultural universals Behavioural phenomena, such as singing, dancing, and mental illness, that are found in almost all human cultures, but are not necessarily exhibited by each member of a cultural group.
crossing over Exchange of genetic material between homologous chromosomes during the first prophase of meiosis; mechanism for genetic recombination.
cytoplasm In a eukaryotic cell, the region within the cell membrane that surrounds the nucleus; it contains organelles, which carry out the essential functions of the cell, such as energy production, metabolism, and protein synthesis.
data The scientific evidence produced by an experiment or by observation, from which scientific conclusions are made.
daughter isotope (product) The isotope that is produced as the result of radioactive decay of the parent isotope.
deduction A conclusion that follows logically from a set of observations.
deletion mutation A change in the base sequence of a gene that results from the loss of one or more base pairs in the DNA.

deme A local, interbreeding population that is defined in terms of its genetic composition (for example, allele frequencies).

dental apes Early apes exhibiting Y-5 molar patterns but monkeylike post cranial skeletons.

dental arcade The parabolic arc that forms the upper or lower row of teeth.

deoxyribonucleic acid (DNA) A double-stranded molecule that is the carrier of genetic information. Each strand is composed of a linear sequence of nucleotides; the two strands are held together by hydrogen bonds that form between complementary bases.

diploid number Full complement of paired chromosomes in a somatic cell. In humans, the diploid number is 46 (23 pairs of different chromosomes).

directional selection Natural selection that drives evolutionary change by selecting for greater or lesser frequency of a given trait in a population.

diurnal Active during daylight hours.

dominance hierarchy Ranking of individual primates in a group that reflects their ability to displace, intimidate, or defeat group mates in contests.

dominant In a diploid organism, an allele that is expressed when present on only one of a pair of homologous chromosomes.

Early Stone Age (or Lower Palaeolithic) The earliest stone tool industries, including the Oldowan and Acheulean industries; called the ESA in Africa and the Lower Palaeolithic outside Africa.

ecological intelligence Hominid intelligence and brain size increase theorized as a result of benefits of navigating and foraging in a complex tropical forest ecosystem.

ecological species concept Defines species based on the uniqueness of their ecological niche.

ecology The study of the interrelationships of plants, animals, and the physical environment in which they live.

electron spin resonance (ESR) Electron trap technique that measures the total amount of radioactivity accumulated by a specimen such as tooth or bone since burial.

electron trap techniques Radiometric techniques that measure the accumulation of electrons in traps in the crystal lattice of a specimen.

encephalization A measure relating brain size to body size in a species.

encephalization quotient (EQ) The ratio of the actual brain size of a species to its expected brain size based on a statistical regression of brain to body size based on a large number of species.

endocast A replica (or cast) of the internal surface of the braincase that reflects the impressions made by the brain on the skull walls. Natural endocasts are formed by the filling of the braincase by sediments.

endoplasmic reticulum (ER) An organelle in the cytoplasm consisting of a folded membrane.

environment of evolutionary adaptedness (EEA) According to evolutionary psychologists, the critical period for understanding the selective forces that shape human behaviour; exemplified by hunter-gatherer lifestyles of hominids before the advent of agriculture.

enzyme A complex protein that is a catalyst for chemical processes in the body.

epidemiology The quantitative study of the occurrence and cause of disease in populations.

ethnic group A human group defined in terms of sociological, cultural, and linguistic traits.

ethnobiology The study of how traditional cultures classify objects and organisms in the natural world.

eukaryote A cell that possesses a well-organized nucleus.

eutheria Mammals that reproduce with a placenta and uterus.

evolution A change in the frequency of a gene or a trait in a population over multiple generations.

evolutionary psychology Approach to understanding the evolution of human behaviour that emphasizes the selection of specific behavioural patterns in the context of the environment of evolutionary adaptedness.

evolutionary species concept Defines species as evolutionary lineages with their own unique identity.

experimentation The testing of a hypothesis.

falsifiable Can be shown to be false.

female philopatry Primate social system in which females remain and breed in the group of their birth, whereas males emigrate.

femoral condyles The enlarged inferior end of the femur that forms the top of the knee joint.

field study Primate behaviour study conducted in the habitat in which the primate naturally occurs.

fission track dating Radiometric technique for dating noncrystalline materials using the decay of ^{238}Ur and counting the tracks that are produced by this fission. Estimates the age of sediments in which fossils are found.

fission–fusion Form of social system seen in chimpanzees, bonobos, and a few other primates in which there are temporary subgroups but no stable, cohesive groups.

flake The stone fragment struck from a core, thought to have been the primary tools of the Oldowan.

folivores Animals who eat a diet composed mainly of leaves, or foliage.

foramen magnum Hole in the occipital bone through which the spinal cord connects to the brain.

forensic anthropology The study of human remains applied to a legal context.

fossils The mineralized or otherwise preserved remnants of once-living things.

founder effect A component of genetic drift theory, stating that new populations that become isolated from the parent population carry only the genetic variation of the founders.

frequency-dependent balanced polymorphism Balanced polymorphism that is maintained because one (or more) of the alternative phenotypes has a selective advantage over the other phenotypes only when it is present in the population below a certain frequency.

frugivorous An animal that eats a diet composed mainly of fruit.

gametes The sex cells: sperm in males and eggs (or ova) in females.

gene The fundamental unit of heredity. It consists of a sequence of DNA bases that carries the information for synthesizing a protein (or polypeptide), and occupies a specific chromosomal locus.

gene flow Movement of genes between populations.

genetic bottleneck Temporary dramatic reduction in size of a population or species.

genetic code The system whereby the nucleotide triplets in DNA and RNA contain the information for synthesizing proteins from the 20 amino acids.

genetic drift Random changes in gene frequency in a population.

genocide The deliberate and systematic killing of members of a particular religious, political, or cultural group.

genome The hereditary information of an organism, encoded in the DNA (or, for some viruses, RNA).

genotype The genetic makeup of an individual. *Genotype* can refer to the entire genetic complement or more narrowly to the alleles present at a specific locus on two homologous chromosomes.

geologic time scale (GTS) The categories of time into which Earth's history is usually divided by geologists and palaeontologists: eras, periods, epochs.

geology The study of the Earth.

geomagnetic polarity time scale (GPTS) Time scale composed of the sequence of palaeomagnetic orientations of sediments through time.

gluteal muscles Gluteus maximus, medius, and minimus, the muscles of walking, which have undergone radical realignment in habitual bipeds.

gradualism Darwinian view of slow, incremental evolutionary change.

gyri (sing., gyrus) Ridges on the surface of the brain that are formed by sulci.

haemoglobin Protein found in red blood cells that transports oxygen.

half-life The time it takes for half of the original amount of an unstable isotope of an element to decay into more stable forms.

hammerstone A stone used for striking cores to produce flakes or bones to expose marrow.

hand axe Type of Acheulean tool, usually teardrop-shaped, with a long cutting edge.

haploid number The number of chromosomes found in a gamete, representing one from each pair found in a diploid somatic cell. In humans, the haploid number is 23.

haplorhine (Haplorhini) Infraorder of the order Primates that includes the anthropoids and the tarsier.

haplotypes Combinations of alleles (or at the sequence level, mutations) that are found together in an individual.

hard object feeding Chewing tough, hard-to-break food items such as nuts or fibrous vegetation.

Hardy–Weinberg equilibrium The theoretical distribution of alleles in a given population in the absence of evolution, expressed as a mathematical equation.

heritability The proportion of total phenotypic variability observed for a given trait that can be ascribed to genetic factors.

heterozygous Having two different alleles at the loci for a gene on a pair of homologous chromosomes (or autosomes).

heterozygous advantage With reference to a particular genetic system, the situation in which heterozygotes have a selective advantage over homozygotes (for example, sickle cell disease); a mechanism for maintaining a balanced polymorphism.

home range The spatial area used by a primate group.

hominid A member of the primate family Hominidae, distinguished by bipedal posture and, in more recently evolved species, large brain.

homologous chromosomes Members of the same pair of chromosomes (or autosomes). Homologous chromosomes undergo crossing over during meiosis.

homology Similarity of traits resulting from shared ancestry.

homozygous Having the same allele at the loci for a gene on both members of a pair of homologous chromosomes (or autosomes).

hormone A natural substance (often a protein) produced by specialized cells in one location of the body that influences the activity or physiology of cells in a different location.

human biology Subfield of biological anthropology dealing with human growth and development, adaptation to environmental extremes, and human genetics.

human evolutionary ecology Approach to understanding the evolution of human behaviour that attempts to explore ecological and demographic factors important in determining individual reproductive success and fitness in a cultural context.

human leukocyte antigen (HLA) system Class of blood group markers formed by proteins expressed on the surface of white blood cells (leukocytes).

hylobatid (Hylobatidae) Member of the gibbon, or lesser ape, family.

hyoid bone A small "floating bone" in the front part of the throat, which is held in place by muscles and ligaments.

hypothesis A preliminary explanation of a phenomenon. Hypothesis formation is the first step of the scientific method.

ilium The blade of the innominate to which gluteal muscles attach.

immunoglobulins Proteins that function as antibodies.

inbreeding Mating between close relatives.

inbreeding depression Lesser fitness of offspring of closely related individuals compared with the fitness of the offspring of less closely related individuals, caused largely by the expression of lethal or debilitating recessive alleles.

incest A violation of cultural rules regulating mating behaviour.

inclusive fitness Reproductive success of an organism plus the fitness of its close kin.

infanticide The killing of infants, either by members of the infant's group or by a member of a rival group.

innominate bones (os coxae) The pair of bones that compose the lateral parts of the pelvis; each innominate is made up of 3 bones that fuse during adolescence.

insertion mutation A change in the base sequence of a gene that results from the addition of one or more base pairs in the DNA.

intelligent design A creationist school of thought that proposes that natural selection cannot account for the diversity and complexity of form and function seen in nature.

ischium Portion of the innominate bone that forms the bony underpinning of the rump.

isotopes Variant forms of an element that differ based on the number of neutrons in the nucleus. Both stable and unstable (radioactive) isotopes exist in nature.

juxtamastoid eminence A ridge of bone next to the mastoid process; in Neandertals, it is larger than the mastoid process itself.

k-selected Reproductive strategy in which few offspring are produced per female, interbirth intervals are long, and maternal investment is high.

kin selection Principle that animals behave preferentially toward their genetic kin.

lactose intolerant The inability to digest lactose, the sugar found in milk; most adult mammals (including humans) are lactose intolerant as adults.

language The unique system of communication used by members of the human species.

linkage Genes that are found on the same chromosome are said to be linked. The closer together two genes are on a chromosome, the greater the linkage and the less likely they are to be separated during crossing over.

lithostratigraphy The study of geologic deposits and their formation, stratigraphic relationships, and relative time relationships based on their lithologic (rock) properties.

locus The location of a gene on a chromosome. The locus for a gene is identified by the number of the chromosome on which it is found and its position on the chromosome.

lumbar vertebrae The five vertebrae of the lower back.

Lysenkoism Soviet-era research program that tried to apply Lamarckian thinking to agricultural production.

macroevolution Evolution of major phenotypic changes over relatively short time periods.

magnetic resonance imaging (MRI) A technique for visualizing body tissues (including the nervous system). It works essentially as a map of water concentration in different tissues of the body.

male philopatry Primate social system in which males remain and breed in the group of their birth, whereas females emigrate.

mastoid process A protrusion from the temporal bone of the skull located behind the ear.

maternal–foetal incompatibility Occurs when the mother produces antibodies against an antigen (for example, a red blood cell surface protein) expressed in the foetus that she does not possess.

matrilineal Pattern of female kinship in a primate social group.

medical examiner A licensed pathologist, a specialist in disease, who specializes in performing autopsies.

meiosis Cell division that occurs in the testes and ovaries that leads to the formation of sperm and ova (gametes).

melanin A dark pigment produced by the melanocytes of the epidermis, which is the most important component of skin colour.

melanocytes Cells in the epidermis that produce melanin.

menarche The onset of a girl's first menstrual period.

Mendel's law of independent assortment Genes found on different chromosomes are sorted into sex cells independently of one another.

Mendel's law of segregation The two alleles of a gene found on each of a pair of chromosomes segregate independently of each other into sex cells.

menopause The postreproductive period in the lives of women, after the cessation of ovulation and menses.

messenger RNA (mRNA) Strand of RNA synthesized in the nucleus as a complement to a specific gene (transcription). It carries the information for the sequence of amino acids to make a specific protein into the cytoplasm, where at a ribosome it is read and a protein molecule is synthesized (translation).

metatarsals Five foot bones that join the tarsals to the toes and form a portion of the longitudinal arch of the foot.

metatheria Mammals that reproduce without a placenta, including the marsupials.

metopic keel Longitudinal ridge or thickening of bone along the midline of the frontal bone.

microevolution The study of evolutionary phenomena that occur within a species.

microliths Small, flaked stone tools probably designed to be hafted to wood or bone; common feature of Upper Palaeolithic and Later Stone Age tool industries.

Middle Palaeolithic (Middle Stone Age) Stone tool industries that used prepared core technologies.

midfacial prognathism The forward projection of the middle facial region, including the nose.

mitochondria Organelles in the cytoplasm of the cell where energy production for the cell takes place. Contains its own DNA.

mitochondrial DNA (mtDNA) Small loop of DNA found in the mitochondria. It is clonally and maternally inherited.

mitosis Somatic cell division in which a single cell divides to produce two identical daughter cells.

molecular clock A systematic accumulation of genetic change that can be used to estimate the time of divergence between two groups if relative rates are constant and a calibration point from the fossil record is available.

monogamy A mating bond; primates can be socially monogamous but still mate occasionally outside the pair bond.

most recent common ancestor (MRCA) In a phylogenetic tree, the MRCA is indicated by the deepest node from which all contemporary variants can be shown to have evolved.

multiregional models Phylogenetic models that suggest that modern humans evolved in the context of gene flow among Middle to Late Pleistocene hominid populations from different regions, so there is no single location where modern humans first evolved.

mutation An alteration in the DNA, which may or may not alter the function of a cell. If it occurs in a sex cell (i.e., sperm or egg), it may be passed from one generation to the next.
natural selection Differential reproductive success over multiple generations.
neocortex The part of the brain that controls higher cognitive function; part of the cerebrum.
nocturnal Active at night.
nondisjunction error The failure of homologous chromosomes (chromatids) to separate properly during cell division. When it occurs during meiosis, it may lead to the formation of gametes that are missing a chromosome or have an extra copy of a chromosome.
nuchal plane Flattened bony area of the occipital posterior to the foramen magnum, to which neck muscles attach.
nucleotide Molecular building block of nucleic acids DNA and RNA; consists of a phosphate, sugar, and base.
nucleus In eukaryotic cells, the part of the cell in which the genetic material is separated from the rest of the cell (cytoplasm) by a plasma membrane.
null hypothesis The starting assumption for scientific inquiry that one's research results occur by random chance. One's hypothesis must challenge this initial assumption.
observation The gathering of scientific information by watching a phenomenon.
occipital bun A backward-projecting bulge on the occipital part of the skull.
occipital torus A thickened horizontal ridge of bone on the occipital bone at the rear of the cranium.
Oldowan The tool industry characterized by simple, usually unifacial core and flake tools.
olfactory bulbs Knoblike structures located on the underside of the frontal lobes that form the termination of olfactory nerves running from the nasal region to the brain.
omomyoids Family of mostly Eocene primates probably ancestral to all haplorhines.
ontogeny The life cycle of an organism from conception to death.
optically stimulated luminescence (OSL) Electron trap technique that uses light to measure the amount of radioactivity accumulated by crystals in sediments (such as sand grains) since burial.
osteobiography A biological profile of aspects of a person's life history that are recorded in the individual's skeleton.
osteology The branch of anatomy that deals with the structure and function of bones.
osteology The study of the skeleton.
palaeoanthropology The study of the fossil record of ancestral humans and their primate kin.
Palaeodemography Analyzes the osteobiographical data for all the individuals in an archaeological sample to learn something about a past population.
palaeomagnetism The magnetic polarity recorded in ancient sediments. Reversed or normal direction is used to correlate with the geomagnetic polarity time scale to infer an age for a site.
palaeoneurology The study of the evolution of brain structure and function.
palaeontology The study of extinct organisms, based on their fossilized remains.
palaeopathology The study of disease and injury in antiquity.
palaeosol Ancient soil.
paradigm A conceptual framework useful for understanding a body of evidence.
parapatric speciation Speciation occurring when two populations have continuous distributions and some phenotypes in that distribution are more favourable than others.
parent isotope The original radioactive isotope in a sample.
pathogens Organisms and entities that can cause disease.
pedigree A diagram used in the study of human genetics that shows the transmission of a genetic trait over several generations of a family.
perimortem trauma Perimortem trauma is the physical evidence of activity that happened around the time of death, either slightly before or slightly after. We can differentiate it from premortem injury because in perimortem trauma no healing is evident at the trauma site.
phalanges Bones that form the fingers and toes.
phenotype An observable or measurable feature of an organism. Phenotypes can be anatomical, biochemical, or behavioural.
phenylketonuria (PKU) Autosomal recessive condition that leads to the accumulation of large quantities of the amino acid phenylalanine, which causes mental retardation and other phenotypic abnormalities.
phylogeny An evolutionary tree indicating relatedness and divergence of taxonomic groups.
physical anthropology The study of humans as biological organisms, considered in an evolutionary framework. Now also referred to as biological anthropology.
phytoliths Silica bodies produced by some plants, especially grasses, that can be used to indicate the presence of certain types of vegetation at a fossil site.
Platyrrhini Infraorder of the order Primates that is synonymous with the New World monkeys, or ceboids.
pleiotropy The phenomenon of a single gene having multiple phenotypic effects.
plesiadapiforms Fossil mammals of the Palaeocene Epoch that appear primate-like, but lack certain features of the skull that are common to living primates. Thus they are referred to as "questionable" primates.
point mutation A change in the base sequence of a gene that results from the change of a single base to a different base.
polyandry Mating system in which one female mates with multiple males.
polygenic traits Phenotypic traits that result from the combined action of more than one gene; most complex traits are polygenic.
polygynandrous Primate social system consisting of multiple males and multiple females.
polygynous Mating system consisting of at least one male and more than one female.

polymerase chain reaction (PCR) Method for amplifying DNA sequences using the Taq polymerase enzyme. Can potentially produce millions or billions of copies of a DNA segment starting from a very small number of target DNA.

polymorphic Two or more distinct phenotypes (at the genetic or anatomical levels) that exist within a population.

polypeptide A molecule made up of a chain of amino acids.

polytypic species Species that consist of a number of separate breeding populations, each varying in some genetic trait.

pongid (Pongidae) One of the four great apes species: gorilla, chimpanzee, bonobo, or orangutan.

population An interbreeding group of organisms.

population genetics The study of genetic variation within and among groups of organisms.

potassium–argon (K–Ar) dating Radiometric technique using the decay of ^{40}K to ^{40}Ar in potassium-bearing rocks; estimates the age of sediments in which fossils are found.

prehensile tail Grasping tail possessed by some species of New World monkeys.

primary cortex Regions of the cerebral cortex that are involved directly with motor control or sensory input.

primate Member of the mammalian order Primates, including prosimians, monkeys, apes, and humans, defined by a suite of anatomical and behavioural traits.

primatology The study of the nonhuman primates and their anatomy, genetics, behaviour, and ecology.

progesterone A steroid hormone produced by the corpus luteum and the placenta, which prepares the uterus for pregnancy and helps maintain pregnancy once fertilization has occurred.

prokaryotes Single-celled organisms, such as bacteria, in which the genetic material is not separated from the rest of the cell by a nucleus.

prosimian Member of the primate suborder Prosimii that includes the lemurs, lorises, galagos, and tarsiers.

protein synthesis The assembly of proteins from amino acids, which occurs at ribosomes in the cytoplasm and is based on information carried by messenger RNA.

proteins Complex molecules formed from chains of amino acids (polypeptide) or from a complex of polypeptides. They function as structural molecules, transport molecules, antibodies, enzymes, and hormones.

prototheria Mammals that reproduce by egg-laying, then nurse young from nipples. The Australian platypus and echidna are the only living monotremes.

provenience The origin or original source (as of a fossil).

pubis Portion of the innominate that forms the anterior part of the birth canal.

punctuated equilibrium Model of evolution characterized by rapid bursts of change, followed by long periods of stasis.

qualitative variation Phenotypic variation that can be characterized as belonging to discrete, observable categories.

quantitative variation Phenotypic variation that is characterized by the distribution of continuous variation (expressed using a numerical measure) within a population (for example, in a bell curve).

r-selected Reproductive strategy in which females have many offspring, interbirth intervals are short, and maternal investment per offspring is low.

race In biological taxonomy, it is the same thing as a subspecies; when applied to humans, it sometimes incorporates both cultural and biological factors. The term is not used by biological anthropologists today.

racism A prejudicial belief that members of one group are superior in some way to those of another because of their ancestry. Usually geographically or ethnically defined.

radiocarbon dating Radiometric technique that uses the decay of ^{14}C in organic remains such as wood and bone to estimate the time since death of the organism.

radiometric dating Chronometric techniques that use radioactive decay of isotopes to estimate age.

recessive In a diploid organism refers to an allele that must be present in two copies (homozygous) in order to be expressed.

recognition species concept Defines species based on unique traits or behaviours that allow members of one species to identify each other for mating.

recombination The rearrangement of genes on homologous chromosomes that occurs during crossing over in meiosis. It is the source of variation arising out of sexual reproduction; it is important for increasing rates of natural selection.

reductionism Paradigm that an organism is the sum of many evolved parts and that organisms can best be understood through an adaptationist approach.

regulatory genes Genes that guide the expression of structural genes, without coding for a protein themselves.

relative dating techniques Dating techniques that establish the age of a fossil only in comparison to other materials found above and below it.

replacement models Phylogenetic models that suggest that modern humans evolved in one location and then spread geographically, replacing other earlier hominid populations without or with little admixture.

reproductive isolating mechanisms (RIMS) Any factor—behavioural, ecological, or anatomical—that prevents a male and female of two different species from hybridizing.

reproductive potential The possible offspring output by one sex.

reproductive variance A measure of variation from the mean of a population in the reproductive potential of one sex compared with the other.

rhesus (Rh) system Blood type system that can cause haemolytic anaemia of the newborn through maternal-foetal incompatibility if the mother is Rh-negative and the child is Rh-positive.

ribonucleic acid (RNA) Single-stranded nucleic acid that performs critical functions during protein synthesis and comes in three forms: messenger RNA, transfer RNA, and ribosomal RNA.

ribosomes Structures composed primarily of RNA, which are found on the endoplasmic reticulum. They are the site of protein synthesis.

sacrum The fused vertebrae that form the back of the pelvis.
sagittal crest Bony crest running lengthwise down the centre of the cranium on the parietal bones; for the attachment of the temporalis muscles.
sagittal keel Longitudinal ridge or thickening of bone on the sagittal suture not associated with any muscle attachment.
scientific method Standard scientific research procedure in which a hypothesis is stated, data are collected to test it, and the hypothesis is either supported or refuted.
secondary compounds Toxic chemical compounds found in the leaves of many plants which the plants use as a defence against leaf-eating animals.
sectorial premolar complex Combination of canine and first premolar teeth that form a self-sharpening apparatus.
semi–free-ranging Primate behaviour study conducted in a large area that is enclosed or isolated in some way so the population is captive.
senescence Age-related decline in physiological or behavioural function in adult organisms.
sex chromosomes In mammals, chromosomes X and Y, with XX producing females and XY producing males.
sexual dimorphism Difference in size, shape, or colour, between the sexes.
sexual receptivity Willingness and ability of a female to mate, also defined as fertility.
sexual selection Differential reproductive success within one sex of any species.
shovel-shaped incisors Anterior teeth that on their lingual (tongue) surface are concave with two raised edges, which makes them look like tiny shovels.
sickle cell disease An autosomal recessive disease caused by a point mutation in an allele that codes for one of the polypeptide chains of the haemoglobin protein.
social intelligence Hominid intelligence and brain size increase theorized as a result of benefits of being politically or socially clever when living with others; sometimes called Machiavellian intelligence.
social system The grouping pattern in which a primate species lives, including its size and composition, evolved in response to natural and sexual selection pressures.
sociality Group living, a fundamental trait of haplorhine primates.
sociobiology Name popularized by E.O. Wilson for the evolutionary study of animal social behaviour.
somatic cells The cells of the body that are not sex cells.
speciation Formation of one or more new species via reproductive isolation.
species An interbreeding group of animals or plants that are reproductively isolated through anatomy, ecology, behaviour, or geographic distribution from all other such groups.
stabilizing selection Selection that maintains a certain phenotype by selecting against deviations from it.
stem cells Undifferentiated cells found in the developing embryo that can be induced to differentiate into a wide variety of cell types or tissues. Also found in adults, although adult stem cells are not as totipotent as embryonic stem cells.
strata Layers of rock.
stratigraphy The study of the order of rock layers and the sequence of events they reflect.
strepsirhine (Strepsirhini) Infraorder of the order Primates that includes the prosimians, excluding the tarsier.
structural genes Genes that contain the information to make a protein.
subspecies A group of local populations that share part of the geographic range of a species, and can be differentiated from other subspecies based on one or more phenotypic traits.
sulci (sing., sulcus) Grooves on the surface of the brain that divide the hemispheres into gyri.
supraorbital torus Thickened ridge of bone above the eye orbits of the skull; a browridge.
sympatric speciation Speciation occurring in the same geographic location.
systematics Branch of biology that describes patterns of organismal variation.
taphonomy The study of what happens to the remains of an animal from the time of death to the time of discovery.
tarsals Foot bones that form the ankle and arches of the foot.
taurodontism Molar teeth that have expanded pulp cavities and fused roots.
taxon A group of organisms assigned to a particular category.
taxonomy The science of biological classification.
technical intelligence Hominid intelligence and brain size increase modelled as a result of tool use and extractive foraging.
tephrostratigraphy A form of lithostratigraphy in which the chemical fingerprint of a volcanic ash is used to correlate across regions.
teratogens Substances that cause birth defects or other abnormalities in the developing embryo or foetus during pregnancy.
territory The part of a home range that is defended against other members of the same species.
theory of inheritance of acquired characteristics Discredited theory of evolutionary change proposing that changes that occur during the lifetime of an individual, through use or disuse, can be passed on to the next generation.
theory of mind Ability to place oneself into the mind of others; necessary for possessing an awareness of the knowledge or cognitive ability of others and for imitating or teaching others.
thermoluminescence (TL) Electron trap technique that uses heat to measure the amount of radioactivity accumulated by a specimen such as a stone tool since its last heating.
thoracic vertebrae The twelve vertebrae of the thorax that hold the ribs.
tool industry A particular style or tradition of making stone tools.
transfer RNA (tRNA) RNA molecules that bind to specific amino acids and transport them to ribosomes to be used during protein synthesis.

trinucleotide repeat diseases A family of autosomal dominant diseases that is caused by the insertion of multiple copies of a three-base pair sequence (CAG) that codes for the amino acid glutamine. Typically, the more copies inserted into the gene, the more serious the disease.

twin method A method for estimating the heritability of a phenotypic trait by comparing the concordance rates of identical and fraternal twins.

type specimen According to the laws of zoological nomenclature, the anatomical reference specimen for the species definition.

uniformitarianism Theory that the same gradual geological process we observe today was operating in the past.

Upper Palaeolithic (Later Stone Age) Stone tool industries that are characterized by the development of blade-based technology.

uranium series (U-series) techniques Radiometric techniques using the decay of uranium to estimate an age for calcium carbonates including flowstones, shells, and teeth.

vertebral column The column of bones and cartilaginous discs that houses the spinal cord and provides structural support and flexibility to the body.

visual predation hypothesis Hypothesis for the origin of primate adaptation that focuses on the value of grasping hands and stereoscopic vision for catching small prey.

X-linked disorders Genetic conditions that result from mutations to genes on the X chromosome. They are almost always expressed in males, who have only one copy of the X chromosome; in females, the second X chromosome containing the normally functioning allele protects them from developing X-linked disorders.

zygote A fertilized egg.

BIBLIOGRAPHY

Abbate E, Albianelli A, Azzaroli A, et al. 1998. A one million year old *Homo* cranium from the Danakil (Afar) depression of Eritrea. *Nature* 393:458–460.

Adachi, K. 1977. *The Enemy That Never Was: A History of the Japanese Canadians*. McClelland and Stewart Ltd., Toronto.

Adcock GJ, Dennis ES, Easteal S, et al. 2001. Mitochondrial DNA sequences in ancient Australians: Implications for modern human origins. *Proceedings of the National Academy of Sciences* 98:537–542.

Aiello L, Dean C. 1990. *An Introduction to Human Evolutionary Anatomy*. Academic Press, London.

Aiello LC, Wheeler P. 1995. The expensive-tissue hypothesis. *Current Anthropology* 36:199–221.

Alcock J. 2001. *The Triumph of Sociobiology*. Oxford University Press, New York.

Allen JS. 1989. Franz Boas's physical anthropology: The critique of racial formalism revisited. *Current Anthropology* 30:79–84.

Allen JS. 1997. Are traditional societies schizophrenogenic? *Schizophrenia Bulletin* 23:357–364.

Allen JS, Cheer SM. 1996. The non-thrifty genotype. *Current Anthropology* 37:831–842.

Allen JS, Damasio H, Grabowski TJ. 2002. Normal neuroanatomical variation in the human brain: An MRI-volumetric study. *American Journal of Physical Anthropology* 118:341–358.

Allen JS, Damasio H, Grabowski TJ, et al. 2003. Sexual dimorphism and asymmetries in the gray-white composition of the human cerebrum. *NeuroImage* 18:880–899.

Allen JS, Sarich VM. 1988. Schizophrenia in an evolutionary perspective. *Perspectives in Biology and Medicine* 32:132–153.

Allison AC. 1954. Protection afforded by sickle-cell trait against malarial infection. *British Medical Journal* 1:290–294.

Altmann J. 1980. *Baboon Mothers and Infants*. Harvard University Press, Cambridge, MA.

Alvarez LW, Alvarez W, Asaro F, Michel HV. 1980. Extraterrestrial cause for the Cretaceous–Tertiary extinction. *Science* 208:1095–1108.

Alvarez W. 1997. *T. rex and the Crater of Doom*. Princeton University Press, Princeton, NJ.

Ambrose SH. 2001. Paleolithic technology and human evolution. *Science* 291:1748–1753.

American Psychiatric Association. 1994. *Diagnostic and Statistical Manual of Mental Disorders*, 4th ed. American Psychiatric Association, Washington, DC.

Anderson R. 1999. Human evolution, low back pain, and dual-level control. In *Evolutionary Medicine* (WR Trevathan, EO Smith, JJ McKenna, eds.), pp. 333–349. Oxford University Press, Oxford.

Andersson S. 1992. Female preference for long tails in lekking Jackson's widow-birds: Experimental evidence. *Animal Behavior* 43:379–388.

Andrews PJ. 1989. Palaeoecology of Laetoli. *Journal of Human Evolution* 18:173–181.

Antón SC. 1996. Tendon-associated bone features of the masticatory system in Neandertals. *Journal of Human Evolution* 31:391–408.

Antón SC. 2002. Evolutionary significance of cranial variation in Asian *Homo erectus*. *American Journal of Physical Anthropology* 118:301–323.

Antón SC. 2003. A natural history of *Homo erectus*. *Yearbook of Physical Anthropology* 46:126–170.

Antón SC, Leonard WR, Robertson M. 2002. An ecomorphological model of the initial hominid dispersal from Africa. *Journal of Human Evolution* 43:773–785.

Antón SC, Swisher CC III. 2001. Evolution and variation of cranial capacity in Asian *Homo erectus*. In *A Scientific Life: Papers in Honor of Professor Dr. Teuku Jacob* (E Indriati, SC Antón, J Kurtz, eds.), pp. 25–39. Bigraf Publishing, Yogyakarta, Indonesia.

Aoki K. 1986. A stochastic model of gene-culture coevolution suggested by the "cultural-historical hypothesis" for the evolution of adult lactose absorption in humans. *Proceedings of the National Academy of Sciences* 83:2929–2933.

Ardrey R. 1966. *The Territorial Imperative*. Atheneum, New York.

Arensburg B, Schepartz LA, Tillier AM, et al. 1990. A reappraisal of the anatomical basis for speech in Middle Paleolithic hominids. *American Journal of Physical Anthropology* 83:137–146.

Armelagos G. 1997. Disease, Darwin, and medicine in the third epidemiological transition. *Evolutionary Anthropology* 5:212–220.

Arsuaga JL. 2002. *The Neanderthal's Necklace*. Four Wall Eight Windows, New York.

Arsuaga JL, Martines A, Garcia A, Lorenzo C. 1997. The Sima de los Huesos crania (Sierra de Atapuerca, Spain). A comparative study. *Journal of Human Evolution* 33:219–281.

Arsuaga JL, Martínez I, Lorenzo C, et al. 1999. The human cranial remains from Gran Dolina Lower Pleistocene site (Sierra de Atapuerca, Spain). *Journal of Human Evolution* 37:431–457.

Asfaw B, Gilbert WH, Beyene Y, et al. 2002. Remains of *Homo erectus* from Bouri, Middle Ethiopia. *Nature* 416:317–320.

Asfaw B, White TD, Lovejoy CO, et al. 1999. *Australopithecus garhi:* A new species of early hominid from Ethiopia. *Science* 284:629–635.

Atran S. 1998. Folk biology and the anthropology of science: Cognitive universals and cultural particulars. *Behavioral and Brain Sciences* 21:547–609.

Barkow JH, Cosmides L, Tooby J, eds. 1992. *The Adapted Mind: Evolutionary Psychology and the Generation of Culture*. Oxford University Press, New York.

Barquet N, Domingo P. 1997. Smallpox: The triumph over the most terrible ministers of death. *Annals of Internal Medicine* 127:635–642.

Bateson W. 1900–1901. Problems of heredity as a subject for horticultural investigation. *Journal of the Royal Horticultural Society* 25:54–61.

Bateson W. 1902. *Mendel's Principles of Heredity: A Defence*. Cambridge University Press, Cambridge.

Beall CM. 2001. Adaptations to altitude: A current assessment. *Annual Review of Anthropology* 30:423–456.

Beall CM, Decker MJ, Brittenham GM, et al. 2002. An Ethiopian pattern of human adaptation to high-altitude hypoxia. *Proceedings of the National Academy of Sciences* 99:17215–17218.

Beall CM, Steegman AT. 2000. Human adaptation to climate: Temperature, ultraviolet radiation, and altitude. In *Human Biology: An Evolutionary and Biocultural Perspective* (S Stinson, B Bogin, R Huss-Ashmore, D O'Rourke, eds.), pp. 163–224. Wiley-Liss, New York.

Beals KL, Smith CL, Dodd SM. 1984. Brain size, cranial morphology, climate, and time machines. *Current Anthropology* 25:301–330.

Beard CK, Qi T, Dawson MR, Wang B, Li C. 1994. A diverse new primate fauna from middle Eocene fissure fillings in southeastern China. *Nature* 368:604–609.

Bearder SK, Honess PE, Ambrose L. 1995. Species diversity among galagos with special reference to mate recognition. In *Creatures of the Dark: The Nocturnal Prosimians* (L Alterman, GA Doyle, MK Izard, eds.), pp. 1–22. Plenum, New York.

Beattie O, Geiger J. 2005. *Frozen in Time: The Fate of the Franklin Expedition*. Douglas and McIntyre, Vancouver, BC.

Bednarik RG. 2003. A figurine from the African Acheulian. *Current Anthropology* 44:405–413.

Behe M. 1996. *Darwin's Black Box*. The Free Press, lNew York.

Behrensmeyer AK, Hill A, eds. 1980. *Fossils in the Making*. University of Chicago Press, Chicago.

Bellomo RV. 1994. Methods of determining early hominid behavioral activities associated with the controlled use of fire at FxJj 20 Main, Koobi Fora, Kenya. *Journal of Human Evolution* 27:173–195.

Benefit BR. 1999. *Victoriapithecus*, the key to Old World monkey and catarrhine origins. *Evolutionary Anthropology* 7:155–174.

Benefit BR, McCrossin ML. 1995. Miocene hominoids and hominid origins. *Annual Review of Anthropology* 24:237–256.

Benefit BR, McCrossin ML. 2002. The Victoriapithecidae, Cercopithecoidea. In *The Primate Fossil Record* (WC Hartwig, ed.), pp. 241–253. Cambridge University Press, Cambridge.

Benit P, Rey F, Blandin-Savoja F, et al. 1999. The mutant genotype is the main determinant of the metabolic phenotype in phenylalanine hydroxylase deficiency. *Molecular Genetics and Metabolism* 68:43–47.

Berger T, Trinkaus E. 1995. Patterns of trauma among the Neandertals. *Journal of Archaeological Science* 22:841–852.

Berlin B. 1992. Ethnobiological Classification: Principles of Categorization of Plants and Animals in Traditional Societies. Princeton University Press, Princeton, NJ.

Berlin B, Kay P. 1969. *Basic Color Terms: Their Universality and Evolution*. University of California Press, Berkeley.

Bermudez de Castro JM, Arsuaga JL, Carbonell E, et al. 1997. A hominid from the lower Pleistocene of Atapuerca, Spain: Possible ancestor to Neandertals and modern humans. *Science* 276:1392–1395.

Berry WBN. 1968. *Growth of a Prehistoric Time Scale Based on Organic Evolution*. WH Freeman, San Francisco.

Betzig L, ed. 1997. *Human Nature: A Critical Reader*. Oxford University Press, New York.

Beyerstein BL. 1999. Whence cometh the myth that we only use 10% of our brains? In *Mind Myths* (S Della Sala, ed.), pp. 3–24. Wiley, New York.

Bickerton D. 1983. Pidgin and creole languages. *Scientific American* 249:116–122.

Bickerton D. 1990. *Language and Species*. University of Chicago Press, Chicago.

Bird R. 1999. Cooperation and conflict: The behavioral ecology of the sexual division of labor. *Evolutionary Anthropology* 8:65–75.

Bix HP. 2000. *Hirohito and the Making of Modern Japan*. HarperCollins, New York.

Blixt S. 1975. Why didn't Gregor Mendel find linkage? *Nature* 256:206.

Bloch JI, Silcox MT. 2001. New basicrania of Paleocene–Eocene *Ignacius*: Re-evaluation of the Plesiadapiform–Dermopteran link. *American Journal of Physical Anthropology* 116:184–198.

Blum K, Cull JG, Braverman ER, Comings DE. 1996. Reward deficiency syndrome. *American Scientist* 84:132–145.

Blumenschine RJ. 1986. Carcass consumption sequences and the archaeological distinction of scavenging and hunting. *Journal of Human Evolution* 15:639–659.

Blumenschine RJ. 1987. Characteristics of an early hominid scavenging niche. *Current Anthropology* 28:383–407.

Boas F. 1912. Changes in the bodily form of descendants of immigrants. *American Anthropologist* 14:530–533.

Boas F. 1938 (1911). *The Mind of Primitive Man*, rev. ed. Macmillan, New York.

Boas F. 1940. *Race, Language, and Culture*. University of Chicago Press, Chicago.

Bobe R, Behrensmeyer AK. 2004. The expansion of grassland ecosystems in Africa in relation to mammalian evolution and the origin of the genus *Homo*.

Palaeogeography, Palaeoclimatology, Palaeoecology. 207 (3/4):399–420.

Boesch C, Boesch H. 1989. Hunting behavior of wild chimpanzees in the Taï National Park. *American Journal of Physical Anthropology* 78:547–573.

Bogin B. 1993. Why must I be a teenager at all? *New Scientist* 137:34–38.

Bogin B. 1995. Plasticity in the growth of Mayan refugee children living in the United States. In *Human Variability and Plasticity* (CGN Mascie-Taylor, B Bogin, eds.), pp. 46–74. Cambridge University Press, Cambridge.

Bogin B. 1999. Evolutionary perspective on human growth. *Annual Review of Anthropology* 28:109–153.

Boinski S. 1987. Mating patterns in squirrel monkeys (*Saimiri oerstedi*). *Behavioral Ecology & Sociobiology* 21:13–21.

Boinski S. 1994. Affiliation patterns among male Costa Rican squirrel monkeys. *Behaviour* 130:191–209.

Bookstein F, Schäfer K, Prossinger H, et al. 1999. Comparing frontal cranial profiles in archaic and modern *Homo* by morphometric analysis. *Anatomical Record (New Anat.)* 257:217–224.

Borgerhoff Mulder M. 1987. On cultural and reproductive success: Kipsigis evidence. *American Anthropologist* 89:617–634.

Borgerhoff Mulder M. 1990. Kipsigis women's preferences for wealthy men: Evidence for female choice in mammals. *Behavioral Ecology and Sociobiology* 27:255–264.

Borries C, Launhardt K, Epplen C, et al. 1999. DNA analyses support the hypothesis that infanticide is adaptive in langur monkeys. *Proceedings of the Royal Society of London* B 266:901–904.

Bottini N, Meloni GF, Finocchi A, et al. 2001. Maternal-fetal interaction in the ABO system: A comparative analysis of healthy mothers and couples with recurrent spontaneous abortion suggests a protective effect of B incompatibility. *Human Biology* 73:167–174.

Bowler JM, Johnston H, Olley JM, et al. 2003. New ages for human occupation and climatic change at Lake Mungo, Australia. *Nature* 421:837–840.

Boyd R, Richerson P. 1988. *Culture and the Evolutionary Process*. University of Chicago Press, Chicago.

Boyd WC. 1950. *Genetics and the Races of Man*. Little, Brown, Boston.

Brace CL, Xinag-qing S, Zhen-biao Z. 1984. Prehistoric and modern tooth size in China. In *The Origins of Modern Humans: A World Survey of the Fossil Evidence* (F Smith, F Spencer, eds.), pp. 485–516. Alan R. Liss, New York.

Brain CK. 1981. *The Hunters or the Hunted? Introduction to African Cave Taphonomy*. University of Chicago Press, Chicago.

Branda RF, Eaton JW. 1978. Skin color and nutrient photolysis: An evolutionary hypothesis. *Science* 201:625–626.

Bräuer G. 1984. The "Afro-European *sapiens* hypothesis" and hominid evolution in East Asia during the Late Middle and Upper Pleistocene. *Courier Forschunginstitut Senckenberg* 69:145–165.

Britten RJ. 2002. Divergence between samples of chimpanzee and human DNA sequences is 5%, counting indels. *Proceedings of the National Academy of Sciences* 99:13633–13635.

Broadfield DC, Holloway RL, Mowbray K, et al. 2001. Endocast of Sambungmacan 3: A new *Homo erectus* from Indonesia. *The Anatomical Record* 262:369–379.

Broca P. 1861. Remarks on the seat of the faculty of articulated language, following an observation of aphemia (loss of speech) [in French]. *Bulletin de la Société Anatomique* 6:330–357. English translation by CD Green available at psychclassics.yorku.ca/Broca/aphemie-e.htm.

Brockelman WY, Reichard U, Treesucon U, Raemakers JJ. 1998. Dispersal, pair formation, and social structure in gibbons (*Hylobates lar*). *Behavioral Ecology and Sociobiology* 42:329–339.

Brooks J Langdon. 1984. *Just Before the Origin*. ToExcel Publishing, New York.

Broom R. 1947. Discovery of a new skull of the South African ape-man, *Plesianthropus*. *Nature* 159:672.

Brown DE. 1991. *Human Universals*. McGraw-Hill, New York.

Brown FH. 1983. Correlation of Tulu Bor Tuff at Koobi Fora with the Sidi Hakoma Tuff at Hadar. *Nature* 306:210.

Brown FH. 1992. Methods of dating. In *The Cambridge Encyclopedia of Human Evolution* (S Jones, R Martin, D Pilbeam, eds.), pp. 179–186. Cambridge University Press, Cambridge.

Brown KH, Gilman R. 1986. Nutritional effects of intestinal helminths with special reference to ascariasis and strongyloidiasis. In *The Interaction of Parasitic Diseases and Nutrition* (C Chagas, GT Keusch, eds.), pp. 213–232. Pontifica Academia Scientarium, Vatican City.

Brown P, Sutikana T, Morwood MJ, et al. Due (2004) A new small-bodied hominid from the Late Pleistocene of Flores, Indonesia. *Nature* 431:1055–1061.

Browner CH, Ortiz de Montellano BR, Rubel AJ. 1988. A methodology for cross-cultural ethnomedical research. *Current Anthropology* 29:681–702.

Brues AM. 1977. *People and Races*. Macmillan, New York.

Brunet M, Beauvilain A, Coppens Y, et al. 1995. The first australopithecine 2,500 kilometres west of the Rift Valley (Chad). *Nature* 378:273–275.

Brunet M, Beauvilain A, Coppens Y, et al. 1996. *Australopithecus bahrelghazali*, une nouvelle espece d'hominide ancien de la region de Koro Toro (Tchad). *Comptes Rendus des Seances de l'Academie des Sciences* 322:907–913.

Brunet M, Guy F, Pilbeam D, et al. 2002. A new hominid from the Upper Miocene of Chad, Central Africa. *Nature* 418:145–151.

Bshary R, Noë R. 1997. The formation of red colobus–diana monkey associations under predation pressure from chimpanzees. *Proceedings of the Royal Society of London* B 264:253–259.

Buckley GA. 1997. A new species of *Purgatorius* (Mammalia; Primatomorpha) from the Lower Paleocene Bear Formation, Crazy Mountains Basin, South-Central Montana. *Journal of Palaeontology* 71:149–155.

Bumpus HC. 1899. The elimination of the unfit as illustrated by the introduced sparrow, *Passer domesticus*. *Biol. Lectures, Marine Biological Laboratory, Woods Hole* 209–226.

Bunn HT, Ezzo JA. 1993. Hunting and scavenging by Plio-Pleistocene hominids: Nutritional constraints, archaeological patterns, and behavioural implications. *Journal of Archaeological Science* 20:365–398.

Buss DM. 2003. *The Evolution of Desire*. Basic Books, New York.

Buzon MR. 2006. The relationship between biological and ethnic identity in New Kingdom Nubia. *Current Anthropology* 47:683–695.

Buzon MR, Simonetti A, Creaser RA. 2007. Migration in the Nile Valley during the New Kingdom period: a preliminary strontium isotope study. *Journal of Archaeological Science* 34:1391–1401.

Buzon MR, Richman R. 2007. Traumatic injuries and imperialism: the effects of Egyptian colonial strategies at Tombos in Upper Nubia. *American Journal of Physical Anthropology* 133 (2):783–791.

Byrne RW. 1995. *The Thinking Ape*. Oxford University Press, Oxford.

Byrne RW, Whiten A, eds. 1988a. Machiavellian Intelligence: Social Expertise and the Evolution of Intellect in Monkeys, Apes, and Humans. Clarendon, Oxford.

Byrne RW, Whiten A. 1988b. Towards the next generation in data quality: A new survey of primate tactical deception. *Behavioral and Brain Sciences* 11:267–273.

Calvin WH. 1982. Did throwing stones shape hominid brain evolution? *Ethology and Sociobiology* 3:115–124.

Calvin WH. 1983. *The Throwing Madonna*. McGraw-Hill, New York.

Calvin WH, Ojemann GA. 1994. Conversations with Neil's Brain: The Neural Nature of Thought and Language. Perseus Books, Reading, MA.

Canadian Institutes of Health Research, Natural Sciences and Engineering Research Council of Canada, Social Sciences and Humanities Research Council of Canada. *Tri-Council Policy Statement: Ethical Conduct for Research Involving Humans*. 1998 (with 2000, 2002, and 2005 amendments).

Cande SC, Kent DV. 1995. Revised calibration of the geomagnetic polarity timescale for the Late Cretaceous and Cenozoic. *Journal of Geophysical Research* 100:6093–6095.

Cann RL. 2001. Genetic clues to dispersal in human populations: Retracing the past from the present. *Science* 291:1742–1748.

Cann RL. 2002. Tangled genetic routes. *Nature* 416:32–33.

Cann RL, Stoneking M, Wilson AC. 1987. Mitochondrial DNA and human evolution. *Nature* 325:31–36.

Caramelli D, Lalueza-Fox C, Vernesi C, et al. 2003. Evidence for a genetic discontinuity between Neandertals and 24,000-year-old anatomically modern Europeans. *Proceedings of the National Academy of Sciences* 100:6593–6597.

Cartmill M. 1974. Rethinking primate origins. *Science* 184:436–443.

Caspi A, Sugden K, Moffitt TE, et al. 2003. Influence of life stress on depression: Moderation by a polymorphism in the 5-HTT gene. *Science* 301:386–389.

Cavalli-Sforza LL, Bodmer WF. 1999 (1971). *The Genetics of Human Populations*. Dover, Mineola, New York.

Cavalli-Sforza LL, Feldman MS. 2003. The application of molecular genetic approaches to the study of human evolution. *Nature Genetics* (suppl.) 33:266–275.

Cavalli-Sforza LL, Menozzi P, Piazza A. 1994. *The History and Geography of Human Genes*. Princeton University Press, Princeton, NJ.

Chagnon NA. 1988. Life histories, blood revenge, and warfare in a tribal population. *Science* 239:985–992.

Chagnon NA. 1997. *Yanomamö: The Fierce People*. Holt, Rinehart, and Winston, New York.

Chakravarti A, Chakraborty R. 1978. Elevated frequency of Tay–Sachs disease among Ashkenazic Jews unlikely by drift alone. *American Journal of Human Genetics* 30:256–261.

Chargaff E. 1950. Chemical specificity of nucleic acids and mechanism for their enzymatic degradation. *Experientia* 6:201–209.

Charles-Dominique P. 1977. *Ecology and Behaviour of Nocturnal Prosimians*. Columbia University Press, New York.

Cheney DL, Seyfarth RM. 1991. *How Monkeys See the World*. University of Chicago Press, Chicago.

Cheney D, Seyfarth RM, Andelman SJ, Lee PC. 1988. Reproductive success in vervet monkeys. In *Reproductive Success* (TH Clutton-Brock, ed.), pp. 384–402. University of Chicago Press, Chicago.

Chomsky N. 1967. The formal nature of language (Appendix A). In *Biological Foundations of Language* (EH Lenneberg, ed.), pp. 397–442. Wiley, New York.

Clark WEL. 1975. *The Fossil Evidence for Human Evolution*. University of Chicago Press, Chicago.

Clarke RJ. 1998. First ever discovery of a well-preserved skull and associated skeleton of *Australopithecus*. *South African Journal of Science* 94:460–464.

Clarke RJ, Tobias PV. 1995. Sterkfontein Member 2 foot bones of the oldest South African hominid. *Science* 269:521–524.

Coghlan A. 2003. A sad farewell for Dolly the sheep, the world's first cloned mammal. *New Scientist* 177:5.

Cohen MN, Armelagos GJ. 1984. *Paleopathology at the Origins of Agriculture*. Academic Press, New York.

Coleman L, Coleman J. 2002. The measurement of puberty: A review. *Journal of Adolescence* 25:535–550.

Collard M, Wood B. 2000. How Reliable Are Human Phylogene Hypothesis? *Proceedings of the National Academy of Sciences*. Vol. 97:5003–5006

Conroy GC. 1997. *Reconstructing Human Origins*. Norton, New York.

Conroy GC, Jolly CJ, Cramer D, Kalb JE. 1978. Newly discovered fossil hominid skull from the Afar depression, Ethiopia. *Nature* 275:67–70.

Cook D. 1979. Subsistence base and health in the lower Illinois Valley: Evidence from the human skeleton. *Medical Anthropology* 4:109–124.

Cook D, Buikstra JE. 1979. Health and differential survival in prehistoric populations: Prenatal dental defects. *American Journal of Physical Anthropology* 51:649–664.

Cooke GS, Hill AVS. 2001. Genetics of susceptibility to human infectious disease. *Nature Reviews: Genetics* 2:967–977.

Cords M. 1990. Vigilance and mixed-species association of some East African forest monkeys. *Behavioral Ecology and Sociobiology* 26:297–300.

Covert HH. 2002. The earliest fossil primates and the evolution of the prosimians: Introduction. In *The Primate Fossil Record* (WC Hartwig, ed.), pp. 13–20. Cambridge University Press, Cambridge.

Crews DE, Gerber L. 1994. Chronic degenerative diseases and aging. In *Biological Anthropology and Aging* (DE Crews, R Garruto, eds.), pp. 154–181. Oxford University Press, New York.

Crooks D. 1999. Child growth and nutritional status in a high-poverty community in eastern Kentucky. *American Journal of Physical Anthropology* 109:129–142.

Cuatrecasas PD, Lockwood H, Caldwell J. 1965. Lactase deficiency in the adult: A common occurrence. *Lancet* 1:14–18.

Curtin RA, Dolhinow P. 1978. Primate behavior in a changing world. *American Scientist* 66:468–475.

Dagosto M. 1993. Postcranial anatomy and locomotor behavior in Eocene primates. In *Postcranial Adaptation in Nonhuman Primates* (DL Gebo, ed.), pp. 567–593. Northern Illinois University Press, DeKalb.

Damasio A. 1994. *Descartes' Error*. Avon Books, New York.

Damasio H, Damasio AR. 1989. *Lesion Analysis in Neuropsychology*. Oxford University Press, New York.

Dart RA. 1925. *Australopithecus africanus:* The man-ape of South Africa. *Nature* 115:195–199.

Darwin C. 1839. Journal of Researches into the Geology and Natural History of the Various Countries Visited by H.M.S. *Beagle*. Colburn, London.

Darwin C. 1859. On the Origin of Species by Means of Natural Selection; or, The Preservation of Favoured Races in the Struggle for Life. John Murray, London.

Darwin C. 1871. The Descent of Man and Selection in Relation to Sex. J. Murray, London.

Da Silva OP. 1994. Prevention of low birthweight/preterm birth. In *Canadian Task Force on the Periodic Health Examination*. Canadian Guide to Clinical Preventive Health Care. Health Canada, Ottawa, ON:38–50.

Dawkins R. 1976. *The Selfish Gene*. Oxford University Press, New York.

Deacon TW. 1990. Fallacies of progression in theories of brain-size evolution. *International Journal of Primatology* 11:193–236.

Deacon TW. 1997. The Symbolic Species: The Co-Evolution of Language and the Brain. Norton, New York.

De Bonis L, Koufos G. 1993. The face and mandible of *Ouranopithecus macedoniensis:* Description of new specimens and comparisons. *Journal of Human Evolution* 24:469–491.

Dedrick D. 1996. Color language universality and evolution: On the explanation for basic color terms. *Philosophical Psychology* 9:497–524.

Defleur A, White T, Valensi P, Slimak L, Crégut-Bonnoure E. 1999. Neanderthal cannibalism at Moula-Guercy, Ardèche, France. *Science* 286:128–131.

Dehaene S. 2003. Natural born readers. *New Scientist* 179:30–33.

Dehaene S, Dupoux E, Mehler J, et al. 1997. Anatomical variability in the cortical representation of first and second language. *NeuroReport* 8:3809–3815.

De Heinzelen J, Clark JD, White T, et al. 1999. Environment and behavior of 2.5 million-year-old Bouri hominids. *Science* 284:625–628.

Deino AL, Renne PR, Swisher CC. 1998. $^{40}Ar/^{39}Ar$ dating in paleoanthropology and archaeology. *Evolutionary Anthropology* 6:63–75.

Delgado RA, van Schaik CP. 2000. The behavioral ecology and conservation of the orangutan (*Pongo pygmaeus*): A tale of two islands. *Evolutionary Anthropology* 9:201–218.

Delson E. 1980. Fossil macaques, phyletic relationships and a scenario of deployment. In *The Macaques: Studies in Ecology, Behavior, and Evolution* (DG Lindburg, ed.), pp. 10–30. Van Nostrand Reinhold, New York.

Department for Culture, Media, and Sport. 2005. *Guidance for the Care of Human Remains in Museums*. London.

d'Errico F, Blackwell LR, Berger LR. 2001. Bone tool use in termite foraging by early hominids and its impact on understanding early hominid behaviour. *South African Journal of Science* 97:71–75.

Dettwyler KA. 1991. Can paleopathology provide evidence for "compassion"? *American Journal of Physical Anthropology* 84:375–384.

de Waal FBM. 1982. *Chimpanzee Politics*. Johns Hopkins University Press, Baltimore.

de Waal FBM, Lanting F. 1997. *Bonobo: The Forgotten Ape*. University of California Press, Berkeley.

de Waal Malefijt A. 1968. *Homo monstrosus. Scientific American* 219:112–118.

Di Fiore A, Rendall D. 1994. Evolution of social organization: A reappraisal for primates by using phylogenetic methods. *Proceedings of the National Academy of Sciences* 91:9941–9945.

Digby L. 1995. Infant care, infanticide, and female reproductive strategies in polygynous groups of common marmosets (*Callithrix jacchus*). *Behavioral Ecology and Sociobiology* 37:51–61.

Disotell TR. 1999. Human evolution: Origins of modern humans still look recent. *Current Biology* 9:R647–R650.

Dobzhansky T. 1973. Nothing in biology makes sense except in the light of evolution. *American Biology Teacher* 35:125–129.

Dunbar RIM. 1983. Reproductive Decisions: An Economic Analysis of Gelada Baboon Social Strategies. Princeton. Princeton University Press.

Dunbar RIM. 1992. Neocortex size as a constraint on group size in primates. *Journal of Human Evolution* 20:469–493.

Dunbar RIM. 1993. Coevolution of neocortical size, group size, and language in humans. *Behavioral and Brain Sciences* 16:681–735.

Dunbar R. 1997. *Grooming, Gossip, and the Evolution of Language.* Harvard University Press, Cambridge, MA.

Durham WH. 1991. *Coevolution: Genes, Culture, and Human Diversity.* Stanford University Press, Stanford, CA.

Eaton SB, Eaton SB III, Konner MJ. 1999. Paleolithic nutrition revisited. In *Evolutionary Medicine* (WR Trevathan, EO Smith, JJ McKenna, eds.), pp. 313–332. Oxford University Press, Oxford.

Eaton SB, Konner MJ. 1985. Paleolithic nutrition. A consideration of its nature and current implications. *New England Journal of Medicine* 312:283–289.

Eldredge N, Gould SJ. 1972. Punctuated equilibrium: An alternative to phyletic gradualism. In *Models in Paleobiology* (TJM Shopf, ed.), pp. 82–115. Freeman, Cooper, and Co., San Francisco.

Elford, RW. 1994. Prevention of Motor Vehicle Accident Injuries. In *Canadian Guide to Clinical Preventive Health Care* (Canadian Task Force on the Periodic Health Examination), pp. 514–524. Health Canada, Ottawa.

Ellison PT. 1990. Human ovarian function and reproductive ecology: New hypotheses. *American Anthropologist* 92:933–952.

Ellison PT. 1994. Advances in human reproductive ecology. *Annual Review in Anthropology* 23:255–275.

Endler J. 1983. Natural and sexual selection on color patterns in poeciliid fishes. *Environmental Biology of Fishes* 9:173–190.

Endler J. 1986. *Natural Selection in the Wild.* Princeton University Press, Princeton, NJ.

Engels F. 1896. The part played by labor in the transition from ape to man.

Ennattah NS, Sahi T, Savilahti E, et al. 2002. Identification of a variant associated with adult-type hypolactasia. *Nature Genetics* 30:233–237.

Enoch MA, Goldman D. 1999. Genetics of alcoholism and substance abuse. *Psychiatric Clinics of North America* 22:289–299.

Etler DA. 1996. The fossil evidence for human evolution in Asia. *Annual Review of Anthropology* 25:275–301.

Everett DL. 2005. Cultural constraints on grammar and cognition in Pirahã. *Current Anthropology* 46(4):621–646.

Evernden JF, Curtis GH. 1965. Potassium–argon dating of Late Cenozoic rocks in East Africa and Italy. *Current Anthropology* 6:643–651.

Eyre-Walker A, Keightley PD. 1999. High genomic deleterious mutation rates in hominids. *Nature* 397:344–347.

Fagan BM. 2001. *People of the Earth*, 10th ed. Prentice Hall, Upper Saddle River, NJ.

Fairbanks DJ, Rytting B. 2001. Mendelian controversies: A botanical and historical review. *American Journal of Botany* 88:737–752.

Fairburn HR, Young LE, Hendrich BD. 2002. Epigenetic reprogramming: How now, cloned cow? *Current Biology* 12:R68–R70.

Falk D. 1975. Comparative anatomy of the larynx in man and chimpanzee. *American Journal of Physical Anthropology* 43:123–132.

Falk D. 1980. A reanalysis of South African australopithecine natural endocasts. *American Journal of Physical Anthropology* 53:525–539.

Falk D. 1983a. Cerebral cortices of East African early hominids. *Science* 221:1072–1074.

Falk D. 1983b. The Taung endocast: A reply to Holloway. *American Journal of Physical Anthropology* 60:479–489.

Falk D. 1985a. Apples, oranges, and the lunate sulcus. *American Journal of Physical Anthropology* 67:313–315.

Falk D. 1985b. Hadar AL 162-28 endocast as evidence that brain enlargement preceded cortical reorganization in hominid evolution. *Nature* 313:45–47.

Falk D. 1989. Ape-like endocast of "ape-man" Taung. *American Journal of Physical Anthropology* 80:335–339.

Falk D. 1990. Brain evolution in *Homo*: The "radiator" theory. *Behavioral and Brain Sciences* 13:333–381.

Falk D. 1991. Reply to Dr. Holloway: Shifting positions on the lunate sulcus. *American Journal of Physical Anthropology* 84:89–91.

Falk D, Conroy G. 1983. The cranial venous sinus system in early hominids: Phylogenetic and functional implications for *Australopithecus afarensis. Nature* 306:779–781.

Falk D, Froese N, Sade DS, Dudek BC. 1999. Sex differences in brain/body relationships of rhesus monkeys and humans. *Journal of Human Evolution* 36:233–238.

Feathers JK. 1996. Luminescence dating and modern human origins. *Evolutionary Anthropology* 5:25–36.

Fedje DW, Mackie AP, Wigen RJ, et al. 2005. Kilgii Gwaay: An Early Maritime Site in the South of Haida Gwaii. In *Haida Gwaii: Human History and Environment from the Time of Loon to the Time of the Iron.* (DW Fedje, RW Mathewes, eds.), University of British Columbia Press, Vancouver, BC, pp. 187–203.

Feibel CS. 1999. Tephrostratigraphy and geological context in paleoanthropology. *Evolutionary Anthropology* 8:87–100.

Feibel CS, Brown FH, McDougall I. 1989. Stratigraphic context of fossil hominids from the Omo Group deposits, northern Turkana Basin, Kenya and Ethiopia. *American Journal of Physical Anthropology* 78:595–622.

Feldman MW, Cavalli-Sforza LL. 1989. On the theory of evolution under genetic and cultural transmission with application to the lactose absorption problem. In *Mathematical Evolutionary Theory* (MW Feldman, ed.), pp. 145–173. Princeton University Press, Princeton, NJ.

Ferguson CA. 1964. Baby talk in six languages. *American Anthropologist* 66:103–114.

Fernald A. 1992. Human maternal vocalizations to infants as biologically relevant signals: An evolutionary perspective. In *The Adapted Mind* (JH Barkow, L Cosmides, J Tooby, eds.), pp. 391–428. Oxford University Press, New York.

Fernald A, Taeschner T, Dunn J, et al. 1989. A cross-language study of prosodic modifications in mothers' and fathers' speech to preverbal infants. *Journal of Child Language* 16:477–501.

Finkel T, Holbrook NJ. 2000. Oxidants, oxidative stress and the biology of ageing. *Nature* 408:239–247.

Finlay BL, Darlington RB. 1995. Linked regularities in the development and evolution of mammalian brains. *Science* 268:1578–1584.

Fischbeck KH. 2001. Polyglutamine expansion neurodegenerative disease. *Brain Research Bulletin* 56:161–163.

Fisher H. 1992. *Anatomy of Love.* Fawcett Columbine, New York.

Fisher RA. 1958. *The Genetical Theory of Natural Selection*, 2nd ed. Dover Publications, New York.

Fleagle JG. 1998. *Primate Adaptation and Evolution*, 2nd ed. Academic Press, San Diego, CA.

Fleagle JG, Kay RF. 1987. The phyletic position of the Parapithecidae. *Journal of Human Evolution* 16:483–532.

Fleagle JG, Rosenberger AL, eds. 1990. The platyrrhine fossil record. *Journal of Human Evolution* 19:1–254.

Fleagle JG, Stern JT, Jungers WL, et al. 1981. Climbing: A bio-mechanical link with brachiation and with bipedalism. *Symposia of the Zoological Society of London* 48:359–375.

Fleagle JG, Tejedor MF. 2002. Early platyrrhines of southern South America. In *The Primate Fossil Record* (WC Hartwig, ed.), pp. 161–173. Cambridge University Press, Cambridge.

Foley RA, Lee PC. 1991. Ecology and energetics of encephalization in hominid evolution. *Philosophical Transactions of the Royal Society of London* B 334:223–232.

Fossey D. 1983. *Gorillas in the Mist.* Houghton Mifflin, Boston.

Franciscus RG. 1999. Neandertal nasal structures and upper respiratory tract "specialization." *Proceedings of the National Academy of Sciences* 96:1805–1809.

Franciscus RG. 2003. Internal nasal floor configuration in *Homo* with special reference to the evolution of Neandertal facial form. *Journal of Human Evolution* 44:701–729.

Fratkin E, Roth E, Nathan M. 2004. Pastoral sedentarization and its effects on children's diet, health, and growth among Rendille of northern Kenya. *Human Ecology* 32(5):531–559.

Frayer D, Wolpoff MH, Smith FM, et al. 1993. Theories of modern human origins: The paleontological test. *American Anthropologist* 95:14–50.

Frisancho AR, Baker PT. 1970. Altitude and growth: A study of the patterns of physical growth of a high altitude Peruvian Quechua population. *American Journal of Physical Anthropology* 32:279–292.

Frosk P, Greenberg CR, Tennese AAP, et al. 2005. The most common mutation in FKRP causing limb girdle muscular dystrophy type 2I (LGMD2I) may have occurred only once and is present in Hutterites and other populations. *Human Mutation* 25:38–44.

Fuller BT, Molleson TI, Harris DA, et al. 2006. Isotopic evidence for breastfeeding and possible adult dietary differences from Late/Sub-Roman Britain. *American Journal of Physical Anthropology* 129:45–54.

Furuichi T. 1987. Sexual swelling, receptivity, and grouping of wild pygmy chimpanzee females at Wamba, Zaïre. *Primates* 28:309–318.

Gabunia L, Antón SC, Lordkipanidze D, et al. 2001. Dmanisi and dispersal. *Evolutionary Anthropology* 10:158–170.

Gabunia L, Vekua A, Lordkipanidze D, et al. 2000. Earliest Pleistocene cranial remains from Dmanisi, Republic of Georgia: Taxonomy, geological setting, and age. *Science* 288:1019–1025.

Gagneux P, Wills C, Gerloff U, et al. 1996. Mitochondrial sequences show diverse evolutionary histories of African hominoids. *Proceedings National Academy Sciences* 96:5077–5082.

Gajdusek DC, Gibbs CJ Jr, Alpers M. 1966. Experimental transmission of a kuru-like syndrome to chimpanzees. *Nature* 209:794–796.

Gajdusek DC, Zigas V. 1957. Degenerative disease of the central nervous system in New Guinea: The endemic occurrence of "kuru" in the native population. *New England Journal of Medicine* 257:974–978.

Galdikas BMF. 1985. Subadult male sociality and reproductive tactics among orangutans at Tanjung Putting. *American Journal of Primatology* 8:87–99.

Galdikas BMF, Wood JW. 1990. Birth spacing patterns in humans and apes. *American Journal of Physical Anthropology* 83:185–191.

Galik K, Senut B, Pickford M, et al. 2004. External and internal morphology of the BAR 1002'00 *Orrorin tugenensis* femur. *Nature* 305:1450–1453.

Gambier D. 1989. Fossil hominids from the early Upper Paleolithic (Aurignacian) of France. In *The Human Revolution: Behavioral and Biological Perspectives on the Origins of Modern Humans* (P Mellars, C Stringer, eds.), pp. 194–211. Princeton University Press, Princeton, NJ.

Ganzhorn HU, Kappeler PM. 1993. *Lemur Social Systems and Their Ecological Basis*. Plenum, New York.

Garber PA. 1989. Role of spatial memory in primate foraging patterns: *Saguinus mystax* and *Saguinus fuscicollis*. *American Journal of Primatology* 19:203–216.

Garber P. 1997. One for all and breeding for one: Cooperation and competition as a tamarin reproductive strategy. *Evolutionary Anthropology* 5:187–199.

Gardner H. 1993. *Frames of Mind: The Theory of Multiple Intelligences*, 2nd ed. Basic Books, New York.

Gargett RH. 1989. Grave shortcomings: The evidence for Neandertal burial. *Current Anthropology* 30:157–190.

Gargett RH. 1999. Middle Paleolithic burial is not a dead issue: The view from Qafzeh, Saint-Césaire, Amud, and Dederiyeh. *Journal of Human Evolution* 37:27–90.

Garner KJ, Ryder OA. 1996. Mitochondrial DNA diversity in gorillas. *Molecular Phylogenetics and Evolution* 6:39–48.

Gautier-Hion A, Quris R, Gautier JP. 1983. Monospecific vs. polyspecific life: A comparative study of foraging and antipredatory tactics in a community of *Cercopithecus* monkeys. *Behavioral Ecology and Sociobiology* 12:325–335.

Gazzaniga MS, Ivry RB, Mangun GR. 1998. *Cognitive Neuroscience: The Biology of the Mind*. Norton, New York.

Gebo DL. 1996. Climbing, brachiation, and terrestrial quadrupedalism: Historical precursors of hominid bipedalism. *American Journal of Physical Anthropology* 101:55–92.

Gebo DL, MacLatchy L, Kityo R, et al. 1997. A hominoid genus from the early Miocene of Uganda. *Science* 276:401–404.

Gerber LM, Crews DE. 1999. Evolutionary perspectives on chronic degenerative diseases. In *Evolutionary Medicine* (WR Trevathan, EO Smith, JJ McKenna, eds.), pp. 443–469. Oxford University Press, Oxford.

Gibbons A. 1991. Déjà vu all over again: Chimp-language wars. *Science* 251:1561–1562.

Giedd JN, Blumenthal J, Jeffries NO, et al. 1999. Brain development during adolescence: A longitudinal MRI study. *Nature Neuroscience* 2:861–863.

Gingerich PD. 1976. Cranial anatomy and evolution of early Tertiary Plesiadapidae (Mammalia, Primates). *Museum of Paleontology, University of Michigan, Papers on Paleontology* 15:1–140.

Gislén A, Dacke M, Kröger RHH, et al. 2003. Superior underwater vision in a human population of sea gypsies. *Current Biology* 13:833–836.

Glander KE, Wright PC, Seigler DS, Randrianasolo VB. 1989. Consumption of cyanogenic bamboo by a newly discovered species of bamboo lemur. *American Journal of Primatology* 19:119–124.

Gleason TM, Norconk MA. 2002. Predation risk and antipredator adaptation in white-faced sakis, *Pithecia pithecia*. In *Eat or Be Eaten: Predation Sensitive Foraging among Primates* (LE Miller, ed.), pp. 169–186. Cambridge University Press, Cambridge.

Godfrey LR, Jungers WL. 2002. Quaternary fossil lemurs. In *The Primate Fossil Record* (WC Hartwig, ed.), pp. 97–121. Cambridge University Press, Cambridge.

Godinot M, Dagosto M. 1983. The astragalus of *Necrolemur* (Primates, Microchoerinae). *Journal of Paleontology* 57:1321–1324.

Goldberg A, Wrangham RW. 1997. Genetic correlates of social behaviour in chimpanzees: Evidence from mitochondrial DNA. *Animal Behaviour* 54:559–570.

Goldberg E. 2001. *The Executive Brain: Frontal Lobes and the Civilized Mind*. Oxford University Press, New York.

Goldberg P, Weiner S, Bar-Yosef O, Xu Q, Liu J. 2001. Site formation processes of Zhoukoudian, China. *Journal of Human Evolution* 41:483–530.

Goldfarb LG. 2002. Kuru: The old epidemic in a new mirror. *Microbes and Infection* 4:875–882.

Goldsmith ML. 1999. Ranging behavior of a lowland gorilla (*Gorilla g. gorilla*) group at Bai Hokou, Central African Republic. *International Journal of Primatology* 20:1–23.

Golovanova LV, Hoffecker JF, Kharitonov VM, Romanova GP. 1999. Mezmaiskaya Cave: A Neanderthal occupation in the northern Caucasus. *Current Anthropology* 40:77–86.

Goodall J. 1963. Feeding behaviour of wild chimpanzees: A preliminary report. *Symposium of the Zoological Society of London* 10:39–48.

Goodall J. 1968. Behaviour of free-living chimpanzees of the Gombe Stream area. *Animal Behaviour Monographs* 1:163–311.

Goodall J. 1968. *In the Shadow of Man*. National Geographic Society, Washington, DC.

Goodall J. 1986. *The Chimpanzees of Gombe: Patterns of Behavior*. Harvard University Press, Cambridge, MA.

Goodman M. 1962. Immunochemistry of the primates and primate evolution. *Annals of the New York Academy of Sciences* 102:219–234.

Goodman M. 1963. Serological analysis of the systematics of recent hominoids. *Human Biology* 35:377–436.

Goodman M. 1999. The genomic record of humankind's evolutionary roots. *American Journal of Human Genetics* 64:31–39.

Goodman M, Porter CA, Czelusniak J, et al. 1998. Toward a phylogenetic classification of primates based on DNA evidence complemented by fossil evidence. *Molecular Phylogenetics and Evolution* 9:585–598.

Goodman SM, O'Connor S, Langrand O. 1993. A review of predation on lemurs: Implications for the evolution of social behavior in small, nocturnal primates. In *Lemur Social Systems and Their Ecological Basis* (PM Kappeler, JU Ganzhorn, eds.), pp. 51–66. Plenum, New York.

Gossett TF. 1965. *Race: The History of an Idea in America*. Schocken Books, New York.

Gottesman II, Shields J. 1982. *Schizophrenia: The Epigenetic Puzzle*. Cambridge University Press, Cambridge.

Gould L, Sussman RW, Sauther, ML. 1999. Natural disasters and primate populations. The effects of a two-year drought on a naturally occurring population of ring-tailed lemurs (*Lemur catta*) in Southwestern Madagascar. *International Journal of Primatology* 20: 69–84.

Gould L, Sussman RW, Sauther ML. 2003. Demographic and life-history patterns in a population of ringtailed lemurs (*Lemur catta*) at Beza Mahafaly Reserve, Madagascar: a 15-year perspective. *American Journal of Physical Anthropology* 120:182–194.

Gould SJ, Lewontin RC. 1979. The spandrels of San Marco and the Panglossian paradigm. *Proceedings of the Royal Society of London* B 205:581–598.

Grant PR. 1986. *Ecology and Evolution of Darwin's Finches*. Princeton University Press, Princeton, NJ.

Gravlee CC, Bernard HR, Leonard WR. 2003. Heredity, environment, and cranial form: A reanalysis of Boas's immigrant data. *American Anthropologist* 105:125–138.

Groves C. 2001. *Primate Taxonomy*. Smithsonian Institution Press, Washington, DC.

Grün R, Huang PH, Huang W, et al. 1998. ESR and U-series analyses of teeth from the paleoanthropological site of Hexian, Anhui Province, China. *Journal of Human Evolution* 34:555–564.

Grün R, Huang PH, Wu X, et al. 1997. ESR analysis of teeth from the paleoanthropological site of Zhoukoudian, China. *Journal of Human Evolution* 32:83–91.

Grün R, Stringer CB. 1991. Electron spin resonance dating and the evolution of modern humans. *Archaeometry* 33:153–199.

Grün R, Stringer CB, Schwarcz HP. 1991. ESR dating of teeth from Garrod's Tabun Cave collection. *Journal of Human Evolution* 20:231–248.

Guglielmino CR, Desilvesteri A, Berres J. 2000. Probable ancestors of Hungarian ethnic groups: An admixture analysis. *Annals of Human Genetics* 64:145–159.

Gursky S. 1994. Infant care in the spectral tarsier (*Tarsius spectrum*) Sulawesi, Indonesia. *International Journal of Primatology* 15:843–853.

Gursky S. 1995. Group size and composition in the spectral tarsier, *Tarsius spectrum:* Implications for social organization. *Tropical Biodiversity* 3:57–62.

Haile-Selassie Y, Asfaw B, White TD. 2004. Hominid cranial remains from Upper Pleistocene deposits at Aduma, Middle Awash, Ethiopia. *American Journal of Physical Anthropology* 123:1–10.

Haile-Selassie Y, White T, Suwa G. 2004. Late Miocene teeth from Middle Awash Ethiopia and early hominid dental evolution. *Science* 303:1503–1505.

Haller JS. 1970. The species problem: Nineteenth-century concepts of racial inferiority in the origin of man controversy. *American Anthropologist* 72:1321–1329.

Hamilton WD. 1964. The genetical evolution of social behaviour, I and II. *Journal of Theoretical Biology* 7:1–52.

Hammer MF, Redd AJ, Wood ET, et al. 2000. Jewish and Middle Eastern non-Jewish populations share a common pool of Y-chromosome biallelic haplotypes. *Proceedings of the National Academy of Sciences* 97:6769–6774.

Hansson GC. 1988. Cystic fibrosis and chloride-secreting diarrhoea. *Nature* 333:711.

Harcourt AH. 1978. Strategies of emigration and transfer by primates, with particular reference to gorillas. *Zeitschrift für Tierpsychologie* 48:401–420.

Harding RM, Fullerton SM, Griffiths RC, et al. 1997. Archaic African and Asian lineages in the genetic ancestry of modern humans. *American Journal of Human Genetics* 60:772–789.

Hardy GH. 1908. Mendelian proportions in a mixed population. *Science* 28:49–50.

Harpending HC, Batzer MA, Gurven M, et al. 1998. Genetic traces of ancient demography. *Proceedings of the National Academy of Sciences* 95:1961–1967.

Harpending H, Rogers A. 2000. Genetic perspectives on human origins and differentiation. *Annual Review in Genomics and Human Genetics* 1:361–385.

Harrison GA, Tanner JM, Pilbeam DR, Baker PT. 1988. *Human Biology*, 3rd ed. Oxford University Press, Oxford.

Harrison T, Gu Y. 1999. Taxonomy and phylogenetic relationships of early Miocene catarrhines from Sihong, China. *Journal of Human Evolution* 37:225–277.

Hartwig WC. 1994. Patterns, puzzles and perspectives on platyrrhine origins. In *Integrative Paths to the Past: Paleoanthropological Essays in Honor of F. Clark Howell* (RS Corruccini, RL Ciochon, eds.), pp. 69–94. Prentice Hall, Englewood Cliffs, NJ.

Harvey P, Martin RD, Clutton-Brock TH. 1987. Life histories in comparative perspective. In *Primate Societies* (BB Smuts, DL Cheney, RM Seyfarth, RW Wrangham, TT Struhsaker, eds.), pp. 181–196. University of Chicago Press, Chicago.

Hassold T, Hunt P. 2001. To err (meiotically) is human: The genesis of human aneuploidy. *Nature Reviews: Genetics* 3:280–291.

Hauser MD, Sulkowski GM. 2001. Can rhesus monkeys spontaneously subtract? *Cognition* 79:239–262.

Hausfater G. 1975. Dominance and reproduction in baboons (*Papio cynocephalus*). In *Contributions to Primatology*, vol. 7. Karger, Basel.

Hawkes K. 2003. Grandmothers and the evolution of human longevity. *American Journal of Human Biology* 15:380–400.

Hawkes K, O'Connell JF, Blurton Jones NG. 1997. Hadza women's time allocation, offspring production, and the evolution of long postmenopausal life spans. *Current Anthropology* 38:551–577.

Hawkes K, O'Connell JF, Blurton Jones NG. 2001. Hadza meat sharing. *Evolution and Human Behavior* 22:113–142.

Health Canada. 2000. *Diabetes among aboriginals (First Nations, Inuit, and Métis) people in Canada: The evidence.* Ottawa, ON.

Health Canada. 2002. *A report on mental illnesses in Canada.* Ottawa, ON.

Heider ER. 1972. Universals in color naming and memory. *Journal of Experimental Psychology* 93:10–20.

Henshilwood C, d'Errico F, Vanhaeren M, et al. 2004. Middle Stone Age shell beads from South Africa. *Science* 304:404.

Herman-Giddens ME, Slora E, Wasserman RC, et al. 1997. Secondary sexual characteristics and menses in young girls seen in office practice: A study from the Pediatric Research in Office Settings Network. *Pediatrics* 99:505–512.

Herring DA, Saunders SR, Katzenberg MA. 1998. Investigating the weaning process in past populations. *American Journal of Physical Anthropology* 105:425–439.

Hewes GW. 1999. A history of the study of language origins and the gestural primacy hypothesis. In *Handbook of Human Symbolic Evolution* (A Lock, CR Peters, eds.), pp. 571–595. Blackwell, Oxford.

Hey J. 2001. The mind of the species problem. *Trends in Ecology and Evolution* 16:326–329.

Hill EM, Chow K. 2002. Life-history theory and risky drinking. *Addiction* 97:401–413.

Hill EM, Ross L, Low B. 1997. The role of future unpredictability in human risk-taking. *Human Nature* 8:287–325.

Hill K, Hurtado AM. 1991. The evolution of premature reproductive senescence and menopause in human females: An evaluation of the "grandmother hypothesis." *Human Nature* 2:313–350.

Hill K, Hurtado AM. 1996. Aché Life History: The Ecology and Demography of a Foraging People. Aldine de Gruyter, New York.

Hill K, Kaplan H. 1993. On why male foragers hunt and share food. *Current Anthropology* 34:701–706.

Hirszfeld L, Hirszfeld H. 1919. Essai d'application des methods au problème des races. *Anthropologie* 29:505–537.

Hladik CM. 1975. Ecology, diet and social patterns in Old and New World Primates. In *Socioecology and Psychology of Primates* (RH Tuttle, ed.), pp. 3–35. Mouton, The Hague.

Hocket CF. 1960. The origin of speech. *Scientific American* 203:88–111.

Hodgen MT. 1964. *Early Anthropology in the Sixteenth and Seventeenth Centuries.* University of Pennsylvania Press, Philadelphia.

Hofman M. 1988. Size and shape of the cerebral cortex. II. The cortical volume. *Brain, Behavior and Evolution* 32:17–26.

Hohmann G, Fruth B. 1993. Field observations on meat sharing among bonobos (*Pan paniscus*). *Folia Primatologica* 60:225–229.

Holick MF, MacLaughlin JA, Doppelt SH. 1981. Regulation of cutaneous previtamin D3 photosynthesis in man: Skin pigment is not an essential regulator. *Science* 211:590–593.

Holliday TW. 1995. Body size and proportions in the late Pleistocene western Old World and the origins of modern humans. PhD dissertation, University of New Mexico, Albuquerque.

Holloway RL. 1968. The evolution of the primate brain: Some aspects of quantitative relations. *Brain Research* 7:121–172.

Holloway RL. 1976. Paleoneurological evidence for language origins. *Annals of the New York Academy of Sciences* 280:330–348.

Holloway RL. 1980. Within-species brain–body weight variability: A reexamination of the Danish data and other primate species. *American Journal of Physical Anthropology* 53:109–121.

Holloway RL. 1981. Revisiting the South African Taung australopithecine endocast: The position of the lunate sulcus as determined by stereoplotting technique. *American Journal of Physical Anthropology* 56:43–58.

Holloway RL. 1984. The poor brain of *Homo sapiens neanderthalensis:* See what you please. In *Ancestors: The Hard Evidence* (E Delson, ed.), pp. 319–324. Alan R. Liss, New York.

Holloway RL. 1984. The Taung endocast and the lunate sulcus: A rejection of the hypothesis of its anterior position. *American Journal of Physical Anthropology* 64:285–287.

Holloway RL. 1991. On Falk's 1989 accusations regarding Holloway's study of the Taung endocast: A reply. *American Journal of Physical Anthropology* 84:87–88.

Holloway RL. 1999. Evolution of the human brain. In *Handbook of Human Symbolic Evolution* (A Lock, CR Peters, eds.), pp. 74–125. Blackwell, Oxford.

Holloway RL, de LaCoste-Lareymondie MC. 1982. Brain endocast asymmetry in pongids and hominids: Some preliminary findings on the paleontology of cerebral dominance. *American Journal of Physical Anthropology* 58:101–110.

Holloway RL, Kimbel WH. 1986. Endocast morphology of Hadar hominid AL 162-28. *Nature* 321:536–537.

Hollox EJ, Poulter M, Zvarik M, et al. 2001. Lactase haplotype diversity in the Old World. *American Journal of Human Genetics* 68:160–172.

Hooton EA. 1916. The relation of physical anthropology to medical science. *Medical Review of Reviews* April:260–264.

Hooton EA. 1946. *Up from the Ape*, rev. ed. Macmillan, New York.

Hovers E, Ilani S, Bar-Yosef O, Vandermeersch B. 2003. An early case of color symbolism: Ochre use by modern humans in Qafzeh Cave. *Current Anthropology* 44:491–522.

Hovers E, Kimbel WH, Rak Y. 2000. The Amud 7 skeleton: Still a burial. Response to Gargett. *Journal of Human Evolution* 39:253–260.

Howell FC. 1964. Pleistocene glacial ecology and the evolution of "classic Neandertal" man. *Southwestern Journal of Anthropology* 8:377–410.

Howell FC. 1966. Observations on the earlier phases of the European Lower Paleolithic. *American Anthropologist* 68:111–140.

Howell FC. 1994. A chronostratigraphic and taxonomic framework of the origins of modern humans. In *Origins of Anatomically Modern Humans* (MH Nitecki, DV Nitecki, eds.), pp. 253–319. Plenum, New York.

Howell WM, Calder PC, Grimble RF. 2002. Gene polymorphisms, inflammatory diseases and cancer. *Proceedings of the Nutritional Society* 61:447–456.

Howells WW. 1973. *Cranial Variation in Man.* Papers of the Peabody Museum, Cambridge, MA.

Hrdy SB. 1977. *The Langurs of Abu.* Harvard University Press, Cambridge, MA.

Hrdy SB, Whitten PL. 1987. Patterning of sexual activity. In *Primate Societies* (BB Smuts, DL Cheney, RM Seyfarth, RW Wrangham, TT Struhsaker, eds.), pp. 370–384. University of Chicago Press, Chicago.

Hublin JJ. 1985. Human fossils from the North African Middle Pleistocene and the origin of *Homo sapiens.* In *Ancestors: The Hard Evidence* (E Delson, ed.), pp. 283–288. Alan R. Liss, New York.

Hublin JJ, Spoor F, Braun M, et al. 1996. A late Neanderthal associated with Upper Paleolithic artefacts. *Nature* 381:224–226.

Hudjashov J, Kivisild T, Underhill PA, et al. 2007. Revealing the prehistoric settlement of Australia by Y chromosome and mtDNA analysis. *Proceedings of the National Academy of Sciences* 104(21):8726–8730.

Hunt KD. 1996. The postural feeding hypothesis: An ecological model for the evolution of bipedalism. *South African Journal of Science* 92:77–90.

Hurford JR. 1991. The evolution of the critical period for language acquisition. *Cognition* 40:159–201.

Huxley J, Kettlewell HBD. 1965. *Charles Darwin and His World.*

Huxley J, Mayr E, Osmond H, Hoffer A. 1964. Schizophrenia as a genetic morphism. *Nature* 204:220–221.

Ingman M, Kaessmann H, Pääbo S, Gyllensten U. 2000. Mitochondrial genome variation and the origin of modern humans. *Nature* 408:708–713.

Irons W. 1979. Cultural and biological success. In *Evolutionary Biology and Human Social Behavior* (NA Chagnon, W Irons, eds.), pp. 257–272. Duxbury Press, North Scituate, MA.

Irwin G. 1992. *The Prehistoric Exploration and Colonisation of the Pacific.* Cambridge University Press, New York.

Isaac GL. 1978. The food-sharing behavior of protohuman hominids. *Scientific American* 238:90–108.

Isbell L, Young T. 1996. The evolution of bipedalism in hominids and reduced group size in chimpanzees: Alternative responses to decreasing resource availability. *Journal of Human Evolution* 30:389–397.

Ishida H, Pickford M. 1997. A new late Miocene hominoid from Kenya: *Samburupithecus kiptalami* gen et sp. nov. *Comptes Rendus de l'Academie des Sciences de Paris* 325:823–829.

Jablensky A, Sartorius N, Ernberg G, et al. 1992. Schizophrenia: Manifestations, incidence and course in different cultures: A World Health Organization Ten-Country Study. *Psychological Medicine* 20(suppl.):1–97.

Jablonski NG, Chaplin G. 1993. Origin of habitual terrestrial bipedalism in the ancestor of the Hominidae. *Journal of Human Evolution* 24:259–280.

Jablonski NG, Chaplin G. 2000. The evolution of human skin coloration. *Journal of Human Evolution* 39:57–106.

Jablonski NG, Chaplin G. 2002. Skin deep. *Scientific American* 287:74–81.

Jackendoff R. 1994. *Patterns in the Mind: Language and Human Nature.* Basic Books, New York.

Jackson FLC. 2000. Human adaptations to infectious disease. In *Human Biology: An Evolutionary and Biocultural Perspective* (S Stinson, B Bogin, R Huss-Ashmore, D O'Rourke, eds.), pp. 273–293. Wiley-Liss, New York.

Janson CH. 1985. Aggressive competition and individual food consumption in wild brown capuchin monkeys (*Cebus apella*). *Behavioral Ecology and Sociobiology* 18:125–138.

Janson CH, Goldsmith ML. 1995. Predicting group size in primates: Foraging costs and predation risks. *Behavioral Ecology* 6:326–336.

Jantz RL, Owsley DW. 2001. Variation among early North American crania. *American Journal of Physical Anthropology* 114:146–155.

Jarman PJ. 1974. The social organization of antelope in relation to their ecology. *Behaviour* 48:215–267.

Jeffreys AJ, Wilson V, Thein SL. 1985. Hypervariable "minisatellite" regions in human DNA. *Nature* 314:67–73.

Jensen-Seaman M, Kidd KK. 2001. Mitochondrial variation and biogeography of eastern gorillas. *Molecular Ecology* 10:2240–2247.

Jerison HJ. 1991. Brain size and the evolution of mind. In *59th James Arthur Lecture on the Evolution of the Human Brain, 1989*. Columbia University Press, New York.

Jobling MA, Tyler-Smith C. 2003. The human Y chromosome: An evolutionary marker comes of age. *Nature Reviews Genetics* 4:598–612.

Johannsen W. 1911. The genotype conception of heredity. *American Naturalist* 45:129–159.

Johanson D, Edey M. 1981. *Lucy: The Beginnings of Humankind*. Simon & Schuster, New York.

Johanson DC, Lovejoy CO, Kimbel WH, et al. 1982. Morphology of the Pliocene partial hominid skeleton (AL 288-1) from the Hadar Formation, Ethiopia. *American Journal of Physical Anthropology* 57:403–452.

Johanson DC, Taieb M. 1976. Plio-Pleistocene hominid discoveries in Hadar, Ethiopia. *Nature* 260:293–297.

Johanson DC, White TD. 1979. A systematic assessment of early African hominids. *Science* 202:321–330.

Johnson AL, Lovell NC. 1994. Biological differentiation at Predynastic Naqada, Egypt: An analysis of dental morphological traits. *American Journal of Physical Anthropology* 93:427–433.

Jolly CJ. 1970. The seed-eaters: A new model of hominid differentiation based on a baboon analogy. *Man* 5:1–26.

Jones FW. 1916. *Arboreal Man*. Edward Arnold, London.

Jordan P. 1999. *Neanderthal*. Sutton Publishing, Phoenix Mill, Gloucestershire.

Judd MA. 2004. Trauma in the city of Kerma: ancient versus modern injury patterns. *International Journal of Osteoarchaeology* 14:34–51.

Judd MA. 2006. Continuity of interpersonal violence between Nubian communities. *American Journal of Physical Anthropology* 131:432–433.

Kaessmann H, Heissig F, von Haeseler A, Pääbo S. 1999. DNA sequence variation in a non-coding region of low recombination on the human X chromosome. *Nature Genetics* 22:78–81.

Kandel ER, Schwartz JH, Jessell TM. 2000. *Principles of Neural Science*, 4th ed. McGraw-Hill, New York.

Kano T. 1992. *The Last Ape*. Stanford University Press, Stanford, CA.

Kaplan H, Hill K, Lancaster J, Hurtado AM. 2000. A theory of human life history evolution: Diet, intelligence, and longevity. *Evolutionary Anthropology* 9:156–185.

Kappelman J. 1996. The evolution of body mass and relative brain size in hominids. *Journal of Human Evolution* 30:243–276.

Karn MN, Penrose LS. 1951. Birth weight and gestation time in relation to maternal age, parity, and infant survival. *Annals of Eugenics* 16:147–161.

Katzman MA, Lee S. 1997. Beyond body image: The integration of feminist and transcultural theories in the understanding of self starvation. *International Journal of Eating Disorders* 22:385–394.

Kay P, Berlin B. 1997. Science imperialism: There are nontrivial constraints on color naming. *Behavioral and Brain Science* 20:196–201.

Keith A. 1923. Man's posture: Its evolution and disorders. *British Medical Journal* 1:451–454, 499–502, 545–548, 587–590, 624–626, 669–672.

Keith A. 1940. Blumenbach's centenary. *Man* 40:82–85.

Kennedy KA, Sonakia A, Chiment J, Verma KK. 1991. Is the Narmada hominid an Indian *Homo erectus*? *American Journal of Physical Anthropology* 86:475–496.

Kessler RC, Berglund P, Demler O, et al. 2003. The epidemiology of major depressive disorder. *Journal of the American Medical Association* 289:3095–3105.

Kevles DJ. 1985. *In the Name of Eugenics*. Alfred A. Knopf, New York.

Kidd K. 1975. On the magnitude of selective forces maintaining schizophrenia in the population. In *Genetic Research in Psychiatry* (R Fieve, D Rosenthal, H Brill, eds.), pp. 135–145. Johns Hopkins University Press, Baltimore.

Kimbel WH, Rak Y, Johanson DC. 2004. *The Skull of* Australopithecus afarensis. Oxford University Press, New York.

Kirch PV. 2001. *On the Road of the Winds: An Archaeological History of the Pacific Islands before European Contact*. University of California Press, Berkeley.

Kirkpatrick M. 1982. Sexual selection and the evolution of female choice. *Evolution* 36:1–12.

Kirkpatrick RC. 1998. Ecology and behavior of the snub-nosed and douc langurs. In *The Natural History of the Doucs and Snub-Nosed Langurs* (NG Jablonski, ed.), pp. 155–190. World Scientific, Singapore.

Kirkwood TBL. 2002. Evolution theory and the mechanisms of aging. In *Brocklehursts' Textbook of Geriatric Medicine and Gerontology*, 6th ed. (R Tallis, HM Fillit, eds.), pp. 31–35. Churchhill Livingstone, Edinburgh and New York.

Kirkwood TBL, Austad SN. 2000. Why do we age? *Nature* 408:233–238.

Klaus MH, Kennell JH. 1997. The doula: An essential ingredient of childbirth revisited. *Acta Paediatrica* 86:1034–1036.

Klein RG, Edgar B. 2002. *The Dawn of Human Culture*. Wiley, New York.

Klug WS, Cummings MR. 2003. *Concepts of Genetics*. Prentice Hall, Upper Saddle River, NJ.

Knott CD. 1998. Social system dynamics, ranging patterns, and male and female strategies in wild Bornean orangutans (*Pongo pygmaeus*). *American Journal of Physical Anthropology* 26(suppl.):140.

Koda Y, Tachida H, Liu Y, et al. 2001. Contrasting patterns of polymorphisms at the ABO-secretor gene

(FUT2) and plasma (1,3)fucosyltransferase gene (FUT6) in human populations, pp. 747–756.

Kornberg A. 1960. Biological synthesis of DNA. *Science* 131:1503–1508.

Kostianovsky M. 2000. Evolutionary origin of eukaryotic cells. *Ultrastructural Pathology* 24:59–66.

Krings M, Capelli C, Tschentscher F, et al. 2000. A view of Neandertal genetic diversity. *Nature Genetics* 26:144–146.

Krings M, Geisert H, Schmitz RW, et al. 1999. DNA sequence of the mitochondrial hypervariable region II from the Neandertal type specimen. *Proceedings of the National Academy of Sciences* 96:5581–5585.

Krings M, Stone A, Schmitz RW, et al. 1997. Neandertal DNA sequences and the origin of modern humans. *Cell* 90:19–30.

Kuhn SL, Stiner MC. 2006. What's a Mother to Do? The division of labor among Neandertals and modern humans in Eurasia. *Current Anthropology* 47(6):953–980.

Kummer H. 1968. *Social Organization of Hamadryas Baboons*. University of Chicago Press, Chicago.

Lahdenpera M, Lummaa V, Helle S, et al. 2004. Fitness benefits of prolonged post-reproductive lifespan in women. *Nature* 428:178–181.

Laidlaw SA, Kopple JD. 1987. Newer concepts of the indispensable amino acids. *American Journal of Clinical Nutrition* 46:593–605.

Laitman J. 1984. The anatomy of human speech. *Natural History* 92:20–27.

Laitman JT, Heimbuch RC. 1982. The basicranium of Plio-Pleistocene hominids as an indicator of their upper respiratory systems. *American Journal of Physical Anthropology* 59:323–343.

Laitman JT, Reidenberg JS. 1988. Advances in understanding the relationship between skull base and larynx, with comments on the origins of speech. *Human Evolution* 3:101–111.

Lalueza C, Perez-Perez A, Turbon D. 1996. Dietary inferences through buccal microwear analysis of middle and upper Pleistocene human fossils. *American Journal of Physical Anthropology* 100:367–387.

Larick R, Ciochon RL, Zaim Y, et al. 2001. Early Pleistocene $^{40}Ar/^{39}Ar$ ages for Bapang Formation hominids, Central Java, Indonesia. *Proceedings of the National Academy of Science* 98:4866–4871.

Larsen CS, ed. 2002. *Bioarchaeology of Spanish Florida: The Impact of Colonialism*. University Press of Florida, Gainesville, FL.

Larsen CS, Milner GR. 1993. *In the Wake of Contact: Biological Responses to Conquest*. Wiley-Liss, New York.

Larsen CS, Matter RM, Gebo DL. 1998. *Human Origins: The Fossil Record*, 3rd ed. Waveland Press, Prospect Heights, IL.

Larson E. 1997. Summer of the Gods: The Scopes Trial and America's Continuing Debate over Science and Religion. Harvard University Press, Cambridge, MA.

Larson E. 2001. Evolution's Workshop: God and Science on the Galapagos Islands. Basic Books, New York.

Latimer B, Ward C. 1993. The thoracic and lumbar vertebrae. In *The Nariokotome* Homo erectus *Skeleton* (A Walker, R Leakey, eds.), pp. 266–293. Harvard University Press, Cambridge, MA.

***Homo erectus* Skeleton** (A Walker, R Leakey, eds.), pp. 266–293. *Harvard University Press*, Cambridge, MA.

Leakey LSB. 1959. A new fossil skull from Olduvai. *Nature* 184:491–493.

Leakey LSB. 1962. A new lower Pliocene fossil primate from Kenya. *Annals of the Magazine of Natural History* 4:689–696.

Leakey MG, Feibel CS, McDougall I, Walker A. 1995. New four-million-year-old hominid species from Kanapoi and Allia Bay, Kenya. *Nature* 376:565–571.

Leakey MG, Spoor F, Brown FH, et al. 2001. New hominid genus from eastern Africa shows diverse middle Pliocene lineages. *Nature* 410:433–440.

Leakey MG, Spoor F, Brown FH, et al. 2003. A new hominid calvaria from Ileret (Kenya). *American Journal of Physical Anthropology* 36(suppl.):136.

Leakey R, Lewin R. 1978. *People of the Lake: Mankind and Its Beginnings*. Doubleday, New York.

LeBlanc S, Register K. 2003. *Constant Battles: The Myth of the Peaceful, Noble Savage*. St. Martin's Press, New York.

Ledoux J. 1996. *The Emotional Brain*. Touchstone, New York.

Lee RB, DeVore I, eds. 1968. *Man the Hunter*. Aldine, Chicago.

Lee-Thorp JA, van der Merwe NJ, Brain CK. 1994. Diet of *Australopithecus robustus* at Swartkrans from stable carbon isotope analysis. *Journal of Human Evolution* 27:361–372.

Le Gros Clark WE, Thomas DP. 1952. The Miocene lemuroids of East Africa. *Fossil Mammals of Africa* 5:1–20.

Leigh SR. 1992. Cranial capacity evolution in *Homo erectus* and early *Homo sapiens*. *American Journal of Physical Anthropology* 87:1–13.

Leighton M. 1993. Molding diet selectivity by Bornean orangutans: Evidence for integration of multiple criteria for fruit selection. *International Journal of Primatology* 14:257–313.

LeMay M. 1985. Asymmetries of the brains and skulls of non-human primates. In *Cerebral Lateralization in Nonhuman Species* (SD Glick, ed.), pp. 233–245. Academic Press, Orlando, FL.

Leonard WR, Robertson ML. 1997. Rethinking the energetics of bipedality. *Current Anthropology* 38:304–309.

Li T, Etler DA. 1992. New Middle Pleistocene hominid crania from Yunxian in China. *Nature* 357:484–487.

Lieberman P. 1984. *The Biology and Evolution of Language*. Harvard University Press, Cambridge, MA.

Lieberman P. 1991. Uniquely Human: The Evolution of Speech, Thought, and Selfless Behavior. Harvard University Press, Cambridge, MA.

Lifton RJ. 1986. *The Nazi Doctors*. Basic Books, New York.

Lindee MS. 2000. Genetic disease since 1945. *Nature Reviews Genetics* 1:236–241.

Lindenbaum S. 2001. Kuru, prions, and human affairs: Thinking about epidemics. *Annual Review in Anthropology* 30:363–385.

Littlefield A, Lieberman L, Reynolds LT. 1982. Redefining race: The potential demise of a concept in physical anthropology. *Current Anthropology* 23:641–655.

Livingstone FB. 1958. Anthropological implications of sickle cell gene distribution in West Africa. *American Anthropologist* 60:533–562.

Ljung BO, Bergsten-Brucefors A, Lindgren G. 1974. The secular trend in physical growth in Sweden. *Annals of Human Biology* 1:245–256.

Loomis WF. 1967. Skin-pigment regulation of vitamin D biosynthesis in man. *Science* 157:501–506.

Lovejoy CO. 1978. A biomechanical review of the locomotor diversity of early hominids. In *Early Hominids of Africa* (CJ Jolly, ed.), pp. 403–429. St. Martin's, New York.

Lovejoy CO. 1988. The evolution of human walking. *Scientific American* 259:118–125.

Lovejoy OW. 1981. The origin of man. *Science* 211:341–350.

Low BS. 2000. *Why Sex Matters*. Princeton University Press, Princeton, NJ.

Lowe JJ, Walker MJC. 1997. *Reconstructing Quaternary Environments*, 2nd ed. Prentice Hall, Essex, England.

Ludwig KR, Renne PR. 2000. Geochronology on the paleoanthropological time scale. *Evolutionary Anthropology* 9:101–110.

MacDorman MF, Minino AM, Strobino DM, Guyer B. 2002. Annual summary of vital statistics: 2001. *Pediatrics* 110:1037–1052.

Mackintosh NJ. 1998. *IQ and Human Intelligence*. Oxford University Press, Oxford.

MacLatchy L, Gebo D, Kityo R, Pilbeam D. 2000. Postcranial functional morphology of *Morotopithecus bishopi*, with implications for the evolution of modern ape locomotion. *Journal of Human Evolution* 39:159–183.

Maggioncalda AN, Sapolsky RM, Czekala NM. 1999. Reproductive hormone profiles in captive male orangutans: Implications for understanding development arrest. *American Journal of Physical Anthropology* 109:19–32.

Malenky RK, Kuroda S, Vineberg EO, Wrangham RW. 1994. The significance of terrestrial herbaceous foods for bonobos, chimpanzees and gorillas. In *Chimpanzee Cultures* (RW Wrangham, WC McGrew, FB de Waal, PG Heltne, eds.), pp. 59–75. Harvard University Press, Cambridge, MA.

Mandryk C. 1992. Paleoecologist finds corridor ice-free but forbidding. *Mammoth Trumpet March* 1992.

Maples WR, Browning M. 1994. *Dead Men Do Tell Tales*. Broadway Books, New York.

Marcus G. 2004. *The Birth of the Mind*. Basic Books, New York.

Marean C. 1989. Sabertooth cats and their relevance for early hominid diet. *Journal of Human Evolution* 18:559–582.

Marean CW, Assefa Z. 1999. Zooarcheological evidence for the faunal exploitation behavior of Neandertals and early modern humans. *Evolutionary Anthropology* 8:22–37.

Marks J. 1992. Chromosomal evolution in primates. In *The Cambridge Encyclopedia of Human Evolution* (S Jones, R Martin, D Pilbeam, eds.), pp. 298–302. Cambridge University Press, Cambridge.

Marks J, Schmid CW, Sarich VM. 1988. DNA hybridization as a guide to phylogeny: Relations of the Hominoidea. *Journal of Human Evolution* 17:769–786.

Marshack A. 1996. A Middle Paleolithic symbolic composition from the Golan Heights: The earliest known depictive image. *Current Anthropology* 37:357–365.

Martin RD. 1983. Human brain evolution in an ecological context. In *52nd James Arthur Lecture on the Evolution of the Human Brain, 1982*. Columbia University Press, New York.

Mascie-Taylor CGN. 1993. The biological anthropology of disease. In *The Anthropology of Disease* (CGN Mascie-Taylor, ed.), pp. 1–72. Oxford University Press, Oxford.

Mascie-Taylor CGN, Bogin B, eds. 1995. *Human Variability and Plasticity*. Cambridge University Press, Cambridge.

Matisoo-Smith E, Roberts RM, Allen JS, et al. 1998. Patterns of prehistoric mobility in Polynesia revealed by mitochondrial DNA from the Pacific rat. *Proceedings of the National Academy of Sciences* 95:15145–15150.

Mayr E. 1942. *Systematics and the Origin of Species*. Columbia University Press, New York.

Mayr E. 1963. *Animal Species and Evolution*. Harvard University Press, Cambridge, MA.

Mayr E. 1983. How to carry out the adaptationist program. *American Naturalist* 121:324–334.

Mazurek R. 1999. Back from the dead. *New Scientist* 164:40.

McBrearty S, Brooks AS. 2000. The revolution that wasn't: A new interpretation of the origin of modern human behavior. *Journal of Human Evolution* 39:453–563.

McConkey K. 2005. Sumatran orangutan (*Pongo abelii*). In *World Atlas of Great Apes and Their Conservation*. (J Caldecott, L. Miles eds.). University of California Press, Berkeley, pp. 185–204.

McCown TD, Kennedy KAR, eds. 1971. *Climbing Man's Family Tree*. Prentice Hall, Englewood Cliffs, NJ.

McCracken RD. 1971. Lactase deficiency: An example of dietary evolution. *Current Anthropology* 12:479–517.

McCrossin ML, Benefit BR. 1993. Recently recovered *Kenyapithecus* mandible and its implications for great ape and human origins. *Proceedings of the National Academy of Sciences USA* 90:1962–1966.

McCrossin ML, Benefit BR, Gitau S, Blue KT. 1998. Fossil evidence for the origins of terrestriality among Old World higher primates. In *Primate Locomotion: Recent Advances* (EL Strasser, JG Fleagle, AL Rosenberger, HM McHenry, eds.), pp. 353–396. Plenum, New York.

McDermott F, Grün R, Stringer CB, Hawkesworth CJ. 1993. Mass-spectrometric U-series dates for Israeli Neanderthal/early modern hominid sites. *Nature* 363:252–255.

McDougall I. 1985. K–Ar and $^{40}Ar/^{39}Ar$ dating of the hominid-bearing Pliocene–Pleistocene sequence at Koobi Fora, Lake Turkana, northern Kenya. *Geological Society America Bulletin* 96:159–175.

McElroy A, Townsend PK. 1996. *Medical Anthropology in Ecological Perspective*, 3rd ed. Westview Press, Boulder, CO.

McFadden et al. 1999. Global ecology and biogeography Journal of 8:137–149.

McGrew WC. 1992. *Chimpanzee Material Culture.* Cambridge University Press, Cambridge.

McHenry HM. 1991. Sexual dimorphism in *Australopithecus afarensis. Journal of Human Evolution* 20:21–32.

McHenry HM. 1992. Body size and proportions in early hominids. *American Journal of Physical Anthropology* 87:407–431.

McHenry HM. 1994. Behavioral ecological implications of early hominid body size. *Journal of Human Evolution* 27:77–87.

McHenry HM, Coffing K. 2000. *Australopithecus* to *Homo:* Transformations in body and mind. *Annual Review of Anthropology* 29:125–146.

McKusick VA, Eldridge R, Hostetler JA, Egeland JA. 1964. Dwarfism in the Amish. *Transactions of the Association of American Physicians, Philadelphia* 77:151–168.

McMillan CJ. 2006. Study on Childhood Obesity. Presentation to the House of Common Standing Committee on Health, October 19, 2006. Canadian Medical Association, Ottawa. URL: www.cma.ca/multimedia/cma/content_images/Inside_cma/Submissions/2006/presentation-child-en.pdf.

McNeil WH. 1976. *Plagues and People.* Doubleday, New York.

Meehan JP. 1955. Individual and racial variations in vascular response to cold stimulus. *Military Medicine* 116:330–334.

Meier B, Albibnac R, Peyrieras A, et al. 1987. A new species of Hapalemur (Primates) from South East Madagascar. *Folia Primatologica* 48:211–215.

Meindl RS. 1987. Hypothesis: A selective advantage for cystic fibrosis heterozygotes. *American Journal of Physical Anthropology* 74:39–45.

Mellars P. 2006. Why did modern human populations disperse from Africa ca. 60 000 years ago? A new model. *Proceedings of the National Academy of Sciences* 103(25):9381–9386.

Melnick D, Hoelzer GA. 1996. Genetic consequences of macaque social organization and behavior. In *Evolution and Ecology of Macaque Societies* (JE Fa, DG Lindburg, eds.), pp. 412–442. Cambridge University Press, Cambridge.

Mendel G. 1866. Versuche über Pflanzenhybriden [Experiments in plant hybridization]. *Verhandlungen des Naturforschenden Vereines in Brünn, Bd. IV für das Jahr 1865*, 3–47.

Menzel CR. 1991. Cognitive aspects of foraging in Japanese monkeys. *Animal Behaviour* 41:397–402.

Merrifield R. 2007. *Healthy Weights for Healthy Kids. Report of the Standing Committee for Health, March 2007, 39th Parliament, 1st Session.* House of Commons of Canada, Ottawa, ON. URL: http://cmte.parl.gc.ca/Content/HOC/committee/391/hesa/reports/rp2795145/hesarp07-e.html.

Mettler LE, Gregg TG, Schaffer HE. 1988. *Population Genetics and Evolution.* Prentice Hall, Upper Saddle River, NJ.

Meyer D, Thomson G. 2001. How selection shapes variation of the human major histocompatibility complex: A review. *Annals of Human Genetics* 65:1–26.

Milton K. 1980. The Foraging Strategy of Howler Monkeys: A Study in Primate Economics. Columbia University Press, New York.

Milton K. 1981. Distribution patterns of tropical food plants as a stimulus to primate mental development. *American Anthropologist* 83:534–548.

Milton K. 1982. Dietary quality and demographic regulation in a howler monkey population. In *The Ecology of a Tropical Forest* (EG Leigh, AS Rand, DM Windsor, eds.), pp. 273–289. Smithsonian Institution Press, Washington, DC.

Milton K. 1999. A hypothesis to explain the role of meat-eating in human evolution. *Evolutionary Anthropology* 8:11–21.

Mintz L. 1977. *Historical Geology: The Science of a Dynamic Earth.* Charles E. Merrill, Columbus, OH.

Mitani JC. 1985. Responses of gibbons (*Hylobates muelleri*) to self, neighbor and stranger song duets. *International Journal of Primatology* 6:193–200.

Mitani JC, Gros-Louis J, Manson JH. 1996. Number of males in primate groups: Comparative tests of competing hypotheses. *American Journal of Primatology* 38:315–332.

Mitchell RJ, Hammer MF. 1996. Human evolution and the Y chromosome. *Current Opinion in Genetics and Development* 6:737–742.

Mithen S. 1996. *The Prehistory of the Mind.* Thames and Hudson, London.

Mittermeier RA, Konstant WR, Rylands AB. 2002. Priorities for primate conservation in the first decade of the 21st century. XIXth Congress of International Primatological Society, Beijing, China (abstract).

Molnar S. 2002. *Human Variation*, 5th ed. Prentice Hall, Upper Saddle River, NJ.

Montagu A. 1974. *Man's Most Dangerous Myth: The Fallacy of Race*, 5th ed. Oxford University Press, London.

Moran EF. 2000. *Human Adaptability*, 2nd ed. Westview Press, Boulder, CO.

Morell V. 1995. Ancestral Passions: The Leakey Family and the Quest for Humankind's Beginnings. Simon & Schuster, New York.

Moya-Sola S, Kohler M. 1996. The first *Dryopithecus* skeleton: Origins of great ape locomotion. *Nature* 379:156–159.

Mullis K. 1990. The unusual origins of the polymerase chain reaction. *Scientific American* April:56–65.

Murphy J. 1976. Psychiatric labeling in cross-cultural perspective. *Science* 191:1019–1028.

Murray FG. 1934. Pigmentation, sunlight, and nutritional disease. *American Anthropologist* 36:438–445.

Myrianthopoulos NC, Aronson SM. 1966. Population dynamics of Tay–Sachs disease. I. Reproductive fitness and selection. *American Journal of Human Genetics* 18:313–327.

Nafte M. 2000. *Flesh and Bone: An Introduction to Forensic Anthropology*. Carolina Academic Press, Durham, NC.

Neel JV. 1962. Diabetes mellitus: A thrifty genotype rendered detrimental by "progress"? *American Journal of Human Genetics* 14:353–362.

Neel JV. 1982. The thrifty genotype revisited. In *The Genetics of Diabetes Mellitus* (J Kobberling, R Tattersall, eds.), pp. 283–293. Academic Press, London.

Nesse RM. 1994. An evolutionary perspective on substance abuse. *Ethology and Sociobiology* 15:339–348.

Nesse RM. 2000. Is depression an adaptation? *Archives of General Psychiatry* 57:14–20.

Nesse RM, Berridge KC. 1997. Psychoactive drug use in evolutionary perspective. *Science* 278:63–66.

Nesse RM, Williams GC. 1994. *Why We Get Sick: The New Science of Darwinian Medicine*. Times Books, New York.

Newman RW, Munroe EH. 1955. The relation of climate and body size in U.S. males. *American Journal of Physical Anthropology* 13:1–17.

Newton PN. 1987. The variable social organization of Hanuman langurs (*Presbytis entellus*), infanticide, and the monopolization of females. *International Journal of Primatology* 9:59–77.

Nichter M, Ritenbaugh C, Nichter M, Vuckovic N, Aickin M. 1995. Dieting and "watching" behaviors among adolescent females: Report of a multimethod study. *Journal of Adolescent Health* 17:153–162.

Nielsen S. 2001. Epidemiology and mortality of eating disorders. *Psychiatric Clinics of North America* 24:201–214.

Nimgaonkar VL, Ward SE, Agarde H, et al. 1997. Fertility in schizophrenia: Results from a contemporary US cohort. *Acta Psychiatrica Scandinavica* 95:364–369.

Nishida T. 1990. *The Chimpanzees of the Mahale Mountains*. University of Tokyo Press, Tokyo.

Noble W, Davidson I. 1996. *Human Evolution, Language and Mind*. Cambridge University Press, Cambridge.

Nolte J. 2002. The Human Brain: An Introduction to Its Functional Anatomy, 5th ed. Mosby, St. Louis.

Nordborg M. 1998. On the probability of Neanderthal ancestry. *American Journal of Human Genetics* 63:1237–1240.

Nowak RM, Paradiso JL. 1983. *Walker's Mammals of the World*, 4th ed. John Hopkins University Press, Baltimore.

Oakley K. 1963. Analytical methods of dating bones. In *Science in Archaeology* (D Brothwell, E Higgs, eds.). Basic Books, New York.

O'Connell JF, Hawkes K, Blurton Jones NG. 1992. Patterns in the distribution, site structure, and assemblage composition of Hadza kill-butchering sites. *Journal of Archaeological Science* 19:319–345.

Ogonuki N, Inoue K, Yamamoto Y, et al. 2002. Early death of mice cloned from somatic cells. *Nature Genetics* 30:253–254.

Omran AR. 1971. The epidemiologic transition: A theory of the epidemiology of population change. *Milbank Memorial Fund Quarterly* 49:509–538.

O'Neill A, Fedigan L, Ziegler T. 2004. Ovarian cycle phase and same-sex mating behavior in Japanese macaque females. *American Journal of Primatology* 63(1):25–31.

O'Neill A, Fedigan L, Ziegler T. 2004. The relationship between ovarian cycle phase and sexual behavior in female Japanese macaques. *American Journal of Physical Anthropology* 125(4):352–362.

Online Mendelian Inheritance in Man. 2000. McKusick-Nathans Institute for Genetic Medicine, Johns Hopkins University, Baltimore, and National Center for Biotechnology Information, National Library of Medicine, Bethesda. URL: www.ncbi.nlm.nih.gov/omim/.

Ovchinnikov IV, Götherström A, Romanova GP, et al. 2000. Molecular analysis of Neanderthal DNA from the northern Caucasus. *Nature* 404:490–493.

Paine RR, Mancinelli D, Ruggieri M, Coppa A. 2006. Cranial trauma in iron age Samnite agriculturalists, Alfedena, Italy: implications for biocultural and economic stress. *American Journal of Physical Anthropology* 132:48–58.

Palombit RA. 1994. Extra-pair copulations in a monogamous ape. *Animal Behaviour* 47:721–723.

Panter-Brick C. 2002. Sexual division of labor: Energetic and evolutionary scenarios. *American Journal of Human Biology* 14:627–640.

Parish AR. 1996. Female relationships in bonobos (*Pan paniscus*). *Human Nature* 7:61–96.

Parra EJ, Marcini A, Akey J, et al. 1998. Estimating African American admixture proportions by use of population-specific alleles. *American Journal of Human Genetics* 63:1839–1851.

Partridge TC, Granger DE, Caffee MW, Clarke RJ. 2003. Lower Pliocene hominid remains from Sterkfontein. *Science* 300:607–612.

Paterson HEH. 1986. Environment and species. *South African Journal of Science* 82:62–65.

Paterson JD. 1996. Coming to America: Acclimation in macaque body structures and Bergmann's rule. *International Journal of Primatology* 17:585–611.

Pavelka M, Fedigan L, Zohar S. 2002. Availability and adaptive value of reproductive and postreproductive Japanese macaque mothers and grandmothers. *Animal Behaviour* 64:407–414.

Pavelka MSM, Fedigan LM. 1999. Reproductive termination in female Japanese monkeys: a comparative life history perspective. *American Journal of Physical Anthropology* 109:455–464.

Pavelka MSM, Brusselers O, Nowak D, Behie AM. 2003. Population reduction and social disorganization in *Alouatta pigra* following a hurricane. *International Journal of Primatology* 24:1037–1055.

Pearson OM. 2000. Postcranial remains and the origin of modern humans. *Evolutionary Anthropology* 9:229–247.

Peccei JS. 1995. The origin and evolution of menopause: The altriciality–lifespan hypothesis. *Ethology and Sociobiology* 16:425–449.

Peccei JS. 2001a. A critique of the grandmother hypothesis: Old and new. *American Journal of Human Biology* 13:434–452.

Peccei JS. 2001b. Menopause: Adaptation or epiphenomenon? *Evolutionary Anthropology* 10:43–57.

Peschken CA, Esdaile JM. 1999. Rheumatic diseases in North America's indigenous peoples. *Seminars in Arthritis and Rheumatism* 28:368–391.

Petitto LA, Marentette PF. 1991. Babbling in the manual mode: Evidence for the ontogeny of language. *Science* 251:1493–1496.

Pickford M, Senut B. 2001. "Millennium Ancestor," a 6-million-year-old bipedal hominid from Kenya: Recent discoveries push back human origins by 1.5 million years. *South African Journal of Science* 97:2–22.

Pickford M, Senut B, Gommery D, Treil J. 2002. Bipedalism in *Orrorin tugenensis* revealed by its femora. *Concise Review Papers Paleoevolution* 1:191–203.

Pilbeam D. 1982. New hominoid skull material from the Miocene of Pakistan. *Nature* 295:232–234.

Pinker S. 1994. *The Language Instinct.* HarperPerennial, New York.

Pinker S, Bloom P. 1990. Natural language and natural selection. *Behavioral and Brain Sciences* 13:707–784.

Polimeni J, Reiss JP. 2003. Evolutionary perspectives on schizophrenia. *Canadian Journal of Psychiatry* 48:34–39.

Potts R. 1984. Home bases and early hominids. *American Scientist* 72:338–347.

Potts R. 1988. Early Hominid Activities at Olduvai. Aldine, Chicago.

Pritzker BM. 2000. *A Native American Encyclopedia.* Oxford University Press, New York.

Prowse TL, Lovell NC. 1996. Concordance of cranial and dental morphological traits and evidence for endogamy in ancient Egypt. *American Journal of Physical Anthropology* 101:237–246.

Prowse TL, Schwarcz HP, Garnsey P, et al. 2007. Isotopic Evidence for Age-Related Immigration to Imperial Rome. *American Journal of Physical Anthropology* 132:510–519.

Pusey A, Williams J, Goodall J. 1997. The influence of dominance rank on the reproductive success of female chimpanzees. *Science* 277:828–831.

Radinsky L. 1979. The fossil record of primate brain evolution. In *49th James Arthur Lecture on the Evolution of the Human Brain, 1979.* American Museum of Natural History, New York.

Rak Y, Kimbel WH, Hovers E. 1994. A Neandertal infant from Amucd Cave, Israel. *Journal of Human Evolution* 26:313–324.

Randerson J. 2007. Give us back our bones, pagans tell museums. *The Guardian:* February 5, 2007.

Rasmussen DT. 2002. The origin of primates. In *The Primate Fossil Record* (WC Hartwig, ed.), pp. 5–9. Cambridge University Press, Cambridge.

Ratjen F, Döring G. 2003. Cystic fibrosis. *Lancet* 361:681–689.

Reed KE. 1997. Early hominid evolution and ecological change through the African Plio-Pleistocene. *Journal of Human Evolution* 32:289–322.

Reed TE. 1969. Caucasian genes in American Negroes. *Science* 165:762–768.

Relethford JH. 2001. Absence of regional affinities of Neandertal DNA with living humans does not reject multiregional evolution. *American Journal of Physical Anthropology* 115:95–98.

Remis MJ. 1997a. Ranging and grouping patterns of a western lowland gorilla group at Bai Hokou, Central African Republic. *American Journal of Primatology* 43:111–133.

Remis MJ. 1997b. Western lowland gorillas (*Gorilla gorilla gorilla*) as seasonal frugivores: Use of variable resources. *American Journal of Primatology* 43:87–109.

Richard A. 1992. Aggressive competition between males, female-controlled polygyny and sexual monomorphism in a Malagasy primate, *Propithecus verreauxi. Journal of Human Evolution* 22:395–406.

Richards MP, Mays S, Fuller BT. 2002. Stable carbon and nitrogen isotope values of bone and teeth reflect weaning age at the Medieval Wharram Percy site, Yorkshire, UK. *American Journal of Physical Anthropology* 119:205–210.

Richards MP, Pettitt PB, Stiner MC, Trinkaus E. 2001. Stable isotope evidence for increasing dietary breadth in the European mid–Upper Paleolithic. *Proceedings of the National Academy of Sciences* 98:6528–6532.

Richards MP, Pettitt PB, Trinkaus E, et al. 2000. Neanderthal diet at Vindija and Neanderthal predation: The evidence from stable isotopes. *Proceedings of the National Academy of Sciences* 97:7663–7666.

Richmond BG, Strait DS. 2000. Evidence that humans evolved from a knuckle-walking ancestor. *Nature* 404:382–385.

Rightmire GP. 1993. *The Evolution of Homo erectus,* Comparative Anatomical Studies of an Extinct Human Species. *Cambridge University Press, New York.*

Rightmire GP, Deacon HJ. 1991. Comparative studies of Late Pleistocene human remains from Klasies River Mouth, South Africa. *Journal of Human Evolution* 20:131–156.

Ristau CA. 1999. Animal language and cognition projects. In *Handbook of Human Symbolic Evolution* (A Lock, CR Peters, eds.), pp. 644–685. Blackwell, Oxford.

Roberts DF. 1978. *Climate and Human Variability.* Cummings, Menlo Park, CA.

Roberts MB, Parfitt SA. 1999. *A Middle Pleistocene Hominid Site at Eartham Quarry, Boxgrove, West Sussex.* English Heritage Archaeological Report 17. English Heritage, London.

Roberts MB, Stringer CB, Parfitt SA. 1994. A hominid tibia from Middle Pleistocene sediments at Boxgrove, U.K. *Nature* 369:311–313.

Robins AH. 1991. *Biological Perspectives on Human Pigmentation.* Cambridge University Press, Cambridge.

Rodman PS, McHenry HM. 1980. Bioenergetics and the origin of hominid bipedalism. *American Journal of Physical Anthropology* 52:103–106.

Rose MD. 1984. Food acquisition and the evolution of positional behavior: The case of bipedalism. In *Food Acquisition and Processing in Primates* (DJ Chivers, BA Wood, A Bilsborough, eds.), pp. 509–524. Plenum, New York.

Rosenberg KR, Trevathan WR. 1996. Bipedalism and human birth: The obstetrical dilemma revisited. *Evolutionary Anthropology* 4:161–168.

Rosenberger AL. 2002. Platyrrhine paleontology and systematics: The paradigm shifts. In *The Primate Fossil Record* (WC Hartwig, ed.), pp. 151–159. Cambridge University Press, Cambridge.

Ross C, Williams B, Kay RF. 1998. Phylogenetic analysis of anthropoid relationships. *Journal of Human Evolution* 35:221–306.

Rowe JH. 1965. The Renaissance foundations of anthropology. *American Anthropologist* 67:1–20.

Rowell TE. 1988. Beyond the one-male group. *Behaviour* 104:189–201.

Russell MD. 1987. Bone breakage in the Krapina hominid collection. *American Journal of Physical Anthropology* 72:373–379.

Ruvolo M. 1997. Molecular phylogeny of the hominoids: Inferences from multiple independent DNA sequence data sets. *Molecular Biology and Evolution* 14:248–265.

Ryan MJ. 1990. Sexual selection, sensory systems, and sensory exploitation. *Oxford Surveys in Evolutionary Biology* 7:156–195.

Sabater-Pi J, Bermejo M, Ilera G, Vea JJ. 1993. Behavior of bonobos (*Pan paniscus*) following their capture of monkeys in Zaïre. *International Journal of Primatology* 14:797–804.

Sanders WJ, Bodenbender BE. 1994. Morphometric analysis of lumbar vertebra UMP 67-28: Implications for spinal function and phylogeny of the Miocene Moroto hominoid. *Journal of Human Evolution* 26:203–237.

Sarich VM, Wilson AC. 1967. Immunological time scale for hominid evolution. *Science* 158:1200–1203.

Sauther ML. 2002. Group size effects on predation sensitive foraging in wild ring-tailed lemurs (*Lemur catta*). In *Eat or Be Eaten: Predation Sensitive Foraging among Primates* (LE Miller, ed.), pp. 107–125. Cambridge University Press, Cambridge.

Sauther ML, Sussman RW, Gould L. 1999. The socioecology of the ringtailed lemur: Thirty-five years of research. *Evolutionary Anthropology* 8:120–132.

Savage-Rumbaugh S, Lewin R. 1994. *Kanzi: The Ape at the Brink of the Human Mind.* New York: Wiley.

Savage-Rumbaugh S, Rumbaugh D. 1993. The emergence of language. In *Tools, Language, and Cognition in Human Evolution* (KR Gibson, T Ingold, eds.), pp. 86–108. Cambridge University Press, Cambridge.

Savage-Rumbaugh S, Shanker SG, Taylor TJ. 1998. *Apes, Language, and the Human Mind.* Oxford University Press, New York.

Schaaffhausen H. 1858. Zur Kentiss der ältesten Rassenschädel. *Archiv für Anatomie* 5:453–488.

Schell L. 1991. Pollution and human growth: Lead, noise, polychlorobiphenyl compounds and toxic wastes. In *Applications of Biological Anthropology to Human Affairs* (CGN Mascie-Taylor, GW Lasker, eds.), pp. 83–116. Cambridge University Press, Cambridge.

Schell L. 1995. Human biological adaptability with special emphasis on plasticity: History, development and problems for future research. In *Human Variability and Plasticity* (CGN Mascie-Taylor, B Bogin, eds.), pp. 213–237. Cambridge University Press, Cambridge.

Schell LM, Hills EA. 2002. Polluted environments as extreme environments. In *Human Growth from Conception to Maturity* (G Gilli, LM Schell, L Benso, eds.), pp. 249–261. Smith-Gordon, London.

Schick K, Toth N. 1993. Making Silent Stones Speak: Human Evolution and the Dawn of Technology. Simon & Schuster, New York.

Schick KD, Toth N, Garufi G, et al. 1999. Continuing investigations into the stone tool-making and tool-using capabilities of a Bonobo (*Pan paniscus*). *Journal of Archaeological Science* 26:821–832.

Schiller F. 1979. *Paul Broca: Founder of French Anthropology, Explorer of the Brain.* University of California Press, Berkeley.

Schmitz RW, Serre D, Bonani G, et al. 2002. The Neandertal type site revisited: Interdisciplinary investigations of skeletal remains from the Neander Valley, Germany. *Proceedings of the National Academy of Sciences* 99:13342–13347.

Schoenemann PT. 1999. Syntax as an emergent characteristic of the evolution of semantic complexity. *Mind and Machines* 9:309–346.

Schoenemann PT, Budinger TF, Sarich VM, Wang WSY. 2000. Brain size does not predict general cognitive ability within families. *Proceedings of the National Academy of Sciences* 97:4932–4937.

Schoetensack O. 1908. Der unterkiefer des *Homo heidelbergensis* aus den Sanden von Mauer bei Heidelberg. W. Engelmann, Leipzig.

Schultz AH. 1969. *The Life of Primates.* Universe Books, New York.

Schulz R, Salthouse T. 1999. *Adult Development and Aging: Myths and Emerging Realities.* Prentice Hall, Upper Saddle River, NJ.

Schuman LM. 1953. Epidemiology of frostbite: Korea. In *Cold Injury: Korea 1951–52*, pp. 205–568. Army Medical Research Laboratory Report 113, Ft. Knox.

Schurr TG. 2004. The peopling of the New World: perspectives from molecular anthropology. *Annual Review of Anthropology* 33:551–583.

Schurr TG, Sherry ST. 2004. Mitochondrial DNA and Y-chromosome diversity and the peopling of the Americas: evolutionary and demographic evidence. *American Journal of Human Biology* 16:420–439.

Scriver CR, Gregory DM, Sovetts D, et al. 1985. Normal plasma free amino acid values in adults: The influence of some common physiological variables. *Metabolism* 34:868–873.

Segerstråle U. 2000. *Defenders of the Truth: The Battle for Science in the Sociobiology Debate.* Oxford University Press, New York.

Seielstad M, Yuldasheva N, Singh N, et al. 2003. Novel Y-chromosome variant puts an upper limit on the timing of first entry into the Americas. *American Journal of Human Genetics* 73(3):700–705.

Seiffert ER, Simons EL, Attia Y. 2003. Fossil evidence for an ancient divergence of lorises and galagos. *Nature* 422:421–424.

Semendeferi K, Damasio H. 2000. The brain and its main anatomical subdivisions in living hominoids using magnetic resonance imaging. *Journal of Human Evolution* 38:317–332.

Semendeferi K, Damasio H, Franks R, Van Hoesen GW. 1997. The evolution of the frontal lobes: A volumetric analysis based on three-dimensional reconstructions of magnetic resonance scans of human and ape brains. *Journal of Human Evolution* 32:375–388.

Semendeferi K, Lu A, Schenker N, Damasio H. 2002. Humans and large apes share a large frontal cortex. *Nature Neuroscience* 5:272–276.

Serre D, Langaney A, Chech M, et al. 2004. No evidence of Neandertal mtDNA contribution to early modern humans. *PLoS Biology* 2:E57.

Seymour RM, Allan MJ, Pomiankowski A, Gustafsson K. 2004. Evolution of the human ABO polymorphism by two complementary selective pressures. *Proceedings of the Royal Society of London* B 22:1065–1072 Vol. 22:1065–1072

Shapiro HL. 1939. *Migration and Environment.* Oxford University Press, Oxford.

Shell ER. 2002. *The Hungry Gene: The Science of Fat and the Future of Thin.* Atlantic Monthly Press, New York.

Shen G, Wang J. 2000. Chronological studies on Chinese middle–late Pleistocene hominid sites, actualities and prospects. *Acta Anthropologica Sinica* 19(suppl.):279–284.

Shen G, Wang W, Wang Q, et al. 2002. U-series dating of Liujiang hominid site in Guangxi, southern China. *Journal of Human Evolution* 43:817–829.

Shepher J. 1983. *Incest: A Biosocial View.* Academic Press, New York.

Sherman PW. 1977. Nepotism and the evolution of alarm calls. *Science* 197:1246–1253.

Shipman P. 1981. *Life History of a Fossil.* Harvard University Press, Cambridge, MA.

Shipman P. 1986. Scavenging or hunting in early hominids. *American Anthropologist* 88:27–43.

Shipman P. 2001. *The Man Who Found the Missing Link.* Harvard University Press, Cambridge, MA.

Shipman P, Rose J. 1983. Evidence of butchery and hominid activities at Torralba and Ambrona. *Journal of Archaeological Science* 10:475–482.

Shipman P, Walker A. 1989. The costs of becoming a predator. *Journal of Human Evolution* 18:373–392.

Shipman P, Walker AC, Van Couvering JA, et al. 1981 The Fort Ternan hominoid site, Kenya: Geology, age, taphonomy and paleoecology. *Journal of Human Evolution* 10:49–72.

Sibley CG, Ahlquist JE. 1984. The phylogeny of the hominoid primates, as indicated by DNA–DNA hybridization. *Journal of Molecular Evolution* 20:2–15.

Sikes N. 1994. *Journal of Human Evolution* 27:25–45.

Sillen A. 1988. Elemental and isotopic analyses of mammalian fauna from southern Africa and their implications for paleodietary research. *American Journal of Physical Anthropology* 76:49–60.

Simons EL. 1987. New faces of *Aegyptopithecus* from the Oligocene of Egypt. *Journal of Human Evolution* 16:273–290.

Simons EL. 1995. Egyptian Oligocene primates: A review. *Yearbook of Physical Anthropology* 38:199–238.

Simoons FJ. 1970. Primary adult lactose intolerance and the milking habit: A problem in biological and cultural interrelations. 2. A cultural historical hypothesis. *American Journal of Digestive Diseases* 15:695–710.

Simpson GG. 1961. *Principles of Animal Taxonomy.* Columbia University Press, New York.

Small MF. 1989. Female choice in nonhuman primates. *Yearbook of Physical Anthropology* 32:103–127.

Smith CI, Chamberlain AT, Riley MS, et al. 2003. The thermal history of human fossils and the likelihood of successful DNA amplification. *Journal of Human Evolution* 45:203–217.

Smith EO. 1999. Evolution, substance abuse, and addiction. In *Evolutionary Medicine* (WR Trevathan, EO Smith, JJ McKenna, eds.), pp. 375–406. Oxford University Press, New York.

Smith FH. 1984. Fossil hominids from the Upper Pleistocene of central Europe and the origin of modern Europeans. In *The Origins of Modern Humans* (FH Smith, F Spencer, eds.), pp. 137–210. Alan R. Liss, New York.

Smith GE. 1913. The evolution of man. Annual Report of the Board of Regents of the Smithsonian Institution 1912:553–572.

Smith MT. 1998. Genetic adaptation. In *Human Adaptation* (GA Harrison, H Morphy, eds.), pp. 1–54. Berg, Oxford.

Smith SS. 1965 (1810). An Essay on the Causes of the Variety of Complexion and Figure in the Human Species. Belknap Press-Harvard University Press, Cambridge, MA.

Smuts BB. 1985. *Sex and Friendship in Baboons.* Aldine, New York.

Snow CC. 1982. Forensic anthropology. *Annual Review of Anthropology* 11:97–131.

Solecki R. 1971. *Shanidar: The First Flower People.* Knopf, New York.

Solter D. 2000. Mammalian cloning: Advances and limitations. *Nature Reviews: Genetics* 1:199–207.

Sommer V. 1994. Infanticide among the langurs of Jodhpur: Testing the sexual selection hypothesis with a long-term record. In *Infanticide and Parental Care* (S Parmigiani, F vom Saal, eds.), pp. 155–198. Harwood Academic Publishers, London.

Sommer V, Reichard U. 2000. Rethinking monogamy: the gibbon case. In *Primate Males: Causes and Consequences of Variation in Group Composition* (PM Kappeler, ed.), pp. 159–168. Cambridge University Press, Cambridge.

Sorensen M, Leonard WR. 2001. Neandertal energetics and foraging efficiency. *Journal of Human Evolution* 40:483–495.

Sowell ER, Thompson PM, Holmes CJ, et al. 1999. *In vivo* evidence for post-adolescent brain maturation in frontal and striatal regions. *Nature Neuroscience* 2:859–861.

Sparks CS, Jantz RL. 2002. A reassessment of human cranial plasticity: Boas revisited. *Proceedings of the National Academy of Sciences* 99:14636–14639.

Spencer F, ed. 1997. *History of Physical Anthropology.* Garland, New York.

Speth JD, Tchernov E. 2001. Neandertal hunting and meat-processing in the Near East. In *Meat-Eating and Human Evolution* (CB Stanford, HT Bunn, eds.), pp. 52–72. Oxford University Press, New York.

Spigelman M, Matheson C, Lev G, et al. 2002. Confirmation of the presence of *Mycobacterium tuberculosis* complex-specific DNA in three archaeological specimens. *International Journal of Osteoarchaeology* 12:393–401.

Spoor F, Leakey MG, Gathogo PN, et al. 2007 Implications of new early *Homo* fossils from Ileret, east of Lake Turkana, Kenya. *Nature* 448:688–691.

Spoor F, Hublin JJ, Braun M, Zonneveld F. 2003. The bony labyrinth of Neanderthals. *Journal of Human Evolution* 44:141–165.

Spurdle AB, Jenkins T. 1996. The origins of the Lemba "Black Jews" of southern Africa: Evidence from p12F2 and other Y-chromosome markers. *American Journal of Human Genetics* 59:1126–1133.

Stanford, C. 2008. *Apes of the Impenetrable Forest: The behavioural ecology of sympatric chimpanzees and gorillas.* Pearson Education, Upper Saddle River, NJ.

Stanford CB. 1998a. *Chimpanzee and Red Colobus: The Ecology of Predator and Prey.* Harvard University Press, Cambridge, MA.

Stanford CB. 1998b. The social behavior of chimpanzees and bonobos: Empirical evidence and shifting assumptions. *Current Anthropology* 39:399–420.

Stanford CB. 1999. *The Hunting Apes.* Princeton University Press, Princeton, NJ.

Stanford CB. 2001. The subspecies concept in primatology: The case of mountain gorillas. *Primates* 42:309–318.

Stanford CB. 2002. Arboreal bipedalism in Bwindi chimpanzees. *American Journal of Physical Anthropology* 119:87–91.

Stanford CB, Nkurunungi JB. 2003. Sympatric ecology of chimpanzees and gorillas in Bwindi Impenetrable National Park, Uganda. Diet. *International Journal of Primatology* 24:901–918.

Stanford CB. 2003. *Upright.* Houghton Mifflin, Boston.

Stanton W. 1960. *The Leopard's Spots: Scientific Attitudes toward Race in America 1815–59.* University of Chicago Press, Chicago.

Steadman DW. 2003. *Hard Evidence: Case Studies in Forensic Anthropology.* Prentice Hall, Upper Saddle River, NJ.

Steckel RH, Rose JC, eds. 2002. *The Backbone of History: Health and Nutrition in the Western Hemisphere.* Cambridge University Press, New York.

Stedman HH, Kozyak BW, Nelson A, et al. 2004. Myosin gene mutation correlates with anatomical changes in the human lineage. *Nature* 428:415–418.

Steegman AT. 2003. Climate, racial category, and body proportions in the U.S. *American Journal of Physical Anthropology* 36(suppl.):199–200.

Steno N. 1669. *De Solido intra Solidum Naturaliter Contento.* Dissertatio Prodromus, Florence.

Stephan H, Frahm H, Baron G. 1981. New and revised data on volumes of brain structures in insectivores and primates. *Folia Primatologica* 35:1–29.

Stern JT, Susman RL. 1983. The locomotor anatomy of *Australopithecus afarensis. American Journal of Physical Anthropology* 60:279–317.

Sternberg R. 1990. *Metaphors of Mind: Conceptions of the Nature of Intelligence.* Cambridge University Press, Cambridge.

Steudel KL. 1996. Limb morphology, bipedal gait, and the energetics of hominid locomotion. *American Journal of Physical Anthropology* 99:345–355.

Stewart C, Disotell TR. 1998. Primate evolution: in and out of Africa. *Current Biology* 8:R582–R588.

Stewart R, Pryzborski S. 2002. Non-neural adult stem cells: Tools for brain repair? *BioEssays* 24:708–713.

Stine GJ. 2003. *AIDS Update 2003*. Prentice Hall, Upper Saddle River, NJ.

Stock J, Pfeiffer S. 2001. Linking structural variability in long bone diaphyses to habitual behaviors: foragers from the southern African Later Stone Age and the Andaman Islands. *American Journal of Physical Anthropology*, 115 (4):337–348.

Stock JT, Pfeiffer S. 2004. Long bone robusticity and subsistence behavior among Later Stone Age foragers of the forest and fynbos biomes of South Africa. *Journal of Archaeological Science* 31:999–1013.

Stocking GW. 1987. *Victorian Anthropology*. The Free Press, New York.

Strickland M, Hardy R. 2005. *The Great Warbow: From Hastings to the Mary Rose*. Sutton Publishing, Stroud, UK.

Stringer CB. 1994. Out of Africa: A personal history. In *Origins of Anatomically Modern Humans* (MH Nitecki, DV Nitecki, eds.), pp. 149–172. Plenum, New York.

Stringer CB, Andrews P. 1988. Genetic and fossil evidence for the origin of modern humans. *Science* 239:1263–1268.

Stringer CB, Gamble C. 1993. *In Search of the Neanderthals*. Thames and Hudson, New York.

Stringer CB, Grün R, Schwarcz HP, Goldberg P. 1989. ESR dates for the hominid burial site of Es Skhul in Israel. *Nature* 338:756–758.

Stringer CB, Hublin JJ, Vandermeersch B. 1984. The origin of anatomically modern humans in Western Europe. In *The Origins of Modern Humans* (FH Smith, F Spencer, eds.), pp. 51–136. Alan R. Liss, New York.

Stringer CB, Trinkaus E, Roberts MB, et al. 1998. The Middle Pleistocene human tibia from Boxgrove. *Journal of Human Evolution* 34:509–547.

Strum SC. 1981. Processes and products of change: Baboon predatory behavior at Gilgil, Kenya. In *Omnivorous Primates*. (RSO Harding, G Teleki, eds.), pp. 255–302. Columbia University Press, New York.

Stumpf MPH, Goldstein DB. 2001. Genealogical and evolutionary inference with the human Y chromosome. *Science* 291:1738–1742.

Sullivan RJ, Hagen EH. 2002. Psychotropic substance-seeking: Evolutionary pathology or adaptation? *Addiction* 97:389–400.

Sunahara A. 2000. *The Politics of Racism: The Uprooting of Japanese Canadians During the Second World War*. Originally published by James Lorimer & Company, 1981. (Updated 2000, re-released under a Creative Commons license, 2004.)

Susman R, ed. 1984. *The Pygmy Chimpanzee*. Plenum, New York.

Susman RL, Stern JT, Jungers WL. 1984. Arboreality and bipedality in the Hadar hominids. *Folia Primatologica* 43:113–156.

Sussman RL. 1991. Primate origins and the evolution of angiosperms. *American Journal of Primatology* 23:209–223.

Sussman RL. 1992. Male life history and intergroup mobility among ringtailed lemurs (*Lemur catta*). *International Journal of Primatology* 13:395–413.

Suwa G, Asfaw B, Beyene Y, et al. 1997. The first skull of *Australopithecus boisei*. *Nature* 389:489–492.

Swisher CC, Curtis GH, Jacob T, et al. 1994. Age of the earliest known hominids in Java, Indonesia. *Science* 263:1118–1121.

Swisher CC III, Rink WJ, Antón SC, et al. 1996. Latest *Homo erectus*, in Java: Potential contemporaneity with *Homo sapiens* in Southeast Asia. *Science* 274:1870–1874.

Sy MS, Gambetti P, Wong BS. 2002. Human prion diseases. *Medical Clinics of North America* 86:551–571.

Symons D. 1979. *The Evolution of Human Sexuality*. Oxford University Press, New York.

Szalay FS. 1975. Where to draw the nonprimate–primate taxonomic boundary. *Folia Primatologia* 23:158–163.

Szalay FS. 1981. Phylogeny and the problems of adaptive significance: The case of the earliest primates. *Folia Primatologica* 34:1–45.

Szalay FS, Delson E. 1979. *Evolutionary History of the Primates*. Academic Press, New York.

Takahata N, Lee SH, Satta Y. 2001. Testing multiregionality of modern human origins. *Molecular Biology and Evolution* 18:172–183.

Tan CL. 1999. Group composition, home range size, and diet of three sympatric bamboo lemur species (genus *Hapalemur*) in Ranomafana National Park, Madagascar. *International Journal of Primatology* 20:547–566.

Tanner JM. 1978. *Fetus into Man*. Harvard University Press, Cambridge, MA.

Tanner NM, Zihlman AL. 1976. Women in evolution part 1: Innovation and selection in human origins. *Signs: Journal of Women, Culture, and Society* 1:585–608.

Tappen M. 2001. Deconstructing the Serengeti. In *Meat-Eating and Human Evolution* (CB Stanford, HT Bunn, ed.), pp. 13–32. Oxford University Press, New York.

Tattersall I. 1986. Species recognition in human paleontology. *Journal of Human Evolution* 15:165–175.

Taylor RE. 2000. Fifty years of radiocarbon dating. *American Scientist* 88:60–67.

Templeton AR. 2002. Out of Africa again and again. *Nature* 416:45–51.

Terborgh J. 1983. *Five New World Primates*. Princeton University Press, Princeton, NJ.

Terrace H. 1979. *Nim*. Knopf, New York.

Thackray HM, Tifft C. 2001. Fetal alcohol syndrome. *Pediatrics in Review* 22:47–55.

Thieme H. 1997. Lower palaeolithic hunting spears from Germany. *Nature* 385:807–810.

Thornhill NW. 1991. An evolutionary analysis of rules regulating human inbreeding and marriage. *Behavioral and Brain Sciences* 14:247–293.

Tobias PV. 1971. *The Brain in Hominid Evolution.* Columbia University Press, New York.

Tobias PV. 1987. The brain of *Homo habilis:* A new level of organization in cerebral evolution. *Journal of Human Evolution* 16:741–761.

Tomasello M, Savage-Rumbaugh S, Kruger A. 1993. Imitative learning of actions on objects by children, chimpanzees and enculturated chimpanzees. *Child Development* 64:1688–1705.

Tooby J, Cosmides L. 2000. Toward mapping the evolved functional organization of mind and brain. In *The New Cognitive Neurosciences*, 2nd ed. (MS Gazzaniga, editor-in-chief), pp. 1167–1178. MIT Press, Cambridge, MA.

Torres-Rouff C, Costa Junqueira MA. 2006. Interpersonal violence in prehistoric San Pedro de Atacama, Chile: behavioral implications of environmental stress. *American Journal of Physical Anthropology* 130:60–70.

Toth N. 1985. Archaeological evidence for preferential right-handedness in the Lower and Middle Pleistocene, and its possible implications. *Journal of Human Evolution* 14:607–614.

Toth N, Schick K, Savage-Rumbaugh S. 1993. *Pan* the tool-maker: Investigations into the stone tool-making and tool using capabilities of a bonobo (*Pan paniscus*). *Journal of Archaeological Science* 20:81–91.

Trainor LJ, Austin CM, Desjardins RN. 2000. Is infant-directed speech prosody a result of the vocal expression of emotion? *Psychological Science* 11:188–195.

Trehub SE, Unyk AM, Trainor LJ. 1993. Maternal singing in cross-cultural perspective. *Infant Behavior and Development* 16:285–295.

Trevathan WR. 1987. *Human Birth: An Evolutionary Perspective.* Aldine de Gruyter, Hawthorne, NY.

Trevathan WR. 1999. Evolutionary obstetrics. In *Evolutionary Medicine* (WR Trevathan, EO Smith, JJ McKenna, eds.), pp. 183–207. Oxford University Press, Oxford.

Trevathan W, Smith EO, McKenna JJ, eds. 1999. *Evolutionary Medicine.* Oxford University Press, Oxford.

Trinkaus E. 1983. *The Shanidar Neandertals.* Academic Press, New York.

Trinkaus E. 1995. Neanderthal mortality patterns. *Journal of Archaeological Science* 22:121–142.

Trinkaus E. 2003. Neandertal faces were not long; modern human faces were short. *Proceedings of the National Academy of Sciences* 100:8142–8145.

Trinkaus E. 2007. European early modern humans and the fate of the Neandertals. *Proceedings of the National Academy of Sciences* 104(18):7367–7372.

Trinkaus E, Moldovan O, Milota S, et al. 2003. An early modern human from the Petera cu Oase, Romania. *Proceedings of the National Academy of Sciences* 100:11231–11236.

Trinkaus E, Shipman P. 1992. *The Neandertals.* Vintage Press, New York.

Turner CG. 1989. Teeth and prehistory in Asia. *Scientific American* 260:88–91, 94–96.

Turner CG. 1990. Major features of Sundadonty and Sinodonty, including suggestions about East Asian microevolution, population history, and late Pleistocene relationships with Australian aboriginals. *American Journal of Physical Anthropology* 82:295–317.

Tutin CEG. 1996. Ranging and social structure of lowland gorillas in the Lopé Reserve, Gabon. In *Great Ape Societies* (WC McGrew, LF Marchant, T Nishida, eds.), pp. 58–70. Cambridge University Press, Cambridge.

Tuttle RH. 1981. Evolution of hominid bipedalism and prehensile capabilities. *Philosophical Transactions of the Royal Society of London* B 292:89–94.

Tyson E. 1972 (1699). *Orang-outang sive Homo sylvestris:* or the anatomy of a pygmie. In *Climbing Man's Family Tree* (TD McCown, KAR Kennedy, eds.), pp. 41–48. Prentice Hall, Englewood Cliffs, NJ.

Van den Berghe PL. 1983. Human inbreeding avoidance: Culture in nature. *Behavioral and Brain Sciences* 6:91–123.

Vandermeersch B. 1985. The origin of the Neandertals. In *Ancestors: The Hard Evidence* (E Delson, ed.), pp. 306–309. Alan R. Liss, New York.

van Schaik CP, Hörstermann M. 1994. Predation risk and the number of adult males in a primate group: A comparative test. *Behavioral Ecology and Sociobiology* 35:261–272.

van Schaik CP, Monk KR, Yarrow Robertson JM. 2001. Dramatic decline in orang-utan numbers in the Leuser ecosystem, northern Sumatra. *Oryx* 35:14–25.

van Schaik CP, van Hoof JARAM. 1983. On the ultimate causes of primate social systems. *Behaviour* 85:91–117.

Van Valen L. 1976. Ecological species, multispecies, and oaks. *Taxon* 25:233–239.

Van Valen L, Mellin GW. 1967. Selection in natural populations. VII. New York babies (fetal life study). *Annals of Human Genetics* 31:109–127.

Vasey N. 1996. Feeding and ranging behavior of red ruffed lemurs (*Varecia variegata rubra*) and white-fronted lemurs (*Lemur fulvus albifrons*). *American Journal of Physical Anthropology* (suppl. 22):234–235.

Vekua A, Lordkipanidze D, Rightmire GP, et al. 2002. A new skull of early *Homo* from Dmanisi, Georgia. *Science* 297:85–89.

Venter JC, Adams MD, Myers EW, et al. 2001. The sequence of the human genome. *Science* 291:1304–1351.

Vervaecke H, van Elsacker L, Möhle U, et al. 1999. Intermenstrual intervals in captive bonobos (*Pan paniscus*). *Primates* 40:283–289.

Videan E, McGrew WC. 2001. Are bonobos (*Pan paniscus*) really more bipedal than chimpanzees (*Pan troglodytes*)? *American Journal of Primatology* 54:233–239.

Vollrath D, Nathans J, Davis RW. 1988. Tandem array of human visual pigment genes at Xq28. *Science* 240:1669–1672.

Volta U, Bellentani S, Bianchi G, et al. 2001. High prevalence of celiac disease in Italian general population. *Digestive Diseases and Sciences* 46:1500–1505.

Von Koenigswald GHR. 1952. *Gigantopithecus blacki* von Koenigswald, a giant fossil hominoid from the Pleistocene of southern China. *Anthropological Papers of the American Museum of Natural History* 43:291–326.

Walker A, Leakey R, eds. 1993a. *The Nariokotome* Homo erectus *Skeleton. Harvard University Press, Cambridge*, MA.

Walker AC, Leakey RE, Harris JM, Brown FH. 1986. 2.5-myr *Australopithecus boisei* from west of Lake Turkana, Kenya. *Nature* 322:517–522.

Walker A, Shipman P. 1996. *The Wisdom of the Bones.* Vintage Books, New York.

Walker AC, Teaford M. 1989. The hunt for *Proconsul. Scientific American* 260:76–82.

Walker A, Zimmerman MR, Leakey REF. 1982. A possible case of hypervitaminosis A in *Homo erectus. Nature* 296:248–250.

Walker R, Hill K, Kaplan H, McMillan G. 2002. Age-dependency in hunting ability among the Ache of eastern Paraguay. *Journal of Human Evolution* 42:639–657.

Walsh PD, Abernethy KA, Bermejo M, et al. 2003. Catastrophic ape decline in western equatorial Africa. *Nature* 422:611–614.

Walter RC, Aronson JL. 1982. Revisions of K/Ar ages for the Hadar hominid site, Ethiopia. *Nature* 296:122–127.

Ward CV. 1997. Functional anatomy and phylogenetic implications of the hominoid trunk and hindlimb. In *Function, Phylogeny and Fossils: Miocene Hominoid Evolution and Adaptation* (DR Begun, CV Ward, MD Rose, eds.), pp. 101–130. Plenum, New York.

Ward WP. 1990. *White Canada Forever: Popular Attitudes and Public Policy Toward Orientals in British Columbia*, 2nd ed. McGill-Queen's University Press, Montreal, QC.

Washburn SL. 1968. Speculation on the problem of man's coming to the ground. In *Changing Perspectives on Man* (B Rothblatt, ed.), pp. 191–206. University of Chicago Press, Chicago.

Watanabe H, Fujiyama A, Hattori M, et al. 2004. DNA sequence and comparative analysis of chimpanzee chromosome 22. *Nature* 429:382–388.

Watson JD, Crick FHC. 1953a. Genetical implications of the structure of deoxyribonucleic acid. *Nature* 171:964–967.

Watson JD, Crick FHC. 1953b. A structure for deoxyribonucleic acid. *Nature* 171:737–738.

Watts DP. 1989. Infanticide in mountain gorillas: New cases and a reconsideration of the evidence. *Ethology* 81:1–18.

Wayne RK, Leonard JA, Cooper A. 1999. Full of sound and fury: The recent history of ancient DNA. *Annual Review in Ecology and Systematics* 30:457–477.

Weidenreich F. 1943. The skull of *Sinanthropus pekinensis:* A comparative study of a primitive hominid skull. *Palaeontologica Sinica* D10:1–485.

Weiner A. 1988. *The Trobrianders of Papua New Guinea.* Holt, Rinehart, and Winston, New York.

Weiner J. 1994. *The Beak of the Finch.* Vintage Books, New York.

Weiss KM. 2002. Goings on in Mendel's garden. *Evolutionary Anthropology* 11:40–44.

Wertz RC, Wertz DC. 1989. *Lying-In: A History of Childbirth in America.* Yale University Press, New Haven, CT.

Westermarck EA. 1891. *The History of Human Marriage.* Macmillan, New York.

Wheeler PE. 1991. The thermoregulatory advantages of hominid bipedalism in open equatorial environments: The contribution of increased convective heat loss and cutaneous evaporative cooling. *Journal of Human Evolution* 21:107–115.

White C. 1993. Isotopic determination of seasonality of diet and death in ancient Nubian hair. *Journal of Archaeological Science* 20:657–666.

White C, Spence M, Longstaffe F. 2002. Geographic identities of the sacrificial victims at the Temple of Quetzalcoatl: implications for the nature of state power. *Latin American Antiquity* 13:217–236.

White C, Spence M, Longstaffe F. 2004. Demography and ethnic continuity in the Tlailotlacan enclave of Teotihuacan: the evidence from stable oxygen isotopes. *Journal of Anthropological Archaeology* 23(4):385–403.

White C, Spence M, Stuart-Williams H.LeQ. 1998. Oxygen isotopes and the identification of geographical origin: the Valley of Oaxaca vs. the Valley of Mexico. *Journal of Archaeological Science* 25(7):643–657.

White TD, Moore RV, Suwa G. 1984. Hadar biostratigraphy. *Journal of Vertebrate Paleontology* 4:575–581.

White M. 2001. *Leonardo: The First Scientist.* Griffin, New York.

White R. 2001. Personal ornaments from Grotte du Renne at Arcy-sur-Cure. *Athena Review* 2:41–46.

White TD. 1986. Cut marks on the Bodo cranium: A case of prehistoric defleshing. *American Journal of Physical Anthropology* 69:503–509.

White TD, Asfaw B, DeGusta D, et al. 2003.Pleistocene *Homo sapiens* from Middle Awash, Ethiopia. *Nature* 423:742–747.

White TD, Harris JM. 1977. Suid evolution and correlation of African hominid localities. *Science* 198:13–21.

White TD, Suwa G, Asfaw B. 1994. *Australopithecus ramidus*, a new species of early hominid from Aramis, Ethiopia. *Nature* 371:306–312.

Whiten A, Goodall J, McGrew WC, et al. 1999. Cultures in chimpanzees. *Nature* 399:682–685.

Wiens JJ. 2001. Widespread loss of sexually selected traits: How the peacock lost its spots. *Trends in Ecology and Evolution* 16:517–523.

Wiley A. 1992. Adaptation and the biocultural paradigm in medical anthropology: A critical review. *Medical Anthropology Quarterly* 6:216–236.

Wiley AS. 2004. *An Ecology of High-Altitude Infancy: A Biocultural Perspective.* Cambridge University Press, Cambridge.

Willey P, Leach P. 2003. The skull on the lawn: trophies, taphonomy and forensic anthropology. In *Hard Evidence: Case Studies in Forensic Anthropology* (DW Steadman, ed.), pp. 176–188. Prentice Hall, Upper Saddle River, NJ.

Williams DR. 2003. The biomedical challenges of space flight. *Annual Review in Medicine* 54:245–256.

Williams GC. 1957. Pleiotropy, natural selection, and the evolution of senescence. *Evolution* 11:398–411.

Williams GC. 1966. *Adaptation and Natural Selection.* Princeton University Press, Princeton, NJ.

Williams JS, White CD, Longstaffe FJ. 2005. Trophic level and macronutrient shift effects associated with the weaning process in the Postclassic Maya. *American Journal of Physical Anthropology* 128:781–790.

Williams RJ. 1956. *Biochemical Individuality.* University of Texas Press, Austin.

Wilson EO. 1975. *Sociobiology: The New Synthesis.* Harvard University Press, Cambridge, MA.

Wise RJ, Greene J, Buchel C, Scott SK. 1999. Brain regions involved in articulation. *Lancet* 353:1057–1061.

WoldeGabriel G, White TD, Suwa G, et al. 1994. Ecological and temporal placement of early Pliocene hominids at Aramis, Ethiopia. *Nature* 371:330–333.

Wolf AP. 1966. Childhood association, sexual attraction, and the incest taboo: A Chinese case. *American Anthropologist* 68:883–898.

Wolf AP. 1970. Childhood association and sexual attraction: A further test of the Westermarck hypothesis. *American Anthropologist* 72:503–515.

Wolff G, Wienker T, Sander H. 1993. On the genetics of mandibular prognathism: Analysis of large European noble families. *Journal of Medical Genetics* 30:12–16.

Wolpoff MH. 1999. *Paleoanthropology*, 2nd ed. McGraw-Hill, New York.

Wolpoff M, Caspari R. 1997. *Race and Human Evolution.* Westview Press, Boulder, CO.

Wolpoff M, Hawks J, Caspari R. 2000. Multiregional, not multiple origins. *American Journal of Physical Anthropology* 112:129–136.

Wolpoff MH, Senut B, Pickford M, Hawks J. 2002. Paleoanthropology: *Sahelanthropus* or "*Sahelpithecus*"? *Nature* 419:581–582.

Wolpoff MH, Thorne AG, Smith FH, et al. 1994. Multiregional evolution: A world-wide source for modern human populations. In *Origins of Anatomically Modern Humans* (MH Nitecki, DV Nitecki, eds.), pp. 175–199. Plenum, New York.

Wolpoff MH, Zhi WX, Thorne AG. 1984. Modern *Homo sapiens* origins: A general theory of hominid evolution involving the fossil evidence from east Asia. In *The Origins of Modern Humans* (FH Smith, F Spencer, eds.), pp. 411–484. Alan R. Liss, New York.

Wood B, Collard M. 1999. The changing face of genus *Homo. Evolutionary Anthropology* 8:195–207.

Worthman CM. 1999. Evolutionary perspectives on the onset of puberty. In *Evolutionary Medicine* (WR Trevathan, EO Smith, JJ McKenna, eds.), pp. 135–163. Oxford University Press, Oxford.

Wrangham RW. 1980. An ecological model of female-bonded primate groups. *Behaviour* 75:262–292.

Wrangham RW, Jones JH, Laden G, et al. 1999. Cooking and human origins. *Current Anthropology* 40:567–594.

Wu R, Dong X. 1985. *Homo erectus* in China. In *Palaeoanthropology and Palaeolithic Archaeology in the People's Republic of China* (R Wu, JW Olsen, eds.), pp. 79–89. Academic Press, New York.

Wu X, Poirer FE. 1995. *Human Evolution in China: A Metric Description of the Fossils and a Review of the Sites.* Oxford University Press, New York.

Wynn TG. 1999. The evolution of tools and symbolic behaviour. In *Handbook of Human Symbolic Evolution* (A Lock, CR Peters, eds.), pp. 263–287. Blackwell, Oxford.

Wynne-Edwards VC. 1962. *Animal Dispersion in Relation to Social Behaviour.* Oliver & Boyd, Edinburgh.

Yamashita N. 2002. Diets of two lemur species in different microhabitats in Beza Mahafaly Special Reserve, Madagascar. *International Journal of Primatology* 23:1025–1051.

Yarrow Robertson JM, van Schaik CP. 2001. Causal factors underlying the dramatic decline of the Sumatran orang-utan. *Oryx* 35:26–38.

Yellen JE. 1991. Small mammals: !Kung San utilization and the production of faunal assemblages. *Journal of Anthropological Research* 10:1–26.

Yule GU. 1902. Mendel's laws and their probable relations to intra-racial heredity. *New Phytologist* 1:193–207, 222–238.

Zahavi A. 1975. Mate selection: A selection for a handicap. *Journal of Theoretical Biology* 53:205–214.

Zerjal T, Xue Y, Bertorelle G, et al. 2003. The genetic legacy of the Mongols. *American Journal of Human Genetics* 72:717–721.

Zhao Z, Jin L, Fu YX, et al. 2000. Worldwide DNA sequence variation in a 10-kilobase noncoding region on human chromosome 22. *Proceedings of the National Academy of Sciences* 97:11354–11358.

Zhu RX, Potts R, Xie F, et al. 2004. New evidence on the earliest human presence at high northern latitudes in northeast Asia. *Nature* 431:559–562.

Zubenko GS, Hughes HB, Maher BS, et al. 2002. Genetic linkage of region containing the *CREB1* gene to depressive disorders in women from families with recurrent, early-onset, major depression. *American Journal of Medical Genetics* 114:980–987.

CREDITS

Cave Art: Parts I, II, III, IV, and V: Berna Villiers/ Douglas Mazonowicz

Part I: 2, © The Natural History Museum of London; AP Wide World Photos; Rikard Larma/Getty Images, Inc, Liaison; Craig Stanford; William F. McComas.

Chapter 1: 3, Craig Stanford; © William F. McComas; **5,** Fig. 1.1, Fred Spoor; **6,** Fig. 1.2, © The Natural History Museum of London; **6,** Fig. 1.3, AP Wide World Photos; **7,** Fig. 1.4, Rickard Larma/Getty Images Inc., Liaison; **8,** Fig. 1.5, AP Wide World Photos; **8,** Fig. 1.6, Craig Stanford; **9,** Fig. 1.7, AP Wide World Photos; **9,** Fig. 1.8, Roger Ressmeyer/Corbis/Bettmann.

Chapter 2: 13, The Granger Collection, New York/ Archive/Photo Researchers, Inc.**; 17,** Fig. 2.2, Corbis/Bettmann; **17,** Fig. 2.3, Leonard de Selva/ Corbis/Bettmann; **18,** Fig. 2.4, © Science Photo Library/Photo Researchers, Inc.; **18,** Fig. 2.5, Stock Montage, Inc./Historical Pictures Collection; **19,** Fig. 2.7, Corbis/Bettmann; **20,** Fig. 2.8, Archive/ Photo Researchers, Inc.; **20,** Fig. 2.9, Dorling Kindersley; **21,** Fig. 2.10, © William F. McComas; **22,** Fig. 2.11, © William F. McComas; **22,** Fig. 2.12, © William F. McComas; **24,** Fig. 2.14a, Craig Stanford; Fig. 2.14b, Craig Stanford/Jane Goodall Research Center; Fig. 2.14c, Craig Stanford; Fig. 2.14d, AP Wide World Photos; **25,** Fig. 2.15, Library of Congress; **25,** Fig. 2.16, Getty Images, Inc./Hulton Archive; **26,** Fig. 2.18b, Yann Arthus-Bertrand/Corbiss/Bettmann; Fig. 2.18c, Michael P. Gadomski/Photo Researchers, Inc.; **28,** Fig. 2.19, Kurt Wilson.

Part II: 32, CNRI/Photo Researchers, Inc.; Oliver Meckes and Nicole Ottawa/Photo Researchers, Inc.; The Ohio Historical Society; Renne Purse/Photo Researchers, Inc.

Chapter 3: 33, Dan McCoy/Rainbow; **35,** Fig. 3.2, Getty Images Inc.-Hulton Archive; **41,** Fig. A, courtesy of the Centre d'insémination artificielle du Québec (CIAQ) www.ciaq.com; **42,** Fig. 3.6a, AP Wide World Photos; Fig. 3.6b, The Novartis Foundation; **48,** Fig. A, Dr. William S. Klug; **50,** Fig. 3.11, reproduced with permission from *Nature Reviews Genetics*, Vol. 2, No. 4, pp. 280–91. © 2001 Macmillan Magazines Ltd.; **52,** Fig. 3.12c, Dr. Elisabeth Matisoo-Smith, University of Auckland.

Chapter 4: 56, Cynthia Hart/Corbis/Bettmann; **59,** Fig. 4.1, Paramount Pictures/Picture Desk, Inc./Kobal Collection; **60,** Fig. 4.2, John Sholtis/Amgen Inc.; **65,** Fig. 4.7, Oliver Meckes and Nichole Ottawa/Photo Researchers, Inc.; **66,** Fig. 4.8, Barent (Bernard) van Orley (c. 1492–1542), *Portrait of Charles V as a boy.* Oil on Wood. Herve Lewandowski/Musee Louvre, Paris. RMN Reunion des Nationaux/Art Resource, NY; **68,** Fig. 4.10, Mary Evans Picture Library/Photo Researchers, Inc.

Chapter 5: 75, American Museum of Natural History; **78,** Fig. 5.2, University of Chicago Divisions of Biological Sciences, Ecology, and Evolution. Reprinted by permission; **79,** Fig. 5.3, Craig Stanford; **82,** Fig. 5.5, Renne Purse/Photo Researchers, Inc.; **88,** Fig B, Craig Stanford; **90,** Fig. 5.11a, Fig. 5.11b, Craig Stanford; **92,** Fig. 5.13, Reuters/Mike Segar/ Corbis/Bettmann; **93,** Fig. A, The Royal Society of London; **94,** Fig. 5.14, Craig Stanford.

Chapter 6: 97, Jose Luis Pelaez/Corbis/Bettmann; **100,** Fig. 6.1, Jeff Greenberg/PhotoEdit; **104,** Fig. A, © Cristina Pedrazzini/Science Photo Library; **105,** Fig. 6.3, Dorling Kindersley; **109,** Fig. 6.5, The Jews of Africa; **111,** Fig. 6.8, Cavalli-Sforza, Luca, *The History and Geography of Human Genes*, © 1994 Princeton University Press. Reprinted by permission of Princeton University Press; **115,** Fig. 6.9, Mathieu Laboureur/Peter Arnold, Inc.; **116,** Fig. 6.10, Dorling Kindersley; **119,** Fig. A, NASA/John F. Kennedy Space Center; **120,** Fig. 6.12a, Michael S. Quinton/National Geographic Image Collection; Fig. 6.12b, Terry W. Eggers/Corbis/Bettmann; **121,** Fig. 6.13a, Adrian Arbib/Corbis/Bettmann; Fig. 6.13b, Yvette Cardozo/ Index Stock Imagery, Inc.; **121,** Fig. 6.14, Dr. Andrea Wiley/James Madison University; **123,** Fig. 6.15, Anna Gislen, Ph.D./Lund University.

Part III: 126, Craig Stanford.

Chapter 7: 127, Craig Stanford; **129,** Fig. 7.1, Craig Stanford; **129,** Fig. 7.2, Craig Stanford; **131,** Fig. 7.5, © Phototake Inc./Alamy; **133–134,** Fig. 7.6a, b (photos), Craig Stanford; **133–134,** Fig. 7.6c, d (photos), Craig Stanford; **137,** Fig. 7.8, Schultz; **140–141,** Fig. 7.10, Craig Stanford; Juergen and Christine Sohns/Animals Animals/Earth Scenes; Michael Dick/Animals Animals/Earth Scenes; Michael and Patricia Fogdon/Corbis/Bettmann; George D.

Lepp/Corbis/Bettmann; **142,** Fig. 7.11, Dorling Kindersley; **142,** Fig. 7.12, Craig Stanford; **142,** Fig. 7.13, Dorling Kindersley; **143,** Fig. 7.14, Michael Dick/Animals Animals/Earth Scenes; **143,** Fig. 7.15, Juergen and Christine Sohns/Animals Animals/Earth Scenes; **143,** Fig. 7.16, Michael and Patricia Fogdon/Corbis/Bettmann; **144,** Fig. 7.17, Dorling Kindersley; **145,** Fig. 7.18, Dorling Kindersley; **145,** Fig. 7.19, Mickey Gibson/Animals Animals/Earth Scenes; **146,** Fig. 7.20, Dorling Kindersley; **146,** Fig. 7.21, Craig Stanford; **147,** Fig. 7.22, Craig Stanford; **147,** Fig. 7.23, Craig Stanford; **147,** Fig. 7.24, © Photodisc/Getty Images; **148,** Fig. 7.25, Dorling Kindersley; **148,** Fig. 7.26, Craig Stanford; **148,** Fig. 7.27, Dorling Kindersley; **149,** Fig. 7.28, George D. Lepp/Corbis/Bettmann; **149,** Fig. 7.29, Craig Stanford; **150,** Fig. A, Craig Stanford; **152,** Fig. 7.31, Craig Stanford; **153,** Fig. 7.32; **153,** Fig. 7.33, Craig Stanford; **154,** Fig. 7.34, Craig Stanford.

Chapter 8: 159, Martin Harvey/Gallo Images; **160,** From *Reflections of Eden* by Biruté Galdikas. Copyright © 1995 by Biruté Galdikas. By permission of Little Brown & Company; **161,** Fig. 8.1, Craig Stanford; **162,** Fig. A, Linda Marie Fedigan, Department of Anthropology, University of Calgary; **163,** Fig. 8.2, Craig Stanford; **163,** Fig. 8.3, Craig Stanford; **163,** Fig. 8.4, Craig Stanford; **164,** Fig. 8.5, Craig Stanford; **165,** Fig. 8.7, Nick Ellwanger; **167,** Fig. 8.9, Craig Stanford; **168,** Fig. 8.10, Craig Stanford; **171,** Fig. 8.12, Craig Stanford; **171,** Fig. 8.13, Craig Stanford; **172,** Fig. 8.14, Craig Stanford; **174,** Fig. 8.15a, b, Craig Stanford; **175,** Fig. 8.16, Strier, K. B., 1994, "Myth of the Typical Primate," *Yearbook of Physical Anthropology* 37:233–71. Copyright © 1994, Wiley-Liss, Inc. Reprinted by permission of Wiley-Liss, Inc., a subsidiary of John Wiley & Sons, Inc.; **176,** Fig. 8.17, Craig Stanford; **177,** Fig. 8.18, Craig Stanford; **178,** Fig. 8.19, reprinted with permission from American Association for the Advancement of Science. Copyright 1991 AAAS. Fig. 2 from Pussey et al., *Science* 277:828–31; **179,** Fig. 8.20, Craig Stanford.

Part IV: 182, © Carr Clifton; Copyright Susan C. Antón; Meave Leakey, Fred Spoor/National Museums of Kenya; John Krigbaum; Randall White.

Chapter 9: 183, David Muench/Muench Photography, Inc.; **186,** Fig. 9.2a, Breck P. Kent; Fig. 9.2b, E. J. Tarbuck; **187,** Fig. 9.3a, © Photos.com/Jupiter Images; Fig. 9.3b, © Gunter Marx/Alamy; **195,** Fig. 9.9a, Fig. 9.9b, copyright Susan C. Antón; **194,** Fig. A, Corbis/Bettmann; **195,** Fig. B, courtesy The Natural History Museum Picture Library; **196,** Fig. 9.10a, copyright Susan C. Antón/Carl Swisher; Fig. 9.10b, copyright Susan C. Antón; **199,** Fig. 9.12, photo courtesy of Craig Feibel; **202,** Fig. 9.14, copyright Susan C. Antón; **205,** Fig. 9.16a, K. D. Rose, 1995, "The Earliest Primates," from Evolutionary Anthropology 3:159–73. Reprinted with permission of Wiley-Liss, Inc., a subsidiary of John Wiley & Sons, Inc.; Fig. 9.16b, illustration courtesy of P. Wynne, Ian Tattersall & American Museum of Natural History; Fig. 9.16c, William K. Sacco, Peabody Museum of Natural History, Yale University; **208,** Fig. 9.18, reprinted with permission of Cambridge University Press; **210,** Fig. 9.19, Dorling Kindersley; **211,** Fig. 9.22a, b, Peabody Museum of Archaeology and Ethnology; **212,** Fig. 9.23a, b, Russell L. Ciochon, University of Iowa; **214–215,** Fig. 9.25, reprinted from "Evolutionary Relationship of New World Monkeys" in Primate Adaptation and Evolution by John G. Fleagle, 1988, by Academic Press; Peabody Museum of Archaeology and Ethnology; William K. Sacco, Peabody Museum of Natural History, Yale University; Monte L. McCrossin, Ph.D.

Chapter 10: 221, Kenneth Garrett Photography; **223,** Fig. 10.1 (left), Stephen Wilkes/Image Bank/Getty Images; Fig. 10.1 (middle), Jonathan Chester/Lonely Planet Images/Photo 20-20; Fig. 10.1 (right), Getty Images/Digital Vision; **223,** Fig. 10.2, AP Wide World Photos; **224,** Fig. 10.3, Milford Wolpoff, *Paleoanthropology,* Second Edition, Figure 38. Reprinted by permission of McGraw Hill Companies; **225,** Fig. 10.4, Kenneth Garrett Photography; **232,** Fig. A, Frank Lane Picture Agency/Michael Gore/Corbis/Bettmann; **234,** Fig. 10.12, Michael Nichols/NGS Image Collection; **236,** Fig. 10.13, Craig Stanford.

Chapter 11: 240, Kenneth Garrett Photography; **243,** Fig. 11.2b, Craig Stanford; **244,** Fig. 11.3, Dorling Kindersley; **245,** Fig. 11.4, Michel Brunet; **246,** Fig. 11.6, © 2003 Tim D. White/Brill Atlanta; **250,** Fig. 11.8, Alan Walker/National Museums of Kenya; **250,** Fig. 11.10, Institute of Human Origins, Arizona State University; **252,** Fig. A, Carl Swisher; **254,** Fig. 11.13, Meave Leakey, Fred Spoor/National Museums of Kenya; **255,** Fig. 11.14, Medical School, University of the Witwatersrand © 1985 David L. Brill;

256, Fig. 11.16, © 1999 David L. Brill/Brill Atlanta; **258,** Fig. 11.19, Jeffrey K. McKee; **258,** Fig. 11.18, Alan Walker/National Museums of Kenya; **259,** Fig. 11.21, Jeffrey K. McKee.

Chapter 12: 265, Javier Trueba/Madrid Scientific Films; **275,** Fig. 12.7, Alan Walker/National Museums of Kenya; **278–279,** Fig. 12.9, Javier Trueba/Madrid Scientific Films; copyright Susan C. Antón; © 2001 David L. Brill/Atlanta; Pat Shipman/Alan Walker/ National Museums of Kenya; Kenneth Garrett Photography, copyright Susan C. Antón; **280,** Fig. 12.10, Kenneth Garrett Photography; **280,** Fig. 12.11, copyright Susan C. Antón; **280,** Fig. 12.12, copyright Susan C. Antón; **281,** Fig. 12.13, Dorling Kindersley; **282,** Fig. 12.14, © John Reader/Science Photo Library; **283,** Fig. A, Carl Swisher; **283,** Fig. B, © John Reader/Science Photo Library; **286,** Fig. 12.16, Dorling Kindersley.

Chapter 13: 288, Kenneth Garrett Photography; **293,** Fig. 13.3a, courtesy of and copyright by Eric Delson; Fig. 13.3b, Kenneth Garrett Photography; **293,** Fig. 13.4, Javier Trueba/Madrid Scientific Films; **294,** Fig. 13.5, courtesy of Donald Johanson, Institute of Human Origins and National Museum of Ethiopia; **296,** Fig. 13.6, F. Clark Howell; **298,** Figure 13.7, Dorling Kindersley; **299,** Fig. A, © Chris Hellier/ CORBIS; **300,** Fig. 13.8, © John Reader/Science Photo Library; **301,** Fig. 13.9a, Prof. Milford Wolpoff/Univ. of Michigan; Fig. 13.9b, John Reader/Science Photo Library; **302,** Fig. 13.11, Prof. Milford Wolpoff/Univ. of Michigan; **307,** Fig. 13.14, Defleur, Alban, Tim White, Patricia Valensi, Ludovic Slimak, Évelyne Crégut-Bonnoure, Neanderthal Cannibalism at Moula-Guercy, Ardeche, France, Science, v.286, no. 5437 (October 1, 1999), pp.128–131, Fig. 2B, p. 130.

Chapter 14: 315, Ulmer Museum; **320,** Fig. 14.2, Dorling Kindersley; **321,** Fig. 14.3, © 2001 David L. Brill/Atlanta; **321,** Fig. 14.4, Kenneth Garrett Photography; **322,** Fig. 14.5, The Natural History Museum, London; **322,** Fig. 14.6, John Krigbaum; **323,** Fig. 14.7, The Granger Collection, New York; **324,** Fig. A, Dr. Peter Brown, University of New England; **325,** Fig. 14.8, Erik Trinkaus/Romanian Academy; **325,** Fig. 14.9, John Reader/Photo Researchers, Inc.; **326,** Fig. 14.10, Randall White; **330,** Fig. 14.13, Randall White; **330,** Fig. 14.14, Kenneth Garrett Photography; **331,** Fig. 14.15, Penny Tweedie/Corbis/Bettman; **331,** Fig. 14.16a, Randall White; Fig. 14.16b, Kenneth Garrett Photography; Fig. 14.16c, Randall White; **332,** Fig. 14.17, Randall White; **335,** Fig. A, The Granger Collection, New York.

Part V: 340–341 Hanna Damasio, M.D.; Cary Wolinsky/Aurora & Quanta Productions Inc.; William Sallaz/Duomo/Corbis/Bettmann.

Chapter 15: 344, Fig. 15.2, Hanna Damasio, M.D.; **345,** Fig. 15.4, National Library of Medicine; **345,** Fig. 15.5, Hanna Damasio, M.D.; **346,** Fig. 15.6, John Reader/SPL/Photo Researchers, Inc.; **348,** Fig. 15.8, Jorg and Petra Wegner/Animals Animals/Earth Scenes; **352,** Fig. 15.11a, b, c, Hanna Damasio, M.D.; **356,** Fig. 15.15, reprinted by permission of the publisher from *Uniquely Human: The Evolution of Speech, Thought, and Selfless Behavior* by Philip Lieberman, p. 55, Cambridge, Mass.: Harvard University Press, © 1991 by the President and Fellows of Harvard College; **358,** Fig. A, © Yerkes Regional Primate Research Center, Emory University.

Chapter 16: 362, Philip de Bay/Corbis/Bettmann; **365,** Fig 16.1, Gabe Palmer/Corbis/Bettmann; **366,** Fig. 16.2, National Library of Medicine; **368,** Fig. 16.4, "Fig. 8.2: Pelvic inlet, midplane, and outlet of chimpanzees and humans" from *Evolutionary Medicine*, edited by Wenda Trevathan and E. O. Smith, copyright 1999 by Oxford University Press, Inc. Used by permission of Oxford University Press, Inc.; **369,** Fig. 16.6, Vo Trung Dung/Corbis/Bettmann; **370,** Fig. 16.7, reprinted by permission of the publisher from *Fetus Into Man: Physical Growth From Conception to Maturity* by J. M. Tanner, p. 16, Cambridge, Mass.: Harvard University Press, copyright 1978, 1989 by J. M. Tanner; **371,** Fig. 16.8, B. Bogin (2001) *The Growth of Humanity*, p. 4. This material is used by permission of Wiley-Liss, a subsidiary of John Wiley & Sons, Inc.; **375,** Fig. 16.11 (top), Corbis/Bettmann; Fig. 16.11 (bottom), Fafael Roa/Corbis/Bettmann; **378,** Fig. 16.13, Dorling Kindersley; **381,** Fig. 16.14 (left), Sheldon Collins/Corbis/Bettmann; Fig. 16.14 (right), Sheldon Collins /Corbis/Bettmann; **382,** Fig. 16.15, Dorling Kindersley; **386,** Fig. 16.16, courtesy of Della Collins Cook.

Chapter 17: 390, National Gallery, London/ SuperStock; **396,** Fig. 17.2, Jack Fields/Corbis/ Bettmann; **397,** Fig. 17.4, Corbis/Bettmann; **400,** Fig. 17.7, George Holton/Photo Researchers, Inc./First

Light; **403,** 17.9, © Comstock/Jupiter Images; **405,** Fig. A, Digital Vision Ltd.; **407,** Fig. 17.11 (left), Peter Turnley/Corbis/Bettmann; Fig. 17.11 (middle), David Turnley/Corbis/Bettmann; Fig. 17.11 (right), Shaul Schwarz/Corbis/Bettmann; **409,** Figure 17.12, Dorling Kindersley.

Chapter 18: 413, Dr. Andrzej Weber, Department of Anthropology, University of Alberta; **415,** Fig. 18.1, Nancy Lovell/Physical Anthropology Collection, Department of Anthropology, University of Alberta; **416,** Fig. 18.2, copyright Susan C. Antón; **416,** Fig. 18.3, Nancy Lovell/Physical Anthropology Collection, Department of Anthropology, University of Alberta; **543,** Fig. A.5, Paul Sledzik; **417,** Fig. 18.4, *Forensic Anthropology Training Manual* by Karen Ramey Burns, illustrations by Joanna Wallington; **418,** Fig. 18.5, Nancy Lovell; **426,** Fig. 18.7, Paul Sledzik; **430,** Fig. 18.8, Paul Sledzik.

Appendix A: 436, Fig. A.4, *Forensic Anthropology Training Manual* by Karen Ramey Burns, illustrations by Joanna Wallington; **437,** Fig. A.5, *Forensic Anthropology Training Manual* by Karen Ramey Burns, illustrations by Joanna Wallington.

INDEX

Note: Entries in **bold** indicate glossary terms. Page numbers followed by *f* indicate figures and by *t,* tables.

N